# STRATEGIC LEADERSHIP

## Managing the Firm in a Turbulent World

**Alfie Morgan**

University of Windsor

**KENDALL/HUNT PUBLISHING COMPANY**
4050 Westmark Drive   Dubuque, Iowa 52002

Copyright © 2001 by Kendall/Hunt Publishing Company

Library of Congress Catalog Card Number: 00-109897

ISBN 0-7872-6712-X

All rights reserved. No part of this publication may be reproduced, stored in a retrieval system, or transmitted, in any form or by any means, electronic, mechanical, photocopying, recording, or otherwise, without the prior written permission of the copyright owner.

Printed in the United States of America
10  9  8  7  6  5  4  3  2  1

# Contents

**CHAPTER 1: INTRODUCTION 1**
TOWARD A CONCEPT OF THE CEO'S WORK 2
OVERVIEW OF THE BOOK 3

**CHAPTER 2: THE CONCEPT OF THE CEO IS WORK IN THEORY 7**
GENERAL MANAGEMENT 8
STRATEGIC MANAGEMENT 9
THEORY VERSUS REALITY 12

**CHAPTER 3: CONCEPT OF THE CEO'S WORK IN PRACTICE 19**
CASE STUDIES IN THE PRACTICES OF PROGRESSIVE CEOs 20
Jack Welch (General Electric) 20
Lars Kolind (Oticon) 21
Fred Smith (FedEx) 23
Ralph Stayer (Johnsonville Foods) 24
Patrick Kelly (PSS/WORLD Medical) 26
Jack Stack (Springfield Remanufacturing Company; SRC) 27
CONCLUSIONS FROM THE CASE STUDIES 29

**CHAPTER 4: STRATEGIC LEADERSHIP: A CONCEPTUAL FRAMEWORK 31**
MODELING STRATEGIC LEADERSHIP 32
STRUCTURING THE FIRM AS A SELF-ORGANIZING SYSTEM 33
GUIDING THE FIRM TOWARD STRATEGIC END-STATES 34
RATIONALE: THE STRATEGIC LEADERSHIP IMPERATIVE 35
Information Technology 36
The E-Economy 37
Molecularization 38
The E-Business Model 38
The Internet Culture 38
Punctuated Chaos/Edge of Chaos 39
The Digital Organization: Doing Business at the Speed of Thought 40
The Virtual Organization 41
Implications for the Job of the Chief Executive 41
IS THE STRATEGIC LEADERSHIP MODEL PRACTICAL? 43
Can Employees Realistically Function as a Self-Organizing System? 44
Can the Self-Organizing System Concept Be Applied in a Unionized Workforce? 44
Limitations of Self-Organization 47
Strategic Leadership and Type of Firm 47

**CHAPTER 5: STRUCTURING THE FIRM AS A SELF-ORGANIZING SYSTEM 51**
TRADITIONAL ORGANIZATIONAL STRUCTURES 52
THE EMERGENCE OF NEW ORGANIZATIONAL PARADIGMS 54
The Emergence of the Virtual Organization Model 55

The Emergence of the E-Organization Model 58
THE SELF-ORGANIZING SYSTEM'S PARADIGM 59
PRINCIPLES OF BUILDING SELF-ORGANIZING SYSTEMS 61
Distributed Being 62
Networked Being 62
Control from the Bottom Up 62
Cultivation of Increasing Returns 62
Growing by "Chunking" 63
Maximizing the Fringes 63
Honoring Errors 63
Persistent Disequilibrium 63
Pursuing No Optima 64
Self-Changing Change Rules 64
VARIATIONS ON THE THEME OF THE SELF-ORGANIZING SYSTEM 64

## CHAPTER 6: GUIDING THE FIRM TOWARD STRATEGIC END STATES: AN OVERVIEW 69

ACTIVITIES OF THE SELF-ORGANIZING SYSTEM 70
Turbulence Sensing and Interpretation Activities 70
Response Activities 71
Strategic Renewal Activities 73
GUIDING SELF-ORGANIZATION ACTIVITIES 73
INDUCING AND ORCHESTRATING STRATEGIC COLLABORATION 75
Creating an Environment Conducive to Strategic Collaboration 75
Inducing and Stimulating Strategic Conversation 77
Marshalling Strategic Conversation to Strategic Action 79
Acknowledging and Rewarding the Achievements of Strategic Collaboration 81
Affirming Accountability and Governance 81
Exercising Personal Influence 81

## CHAPTER 7: TURBULENCE SENSING AND INTERPRETATION: AN OVERVIEW 85

THE CONCEPT OF TURBULENCE 86
THE NATURE OF TURBULENCE 86
An Academic Perspective on Turbulence 87
A CEO's Perspective on Turbulence 88
A Complexity Science Perspective on Turbulence 89
EXPERIENCING TURBULENCE 92
GUIDING TURBULENCE SENSING ACTIVITIES 93
Creating an Environment Conducive to Collaboration 93
Inducing and Stimulating Conversation on Sensing Turbulence 94
Marshalling Strategic Conversation to Strategic Action 95
Acknowledging and Rewarding the Achievements of Collaborative Turbulence Sensing 95
Affirming Accountability and Governance 96
Exercising Personal Influence 96

## CHAPTER 8: SENSING PRESENT TURBULENCE 99

ANALYSIS 100
Macro-Environmental Analysis 101
Industry Analysis 103
Competitor Analysis 105
MICROANALYSIS: ANALYSIS OF THE FIRM 107
Financial Analysis 107
SWOT/WOTS-UP ANALYSIS 107

PATTERN RECOGNITION 111
MAPPING 113

## CHAPTER 9: SENSING FUTURE TURBULENCE 117

THINKING ABOUT THE FUTURE 118
APPROACHES FOR SENSING FUTURE TURBULENCE 119
I. Intuitive Approaches 119
FLASH OF GENIUS 119
INTUITION 120
EXPERIENCE 121
EXPERT OPINION 122
GROUP METHODS 123
II. Forecasting 123
THE FORECASTING PROCESS 123
FORECASTING METHODS 125
APPLICATIONS OF FORECASTING 128
III. Scenario Construction: Alternative Futures 128
THE CONCEPT OF "ALTERNATIVE FUTURES" 129
THE NATURE OF SCENARIOS 130
PROCESS OF CONSTRUCTING SCENARIOS 132
USING SCENARIOS 137

## CHAPTER 10: INTERPRETING TURBULENCE 139

THE NATURE OF INTERPRETATION 140
FACTORS COMPLICATING THE INTERPRETATION PROCESS 141
Ambiguity 142
NATURE OF AMBIGUITY 142
APPROACHES FOR TACKLING AMBIGUITY 142
Complexity 145
NATURE OF COMPLEXITY 145
Reduction: An Approach for Tackling the "Too Many Factors" Complexity 146
Approaches for Dealing with "Tip-of-the-Iceberg" Complexity 149
A FRAMEWORK FOR TURBULENCE INTERPRETATION: ISSUES ANALYSIS 149
The Concept of Issues 150
ANATOMY OF AN ISSUE 150
WHAT MAKES AN ISSUE STRATEGIC? 151
ISSUES ANALYSIS METHODOLOGY 152
Phase I: Developing the Issue Pool 152
Phase II: Impact Analysis 154
1. PRELIMINARY IMPACT ANALYSIS 154
2. CROSS IMPACT ANALYSIS 155
3. SCOPE ANALYSIS 157
Phase III: Prioritization and Diagnosis 159
1. PRIORITIZATION 159
2. DIAGNOSIS: TRACING ISSUES TO THEIR UNDERLYING CAUSES 159

## CHAPTER 11: FORMULATING STRATEGIC RESPONSE: AN OVERVIEW 163

A CONCEPT OF STRATEGIC RESPONSE 164
Anatomy of Strategic Response 164
SCENARIO PLANNING 167
1. Determining Strategic Issues 168
2. Formulating Alternative Responses to Each Issue: 168
3. Formulating Alternative Complete Strategies to Address the Situation in its Totality 171
4. Evaluating Alternative Strategies 171
5. Choosing from among Alternative Strategies 173
Contingency Planning 174
Implementation Planning 176

FURTHER APPLICATIONS OF SCENARIO PLANNING 176
Scenario Planning for an Overarching Goal 177
Scenario Planning for a Particular Future 179
Scenario Planning for Strategy Experimentation 182

## CHAPTER 12: STRATEGIC RESPONSE: MANEUVER 189
CONCEPT OF MANEUVER 190
MANEUVER: THE FOCAL ELEMENT OF BUSINESS STRATEGY 191
BUSINESS MANEUVER: A CONCEPTUAL FRAMEWORK 193
Establishing Corporate Objectives 193
Structure of Maneuver 195
I. OPPORTUNITIES AND CHALLENGES/ NEW STRATEGIC END-STATE 196
II. THE STRATEGIC THRUST 197
III. PERIPHERAL STRATEGIC THRUSTS 209
IV. THE BUSINESS MODEL 209
V. SYSTEM OF MOVES 213
Formulating Maneuver in the Single Business Firm 215
Maneuver in the Context of the Multi-Business Firm 217
GUIDING MANEUVER FORMULATION 221
Creating an Environment Conducive to Collaboration 222
Inducing and Stimulating Conversation on Maneuver 222
Marshalling Strategic Conversation to Strategic Action 222
Affirming Accountability and Governance 223
Exercising Personal Influence 223

## CHAPTER 13: GUIDING MANEUVER AS IT UNFOLDS IN THE MARKETPLACE 227
REALITIES OF IMPLEMENTATION 228
GUIDING MANEUVER IMPLEMENTATION 230
Coordination and Integration 230
1. ASSURANCE OF A CONTINUOUS SUPPLY OF RESOURCES 231
2. KEEPING THE VISION 231
3. MOBILIZING VALUES AND BELIEF SYSTEMS 232
4. POWERING THE INFORMATION NETWORK 233
5. SPREADING BEST PRACTICES 233
Nurturing Self-organization 233
1. ASSURING INDIVIDUAL AUTONOMY 234
2. MANAGING CONTENTION 235
3. REWARDING 236
4. PRACTICING DELIBERATE AMBIGUITY 237
5. ENABLING 238
Maintaining a Supportive Climate 238
1. MAINTAINING VISIBILITY 238
2. BUILDING TRUST 239
3. KEEPING MORALE HIGH 239
Monitoring the Unfolding Maneuver 243
1. PIECING TOGETHER THE EMERGING MANEUVER 243
2. CHALLENGING RESULTS 243
3. CHALLENGING PARADIGMS 244

## CHAPTER 14: STRATEGIC RESPONSE: CAPABILITY 247
THE NATURE OF CAPABILITY 248
Managerial/Organizational Capability 248
Process Capability 248
Capability As Capacity for Action 250
Capability As Competencies 250

A PROPOSED CONCEPT OF CAPABILITY FOR THE SINGLE BUSINESS FIRM 251
Capacity for Action 251
Resources, Processes, and Functions 253
Manner of Using Resources 255
Competencies 256
CAPABILITY DEVELOPMENT 257
Capability Planning 257
Acquisition of Resources 257
Timing of Resource Acquisition 259
Capability of the Multi-Business Firm 259
Capacity to Add New Entries to the Portfolio 260
Capacity to Position Entries within the Portfolio 260
Capacity to Control the Sizes of Entries 260
GUIDING CAPABILITY ACTIVITIES 262
Creating an Environment Conducive to Collaboration for Capability Building 262
Inducing and Stimulating Conversation on Capability 263
Marshalling Strategic Conversation to Strategic Action 263
Affirming Accountability and Governance 263
Exercising Personal Influence 263

## CHAPTER 15: STRATEGIC RESPONSE: STRUCTURE 267
ORGANIZATIONAL STRUCTURE 268
The Horizontal Dimension 268
The Vertical Dimension 269
Activity Flows 269
STRUCTURE ACTIVITIES IN THE SELF-ORGANIZING FIRM 272
Formation of Modules 272
The Project Concept 275

Distributing Power: Empowerment 276
Coordination and Integration 277
GUIDING STRUCTURE ACTIVITIES 279
Creating an Environment Conducive to Collaboration 279
Inducing and Stimulating Conversation on Structure 280
Marshalling Strategic Conversation to Action on Structure 281
Affirming Accountability and Governance 281
Exercising Personal Influence 281

## CHAPTER 16: STRATEGIC RESPONSE: VISION 283
THE CONCEPT OF VISION 284
A PROPOSED CONCEPT OF VISION 288
A WORLDVIEW 290
1. View of the Macro-Environment 290
2. View of the Industry 290
3. Opportunity Arena 291
4. Key Success Factors (KSG's) 292
VISION OF THE FIRM 293
1. Purpose 293
2. Business Model 294
3. Competencies 294
4. Character 295
5. Envisioned Outcomes: Desired Strategic End-State 296
The Difference between Vision, Mission, and Strategic Intent 296
Vision in the Context of the Multi-Business Firm 297
Vision of the Firm 299
VISIONING 302
Approaches for Structuring Organizational Visioning 302
Visioning Activities in the Self-Organizing Firm: A Proposed Framework 307

GUIDING VISIONING ACTIVITIES 310

Creating an Environment Conducive to Collaboration for Visioning 310

Inducing and Stimulating Conversation on Vision 311

Marshalling Strategic Conversation to Vision Action 311

Affirming Accountability and Governance 311

Exercising Personal Influence 311

## CHAPTER 17: STRATEGIC RENEWAL 317

CORPORATE RENEWAL 319

RENEWAL ACTIVITIES OF THE SELF-ORGANIZING FIRM 320

CONNECTING WITH THE CHANGING ENVIRONMENT 321

Mapping the Unfolding Environment 321

Mapping the Firm's Strategic Configuration 321

Mapping the Firm's Strategic End-State 323

Assessing Unfolding End-States 331

ENVISIONING THE NEXT GENERATION COMPANY 333

Envisioning the Trajectory of the Changing Environment 333

Envisioning the Next Generation Company 334

TRANSFORMATION: BECOMING THE NEXT GENERATION COMPANY 334

Renewal Platforms 335

GUIDING STRATEGIC RENEWAL ACTIVITIES 337

Creating an Environment Conducive to Renewal Collaborative Action 338

Inducing and Stimulating Renewal Conversation 339

Marshalling Conversation to Collaborative Renewal Action 340

Acknowledging and Rewarding Collaborative Renewal Action 340

Fusing Renewal into Accountability and Governance 341

Exercising Personal Leadership of the Renewal Effort 341

## APPENDIX I: A RESEARCH NOTE 345

## SELECTED BIBLIOGRAPHY 351

# CHAPTER 1

# INTRODUCTION

This book is about how to run the business firm in today's turbulent world. It is essentially a body of concepts and conceptual frameworks or simply blueprints for managing the contemporary firm. To ground such concepts and frameworks in reality, they were derived from an examination of the "work" of progressive CEOs, for they are the people who actually run companies. They have also pioneered new approaches for leading their organizations.

The work of the CEO has always been the subject of study, starting with Chester L. Bernard's seminal work on the functions of the executive published in the 1930s. Current developments in the new economy behoove us to reopen the subject one more time. Developments like the Internet, the e-business revolution, the digital organization, and the virtual corporation, among others, have altered the fundamentals of doing business and running a business. In the process, they restructured the work the CEO in substantial ways. To appreciate the extent of the change, let us briefly examine the history of the CEO's job.

Until the 1970s, the content of the chief executive's job had a clear-cut theme: to command and control the firm in order to maximize return to shareholders. The business world was stable and predictable. The CEO established objectives and strategies to realize the intended return and then proceeded to impose them on the marketplace. To do so, the primary instrument was the organization. To that end, the chief executive designed an organization inspired by the machine model. The parts of the machine were configured using the principles of division of labor, specialization, and departmentalization. These parts functioned according to procedures inspired by scientific management and bureaucracy. To ensure employees' compliance with the prescribed strategy and procedures, an extensive chain of command was installed based on the principle of span of control, which resulted in an elaborate hierarchy. Nothing is to be left to the discretion of the employees for they were mainly a factor of production. Good results materialized in those days thus reinforcing this management model. The chief executive was the general, the supreme commander, the well of all wisdom, and the source of creative strategic thoughts.

In the decade of the 1980s, the business world turned somewhat chaotic. The age of globalization began. Foreign competitors made serious inroads in the major industries. High Tech reformatted the way business does business. The success of Japanese firms (at the expense of domestic firms) triggered considerable interest in Japanese management practices. The thrust of the CEO's work turned to changing their companies to cope with a changing world. CEOs thought that their job was managing strategic change or transforming the company to be a fast, agile competitor. Although they sought to transform the company, CEOs continued to practice as if they were in the 1970s. They worked to maximize shareholders' wealth and continued to chart strategy and control the organization. There were attempts to apply Japanese management methods. Some were implemented at the lower echelons of the organization, but the chief executive's job did not change much.

Interestingly enough, there was another model of the CEO's job at that time, the Silicon Valley CEO. This type of CEO viewed the chief executive as just another team member rather than supreme commander. In the Silicon Valley model, knowledge workers exercised considerable powers accorded to them willingly by the CEO. To the traditional CEO, Silicon Valley companies were described as a camp run amuck. Most CEOs felt that the Silicon Valley model could not be applied to their firms.

In the 1990s, the business world became more chaotic. Globalization accelerated and in the process altered the way companies did business. Information technology transformed the economy and society. The substance and rate of change increased to a dizzying speed. It was becoming clear that the CEO and the top management team could not stay abreast of a rapidly changing business world. The job of the CEO, for the first time, underwent some radical restructuring. Ownership of many of the strategic matters, along with the power to deal with them, was transferred to those close to the customer. The company's organization was downsized and delayered. Bureaucracy (systems and procedures) was simplified, if not abolished.

In the 2000s, the business world is brimming with unprecedented trends that are radically restructuring it. Such dynamics will press for a continued reconfiguration of the roles and functions of the chief executive. Notable among these trends are: the emergence of the Internet as a major marketplace; the e-business revolution; the movement from the mass to the molecular (mass customization); the entry of a generation of people growing up connected to the Internet; the spread of the digital organization that does business at the speed of thought; and, last but not least, the growing popularity of the virtual corporation (a company that appears to exist but in reality does not). All of these developments are altering how the CEO runs the firm. As a *Fortune Magazine* article observed, the power of the position has been eroded so much so, that ". . . corporate leaders are going to resemble not so much captains of ships as candidates running for office."[1] There is a need for a concept that reflects these new realities.

## TOWARD A CONCEPT OF THE CEO'S WORK

Our contemporary business world appears to assume a state of punctuated chaos, ". . . a state of constant upheaval marked by brief respites."[2] Others described this state as "edge of chaos," a condition where things are neither totally chaotic nor orderly; a mix of chaos and order in one stream.[3] Both these descriptors seem to depict the business world of the 2000s.

In an edge-of-chaos world, the marketplace changes constantly. It is turbulent. The parts of the firm that interface with this marketplace (e.g., sales, purchasing, production, financing, human resources, etc.) receive the brunt of the continuous pounding by relentless turbulence. It is not humanly possible for the CEO and the management team to stay on top of things inside and/or outside the firm. Progressive CEOs soon discovered that if the firm is to cope with the chaos of the marketplace, its parts must be freed to arrange and rearrange themselves so that they may align themselves with the changing conditions in a timely fashion. Employees (who make up the parts) must be empowered to become frontline entrepreneurs with full decision making powers and control over resources. They are close to the market and hence they know what needs to be done and how it should be done. Some CEOs went as far as to let the employees lead.[4] These CEOs worked to build a self-managing company that is not dependent on the CEO. They saw themselves as "support personnel" or "resource persons" to these frontline entrepreneurs. They strove to make the company a self-organizing system, a model borrowed from natural systems. The main feature of self-organizing systems is their capacity to recover after every environmental disruption grabbing on to new opportunities while preserving their wholeness.

Once these CEOs structure the company as a self-organizing system, they step back and let the frontline entrepreneurs function in a self-organizing manner. They trust them to decide what needs to be done and to carry it out, without frequent referral to and intervention from the top. In such a set-up, strategy (the traditional prerogative of the CEO) evolves as a semicoherent direction out of the numerous initiatives of empowered people.[5] The CEO "spots" it from these diverse initiatives rather than dictate it in advance.

Now that the CEO has transferred power to frontline entrepreneurs and he/she no longer dictates strategy, what is left for him/her to do? As autonomous frontline entrepreneurs self-organize (i.e., do things their way), there will be a multitude of visions, positions, and initiatives in the firm. This situation might even border on anarchy. There is the potential for conflict, loss of unity, and erratic direction. These are the risks of making the firm self-organizing. However, no CEO can afford loss of direction in a changing world. To compensate for these consequences, progressive CEOs act as the coordinating and unifying force that brings these diverse individuals and units together. They do so by inducing strategic collaboration among those frontline entrepreneurs and then they orchestrate this collaboration by steering it in the direction of a promising strategic end-state for the firm. A strategic end-state is a profitable, defensible position in the marketplace that a firm arrives at after an episode of struggle with turbulence. As some CEOs refer to it, orchestrating strategic collaboration in a self-organizing setting is like "steering a mob" or "riding a wild tiger." In essence, the work of the CEO is to guide a self-organizing company toward a strategic end-state that would please its stakeholders.

To summarize, the new paradigm of managing the firm in the turbulent world of the 2000s views the work of the chief executive as twofold: (1) structuring the firm as a self-organizing system; and (2) guiding this system toward strategic end-states that would please its stakeholders.

## OVERVIEW OF THE BOOK

This book consists of seventeen chapters. Exhibit 1.1 shows the sequence and arrangement of these chapters. The current chapter sets the stage by introducing the overall thrust of the book, presenting its layout, and previewing its content. Since the thrust of this book represents a point of departure from current theory, it is crucial to survey theory at the outset. Accordingly, in Chapter 2, we examine the two popular constructs that reportedly capture the essence of the CEO's work, namely strategic management, and general management. The point of departure begins in Chapter 3 when we survey the practices of actual CEOs to see if they conform to theory. A small sample drawn from the database of this study is presented in the form of mini-case studies. The cases suggest that CEOs practices are driven by a different paradigm. Some writers like Wilson, called this new paradigm "strategic leadership."[6] In Chapter 4, we present a model of strategic leadership. The model is a conceptual framework derived from a larger study, as outlined in the research note in the appendix. As suggested earlier, the model comprises two broad variables: structuring the firm as a self-organizing system; and, guiding this system toward strategic end-states. The presentation in Chapter 4 is only an overview of the model. Its components are described in more detail in Chapters 5 and 6.

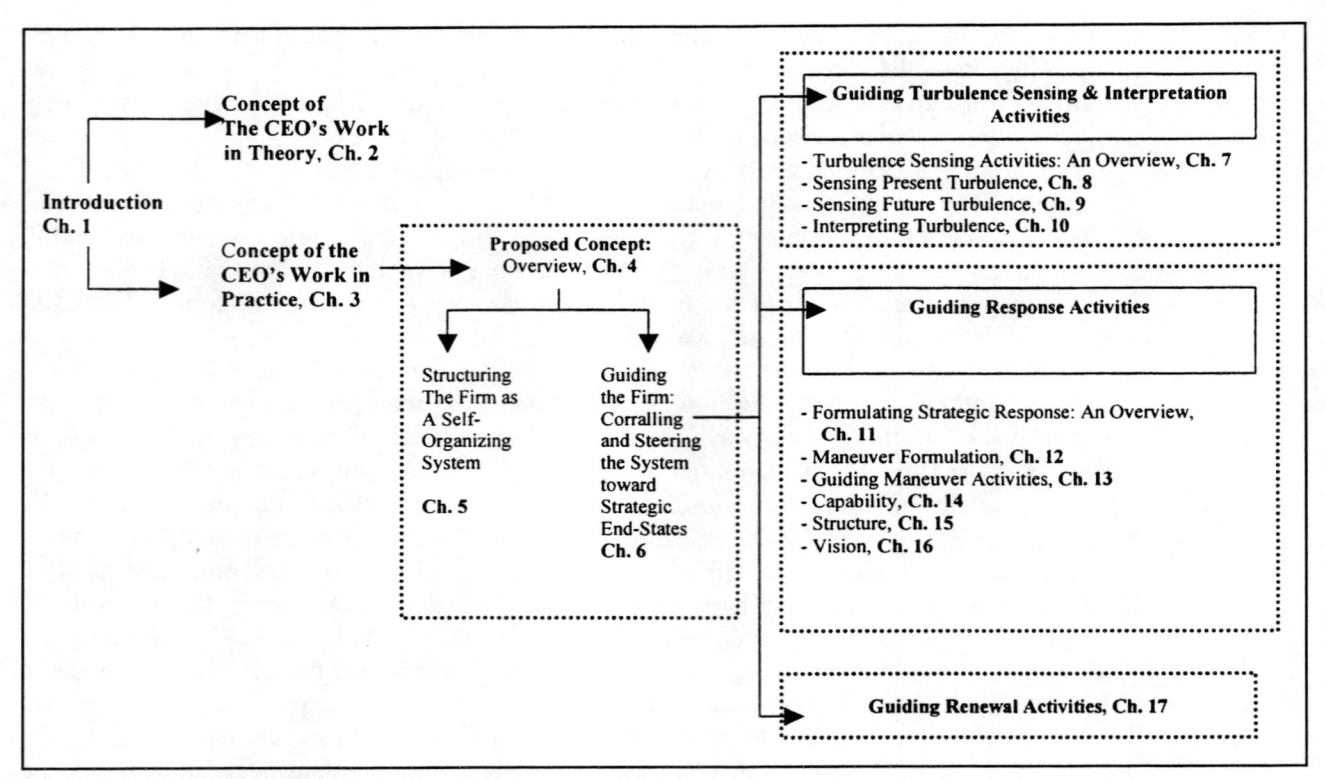

Exhibit 1.1: Flow of the Presentation of Chapters

Chapter 5 introduces the concept of the self-organizing system and describes the principles of configuring or reconfiguring a firm to make it self-organizing. In Chapter 6, we get into the details of the CEO's work in guiding the firm toward a strategic end-state. The focal topic of that chapter is inducing and orchestrating strategic collaboration. There, we present a framework that organizes the various activities in which the progressive CEO engages to bring about strategic collaboration in a self-organizing firm.

Inducing and orchestrating strategic collaboration is about corralling and steering the diverse activities by various empowered individuals and groups operating in a self-organizing fashion. These activities pertain to sensing turbulence in the firm's environment and responding to it, without an externally imposed plan or directive. They fall into three categories: turbulence sensing and interpretation, responding to turbulence, and strategic renewal. Chapters 7 to 17 explore each category and its subsets. At all times, our objective is to understand these activities with a view toward guiding them.

Chapters 7 to 10 deal with turbulence sensing and interpretation. In Chapter 7, this category and its subset are overviewed. It starts with a study of the phenomenon of turbulence and how it affects the business firm. Then, it describes the various activities involved in sensing and interpreting turbulence. Chapter 8 delves into the topic of sensing impending turbulence and techniques for mapping it such as environmental analysis, industry analysis, SWOT analysis, vulnerability analysis, and the like. Because the future is crucial in every business decision, the topic of anticipating future turbulence is examined in Chapter 9. In it, we present methods for anticipating the future, particularly forecasting and scenarios construction. Once mapped, present and future turbulence must be peered through to determine what ramifications they have for the firm. This is the topic of Chapter 10, interpreting turbulence. The focal methodology here is issues analysis, which boils turbulence information down to a set of top-priority strategic issues to which the firm must respond.

Given these strategic issues, the activities involved in responding to turbulence are triggered. They generally revolve around formulating and implementing a strategy that would embody an intelligent response. This strategy has four interdependent, interlocking aspects: maneuver, capability, structure, and vision. The presentation of response activities spans chapters 11–16. Chapter 11 sets the stage for formulating a good strategic response using the methodology of scenario planning. Maneuver is a calculated scheme or game plan designed to keep the non-controllable forces of turbulence at bay while the firm proceeds toward its desired end-state. It is the subject of chapters 12 and 13. Chapter 12 deals with three critical aspects of maneuver: (1) formulating a strategic thrust to focus the firm's resources; (2) translating this thrust into a business model or a design to create and deliver superior value to the customers, to win them over despite competitors; and, (3) translating this model into a coherent system of moves to be carried out in the marketplace. Chapter 13 surveys the various tasks of the CEO as he/she induces and orchestrates strategic collaboration during the course of implementing a planned maneuver. The discussion gets into matters such as maintaining a supportive climate, coordination, integration, monitoring implementation, and assessing ensuing results.

Maneuver prerequires two sets of activities as its underpinnings: building capability, and, structuring the organization. Capability activities are the topic of Chapter 14 where a framework that organizes them is introduced. The framework not only takes into account resources but also the manner of using them to ignite the energy in them, particularly the use of improvisation, stretch, and leverage. Chapter 15 deals with the activities involved in structuring the organization of the firm so that capability may be deployed effectively and efficiently as the maneuver is implemented. In that chapter, principles are introduced for building a fluid structure such as the modular concept, the project concept, governance systems, and the like.

Maneuver, along with capability and structure, do not happen in a vacuum. Maneuver is the path toward a strategic end-state (a destination, or simply a vision), at which the firm aspires to arrive. Although the strategic end-state is often established in advance to guide maneuver, it is sometimes discovered *en route* or on the way to a pre-established one. Vision is the subject of Chapter 16 where the literature will be reviewed and a framework for vision will be proposed.

The third set of activities of the self-organizing firm pertains to renewing itself, or evolving into the "next-generation company." We label this strategic renewal. Renewal is the capacity of the firm to evolve with its evolving environment. It amounts to reinventing the firm every now and then since turbulence periodically restructures the environment in a radical manner.

In concluding, it is worth stressing that the concepts, tools, and techniques presented in this book are derived from two sources. First, the research study undertaken by the author provided conceptual frameworks that served as skeletons or conceptual maps. Second, these conceptual frameworks were fleshed out by including findings and ideas from the literature, particularly the writings of CEOs, management consultants, and researchers in the fields of strategic management, general management, and business policy.

# ENDNOTES

1. Huey, J., "The New Post-Heroic Leadership," *Fortune*, February 21, 1994, pp. 42–44.
2. Gates III, W.H., *Business @ the Speed of Thought: Using a Digital Nervous System*, New York, NY: Warner Books, 1999.

3. Brown, S.L. and K.M. Eisenhardt, *Competing on the Edge,* Boston, MA: Harvard Business School Press, 1998.

4. Belasco, J.A., and R.C. Stayer, *Flight of the Buffalo: Soaring to Excellence; Learning to Let Employees Lead*, New York, NY: Warner Books, 1993.

5. Brown and Eisenhardt, op. cit.

6. Wilson, I., "The 5 Compasses of Strategic Leadership," *Strategy & Leadership*, Vol. 24, No. 4, July/August, 1996, pp. 26–31.

# CHAPTER 2

# Concept of the Work of the CEO in Theory

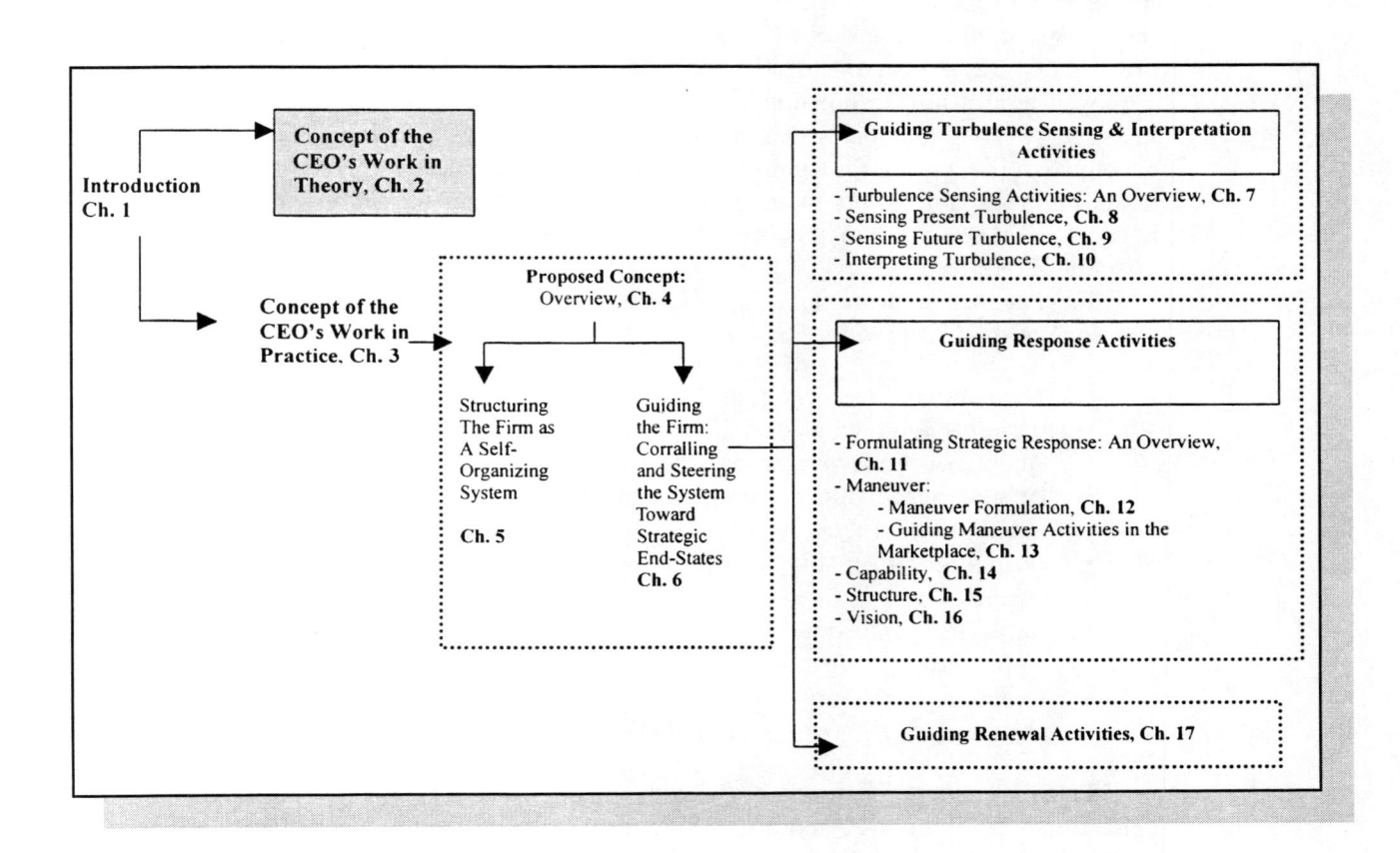

```
Introduction          Concept of the
Ch. 1                 CEO's Work in
                      Theory, Ch. 2                    Guiding Turbulence Sensing & Interpretation
                                                                         Activities

                                                  - Turbulence Sensing Activities: An Overview, Ch. 7
                                                  - Sensing Present Turbulence, Ch. 8
                      Proposed Concept:           - Sensing Future Turbulence, Ch. 9
                      Overview, Ch. 4             - Interpreting Turbulence, Ch. 10
     Concept of the
     CEO's Work in
     Practice, Ch. 3                                        Guiding Response Activities


              Structuring    Guiding
              The Firm as    the Firm:
              A Self-        Corralling
              Organizing     and Steering      - Formulating Strategic Response: An Overview,
              System         the System          Ch. 11
                             Toward            - Maneuver:
              Ch. 5          Strategic             - Maneuver Formulation, Ch. 12
                             End-States            - Guiding Maneuver Activities in the
                             Ch. 6                   Marketplace, Ch. 13
                                               - Capability, Ch. 14
                                               - Structure, Ch. 15
                                               - Vision, Ch. 16


                                                          Guiding Renewal Activities, Ch. 17
```

This chapter begins our exploration of the work of the CEO. To establish a benchmark, we examine the concept of the CEO's work in theory as presented in business management literature. It is worth noting that a firm theory is yet to emerge. As Bower *et al* noted, "Many attempts to characterize executive roles and functions come to very little."[1] With regard to the job of the chief executive, there are two main schools of thought: general management and strategic management. Each will be described briefly below. The emphasis will be on strategic management since it seems to be the most popular.

# GENERAL MANAGEMENT

Pioneered by the Harvard Business School's faculty, the general management view was perhaps the first attempt to conceptualize the work of the CEO. The CEO is viewed as a generalist whose responsibility is to run the entire business as opposed to a singular function (e.g., marketing or finance) or a process (e.g., human resource management). The general management school once articulated a concept of the chief executive's work as comprising three roles and four groups of functions.[2] The three roles were stated as (1) the leader of the organization, (2) the personal leader for subordinates, and (3) the architect of organizational purpose—establishing or presiding over goal setting, resource allocation, and making/ratifying strategy. They then described the functions of the CEO as follows: "The four functions encompass (1) securing the attainment of planned results in the present, (2) developing an organization capable of producing both technical achievement and human satisfaction, (3) making a distinctive personal contribution, and (4) planning and executing policy decisions affecting future results."[3]

In a later work, Bower *et al*, offered this sample of responsibilities as an illustration of the scope of the CEO's work:[4]

- The results of the behavior of the corporation.
- Earnings and the balance sheet.
- Quality of products and services.
- Personal leadership to the employees in the firm.
- Safety of plant facilities.
- Corporate citizenship of the company in the towns and countries where it does business.
- Explaining and dealing with gaffs and crimes committed by the company's employees.
- Explaining problems such as decreased earnings, an environmental disaster, or a change in some government policy—in a knowledgeable way.

Further, Bower *et al* conceptualized the work of the CEO in terms of three roles: strategist, organization builder, and doer.[5] They further identified the tasks that are involved in performing these three roles as follows:

"- crafting the strategy of the organization and communicating it to the organization
- managing the resource allocation process so that it reflects the strategy
- managing the selection, training, and progress of the people and building a positive work environment, designing the structure and systems that provide context for the operations—both so that capabilities increase in areas that permit moving toward strategic objectives
- intervening personally where necessary to drive forward and raise the quality of day-to-day performance"[6]

# STRATEGIC MANAGEMENT

The concept of strategic management dates back to the late 1970s when Schendel and Hofer introduced it as an alternative to general management.[7] Rowe, *et al* distinguished between general management and strategic management as follows:

> "Unlike general management, which is primarily concerned with internal operations, strategic management is equally concerned with the external and the internal environment. An essential objective of strategic management is to match the organization's internal capability with the external opportunities and threats in order to formulate strategies that will achieve basic goals and maintain organizational values. Strategic management also enables the organization to adapt profitably to the vagaries of an unpredictable environment."[8]

## Schendel and Hofer

Schendel and Hofer viewed the essence of strategic management as ". . . developing and utilizing the strategy which is to guide the organization's operations."[9] They believed that five major themes form a paradigm or a model of strategic leadership as follows:[10]

1. Organizational Goal Formation: The first task of strategic management is to formulate a set of goals for the organization.
2. Environmental Analysis: The second step in strategic management is to analyze the environment in which the firm operates in order to forecast it and to come to grips with any discontinuities that the firm might encounter in the future.
3. Strategy Formulation: This step begins with the evaluation of existing strategy to assess its viability as a future strategy. Failing that, a new strategy is then formulated by generating alternatives and evaluating them to arrive at the best option. The essence of strategy formulation is creating designs for matching the firm's strengths and weaknesses with the environmental opportunities and threats.
4. Strategy Implementation: The fourth step is to translate the strategy into action and to achieve integration among parts of the organization. Often this involves the formulation of operational plans (or implementation plans), the designing or configuring of the organizational structure, instituting and enforcing strategic control, and creating a corporate culture conducive to efficient and effective implementation.
5. Strategic Control: This is the last task of the strategic management process. It focuses on ascertaining whether (1) the strategy is being carried out as planned, and (2) whether the results achieved are those intended. Based on this, corrective action is to be taken.

Schendel and Hofer further presented a conceptual framework that shows the various components of strategic management and how they hang together. This is shown in Exhibit 2.1.[11]

Since its introduction in 1979, Schendel and Hofer's model has gained wide acceptance among academics. Over the years, the concept was articulated and interpreted further by many writers as can be seen from the following sample of "newer" derivative conceptualizations.

## Thompson and Strickland

Thompson and Strickland view strategic management as ". . . the managerial tasks of crafting, implementing, and executing company strategies."[12] They amplified the concept as comprising five interrelated managerial tasks as follows:

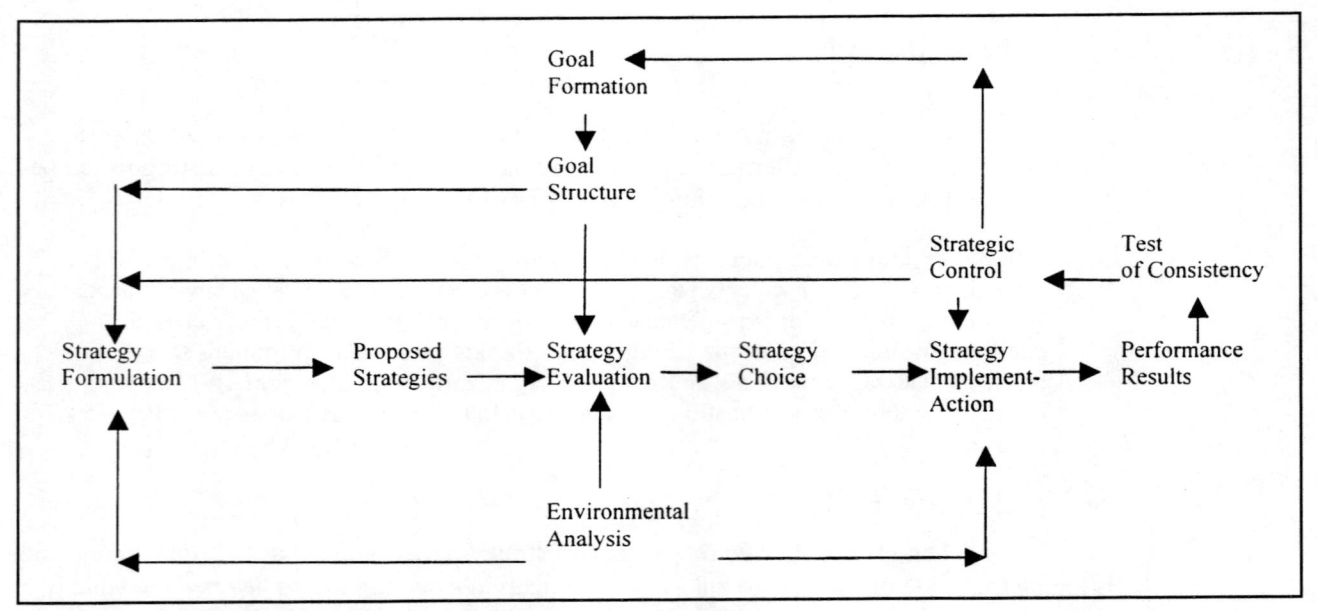

Exhibit 2.1: Schendel and Hofer's Model of Strategic Management

> "1. *Forming a strategic vision of what the company's future business make up will be and where the organization is headed*—so as to provide long-term direction, delineate what kind of enterprise the company is trying to become, and infuse the organization with a sense of purposeful action.
> 2. *Setting objectives*—converting the strategic vision into specific performance outcomes for the company to achieve.
> 3. *Crafting a strategy to achieve the desired outcomes.*
> 4. *Implementing and executing the chosen strategy efficiently and effectively.*
> 5. *Evaluating performance and initiating corrective adjustments in vision, long-term direction, objectives, strategy, or implementation in light of actual experience, changing conditions, new ideas, and new opportunities.*"[13]

Thompson and Strickland organized the components of strategic management in the form of a model as shown in Exhibit 2.2.[14]

## Hitt, Ireland and Hoskisson

According to Hitt, Ireland and Hoskisson, strategic management is ". . . the full set of commitments, decisions, and actions required by a firm to achieve strategic competitiveness and earn above average returns."[15] They also developed the conceptual framework presented in Exhibit 2.3.[16]

## Fahey and Randall

Fahey and Randall reduced strategic management to three main interrelated tasks:

> "1. Managing strategy in the marketplace: designing, executing, and refining strategies that 'win' in a changing marketplace. Strategy is the means by which the organization creates and leverages change in and around the marketplace.
> 2. Managing the organization: continually reconfiguring the organization—how it thinks, how it operates. Without such internal change, the organization cannot hope to hone its capacity to identify, adapt to, and leverage environmental change.

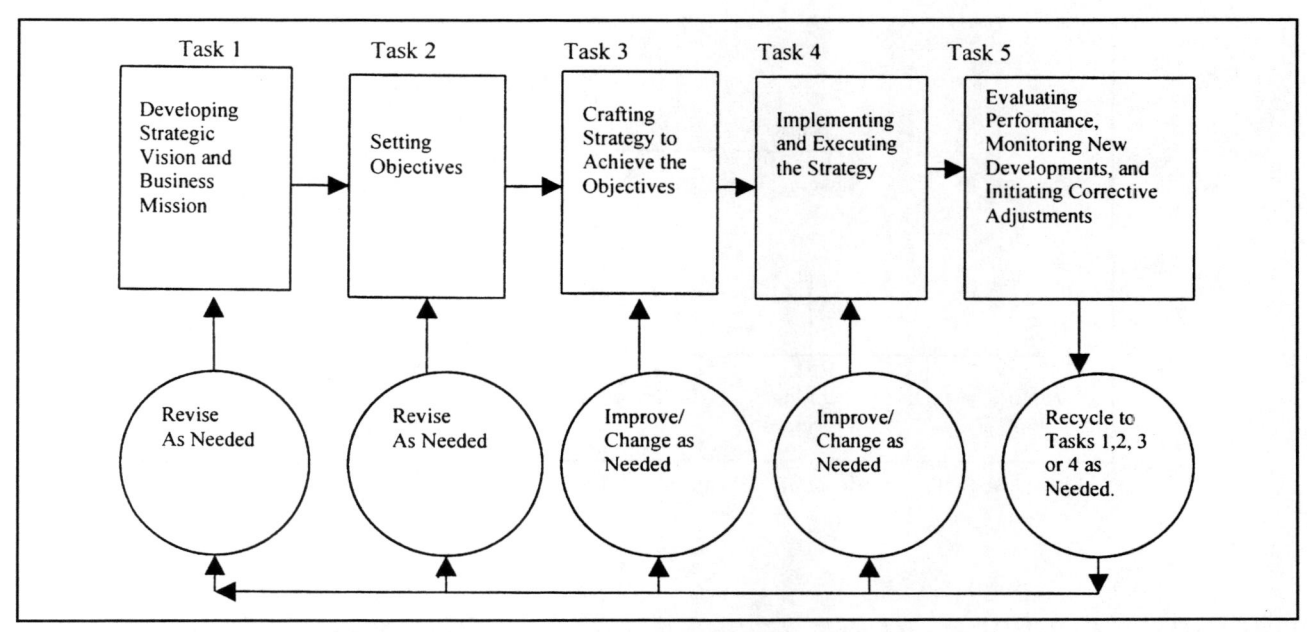

Exhibit 2.2: Thompson and Strickland Model of Strategic Management

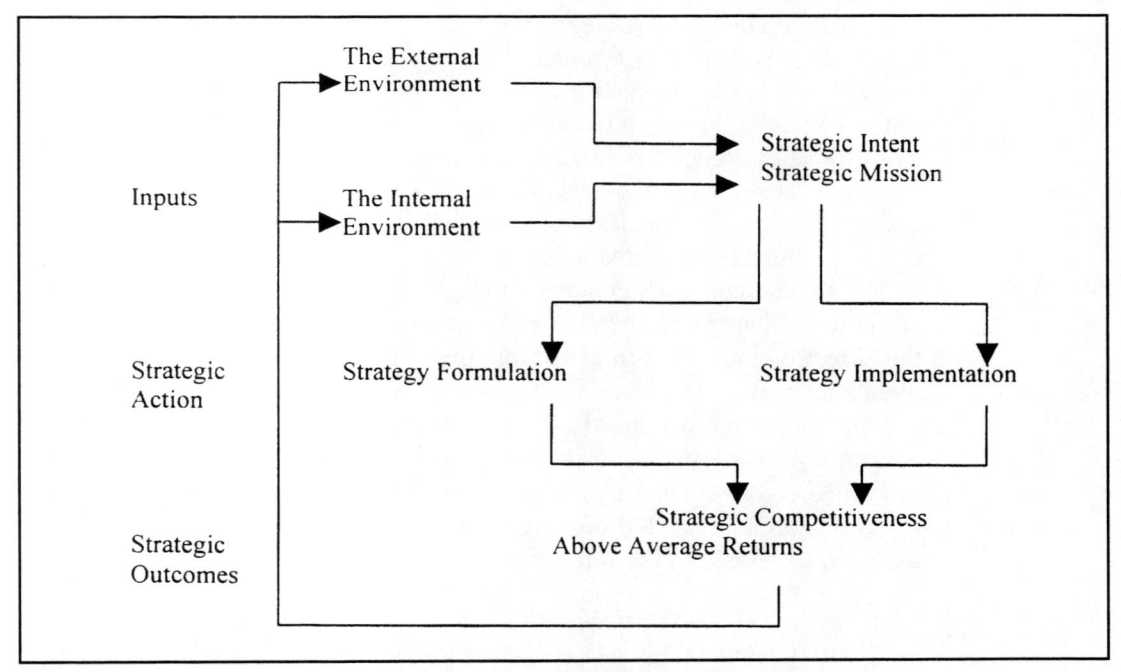

Exhibit 2.3: Hitt, Ireland, and Hoskison's Model of Strategic Management

3. Practicing strategic management: continually enhancing the linkages or 'interface' between strategy (what the organization does in the market place) and organization (what takes place within the organization)."[17]

Their conceptual framework for strategic management is presented as a hierarchy of concepts as shown in Exhibit 2.4.

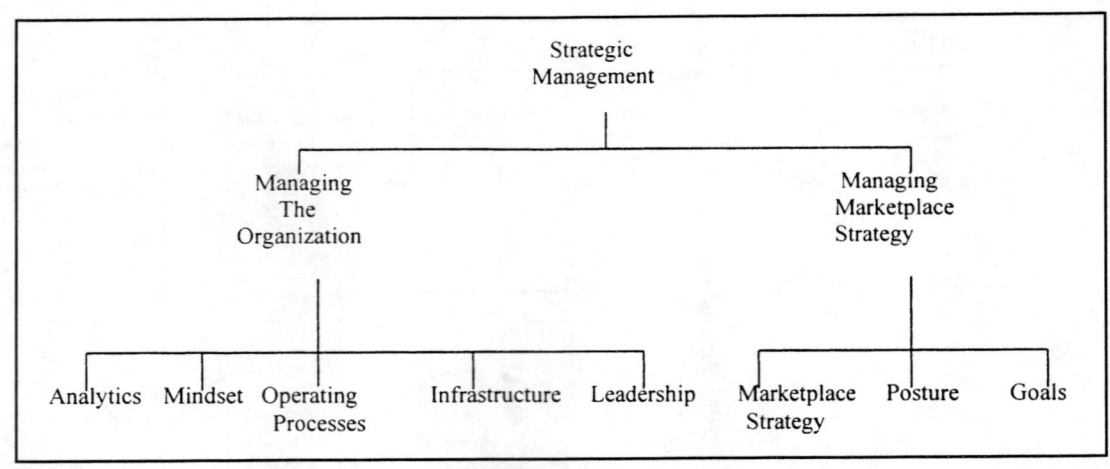

Exhibit 2.4: Fahey and Randall's Strategic Management Model

# THEORY VERSUS REALITY

The preceding brief exploration sheds light on the extent and complexity of the CEO's work. According to the strategic management school, the essence of the CEO's work is aligning the firm with its environment. The purpose of this alignment is to achieve a high degree of goodness of fit between the firm (its resources, strengths, and weaknesses) and the opportunities and the threats in the environment. Such goodness of fit is assumed to translate into a profitable existence for the firm. The process of achieving this fit has been modeled in various ways as shown in the previous exhibits. In most cases, it is viewed as comprising a sequence of steps encompassing the key elements of goal setting, strategy formulation, strategy implementation, and strategic control.

The strategic management paradigm appears to capture the essence of the CEO's work at the time it surfaced, the 1970s. A direction has to be set for the firm. Strategies to pursue this direction must be formulated and implemented. Results must be assessed and this assessment shapes the next round of strategy formulation and implementation. However, one important question must be raised: Is the strategic management paradigm still valid given the current upheavals in the business world in the 2000s? The current business world has been described as punctuated chaos or edge of chaos. Can a paradigm from the 1970s still hold true? Wilson, a respected observer of the business world, was among the first to alert us to the need to revisit and to rethink the concept of strategic management.[18] He wrote:

> "In the 1970s, strategic planning was the corporate mantra in most companies. But as we moved into a new decade, strategic planning was tarred with the brush of 'failure to implement.' In the 1980s, the corporate and consulting world was abuzz with strategic management—the new and improved version of setting direction and creating shareholder wealth. Now, in the 1990s, the focus is strategic leadership."[19]

Wilson's thesis is that there has been a paradigm shift in corporate practice, a shift from strategic management to strategic leadership. He urges us to make a distinction between strategic management and strategic leadership. Why worry about the difference between the two terms "strategic management" and "strategic leadership"? Is it just semantics? Does it really matter? He stresses that the difference is real, concrete, and significant. To visualize the difference, he offers the contrast between "management" and "leadership" shown in Exhibit 2.5.

| MANAGEMENT | LEADERSHIP |
|---|---|
| • Focuses on the present<br>• Deals with "what is"<br>• Executes—controls<br>• Manages things/programs/resources<br>• Focuses on organizational efficiency<br>• Emphasizes hierarchy: chain of command | • Emphasizes the future<br>• Emphasizes setting direction for "what will be"<br>• Gives vision and inspiration<br>• Leads people<br>• Builds the effectiveness of the organization<br>• Emphasizes hierarchy: diffused authority |

Exhibit 2.5: The Paradigm Shift from Management to Leadership

Hargrove also observed a paradigm shift from the traditional top-down (hierarchical) management to lateral leadership.[20] Traditional management rested on two pillars: specialists (e.g., salespersons, engineers, accountants, etc.) and strong managers. In the traditional, hierarchical model, problems are addressed and decisions are made by strong CEOs commanding an organization of specialists. However, he maintains that top-down management and specialization were sound answers for a simpler world, e.g., the world of the 1960s and 1970s. However, hierarchical management is not the most suitable model for the realities of today's world. The contemporary business world is moving toward lateral leadership where the CEO leads from the middle. The lateral CEO manages by stimulating creative collaboration. To help us understand the difference between the two approaches, he developed the contrast shown in Exhibit 2.6.

Citrin and Nef observed a major change in the content of the CEO's job in our current era, the digital age.[21] The digital age has altered the business world radically. It has restructured the economy and made the Internet the new marketplace. It has changed the way business is organized and managed. We now have the digital organization and even "digital leadership." The contrast in Exhibit 2.7 is constructed from their work. It compares the CEO of 1998 and the digitally driven CEO of the 2000s.

The CEOs of the digital age display characteristics that are different from the progressive CEOs of traditional, non-digital corporations. First, they tend to be obsessed about the customer. The customer resides at the very top of the CEO's priority list. Second, they build

| THE HIERARCHICAL CEO | THE LATERAL CEO |
|---|---|
| • Presides over status quo; pursues own agenda; seeks predictable results | • Designates new possibilities; promotes shared understood goals, seeks creative, entrepreneurial results |
| • Relies on traditional structures of organization; views emotions as sign of weakness | • Builds collaborative networks and new patterns of relationships and interactions; shows authenticity and vulnerability |
| • Acts as a know-it-all; is a specialist; equates success with knowing | • Attitude of learning; is a specialist and generalist; equates success with questions |
| • Passionately advocates view in order to win and discourages inquiry; listens as if "out to lunch" or reactively. | • Balances advocacy of views with inquiry into own and others' thinking; listens deeply; understand others |
| • Controls others by diminishing their talents; takes care of others so they will submit | • Empowers others on the job by acknowledging talents and gifts; provides an enabling environment |

Exhibit 2.6: Comparing the Top-Down and the Lateral CEOs

| Profile of the Job of the Progressive CEO of the 1990s | Profile of the Job of the CEO of the Digital Age |
|---|---|
| • Living with integrity and leading by example<br>• Developing a winning strategy or "big ideas"<br>• Building a great management team<br>• Inspiring employees to achieve greatness<br>• Creating a flexible, responsive organization<br>• Tying it all together with reinforcing management and compensations systems | • Obsessing about the customer<br>• Building a flat, cross-functional organization<br>• Managing via business model<br>• Evangelizing and generating positive buzz<br>• Encouraging risk taking for real<br>• Rolling up the sleeves and working hard |

Exhibit 2.7: The CEO of the 1990s and the CEO of the 2000s

flat, cross-functional organizations. They insist on having the employees work together across functional disciplines and on giving them all the information they need to make decisions. The organization is so flat that no employee will be more than three clicks away from others above, below, or at the same level. Third, they manage via a business model rather than detailed strategic plans and programs. They insist on fluid strategy to allow changing with the changing marketplace. In doing so, they create business models which serve as platforms from which many different strategies can be generated. Fourth, they are evangelical on their zeal for the firm's business model and cause. To that extent, they generate a positive buzz inside and outside the firm, particularly with the financial markets. Fifth, they encourage risk taking as a way of doing business. They realize that barriers to entry in the digital economy are low. The only protection is for the company to stay creative and ahead of its competitors. Finally, they are hands-in CEOs. They roll up their sleeves and work side-by-side with everyone else in the organization.

The term "paradigm" was mentioned several times so far. It is worth clarifying at this point. A paradigm is "a constellation of concepts, values, perceptions and practices shared by a community which forms a particular vision of reality that is the basis of the way a community organizes itself."[22]

A paradigm thus becomes a belief system that becomes our "worldview." Paradigms somehow tend to remain unchanged even though the world has changed. Even when they lose touch with the real world, they continue to pose as if they still reflect it. Pascale alerted us to this danger:

> "What gives paradigms their insidious power is that we generally don't distinguish between what's being thought and the paradigm it's being thought through. . . . First, a dominant paradigm is seldom, if ever, stated explicitly; it exists unquestioned. Second, paradigms, once accepted, are clung to tenaciously by our mental apparatus. When questions arise that the older belief system can't answer, the rationalization is: 'We're not clever enough to figure out how it applies yet,' or 'We don't have the right measuring equipment.' . . . Third, the unfolding of a new paradigm is always discontinuous. Intellectual and emotional resistance inevitably arise when a radical way of looking at the world is presented."[23]

During a period of paradigm shift (like our current era), old paradigms continue to linger on as truths. Is this the case of the strategic management paradigm? Aside from the paradigm shift, there are five major concerns that raise further questions about strategic management as a paradigm for the chief executive's work.

In the first place, strategic management refers to management of strategy or management by strategy. Both viewpoints assume that strategy exists. However, research by Inkpen and Choudhary showed that there are many situations where strategy does not exist.[24] There are firms that cannot or will not have a strategy because of the particulars of the situation they are in, e.g., in rapidly changing industries.

Second, strategic management assumes that strategy is something to be "crafted." The implication here is that strategy can be "engineered." Once it is constructed, it will be concrete and clear. However, in today's volatile business world, this is not feasible and may even be undesirable. Research by Brown and Eisenhardt portrays strategy as a semi-coherent direction, an uncertain (possibly fuzzy) concept that evolves from repeated, numerous, diverse, trial-and-error type of initiatives by empowered people.[25] If this is the case, then strategy cannot be crafted. If it is crafted, it will be irrelevant in no time because new chaos and new initiatives will render it obsolete. Many CEOs found that out. Their elaborate strategic plans were not implemented, as intended, by frontline units. If CEOs insist on crafting strategy and on implementing it (as formulated), they are in essence imposing their will on a world beyond their control. This is unrealistic. As Winston Churchill remarked: "[We] assign a larger importance to opportunism and improvisation, seeking to live and conquer in accordance with the unfolding event than to aspire to dominate it often by fundamental decisions."[26]

Third, strategic management models may give the impression that the CEO, as the ultimate strategic manager, performs the sequence of steps in the strategic management process. The reality is that CEOs do not perform all these steps. Evidence from CEOs' practices show that they set boundaries or frameworks and then let employees formulate and implement strategy within such boundaries. As Robert Eaton (former CEO of Chrysler) put it: "My philosophy is, I want to know where we're going and how we're gonna get there. Then I want to get out of the way."[27]

Fourth, strategic management is pivoted on the concept of strategy as a competitive tool. The firm is perceived to be in conflict with its competitors in a zero-sum game. It needs strategy to win this conflict. That is why the concept of strategy was borrowed from the military in the first place. In military literature, strategy refers to "the art of the general." As such, it is predicated on a particular type of conflict, war. However, the military general/war model is designed to deal with a *singular event*, a war. A war erupts in a specific location in time and space, and then it ends. In such a model, strategy is a set of moves and counter moves that end at a specific point in time, the date of cessation of hostilities. This, however, is not the case of the business firm. The business firm is a going concern. Its life is a marathon without a finish line. It does not live and die for or by a single campaign.

Fifth, the strategy model, the core of the strategic management paradigm, assumes that business is a zero-sum game. If one competitor wins, another loses. This is not necessarily so. There are times when all competitors win. Their activities expand the overall market and each obtains an increasing share of a growing pie. In many situations competitors discovered that they all could win if they cooperate and pool resources instead of wasting them fighting one another. The popularity of strategic alliances confirms this conclusion. Competitors like IBM and Apple or GM and Toyota are now collaborators. Where does this leave the basic premise of strategy as a tool for resolving competitive conflict?

Finally, the thrust of strategic management is the deliberate matching of the firm with its environment. This is not a feasible ideal. In our current era, the environment is rapidly changing. The firm itself is rapidly changing. When we have two entities spinning in this fashion, how is a match possible? By the time one comes to grips with a picture of either, it would have changed. Reality is outpacing our ability to grasp it.

## CONCLUSION

General management and strategic management offer conceptualizations of the work of the CEO. The two concepts, however, were products of a different era and as such they were based on a different paradigm. Times have changed. Other paradigms of business management are emerging. A good starting point is to examine the practices of contemporary CEOs. They are the ultimate persons who can define the work of the CEO. Many have written extensively about what they do. Their writings present concepts and paradigms that are truly interesting.[28] We sample them in the next chapter.

## ENDNOTES

1. Bower, J.L., C.A. Bartlet, C.R. Christensen, A.E. Pearson, and K.R. Andrews, *Business Policy: Text and Cases*, (7th ed.), Homewood, IL: Irwin, 1991, p. 14.
2. Ibid., p. 22.
3. Ibid., p. 22.
4. Bower, J. L., C.A. Bartlet, H.E.R. Uyterhoeven, and R.E. Walton, *Business Policy: Managing Strategic Processes,"* Chicago, Ill.: Irwin, 1995, pp. 1–2.
5. Ibid., p. 3.
6. Ibid., p. 3.
7. Schendel, D.E. and C.W. Hofer (editors), *Strategic Management: A New View of Business Policy and Planning*, Boston, MA: Little, Brown, and Company, 1979, pp. 3–22.
8. Rowe, A.J., R.O. Mason, E.E. Dickel, R.B. Mann, and R.J. Mockler, *Strategic Management: A Methodological Approach*, (4th ed.), Reading, MA: Addison-Wesley Publishing Company, 1994, pp. 29–31.
9. Schendel and Hofer, op. cit., p. 11.
10. Schendel, D.E. and C.W. Hofer, op. cit., pp. 14–18.
11. Ibid., p. 15.
12. Thompson, A.A. and A.J. Strickland, *Strategic Management: Concepts and Cases*, 10th ed., Boston, MA: Irwin/McGraw-Hill, 1998, p. 1.
13. Ibid., p. 3.
14. Ibid., p. 4.
15. Hitt, M.A., R.D. Ireland, and R.E. Hoskisson, *Strategic Management: Competitiveness and Globalization*, Minneaopolis/St.Paul, Minn.: West Publishing Company, 1997, p. 5.
16. Ibid., p. 6.
17. Fahey, L., and R.M. Randall, *The Portable MBA in Strategy*, New York, NY: John Wiley & Sons, 1994, pp. 5–7.
18. Wilson, I., "The 5 Compasses of Strategic Leadership," *Strategy & Leadership*, Vol. 24, No. 4, July/August, 1996, pp. 26–31.
19. Ibid.
20. Hargrove, R., *Mastering the Art of Creative Collaboration*, New York, NY: McGraw-Hill, 1998.
21. Citrin, J.M. and T.J. Neff, "Digital Leadership," *Strategy & Business*, First Quarter, 2000, pp. 42–50.
22. Kuhn, T.S., *The Structure of Scientific Revolutions*, Chicago, Ill.: University of Chicago Press, 1970.
23. Pascale, R.T., *Managing On the Edge: How the Smartest Companies Use Conflict to Stay Ahead*, New York, NY: Simon and Schuster, 1990, p. 89.

24. Inkpen, A. and N. Choudhary, "The Seeking of Strategy Where It Is Not: Towards a Theory of Strategy Absence," *Strategic Management Journal,* May 1995, pp. 313–324.

25. Brown, L.S., and K.M. Eisendtadt, *Competing on the Edge: Strategy as Structured Chaos*, Boston, MA: Harvard Business School Press, 1998.

26. As quoted in Humes, J.C., *The Wit & Wisdom of Winston Churchill*, New York, NY: Harper Perennial, 1994, p. 75.

27. As quoted in Puris, M., *Comeback: How Seven Straight-Shooting CEOs Turned Around Troubled Companies*, New York, NY: Times Business, Random House, 1999.

28. See for example Kelly, P., *Faster Company*, New York, NY: Wiley, 1998; Stack, J., *The Great Game of Business*, New York, NY: Doubleday, 1994, Melohn, T., *The New Partnership*, Essex Junction, Vermont: Omneo, 1994, and Kearns, D.T., Belasco, J.A. and R.C. Stayer, *Flight of the Buffalo: Soaring To Excellence, Learning To Let Employees Lead*, New York, NY: Time Warner, 1993; and, D.A. Nadler, *Profits in the Dark: How Xerox Reinvented Itself and Beat Back the Japanese*, New York, NY: Harper Collins, 1992.

# CHAPTER 3

# Concept of the Work in Practice

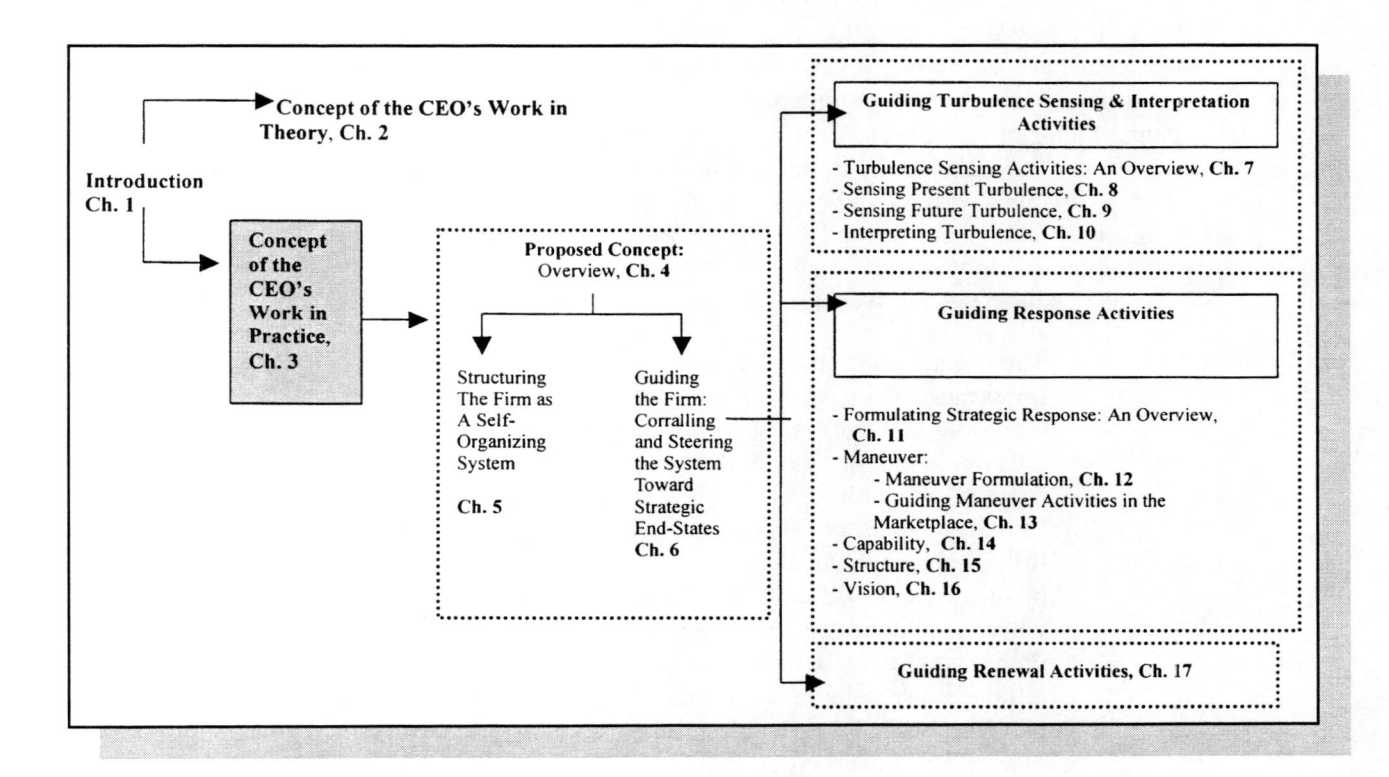

In the previous chapter, the concept of the CEO's work in theory was introduced. Concerns arose regarding the goodness of fit between theory and the realities of today's business world. Clearly, a paradigm shift appears to be taking place. What does the new paradigm look like? To answer this question, we examine the practices of progressive CEOs in this chapter. The practices are presented in the form of mini cases that describe how these CEOs manage their firms in today's turbulent marketplace. The chapter concludes with an attempt to extract the paradigm that underlies these practices.

## CASE STUDIES IN THE PRACTICES OF PROGRESSIVE CEOS

### Jack Welch (General Electric)[1]

Jack Welch took office in 1981 as chairman and CEO of General Electric. Although GE was a successful corporation at the time, Welch sensed the effects of a severe turbulence in the business world. It was becoming a tougher and more competitive world with Japan at the cutting edge of the new competition. He estimated that "competitive toughness has increased by a factor of five or ten." The U.S. economy was in serious decline aggravated by soaring interest rates and a strong dollar. He saw that the solution was to make GE a fast, agile company capable of responding quickly to changing market conditions. To ensure GE's speed and agility, Welch thought that employees must be empowered to make quick response to a changing marketplace.

Welch's leadership design rested on these key principles:

1. The organization must be provided with a vision that can help it focus on what is important. While the vision serves as a general boundary, people should be able to work and achieve freely within that vision. In his words: "Good business leaders create a vision, articulate the vision, passionately own the vision, and relentlessly drive it to completion."[2]
2. Employees must be empowered to make the necessary decisions quickly. For people to feel empowered, they must have "self-confidence." He worked hard to help people acquire self-confidence. He entrenched the principle of "entrepreneurship" where employees are encouraged to undertake new initiatives. Coupled with entrepreneurship is recognition. If they succeeded, success is celebrated. If they failed, failure is also celebrated. His theory behind celebrating failure is that it encourages people to take risks. Besides, failure is an experience that increases the probability of success in the next attempt.
3. The organization has to be "boundaryless." All different entities inside and outside of the company are integrated in a seamless manner. Hence, Welch entrenched the principle of cross-functional teams. Units were asked to work with suppliers and customers as if they were an integrated whole. Concomitant with boundarylessness is the concept of integrated diversity. The company is made up of many diverse groups, but they all must have a common perspective.
4. The organization should have a flat structure. Multiple layers hinder the flow of information and consequently slow the decision making process, which will inhibit quick response.
5. Employees should be freed from rules and procedure (bureaucracy) in order to respond quickly. Thus, he undertook a massive effort to "debureaucratize" General Electric. He drove home the concept of "simplicity" to focus people's attention on the problems and to discourage hiding behind procedure.

6. Employees should feel free to express their view without fear of retribution by superiors. He instituted the concept of "work-out"; a town-hall meeting style designed to encourage freewheeling debates without fear of repercussions. Employees, regardless of rank, are brought together to air gripes and suggestions and mangers are required to take actions on such issues. Work-out sessions build trust as both management and employees obtain more information about one another and their reasoning behind their actions.
7. Learning must circulate around the organization. If one unit has invented effective ways of doing things, then they must be transferred somehow to other units in the company. He thus developed the principle of "best practices" or "benchmarking" that encourages any unit to study the practices of other successful units in GE (and even outside GE) and adapt them to its operation.

## Lars Kolind (Oticon)[3]

Lars Kolind was the CEO of Oticon Holding A/S, a Danish hearing aid manufacturer. Giants such as Siemens, Philips, and Sony have dominated the industry. Since he was hired as CEO in 1988, Kolind has provided leadership for Oticon by concentrating on *two* main activities. His *first* leadership activity was to redefine the business of Oticon as "better hearing solutions" instead of "manufacturing smaller hearing aids." This focused the company on the customer instead of the product.

Kolind's *second* main leadership activity was to develop what he called "the creative organization," an organization that runs itself without his direct supervision and control. He defines his role as a CEO as follows: "I don't see myself as a captain who steers the ship. I see myself as a naval architect who designs the ship." His fundamental leadership premise is "It is more important to design the organization to act in a clever and responsible way than to control every action."

Kolind's management model can be summarized as follows:

- The company is "a network of experts" where each group in the network runs with a chunk of his vision in the form of "projects."
- People are to be trusted in running the organization. His fundamental assumption about people: ". . . all employees are responsible adults, unique individuals, interested in having full information and are fundamentally honest." This allowed him to dispense with the complicated structure (bureaucratic) that was based on many rules and regulations to control people.
- Employees must have a choice in their work. Accordingly, employees are allowed to choose the projects to work on freely as well as determine their own work hours, vacation days, and training needs.
- The company is to be organized as "a free market system" when it comes to allocating resources. Dynamic individuals "compete for resources." Even "less popular individuals get something to do." Workers who consistently fail to seek out project engagements do not survive long.
- With the company viewed as a "network of experts," workers are valued for their particular experience and expertise. They are encouraged to indulge their curiosity.
- Kolind instituted the principle of "multijob" in Oticon. It extends beyond cross-functional collaboration. It requires employees to "include something they are not qualified for in their roster of activities." For example, a top chip designer in a chip design project who performs a marketing function in one project becomes a better chip designer. As Kolind observes, the chip designer then "sees the world stereophonically."

- Kolind instituted the principle of "transparency" in all organizational dealings. The principle requires that "every piece of information, with very few exceptions, is available to everybody" in the company. "Anyone can click on our strategic plan in the computer and see what we intend to do to beat Siemens." His premise is that through such access to sensitive information, Oticon will possess greater agility and integration. This would offset the danger of exposure. "If people know what we are doing and why we are doing it, they know exactly which project to work on," he stresses.
- To increase the company's agility and speed, Kolind fights documentation. He believes that "documentation seriously hampers the vital exchange of information within the organization . . . There is absolutely no doubt that oral communication is ten times more powerful, more creative, quicker, and nicer than writing memos." Even electronic mail is not welcome. Although he, as a CEO, receives from five to eight e-mail messages daily, he sends unnecessary messages back to the sender.
- Kolind practices the principle of "no controls." He notes that the firm's employees may be working on about one hundred projects at any one time. He further states, "projects emerge quite chaotically." Even when a project is formalized, Kolind affirms, "there is no mechanism that prevents project leaders from using too many resources." His commandment to his people: "If you are in doubt, do it. If it works, fine. If not, we forgive you."

To ensure Oticon's agility and speed in the marketplace, Kolind views, and gets his employees to view, the company as three-dimensional chaos. He uses the metaphor of "a one-day old can of well boiled spaghetti" to visualize Oticon's organization. The behaviour of the spaghetti resembles the relationships in Oticon. The organization consists of three dimensions: "project management," "specialists," and "people." Project management involves project leaders and project owners. Project owners are senior management, about ten people in a head office function. They are not involved directly in the project's work, but are very seriously interested in supporting the project's success. Specialists coordinate the diverse professions involved in hearing care. The specialists are the links to the market. Project managers interact continuously with these specialists. The third dimension is "people" including all project leaders, owners, participants, and professionals. Every employee chooses a mentor from the management group whose tasks are (1) to make the employee happy, productive, and creative, and (2) to coordinate annual salary adjustments in conjunction with each employee's previous project leaders and peers.

In this "spaghetti organization," the project, not the function or department, is the defining unit of work. At Oticon, teams form, disband, and form again, as the work dictates. Project leaders (anyone with a compelling idea) compete to obtain and attract the required resources and people in a "free market arena" to get their project underway. Project owners, by contrast, provide advice and support, but do not make the operating decisions. Kolind asserts, "We want each project to feel like a company, the project leader to feel like a 'CEO.' We allow a lot of freedom. We don't worry if we use more resources than planned. Deadlines are what really matter."

At any one point, there may be as many as one hundred projects and most employees work on several projects concurrently. It is hard to tell who is working where. A marketing team writing product brochures sits next to software engineers writing code. The chip design center is a cluster of workstations that is virtually indistinguishable from the audiology research group. A machine shop that builds tools for Oticon's factory is located just outside the cafeteria.

According to Kolind, Oticon is a tangle of relationships in which each person performs a variety of roles in more than one dimension. Although the structure is unfathomable, Kolind insists that it is exactly the kind of structure "in which intelligent people work well, feel good, and are very productive and creative." To facilitate this "three-dimensional chaos," Kolind designed the physical facility to allow for the needed interaction, especially face-to-face communication. First, there are slogans that communicate effectively, e.g., "Think the unthinkable." Work areas are set up with workstations around which individuals and groups are able to move fluidly. The hindrances are caddies containing a maximum of thirty files and a few binders. He removed the "mental restrictions" of paper and belongings. Kolind observes that by removing individual physical territories, "people shift their focus from their power base and backgrounds to focus on the task, the customer, the new product."

To discourage documentation and paper work, Kolind created "the paper room, the only place where paper is safe at Oticon." The mail enters. Next, it is scanned into the computer. Next, it is temporarily placed in individual pigeonholes for reading. After that, it is shredded.

Coffee bars are spread throughout the building with counters to facilitate stand-up meetings. The belief is that "people think and work better, faster, and are more flexible while they are standing up." All throughout the building, there are "dialogue rooms" of various sizes, furnished with circular sofas and tiny coffee tables. Kolind's idea is to remind the employees "that it is much more important to simply talk to your colleagues about what to do, rather than protect yourself behind paper or the table." Even the stairwells are designed to induce interaction. Kolind maintains that this is "a superb invention because while you are passing on the staircase you are often talking to each other."

The physical facility layout is designed to increase interaction. Important facilities have been located in the corners of the building to induce employees to walk about. This way, no employee is "a stranger anywhere and that stimulates dialogue" as Kolind insists. Dialogue is thus taking place everywhere: at the coffee bars, dialogue rooms, and stairwells.

What were the outcomes of the "spaghetti" structure and "chaotic" mode of operation? When Kolind took over in 1988, Oticon was a company in trouble; losing money and market share. During Kolind's reign, Oticon had more than doubled in size, with sales of $160 million in the world market of $1 billion. Operating profits increased by ten times. The Company introduced ten major new products. It also went public and its shares traded at double the initial public offering price. It has become the third largest hearing aid manufacturer in the world.

## Fred Smith (FedEx)[4]

Fred Smith, CEO of Federal Express, has long prided himself on creating an organization where employees are "mavericks." He once proudly announced "I have 40,000 mavericks working for me." There is a true story about a FedEx employee who, upon observing that a blizzard downed power and telephone lines (which halted business at his branch), chartered a helicopter, flew to the power line location, and fixed it. Business continued despite the storm. The employee felt empowered to act, without permission from his superiors.

Smith's leadership design is to have a self-directed organization that is able to respond on its own, as exemplified by the above employee. He institutionalized the principle: "everyone pitches in." The principle is not confined to any department or function. Employees are expected to reach across boundaries, working together to find solutions and resolve problems. In Smith's view, employees cannot have blinders on at work, focusing only on their particular task. If they develop a big picture perspective, they will recognize that their function is not to complete a task, but to help the company achieve its goals. Thus, they are asked to take care of "the trees," and at the same time, keep "the forest" in focus. This "forest and trees" thinking encourages workers to pitch in and help the company wherever help is needed.

In applying the principle of "everyone pitches in," all employees are expected to market FedEx services to customers whether or not marketing is their job. To reinforce this point, FedEx compensates employees who bring in new business.

Smith is able to create this kind of organization by following some key principles that can be summarized as follows:

- Defining the company's mission in terms that everyone can grasp: Smith coined FedEx's goal as "to deliver packages, intact and on time."
- Creating an atmosphere in which employees can advance ideas that add value to the company, and can extend even beyond that employee's organizational unit.
- Entrenching policies that encourage crossing boundaries.
- Avoiding rigid job boxes that inhibit employees from crossing departmental lines and stifle their creative thinking beyond their particular job.
- Encouraging cooperative learning by letting employees from different functions learn about each other's jobs. Thus, couriers learn from customer service representatives and both groups learn from inventory control specialists.
- Supporting the various microcultures in the company. Different job responsibilities and goals require different cultures. No established microculture should crush another. FedEx's speed is enhanced because innovation is also allowed to flourish. New microcultures are encouraged to emerge and are not to be suppressed. For example, FedEx Logistics, Electronic Commerce, and Catalog (LECC) started as an internal service. It grew to become a full-blown consulting service and a profit center. Smith could have chosen to keep it small and internal given the fact that the primary business of the company is package distribution, and not consulting. However, Smith recognized that this new culture could provide added revenues while enhancing FedEx's core service.
- Encouraging people to follow their hunches. Hunches are not wild shots in the dark. They are educated guesses based on knowledge and experience. At FedEx, pursuing hunches is for everybody. For example, the next day afternoon service was created based on the hunches of the marketing managers. Financial analysts argued against it, fearing that it may cannibalize the core overnight service business. Nevertheless, marketing managers insisted that the new service would create a larger pie, not cut the existing pie up. They were allowed to act and the new service became a success. Smith's leadership grants employees the time to develop ideas, and persist with them without giving in to doubts.

## Ralph Stayer (Johnsonville Foods)[5]

Ralph Stayer co-authored a national best selling book in which he eloquently presented his leadership paradigm. Stayer begins by describing the old leadership paradigm: the leader's job is to plan, organize, command, coordinate, and control. Employees do exactly what the leader, as the center of power, tells them to do. Stayer then notes that the old paradigm presents a misleading picture of life. He asserts that in reality the CEO is powerless. To illustrate, he narrated the situation that one CEO faced:

> "Although, he sat in the CEO's chair, he was powerless to accomplish the change he knew had to be made. He saw clearly what had to be done. The management mantra of the nineties was familiar: teamwork, better quality, improved service, and faster time to market. He knew them well. He preached them to anyone who would listen. Yet, he was unable to produce any of these vital outcomes in his organization.

". . . In the last six years he'd instated programs designed to stimulate quality, customer service, and teamwork. He'd trimmed the organization; reorganized functional groups into product/customer focused units, and reduced the number of management layers. Yet, he continued to lose market share, competitors continued to beat him to the market, and he'd lost 50 percent of his market value. He just couldn't move his people to do what he knew had to be done."[6]

Stayer then declares: "All leaders face a challenge of leadership. The old models and paradigms no longer work."[7] He likened the leader following the old paradigm to the lead buffalo in a buffalo herd. Buffalo are loyal followers of one leader. Because of that, they stand around and wait for the leader's commands. If the leader is not around, they wait for it to show up. Early settlers took advantage of this phenomenon. They were able to decimate a herd by killing the lead buffalo. The rest of the herd stood around, waiting for the leader to lead them, while they were being slaughtered. Stayer observed that this also happens in corporations. He found "a lot of waiting around" in his company. The firm was being "slaughtered" in the marketplace because he could not respond quickly enough and give the necessary commands. He also came to the revelation that it was humanly impossible to be the lead buffalo in a modern corporation operating in today's volatile environment. He thinks that the leader, the CEO, is the problem: "In most cases, 'I am the problem.' My desire to be the head buffalo, my wanting to rescue people, my previous successes all got in the way of successfully handling the current situation."[8]

He discovered a new leadership paradigm, the flock of geese:

"Then one day I got it. What I really wanted in the organization was a group of responsible, interdependent workers, similar to a flock of geese. I could see the geese flying in their 'V' formation, the leadership changing frequently, with different geese taking the lead. I saw every goose being responsible for getting itself to wherever the gaggle was going, changing roles whenever necessary, alternating as a leader, a follower, or a scout. And when the task changed, the geese would be responsible for changing the structure of the group to accommodate, . . . fly in a 'V' but land in waves. I could see each goose being a leader."[9]

Inspired by the phenomenon of leadership in a flock of geese, Stayer developed his own new leadership paradigm that can be summed up in one phrase: "letting employees lead." Stayer developed a model of the new paradigm.[10] It is presented in Exhibit 3.1. Stayer's paradigm has four main components as follows:

- Determining focus and direction: This is done by developing a vision for the company. The vision should focus everyone's attention on the customer. It must define individual and company performance in terms of customer satisfaction. It should also stress creating value added for the customers and for the company.
- Removing the obstacles that inhibit the creativity and initiatives of employees: Most notable among these obstacles is the bureaucracy in the form of systems, structures, and procedures which cause people to waste precious time and energy "waiting around."
- Developing ownership: This involves transferring ownership of responsibility for work from the leader to the employees. A key leadership task is to create the environment in which employees own the problems facing the company and the solutions to such problems.
- Stimulating self-directed action: The focus here is on empowering employees to "lead" by practicing ownership. The new paradigm leader involves employees in defining direction, identifying obstacles, developing ownership, and taking self-

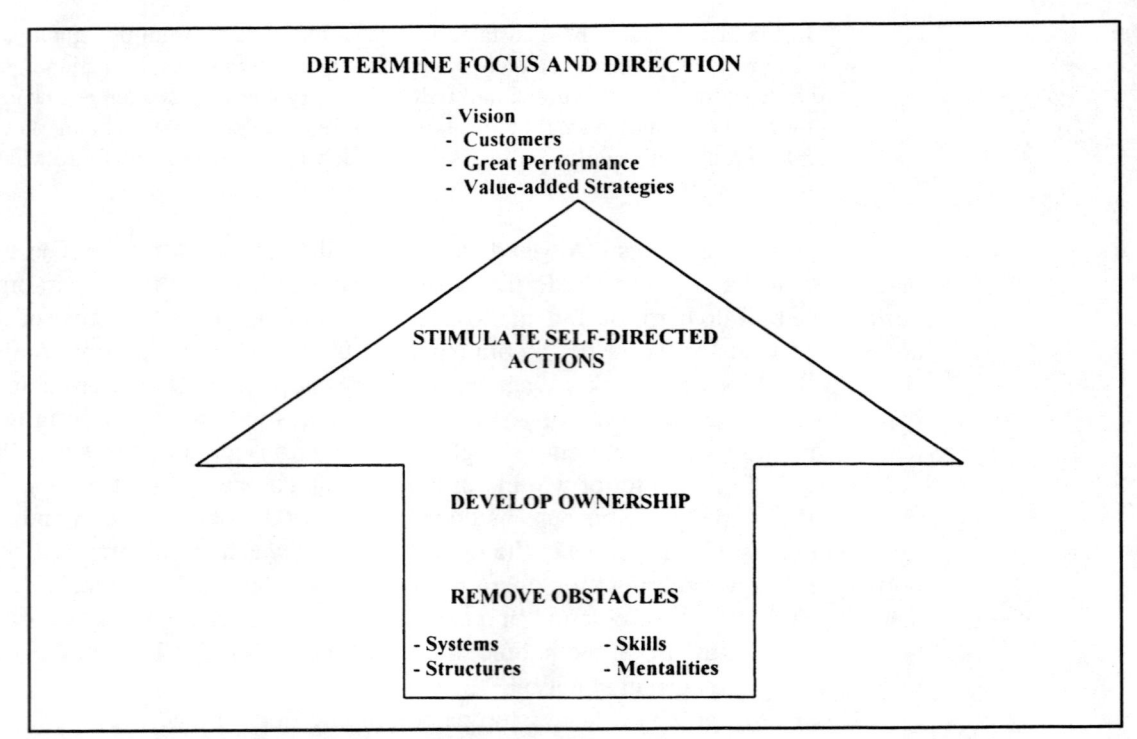

```
                    DETERMINE FOCUS AND DIRECTION
                         - Vision
                         - Customers
                         - Great Performance
                         - Value-added Strategies


                     STIMULATE SELF-DIRECTED
                            ACTIONS


                        DEVELOP OWNERSHIP

                        REMOVE OBSTACLES

                   - Systems      - Skills
                   - Structures   - Mentalities
```

Exhibit 3.1: Stayer's New Leadership Paradigm

directed actions. This applies to all situations in order to reinforce correct ownership of the responsibility for performance.

## Patrick Kelly (PSS/WORLD Medical)[11]

By 1999, Patrick Kelly has founded a billion dollar company, PSS/World Medical (in the business of providing medical supplies and equipment to doctors and hospitals). Kelly's management focus has been on building a "faster" company. He believed that only a faster company could survive in today's business environment.

He described the "faster" company as follows:

> "This kind of company can spot changes in the marketplace and turn on a dime without losing its focus or its people. . . . It can get things done fast because its people march to the same drum and don't need anybody looking over their shoulder telling them what to do. It does a whole lot better than the other guys . . . it leaves them in the dust."[12]

Here is a brief overview of Kelly's work at PSS/World Medical:

1. Setting Gutsy Goals: This involves choosing overarching goals that are beyond easy reach of the organization. He first set a goal of $500 million for PSS/World. Later, this was increased to $1 billion. Both goals were considerably higher than what the company was capable of doing at the time. Both goals were met.
2. Creating a Competitive Edge: The competitive edge lies only in delivering better value to customers by knowing what the customer values; setting up systems to deliver the value consistently; communicating this value to customers continuously; and, changing with the changing needs of customers.
3. Building a Company of CEOs: Employees require the power to address customer needs and concerns on the spot and without authorization from the higher-ups in

the company. Kelly reaffirms this empowerment; "We put CEO on truck drivers' business cards. . . . We take the notion of every man and woman CEO, very, very seriously."[13]

4. Establishing Values: Kelly is a strong believer in values as forces that shape behavior. PSS publishes a list of values "PSS's Top 20."[14] They prescribe how a CEO employee is expected to behave and act. Kelly persistently communicates the values to everyone and acts vigilantly to ensure that they are implemented.

In building a company of CEOs, Kelly practices the following principles:

- Running an open company: Kelly practices "open-book" management where all information including financial statement, cost figures, operating data, etc, are made available regularly to all employees.
- Giving people authority and accountability: The employee is given full authority to act on his/her own to solve whatever problem he/she encounters in delivering value to the customer. The principle here is "it is easier to ask for forgiveness than permission."[15] At the same time, the employee is responsible for the consequences of the decision taken and implemented. The ultimate testimony to employee empowerment is that employees can fire their boss. "At PSS, we believe in real empowerment—to the point where we expect employees to fire their bosses if they have to."[16]
- Sharing the wealth: Concomitant with authority and accountability is the principle of sharing the company's gains with the employees. Kelly instituted an employee ownership and generous profit sharing plans.
- Having leaders, not managers: In applying the principle of a company of CEOs, Kelly believes that "People who think of themselves as CEOs don't really want to be told what to do . . . At PSS, we expect people to figure out for themselves what to do. We also don't have managers. Managers tell people what to do, and people at PSS don't need to be told what to do. What do they need? They need leadership . . . inspiration and guidance . . . advice and teaching . . . A leader at PSS is expected to provide all that."[17]
- Exceptional performance: As CEOs, employees are urged to seek exceptional performance. Rewards follow accordingly.
- Continuous improvement: To ensure changing with the changing customer needs and offering better-than-anyone customer value, employees are expected to improve and change operating procedures and work on a continuous basis. Continuous improvement extends to restructuring the organization, not just work.
- Loyalty and commitment: As CEOs, employees are expected not ". . . to quit when the going get tough. They stick around, pitch in, work harder."[18]

## Jack Stack (Springfield Remanufacturing Company; SRC)[19]

In 1983, International Harvester had a plant in Springfield, Missouri that rebuilt truck and bulldozer engines. Management believed that the plant was losing money and that it could not be turned around and decided to shut it down. Jack Stack, one of the managers, organized a leveraged buyout. Stack and colleagues invested $100,000. The rest of the deal, $9 million, was a debt to International Harvester. The new company, Springfield Remanufacturing (SRC) was undercapitalized. Its financial situation was very tight. It could not afford to miss one interest payment ($90,000 a month). Stack had to figure out a way to increase revenue and cut costs. It was crucial for SRC to generate enough cash to meet debt and other current obligations. His solution was to turn workers into businesspersons who think about the company in its entirety every minute of the day. Out of these circumstances, a new approach for managing the company emerged. It rests on five main principles. These are described briefly below.

### 1. The Big-Picture

From the start, Stack insisted that the employees know exactly the company's situation and where it is heading. He invited them to shape the destiny of the new firm. He maintained that helping the employees develop a big picture perspective is ". . . all about motivation. It's giving people the reason for doing the job, the purpose of working. If you are going to play the game, you have to understand what it means to win. When you show people the Big Picture, you define winning."[20]

### 2. Open-Book Management

To reinforce knowledge of the big picture, Stack insisted that all employees must have all the necessary information about the company finances. All employees, whether they are machinists, truck drivers, or secretaries were provided all the information about the company's financial position so that they may act in a way to improve the big picture. He started with the income statement. Next, all spending categories where the majority of money is spent were highlighted. Then, the various categories of expenses were broken down into controllable elements. Armed with all this information, employees were then educated about the balance sheet. The company had financial management courses for all employees. According to Stack, "The payoff comes from getting the people who create the numbers to understand the numbers. When that happens, the communication between the bottom and the top of the organization is just phenomenal."[21]

### 3. Empowering People

Now that people had the numbers, they were given the authority to act in a way that would impact positively on the income statement and the balance sheet. They were given free reign and this unleashed their creativity and commitment. Accountability was already built into the process since people who created the numbers, made the numbers. With all information available to everyone, it was difficult for anyone to avoid responsibility for the final numbers. To reinforce and support people's creativity, the company developed "the great huddle" where people gather to develop a game plan and execute it together.

### 4. Turning Employees into Entrepreneurs

With creativity unleashed, financial information at hand, and empowerment, employees became *de facto* entrepreneurs who were responsible for the bottom line of the company. Stack went even further. If a group of employees developed a business idea, they were encouraged to build it into a separate business with the financial backing of SRC. As a result, a number of subsidiaries were formed and this gave SRC considerable diversification. In doing R&D for new ideas, employees used pizza parlors and their own stoves to test different heat treatment methods. This improvisation in R&D produced many innovations that evolved into new divisions.

### 5. Sharing the Gain

Early in the game, employees told Stack "spare the praise, give us the raise." This firmed up the principle of sharing the gain and providing people with concrete financial rewards based on a transparent system for allocating them. Since employees have the financial statements, distributing the earnings becomes easier. Relative contributions are assessed on a group basis and the gains are distributed in an equitable manner.

What outcomes did Stack's leadership design bring about? Stack started SRC (1983) from the remnants of a plant that was losing money and targeted for closure. As of 1998, SRC reached a sales volume of $83 million with an after-tax profit of $1.8 million. Although SRC initially was a one-product company, it now does business in many fields including oil coolers, starters and alternators, torque amplifiers, natural gas power conversion, do-it-yourself engine-overhaulers, seminars, training material, and even publishing.

## CONCLUSIONS FROM THE CASE STUDIES

The six CEOs discussed above are not unique. There are many more CEOs whose practices are just as interesting. The six presented here form more or less a representative sample of this new breed of CEO. Even a cursory analysis of the above sample reveals a different kind of concept of the work of the CEO. A certain type of paradigm appears to underlie their actions. This paradigm comprises two fundamental elements:

1. The six CEOs seem to structure their companies as "employee-led," "self-managing" organizations. They organized the company in such a way that employees were empowered to do things—on their own—without waiting to be told by their bosses. Kelly called this type of organization "a company of CEOs."

Why do these CEOs structure their firms as employee-led organizations? The obvious answer is to ensure quick response to turbulence in the marketplace. If, as Stayer asserts, employees had to wait around (like a herd of buffalo) for the CEO (the head buffalo) to tell them what to do, the competition will move in and slaughter the firm. Along the same line, Kelly thought this type of organization would make his company a "faster" company—able to turn on a dime. Make no mistake about it, these CEOs realize that empowering people will create a state of anarchy. However, they also realize that this anarchy is constructive in that it often yields a semicoherent direction. The anarchy is useful because it empowers individuals to respond to market conditions; thereby enabling the firm as a whole to respond quickly to changes in the marketplace.

2. With an employee-led organization in place, these CEOs concentrated on nudging the employees so that the firm may arrive at a strong strategic position in the marketplace. For example, Kelly challenged the employees to make PSS a $500 million company and later a billion-dollar company. Welch challenged all GE's units to become number one or number two in their respective fields. The CEOs here appear to focus on corralling and steering the diverse positions of empowered people.

Why do these CEOs practice "nudging" instead of micromanaging? Kelly answered the question best when he stressed that if you want to have a company of CEOs, then you had better leave it up to them, "People who think of themselves as CEOs don't really want to be told what to do."[22] To have a true employee-led organization, the CEO will have to "transfer ownership" as stayer suggested. Nudging involves establishing overarching visions for the people and then supporting, enabling, and rewarding them for attaining such visions.

Clearly, the practices of *avant-garde* CEOs reveal a certain concept of the CEO's work. The concept differs from the one portrayed in strategic management and general management. These CEOs seem to see themselves as builders of employee-led organizations where their job is to influence or nudge the people toward a semicoherent direction that emerges out of their diverse positions and actions. We will use Wilson's terminology and call this concept "strategic leadership."[23] In the next chapter, we will attempt to formulate a model of strategic leadership in the hope that it will capture the new paradigm.

# ENDNOTES

1. This case is abstracted from the following Harvard Business School cases: "Jack Welch: General Electric's Revolutionary," (case no. 9-394-065), 1994; "GE—Preparing for the 1990s, (case no. 9-390-91), 1990; "General Electric: Jack Welch's Second Wave (A), (case no. 9-391-248), 1991; and "General Electric, 1984" (case no. 9-385-315), 1985. Further material was abstracted from Tichy, N.M., and S. Sherman, *Control Your Destiny or Someone Else Will: How Jack Welch Is Making General Electric The World's Most Competitive Company*, New York, NY: 1993.

2. Tichy, N. and R. Charan, "Speed, Simplicity, Self-Confidence: An Interview with Jack Welch," *Harvard Business Review*, September–October, 1989, p. 114.

3. The case of Lars Kolind is abstracted from the work of Labarre, P., including her article "The Disorganization of Oticon," *Industry Week*, July 16, 1994, pp. 23–28, and from Oticon's web site on the Internet.

4. The case is abstracted from Wetherbe, J.C., *The World On Time: The 11 Management Principles That Made FedEx an Overnight Sensation*, Santa Monica, CA: Knowledge Exchange, 1996.

5. The material for this case is abstracted from Stayer's writing in Belasco, J.A., and R.C. Stayer, *Flight of The Buffalo: Soaring To Excellence, Learning To Let Employees Lead*, New York, NY: Warner Books, 1993.

6. Ibid., p. 16.

7. Ibid., p. 16.

8. Ibid., p. 22.

9. Ibid., p. 18.

10. Ibid., p. 22.

11. Kelly, P., *Faster Company: Building the World's Nuttiest Turn-on-a-Dime Home-Grown Billion-Dollar Business*, New York, NY: Wiley, 1998.

12. Ibid., p. 18.

13. Ibid., p. 86.

14. Ibid., p. 112.

15. Ibid., p. 96.

16. Ibid., p. 187.

17. Ibid., pp. 98–99.

18. Ibid., p. 102.

19. Stack, J., *The Great Game of Business: Unlocking the Power and Profitability of Open-Book Management*, New York, NY: Doubleday, 1992.

20. Ibid., p. 57.

21. Ibid., p. 93.

22. Kelly, op. cit, p. 98.

23. Wilson, I., "The Five Compasses of Strategic Leadership," *Strategy & Leadership*, Vol. 24, No. 4, July–August, 1996, pp. 26–31.

# CHAPTER 4

# Strategic Leadership: A Conceptual Framework

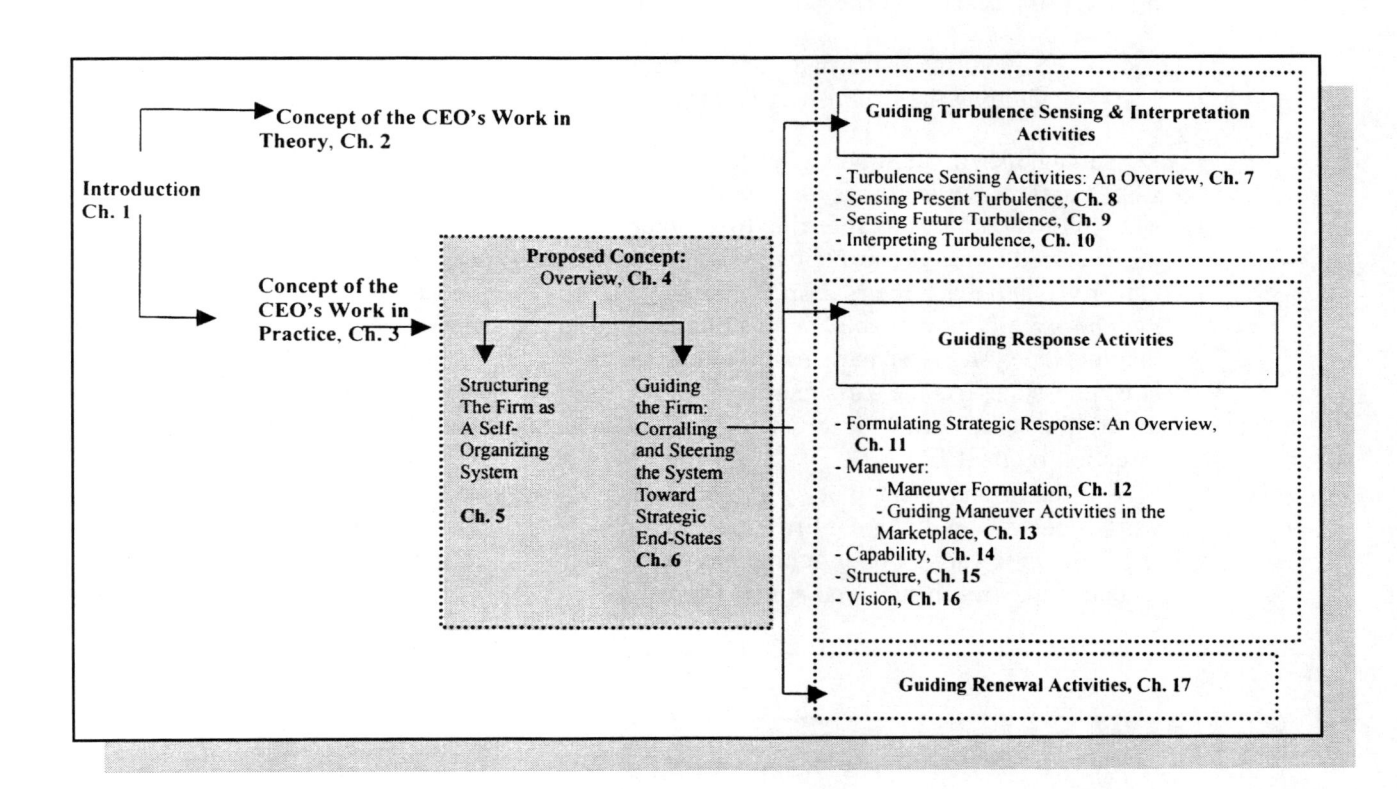

In the preceding two chapters, the work of the CEO was examined from two perspectives: theory and practice. Interestingly, CEOs' practices revealed a corporate management paradigm that is different from the one that underlies theory. We labeled this new paradigm "strategic leadership." In this chapter, we attempt to conceptualize strategic leadership. A conceptual framework will be presented. This framework will show the various elements of strategic leadership and how they "hang together" to make up this important phenomenon.

## MODELING STRATEGIC LEADERSHIP

The individual practices of a large sample of progressive CEOs were gathered and grouped into elemental categories. These, in turn, were related to one another and then grouped into broader categories. These, in turn, were grouped again into more broad categories. This process was repeated until no further grouping was possible. The research note in the appendix explains the details of this procedure. This process yielded two major categories of practices that seem to represent the essence of strategic leadership. As shown in Exhibit 4.1, the two categories are:

- Structuring the firm as a self-organizing system.
- Guiding the firm toward strategic end-states.

In a nutshell, the strategic leadership model portrays the work of the CEO like this: The CEO configures the firm as an organization that manages itself by itself and then lets it do so, without continuously referring to him/her for directions. The theory is that when the firm is structured as a self-organizing system, it will search for strategic end-states and will find clever ways to reach them, despite disruption by the turbulence in its environment. A strategic end-state is a profitable, defensible position in the marketplace. Every time turbulence disrupts the system, the parts pull together to preserve its integrity and resolve to pursue desired end-states. As the parts rearrange themselves, the firm as a whole would be responding to turbulence in a timely fashion. All this can happen without strict supervision and detailed direction by the CEO.

If the firm is going to be self-managing, then what is left for the CEO to do? The CEO's work focuses on guiding the firm toward promising strategic end-states. This includes nudging the firm toward more enriching end-states as well as corralling and steering its activities so that it may reach such end-states.

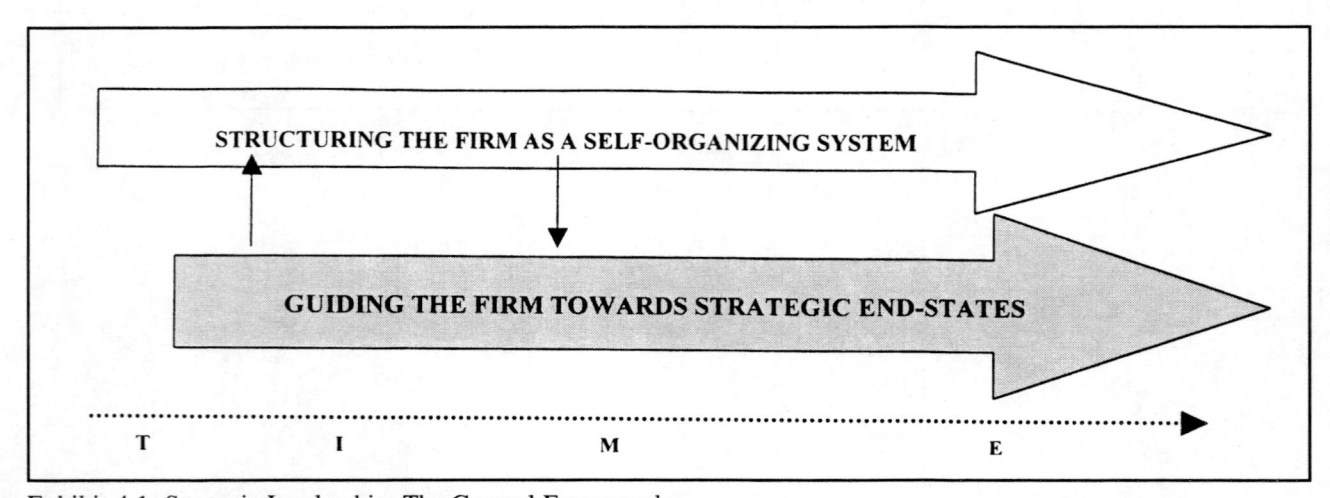

Exhibit 4.1: Strategic Leadership: The General Framework

The two categories of CEO tasks display three important properties. First, each category is a stream of activities that goes on indefinitely. The CEO's work in this regard never ceases since turbulence continuously disrupts all arrangements. Second, both streams take place concurrently, not sequentially. However, structuring the firm as a self-organizing system has to be in place first. Third, both streams are interdependent; each affects and is affected by the other simultaneously. Each element will be overviewed briefly below. Further details will be provided in Chapters 5 and 6.

# STRUCTURING THE FIRM AS A SELF-ORGANIZING SYSTEM

CEOs often refer to structuring the firm as a self-organizing system using terms such as "the employee-led organization," "the employee-driven organization," "a company of CEOs," or the "entrepreneurial organization." Clearly, the underlying principle is the concept of the self-organizing system.

The self-organizing system is an excellent model for structuring the business firm. As Wheatly and Keliner-Rogers suggested:[1]

> *"It is time to change the way we think about organizations.* Organizations are living systems. All living systems have the capacity to self organize, to sustain themselves and move toward greater complexity and order as needed. They can respond intelligently to the need for change. They organize (and then reorganize) themselves into adaptive patterns and structures without any externally imposed plan or direction.
>
> Self-organizing systems have what all leaders crave. The capacity to respond continuously to change . . ."

As a broad category, structuring the firm as a self-organizing system comprises many sub-categories of CEO tasks. Foremost among these, is the restructuring of the company as a collection of modules that can be "snapped together" to develop and deliver a quick response to the challenges posed by turbulent conditions. A module can be as small as a business-minded employee, or as large as a market scale unit, e.g., a division or a subsidiary. Coupled with the principle of modules is the concept of empowering them to act in their own sphere without frequent referral to the center for approval. In essence, the firm is to become a "centerless" organization where the authority resides in the modules at the firing line rather than at the top. This calls for a different type of governance system where the modules are steeped into values rather than being programmed and constrained by detailed regulations. A key principle here is the idea of concrete rewards to spark and reinforce entrepreneurial action by the modules.

A crucial part of structuring the firm as a self-organizing system is redefining the "work" of the organization as "projects." A project is a strategic undertaking (conceived and carried out collectively) to address a certain strategic issue facing the firm. As such, it involves and energizes the modules (the people) and this makes the response vigorous. As a project is accomplished, the bar is raised for the next one, thus causing the firm to reach an ever-increasing level of achievement. Business activities in the firm assume the form of one project after another. Organizational life becomes one wave after another of excitement, rejuvenation, and renewal.

The task of structuring the firm as a self-organizing system is an ongoing process. Every structure is an experiment born out of interfacing with a certain episode of turbulence. It never stops. This topic will be examined in more depth in Chapter 5.

# GUIDING THE FIRM TOWARD STRATEGIC END-STATES

Once the CEO structures the firm as a self-organizing system, he/she steps back and lets it operate autonomously. Robert Eaton, (then CEO of the Chrysler Corporation) stated this phenomenon as follows: "My philosophy is, I want to know where we're going and how we're gonna get there. Then I want to get out of the way."[2] Another CEO, Paul Fentener van Vlissingen (SHV Holdings, Holland) expressed it this way: "It's very important all the time to tell people to do it themselves. You don't have to stimulate an athlete who is running the thousand meters. You don't have to tell them that they have to win. They know that. But you can ask them, 'Have you checked your diet? Have you got the best trainer? That you can do.'"[3]

The focus of the CEO's work here is on guiding the firm to search for strategic end-states and to reach them unimpeded by turbulence. Guiding is essential for two reasons. First, as employees function as a self-organizing system, they will undertake numerous initiatives that they believe would help the firm survive and thrive in the turbulent marketplace. As they do so, the firm might resemble a hodge-podge of diverse visions, initiatives, and actions that may border on anarchy. To what end will this anarchy lead? The progressive CEO does not wait too long to find out if it is the wrong end. Rather, he/she focuses on guiding these activities toward strategic end-states. These are points of arrival where the firm would have successfully negotiated the forces of turbulence and reached a profitable, defensible position. Second, guiding is essential because it is the most suitable mode for managing a self-organizing system. By choosing guiding, the CEO avoids micromanaging the firm. As present experience shows, micromanaging is not constructive.

So, how does a CEO guide the self-managing firm under such circumstances? An analysis of progressive CEOs' practices reveals that guidance boils down to inducing and orchestrating strategic collaboration among the empowered employees in the self-managing firm.[4] First, the CEO induces employees (management and workers alike) to collaborate so that they may function as a genuine self-organizing system. Second, once collaboration occurs, he/she steers or nudges collaboration in the direction of finding more profitable end-states, discovering clever ways to reach them, and actually arriving at the most desirable end-state.

Four terms need to be defined at this point. The first is the term "collaboration" and this refers to the joining of forces and resources by different units and individuals to advance toward a common goal. The second is the adjective "strategic" that qualifies collaboration, and it signifies a special type of collaboration; one that is focused on discovering strategic end-states for the firm that please its stakeholders, and on negotiating the non-controllable forces of turbulence to get to a desired end-state unimpeded by them. Strategic collaboration is creative in that it revolves around searching for new and promising end-states and for breakthrough ways to reach them. The third is the term "inducing" and it refers to motivating collaboration by creating the environment conducive to it. The fourth is the term "orchestrating" and it refers to steering or pointing collaboration in the direction of finding desirable strategic end-states and actually reaching them.

Inducing and orchestrating strategic collaboration involves a range of CEO activities as follows:

- Building the Infrastructure for Strategic Collaboration: This involves cultivating paradigms to help people develop a common perspective, building shared goals, defining roles, institutionalizing dialogue among different groups, and instilling a climate suitable for collaborative action.
- Inducing and Stimulating Strategic Conversation: This focuses on getting divergent groups to talk to one another in the spirit of discovery (of end-states and of innovative ways to reach them). This includes clarification of purpose, building shared

understanding, developing frameworks for action (as common processes for doing things), setting the strategic agenda (desirable end-states), creating new options, recasting desired achievements as projects, arbitrating and balancing advocacy (divergent positions), incorporating implementation into plans, and providing incentives for conversation.

- Marshalling Strategic Conversation Toward Strategic Action: The CEO's work here centers on transforming conversations into action; actually undertaking the moves that would place the firm in the path toward a desirable strategic end-state. The CEO has a host of tools for accomplishing this task. These include transferring decision-making powers, resource allocation, removing obstacles, and, giving ascent.
- Ingraining Accountability: This task is twofold. First, collaboration is instilled as a duty, as a part of the overall accountability scheme in the firm. Everyone is expected to collaborate. Second, collaboration must aim at protecting the firm's assets. It must produce effective results efficiently. The CEO has more tools at his/her disposal including keeping score (of the results of collaborative ventures), performance evaluation, and a governance system.
- Exercising Personal Influence: Strategic collaboration can be further corralled and steered through the personal touch of the CEO himself/herself. The CEO is the personal leader of members of the organization. Personal influence can be delivered in many ways including going first, example setting, preaching, and coaching (to nudge employees toward certain end-state and ways to get to them).
- Acknowledging and Celebrating the Achievements of Strategic Collaboration: To reinforce and induce further strategic collaboration, progressive CEOs acknowledge and celebrate collaborative accomplishments in order to reinforce collaboration and elevate it to higher levels. The theory is that the more the celebration and recognition, the more the collaboration. This is often done by publicizing the accomplishment, acknowledging the key persons and the units that brought it about, and distributing tangible rewards to all participants.

## RATIONALE: THE STRATEGIC LEADERSHIP IMPERATIVE

Why is it necessary to view the work of the CEO as structuring the firm as a self-organizing system and then guiding it toward strategic end-states? Why must CEOs practice strategic leadership instead of traditional top-down management? Strategic leadership is a different style of managing the firm. It is a virtual or lateral leadership model, letting the employees lead. Virtual leadership is a concept the time of which has come. In a *Fortune** article, Huey confirmed the emergence of virtual leadership as a new business reality in the corporate world:

> "Corporate leadership used to be simple. You had it, or you didn't . . . And if you had it, you certainly didn't share it. The surest way to tell if you had it was to look behind you to see if anyone was following. If no one was, you fell back to flogging the chain of command. Because the buck stopped with you, your ass was on the line. Your job was to kick ass and take names. These were the immutable truths of leadership that you learned as you progressed from the Boy Scouts to Officer Candidate School to the Harvard B-School, and they worked. God was in his heaven, and the ruling class . . . ruled.

---

*© 1994 Time, Inc. Reprinted by permission.

Then, of course, the world turned upside down. Global competition wrecked stable markets and whole industries. Information technology created *ad hoc* networks of power within the corporation. Lightning fast innovative entrepreneurs blew past snoozing corporate giants. Middle managers disappeared, along with corporate loyalty . . . Some time after restructuring, but before reengineering and reinvention, you accepted the new dizzying truth: that the only constant in today's world is exponentially increasing change.

The few corporate chiefs who saw all this coming declared themselves 'transformational' and embraced such concepts as 'empowerment,' 'workout,' 'quality,' and 'excellence.' What they didn't do deep down inside—was actually give up much control or abandon their fundamental beliefs about leadership.

The pressure is building to walk the talk. Call it whatever you like: post-heroic leadership, servant leadership, distributed leadership, or, to suggest a tag, virtual leadership. But, don't dismiss it as just another touchy-feely flavor of the month. It's real, it's radical, and it's challenging the very definition of corporate leadership for the 21st century."[5]

Huey goes on further to give us a sense of what virtual leadership is:[6]

"Business already is moving to organize itself into virtual corporations: modules built around information networks, flexible work forces, outsourcing, and webs of strategic partnerships. Virtual leadership is about keeping everyone focused as old structures, including old hierarchies, crumble.

As the power of the position continues to erode, corporate leaders are going to resemble not so much captains of ships as candidates running for office. They will face two fundamental tasks: first to develop and articulate exactly what the company is trying to accomplish, and second, to create an environment in which employees can figure out what needs to be done and then do it well.[7]

If Huey's observation is valid, then effective CEOs must practice virtual leadership. The term "virtual" refers to something that appears to exist, but really does not. The strategic leadership model presented here is a model of virtual leadership. It sees the role of the CEO as creating the environment for self-management, and then letting employees operate as a self-organizing system, as an employee led organization.

Perhaps the following quote by the ancient Chinese philosopher, Lao-Tzu, captures the spirit of virtual leadership: "As for the best of leaders, the people do not notice their existence. The next best, the people honor and praise. The next, the people fear, and the next, the people hate. When the best leader's work is done, the people say 'we did it ourselves'."

The most compelling argument for strategic leadership lies in the new realities of the 2000s. These realities reveal some definite trends that would make strategic leadership inevitable as the paradigm for managing the firm in the 21st Century. These trends and the relationships among them are shown in Exhibit 4.2.

## Information Technology

The pressure towards strategic leadership originated with the emergence of the information technology revolution in the 1980s. Information technology is the result of the convergence of telecommunication, computing, and hi-tech. Telecommunication provided technologies for transmitting information to extensive networks of organizations and persons. Computing, especially digitization, allowed the use of desktop computers to become the nodes in these networks sending and receiving data to and from one another and then processing the masses of data. Hi-tech transferred energy from muscle to machine allowing the automation of virtually everything. The convergence of the three resulted in important developments such as the Internet, the e-economy, molecularization, and the digital organization.

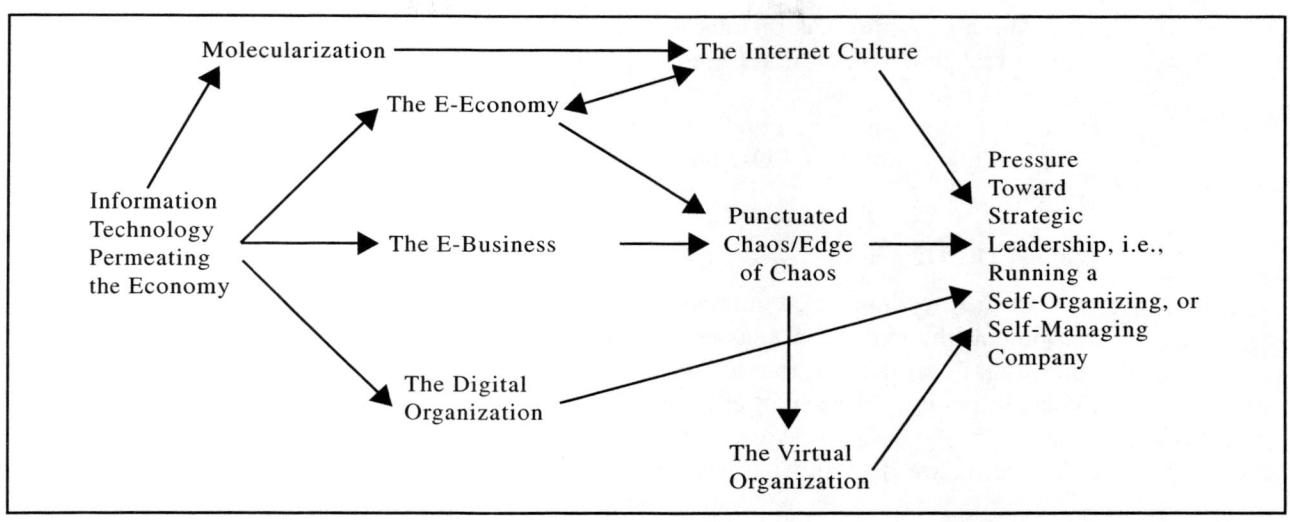

Exhibit 4.2: The Inevitability of Strategic Leadership

## The E-Economy

Information technology led to the emergence of the Internet as the electronic marketplace where buyers and sellers conduct business in cyberspace rather in the traditional brick-and-mortar physical space. We now have an e-economy consisting of e-agents (producers, suppliers and customers) conducting economic transactions on the Web. A CEO described the e-economy as follows:

> "The Web has forever changed the way companies and customers (whether they be consumers or other businesses) buy and sell to each other, learn about each other, and communicate. The best companies will now build systems to pick and pack products that are shipped individually, keep track of those shipments, and make sure the stuff gets delivered to our houses or businesses. They will integrate those systems with the manufacturing, distribution, and computer networks already in place."[8]

Hamel and Sampler note, "The Web will fundamentally change customers' expectations about convenience, speed, comparability, price, and service."[9] As leisure time becomes more valued, customers would rather shop via the Web than visit malls and shopping centers. The Internet provides a wide range of choice of goods and services unmatched by physical stores and malls. It allows customers the luxury of shopping at home at any time of the day. This marks the end of geography as a determining factor in business strategy. Some Internet marketers are turning the marketplace into an auction where customers are actually bidding on products ranging from computers to airline tickets (Priceline.com). In a way, customers, not producers, are setting the price. Because of the low cost of Internet advertising, sellers are becoming generous with comparative product/service data. By surfing the Net, customers are able to compare many producers. Producers cannot hide and hedge through advertising. Producers are being forced to become more objective and to give customers the plain truth. More interesting is the hyper-customization (one-on-one marketing and one-on-one production customized to customer specifications) where vendors will be able to build to demand rather than in anticipation of demand. For example, Dell Computer allows customers to configure their PC to their liking from its pull-down menu on its Website.

The e-economy has serious implications for the job of the CEO. Strategy will have to be a real-time response, *ad hoc*, and fast paced so much so that it cannot be left to one (or few individuals), even if it is the CEO. It will have to be delegated to those close to the customers who can make quick responses. Strategy will become the choices that these individuals make, not the CEOs. The CEO's traditional prerogative in strategy formulation is eroding.

## Molecularization

In the e-economy, e-commerce and e-corporations are creating another important development, the shift from mass to molecular.[10] Mass production becomes molecular as it changes into production runs of one; from jeans to bread. E-corporations already practice molecularization. Mass marketing is turning molecular when one-on-one marketing takes place on the Web. On the Web, every customer is treated as a separate market segment. The mass media are becoming molecular as every PC becomes a channel of communication where newspapers and magazines are available online. Mass education can become molecular where every student can be a learning center through tele-teaching, video conferencing, and books on CD-ROMs. Even mass transit can become molecular where cars, connected via the Internet, can become information appliances in smart roads that manage their movements.

## The E-Business Model

The spread of the Web is leading to the creation of a new way of doing business, the e-business model. The e-business model combines computers, the Web, and massively complex programs known as enterprise software to create a new way of doing business."[11] The e-business model forces a firm to define its business as a brokering process. As Jeff Bezos (founder and CEO of an e-corporation, Amazon.Com) stated it, "Ultimately, we're an information broker. On the left side, we have lots of products; on the right side, we have lots of customers. We're in the middle making the connection."[12] The e-business model is a unique, superior way of creating and delivering value to customers. Hamel and Sampler observe that ". . . competition today is not between products, it's between business models."[13] Amazon.com is a business model for selling books where customers shop and pay in cyberspace, no brick-and-mortar and no geographical boundary. Traditional booksellers, e.g., Chapters, Barnes and Noble, B. Dalton, and Waldenbooks represent another business model based on having brick-and-mortar type bookstores with a geographically defined territory where customers shop in physical space.

## The Internet Culture

For the first time in history, a new generation is evolving with a new culture, people growing up surrounded by home computers, video games, CD-ROMs, and the Internet. Tapscott labeled these people as the Net generation and profiled its culture as follows:[14]

- Independence and autonomy: They initiate communication and information. Unlike their predecessors, the Net generation would not want to work as a cog in a wheel. They are only comfortable working more like autonomous molecules.
- Intellectual openness: They insist on sharing ideas. They have a strong sense of self-esteem.
- Inclusion: They show a strong interest in ideas rather than social and gender differences. They judge others based on their contribution. The Net people are predisposed toward collaboration based on interdependence of contributions.
- Expression of strong views: The net culture is based in the networking of knowledge or the networking of humans through technology. In this regard, they may be

the first generation to network intellect for problem solving, creativity, and innovation; and in the process extend consciousness from individuals to organizations.
- Innovation: Their thinking appears utterly unfettered. They have new tools for exploration and collaboration. They will ask *"Why not?"*
- Preoccupation with maturity: They display an unwavering desire to be treated like an adult (with due respect) and to be judged on contribution rather than age. They also judge others mainly on contribution, not experience, or position in the hierarchy.
- Investigation of everything and challenging the underlying assumptions: They will "look under the hood"; not necessarily for technical details, but to understand the assumptions underlying the design. They have no sacred cows. Just as they hack video games to eliminate hierarchical levels of play, they will be prone to hack corporate hierarchy and culture too.
- Desire for immediacy: They think and act at the electronic speed that shapes the tools of their world from video games to Web sites. The Net-generation world is a real time world. They have minimum patience for procedural delays.
- Uneasiness with corporations: They tend to be distrustful of the corporate way of doing things; perhaps because of their desire to investigate and question things. As customers, they are hard to please. As employees, they are hard to manage.
- Trust: They are trusting individuals. They are committed to promise-keeping and to the sharing of ideas and wisdom. They value authenticity for they have honed their authentication skills online.

The culture of the Net generation has serious implications for redefining the job of the CEO. As employees, they will not submit easily to command-and-control management. Their predisposition toward autonomy will cause strategic thinking and action to be dissipated throughout the organization instead of being held centrally by the CEO. Their culture of independence, investigation, and immediacy will create a measure of anarchy in the organization that the CEO must learn how to corral and steer.

## Punctuated Chaos/Edge of Chaos

Clearly, the dynamics of the e-economy, molecularization, e-business, and the Internet culture have created a condition in the business environment known as punctuated chaos. The term "punctuated chaos" refers to a condition where a system is in a state of constant upheaval marked by brief respites.[15] Another term for describing this state is "edge of chaos," a state that is a mix between order and chaos; neither completely chaotic nor entirely orderly.[16] Here is how one CEO described this state:

> "We live in erratic times. We fly in turbulent business skies. In the past few years we have seen more dramatic political and economic shifts in the world than have occurred in all the decades since World War II. Some of these shifts have already affected our businesses, others will make themselves felt in the future—and nobody can predict with any certainty just how. As the world's business environment continues to undulate relentlessly, success will depend on our ability to channel the raw energy of this turbulence in productive and profitable ways.
>
> I have long used the term turbulence to describe the agitation that is a constant in business. These unsettling winds are felt more acutely today than ever before. . . . I can think of no better term to portray the sudden, frequently unexpected, movement that characterizes the environment in which we all do business."[17]

To get a feel for what an edge of chaos state looks like, consider the changes in our business world in Exhibit 4.3, as identified by Kiernan.[18]

- The explosive and accelerating power of the information and communication technologies. These newly converging technologies are shattering organizational and political barriers, empowering new players, and completely rewriting the rules of international business competition for both individual companies and entire countries.
- The rapid globalization of markets, competition, trading patterns, finance, capital, and management innovation. . . . The explosion and convergence of computing, communications, and financial technologies have created a world of instantaneous interdependence.
- The fundamental shift from a world economy based on manufacturing and natural resource exploitation to one based on knowledge-value, information and innovation. . . . competitive advantage based on natural resource endowments and 'economies of scale' manufacturing capacity is eroding dramatically, both for individual companies and for entire countries.
- The accelerated de-coupling of the 'real' economy from the 'virtual' economy of synthetic financial instruments and transactions. . . . over $1 trillion of 'hot' money, crosses national borders every day in search of the next microscopic edge in the computerized global casino of foreign exchange trading. These . . . are almost entirely unconnected to the production of real value or wealth. They are also beyond the reach and effective control of both individual governments and international institutions.
- Geopolitical re-balancing: the emergence of a new economic order. Double digit real GDP growth rates (in the Pacific Rim countries) coupled with the relative stagnation of the OECD (Organization for Economic Cooperation and Development) economies has created a whole new international economic architecture. The balance of economic power and dynamism has shifted unmistakably and probably irreversibly.
- The 'twilight' of government. The globalization of markets and capital, massive privatization, and the financial and credibility crisis of governments worldwide have all severely reduced the capacity of national governments to control their own economic and political destinies.
- Sectoral and industrial convergence. . . . an unprecedented convergence and blurring of the formerly sharp distinctions between the public and private sectors. . . . a rapid convergence and blurring of once distinct industries into a fluid, constantly changing gestalt of competitors, suppliers, and strategic alliances.
- The emergence of unprecedented new forms of business organization, both within and between firms. . . . Among the most conspicuous ones are the hierarchical, interdisciplinary teams, the proliferation of strategic alliances, the rise of the 'virtual' organization (an organization that exists but in reality it does not), and the emergence of mega-competition between rival alliances in industries as disparate as automobiles, aerospace, and computer chips.
- A shift in the economic 'center of gravity' of the business world from large multinational companies to smaller, nimbler, and more entrepreneurial firms. Technological change has obliterated the traditional balance of power between established corporate behemoths and tiny, but innovative upstarts. Corporate mass and size have even turned from a competitive advantage into a serious liability, as the executives of companies like IBM, Sears, and American Express can attest to.
- The geometric increase in the social, political and commercial significance of environmental considerations in both OECD and industrializing countries. An exponential increase in the velocity, complexity, and unpredictability of change. Together, all these trends are creating a hyper-competitive international business environment that bears little resemblance to the one the that existed five years ago—or that awaits us two years hence.

Exhibit 4.3: Markers of a Business World at the Edge of Chaos. (From *Get Innovative or Get Dead* by M. Kiernan. Reprinted by permission.)

## The Digital Organization: Doing Business at the Speed of Thought

CEO Bill Gates (Microsoft) alerts us to another major trend, the emergence of the digital organization. His argument goes like this: Today's business environment changes in the form of "punctuated chaos." To succeed in such an environment, firms need to act fast to respond quickly to sudden market change. To enable quick response, strategic thinking and strategic decision-making will have to move from the center (the CEO and top management) to the peripheries, i.e., to the people on the firing line. Empowering these employees is inevitable.

For people on the firing line to make these decisions, they must have information instantaneously and must be able to relay it to others (e.g., peers, and customers) in real time. Information technology has advanced to the stage where it can network these individuals providing them with the information inputs they need and disseminating the information outputs they produce. Information can move vertically and horizontally to anyone inside the company or around the world. The tools of the Digital Age extend the capabilities of the mind. A business organization must become digital. When it becomes digital, its members can do business at the speed of thought.

The digital organization has serious implications for defining the work of the CEO. It restructures what CEOs do. Gates stated this impact as follows:

> "However you organize your company . . ., one thing is clear: it is impossible to manage a company totally from the center. It is impossible for a single person or single committee to stay on top of every issue in every business unit or subsidiary. Leaders need to provide strategy and direction and to give employees tools that enable them to gather information and insight from around the world. Leaders shouldn't try to make every decision. Companies that try to direct every action from the center will simply not be able to move fast enough to deal with the tempo of the new economy."[19]

## The Virtual Organization

The term "virtual" refers to something that appears to exist although it really does not. The virtual company may appear to have production and marketing facilities but it really does not own any. The virtual way of doing business calls for teaming up a number of independent businesses that provide the firm with all the capacities it needs from product design and manufacturing to distribution and retailing. Even traditional manufacturing firms such as automakers are going virtual. For example, Ford and Chrysler rely on independents from design service to parts manufacturing and sub-assemblies. Selling has always been performed by independents, the dealers.

The virtual corporation concept is not a new one. For years, the well-known Italian fashion company Benneton coordinated the work of thousands of independents that made, distributed, and retailed garments for it. The concept is gaining considerable momentum nowadays. The momentum has been accelerated by the trends of e-commerce, the e-business model, and molecularization. The e-economy is quickly turning into virtual webs of companies that are integrated by other companies. Independents everywhere are snapped together into networks that are brought together by another corporation that coordinates them and gives them the semblance of one large company. This has significant implications for the CEO's job. With minimal control over independents, the CEO becomes more of a coordinator/integrator rather than supreme commander.

## Implications for the Job of the Chief Executive

The eight forces described above clearly lead to one conclusion: The prudent CEO must run the company as a self-managing organization (a self-organizing system). If the company is to survive in this chaotic environment, it will have to be fluid enough to change continuously (to stay in synch with a continuously changing world). The firm can only become fluid if its parts (employees in the form of teams or units) are freed to become fluid, i.e., given the authority and the resources to interpret the turbulence around them, figure out what needs to be done, and do it without intervention by the top. That is why contemporary CEOs organize their people to become "frontline entrepreneurs."[20] Employees will have to be trusted to lead the company.[21] They discovered the benefits of self-organization as noted by Wheatly and Keliner-Rogers above: responding intelligently to change; and, organizing and reorganizing into adaptive patterns and structures without an externally imposed plan or direction.

When the firm becomes self-organizing, a number of positive conditions happen. Self-organization calls into play the intelligence of all people in the firm, not just the few at the top. This enriches the pool of strategic thoughts available inside the firm. Employees become committed and emotionally involved. They own into problems and into solutions. Because employees are empowered, they respond quickly to whatever changes they encounter. As they do so, the firm becomes spontaneous and fluid. Opportunities are exploited. Negative impacts are evaded or minimized.

However, because employees are empowered, an anarchy-like condition may arise. There will be many visions and positions. People will fight for their positions with all the power they have. Now, will the company fall apart because of this anarchy? The answer is a strong no. As it turns out, anarchy among empowered, competent people turns constructive. A shared vision emerges and a semicoherent direction surfaces. Something like an invisible hand evolves and turns anarchy constructive. Under such circumstances, the organization will have discord and harmony mixed together; chaos and order in one stream. Sagacious CEOs are not intimidated by this situation. Some even encourage it. Take the case of Dee Hock (former CEO of Visa) as one who recognized the importance of mixing discord and harmony. Hock coined the term "chaord" (pronounced kay'ord) to label this paradox. According to Hock a chaord is "any autocatalytic, self-regulating, adaptive, nonlinear, complex organism, organization or system, whether physical, biological or social, the behavior of which harmoniously exhibits characteristics of both order and chaos."[22] He believes that an effective business organization is "chaordic" because it is simultaneously orderly and chaotic. It never quite settles into a stable equilibrium, but it never quite falls apart either.[23]

Although structuring the firm as a self-organizing system is crucial for survival in a turbulent environment, it has serious ramifications for the roles and work of the CEO. In general, the work of the CEO is reduced to guiding the firm or orchestrating strategic collaboration among empowered employees. Traditionally, the CEO led by means of formulating a strategy and driving it down the organization. This is no longer feasible or desirable in a self-organizing firm (a chaord). In a self-organizing setting, strategy making assumes a radically different form and process. In such a firm, people are empowered and are given autonomy to pursue what they envision as best for the company. Consequently, there will be many initiatives and visions. Such initiatives may suggest various strategic directions. Some are worth pursuing and some are not. If the firm is to benefit from all of these initiatives, it will have to let its strategy surface out of this rich pool. It will not make sense to pre-establish a single strategy and implement it ignoring the promising potential of employees' initiatives. It would be wiser to let strategy be dictated by the rich pool of these tactical, opportunistic initiatives. The CEO will have to let go of strategy making. Strategy becomes an employee-driven phenomenon. As Brown and Eisenhardt suggest, strategy emerges as a semicoherent direction or a pattern out of these initiatives.[24] Strategy becomes an unpredictable, uncontrolled, inefficient, proactive, continuous, and diverse entity. It is no longer a clear-cut, precise plan.[25]

If strategy evolves in this fashion, then what role does the CEO play in strategy making? The CEO does not formulate strategy to the last detail as was held before. The role of the CEO in this regard is to stimulate strategic collaboration so that numerous and diverse initiatives will take place inside the organization. When these initiatives take place, the role of the CEO then shifts to "surfing" these waves of activities to see if a strategy (or strategies) suggests itself out of them. Once a strategy surfaces, then he/she proclaims it as the "official" strategy for the firm, albeit for the time being (since new strategies will suggest themselves in the near future). Beyond strategy picking, the CEO plays the role of steward for the strategy who builds, coordinates, and integrates collaborative networks and efforts to see its implementation through.

The peculiarities of the digital age represent another reason for the CEO to let go of strategy making. The e-business world is so fluid and so fast that having a fixed, long-term strategy or a strategic plan is pointless. At best, the firm can have a business model that can be applied in different ways daily depending on the demands of the day. As Citrin and Neff observed,

> "In the Digital Economy, . . . , strategy development must be more fluid. . . . Web sites are linked, traffic moves fluidly from site to site, and business development teams negotiate ferociously for the best placements on highly trafficked sites. As a result a supplier may become a competitor one day, a marketing partner the next day, and an acquisition target soon after that. . . .
>
> The point is that relationships are much more fluid in the Digital Economy. As a result, rather than manage via a detailed annual strategic planning process, the best digital leaders manage via a strategic framework or a business model."[26]

In sum, the CEO still "manages" the firm, but in a different manner from the traditional command-and-control CEO. To illustrate this point, let us take two CEOs who have been judged as among the best CEOs of our times, Jack Welch and Jeff Bezos. Welch leads a traditional economy firm, General Electric. Bezos heads a digital economy company, Amazon.Com. Both structured their firms as self-organizing systems by empowering employees and trusting them to do the right thing the right way. Exhibit 4.4 highlights their practices.

|  | CEO ||
| --- | --- | --- |
| **CEO Practices** | **Jack Welch:** CEO of a traditional Economy company, General Electric Company, revenue, $99.8 billion, capitalization, $427 billion | **CEO: Jeff Bezos** Digital Economy company, Amazon.com Inc., revenue, $1.2 billion, capitalization, $25 billion. |
| **Integrity: lead by example** | Highly competitive, famous for hand writing personal notes, leads training at Crotonville. | Obsessive about customer experience; works on a desk made from a door. |
| **Winning Strategy** | No. 1 or No. 2 in every market, six sigma quality program, each of 12 divisions charged with creating a breakthrough Internet business. | Build the world's largest online department store ($18 items for sale), lowest prices, easiest to use Web site, data mining to target 13 million-and growing-customers. |
| **Great Management Team** | Top general managers of any company. | Hired Joe Galli (COO) ex Black & Decker, Warren Jenson (CFO) ex Delta Airlines, and top logistics team from Wal-Mart. |
| **Employee Inspiration** | "Boundaryless," open idea sharing in town hall meetings, failure scrutinized, not penalized | Tapping into employees' desire to change the way the world shops. |
| **Flexible, Responsive Organization** | Focuses on having the right people solve problems no matter where they are hierarchically, organizationally, geographically, "hate bureaucracy and all the nonsense that comes with it." | Constantly launching businesses and immediately adapting based on customer feedback; taking stakes in early stage companies, e.g., Drugstore.com; Pets.com. |
| **Reinforcing Management Systems** | Ranking of all employees into five quintiles, handsomely rewarding the 4's and the 5's and weeding out the 1's and the 2's. | Significant stock options and low base salaries; extraordinary information management systems. |

Exhibit 4.4: Profiles of Two Leaders of Empowered Organizations[27]

# IS THE STRATEGIC LEADERSHIP MODEL PRACTICAL?

The above rationale leads us to believe that strategic leadership is about the only option for a CEO to build and run a firm that would survive and thrive in today's turbulent world. The strategic leadership model is premised on the principle of letting the firm function as a self-organizing or a self-managing system. Traditional CEOs raise some fundamental objections to this model. These are stated and addressed below.

## Can Employees Realistically Function as a Self-Organizing System?

Employees can and do function as a self-organizing system in many contemporary business firms. The CEOs researched for this study have applied the self-organization philosophy. They report that it works. Two reasons explain why it works. In the first place, nearly all people want to be respected for their intelligence and experience. They want this respect to be translated into trust, i.e., letting them diagnose a situation, develop an action plan, and carry it through on their own without close supervision by superiors. This appeals to many of the higher needs among humans, namely, self-esteem and self-actualization. Many employees want to be "mavericks." In fact, some CEOs encourage this tendency. In explaining the success of Federal Express, Fred Smith once said, "I have 40,000 mavericks working for me." Being a maverick means that the employee has the resources and the authority to act as he/she sees fit without being kept on a short leash. These success stories suggest that self-organization is part of human nature.

Some argue that employees cannot be trusted. They fear that employees will take advantage of trust and misuse the firm's assets. Some even go further to claim that many employees do not really want to be empowered. They maintain that employees just want to do their job and nothing more. These behaviors happen because of the history of management-labor relations, not because employees do not want to be self-organizing or because they are not capable of self-management. In such companies, employees were treated as a factor of production, a resource to be managed just like other resources. Employees learned to follow instructions (like a herd of buffalo). They have become uninvolved and indifferent.

Another reason why employees do not buy into self-organization is that it calls for total involvement on the part of the employee especially hard work, sacrifices, and going beyond the bounds of the job. What is in it for the employees? Strategic leaders realize this factor. They provide materialistic rewards. When the company wins, employees must win too, in the form of higher pay, bonuses, profit sharing, stock options, and the like. One Silicon Valley CEO once said, "My job is to make my employees rich." The clear meaning is that a big portion of the firm's profits is distributed to employees. Jack Stack's employees told him "spare the praise, give us the raise."

## Can the Self-Organizing System Concept Be Applied in a Unionized Workforce?

The above argument goes for employees in a unionized setting as well. Labor-management history is full of episodes in which management took advantage of labor; bordering on exploitation in many cases. In bad times, labor was asked to "share the pain." In good times, labor did not share in the gain; management and shareholders did. The result is mistrust and adversarial relations. Under such conditions, no union leadership would agree to any collective agreement that calls for employees to work more for the same pay under the guise of self-organization. Nevertheless, when management was committed to self-organization and to sharing the gain with labor, self-organization did occur. Herb Kelleher, CEO of Southwest

Airlines, was able to have a self-organizing, unionized workforce. Jack Welch achieved a degree of self-organization at GE and its employees are unionized.

## Can Management Accept the Concept of Self-Organization?

It would seem then that when self-organization does not work, it is not because of the employees. It is primarily because of management. Traditional CEOs find it difficult to buy into the concept. Their fears stem from the false sense of security that the command-and-control structure conveys (the power to give commands about direction and receive unquestioning obedience). They are reluctant to surrender authority and power. It is difficult for them to let go. For some managers, it is difficult to accept the fact that employees can do well without managers looking over their shoulders. They usually raise some fundamental objections such as the following:

- *If the self-organizing system is running itself by itself, then who is in charge?* There is no single person in charge in a self-organizing environment. The system is in charge of itself, just like a swarm system (e.g., a beehive). That is what self-organization is all about. Nevertheless, the CEO still has many tools and weapons at his/her disposal to nudge or corral and steer the system to a mutually acceptable strategic direction and end-state. By law, the CEO is still in charge. What is different here is that the CEO leads from the middle or even from behind by being a "resource person."
- *In a self-organizing setting, employees have power, and this will cause the firm to degenerate into anarchy.* As discussed earlier, there is anarchy, but it is not dysfunctional or destructive. It does not cause the system to fall apart. Anarchy in this case means that people are involved. They are applying themselves to develop strong positions and visions. When people have all the information they need, coordination seems to occur naturally. Nevertheless, the CEO has many tools and weapons for nudging them, including coaching, preaching, allocating resources, staffing key positions, and many others as will be shown in Chapter 6.
- *Given that all parts of the self-organizing system are empowered, how will they stay aligned with the company's vision and mission?* They will be in alignment because they will formulate the company's vision and mission as part of self-organization. Such a vision and mission will have a strong chance of being implemented because employees own into them. This raises another objection: are they capable of forming visions and missions? Is this not the job of the CEO and top management? The CEO and top management are not the only ones who have the wisdom, imaginativeness, and knowledge to formulate vision and mission. The employees "live" on the firing line. They know what works and what does not. Wisdom and insight do not reside only at the top of the organization.
- *If a CEO accepts the self-organizing system's philosophy, how does he/she get the people to assume broad accountability for the firm as a whole, to learn, and to make the decisions?* In a self-organizing setting, people are trusted and valued. Observation suggests that people take this trust seriously in that they feel they are the ones to blame when things go wrong. They can no longer blame management. Furthermore, progressive CEOs build a self-organizing culture. A critical component of this culture is having a "corporate" perspective, i.e., seeing and acting as if the employee were the CEO of the company. In Chapter 3, we saw Patrick Kelly putting the title "CEO" on employees' business cards; and meaning it.
- *The self-organization model ignores employees' need for hierarchy.* Evidence from firms that practice the concept shows that employees enjoy the freedom and respect

that comes with the trust vested in them. Leaders of such firms believe that employees resent hierarchies.
- Because the structure of a self-organizing system is lateral and flat, it ignores employees' need for promotion up the organizational ladder. With the current down-sizing in many firms, promotion opportunities have nearly vanished. Observation suggests that people find intrinsic rewards in being empowered, trusted, and compensated handsomely. These made up for the need for promotion.
- Because it is groupthink and action, individual performance tends to sink to the lowest common denominator in a self-organizing setting. Observation suggests this is not the case. Self-organizing systems (as we will see in Chapter 5) tend to be externally focused on the changing environment. This somehow causes individual performance to have no limits. The individual feels responsible for keeping the company competitive.
- Given its emphasis on being a group or a swarm, the self-organizing environment will cause employees to lose their individualism and creativity. Individualism is more likely to be lost in a hierarchical setting because of close supervision. In a self-organizing setting, everyone pitches in his/her own way thereby encouraging individualism. As Stayer (Johnsonville Foods) suggested, there will be one lead bird after another leading the flock. This will provide ample room for individualism.
- Without close supervision by the higher-ups, there will be no limit to the mistakes made by employees in a self-organizing setting? Actually, in a self-organizing setting, individual mistakes are minimized. First, people are putting their heads together (groupthink). It is difficult for an individual to make a mistake without it being caught by someone else in the group. Second, when mistakes happen, people do pitch in to help one another to keep up group performance levels.
- Because the self-organizing model emphasizes the group rather than management, managers will lose touch with their organization. Managers still have an important role to play. They play a supportive, guiding role. They are resource persons whose input is sought on key issues. They are coaches.
- Making the company self-organizing is not the only way to bring about good results. The same results are also achievable through the hierarchical model as well. In the short-run, the hierarchical approach, through centralization of authority, might bring equal results. However, in the long-run, self-organization assures the firm of continuous adaptation to a changing environment. Hierarchy deprives the firm from the intelligence and wisdom of its employees. It also inhibits them from changing anything without a long wait for management to give orders. This minimizes the firm's capacity to respond to a volatile marketplace.
- With managers' authority diminished in a self-organizing setting, will this take away the fun of being a boss and the firm will lack in management depth? Traditionally, the fun of being a boss resided in pushing people around and the enjoyment of making all the decisions. This, however, resulted in poor performance for the unit as employees outmaneuvered the boss. The manager was blamed for this performance. The fun of being a boss was diminished by the pressure of blame. In a self-organizing setting, there is new type of fun, the fun of building a group, developing it, and seeing it reach an ever increasing level of achievement.

## Limitations of Self-Organization

Is the self-organizing system's model applicable to all organizations? It seems to be applicable to a wide range of organizations even in difficult situations such as a trauma team in an emergency room. Such teams operate in a self-organizing manner. In Chapter 3, we saw the concept practiced in sausage making (Johnsonville Foods), manufacturing (GE and Springfield Remanufacturing), distribution (PSS/World Medical), service (FedEx), and hi-tech (Oticon).

The concept, however, requires a number of necessary and sufficient conditions to be in place. These are:

- A genuine belief that letting the firm function as a self-organizing system is superior to other approaches for running the business.
- Recruiting and selecting the type of employees who are predisposed to self-management, i.e., broad minded (have a big picture perspective), autonomous, willing to be accountable for their actions and for the company.
- Equipping these employees with the skills needed not only to do their job but also to function in a self-organizing setting.
- Genuine sharing of the gains and the pains of self-organization. In an employee-led organization, the employees are a critical factor in bringing about the firm's financial results, good or bad. Therefore, they must share in the gain and the pain. Accordingly, progressive CEOs establish an equitable system that recognizes the contribution of employees in financial terms. Without such a system, there will be no incentive for the employees to undertake the extra work necessitated by self-organization, e.g., coordinating with others, seeking creative solutions, improvising, stretching resources, and piloting their respective units. Financial recognition can take many forms including raises, increments for progression through the ranks, increments for learning new skills, profit sharing, and ownership sharing.

## Strategic Leadership and Type of Firm

Business firms fall into two categories: single business and multi-business. Throughout the chapters to follow, a distinction will be made between the two types. The single business firm is focused on carving and maintaining a defensible, profitable position in a specific product-market segment. It draws most of its revenue from a single product or a product category. It operates primarily in one industry.

The multi-business firm is a constellation or a collection of businesses operating in a number of different industries (often referred to as "strategic business units" or SBUs for short). This type of firm is focused on building and maintaining a "portfolio of businesses" where each carves a good product-market position in an effort to maximize the value of the whole portfolio. All the diversified large corporations and conglomerates in the market today fall into this category. In the multi-business firm, there will be two levels of strategic leadership. At the SBU level, strategic leadership happens as in the case of the single business firm. At the corporate level, there is another level of leadership, the senior chief executive who leads the heads of the SBUs directly, and the whole conglomerate as well.

Clearly, the single businesses firm is the most frequent type in the economy. The majority of firms often deal in one product or a line of related products. The multi-business firms themselves are clusters of single businesses. Because of the preponderance of the single business firm's case, the bulk of the concepts in this work will focus on strategic leadership in this type of firm. The multi-business firm's case will also be addressed but not to the same extent.

# CONCLUSION

In this chapter, an overview of the strategic leadership model was presented. The model comprises two main, concurrent, and interrelated streams of tasks. The first stream encompasses the CEO's tasks in structuring the firm as a self-organizing system. The second involves the CEO's activities in guiding the system toward desired strategic end-states. The two sets of tasks were only introduced here. Further elaboration follows in Chapters 5 and 6.

At this point, we can venture a definition of strategic management. There are two possible ways of defining strategic leadership. First, we can define it operationally just by listing the tasks that constitute it, as shown in Exhibit 4.1. Second, we can define it verbally. In doing so, there are two critical terms in the definition, the adjective "strategic" and the noun "leadership." The term leadership refers to a certain style of leadership, namely virtual leadership, i.e., letting the employees lead. The term strategic signifies that the leadership is about steering the firm toward meeting strategic ends. Putting the two together, one can define strategic leadership as guiding a self-managing organization towards survival and growth in a turbulent marketplace. Clearly, strategic leadership is different from strategic management. To highlight these differences, Exhibit 4.5 was prepared.

| STRATEGIC MANAGEMENT | STRATEGIC LEADERSHIP |
|---|---|
| Presupposition: The firm as a herd of buffalo. The head buffalo leads; the herd follows obediently. | Presupposition: The firm as a flock of geese. Each one takes turns as the leader. |
| The firm as an "apparatus" to be manipulated by the CEO | The firm as a "self-organizing" system that manages itself by itself |
| Flow of power, information, and instructions for the organization: Top-down | Flow of power, information, and instructions for the organization Circular, centerless—diffused throughout the organization. |
| Emphasis on planning and control | Emphasis on "spontaneous" continuous adaptation to continuously changing circumstances |
| Focused on strategy—a predetermined course of action by top management. | Focused on responding intelligently and continuously to turbulence—in ad hoc fashion formulated by various trusted modules (people, teams, units) in their own spheres |
| Focused on developing and sustaining a competitive advantage | Focused on the state of existence of the firm that pleases its stakeholders defined broadly |
| Management | Leadership |
| Hierarchical | Lateral |
| The CEO and top management are the source of all wisdom and intelligence. | People are the source of wisdom and intelligence. |
| The CEO is commander-in-chief. | The CEO is only a member of the system |

Exhibit 4.5: Contrasting Strategic Management and Strategic Leadership

# ENDNOTES

1. Wheatley, M.J. and M. Keliner-Rogers, "Self-Organization: The Irresistible Future Of Organizing," *Strategy & Leadership*, July/August, 1996, p. 18.

2. As quoted in Puris, M., *Comeback: How Seven Straight-Shooting CEOs Turned Around Troubled Companies*, New York, NY: Time Business, Random House, 1999.

3. As quoted in Farkas, C.M. and P. De Backer, *Maximum Leadership: The World's Leading CEOs Share Their Five Strategies for Success*, New York, NY: Henry Holt, 1996.

4. Hargrove, R., *Mastering the Art of Creative Collaboration*, New York, NY: McGraw-Hill, 1998.

5. Huey, J., "The New Post-Heroic Leadership," *Fortune*, vol. 129, no. 4, February 21, 1994, pp. 42–44.

6. Ibid.

7. Huey, J., "The New Post-Heroic Leadership," *Fortune*, vol. 129, no. 4, February 21, 1994, pp. 42–44.

8. Alsop, S., "E or Be Eaten," *Fortune*, November 8, 1999, p. 87.

9. Hamel, G. and J. Sampler, "The e-Corporation," *Fortune*, December 7, 1998, p. 82.

10. Tapscott, D., *Growing Up Digital: The Rise of The Net Generation*, New York, NY: McGraw-Hill, 1998.

11. Ibid., p. 82.

12. Littman, J., "The Book on Amazon.Com," *Los Angeles Times Magazine*, July 20, 1997.

13. Hamel and Sampler, op. cit., p. 81.

14. Tapscott, D., *Growing Up Digital: The Rise of The Net Generation*, New York, NY: McGraw-Hill, 1998.

15. Gates III, W.H., *Business @ the Speed of Thought: Using a Digital Nervous System*, New York, NY: Warner Books, 1999.

16. Brown, S.L. and K.M. Eisenstadt, *Competing on the Edge: Strategy as Structured Chaos*, Boston, MA: Harvard Business School Press, 1998.

17. Putnam, H.D., *The Winds Of Turbulence: A CEO's Reflections on Surviving and Thriving on the Cutting Edge of Corporate Crisis*, New York, NY: Harper Collins, 1998, p. 1.

18. Kiernan, M., *Get Innovative Or Get Dead*, Vancouver, BC: Douglas & McIntyre, 1995, Chapter 1.

19. Schlender, B., "E-Business According to Gates," *Fortune*, April 12, 1999, p. 74.

20. Ghoshal, S. and C.A. Bartlett, *The Individualized Corporation*, New York, NY: HarperCollins, 1997.

21. Belasco, J.A. and R.C. Stayer, *Flight of The Buffalo: Soaring To Excellence, Learning To Let Employees Lead*, New York, NY: Warner Books, 1993.

22. From the Chaordic Alliance Website—The Alliance was founded by Dee Hock to spread the knowledge about Chaordic organizations.

23. Brown, S.L. and K.M. Eisenstadt, *Competing on the Edge: Strategy as Structured Chaos*, Boston, MA: Harvard Business School Press, 1998, p. 12.

24. Ibid.

25. Ibid.

26. Citrin, J.M. and T.J. Neff, "Digital Leadership," *Strategy & Business*, First Quarter, 2000, p. 46–47.

27. Ibid., p. 43.

# CHAPTER 5

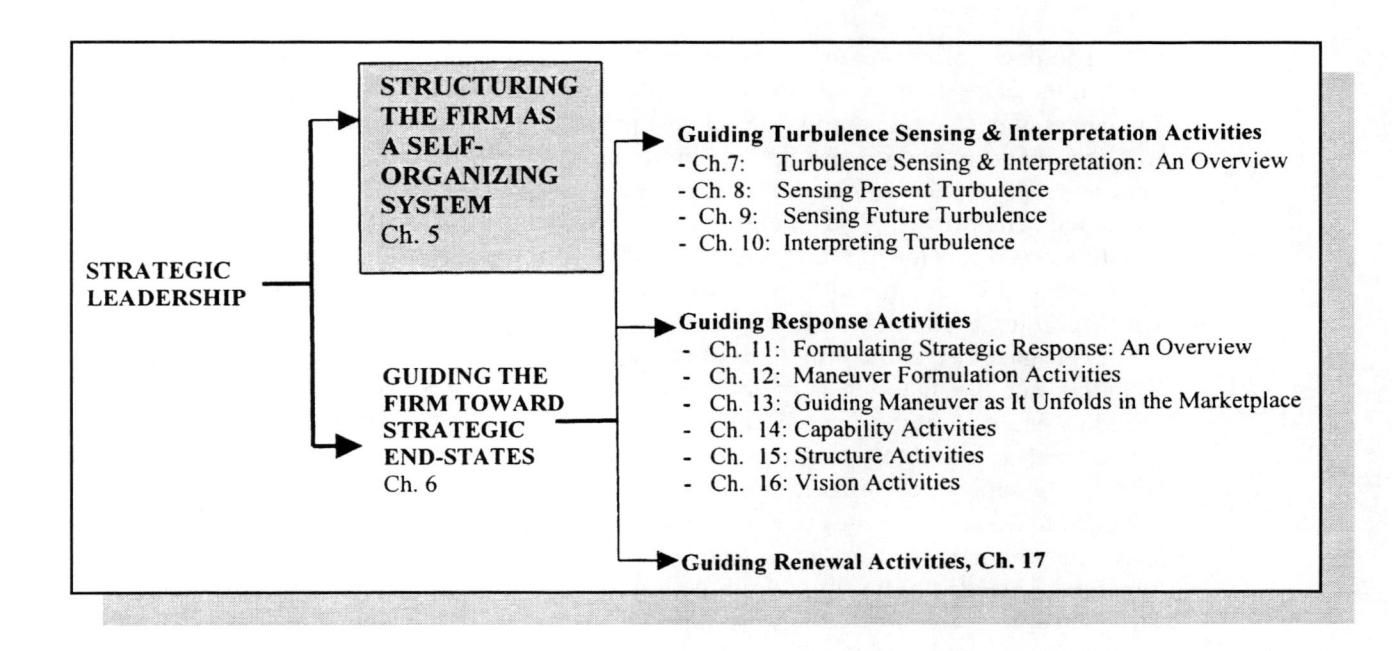

# Structuring the Firm as a Self-Organizing System

```
STRATEGIC
LEADERSHIP
    ├──▶ STRUCTURING THE FIRM AS A SELF-ORGANIZING SYSTEM  Ch. 5
    │         ├──▶ Guiding Turbulence Sensing & Interpretation Activities
    │         │      - Ch. 7:  Turbulence Sensing & Interpretation: An Overview
    │         │      - Ch. 8:  Sensing Present Turbulence
    │         │      - Ch. 9:  Sensing Future Turbulence
    │         │      - Ch. 10: Interpreting Turbulence
    │         │
    │         ├──▶ Guiding Response Activities
    │         │      - Ch. 11: Formulating Strategic Response: An Overview
    │         │      - Ch. 12: Maneuver Formulation Activities
    │         │      - Ch. 13: Guiding Maneuver as It Unfolds in the Marketplace
    │         │      - Ch. 14: Capability Activities
    │         │      - Ch. 15: Structure Activities
    │         │      - Ch. 16: Vision Activities
    │         │
    └──▶ GUIDING THE FIRM TOWARD STRATEGIC END-STATES  Ch. 6
              └──▶ Guiding Renewal Activities, Ch. 17
```

As presented in Chapter 4, the strategic leadership model comprises two interdependent, concurrent streams of CEO activities: structuring the firm as a self-organizing system; and, guiding the firm towards strategic end-states. Because it is so fundamental, we pause to examine the concept of the self-organizing system in greater depth in this chapter. As a background, we begin with an overview of the traditional model of organizing the business firm, primarily the top-down, command-and-control system. However, the turbulence of the 1980s and 1990s rendered this model obsolete. Firms that continue to use it, do so at the risk of being out of touch with their rapidly changing markets.

As of the 1980s, new organizational paradigms started to appear. We highlight this development in the second section. The new paradigms culminated in the emergence of the self-organizing system paradigm. Accordingly, we investigate the concept next. Finally, we conclude with some key principles that the CEO can apply in order to structure the firm as a self-organizing system. This is not the last coverage of the concept. The topic will be taken up again in Chapter 15, where these principles will be applied to the business firm.

# TRADITIONAL ORGANIZATIONAL STRUCTURES

The dawn of professional management began with the scientific management movement in the early 20th century. Scientific management attempted to apply scientific method to managing business operations. Such an approach called for the measurement and control of factor inputs to maximize output and minimize cost. This assumed that the factors of production (capital, people, material, land, etc.) are passive objects that can be manipulated and measured scientifically. Thus, an employee, as a factor of production, is assigned one task. The time to do it is measured. The method of performing it is studied and improved. A standard time/motion combination is set. Henceforth, the employee was expected to perform the task according to this standard repetitively and relentlessly.

This gave rise to the principles of division of labor, specialization, and standardization. They became the main tenets of scientific management. These helped the birth of the high speed or paced assembly line. Further attention was paid to the concept of authority, which was described in military language such as the "chain of command." Since one person can effectively supervise a limited number of subordinates, soon the span of control concept emerged to define how many persons a supervisor can ideally manage. However, supervisors needed to be supervised and a new managerial level was created. Next, the supervisors of the supervisors needed to be supervised. Accordingly, a new, higher managerial level was created. This process continued upward until the organization had a number of echelons forming a hierarchy. Perhaps the CEO who best represents this approach is Alfred P. Sloan, the then CEO of General Motors and architect of its organizational structure.

The typical Sloan type structure was designed along two main dimensions: horizontal and vertical differentiation. Horizontally, the organization was segmented by functions such as marketing, finance, manufacturing, engineering, etc (reflecting the principle of specialization). Vertically, the structure consisted of many layers or echelons reflecting a chain of command that extended downward several levels. This created a "deep" or "tall" organizational structure. These principles were reinforced by Weber's thoughts on bureaucracy, which advocated similar principles and added the emphasis on prescribed procedures for doing everything "right." Hence, bureaucracy's principles such as job descriptions, and procedural manuals were born.

Scientific management thought led to a basic set of beliefs (paradigm) that has been called, "the command-and-control system" or "top-down management." The assumptions include maxims such as:

- Management must manage (management prerogatives).
- Management is the only authority with the expertise to design and make things happen.
- Employees do not have the maturity to participate in strategic matters. For example, a former CEO of a large Airline once warned that allowing employees a seat on the board of directors is like "letting the monkeys be in charge of the zoo."
- The employees are only a "factor of production." There is no difference between humans and machines; both can be manipulated (scientifically) so that they can be integrated in the process of production.
- The employees are only motivated by pay and material rewards.

As of the early 1980s, the age of globalization began and foreign competition changed the dynamics and structure of the business world. The success of the Japanese automakers demonstrated that the command and control system is not as constructive as North American management believed. Soon, North American executives discovered Japanese management, a new model for structuring the organization emphasizing the strategic role of employees. It put into question all the accepted Western principles of managing and organizing people.

Out of alignment with the turbulence of the 1980s, the command-and-control system produced serious problems for many North American manufacturing firms. These problems became dramatic when these firms lost ground to foreign competition, particularly to the Japanese. Here are some examples of such problems:

- Low quality and lack of reliability: Employees performed their job according to procedures and policy manuals (by the book). Beyond this, they did not care. If a crisis developed, it was management's problem. Defects continued to rise but no one took responsibility. Management blamed labor and labor blamed management. Meanwhile, the customer defected to foreign manufacturers.
- High cost of the manufacturing process: Employees did their work, but they did not want to improve the process since "it is not their problem." Even when they wanted to introduce improvements, the bureaucracy and the adversarial roles between management and labor extinguished their interest.
- Long lead-time from concept to market: Command-and-control organizations were stratified along horizontal (functional) and vertical lines (numerous echelons). Its functional units (e.g., sales, manufacturing, engineering, finance, etc.) did not communicate horizontally thus slowing down the movement of information across the organization thus creating coordination problems. Vertically, top echelons were removed from the realities of the firing line and ended up giving instructions that did not make sense to those who were expected to implement them. They in turn ignored the instructions and did what they could. Consequently, the firm became unable to cope with sudden changes in the marketplace.
- Bloated, slow bureaucracy: Management became obsessed with procedures. Following procedure became more important than getting the job done. It took many persons to do the job of one. Often some important tasks were no one's responsibility (not in my job description, somebody else's problem).
- The bureaucracy (layers and layers of middle managers and volumes of detailed procedures) insulated top management from coming to grips with the turbulence of the marketplace. Meanwhile, the rest of the firm waited around for commands from the top. While the organization was waiting around, the firm did not respond to changes in the marketplace. Competitors then moved in to take market share away from the firm. This would appear to be the case of IBM in the early 1990s. The

impact of desktop computers and LANs (local area networks) was underestimated by IBM's top managers who were still focused on the mainframe computer business. Along the same lines, top managers of The Big 3 automakers took years to come up with a realistic appraisal of the invasion of Japanese automakers and to make a strategic response to it.

The above problems were driven by the two features of the traditional organizational structure: (1) horizontal (functional) and vertical segmentation of the firm, and (2) the centralization of authority at the top. Horizontally, there were departments (such as marketing, finance, and manufacturing). Vertically, each department had a deep structure comprising several layers. The organization thus looked like a number of "smoke stacks," "silos," and "chimneys." Due to specialization, each silo operated in isolation with minimum communication with the others, except after the fact, when crises arose. There was little integration among them. For example, if the sales department was granting easy terms and pushed the product, the finance department would experience a bulge in accounts receivable and bad debts. When receivables and bad debts reached undesirable levels, a conflict developed between the two departments. Even then, it was hard to settle the conflict. Every problem was someone else's problem. Interdepartmental conflicts had to be resolved by top management since silos did not talk to one another.

Major decisions naturally had to be made at the top (centralizaton) because the silos could not see the "big picture" as they were focused on their specialty. At the same time, top management was at a considerable organizational distance (several layers) from the firing line where turbulence impacted the firm. By the time the information climbed upward, it was distorted and the response was often misguided. By the time response decisions cascaded down they became distorted in the process, and the response amounted to doing too little (or too much) too late.

## THE EMERGENCE OF NEW ORGANIZATIONAL PARADIGMS

The turbulence of the 1980's and its consequences (as outlined above) prompted many CEOs to think of radically different approaches for managing their corporations. That was the age of reinventing the corporation. The centerpiece of reinventing the corporation was a new paradigm for structuring the organization. Jack Welch of GE pioneered the new paradigm. Realizing that GE could not evolve in the new global economy restrained by the command-and-control paradigm, Welch set out, in the early 1980s, to restructure the company's organization along new principles such as:

- The Flat Organization: Layers upon layers of management make "managing" an end in itself, instead of making the decisions that would help the firm respond quickly to change. Hence, layers of middle management were eliminated to facilitate direct communication between the bottom (where action takes place) and the top.
- Debureaucratization: Emphasis on procedures was eliminated in favor of stressing results and accountability. Thick organizational manuals were abandoned.
- Boundarylessness: The specialization walls and boundaries between silos came down. They were dismantled and rearranged to form smaller integrated units that identify with the company in its entirety (cross functional teams) in addition to their own individual specialty.

Welch articulated these principles in 1983 in the form of a list of ten thoughts. The first thought instructed that each of GE's units must be #1 or #2 in its respective industry or it will be divested. The second thought urged that GE must be a lean, agile corporation; the big corporation that thinks and acts with the speed and agility of a small firm. The rest of the thoughts dealt with the architecture of the desired people's behavior that would make speed and agility possible. These are:[1]

- Ownership: getting people in the trenches to own into the company's problems and to assume responsibility for the company as a whole. This is accomplished by giving them greater power. He elaborated on the concept as follows: "If we can think of ownership as just saying more 'Grab it! Run with it!' Take responsibility. Make the decision. Give the management awards. Make the sales plans. Do the things you want to do to run your business faster everyday, we've got something."
- Stewardship: a responsibility that accompanies ownership. It translates into the obligation to protect GE's assets, and working at capacity to ensure the company's competitive success. As Welch explained: "Stewardship is an obligation. Stewardship is working at 100% to 150%. Stewardship in the end is what your jobs are all about. It's your challenge: to take the assets you have, drive them to newer and better heights through excellence, through taking charge, and make this enterprise better in 1990 than it is today."
- Entrepreneurship: allowing people to experiment and undertake new initiatives and giving them recognition for trying. Welch introduced the principle of "celebrating success as well as celebrating failure." Celebrating failure is crucial to encourage people to take risks experimenting with new initiatives in the hope that success will eventually materialize. This is the essence of entrepreneurship.
- Excellence: driving one's self and demanding the very best from it continuously.
- Quality: accomplished by individual excellence; should be a pervasive way of life, including products, services, fulfillment of citizen responsibilities, and communication with the outside world.
- Reality and Candor: a prerequisite for excellence and quality. They cannot happen unless there is an atmosphere based on reality and candor. It is important to share problems and information to foster trust and facilitate joint problem solving. This principle led to the evolution of the "Work Out" sessions to facilitate a free exchange of ideas between upper and lower levels in the organization.
- Communication: an essential tool for involving people in the overall company success, not just for the purpose of performing their jobs.

## The Emergence of the Virtual Organization Model

In the late 1980s, the concept of the virtual organization gained considerable momentum. As of late, it is rapidly becoming a common model for organizing business. For a variety of reasons, many manufacturing firms are outsourcing parts and assemblies from suppliers instead of making them. Many firms are downsizing relying on outsiders to provide what was made in house traditionally. A new breed of firms has emerged, the virtual corporation. The typical virtual corporation does not produce a product. Instead, it assembles a network of independents and coordinates their outputs so that all together they form what looks and acts like a regular corporation. The increased popularity of e-commerce transformed many businesses into virtual ones, e.g., Amazon.Com; the virtual bookstore.

For years, a major multinational corporation, the Italian fashion firm Benetton, was a model for the virtual organizational structure.[2] Styling, design, manufacturing, logistics distribution, and sales were performed by independents that were assembled and coordinated by Benetton. The features of Benetton's organization were as follows:

- The styling and design of the garments was done outside the firm by a number of international free-lance stylists. A small staff of about 20 people in the Product Development Department interpreted the look created by the stylists and performed the modeling phase.
- Over 80% of manufacturing was done outside the company by 350 sub-contractors who employed 10,000 persons.
- Logistics and distribution activities were also performed mainly by outsiders. The company did the storage.
- The company utilized an external sales organization comprising quasi-independent agents who coordinated the operations of nearly 4000 independently owned retail shops spread all over the world.

The trend towards the virtual organization will gain more momentum as information technology permeates business life. Information technology is becoming the leading cause for the creation of virtual organizations. Because of information technology, phenomena such as "telecommuting," "telework," and, "teleconferencing" have rendered many operations virtual. The virtual organizational structure provides the ultimate in fluidity in a turbulent world. As the business world becomes more turbulent, this trend will become a popular way of doing business and structuring organizations.

Interestingly, the virtual organization is not an entirely new concept. Voss[3] traced the early signs of the trend to the 1970's in the Prato Region in Italy. He reported the case of Massimo Menichetti as one of the early cases of the virtual organization, Exhibit 5.1. Voss identified the characteristics of the virtual structure as follows:

"The characteristics of the emerging virtual organizations . . . are significantly different from those we find in old-fashioned, hierarchical companies. Virtual organizations seem to have five overarching characteristics in common.

- They have a shared vision and goal and/or a common protocol of cooperation.
- They cluster activities around their core competencies.
- They work jointly in teams of core-competence groups to implement their activities in one holistic approach throughout the value chain.
- They process and distribute information in real time throughout the network, which allows them to make decisions and coordinate actions quickly.
- They tend to delegate from the bottom up whenever economies of scale can be achieved, new conditions arise, or a specific competence is required for serving the needs of the whole group."[4]

A forum of business executives, labor leaders, public administrators, and researchers on the topic of the virtual organization arrived at the conclusion that "The virtual corporation or organization is a mosaic (usually temporary) of independent companies or people linked together by information technology to pursue a market opportunity."[5] Speakers at the forum started by recognizing a fundamental shift in the economy. In the old economic model, organizations were stable. They operated from the premise that the environment is stable also and hence committed themselves to constant strategies. Accordingly, they produced predetermined product and services utilizing a stable mix of assets, capital, technology, and people. In the new economy, organizations are much more fluid. There is an infinite variety of configurations that they can assume depending on the circumstances. Although they have core missions and core competencies, their boundaries, inputs, technologies, expertise, and people will always be changing.

> Massimo Menichetti*
>
> "Massimo Menichetti may have been one of the first to move away from a large, hierarchical organization when he changed the way business was done in the textile industry. . . After three succeeding years of loss, he decided to disassemble the company into functionally specialized groups as a way of meeting the challenge of rising internal cost, lower market prices, and the need to create greater product variety.
>
> Menichetti created eight separate functionally specialized companies. He said, 'I wanted the finishing departments to specialize in what they were good at; I broke up the spinning and weaving departments and let them excel in whatever they wanted to specialize in, unencumbered by the rest of the specialties. If they innovate and are good at what they are doing, they can always sell their products to somebody in Prato.' Menichetti sold one third to one half of the stock in the companies to key employees. By allowing them to pay with profits over a period of three years, he arranged that these new shareholders wouldn't have to show their own money up front. Each of the independent companies was expected to achieve more than 50 percent of its turnover through its own sales activities or by subcontracting to other firms. Menichetti, himself, founded Italfabrics, a New York marketing company that specializes in fashion fabrics, he stipulated that it would order no more than 30 percent of its manufacturing volume from companies in the Menichetti group.
>
> The dissaggretation was extremely successful. After three years, machine utilization was greater than 90 percent, including new machines that increased production by 25 percent; labor and machine productivity increased significantly; and over a period of five years, the labor force was reduced by 30 percent through natural attrition.
>
> This pattern of success spread throughout the entire Prato region, and by the 80's there were more than 15,000 independent firms with an average of five employees. Their textiles and yarns produced revenues of about $1.6 million, $1.1 million of which was from export.
>
> While there was competition among these small, independent companies, at the same time they established cooperatives for tasks in which economies of scale or a monopolistic structure would be more efficient, as in purchasing, logistics, technological innovation, and product development.
>
> The design and installation of plants with the most modern looms, computer-aided designs, special applications to translate colors into formulas for dyeing with high fidelity color reproduction, and the world's most modern, fully computerized warehouses—all can be found in the Prato region. These companies work together jointly to solve common problems. They are cooperating and in fierce competition at the same time".

Exhibit 5.1: An Early Case of the Virtual Organizational Structure

The views expressed in the forum can be summarized as follows:

- The virtual corporation is comprised of individuals who have certain visions and unique skills and equipment who are brought together to exploit short-lived opportunities by creating and delivering value to their customers.
- The virtual corporation has an agile organization capable of adapting to its market conditions.
- The operating pattern of the virtual corporation is predominantly project based. They arrange and rearrange themselves according to the challenge at hand, which is pursued as a project. Life for these firms is the pursuit of one project after another.
- The virtual corporation has a transient character and its structure is rather fluid. Virtual companies tend to be *ad hoc*, i.e., their formation is tailored to opportunity.
- The organization of the virtual corporation has a vaguely defined hierarchy. In most cases, the hierarchy is a non-issue for the people involved. They are externally focused. In such organizations, the nature of the relationship among people is more important than status through formal relationships of bosses and subordinates.

---

*From *Strategy & Leadership*, July/August 1996 by H. Voss. Copyright 1996 by Strategic Leadership Forum. Reprinted by permission.

- In the virtual corporations, competencies are distributed throughout the entire organization. After all, it is an assortment or a coalition of people who have something unique to offer.
- Virtual corporations achieve significant competitive advantages in terms of speed, cost, and innovation because they tend to focus on such advantages. To them, the traditional differentials in price, quality, and productivity are viewed as insignificant or marginal at best.

Why is the virtual form of doing business increasing in popularity? According to the participants at the forum, the most important driving force behind the virtual form of business organization is the changing role of the customers. Instead of being on the periphery of the organization (as an external factor), they are now the center of action. Corporations now want to be market-driven. This realization was fueled by unprecedented change and volatility in customers' demands. Because of this volatility, windows of opportunity tend to be short lived. Only nimble, agile, and fast companies can survive and thrive in such an environment. The virtual organization structure does provide the firm with these advantages since it is a fluid, transient structure.

Besides the changing customer, there are intrinsic advantages to the virtual corporation comprised of numerous firms. These advantages act as attractors for many firms to come together to function as a virtual organization. These include:

- The virtual form of doing business provides unique advantages for all participants. It assures the participating firms a certain volume of business. It provides the overall virtual corporation with a steady supply of products and services. It is a win-win arrangement for all concerned.
- When many players come together, business risk and cost are spread among them thereby reducing the risk for each.
- The virtual form of doing business addresses the issue of intellectual capital. Participants come to the table, but they maintain their autonomy including their intellectual capital.

## The Emergence of the E-Organization

With the e-business revolution taking hold in the 2000s, a new organizational model has emerged, "the e-org," the structure most suitable for e-businesses. Neilson, Pasternack and Viscio mapped out the e-org and contrasted it with the traditional organization of the 1990s.[6] The comparison is shown in Exhibit 5.2. The e-org displays different properties. First, its structure tends to be centerless, networked, and easily modifiable. Second, in the e-org, everyone is a leader. Leadership focuses on creating the environment for success and on developing the firm's capacity for change. Third, people operate in a different mode. They have delegated authority, but they are expected to collaborate so that the organization may have a unity of direction. Fourth, e-orgs have coherence because a shared vision is embedded in it. It measures itself by the impact it makes on the marketplace. Fifth, the e-org is a knowledge-based organization. Information is institutionalized so that everyone may have the information to make decisions. Sixth, the e-org is a boundaryless organization. It will ally with anyone who will help it advance whether it is a competitor, a customer, or a supplier. It builds networks through partnerships. It even allies with its competitors at some level to develop extraordinary capabilities. Finally, the e-org displays a different governance pattern from traditional organizations. Governance is distributed rather than centralized at the top. It organizes its governance internally by having inter-company governance boards. At the same time, there is an external focus to governance, as these companies tend to have outside boards that bring in external perspective and challenge the firm's paradigms and strategies.

| Organizational Dimension | The Organization of the 1990s | The E-Organization |
| --- | --- | --- |
| Structure | • Hierarchical<br>• Command-and-Control | • Centerless, networked<br>• Flexible structure that is easily modified |
| Leadership | • Selected "stars" step above<br>• Leaders set the agenda<br>• Leaders force change | • Everyone is a leader<br>• Leaders create environment for success<br>• Leaders create capacity for change |
| People & Culture | • Long term rewards<br>• Vertical decision-making<br>• Individuals and small teams are rewarded | • "Own your own career" mentality<br>• Delegated authority<br>• Collaboration expected and rewarded |
| Coherence | • Hard wired into processes<br>• Internal relevance | • Embedded vision in individuals<br>• Impact projected externally |
| Knowledge | • Focused on internal processes<br>• Individualistic | • Focused on customers<br>• Institutional |
| Alliances | • Complement current gaps<br>• Ally with distant partners | • Create new value and outsource uncompetitive services<br>• Ally with competitors, customers, and suppliers |
| Governance | • Internally focused<br>• Top-down | • Internal and external focus<br>• Distributed |

Exhibit 5.2: Comparing the Traditional Organization of the 1990s and the E-Organization

If we examine the new organizational structures, we can discern one basic paradigm that underlies them and this is the self-organizing system model. The model is explored next.

# THE SELF-ORGANIZING SYSTEM'S PARADIGM

The self-organizing system model is based on the premise that a group of people, like a business firm, can manage its own affairs without an externally imposed directive, just like natural systems, e.g., swarms, flocks of geese, or ant colonies. These natural systems have a structure that can serve as a possible model for human organizations. The most important attraction of this structure is its capacity to respond quickly and continuously to a turbulent marketplace. Wheatly and Keliner-Rogers stated the argument as follows:[7]

"These days, a different ideal for organizations is surfacing. We want organizations to be adaptive, flexible, self-renewing, resilient, learning, and intelligent—attributes found only in living systems. The tension of our times is that we want our organizations to behave as living systems, but we only know how to treat them as machines.

*It is time to change the way we think about organizations.* Organizations are living systems. All living systems have the capacity to self organize, to sustain themselves and move toward greater complexity and order as needed. They can respond intelligently to the need for change. They organize (and then reorganize) themselves into adaptive patterns and structures without any externally imposed plan or direction.

Self-organizing systems have what all leaders crave. The capacity to respond continuously to change . . ."

Kelly's work provides valuable insights into the concept of self-organization.[8] He contrasted two fundamental approaches for structuring human organizations. At one end of the spectrum, there is a structure that is like a long string of sequential operations designed with the logic of a clock operating as a "complicated parade of movements." He called this the "sequential system." The sequential system is the equivalent of the command-and-control system or scientific management discussed earlier in this presentation.

At the other end of the spectrum, there is another structure that he articulated as follows:

". . . a patchwork of parallel operations, very much as in the neural network of a brain or in a colony of ants. Action in these systems proceeds in a messy cascade of interdependent events. Instead of discrete ticks of cause and effect that run a clock, a thousand clock springs try to simultaneously run a parallel system. Since there is no chain of command, the particular action of any single spring diffuses into the whole, making it easier for the sum of the whole to overwhelm the parts of the whole. What emerges from the collective is not a series of critical individual actions but a multitude of simultaneous actions whose collective pattern is far more important."[9]

Kelly called this type of structure "the swarm model." It is also known as a "self-organizing" living system. Kelly noted that the swarm model is known by a variety of names including "parallel-operating wholes, networks, complex adaptive systems, vivisystems, and collective systems."

As Kelly noted, studies of ant colonies and beehives reveal an interesting phenomenon. As individual entities act autonomously with no one in control, a "hive mind" appears to be in charge. "The marvel of the 'hive mind' is that no one is in control, and yet an invisible hand governs, a hand that emerges from very dumb members."[10] The "hive mind" or the "invisible hand" is the mechanism of self-organization. The secret of self-organization "resides" in the hive mind and the "invisible hand."

Kelly defines the self-organizing structure as follows:

". . . a collection of many (thousands) autonomous members. 'Autonomous' means that each member reacts individually according to internal rules and the state of the local environment. This is opposed to obeying orders from a center, or reacting in lock step to the overall environment.

These autonomous members are highly connected to each other, but not to a central hub. They thus form a peer network. Since there is no center of control, the management and heart of the system are said to be decentrally distributed within the system, as a hive is administered."[11]

The phenomenon of "autonomous, parallel peer networks concurrently functioning without a center" is called "distributed being" by Kelly. He further stresses these four aspects for distributed being:

- The absence of imposed centralized control.
- The autonomous nature of subunits.
- The high connectivity between the subunits.
- The webby nonlinear causality of peers influencing peers, i.e., they are all operating individually and concurrently without being triggered and ordered by a center.

The swarm system is not a perfect model. It has its own strengths and drawbacks. Kelly summarizes its strengths as follows:

- Adaptable: Only a whole containing many parts can persist while the parts die off or change to fit the new stimuli
- Evolvable: It can shift the locus of adaptation over time from one part of the system to another
- Resilient: Small failures are lost in the hubbub. Big failures are held in check by becoming merely small failures at the next highest level on a hierarchy.
- Boundless: It incrementally extends a new structure beyond the bounds of its initial state, a swarm can build its own scaffolding to build further structure. Spontaneous order helps create more order. Life begets more life, wealth creates more wealth, information breeds more information, all bursting the original cradle. And with no bounds in sight.
- Novelty: It exists for three reasons: (1) These systems are 'sensitive to initial conditions'—a scientific shorthand for saying that the size of the effect is not proportional to the size of the cause. Thus, they can make a surprising mountain out of a molehill. (2) They hide countless novel possibilities in the exponential combinations of many interlinked individuals. (3) They do not reckon individuals, so therefore individual variations and imperfections can be allowed."[12]

For those considering the swarm model as blueprints for structuring organizations, Kelly has some warnings. Some of its properties represent disadvantages. These include:

- Nonoptimal: There is redundancy due to lack of central control. Resources are allotted "higgledy-piggledy." Duplication is expected due to varied individual initiatives.
- Noncontrollable: There is no authority in charge. "Guiding a swarm system can only be done as a shepherd would drive a herd; by applying force at crucial leverage points, and by subverting the natural tendencies of the system to new ends."[13]
- Nonpredictable: Individual concurrent behaviour creates a great deal of complexity that makes it difficult to predict.
- Nonunderstandable: Lack of causality and non-linearity make it hard to understand exactly why certain things happen.
- Nonimmediate: "Complex swarm systems with rich hierarchies take time to boot up; organic time."[14]

Is the swarm structure applicable to all types of organizations? For organizations and operations requiring absolute control, the command-and-control system is better suited. Examples of these include operating rooms and emergency rooms in hospitals, NASA's space missions, and the like. Such organizations need to operate with clockwork precision. The problem, however, is organizations where supreme adaptability is demanded. These organizations operate in a turbulent, volatile environment that changes continuously. The absolute majority of business firms fall into this category. The swarm system or the parallel-operating whole model is best suited for them. It has disadvantages as mentioned above, but one should consider the trade-off: stay with the command-and-control system and suffer, or change over to the swarm model and prosper.

# PRINCIPLES OF BUILDING SELF-ORGANIZING SYSTEMS

Kelly's analysis of "natural" living systems led him to identify ten principles that define the self-organizing system's paradigm. Kelly's ten principles are adapted here for the business firm.

## Distributed Being

"Distributed being" means that the company exists as "a parallel operating whole," i.e., it consists of a number of empowered autonomous groups that operate in their own sphere according to their internal logic. When each unit has the power to operate as it sees fit in its own sphere, it will be able to adapt quickly and automatically. As each unit adapts quickly, the whole firm would then respond quickly to its changing environment. When the firm exists as a group of separate units, it will not fall apart. Rather, a hive-mind or group-mind emerges, embodying the invisible hand phenomenon, which ensures that all parts move toward the common good although they are independent.

The principle of distributed being is easily applicable to the business firm. The business of any firm is to create value for customers. The attribute of distributed being can be achieved by structuring the firm as a number of autonomous market scale units (Chapter 15) each performing a certain value creating function through a distinctive business model.

## Networked Being

The hive-mind that actualizes self-organization occurs only when all units in the organization are interconnected or "wired" with one another. "Networkedness" causes the hive-mind (group mind) or the invisible hand to emerge. When each unit in the distributed being structure has full information about what all the other units are doing, it somehow starts to coordinate its actions with them (the effect of the invisible hand). The emergence of the digital organization has made networkedness easy to achieve. If all information is on-line (as Kolind did at Oticon), every unit can tap in to find out about all activities in the corporation. A good example of networked being is Wal-Mart, which has an elaborate satellite system and a fleet of airplanes that connect every store manager with other store managers as well as the corporate office continuously.

## Control from the Bottom Up

Self-organization occurs only when control is from the bottom rather than from the top. The reason is that the units at the bottom (the firing line) are ones that deal with turbulence first hand. If the firm is to respond to turbulence at all, these units must be in control, i.e., they have the power to decide what needs to be done, and do it without referring to the top for approval each time. Should units on the firing line be forced to wait for instructions from the top, the firm will not respond in real time to changes in its environment. It takes a long time for information to travel up to the top and down again and this delays the firm's response. Furthermore, as the information travels up and down the organization, it is subject to considerable distortion (being interpreted by several levels twice). With such distortion, the firm's response might become irrelevant as if being delayed was not bad enough. Thus, in a self-organizing firm, control decisions occur at the bottom; and eventually add up to form the overall control of the firm. As Kelly insists: "A mob can steer itself, and in the territory of rapid, massive, and heterogeneous change, only a mob can steer. To get something from nothing, control must rest at the bottom. . . ."[15]

## Cultivation of Increasing Returns

The architecture of self-organization includes the "law" of increasing returns: reinforcing a certain behavior brings more of this same behavior. Good leads to better. Better leads to best. A critical ingredient of self-organization is the presence of reinforcements for self-organizing behavior. The reinforcement takes many tangible and intangible forms including financial rewards, ownership sharing, celebrations, recognition, encouragement, empowerment, and the like.

## Growing by "Chunking"

As a parallel operating whole in a distributed being format, an organization is comprised of distinct units, or chunks. Therefore, when it grows, it has to do so by adding more discrete, distinct units or chunks. This is crucial. If the organization does not grow by chunks, it will have to grow by stretching the existing structure horizontally, vertically, or both. The expansion causes considerable stress inside the structure. This may lead to breakdowns. As the firm expands by adding more people and resources, it becomes too complicated to manage. People become impersonal and procedure and bureaucracy replace trust and interdependence. Soon, customers become alienated and market share will be lost. Add to this, the stress makes the firm too slow to respond to change in its marketplace. By contrast, growing by adding more chunks preserves the agility of each unit and ultimately the agility of the firm itself.

## Maximizing the Fringes

In a turbulent environment, the fringes (the units on the firing line) play two important roles. First, they do the work of the organization (e.g., making the product, selling it, servicing it, obtaining the funds, doing the R&D, etc.). Second, they are the shock absorbers that feel the turbulence and adjust to it, making the firm responsive in the process. Therefore, they have to be maximized, i.e., empowered and equipped with resources. Maximizing the fringes creates heterogeneity (i.e., many genuinely different, strong organs). This heterogeneity is essential for adaptation. As Kelly notes:

> "A diverse heterogeneous entity can adapt to the world in a thousand daily mini revolutions, staying in a state of permanent, but never fatal, churning . . . a healthy fringe speeds adaptation, increases resilience, and is almost always a source of innovation".[16]

## Honoring Errors

A firm operating in a turbulent environment is enveloped by a fog-like condition resulting from the dearth of information due to the inherent ambiguity, complexity, and uncertainty. Operating under such conditions boils down to experimentation, or trial and error. The hitting and missing in the course of trial and error leads to discovering how best to adapt to a changing environment. Adaptation thus occurs through discovering errors and recognizing them, honoring them if you will. Errors figure heavily in reshaping the organization for the next encounter with its environment. As Kelly notes, "Evolution can be thought of as systematic error management."[17] Error management is essential because the organization is constantly experimenting, and making errors in the process. Managing errors can happen only when the organization has mechanisms for recognizing errors for what they are and building on the experience to change itself to become better. It calls for recognizing errors, analyzing them, and viewing them as steps towards perfection.

## Persistent Disequilibrium

Kelly defines persistent disequilibrium as "a continuous state of surfing forever on the edge between never stopping but never falling."[18] The organization can never be in a state of equilibrium because turbulence would not allow it to happen. In a state of persistent disequilibrium, the organization is constantly reinventing itself and this ensures its adaptation and eventually its survival. Survival thus requires a state of disequilibrium. The system's state can be described as edge-of-chaos or punctuated chaos, just like the environment in which it exists. Many CEOs have practiced persistent disequilibrium. They call it "driving change." We have already observed how Kolind created disequilibrium at Oticon. He called it "the disorganization of Oticon." Others refer to this as "creative destruction," i.e., seeking out aspects of the firm that should be disrupted on purpose.[19]

### Pursuing No Optima

As a parallel-operating whole in a state of distributed being, the self-organizing firm will comprise many "autonomous" sub-units. "Autonomous" means that each unit will be pursuing its own goals and its own internal logic. The organization as a whole will have multiple goals rather than *one* "corporate" goal. There will be many "local" optimal solutions for the various modules rather than one "global" optimal solution for the firm in its entirety. Thus, the organization can survive only by "satisficing" (i.e., settling for less than global optimal solutions) a multitude of functions. As Kelly affirms, "survival is a many-pointed goal."[20]

### Self-Changing Change Rules

The behavior of an organization is always based on certain paradigms or sets of fundamental assumptions that form their worldview. These paradigms tell the organization what is acceptable and what is not; what can be changed and what has to be accepted as a given. They become the "change rules." Paradigms emerge from experience, and as a result, they remain anchored to the past. As such, they force us to look at the rear view mirrors instead of looking ahead. When there is a change in the real world, the paradigm dismisses it as unacceptable. The firm becomes in denial. It does not respond to change in a timely fashion. Often, this results in a major crisis (loss of market position and financial losses). It is only when a crisis occurs that dormant paradigms are exposed and changed. There has to be a better way and this is to have mechanisms that ensure that paradigms change on their own, or become self-changing. Andy Grove (CEO of Intel) instilled a mechanism for changing paradigms when he instilled the seminal thought, "only the paranoid survives" at Intel. His message is that we must not feel secure living with our current paradigms, which could have become obsolete without our conscious mind being aware of them. We must remain paranoid so that we may question our paradigms continuously.

Interestingly enough, self-organization is an excellent mechanism for ensuring that paradigms become self-changing. Because self-organizing systems are always arranging and rearranging themselves, they are restless; full of commotion resulting from the actions of strong fringes. This restlessness calls the system's paradigms into question regularly and they are changed in the process. When this happens, the paradigms (the change rules) would be self-changing. As Kelly noted, "Deeper evolution—as it might be formally defined—is about how the rules for changing entities over time, change over time. To get the most out of nothing, you need to have self-changing rules."[21]

## VARIATIONS ON THE THEME OF THE SELF-ORGANIZING SYSTEM

The concept of the self-organizing system appears to underlie a number of published works. The works of Stayer, Mills, Pasternack and Viscio, and Ghoshal and Bartlet are examples of the call for a form of the self-organizing system as the organizational model for the modern business firm.

In the early 1990s, Mills introduced the concept of the cluster organization. After noting that the new business realities require a different form of organization, he proposed the concept of the cluster organization, a collection of clusters.[22] According to Mills,

> "A cluster is a group of people drawn from different disciplines who work together on a semipermanent basis. The cluster itself handles many administrative functions, thereby divorcing itself from an extensive managerial hierarchy. A cluster develops its own expertise, expresses a strong customer or client orientation, pushes decision making toward the

point of action, shares information broadly, and accepts accountability for its business results."[23]

Clearly, Mills is suggesting that each cluster is a mini self-organizing system that operates on its own without strict instructions from the center. In fact, he refers to the cluster using the word like "a beehive." If each cluster is self-organizing, then the whole organization is self-organizing. Mills goes on to identify several types of clusters that make up the cluster organization. These are: a core team (the CEO and senior executives), business units (that have external customers), staff units (specialists), project teams (assembled for a specific project), alliance teams (builders of joint ventures with other corporations), and change teams (they review and modify the broad aspects of the firm's activities).

Stayer was among the first CEOs to write about the need for new models of organization. While he did not use the term "self-organizing system," he advocated a natural system "the flock of birds" as a model for the business firm.[24] A flock of birds is a self-organizing system. As we saw in Chapter 3, in Stayer's model, there is no leader, but members take turns to lead. Hence, the organization has a continuous flow of refreshed leadership. There is no center or hierarchy. Every member is individually and severally responsible for the whole organization.

Viscio and Pasternack's research at the management consulting firm of Booz, Allen Hamilton, suggested another model, the centerless organization.[25] The centerless organization is without a hierarchy or a center. It is "pancake flat." It is non-linear in that everything flows in all directions depending on where best results lie. It comprises five elements: a global core, business units, services, governance, and linkages. The global core (the CEO and senior executives) is responsible for key missions that cut across the entire organization. The global core is not a hierarchical concept. Rather, it operates at the same plane like the other elements. It is not a center. The global core has five responsibilities: develop and preserve identity (shared visions and value system); providing strategic leadership (providing an overall context for growth, developing the overall business portfolio, assisting in fostering key alliances, creating the overall mandate for growth); developing and maintaining capabilities; managing capital; and, exercising control (i.e., defining targets, monitoring performance, and meeting legal and fiduciary requirements). The business units, like Mills' clusters, act in a boundaryless manner to do business with customers on behalf of the firm. They are expected to act on their own, within the broad boundaries established by the core. Services provide support for the other four elements. Governance pertains to the role of the board of directors in preserving and enforcing accountability by all the other components, including the CEO. Linkages are management processes that connect all components of the centerless corporation.

The centerless organization also appears to be a variant of the concept of the self-organizing system. The notion of centerless underscores the idea of power at the peripheries (the fringes) or the business units. Even though Viscio and Pasternack use the term "core team," they defined it in such a way that it does not imply hierarchy in a command-and-control type of structure. The main attribute here is the interdependence among parts, not the dependence on a center to command all.

Ghoshall and Bartlet advocated an organization model that approaches the concept of the self-organizing system.[26] Their model views the organization as comprising three levels. Interacting with customers is the first level, frontline entrepreneurs who are focused on specific opportunities. They develop and build on the firm's business and competencies. They assume responsibility for short and long term results. They are genuinely empowered to act on their own. Supporting frontline entrepreneurs is another level, middle level managers who coach, coordinate, mentor, guide, and integrate these frontline units. At the foundation of this organization is the level of top management whose responsibility is to provide a sense of purpose, create shared values, and create an environment that enables everyone to do their best.

## CONCLUSION

In this chapter, the concept of the self-organizing system was examined in an attempt to develop the principles that a CEO can use to make his/her firm a self-organizing system. In nature, self-organizing systems are effective in surviving turbulence in their environment. Somehow, they have the capability to arrange and rearrange their parts or organize and reorganize themselves and eventually arrive at a state of existence that represents constructive survival. Although a self-organizing system consists of numerous parts that function autonomously, they do not turn absolutely anarchic and the system does not fall apart. Instead, the parts tend to work with impressive cohesiveness. It is as if there is an "invisible hand" that coordinates and orchestrates the parts and their actions.

## ENDNOTES

1. Aguilar, F.J., "General Electric, 1984," case no. 9-385-315 (rev. 12/87), Harvard Business School, Boston, MA.
2. Benetton S.p.A., Boston, MA: Harvard Business School, Case # 9-389-074.
3. Voss, H., "Virtual Organizations: The Future Is Now," *Strategy & Leadership*, July/August 1996, pp. 12–16.
4. Ibid., p. 14.
5. "The Virtual Organization," *Challenges: Ontario Business: Issues and Opportunities*, Spring, 1996, pp. 1 and 4–9.
6. Ibid., p. 4.
7. Ibid., p. 6.
8. Ibid., p. 7.
9. Ibid., p. 6.
10. Ibid., p. 4.
11. Neilson, G.L., B.A. Pasternack, and A.J. Viscio, "Up the E-Organization," *Strategy & Business*, First Quarter 2000, pp. 52–61.
12. Wheatley, M.J. and M. Keliner-Rogers, "Self-Organization: The Irresistible Future Of Organizing," *Strategy & Leadership*, July/August, 1996, p. 18.
13. Kelly, K., *Out of Control: The New Biology of Machines, Social Systems And The Economic World*, Reading, MA: Addison Wesley, 1994.
14. Ibid., p. 21.
15. Ibid., p. 13.
16. Ibid., p. 22.
17. Ibid., p. 22.
18. Ibid., p. 23.
19. Ibid., p. 24.
20. Kelly, op. cit., p. 469.
21. Ibid., p. 470.
22. Ibid., p. 470.
23. Ibid., p. 470.

24. Peter, T., *Liberation Management: Necessary Disorganization for the Nanosecond Nineties*, New York, NY: Alfred Knopf, 1992.

25. Kelly, op. cit., p. 470.

26. Ibid., p. 471.

27. Mills, D.Q., *Rebirth of the Corporation*, New York, NY: John Wiley & Sons, 1991.

28. Ibid., p. 29–30.

29. Blasco, J.A. and R.C. Stayer, *Flight of the Buffalo: Soaring to Excellence, Learning to Let Employees Lead*, New York, NY: Warner Books, 1993.

30. Viscio, A.J. and B.A. Pasternack, "Toward a New Business Model," *Strategy & Business*, Second Quarter, 1996. See also, Pasternack, B.A. and A.J. Viscio, "The Centerless Corporation: A Model for Tomorrow," *Strategy & Business*, Third Quarter, 1998.

31. Ghoshal, S. and C.A. Bartlet, *The Individualized Corporation: A Fundamentally New Approach to Management*, New York, NY: HarperCollins Publishers, 1997.

CHAPTER
# 6

# Guiding the Firm toward Strategic End-States

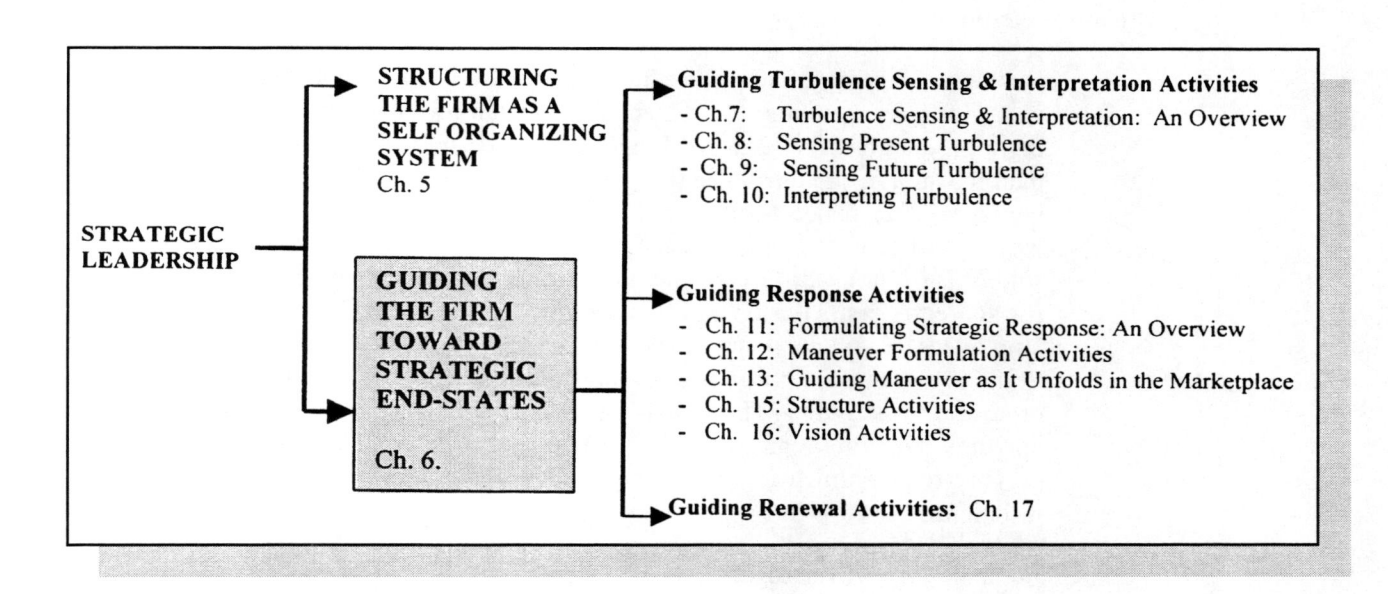

```
STRATEGIC          STRUCTURING           Guiding Turbulence Sensing & Interpretation Activities
LEADERSHIP         THE FIRM AS A           - Ch.7:  Turbulence Sensing & Interpretation: An Overview
                   SELF ORGANIZING         - Ch. 8: Sensing Present Turbulence
                   SYSTEM                  - Ch. 9: Sensing Future Turbulence
                   Ch. 5                   - Ch. 10: Interpreting Turbulence

                   GUIDING               Guiding Response Activities
                   THE FIRM                - Ch. 11: Formulating Strategic Response: An Overview
                   TOWARD                  - Ch. 12: Maneuver Formulation Activities
                   STRATEGIC               - Ch. 13: Guiding Maneuver as It Unfolds in the Marketplace
                   END-STATES              - Ch. 15: Structure Activities
                                           - Ch. 16: Vision Activities
                   Ch. 6.

                                         Guiding Renewal Activities:  Ch. 17
```

The proposed strategic leadership model portrayed the work of the modern CEO as a composite of two interdependent, concurrent streams of CEO tasks: structuring the firm as a self-organizing system; and, guiding the firm towards strategic end-states. In Chapter 5, we explored the concept of the self-organizing system. This chapter is concerned with the second element, guiding or leading the firm towards strategic end-states. It addresses two important questions. First, what is it that the CEO guides? Second, how does the CEO guide it? Clearly, the CEO guides the activities of the self-organizing system. The chapter begins with a delineation of these activities. Given a concept of these activities, the remainder of the presentation will focus on the work of the CEO in guiding them towards promising strategic end-states.

## ACTIVITIES OF THE SELF-ORGANIZING SYSTEM

In order to guide the self-organizing system, we must understand how it works. The activities of a firm structured as a self-organizing system are a composite of two concurrent streams of activities:

- Business Activities: These are the activities involved in creating and delivering value for customers and for stakeholders. Value for customers is created by making a product or service and selling it at a price that customers believe to be less than the sum of the attributes that the product delivers (e.g., quality, service, convenience, etc.). Value for stakeholders refers to the returns that the firm generates when it collects the sale price, the difference between price and the cost of goods sold. It is from this difference that the various stakeholders are paid, e.g., dividends for shareholders, salaries and bonuses for management, wages and bonuses for employees, payments to suppliers, and so on.
- Self-Organization Activities: Intermeshed with business activities are the self-organization activities. These involve sensing turbulence in the firm's environment and then arranging/rearranging the firm's parts to respond to turbulence while preserving the organization's integrity and unity especially after a disruption by turbulence.

Although they are woven together, business activities and self-organization activities are distinguishable. Our focus here is on self-organization activities. These activities start with ascertaining turbulence and unearthing the opportunities and challenges embedded therein. The system next formulates and carries out a strategic response that addresses them. As the system undertakes a sequence of responses over time, it rearranges its parts and eventually evolves into a shape that enhances its chances of long-term survival. Thus, there are three distinguishable categories of self-organization activities as shown in Exhibit 6.1. Each is described briefly next.

### Turbulence Sensing and Interpretation Activities

Because turbulence contains opportunities and threats, a self-organizing system is always reading and interpreting the turbulence surrounding it to determine which opportunities to exploit and which threats to evade or confront. Sensing is simply the gathering of data about turbulence. Turbulence poses a dilemma for the system. On one hand, the firm experiences current or prevailing turbulence and hence it is essential to gather data about the present. On the other, the firm's response is going to take place in the future, possibly under a different set of turbulent conditions. Clearly then, the sensing activities must span the

```
┌─────────────────────────────────────────────────────────────────────┐
│  ┌──────────────────────────┐    ┌──────────────────────────┐       │
│  │ Turbulence Sensing &     │    │ Response Activities:     │       │
│  │ Interpretation Activities:│    │ Strategy Formulation     │       │
│  │                          │    │ and Implementation       │   ┌───────┐
│  │ - Sensing Present        │───▶│                          │──▶│Results│
│  │   Turbulence             │    │ - Maneuver Activities    │   │       │
│  │ - Sensing Future Turbulence│  │ - Capability Activities  │   └───────┘
│  │ - Interpreting Turbulence│    │ - Organization Structuring│      │
│  │                          │    │   Activities             │       │
│  │                          │    │ - Visioning Activities   │       │
│  └──────────▲───────────────┘    └──────────▲───────────────┘       │
│             │                               │                       │
│             │                               │                       │
│  ┌──────────┴───────────────────────────────┴───────────────┐◀──────┘
│  │            Strategic Renewal Activities                  │
│  └──────────────────────────────────────────────────────────┘
└─────────────────────────────────────────────────────────────────────┘
```

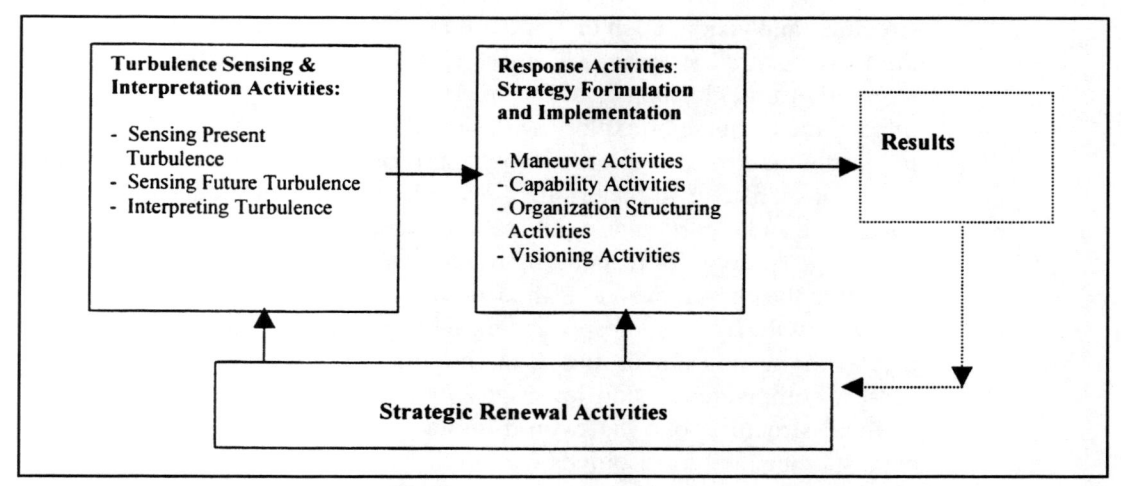

Exhibit 6.1: Self-Organization Activities

present and the future. Turbulence sensing thus falls into two categories: sensing *current* or *present* turbulence, and, sensing *future* turbulence. After gathering data about present and future turbulence comes the task of *interpreting* the collected data. Interpretation means distilling turbulence data to isolate the key challenges embodied in them and determining their impact on the firm, e.g., whether they represent opportunities or threats.

In sum, this set comprises *three* sub-categories of activities: (1) activities involved in sensing present turbulence, (2) activities pertaining to sensing future turbulence; and, (3) interpretation activities, extracting the strategic issues embedded in turbulence.

## Response Activities

Response activities revolve around formulating and implementing a strategy for tackling turbulence. Since the concept of strategy is pivotal here, we pause to examine it. Strategy is a construct, i.e., a concept invented especially to refer to a certain reality or a phenomenon. Because it is a special "invention," a construct tends to mean different things to different people. We need to establish a reference point. In this presentation, strategy refers to a set of intelligent choices.[1]

As Brown and Eisenhardt suggested, strategy comprises two decisions: the choice of where you want to go; and, the choice of how you get there.[2] They view strategy as ". . . the creation of a relentless flow of competitive advantages that, taken together, form a semi-coherent strategic direction."[3] Building on their ideas, we define strategy as a semi-coherent direction that evolves out of the diverse initiatives by numerous empowered people in a business firm structured as a self-organizing system operating in a business environment characterized by punctuated chaos. Strategy will not be viewed in the traditional sense, as a tool for the CEO to impose his/her will on competitors in a zero-sum game. Rather, strategy is thought of as a dynamic, living, and evolving design for outmaneuvering the forces of turbulence by cleverly choosing strategic end-states and routes to them.

Furthermore, strategy is "smart" choices. The term "smart" refers to two characteristics: First, the choice is "robust," i.e., all contingencies have been factored in its conception, and hence it would bring about acceptable outcomes throughout an anticipated range of future conditions. Second, the choice has "intelligence," i.e., it includes rules that allow it to change as the situation itself changes, like the lens of a camera with auto focus, which adjusts itself automatically to distance, and lighting conditions.

As a semicoherent direction, a firm's strategy appears to be multifaceted, comprising four interdependent sets of choices as shown in Exhibit 6.2. These are maneuver, capability, structure, and vision. Each one of them is a strategy in its own right, but combined, they form the firm's overall strategy. The most visible aspect of strategy is *maneuver*, which encompasses the strategic choices of the "physical" moves to be executed in tackling obstacles and threats in the course of exploiting desired opportunities. Maneuver is the wheeling and dealing in the marketplace to outwit, outsmart (or outfox) the forces of turbulence.

For maneuver to materialize, *two* important underpinnings must be in place: a certain *capability* and a particular organizational *structure*. The specification of these two pillars is part of the strategy for responding to turbulence. Capability is the configuration of resources to enable the chosen moves. If the firm has the wherewithal to undertake a certain maneuver action, it will. If not, its response will be impotent. It goes without saying then that a crucial part of the response activities is the building of appropriate capability, i.e., resources, processes, competencies, and leverages. The second enabler of maneuver is a good organizational structure, one that would ignite the energy of people so that they may ignite the energy embedded in resources (capability). A well-conceived structure can translate into a generous range of moves (maneuver) that the firm can undertake.

The bedrock underlying the configuration of maneuver, capability, and structure is another strategic choice, the firm's vision, a concept of its desired end-state. As the system maneuvers its way through and around turbulence, it often comes across a defining moment—the discovery of what it really is and what it wants to become, a strategic end-state. Activities here involve the search and discovery of identity (a concept of self) and a promising position in the scheme of things in the marketplace.

To sum up, we stress the following points:

- The term strategy refers to a composite of the chosen configurations of maneuver, capability, structure, and vision.
- The four elements of strategy make up the self-organizing system's response activities.
- The activities involved in formulating and implementing strategy in each of the four items form a structure of their own composed of four subsets of activities as shown in Exhibit 6.2. Thus, we have (1) maneuver activities, (2) capability-building activities, (3) organization structuring activities, and (4) visioning activities.

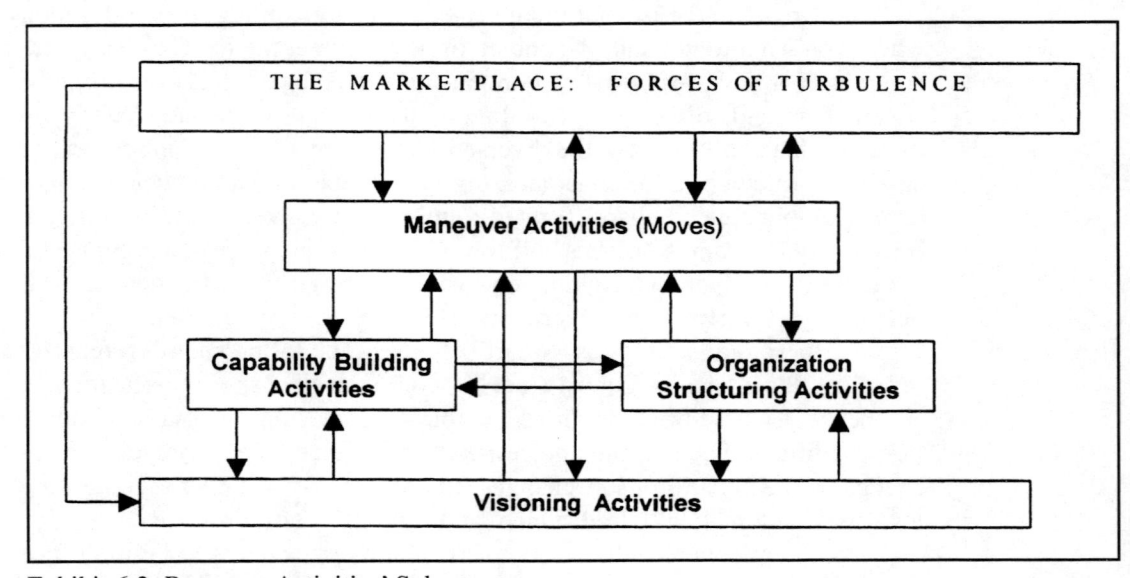

Exhibit 6.2: Response Activities' Subsets

- The four subsets are *interdependent*. They feed on one another. They drive one another simultaneously.

### Strategic Renewal Activities

As stated above, response to turbulence involves the formulation and implementation of a strategy for tackling a certain episode of turbulence. This strategy is essentially a certain configuration of the firm's vision, capability, structure, and maneuver. How long can this configuration last? Turbulence will disrupt it; perhaps sooner than later. It will have to be reorganized or reconfigured again. The self-organizing system, therefore, engages in another set of activities aimed at ensuring that the configuration evolves with the firm's evolving environment; that firm evolves into the "next generation company." We label this set of activities as strategic renewal activities. We define strategic renewal as the firm's capacity to evolve into forms or configurations (without an externally imposed plan or directive) that can withstand successive waves of turbulence.

Renewal activities encompass the following:

- Gathering data about the system's configuration, i.e., seven subsets of activities: These are: (1) present-turbulence sensing, (2) future-turbulence sensing, (3) turbulence interpretation, (4) maneuver, (5) capability, (6) structure, and (7) vision.
- Mapping the configuration: Discerning patterns in the seven sets and assembling them to reconstruct the current configuration. Even though a configuration is first designed as a strategic plan, it might have evolved into something different altogether by the time it is implemented. There is always a difference between things as intended and things after they materialize.
- Determining the consequences of pursuing the present configuration: Activities here pertain to the determination of the strategic end-state at which the firm has arrived, namely strategic position and financial position.
- Assessing the configuration in light of impending and expected turbulence: This involves examining the configuration and challenging it with regard to goodness of fit with the evolving turbulence, its implementation history, and the desirability of results. If the external world evolved as we expected it, implementation was carried as planned, and the results were satisfactory, the configuration may continue as a viable one. However, if the turbulence was severe and surprising, the configuration fell apart during implementation, and the results were undesirable, the configuration is no longer viable.
- Undertaking renewal action: Depending on the severity of disruption, activities here can range from fine-tuning an existing configuration to the reinvention of a new one.

Now that we have a concept of self-organization activities, we turn to the role of the CEO in guiding them so that the firm may arrive at strategic end-states.

## GUIDING SELF-ORGANIZATION ACTIVITIES

Guiding a self-organizing system is difficult. It has been likened to "steering a mob" or "riding a wild tiger." In a self-organization setting, employees are expected to undertake numerous initiatives, which they believe would help the firm survive and thrive in the turbulent marketplace. As they do so, there will be many diverse visions, initiatives, and actions. Because they are all empowered, they will insist on their visions and fight for them. Anarchy may set in. There is a risk of divisiveness and consequent loss of unity of direction. How does the CEO guide the firm under such conditions? Progressive CEOs discovered a way. They focus on inducing and orchestrating strategic collaboration. In this section, we explore the concept of strategic collaboration first and then examine how the CEO induces and orchestrates it.

Collaboration is a mode of operation where empowered players, regardless of their differences, come, stay, and participate such that all of them will have the semblance of one coordinated, integrated whole. Strategic collaboration is labeled "strategic" for two reasons. First, it involves the choice of strategic end-states and paths to them. Second, it involves strategy, i.e., a plotting or scheming type of action that attempts to outmaneuver the non-controllable forces of turbulence (including competition, economic conditions, and the like).

A strategic end-state is a destination towards which the CEO guides the firm. It is a profitable, defensible strategic position in the marketplace that pleases the firm's stakeholders. It has certain characteristics that should be pointed out at the outset:

- A strategic end-state is an evolving entity. It emerges, as a semicoherent aspiration, out of the varied and diverse initiatives of the various individuals and modules as they try to create opportunity in the marketplace. It surfaces opportunistically. A firm might start with a desired end-state, but turbulence may render it undesirable or unattainable. A strategic end-state evolves *en route*; while the firm is pursuing a pre-established end-state. A firm might begin the journey with a certain end-state in mind, but as it maneuvers its way in the marketplace, it discovers a better or a more achievable one. For example, Amazon.com first sought an end-state as an e-business focusing on selling books. However, after venturing in toys and electronic, it now seeks a new end-state, the Wal-Mart of the Internet.
- A strategic end-state is a transient point. The firm does not remain at a certain end-state indefinitely. Turbulence would make this impossible. Today's desirable end-states can be tomorrow's regret. The typical firm then goes through a succession of end-states over time.

Strategic collaboration involves considerable creativity. Creativity is needed in order to discover new and promising end-states that can be easily arrived at unhampered by turbulence. Desirable strategic positions are not just sitting there for the taking. Some are claimed by existing competitors. Some need to be created, e.g., e-business firms carving new positions for themselves. Creativity is also needed for outmaneuvering other firms.

We must stress here that strategic collaboration is the test of whether or not self-organization is taking place. If the firm is operating as a genuine self-organizing system, there will be frequent and intense strategic collaboration. It is through strategic collaboration that the parts of the self-organizing system pull together and help it bounce back after any disruption. That is why strategic collaboration is a focal concern for the CEO. It is the mission of the CEO to ensure that strategic collaboration occurs creatively, purposefully, and continuously.

A critical question at this junction is this: what are the CEO's tasks with regard to strategic collaboration. There are two main tasks:

1. Inducing Strategic Collaboration: Inducing strategic collaboration involves creating an environment and the conditions conducive for people to pool their talents, energies and resources because of their belief that this would advance their ambitions.
2. Orchestrating Strategic Collaboration: Once collaboration is induced, the CEO then focuses it. The term orchestrating here refers to assembling collaborative efforts so that they may have the semblance of unity of direction; and, pointing them in a certain direction, the direction of better strategic end-states.

# INDUCING AND ORCHESTRATING STRATEGIC COLLABORATION

Exhibit 6.3 below presents a systematic framework for inducing and orchestrating strategic collaboration. It shows the relevant categories of CEO tasks. It can be summarized as follows. The centerpieces of strategic collaboration are two processes: inducing and stimulating strategic conversation and then marshalling it toward strategic action, i.e., discovering strategic end-states and ways to reach them. To sustain the two processes, a number of other features have to be in place. The CEO creates the environment that would stimulate and sustain strategic collaboration. Furthermore, the achievements of strategic collaboration must be acknowledged and rewarded. This is essential in order to reinforce collaboration and ensure its continuity. Collaboration must happen within the bounds of accountability since it involves the use of the firm's assets. Finally, penetrating through all these activities is the personal influence of the CEO as the personal leader of the organization. Let us examine these elements further.

## Creating an Environment Conducive to Strategic Collaboration

For strategic collaboration to take place, the CEO must create the environment that would stimulate and sustain it. The CEO undertakes some fundamental tasks in this regard. They can be described as follows:

1. Cultivating Paradigms: In a self-organizing system, individuals are empowered. They are not to be programmed and micromanaged. Nevertheless, it is not a place for destructive anarchy. The system must display some unity in order to survive as one distinctive whole. An effective way of achieving this sense of unity is for members of the system to have a group mind or groupthink. This occurs when all members have the same (or similar) paradigms or worldview. Therefore, it is essential for the CEO to ensure that a common paradigm surfaces.

Progressive CEOs help cultivate common paradigms by formulating certain seminal thoughts (e.g., core values) and promoting them all the time and by all means possible. Seminal thoughts are like the DNA for action. They are like the foreman on the construction site.

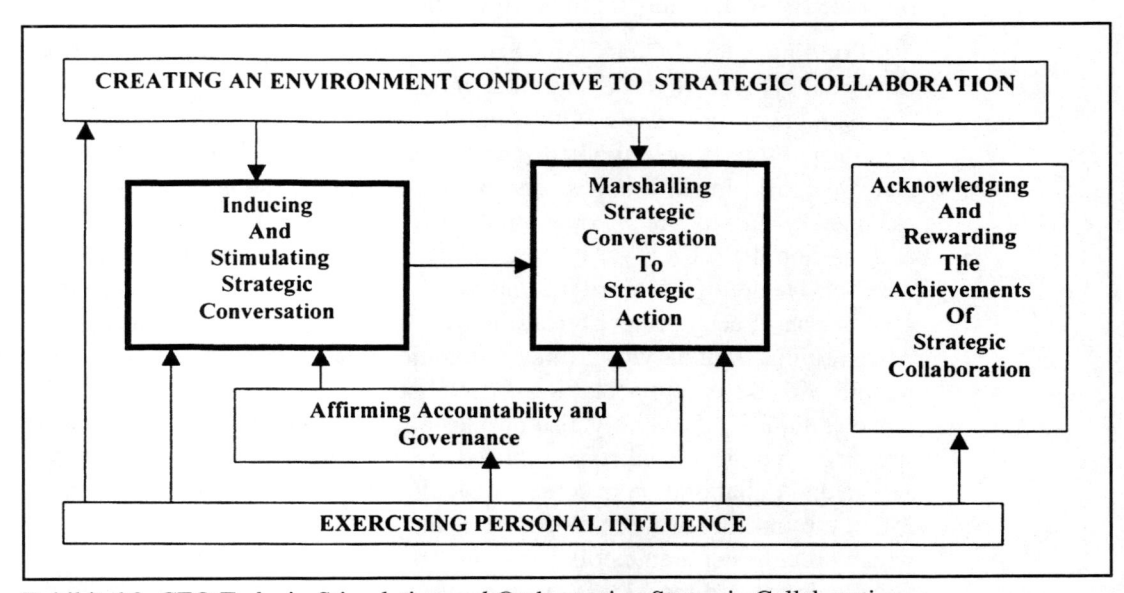

Exhibit 6.3: CEO Tasks in Stimulating and Orchestrating Strategic Collaboration

They remain in the person's mind guiding daily actions. We have seen in Chapter 3 examples of seminal thoughts that CEOs entrench in employees' minds. For example, Patrick Kelly (PSS/World Medical) promoted the thought of "a company of CEOs." As another example, Fred Smith (FedEX) with the thought of "pitch in."

Here is another example of seminal thoughts formulated by Jack Welch (GE) They are intended to shape the mindset of managers.

"GE Leaders throughout the company . . .

- Create a clear, simple, reality-based, customer-focused vision and are able to communicate it straightforwardly to all constituencies.
- Understand accountability and commitment and are decisive . . . set and meet aggressive targets . . . always with unyielding integrity.
- Have the self-confidence to empower others and behave in a boundaryless fashion . . . believe in and are committed to Work-Out as a means of empowerment . . . are open to ideas from anywhere.
- Have, or have the capacity to develop, global brains and global sensitivity and are comfortable building diverse global teams.
- Stimulate and relish change . . . are not frightened or paralyzed by it. See change as an opportunity, not just a threat.
- Have enormous energy and the ability to energize and invigorate others. Understand speed as a competitive advantage and see the total organization benefits that can be derived from a focus on speed."[4]

Where do seminal thoughts come from? In many cases, they come from the CEO himself/herself as part of the leadership act. After all, the CEO is there because he or she has considerable wisdom and experience. He/she has good insights as to what is best for the organization. However, there is a danger here, the temptation to dictate prescriptions for behavior, which might make sense to the CEO, but are not workable from the viewpoint of the people who have to live by them. In such cases, the seminal thoughts are not internalized and the intended mindset does not materialize. Sagacious CEOs employ the seminal thoughts that surface from the people themselves. Such thoughts have a better chance of being carried out. The role of the CEO in this case is to help such thoughts surface, polish them, articulate them, promote them, and implant them throughout the organization.

2. Building Shared Goals: Strategic collaboration happens only if all parties have a common goal. Therefore, an essential foundation for strategic collaboration is the presence of common goals. Progressive CEOs build shared goals by making them surface out of the aspirations of the parties involved. The two main goals to be stressed here are: a desirable end-state, and, arriving at it unimpeded by turbulence. These are too abstract. They are often articulated in various ways. For example, Patrick Kelly set the goal of $500 million for his firm and later on, he set it to $1 billion. An excellent way of building shared goals is the project concept. The journey toward the end-state can be broken down into a number of projects. The completion of each project brings the firm a step closer to this state.

3. Defining Boundaryless Roles: Strategic collaboration is in effect a coalition of different people with different specialties. Specialists are important. Their presence ensures competence and quality. Specialty also defines a role for a certain individual or group in the coalition. However, if specialists are carried away with the standards of their specialty, cocooning sets in and collaboration becomes difficult, just like the isolation among smoke stacks or silos in the traditional hierarchical companies. This inhibits the formation of coalitions and hence preempts strategic collaboration. To achieve strategic collaboration, roles must be defined along two dimensions: the specialty dimension and the corporate dimension. In other words, every member in a collaborative venture would have two roles, as a specialist and as

a member of the coalition. CEOs are aware of this necessity. For example, Jack Welch (GE) invented the concept of the boundaryless organization in which specialists conduct themselves with a sense of responsibility for the whole corporation and not just for the standards of their specialty. Boundarylessness is essential for strategic collaboration.

4. Networking: Clearly, strategic collaboration presupposes the presence of mechanisms for networking all diverse groups in the organization. Networking pre-requires that all information flows freely in the organization. The free flow of information allows networks to form and disband as the need arises. This stimulates collaborative ventures. During a collaborative venture, having complete information allows the various groups to coordinate their actions without the necessity of frequent meetings.

5. Instituting Dialogue: For strategic collaboration to take place, dialogue must precede it. When people and groups can exchange ideas, collaboration has a strong chance of occurring. Therefore, the CEO must create the environment that not only encourages dialogue but also makes it happen. In Chapter 3, we saw how Kolind (Oticon) orchestrated the environment for dialogue by locating coffee bars to interrupt the flow of people traffic. He also introduced the multi-job concept where every employee must find and work on three projects. To generate projects, employees had no option but to dialogue with others.

6. Orchestrating Shared Workspace: An effective tool for instituting dialogue, and hence collaboration, is when employees share workspace by design. Sharing workspace creates opportunities for people to exchange ideas and to think of joint projects. Many firms are now placing employees in an open concept environment where distance among people is minimized. Workspace can also be shared electronically with the help of networked workstations, videoconferencing, and e-mail. Proximity (physical and/or intellectual) enhances the chances of strategic collaboration.

7. Charging Emotions: Strategic collaboration pre-requires an emotional state on the part of people. Employees must feel a compelling need to collaborate. CEOs create this need in ways such as:

- Creating a sense of urgency, a do-or-die type of emotion, demonstrating how vulnerable the firm is in the face of impending turbulence.
- Stressing the need to drive change in order for the firm to stay on top of the game.
- Implanting a sense of paranoia, as in the case of Andy Grove (Intel) when he always stressed that "only the paranoid survive."
- Ingraining the entrepreneurial spirit by encouraging and celebrating the spirit of venturing into uncharted territories. Jack Welch (GE) instituted the principle of rewarding success and failure. Failures were rewarded as long as they were in the spirit of entrepreneurship.

## Inducing and Stimulating Strategic Conversation

Now that the right conditions for strategic collaboration are in place, the next step is to induce strategic conversation. Strategic conversation is the pooling of ideas with the purpose of discovering strategic end-states and formulating strategies to reach them. Conversation is an essential ingredient for collaboration. A strategic planning session is an example of strategic conversation.

Making strategic conversation happen involves a number of CEO tasks as follows:

1. Articulating and Clarifying Purpose: To provide a context for strategic conversation, the CEO articulates the purpose of the firm and its intent. The statement of purpose is an invitation for people to collaborate to help the firm move towards its achievement. Purpose statements tend to be generic and lofty. They need some interpretation to make them concrete and place them within reach of the employees. Purpose is also clarified by breaking it down into

a number of derivative objectives. When the Ford Motor Company adopted the purpose of producing quality cars, this was articulated to employees as "quality is job 1." This somehow opened the door for employees to talk quality and discuss how it can be raised.

2. Developing Shared Understanding: When people have the same referents, constructive conversation occurs easily. If purpose is interpreted in different ways by different people, there will be confusion as to what the purpose is. For people to collaborate, things should have the same meaning. Otherwise, misunderstanding occurs. They will spend the time clarifying terminology instead of conversing to find ways to deal with the issue at hand. To illustrate, we present in Exhibit 6.4 the framework developed by CEO Welch to develop a shared understanding of how GE operates and grows.[5]

Welch developed the diagram to organize the people's perception of how GE hangs together. The flow of ideas in the framework goes like this: The function of the Corporate Executive Office is to multiply the firm's resources, to please stakeholders. The key to multiplying resources is for all business units of the firm to be either number 1 or number 2 in their respective industries. Multiplying resources also happens through:

- Increasing productivity and increasing market growth for each business unit.
- Allocating resources selectively to undertakings and business units that show the promise of being #1 or #2.
- Speeding asset turnover—Total profit is a function of asset turnover. The faster the turnover, the more the profit.
- Coupled with the above is the action to sell business units that cannot be #1 or #2 in their respective industry.
- The result of all of the above is that the supply of cash for the company would increase. Cash can then be used to pay dividends and finance the acquisition of new #1 and #2 businesses that can contribute more growth and more cash for GE.

3. Setting the Firm's Strategic Agenda: Establishing priorities is a good vehicle for stimulating strategic conversation. Priorities are essential because the firm cannot address all the issues facing it due to limited resources. Knowing the priorities is an invitation for self-organizing people to discuss what they can do to help the firm accomplish these pressing tasks.

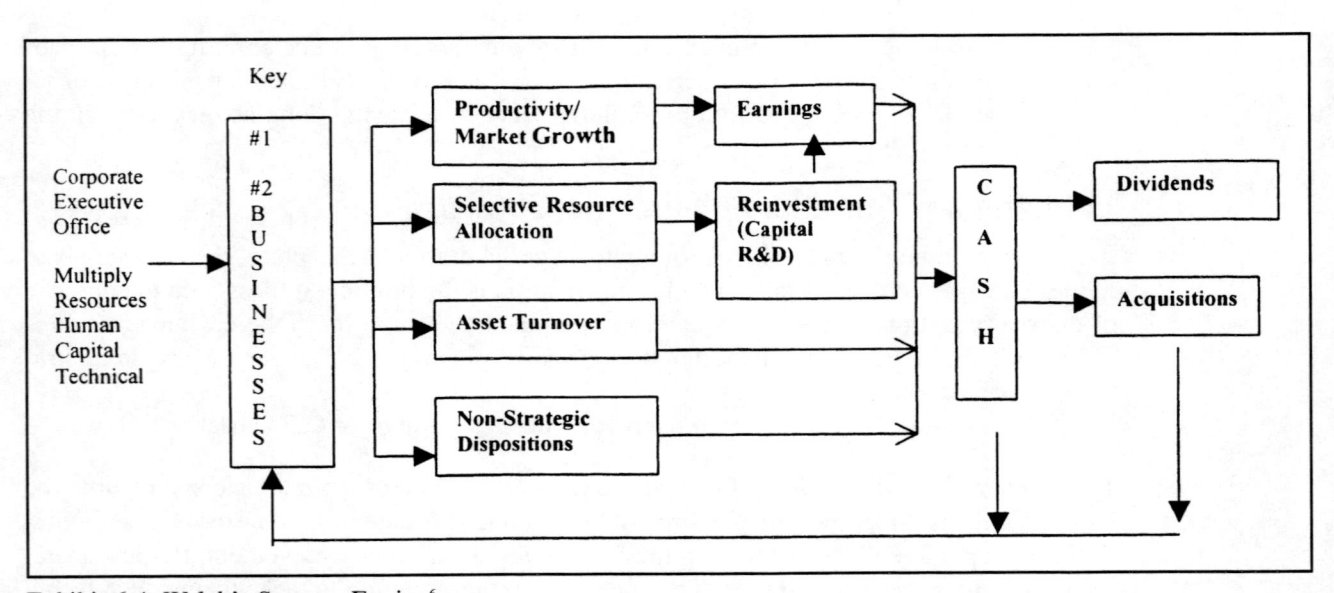

Exhibit 6.4: Welch's Success Engine[6]

4. Creating New Options: When people have only one way to do things, there is no incentive to discuss matters. It is taken at face value and it is not questioned. However, the presentation of new options and alternatives opens the door for people to come together to discuss them. Conversation can focus on the nature of the new options, their viability, the requirements of their implementation and so on.
5. Stimulating and Balancing Advocacy: In a self-organizing firm, people are empowered to function as frontline entrepreneurs. This means that they will have different visions and ventures. They will be advocating for their initiatives. If they are given the opportunity to advocate and persuade others, conversation will take place. If they are silenced, their entrepreneurial spirit diminishes. Nevertheless, some semblance of unity of direction is essential. There is a need for the CEO to balance advocacy without stifling it. The main task here is fair and objective arbitration. Part of the leadership responsibilities is to serve as an arbiter in order to help things move ahead.
6. Institutionalizing the Projects Principle: The work of an organization need not be a continuous, stifling routine. Sagacious CEOs have discovered a way to make organizational life exciting. They introduced the concept of projects. Every now and then, they will think of a major project for the firm to undertake, e.g., project Taurus for Ford. Every time a project is introduced, it galvanizes people and recharges their energies. Once a project is accomplished, it becomes a small win that increases employees' self-confidence. The CEO can stimulate strategic conversation by introducing various projects. Each project is a forum that can bring diverse people together to investigate and plan how to make it happen.
7. Infusing Action into Conversation: Strategic conversation is not just an intellectual exchange of views. It is an action-oriented endeavor. The purpose of conversation is to get things done. Therefore, action and implementation become the topics of conversation. Once the implementation dimension is introduced, conversation moves to another plane. More and more conversation about implementation ensues. Insisting on discussion implementation is thus a crucial forum for conversation.
8. Establishing Incentives: Strategic conversation, like any other organizational activity, needs to have an incentive to attract people to it. There has to be a compelling reason for diverse people to come to the table. If the CEO is to stimulate conversation, he/she must establish a system that rewards engaging in it. The reward system can take a variety of forms that can range from concessions to the respective people to sharing the rewards when the conversation moves to action and eventually to results.

## Marshalling Strategic Conversation to Strategic Action

Strategic collaboration culminates when conversation moves from discussion to action. After all, conversation is only a forum for contemplating and planning strategic action, choosing an end-state and implementing a plan to reach it. The CEO plays a major role in transforming conversation into action as follows.

1. Developing and Cultivating Frameworks for Action: In order to help the transformation of conversation into action, the CEO can help by developing frameworks as templates for people's action. A framework simply outlines how things are to be done. As such, they are guidelines. Deviations are permitted. The general expectation is to stay close to the framework or at least the spirit of it. This leeway is needed to give people the chance to adapt and update the frameworks. This book is full of examples of frameworks for action, e.g., the issues analysis methodology presented in Chapter 10 and the scenario planning methodology introduced in Chapter 11.
2. Keeping the Vision: Strategic collaboration has only one purpose, to help the firm reach its desired end-state or vision. Strategic action has to be conceived and carried out in light

of this vision. A key role for the CEO is to be the keeper of the vision, the one who articulates it, reminds people of it, and the look-out who tells the organization how close it is to the envisioned end-state.

3. Seeking Creative, Entrepreneurial Results: As conversation moves into action, creativity and innovation need to be incorporated in it. The business world is a competitive one. It requires continuous innovation. Innovation emerges when people approach strategic action with an entrepreneurial attitude. If the strategic action is to be helpful at all, it has to display entrepreneurship and creativity. The role of the CEO is to define what entrepreneurial results are and to urge people to be take risks and innovate. At Southwest Air, people are urged to seek forgiveness, not permission. The message for employees is to go ahead and innovate without waiting for permission, as long as the company's interest is served.

4. Building Collaborative Networks: Acting on the results of strategic conversation often requires the pooling of resources and energy of many units. It is crucial for the CEO to look for opportunities for building internal strategic alliances among the various units. Networks ensure that strategic action is carried out properly with a full range of skills drawn from across the organization. It is in this spirit that Welch entrenched the concept of the boundaryless organization at GE. If people think and act in a boundaryless fashion, they can be mobilized into networks, which can be formed and disbanded as needed.

5. Staffing Critical Positions: A good way to move conversation into action is for the CEO to staff critical positions with leaders who champion the action, coordinate networks, and ensure that the action is implemented. In many firms, a new position has been created for this purpose. It is called "project leader." Aside from the project leader, the CEO can provide other key personnel that bring about critical skills, such as financial skills, engineering skills, and so on.

6. Removing Barriers to Action: In every organization, there are always barriers that stall the movement from conversation to action. These can range from lack of resources to lengthy, overwhelming procedure. It is the role of the CEO to ensure that these barriers are removed and do what it takes to remove them, within the overall constraints facing the firm.

7. Allocating Resources: It goes without saying that allocating resources is the most effective means of transforming conversation into action. Committing resources ensures that the action will be carried out.

8. Transferring Decision-Making Powers: Just like resource allocation, action requires numerous decisions to be made and carried out. To transform conversation into action, people need the power to make the necessary decisions without having to wait for a lengthy approval process. The longer the wait for and the more complicated the process of approval, the less the motivation for people to act. Progressive CEOs empower their employees by placing decision making powers in their hands.

9. Promoting and Transferring Best Practices: Best practices are the actions that proved to be successful by other units in (or outside) the organization. As such they serve as models for action. If a group knows about them, they can save time and effort. That is why Welch institutionalized the concept of best practices at GE.

10. Approval: The CEO can help move conversation into action by approving or concurring with the results and decisions of the deliberations. Approval gives the authority for people to carry out the plans formulated during the conversation. It is permission to amass resources and apply them to make the fruits of strategic collaboration happen.

11. Issuing Directives: Finally, the CEO, seeing the results of strategic conversation, gives a directive or an order for the organizations to carry out the plans embodied therein. Like approval, a directive is authority to amass resources and commit them to the respective strategic action.

## Acknowledging and Rewarding the Achievements of Strategic Collaboration

In order to entrench strategic collaboration in the firm, the CEO must reinforce collaborative ventures and behavior. The relevant CEO tasks here include:

- Celebration: Treating the positive results of strategic collaboration as small wins and celebrating them throughout the unit or the organization.
- Recognition: Acknowledging and rewarding the individuals whose strategic collaboration helped the firm to inch closer to its desired strategic end-state.
- Rewards: Establishing a reward system that provides tangible benefits, especially monetary, for those whose strategic collaboration actually brought strategic gains for the firm.

## Affirming Accountability and Governance

Strategic collaboration has to occur within the bounds of accountability and the governance system in the organization in order to protect the firm's assets. There are a number of CEO tasks here including:

- Periodic Audits: These are crucial to ensure that strategic collaboration is actually strategic and a genuine collaboration.
- Keeping Score: Having a bookkeeping system of the various strategic projects that came out of strategic collaboration that highlights their costs and contribution to the firm. Keeping score sends a message that strategic collaboration must yield strategic achievements.
- Challenging Results, Process, and Paradigms: Progressive CEOs do not take the results of strategic collaboration at face value. Rather, they question the resulting achievement in light of what could have been instead of what is. They go even further to challenge the premises (paradigms) underlying the resulting level of achievement. They also question the process that led to it. As they do so, they are pointing out deficiencies in the collaborative efforts. This helps in improving the next round of collaboration.
- Raising the Bar: In order to stimulate more intense strategic collaboration, the CEO can keep raising the standard and expectations. The higher the standards, the better the quality of the next round of collaboration would be.
- Holding Court: This is crucial to enforce and entrench accountability, particularly when the audits show that some persons or groups are taking advantage of the empowerment and freedom that the self-organizing environment provides.

## Exercising Personal Influence

As the leader of the organization, the CEO is expected to exercise personal influence on all phases of strategic collaboration. His/her actions set the tone for collaboration. This requires considerable work on the part of the CEO with regard to all the elements in Exhibit 6.3. Personal influence takes many forms such as:

- Example Setting: If, for example, the CEO believes in dialogue, then he/she should practice dialogue all the time with all concerned. Going first is crucial entrenching the idea of dialogue.
- Coaching: This a non-invasive way of making a point and nudging in a certain direction. It is a vehicle for the CEO to personally steer strategic collaborative efforts.

- Management by Walking Around (MBWA): A good way to exercise personal influence is being visible by being present at the critical points in strategic collaborative ventures. It gives the CEO a chance to steer and to be a participant rather than a "manager."
- Preaching: Repeated preaching to all concerned is another non-invasive way to corral and steer strategic collaboration towards strategic ends.

At this point, we should recall that the six processes of inducing and orchestrating strategic collaboration are the essential CEO tasks in guiding the firm toward desired strategic end-states. We should also keep in mind that the CEO applies them to each of the three sets of self-organizing activities and their subsets. To appreciate the magnitude of the CEO's work in this regard, Exhibit 6.5 was prepared. It is a two dimensional matrix. The rows are the six elements of inducing and orchestrating strategic collaboration. The columns are the categories of self-organization activities in the firm. The cells of the matrix represent the various tasks that the CEO undertakes to guide the respective activity. The remainder of the book is about the activities that should go in each cell. Exhibit 6.5 is the layout for the eleven chapters to follow.

| Elements of Inducing & Orchestrating Strategic Collaboration | Categories of Self-Organization Activities ||||||| Adaptation/ Regeneration |
|---|---|---|---|---|---|---|---|---|
| | Turbulence Sensing & Interpretation ||| Responding to Turbulence |||| |
| | Sensing Present Turbulence | Sensing Future Turbulence | Interpreting Turbulence | Maneuver | Capability | Structure | Vision | |
| Creating the Environment Conducive to Strategic Collaboration | | | | | | | | |
| Inducing and Stimulating Strategic Conversation | | | | | | | | |
| Marshalling Strategic Conversation to Strategic Action | | | | | | | | |
| Acknowledging & Rewarding Achievements of Strategic Collaboration | | | | | | | | |
| Affirming Accountability and the Governance System | | | | | | | | |
| Exercising Personal Influence | | | | | | | | |

Exhibit 6.5: Scope of the CEO's Work in Corralling and Steering the Firm

# CONCLUSION

This chapter concludes the overview of the model of strategic leadership. The model was introduced in Chapter 4. The CEO's work was presented as a composite of two concurrent, interdependent streams of activities: (1) structuring the firm as a self-organizing system; and, (2) guiding it by corralling and steering its activities. Our focus in this chapter was on the category of CEO tasks involved in guiding the firm.

In a self-organizing setting, the CEO has to balance the requirements of self-organization (employee empowerment, autonomy, and freedom) with the need for unity and a common sense of direction. It was suggested here that the CEO can achieve this balance by following a non-invasive approach: to focus on guiding the firm instead of micromanaging it. Guiding the firm, in essence, involves inducing and orchestrating strategic collaboration among its members. Strategic collaboration means that all parts of the system are joining forces (despite their differences) to discover a strategic end-state for the firm, to find a path to it, and to actually follow this path to reach it. Strategic collaboration is thus the vehicle for a self-organizing system to work as one whole, not as a set of isolated, anarchic parts.

Inducing and orchestrating strategic collaboration consumes the bulk of the CEO's time. It is complex and calls for continuous work on his/her part. Such work includes creating the environment that is conducive to strategic collaboration, inducing people to engage in strategic conversation, and to transform this conversation into strategic action. These activities have to occur within an accountability framework that protects the assets of the corporation. At all times, the CEO exerts personal influence by moving around to ensure that the right kind of strategic collaboration is occurring and that it is bringing about strategic achievements that would please the firm's stakeholders.

To help the reader navigate through the remainder of this book, Exhibit 6.6 was developed. It will be reproduced at the beginning of each chapter to place it in the overall perspective.

**GUIDING THE FIRM TOWARDS STRATEGIC END-STATES**

- **Guiding Turbulence Sensing & Interpretation Activities**
  - Ch. 7: Turbulence Sensing & Interpretation: An Overview
  - Ch. 8: Sensing Present Turbulence
  - Ch. 9: Sensing Future Turbulence
  - Ch. 10: Interpreting Turbulence

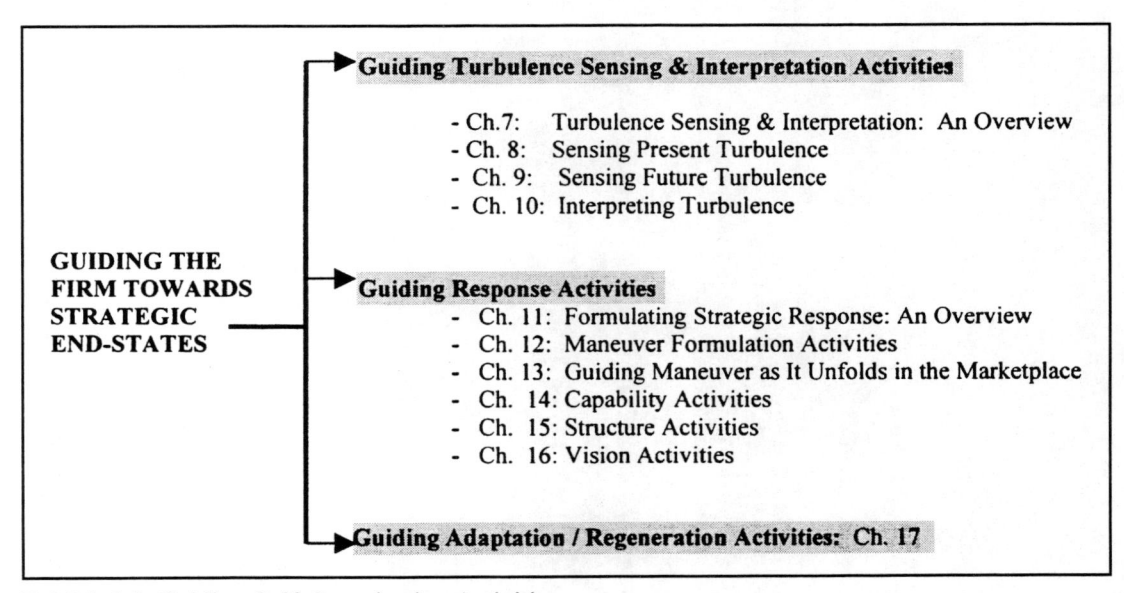

- **Guiding Response Activities**
  - Ch. 11: Formulating Strategic Response: An Overview
  - Ch. 12: Maneuver Formulation Activities
  - Ch. 13: Guiding Maneuver as It Unfolds in the Marketplace
  - Ch. 14: Capability Activities
  - Ch. 15: Structure Activities
  - Ch. 16: Vision Activities

- **Guiding Adaptation / Regeneration Activities: Ch. 17**

Exhibit 6.6: Guiding Self-Organization Activities

## ENDNOTES

1. Bower, J.L., C.A. Bartlet, H.E.R. Uyterhoeven, and R.E. Walton, *Business Policy: Managing Strategic Processes*, Chicago, Ill.: Irwin, 1995, Ch. 1.

2. Brown, S.L. and K.M. Eisenhardt, *Competing on the Edge: Strategy as Structured Chaos*, Boston, MA: Harvard Business School Press, 1998, Ch. 1.

3. Ibid., p. 4.

4. General Electric: Jack Welch's Second Wave (A), Harvard Business School Case # 9-392-247, Boston, MA: Harvard University, 1991, p. 9.

5. General Electric: Jack Welch's Second Wave (B), Harvard Business School Case # 9-392-113, Boston, MA: Harvard University, 1992, p. 4.

6. General Electric: Jack Welch's Second Wave (A), Harvard Business School Case # 9-392-247, Boston, MA: Harvard University, 1991, p. 9.

# CHAPTER 7

# Turbulence Sensing and Interpretation: An Overview

```
STRATEGIC            STRUCTURING           Guiding Turbulence Sensing & Interpretation Activities
LEADERSHIP    ───►   THE FIRM AS A           - Ch.7:   Turbulence Sensing & Interpretation: An Overview
                     SELF ORGANIZING         - Ch. 8:  Sensing Present Turbulence
                     SYSTEM                  - Ch. 9:  Sensing Future Turbulence
                     Ch. 5                   - Ch. 10: Interpreting Turbulence

                                           Guiding Response Activities
                                             - Ch. 11: Formulating Strategic Response: An Overview
                     GUIDING THE             - Ch. 12: Maneuver Formulation Activities
                     FIRM TOWARD             - Ch. 13: Guiding Maneuver as It unfolds in the Marketplace
              ───►   STRATEGIC               - Ch. 14: Capability Activities
                     END-STATES              - Ch. 15: Structure Activities
                     Ch. 6                   - Ch. 16: Vision Activities

                                           Guiding Renewal Activities:  Ch. 17
```

85

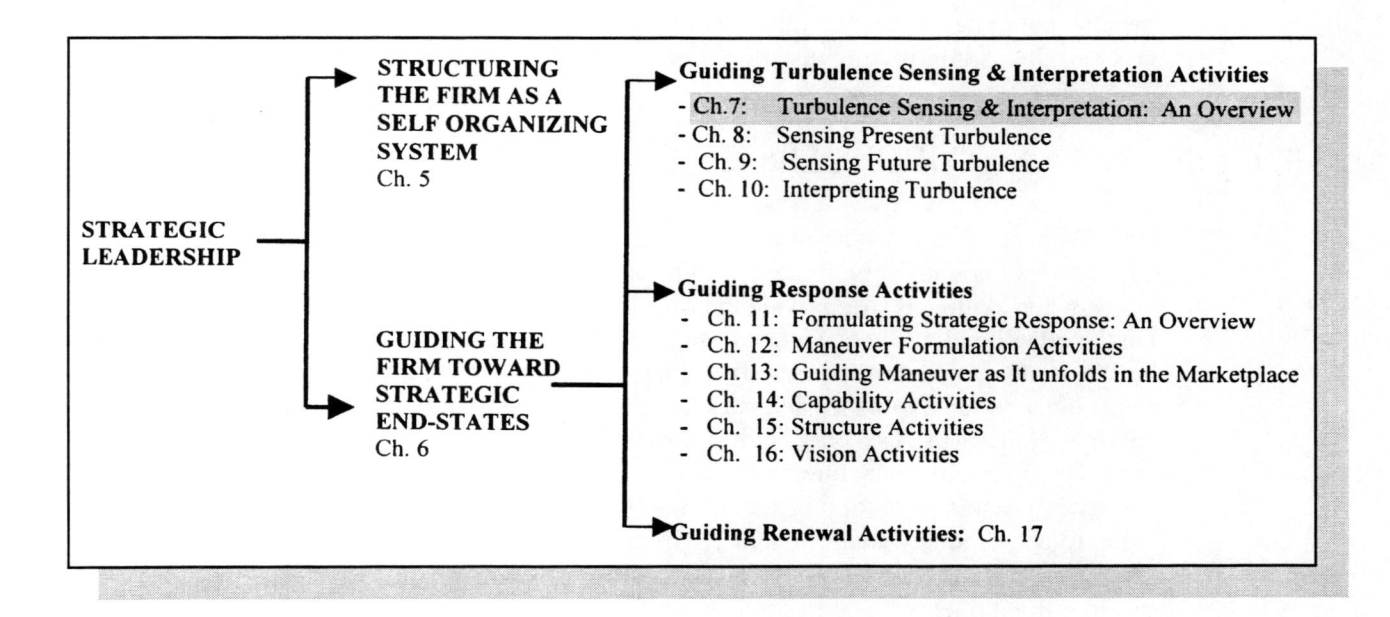

Self-organization activities fall into three categories: turbulence sensing and interpretation, strategic response, and renewal. This chapter is the first of a series of four chapters that present the first category, turbulence sensing and interpretation. It sets the stage for the chapters to follow by introducing the concept of turbulence and the work of the CEO in guiding the firm's activities in sensing and interpreting turbulence.

Simply put, turbulence sensing and interpretation is the act of peering the confusion of turbulence to discover any promising strategic end-states that may be embedded therein as well as any clever paths to them. The typical business firm encounters two types of turbulence, present and future. First, there is the turbulence prevailing at the present, which embodies the current strategic opportunities and challenges facing the firm. This will be the topic of Chapter 8. Understanding present turbulence is not enough. When the firm responds to current challenges, its action will be implemented in the future, possibly under different turbulence conditions. Hence, it is crucial to anticipate future turbulence. This will be the subject of Chapter 9.

Whether it pertains to the present or the future, turbulence sensing is essentially data gathering. The challenge for the firm is to find meaning in the data thus gathered. The developments inherent in turbulence data must be unearthed and their implications for the firm must be computed so that an intelligent response may be formulated. Hence, there is a third task and this is interpreting turbulence data. It will be the concern of Chapter 10.

# THE CONCEPT OF TURBULENCE

Turbulence is the state of affairs in the firm's marketplace. It impacts on the firm in a variety of ways with varying degrees. On one hand, turbulence may embody opportunities, which when exploited will provide the firm with the sustenance needed to survive and thrive. On the other hand, turbulence may pose serious problems, obstacles, and threats. Depending on the content of turbulence, the firm might find itself changing direction: expanding, retrenching, or even exiting the industry altogether. Sensing turbulence is thus essential for the survival of the firm. A self-organizing firm belongs to a class of systems known as open systems. Open systems by nature have built-in mechanisms for scanning their environment and incorporating this external information into their internal workings as part of their predisposition to continuously adapt to their environment.

Thus far, the term turbulence has been used frequently. It is time to pause to examine this important phenomenon in some depth. We do so by raising and answering the following questions. (1) What is turbulence? (2) Where does it come from? (3) How does it happen? (4) How does the CEO experience turbulence in the course of leading the firm? What does it feel like to be in the midst of this phenomenon, turbulence?

# THE NATURE OF TURBULENCE

The Webster's *New Universal Unabridged Dictionary* defines turbulence as "condition of being turbulent." The word "turbulent" has two entries: "full of commotion or disturbance" and "marked by widely irregular motion." The synonyms of "turbulence" were listed as "tumultuousness," "agitation," "disorder," and "commotion." Building on this, we can define turbulence as a set of conditions or a state of the world characterized by commotion, disturbance, agitation, disorder, and widely irregular motion.

In this section, we examine three different perspectives. From an academic perspective, we present the work of Ansoff and McDonnell. From a business perspective, we examine

CEO Putnam's conceptualization of turbulence. From a complexity science perspective, we explore the work of Wolfram and Langton.

## An Academic Perspective on Turbulence

Ansoff and McDonnell identified four attributes of turbulence:[1]

- Complexity or scope, e.g., national, regional or global.
- Familiarity of events or relative novelty: the degree of newness in successive waves of change.
- Rapidity of change: speed of change relative to the firm's speed of response.
- Visibility: adequacy and timeliness of information about the future.

| DIMENSION | LEVEL I | LEVEL II | LEVEL III | LEVEL IV | LEVEL V |
|---|---|---|---|---|---|
|  | Repetitive | Expanding | Changing | Discontinuous | Surprising |
| Complexity | National Economic | + | Regional Technological | + | Global Sociopolitical |
| Familiarity of Events | Familiar | Extrapolable |  | Discontinuous Familiar | Discontinuous Novel |
| Rapidity | Slower than response |  | Comparable to response |  | Faster than response |
| Visibility of future | Recurring Historical | Forecastable | Predictable | Partially Predictable | Unpredictable surprise |

Exhibit 7.1: Ansoff and McDonnell's Typology of Turbulence

Based on those attributes, they developed a typology of turbulence that is presented in Exhibit 7.1. Five levels of turbulence are distinguishable. These are:

- Level I: "Repetitive" Turbulence: In this type of turbulence history repeats itself. Conditions are more or less predictable and hence the CEO can lead under "business as usual" type of conditions. This is a rare condition nowadays.
- Level II: "Expanding" Turbulence: In this type, change is slow and happens in smaller increments that are related to one another in the sequence of progression. Traditional forecasting techniques can pinpoint the next sequence in advance. An example of this level is the demand for automobiles given the behavior of population demographics.
- Level III: "Changing" Turbulence: In this case, change is incremental and happens at increasingly shorter intervals. The increments are not particularly related to one another. The speed makes it difficult to predict the future. Nevertheless, partial predictability is possible. The demand and manufacturing conditions in the personal computer market approximate level III turbulence.
- Level IV: "Discontinuous" Turbulence: Here, change happens in large increments that may or may not be related in sequence but they are somewhat predictable. Examples of level IV turbulence include technological change such as the trend towards miniaturization in computers and electronic equipment. A discontinuous change occurs in big leaps, but its direction is more or less predictable. The trend towards globalization appeared to exhibit this pattern in the late 1980s and 1990s.

- Level V: "Surprising" Turbulence: In this type, change happens in large chunks that are not connected by any means. Turbulence is massive. As a result, even partial predictability is not possible. The decade of the 1990s presented us with many of such surpriseful turbulence. Examples include the fall of the Soviet Union, the democratization of Eastern Europe, the economic liberalization of China, the emergence of the flat, boundaryless organization, cooperative competitors (strategic alliances), the Internet and the rise of electronic commerce, among others.

## CEO's Perspective on Turbulence

To gain a business insight into turbulence, let us examine how a CEO defines it. Howard D. Putnam served twice as the CEO of two large corporations in the aviation industry. In his book, *The Winds of Turbulence*, he defined turbulence as ". . . the agitation that is a constant in business. These unsettling winds. . . ."[2] He classified the turbulence encountered by a business firm into six categories as follows:

- Alpha State: "Forward" Turbulence: In this state, the firm experiences clear skies and smooth progress. The business environment here is characterized by low interest rates, low unemployment, and inflation rates below four percent. It is successfully meeting challenges, handling risks, exploiting opportunities, and tackling business problems.
- Beta State: "Resistive" Turbulence: In this state, the wind picks up or changes direction. Clouds appear overhead. Rain starts to fall. A storm front is visible on the horizon. Such shifts occur when the reality of the environment does not coincide with the company's forecast. Interest rates do not go down, but they increase. Customer orders are canceled or reduced. A company in this state experiences any or all of these conditions: discord among its employees, increased customer complaints, decreased investor interest, lack of cooperation from its suppliers, a slip in market share, and decreased profitability.
- New Alpha State: "Renewed Forward" Turbulence: Such is the case of a firm that made it through a Beta state. It enters a new Alpha state. The external conditions may be almost the same as they were the first time around, but the firm has acquired new skills while it was in the Beta state. Putnam cautions that the peacefulness of the New Alpha is an illusion in that the apparent comfort may mask impending turmoil.
- Gamma State: "Chaotic" Turbulence: The firm's position is like the swirling of dry leaves in a hurricane. This state compels the firm to choose between quitting or smashing through the barriers with every bit of creativity and intelligence it can muster. The company experiences explosive frustration, self-destructive behavior, thievery, embezzlement, sabotage, disintegrating morale, frozen resources, crumbling integrity, festering hostilities, and a growing annihilative momentum. The forces of turbulence are mainly internal. To use a political analogy, this is the equivalent of the breakdown of law and order where armed rebellion, violence, destruction, and death become the order of the day.
- Omega State: "Expansive, Non-directed" Turbulence: According to Putnam, this is ". . . the delicate state that follows a rebellion." The turbulence once again is internal. It is expansive and non-directed like sunrays radiating in all directions. There is the euphoria, exuberance, and relief stemming from having made it through the storm. It is a floating, buzzing, transitory state.
- "New Alpha, After Omega" Turbulence: This is the state that follows the Omega state. The ideas are consolidated. Strengths become stronger. Coping mechanisms

are turned forward. The firm is once again in harmony with its environment. Its market and its industry are assuming a new plateau of business well being.

## A Complexity Science Perspective on Turbulence

Complexity science is an interdisciplinary field that studies the behavior of complex phenomena. Some concepts of complexity theory can shed more light on turbulence. Wolfram's rules describe the behavior of cellular automata as they form an environment. Cellular automata, and the environments they create, generate conditions that approximate the marketplace for a business firm.[3] They are worth examining here. Wolfram categorized the behavior of cellular automata into four categories. He labeled them as classes I, II, III, and IV. It is worth noting that *each category is a type or a model of turbulence*. These four models can help us understand the turbulence facing the firm. Whatever turbulence we face may fall into one of the four categories. The four classes can be described briefly below.

- Class I: Doomsday Behavior: In this environment, no matter what number of living and dead entities it starts with, everything dies within one or two steps. The system is analogous to a marble rolling around a big cereal bowl. Regardless of where it starts, the marble always rolls down quickly to a point in the center—resting in the dead state. Turbulence here is the movement from the top to the bottom. An example of the turbulence modeled after doomsday behavior is the pattern of raw material inventory use or cash burn in the business firm. They build up and then vanish into a dead state; raw materials into finished products, and cash into assets respectively.
- Class II: Periodic Oscillation: In class II, the entities are "somewhat lively." An initial pattern of scattered entities soon coalesces into a set of "static blobs," with perhaps a few other blobs sitting there oscillating too. To use the analogy of the marbles and the cereal bowl, the marble would roll around and around, and up and down the sides of the bowl indefinitely, as if the bottom of the bowl was bumpy. "Periodic oscillation" causes turbulence that may assume the form of cycles, e.g., business cycles and seasonal sales.
- Class III: Chaos: In this case, the entities are "too lively." They produce so much activity that the environment looks as if it is boiling. Nothing is stable. Nothing is predictable. Structures break up almost as soon as they are formed. Using the analogy of the marble in the cereal bowl, the marble would be rolling around from side to side so fast and so hard that it could never settle down. This state is what is known in science as "chaos." Chaos causes extreme turbulence, such as the ones experienced by the business world in the late 1980s, 1990s, and the 2000s. Business observers resorted to strong terms to describe the era, such as: "a world turned upside down," "madness is afoot," and "the age of unreason." The movement towards a borderless world, for example, created considerable Class III type of turbulence.
- Class IV: Complexity or Edge of Chaos: The entities are in a curious state. The conditions are neither chaotic (as in Class III) nor static (as in Class II.). Coherent structures (of entities) grow, split apart, and recombine in a complex way. They essentially never settle down. There are equilibria, but they are only momentary. The environment displays some stability, but at the same time, it is unstable because the old structures are breaking down and new recombinations appear periodically. Class IV appears to describe well the conditions of the business world that Bill Gates referred to as "punctuated chaos." Class IV also describes business behaviors such as strategic alliances (formed and dissolved at the discretion of the par-

| Class of Phenomena | Sequence | | | | |
|---|---|---|---|---|---|
| Cellular Automata | I & II | leading to | IV | ending at | III |
| Dynamical Systems | Order | leading to | Complexity | ending at | Chaos |
| Computation | Halting | leading to | Undecidable | ending at | Nonhalting |
| Life | Too static | leading to | Life/Intelligence | ending at | Too Noisy |

Exhibit 7.2: Patterns in the Behavior of Turbulence

ties involved) and diversification (a single business firm diversifies by building a portfolio of businesses and then manipulating it periodically by adding and dropping business units; acquiring other companies and divesting itself of others, and so on).

Langton studied Wolfram's work further.[4] He added more insights about the sequence of movement from one type of model of turbulence to another. Turbulence tends to move from one type to another in a predictable sequence. Langton examined several systems (Exhibit 7.2) and found that generally they tend to move from Class I or II to Class IV and then rest at Class III. In other words, *they tend to move from order, to complexity, and then to chaos.*

Langton's findings are important in understanding turbulence. If they are valid, the conclusion is that the business world tends to move from order to chaos; from stability to intense illogical disorganization. Business history attests to the validity of Langton's conclusions. Every era started with the business world in some order, but then half way into it, disorganization sets in. For example, mass production and mass marketing became the order of doing business in the 1960s and 1970s. In the 1980s, the order started to change radically with the advent of hi-tech and the emergence of globalization. Since then the business world has been in a state similar to Class III. Typical of Class III is the spread of the Internet and electronic commerce (the e-business revolution) in the 2000s.

# FORMS OF TURBULENCE

From a business perspective, turbulence presents itself in many forms. It is crucial to know these forms so that we can tell when turbulence is present. Here are some examples of the ways in which turbulence reveals itself to us:

1. Complex Behaviors: Complexity is always present in turbulent behavior. Everything appears to be one complication inside another complication, and so on. There are always several patterns and then there are patterns within patterns. Consider cash flows. First, there is the corporate cash flow pattern as shown in consolidated statements. Then, there are different patterns of cash use and generation for every division. Still, there are other patterns for the various departments within the divisional pattern.
2. Randomness: Randomness is one of the most visible aspects of turbulence. The readings of many variables appear erratic. Many do not display a frequency distribution. Consequently, statistical estimates cannot be made of the probability of their occurrences. Events and de-

velopments seem to belong to multiple populations that cannot even be defined let alone sampled. Statistical models did not overcome such problems. Consider the behavior of competitors. If we take each competitor individually, the behavior is virtually random, reflecting the many initiatives that a competitor could take to change the situation in its favor. Taken collectively, one can imagine a wide range of possible moves in a variety of directions that competitors may take.

3. Sudden Leaps: Many business conditions do not change in a gradual fashion. Instead, there is considerable discontinuity, as Ansoff and McDonnell pointed out. Typical of discontinuous change is technological change, which tends to jump from one type of technology to another, and this change may be radical. Consider the changes from electric circuitry to transistor and from transistor to microprocessor. Along the same line, compare the electro-mechanical typewriter to the personal computer (word processor). Stock prices moving in the form of sudden leaps in financial markets depend on the news and rumors of the day. Sudden leaps are also present in the behavior of competitors in the form of "surprise attacks."

4. Reversals: Reversals are frequent in the business world. Consider corporate profits. With a change in market conditions, profits can turn into losses. The same applies for market share gains and losses. Looking at the macro-environment, Peters pointed out a number of reversals, the most important of which is the fragmentation of markets.[5] In the first part of this century, markets were fragmented. From the 1940's on, markets were "mass markets." From the late 1980's onward, markets are becoming fragmented again. More confusing are sudden reversals, as in the case of the "moody" behavior of stock prices.

5. Bifurcation: Many business variables do not behave in a smooth, straight-line progression. Bifurcation is a common occurrence. There are successive splits. Consider an infusion of capital at the corporate level. It starts as a "stream" and then it branches out to divisions and then branches out again to departments. Along the same line is the flow of goods in the distribution of a network of vertical channels. Within the organization, the flow of information bifurcates and branches continuously until it reaches the "final" receivers, if any, since some of it might become public.

6. Rapidity: For many variables, the rate of change is so high that it is not feasible for the firm to respond in a timely fashion. Ansoff and McDonnell observe considerable "acceleration" in the change of many macro-business environmental variables.[6] The two writers further break down acceleration into two components: high frequency of change, and rapid diffusion of change. Consider the rapid rate at which television sets and desktop computers penetrated consumer markets.

7. Perturbance: The business environment is brimming with so many variables, moving in a multitude of directions, and sometimes in a chaotic way. There is hardly a time when the CEO can get a fix on what is going on. Even if he/she succeeds in doing so, the conditions in the marketplace change so quickly that the emerging perception will be outdated and out of touch with the new reality. Perturbances occur all the time, particularly as the globe shrinks and the multitude of players increases exponentially. And, if the turbulence is not caused by human players, there is always nature, which, produces disturbances such as floods and typhoons.

8. Simultaneous Stability and Instability: When plotted, the curves representing various business variables behave like waves of water in a hose. They oscillate, but all of them tend to stay in the boundary of the hose. There is a lot of variation (instability), but the particles stay within the skin of the hose (stability). For example, if one plots cash usage (burn rate) or the specifications of the output of a certain manufacturing process, they appear to be cyclical (deviate from budgets or design specifications), but they stay within an upper and lower boundary. There is a paradox here, namely, instability within stability, but such is life in a private enterprise economy.

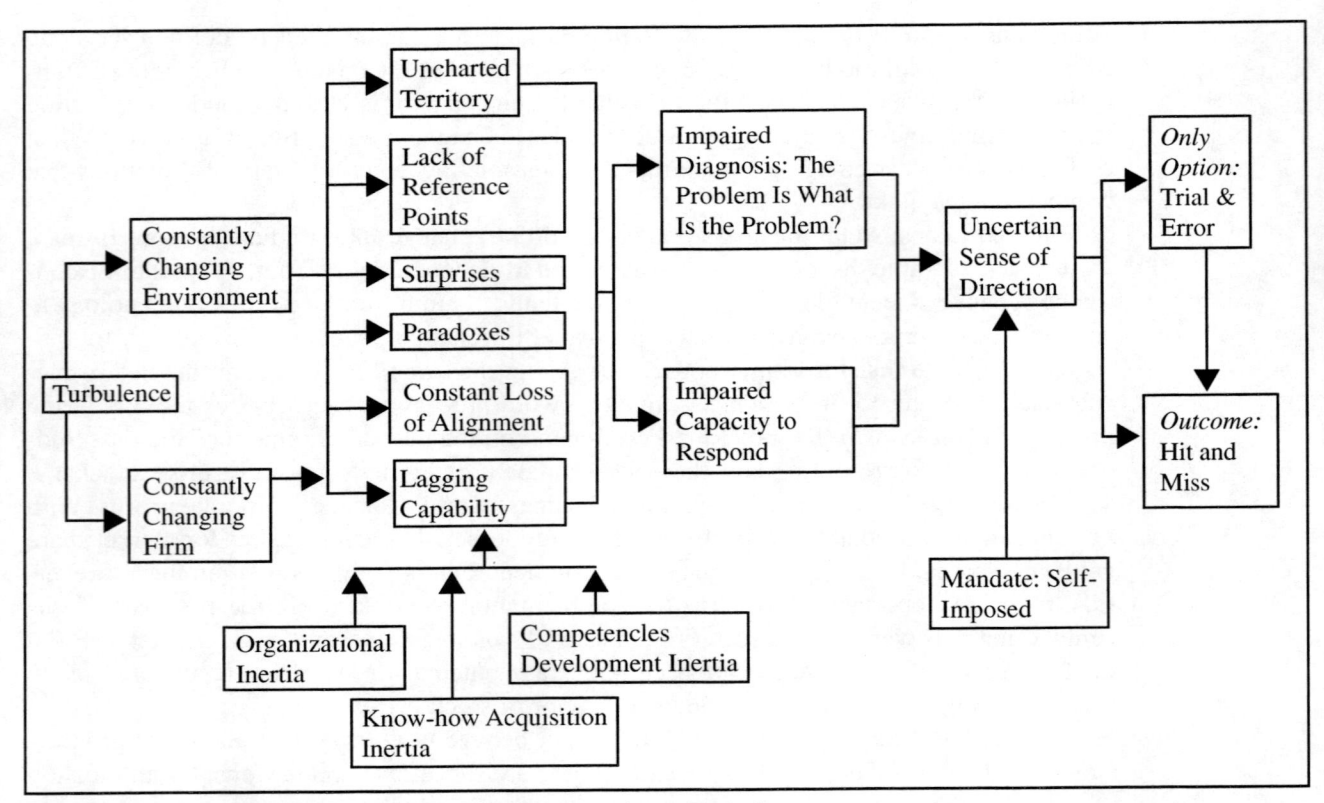

Exhibit 7.3: How the CEO and the Organization Experience Turbulence

## EXPERIENCING TURBULENCE

Exhibit 7.3 attempts to portray how a firm (leaders and employees) experience turbulence first hand. The firm is often encountering uncharted waters, i.e., constant change makes the market and the industry unknowable. In such uncharted waters, there are no reference points. When a new course of action is undertaken, there is little indication whether this direction is the right one. The only sense of direction is suggested by instinct aided by experience.

Turbulence hides developments that are just around the corner. These soon become surprises. Turbulence also produces "paradoxes," situations where two extremes appear to hold true simultaneously. An example of a current paradox is mass customization. How can a market be "mass" and "customized" at the same time? Yet, it is true. Another example is that the elimination of inspection increases quality.

Constant change (turbulence) causes the firm to lose alignment with its environment. By the time it comes to grips with a picture of the market, it would have changed. As the firm loses touch with its markets and industry, its ability to adapt is reduced. Its offering might become obsolete. Its capability will also be misaligned with the changing environment. The lag in responding to environmental change results from "inertia." First, there is organizational inertia resulting from people's inability to comprehend change and their tendency to resist it. Second, there is a time lag in acquiring the needed resources and competencies to update capability. Infusing resources requires huge investments. Time is needed to acquire the necessary capital assets and to train people to work with new technology. There is a third source of inertia that stems from the fact that the know-how needed to cope with the change is not readily available. It too takes a long time to develop. Finally, the firm is a collection of stakeholders (customers, shareholders, employees, community, government, etc.) whose interests are often in conflict. It takes time to understand, reconcile, and unify them. The offshoot of all this is the inertia that robs the firm of its ability to respond quickly to changes in the marketplace.

The sequence of events in Exhibit 7.3 produces two fundamental predicaments. First, is the inability to diagnose and solve problems. Often, the predicament is this: "the problem is what is the problem?" How can one "see" the problem when it is shrouded in ambiguity and uncertainty inherent in rapid change? Second, even when the problem becomes known, the best response might not be readily determined. Being unable to diagnose problems and determine responses quickly, in turn, creates a new problem, an uncertain sense of direction. Turbulence makes it very difficult to define a destination and to chart a course towards it.

This uncertain sense of direction leaves the organization with essentially one option, and this is "trial and error." Consequently, the results are of the "hit and miss" variety. The predicament is that the firm's performance is the outcome of forces that lie beyond its control. Yet, the leader and the people are held accountable for such performance, good or bad.

# GUIDING TURBULENCE SENSING ACTIVITIES

As stated earlier, the respective activities here fall into three subsets. The first pertains to assessing the prevailing turbulence. The second deals with anticipating future turbulence. The third includes the activities involved in making sense of or interpreting turbulence. Clearly, interpretation is the culmination of the turbulence sensing process. In the final analysis, turbulence is sensed when it is translated into a set of strategic issues for the firm. These subsets will be surveyed in the next three chapters. Like the other self-organization activities, the CEO must guide turbulence sensing and interpretation activities in order to ensure that they lead to the discovery of strategic end-states and of intelligent ways to reach them.

The CEO's work in guiding the firm's activities was outlined in Chapter 6. Guiding turbulence sensing and interpretation activities happens along the same line. The crux of the CEO's work is to induce and orchestrate collaboration to sense and interpret turbulence. The relevant tasks are highlighted below:

- Creating an environment conducive to collaboration to sense turbulence.
- Inducing conversation on sensing turbulence.
- Moving conversation to turbulence sensing action.
- Acknowledging and rewarding the achievements of collaborative turbulence-sensing efforts.
- Affirming accountability and governance.
- Exercising personal influence

## Creating an Environment Conducive to Collaboration

1. Cultivating Paradigms: It is crucial that the need for turbulence sensing be engrained in the organization's mindset. It has to be part of the culture. This is accomplished by always pressing few seminal thoughts that charge employees with the responsibility for being on the lookout for developments in the industry and the environment at large. Andy Grove (Intel) succeeded in implanting the thought, "Only the paranoid survive" in the company's culture. Being paranoid suggests being alert and alive to a changing marketplace. Being alert means scanning the industry to be aware of turbulent developments that might threaten the firm.

2. Building Shared Goals: The work of the CEO here involves persuading all diverse groups to have sensing turbulence as a goal. If they all believe in the importance of the continuous surveillance of the firm's environment, chances are they will collaborate to do so. Turbulence sensing can be made a goal by placing it as a derivative of the major goal of surviving and thriving in a turbulent marketplace. Survival cannot be achieved without surveillance.
3. Defining Boundaryless Roles: Sensing turbulence is a massive task. Some units, by virtue of their proximity to the marketplace, can be assigned major roles in surveillance; the sales force for example. Other units can be assigned roles pertaining to analyzing the information and spotting change, e.g., the market research and the finance units. Every unit in the organization must have a well-defined role in sensing turbulence. Nevertheless, the roles have to be interdependent by stressing the importance of passing the information around to all other units so they may benefit from the developments relevant to their operation.
4. Networking: In this age of information technology, this is an easy task. The infrastructure is in place. The challenge is to network everyone with everyone else so that intelligence data can flow freely to all concerned. When information is shared, people become more informed, i.e., more aware of the turbulence around them.
5. Instituting Dialogue: It is crucial to orchestrate forums for diverse groups to discuss changes in the firm's marketplace. Dialogue must be part of the culture: units closer to the marketplace must regularly brief those who are an organizational distance away from it.
6. Orchestrating Shared Workspace: When employees share workspace, they are more likely to collaborate in obtaining helpful information and in sharing it. At Chrysler, for example, the concept of platform teams brings together sales staff along with those in engineering, finance, and manufacturing on the same floor. This allows them to determine their information needs as a team and then work together to gather the necessary data.
7. Charging Emotions: We have seen already Andy Grove creating the emotion of paranoia. Welch (GE) promotes the concept of driving change. The idea of driving change evokes strong feelings. An employee who is practicing the "driving change philosophy" in a "paranoid frame of mind" is more apt to be committed to scanning the environment in search of opportunities for changing the status quo in order to help the firm stay on top of developments in the marketplace.

## Inducing and Stimulating Conversation on Sensing Turbulence

It is crucial for individuals and groups to talk about spotting turbulence. Conversation means that people will dialogue on ways to identify developments and trends in the industry and to monitor them. Getting conversation started involves the following:

1. Articulating and Clarifying Purpose: Knowing the firm's purpose and objectives helps in turbulence sensing. Turbulence affects the achievement of purpose. For example, if the objective is to achieve a certain market share, competition as a force of turbulence will have to be monitored. Employees will be on the alert for competitors' moves and initiatives. They will be more inclined to gather intelligence data.
2. Developing Shared Understanding: The CEO's guidance here focuses on working with the various units to arrive at some unity in defining what is involved in sensing turbulence. For example, the concept "industry" means different things to different people. However, if they all agree on a concept like Porter's model (Chapter 8), then everyone will be attempting to obtain the necessary information to piece together a picture of the industry and the goings-on in it. Thus, marketing personnel can track customers and those in manufacturing can track suppliers, technology, and so on.
3. Placing Turbulence on the Firm's Agenda: Progressive CEOs always place turbulence sensing on the company's agenda. At GE, for example, Welch insisted that unit managers

place the Internet and e-commerce as one of the top three items in the unit's list of priorities. Since the Internet is a major source of turbulence in the 2000s, the units will have to track it.
4. Stimulating and Balancing Advocacy: When units advocate for a certain position, they will have to back up their position with information. If a group is proposing the addition of a new product or service, they will have to collect the relevant information to substantiate their plan. Advocacy is a strong incentive for gathering information about turbulence. Advocates would want to prove that their proposal is timely and in synch with current conditions in the marketplaces.
5. Institutionalizing the Projects Principle: The project concept is a good tool for nudging the organization to stay on top of its environment. A project is born out of developments in the marketplace. Its conception forces people to be externally focused. After a project is completed, it is time to look for another project. This again forces people to look outside for opportunities. In the course of doing this, they will have to collect information about the marketplace.

## Marshalling Strategic Conversation to Strategic Action

Moving discussion about turbulence to actual turbulence sensing activities, involves several CEO's tasks as follows:

1. Developing and Cultivating Frameworks for Sensing Turbulence: To help employees perform turbulence sensing activities properly, they must be provided with frameworks or templates. The next three chapters present many templates for exposing turbulence. These include environmental analysis, industry analysis, SWOT analysis, vulnerability analysis, pattern recognition, mapping, scenarios construction, and issues analysis. Such frameworks systematize turbulence sensing and ensure its exhaustiveness.
2. Keeping the Vision: The vision is the strategic end-state (destination) to which the firm aspires. Keeping it front and center helps in sorting through the mess of turbulence. The search for this destination galvanizes people's energies to assess turbulence and how it impacts on getting to the desired end-state.
3. Building Collaborative Networks: Collaborative networks are crucial for turbulence sensing; the more extensive the network, the more the information. Networks increase people's capacity to collect all sorts of information. They will be in a better position to map out the prevailing turbulence.
4. Staffing Critical Positions: The CEO can help guide turbulence sensing activities by ensuring that the units have qualified individuals who are trained in information gathering and spotting trends. This can include training individual employees to collect and catalogue data, assigning, appointing leaders for various surveillance projects, hiring consultants, or even establishing a unit specialized in data gathering (such as the economic research units in banks).
5. Allocating Resources: Turbulence sensing is not free. Many expenses are incurred in data gathering including research time, travel, report writing, briefing sessions, computer hardware and software, surveillance systems, and the like. If adequate resources are not committed, turbulence sensing cannot happen. The CEO can use resource allocation as a tool for nudging turbulence sensing in a certain direction or another.

## Acknowledging and Rewarding the Achievements of Collaborative Turbulence Sensing

Turbulence defies definition. Understanding it should be viewed as a battle to be won. If the CEO is to entrench turbulence sensing in the culture, then its results must be acknowledged and celebrated. Whenever units come together to gather information about the industry and understand the forces that shape it, they should be recognized and rewarded for it.

### Affirming Accountability and Governance

Because turbulence sensing is crucial for the firm's survival, it must be treated as a responsibility for people, individually and severally. No firm can afford to miss developments in a rapidly changing marketplace. The CEO must affirm and enforce the accountability of all units to work together to help the firm map the turbulence around it. Units that miss certain developments in their industry should be held accountable for these results. Units that did not warn and help other units about changes that might affect them should be held accountable for this as well. The CEO has an arsenal of tools here including periodic audits of collaboration, keeping score, challenging results (intelligence and surveillance reports), and administering rewards and punishments for lack of collaboration.

### Exercising Personal Influence

Finally, the ultimate tool for guiding turbulence sensing is the CEO's personal involvement. "Walking the talk" is the best test. An aware CEO will walk around, discussing things, coaching, and preaching to impress upon the employees the importance of sensing turbulence, doing it right, and pulling together to do a better job. He/she should set the example by scouting around for trends and developments and passing the information to the various units.

## CONCLUSION

In this chapter, the phenomenon of turbulence was examined. Turbulence poses three serious challenges for the CEO and the organization: ambiguity, complexity, and uncertainty. They impact on the firm's ability to sense, anticipate, and interpret turbulence. *Ambiguity* is a lack of information. It results from the swirls and swirls of motion (rapid, erratic, surpriseful change) that camouflage relevant events thus rendering the human mind deprived of data about what lurks inside turbulence. It creates a fog-like condition where visibility is severely impaired. Take, for example, the case of a newly appointed CEO at a large corporation. One of the first things he or she would need to do is to assess the situation of the corporation. He or she will need considerable data to make this assessment. However, getting all the facts about all of the variables is an impossible task. Sometimes the data are not even collectable (e.g., competitors' strategic intentions and plans). If they are, they will take a long time to obtain. After waiting all this time, the issues of reliability and validity remain, particularly if we factor in human error, misinterpretation, organizational politics, etc. Ambiguity is a fact of life.

The second challenge is *complexity*. There are numerous factors fueling the turbulence. Because the universe is interconnected, multitudes of factors converge on the human mind, paralyzing it. This leaves it unable to make sense of all that is coming at it from all directions. Then, there is the *uncertainty* problem. The main challenge here is that the world changes without notice. We do not know for sure which state of affairs will prevail in the future. We do not even have a probability distribution that can help us guess the likelihood of the occurrence of any state of affairs.

Armed with this understanding of turbulence, we proceed next to examine the turbulence sensing and interpretation activities of the self-organizing system. This is the topic of the next three chapters.

# ENDNOTES

1. Ansoff, H.I. and E.J. McDonnell, *Implanting Strategic Management*, 2nd ed., New York, N.Y.: Prentice Hall, 1990, p. 31.

2. Putnam, H.D., *The Winds of Turbulence: A CEO's Reflections on Surviving and Thriving on the Edge of Corporate Crises*, New York, NY: Harper Collins, 1992, pp. 1–19.

3. Waldrop, M.M., *Complexity: The Emerging Science At The Edge Of Order And Chaos*, New York, N.Y.: Simon & Schuster, 1992, Ch. 6.

4. Ibid., p. 234.

5. Peters, T., *Thriving On Chaos*, New York, NY: Alfred A. Knopf, Inc., 1987.

6. Ansoff and McDonnell, op. cit.

CHAPTER
# 8

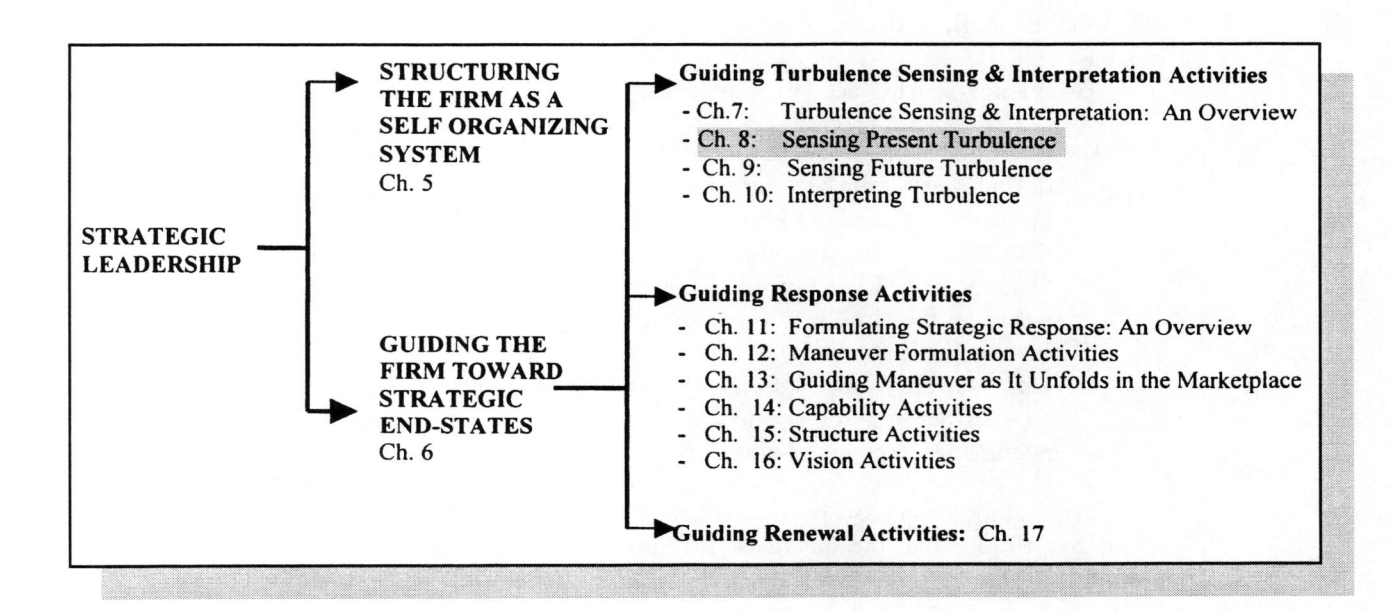

# Sensing Present Turbulence

```
STRATEGIC                STRUCTURING           Guiding Turbulence Sensing & Interpretation Activities
LEADERSHIP  ──┬──▶       THE FIRM AS A           - Ch.7:   Turbulence Sensing & Interpretation: An Overview
              │          SELF ORGANIZING         - Ch. 8:  Sensing Present Turbulence
              │          SYSTEM                  - Ch. 9:  Sensing Future Turbulence
              │          Ch. 5                   - Ch. 10: Interpreting Turbulence
              │
              │                                ▶ Guiding Response Activities
              │                                  - Ch. 11: Formulating Strategic Response: An Overview
              │          GUIDING THE             - Ch. 12: Maneuver Formulation Activities
              │          FIRM TOWARD             - Ch. 13: Guiding Maneuver as It Unfolds in the Marketplace
              └──▶       STRATEGIC               - Ch. 14: Capability Activities
                         END-STATES              - Ch. 15: Structure Activities
                         Ch. 6                   - Ch. 16: Vision Activities

                                               ▶ Guiding Renewal Activities:  Ch. 17
```

One of the major attributes of a self-organizing system is its ability to respond continuously to its changing environment. In order to respond, the system must have a reliable perception of its environment and the forces that make it up along with their dynamics. This chapter is concerned with the topic of sensing impending turbulence. It begins with a survey of the scope of turbulence sensing activities. Next, a number of frameworks for mapping and understanding turbulence will be introduced. Turbulence is a phenomenon that defies a firm grasp. It is like a "blob" with no dimensions and location in time and space. The methods and tools presented in this chapter were designed to help members of a self-organizing system break down this blob into the components that constitute it.

The firm's activities in identifying and assessing turbulence simply amount to intelligence and surveillance, the deliberate gathering of data and organizing them in a manner that facilitates interpretation, the process of extracting the driving forces behind turbulence. Business firms engage in gathering external data all the time. Some firms rely on salespersons and employees in general as the main intelligence and surveillance agents. Others have special units that collect, distill, and disseminate data throughout the organization on a continuous basis.

Turbulence-sensing activities often include these tasks:

- Intelligence and Surveillance: This simply amounts to gathering data. It includes the definition of units of measurements (of various variables); the determination of the kinds of data needed to map out turbulence; the identification of the sources of such data; and, the actual collection of the data from these sources.
- Data Organization: Activities here involve sorting out the data into categories (e.g., based on the similarity of variables or based on their time frame) and plotting the data to facilitate analysis.
- Analysis: Analysis focuses on forcing the tendencies underlying the data to surface, so that they may be spotted, isolated, and noted. The purpose is to identify major events, developments, and trends.

The methods and tools presented next are templates that outline the various components of the main blobs that the business firm has to demystify in order to sense the turbulence around it. In this regard, they help in determining what kind of data that we need to collect. They also help us decide how to organize the data so that we may develop a good picture of the firm's environment. When all the templates are completed, members of the firm will have in front of them a total size-up of the situation facing them, to which they must develop and undertake a response. Three such frameworks will be presented next: analysis, pattern recognition, and mapping.

# ANALYSIS

Analysis begins with the thesis that a phenomenon embedded in turbulence is an ambiguous "blob" that defies precise delineation and that the only way to "see" it (understand it) is to dissect or break it down to its main elemental components. It is like putting a blob under the microscope. The presentation begins with techniques for analyzing the macro-environment. This will be followed by techniques for analyzing the firm itself, microanalysis.

The application of analysis begins with dissecting the world in which the firm exists. This is shown in Exhibit 8.1. There are several components ranging from the micro to the macro as follows:

```
                    THE MACRO-ENVIRONMENT

                          ┌──────────┐
                          │ Economic │
                          │  System  │
                          └────┬─────┘
                               ↕
         ┌──────────────────────────────────────────┐
         │         ECONOMIC SECTOR                  │
┌────────┐│    ┌────────────────────────────┐       │┌─────────────┐
│ Social ││←→ │         INDUSTRY            │   ←→ ││Technological│
│ System ││    │   ┌──────────────────┐     │       ││   System    │
└────────┘│    │   │ Industry Segment │     │       │└─────────────┘
          │    │   │   ┌──────────┐   │     │       │
┌────────┐│    │   │   │ THE FIRM │   │     │       │┌─────────────┐
│Political│←→│   │   └──────────┘   │     │   ←→ ││    Legal    │
│ System  │    │   └──────────────────┘     │       ││   System    │
└────────┘│    └────────────────────────────┘       │└─────────────┘
          └──────────────────────────────────────────┘
                               ↕
                       ┌──────────────────┐
                       │ Global Interfaces│
                       └──────────────────┘
```

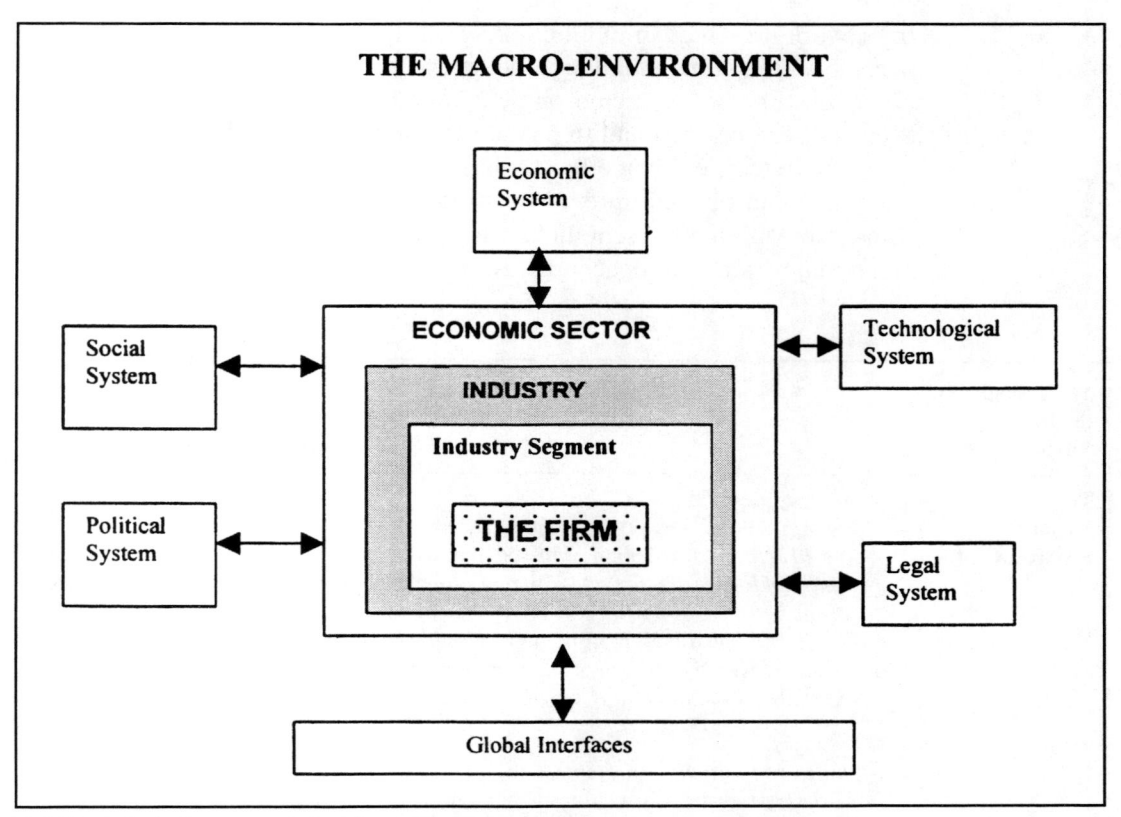

Exhibit 8.1: A Concept of the Firm's Environment

- The *firm* itself.
- Enveloping the firm is *the industry segment*, the specific part of the industry in which the firm exists, e.g., raw material producers, parts makers, assemblers, etc.
- Enveloping a number of segments is *the industry*. The auto industry, for example, has segments such as assembly, original equipment manufacturers (OEM's), and retailing (dealers). This too is hard to grasp because it defies definition in most cases. There is often so much overlap between products and producers that it is difficult to draw a clear boundary around an industry.
- Enveloping a number of industries is *the economic sector*. For example, the aviation, marine, and automobile industries are part of the transportation sector.
- Enveloping an economic sector is the *economic system*.
- Enveloping the economy is the *macro-environment*. Not only does it include the economy, but also the social system, the political system, the legal system, the technological system, and, other countries in the case of the global corporation.

It is worth noting that all of these entities are interrelated. They are all part of one universe. Whatever happens at the macro level trickles (vertically and horizontally) to the firm and affects it. No matter how distant a development may be, it will have an impact of some sort on the firm. Some impacts are significant and immediate. Others are weak and remote.

# Macro-Environmental Analysis

Macro-environmental analysis takes the biggest blob, the so-called "environment," and dissects it in terms of its major components. Fahey and Randall, for example, developed the framework presented in Exhibit 8.2.[1] The key components of the macro environment pertain to society (including population demographics, life styles, social values), the economic environment, the political environment, and the technological environment. Many of the key events, developments, and trends in these arenas eventually trickle down to the level of the firm. These trickle-down effects might represent opportunities, e.g., the use of computers in the classroom opened up enormous opportunities for clone makers and software writing firms. They might represent threats, e.g., society's concern about the effect of cigarette smoking, a major threat to tobacco firms.

| Major Aspect of the Macro-Environment | Sub-Aspect |
|---|---|
| **The Social Environment** | **Demographics:**<br>—*Population size:* in a given geographic area.<br>—*Age structure:* Distribution of the population by age groups.<br>—*Geographic Distribution:* Distribution of the population by region and population shifts among these regions.<br>—*Ethnic mix:* Distribution of the population by ethnic origin and growth rates within the various groups.<br>—*Income level:* Distribution of the population by income groups across age, geographic, ethnic and life style groups such as family type for example. |
|  | **Life Styles:**<br>—*Household formation:* Composition, type, rate of change and size of household.<br>—*Work:* type, place, expectations about work, and work hours.<br>—*Education:* Level reached and type of formal training obtained.<br>—*Consumption:* Classes of products/services people purchase/consume or do not purchase/consume.<br>—*Leisure:* Distribution of hours and expenditure by various types of non-work activities people engage in. |
|  | **Social Values:**<br>—*Political values:* Voting patterns and predisposition towards the key political and social issues.<br>—*Social values:* Attitudes towards work, leisure, participation in organizations, acceptance of other groups, and acceptance of social habits.<br>—*Technological values:* Attitudes toward and acceptance of new technologies and the perception of their costs and benefits.<br>—*Economic values:* Attitudes toward economic growth and position on the trade-off between economic progress and social costs. |
| **The Economic Environment** | —*Structural change:* Changes within and across economic sectors, e.g., growth of some industries coupled with the decline of others as well as the changes in the relationships among the key economic variables, e.g., imports and exports as a per cent of GNP.<br>—*Cyclical change:* The ups and downs of the economic cycle in GNP, interest rates, inflation, price levels, housing starts, and investments. |
| **The Political Environment** | —*The formal system:* The electoral process, the institutions of government, the political parties, the legislation, the judiciary, and the regulatory agencies.<br>—*The informal system:* Arenas outside government where political activity occurs, e.g., the community, the media, etc. |
| **The Technological Environment** | —*Research:* Basic and applied research.<br>—*Development:* Transformation of research findings into a prototype for a product that can be exploited commercially.<br>—*Diffusion:* Making the knowledge gained through research available in a form that facilitates its adoption by others. |

Exhibit 8.2: Macro-Environmental Analysis

## INDUSTRY ANALYSIS

An industry is also a "blob" that is hard to delineate neatly in most cases. To come to grips with what an industry is, analysis is a useful technique. Porter has pioneered the field of industry analysis.[2] We build on his model here to develop a platform for analyzing an industry. The framework is presented in Exhibit 8.3.

If one puts the entity "industry" under the microscope, five major elements can be discerned. These are: the members of the industry or the competitors in a given industry (firms that produce and sell the product/service after which the industry is named); industry suppliers (firms that provide raw material, parts, and services to the industry competitors); buyers (individuals and firms that buy the products/services of the industry competitors); substitutes (products/services that represent alternatives to the industry and hence their producers are competitors to the firms in the industry); and, potential entrants (new firms that judged the industry as attractive and made the decision to enter it in the near or distant future).

The focal element in Porter's industry analysis is rivalry among members of the industry, the competitors themselves. Rivalry is the extent to which the industry's profitability is depressed through aggressive price competition. Rivalry depends on a number of factors. First is concentration, the relative size of competitors. Larger firms can afford to engage in price competition. Second is the diversity of competitors. The more diverse they are, the less the propensity to engage in price reduction battles. Third is product differentiation. If the products are strongly differentiated, then every competitor will have its own quasi-monopoly in the marketplace. This reduces the desire to compete on price. Fourth is the presence of excess capacity. Excess capacity often compels a competitor to reduce price in order to increase volume in an effort to increase the utilization of capacity. Fifth is the presence of exit barriers. If a firm cannot leave the industry (because of size of investment, regulation, political reasons, etc.) it will be tempted to persevere somehow, often resorting to price competition as a way of recovering sunk costs. Finally, cost structures can fuel price competition. For example, firms that have economies of scale enjoy big margins. Such firms sometimes resort to price-cutting as a strategy for gaining market share.

The intensity of rivalry causes the firm to pursue a certain market strategy. Porter suggested three broad (generic) strategies that a firm can follow: cost leadership, differentiation, and focus. A firm can compete by being the lowest-cost producer, e.g., Wal-Mart. Alternatively, a firm can compete by focusing on a certain market or product, e.g., Dell Computers focusing on mail order distribution of PCs. Finally, a firm can compete by differentiating itself from similar competitors through product or service differentiation. Consider, for example, the intensity of differentiation among toothpaste products.

Porter's analysis highlights some key dynamics or conditions that have serious implications for the firm, as a member of an industry or as a rival. These are the bargaining power of suppliers, the bargaining power of buyers, the threat of entrants, and the threat of substitutes. The bargaining power of suppliers determines the firm's cost structure, price levels, and eventually, its ability to compete. Their power can be further analyzed in terms of their numbers, relative size, their power in controlling supply, the impact of what they supply on the firm's cost structure, and the availability of alternative products from a different set of suppliers.

The bargaining power of buyers eventually sets price levels to which the firm must conform. Their power can be analyzed in terms of their price sensitivity and relative bargaining leverage. Their price sensitivity depends on the relative cost of the purchased item in the buyer's cost structure, the degree of product differentiation in the purchased item (which gives the supplying firm a quasi monopoly), and the intensity of competition among the buyers themselves. The relative bargaining power of buyers depends on the size of the buyer

**Suppliers**
- Number of firms
- Products/ services they supply to the industry
- Relative sizes of the various suppliers and the market structure
- Factors affecting supplier behavior: presence of substitutes to the supplier products, intrinsic differences among the products, threat of buyers integrating backward, importance of volume for suppliers, impact of supplier input on the cost structure of buyers, cost relative to making it by buyers, barriers to exit

**Potential Entrants**

- Factors affecting the number of potential entrants:
    - Presence of barriers to entry: economies of scale, investment required to enter the industry, intellectual property barriers, e.g., patents and licenses, fear of retaliation, etc.
    - Access to the distribution system
    - Access to suppliers of inputs
    - Switching cost to compete in a new industry.
    - Availability of technology
    - Ability to withstand Retaliation
- Presence of excess capacity

**Members of the Industry:**

- Number of competing firms
- Products/ services
- Relative sizes of the various competitors
- Relative position in the market
- Factors affecting competitive behavior:
    - Market structure; oligopoly, perfect competition, etc.
    - Intrinsic difference among products
    - Customers' loyalty behavior
    - Innovation capacity
    - Capacity utilization
    - Economics of the business
    - Barriers to exiting the industry

**Substitutes**

- Availability of substitutes
- Number of substitutes
- Factors affecting the impact of substitutes on members of the industry:
    - Relative product performance and quality
    - Relative prices
    - Buyers' willingness to switch to substitutes
    - Cost of switching to substitutes

**Buyers**

- Numbers
- Relative sizes
- Factors affecting buyers' behavior:
    - Relative volume bought by various customers and customer segment
    - Availability of substitutes
    - Sensitivity to price
    - Brand loyalty behavior / relationship with members of the industry
    - Predisposition toward backward integration: acquiring members of the industry
    - Cost of switching to substitutes or making their own product
    - Impact of the product on the cost structure of buyers

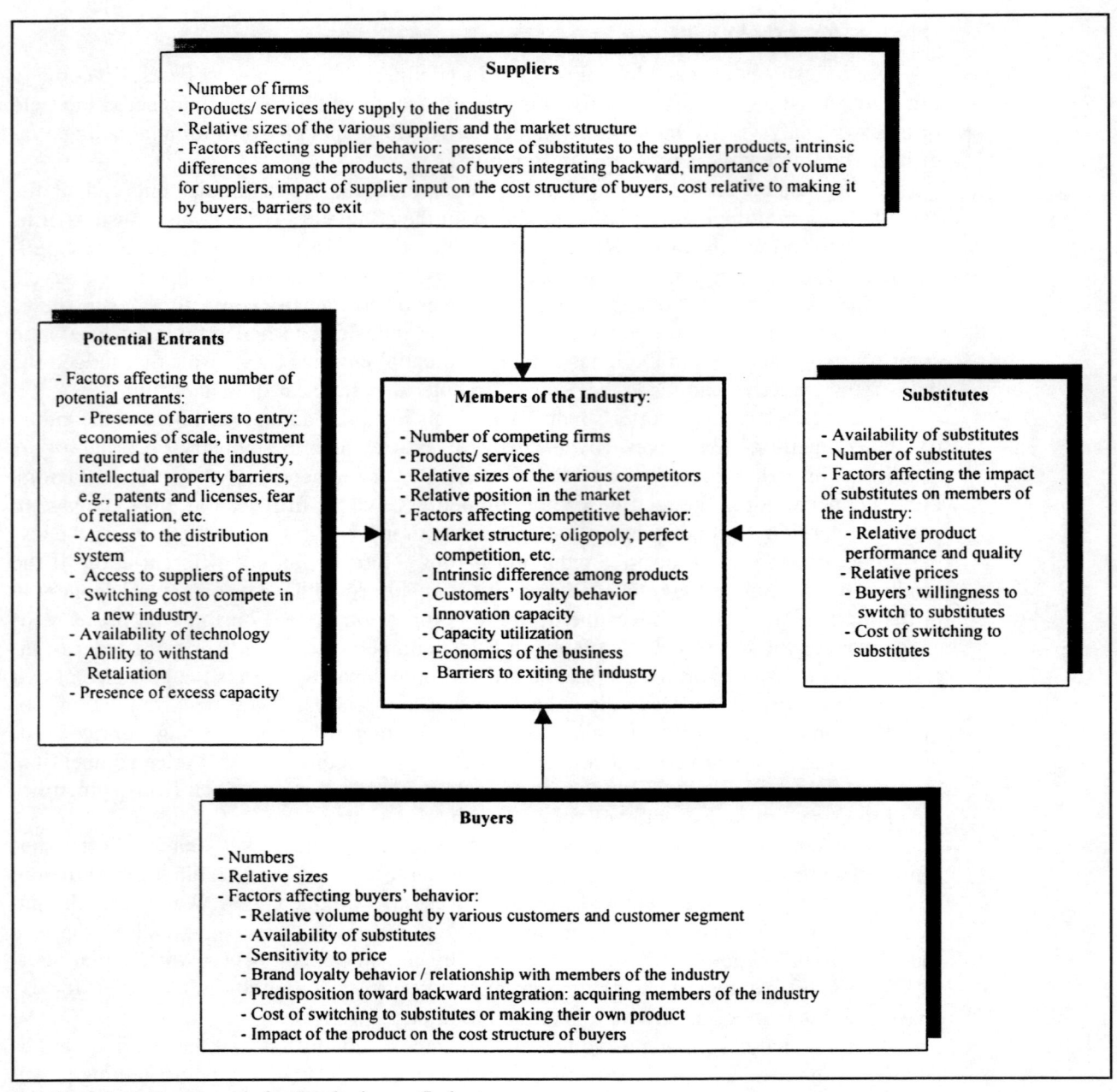

Exhibit 8.3: A Framework for Analyzing an Industry

relative to the seller, their ability to integrate backward (to make what they buy), and the amount of market information available (especially about other suppliers and substitutes). If the firm is squeezed between powerful buyers and powerful suppliers, it might be squeezed out of the market altogether.

Industry analysis is crucial for identifying potential problems, namely, the threat of new entrants and the threat of substitutes. No firm has a total monopoly. There are always substitutes. In the final analysis, a bicycle is a substitute for a car. The dynamics in the substitute-product industries affect the prices and hence the economics of a given industry. Consider, for example, the effect of natural gas on the electricity-generation industry. The effect ranges from price levels for electricity all the way to the design and pricing of appliances that consume it.

The threat of substitutes can be analyzed further into two main elements. The first is the buyer's propensity to use substitutes. A substitute may be available, but the buyer is not inclined to buy it. The second is the price and performance of substitutes. If a substitute's performance and price are better than the original, customers will migrate to the substitute. The original product will lose sales and market share.

Along the same line, new and potential entrants pose an important threat to the firm. If a firm is realizing high profits, this will be a magnet for new entrants. If a market has tremendous potential, it will attract new entrants. For example, Apple Computer's success with the desktop computer demonstrated its enormous market potential, a matter that attracted IBM, and the clone manufacturers.

The threat of entry can be dissected into a number of factors as follows:

- The capital requirements for an entrant to get into the business. The higher the requirements, the less the threat.
- Economies of scale required for entering the industry. If the required scale is enormous, the new entrant will have to sell a considerable volume almost instantly to become viable. This by itself becomes a big barrier.
- If the existing players have an absolute cost advantage, this can be a barrier. A new entrant will not have such an advantage unless it achieves enormous economies of scale, which in itself is a barrier.
- Laws and regulations are barriers to entry in many cases, e.g., patents, or regulated routes for airlines.
- Product differentiation may be a barrier if it is compelling enough to create strong loyalty among customers, e.g., Rolls Royce.
- Access to channels of distribution can be a barrier. If the existing firms can obstruct a new entrant's access to such channels, that will be a strong barrier. The entrants will not be able to sell the product or it will end up creating a new channel, a big expense.
- Finally, one important barrier is the existing firm's ability to retaliate. If it can retaliate (e.g., price cutting), it can make it undesirable for a new entrant to even think about getting into the business.

## COMPETITOR ANALYSIS

Competitors also form a blob. They largely remain unknown because they keep their strategic decisions secret from us. Analysis can be applied here so that we may understand them better. Competitor analysis begins with the definition of what a genuine competitor is. A competitor is not just a direct rival. A competitor can be a supplier that is integrating forward by getting into the firm's field. A competitor can be a customer that is integrating backward by getting into the firm's field. A competitor who produces close substitutes is a potential entrant, just waiting around the corner. Competitors can thus come from all walks of business life. It is important to determine who and how many of them there are.

Porter developed a framework for competitor analysis.[3] An adaptation of his framework is presented in Exhibit 8.4. There are two major components in the framework: forces driving the competitor and its strategic behavior. These, in turn determine the competitor's response behavior, which is critical for the firm as it tackles this competitor. The forces driving the competitor include its future direction (particularly its ambitions with respect to strategic position and its concept of itself and what it ought to be in the scheme of things in the industry), and its view of the world and assumptions about other competitors. The sec-

| **Forces Driving the Competitor** | | **Competitor's Strategic Behavior** |
|---|---|---|
| **Future Strategic Direction**:<br>- Desired strategic position<br>- Assumptions about self | **Competitor's Response Profile:**<br>- Competing mode: Prefers offense, defense, surprise, evasive action, etc.<br>- Propensity to retaliate<br>- Degree of satisfaction with present strategic position<br>- What will provoke it?<br>- Vulnerability: constraints on ability to respond. | **Competitive Strategy:**<br>- Chosen basis of Competition<br>- Strategic thrust<br>- Business model |
| **Worldview**:<br>- Assumptions about the industry<br>- Assumptions about the future | | **Capabilities:**<br>- Resources<br>- Strengths<br>- Weaknesses |

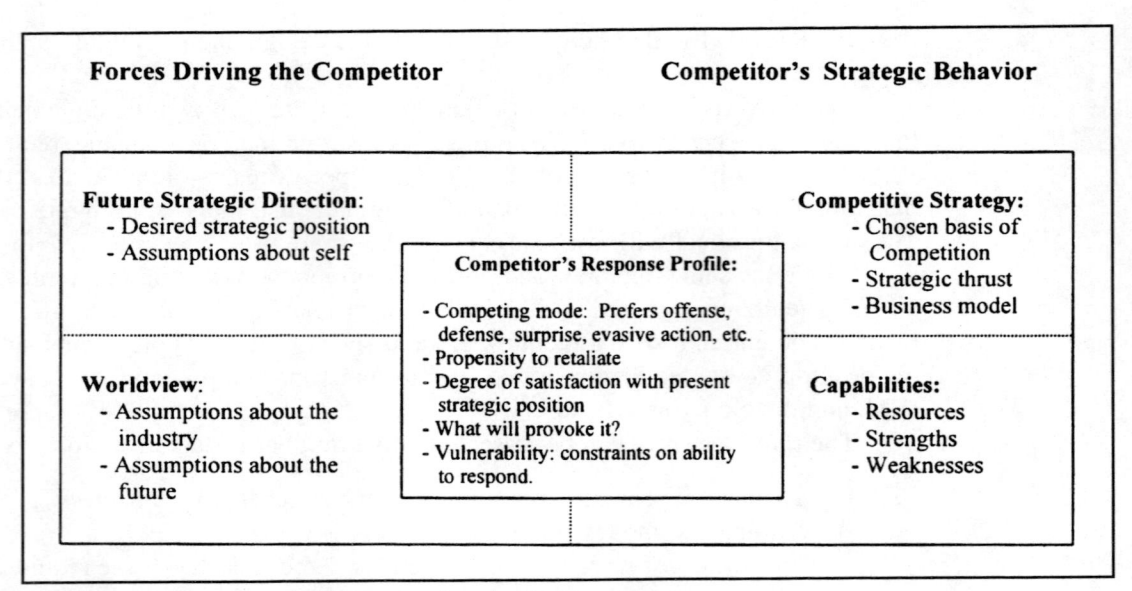

Exhibit 8.4: A Framework for Competitor Analysis

ond component pertains to the competitor's strategic behavior, namely, its strategy (as indicated by its strategic thrust and business model), and capabilities. The competitor's response profile includes its preferred mode for competing, propensity to retaliate, and satisfaction with present position, provocation, and vulnerabilities that will impede a response from it.

To conduct a competitor analysis, the beginning step is to determine their identity and develop a list of them. Once a list of competitors is developed, the next task is to profile each competitor using the framework in Exhibit 8.4. This involves dissecting this entity "competitor" into a number of variables about which we can collect data. These are:

- Definition of the business and its vision: This is important to know the competitor's strategic intent and whether it is heading towards a collision with us.
- Maneuver in the marketplace: This includes the competitor's target market, product-market position, and the strategy or design that underlies its current moves in the marketplace.
- Capability: This includes its resources and capacity to undertake moves that can place them on a head-on collision course with us. This includes any recent proprietary technology that it has developed.
- Organizational structure: It is crucial to know whether a competitor's organizational structure unleashes its people's creativity and commitment to fight hard with tenacity in the marketplace.
- Financial position: This is a good predictor of its ability to fund ventures that encroach on our market niche.
- Quality of its leadership: This is crucial for anticipating what direction a competitor might take and whether it will be on a head-on collision course with us.
- Strengths and weaknesses: A SWOT analysis and a vulnerability analysis for a competitor can help in assessing its ability to compete and retaliate.
- The presence of any "Loose bricks": These are market segments that are poorly served by the competitor (dissatisfied customers).

The above items are to be gleaned (inferred) from information collected from a variety of sources. These include:

- Industry studies: These include industry surveys (like Moody's and Standard & Poor's surveys), analyses by investment firms, books, reports by industry associations, and deliberate market research.
- Reports in the business media, such as the Wall Street Journal, Fortune, trade publications, newspaper, online services (e.g., Bloomberg, Compustat, AOL, and the various search engines).
- Government sources including census, various business and economics statistics, court proceedings, and other government documents.
- Finally, there is a wide range of information available from the companies themselves, such as annual reports, press releases, web sites, and filings with various government agencies.

# MICROANALYSIS: ANALYSIS OF THE FIRM

## Financial Analysis

Financial analysis breaks down the firm's financial position into a number of components that are examined individually and collectively as a way of assessing the financial health of the firm. The income statement dissects the firm's financial performance into a set of variables such as sales, net sales, cost of goods sold, various categories of expenses, gross profit, and net profit. The balance sheet breaks down the firm's financial position in terms of assets, liabilities, and owners' equity. A cash flow statement decomposes cash into inflows, outflows, and a resulting cash position. The topic of financial analysis is covered extensively in books on the topics of corporate finance, financial accounting, and financial statement analysis.

A useful analysis tool is the Du Pont system, a graphic device for showing the key drivers of profitability and returns. It is presented in Exhibit 8.5. Return on equity (ROE) is a function of return on assets (ROA) and the asset to equity ratio. Return on assets, in turn, is a function of profit margin and asset turnover. The faster the asset turnover, the higher the ROA even if the profit margin remains the same. The profit margin is a function of sales and net income. Net income, as we know, is a function of sales and total cost (including operating costs, interest charges, depreciation, and taxes). Asset turnover is a function of sales and total assets (including fixed and current assets which include cash, receivables, inventories, and marketable securities).

Financial analysis further exposes elements that are hidden in the balance sheet and income statement. Ratio analysis is a useful technique in this regard. There are six aspects of the firm's financial performance that are assessed through ratio analysis, namely, liquidity, debt management, asset management, profitability, growth, and valuation as shown in Exhibit 8.6. To conduct ratio analysis, one must also add the measurement of *working capital* (current assets minus current liabilities) and cash flow patterns.

## SWOT/WOTS-UP Analysis

The letters SWOT stand for *s*trengths, *w*eaknesses, *o*pportunities, and *t*hreats. SWOT analysis is also known as WOTS-UP (*w*eaknesses, *o*pportunities, *t*hreats, *s*trengths, and *p*roblems). SWOT/WOTS-UP analysis is a technique for decomposing and visualizing the situation facing the firm. The application of SWOT analysis calls for two steps. In the first step, we take stock of the firm's strengths and weaknesses as well as the opportunities and threats it faces. This is shown in Exhibit 8.7. The contents of the four sections of the exhibit are extracted from other analyses such as the environmental analysis, industry analysis, and financial analysis, as well as from the direct judgment of the persons involved.

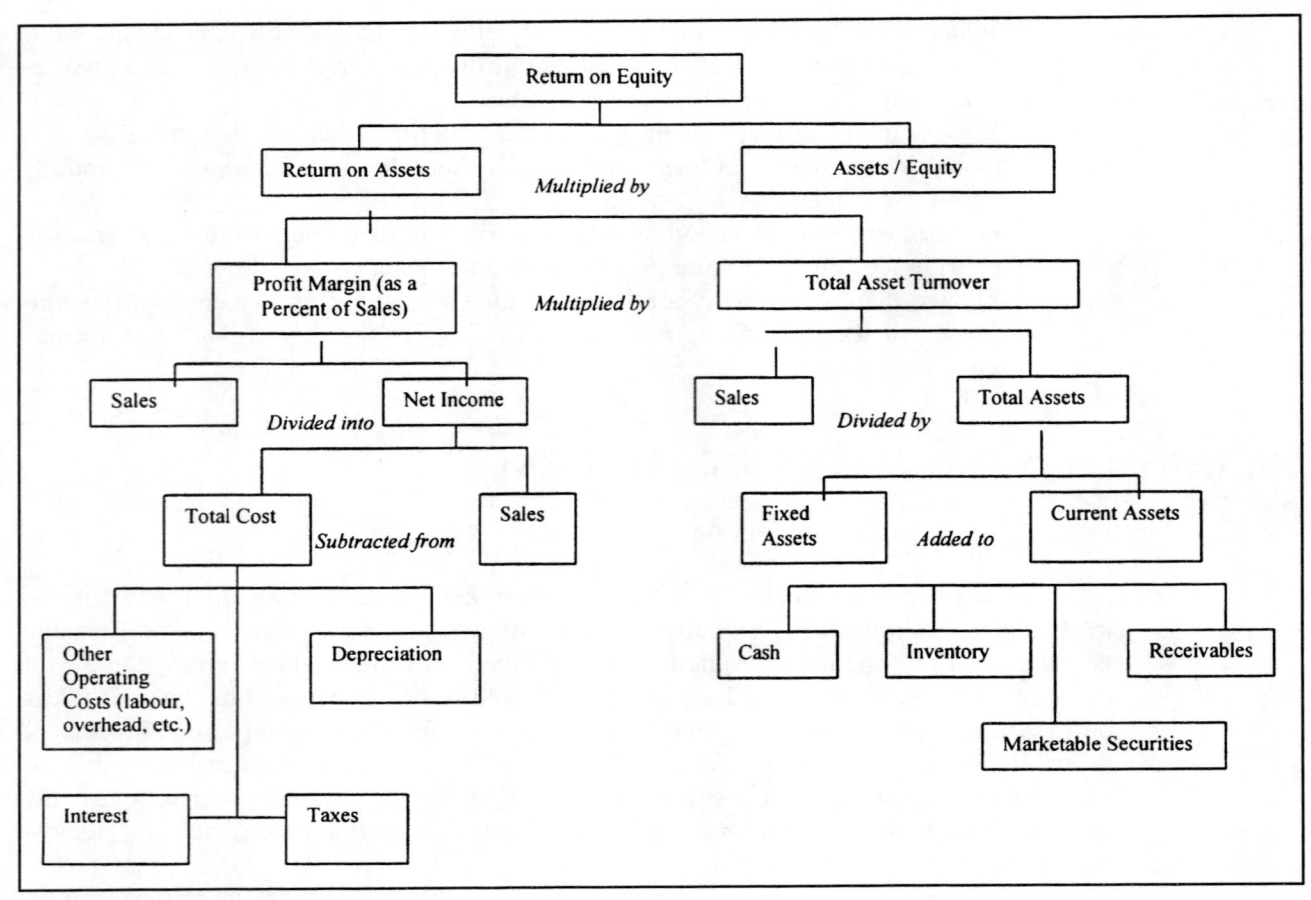

Exhibit 8.5: Du Pont Analysis[4]

In the second step of SWOT analysis, we start by constructing a graph like the one shown in Exhibit 8.8. It consists of two continua: an opportunity-threat continuum (vertical) where the lower end is termed "devastating threats and the higher end is labeled "enormous opportunities." The second continuum (horizontal) has at its lower end "crippling weaknesses" and at the high end "substantial strengths." Next, we plot the opportunities, threats, strengths, and weakness of Exhibit 8.7, where each issue is represented by a symbol in the graph, an x in this presentation.

Once plotted, some clusters of the xs are bound to occur. Where the clusters lie, will suggest observations about the overall position and health of the firm. If the opportunities, threats, strengths, and weaknesses cluster around the high ends of the weaknesses-strengths and the threats-opportunities continua (the upper right hand corner in Exhibit 8.8), the firm is in an excellent position. If, on the other hand, the cluster falls in the lower left corner (weaknesses and threats), the firm is in bad shape. Recognizing this is very crucial. As we will see in the next chapter, this might turn out to be a strategic issue with which the firm must deal.

## Vulnerability Analysis

As the name implies, this analysis takes the blob "vulnerability" and breaks it down into two main elements or dimensions: impact of a threat, and the firm's ability to respond to it. A threat's impact can be rated on a scale of one (improbable) to five (almost cer-

| Aspect of Financial Position | Ratio | Description | Actual Ratio | Industry Ratio | Evaluation |
|---|---|---|---|---|---|
| Liquidity | Current Ratio | Current Assets/Current Liabilities | | | |
| | Quick Ratio or Acid Test | [Current Assets – Inventory]/Current Liabilities | | | |
| Debt Management | Debt | Total Debt/Total Assets | | | |
| | Times Interest Earned, Interest Coverage | Earnings before Interest and Taxes/Interest Charges | | | |
| | Fixed Charge Coverage | [Net Income before Taxes + Interest Charges + Lease Obligations]/[Interest Charges + Lease Obligations] | | | |
| | Cash Flow Coverage | Cash Inflows/[Fixed Charges + Preferred Shares Dividend/(1-T) + Debt Repayment/(1-T)] | | | |
| Asset Management | Inventory Turnover | Sales/Inventory | | | |
| | Days Sales Outstanding | Receivables/Sales per Day | | | |
| | Fixed Asset Turnover | Sales/Fixed Assets | | | |
| | Total Asset Turnover | Sales/Total Assets | | | |
| Profitability | Profit Margin on Sales | Net Income after Taxes/Sales | | | |
| | Basic Earning Power | Earnings before Interest and Taxes/Total Assets | | | |
| | Return on Total Assets | Net Income after Taxes/Total Assets | | | |
| | Return on Common Equity | Net Income after Taxes/Net Worth | | | |
| Growth | Sales | Ending Value/Beginning Value | | | |
| | Net Income | Ending Value/Beginning Value | | | |
| | Earnings per Share | Ending Value/Beginning Value | | | |
| | Dividend per Share | Ending Value/Beginning Value | | | |
| Valuation | Price-to-Earnings Ratio | Price per Share/Earnings per Share | | | |
| | Market-to-Book Ratio | Market Value/Book Value | | | |

Exhibit 8.6: Application of Ratio Analysis[5]

tain). Similarly, the firm's ability to respond can be rated on a scale of one (nil) to five (massive and swift). The two dimensions form a 2x2 matrix as shown in Exhibit 8.9. At their intersection lies four possible states and each state is an indication of the degree of the firm's vulnerability.

To conduct a vulnerability analysis, we simply take every event, development, or trend that is deemed to be a threat by members of the organization and then rate it with respect to magnitude of impact on the firm, and the firm's ability to respond to it. The result of this is that the threats will be categorized in the four quadrants. We are mainly interested in the quadrant that contains the threats to which the firm is totally exposed.

| STRENGTHS | WEAKNESSES |
|---|---|
| Enter here a list of characteristics of the firm's patterns that translate into disproportionate strategic advantage in the market place and those that will position it to take advantage of opportunities including but not restricted to:<br>• Being in synch in the market (a talent for reading turbulence)<br>• A deeply entrenched strategic position, relative high quality<br>• A healthy financial position<br>• Ingenious maneuver<br>• Advanced, unique capability including competencies, proprietary technology, economies of scale, cost structure, cost savings designs<br>• An organizational structure that capitalizes on the talents of every member<br>• A perceptive vision<br>• Talented leadership<br>• Alliances<br>• Leverages | Enter here a list of characteristics of the firm's patterns that translate into disproportionate strategic disadvantage in the market place and those that will deprive the firm from exploiting opportunities as well increase its vulnerability to threat including but not restricted to:<br>• Being out of touch with the market<br>• A weak, easy to dislodge strategic position<br>• An impoverished firm starved for cash<br>• Maneuver that does not outsmart adversarial forces<br>• An outdated capability, lacking in competencies<br>• An organizational structure that inhibits individual initiative<br>• Lack of vision, mediocre vision<br>• Uninspired and uninspiring leadership<br>• Lagging, inferior product quality<br>• Occupying a weak position in a mature, declining industry<br>• Absence of leverages<br>• Being isolated in the industry, no allies |
| **OPPORTUNITIES** | **THREATS** |
| Enter here a list of environmental characteristics that embody opportunities that can be exploited by the firm including:<br>• The emergence of new opportunity arenas<br>• The growth of existing opportunities<br>• Vacuums created by competitors who exited the field<br>• "Loose bricks," current market segments poorly served by existing competitors<br>• Opportunities created by our strengths<br>• Being favourably positioned for forward or backward integration<br>• Being favourably positioned to acquire or merge with rival firms<br>• Being favourably positioned for alliances with other businesses inside and outside the industry | Enter here a list of environmental characteristics that embody threats or potential developments that can weaken the firm's strategic position or possibly wipe it out altogether including:<br>• The emergence of adversarial forces in the market place, e.g., entry of new competitors or increases in the bargaining power of customers and suppliers.<br>• Emergence of proprietary technology by another firm that may revolutionize the industry and give it a strong advantage that we don't have<br>• Leading indicators pointing to the gradual disappearance of the market that the firm is pursuing, loss of sales to substitutes<br>• Leading indicators showing decline in the firm's strategic and financial positions<br>• Excessive vulnerability and sensitivity to changes in the firm's environment |

Exhibit 8.7: A Framework for SWOT Analysis, Step I

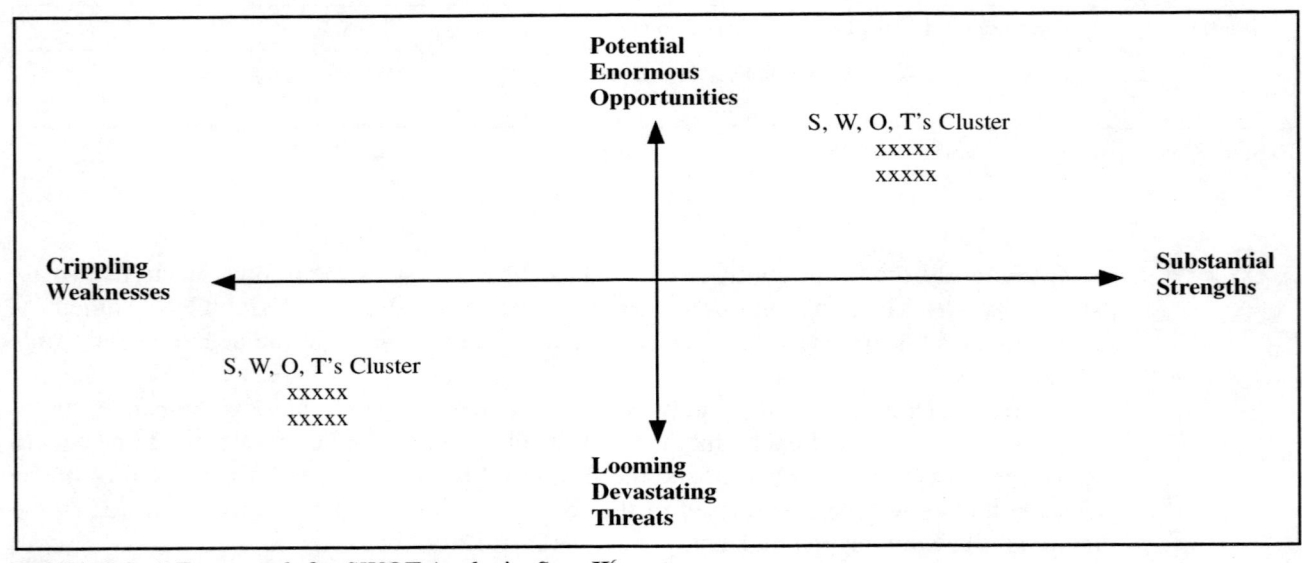

Exhibit 8.8: A Framework for SWOT Analysis, Step II[6]

|  |  | **FIRM'S ABILITY TO REACT** | |
|---|---|---|---|
|  |  | **LOW** | **HIGH** |
| **IMPACT OF THREATS** | **HIGH** | *Conclusion: The firm is defenseless*<br><br>• Enter here all the threats that rated high with respect to impact and for which the firm is in no position to act *when* they happen. | *Conclusion: The firm is endangered*<br><br>• Enter here all the threats that rated high with respect to impact and for which the firm is in a strong position to act quickly *to deal with them* |
|  | **LOW** | *Conclusion: The firm is potentially vulnerable*<br><br>• Enter here all the threats that rated low with respect to impact and for which the firm is in no position to act *if* they happen. | *Conclusion: The firm is prepared*<br><br>• Enter here all the threats that rated low with respect to impact and for which the firm is in a strong position to act quickly *if* they happen. |

Exhibit 8.9: Vulnerability Analysis

# PATTERN RECOGNITION

Given a breakdown of the phenomenon through analysis, pattern recognition is the search for some order, system, or organization among the elemental components. This organization or system is a pattern. This pattern suggests itself during the course of arranging and rearranging the elements in many ways. The process involves arranging and rearranging the elements in a data set in the hope of discovering a pattern.

To illustrate, let us consider an example. Upon performing an industry analysis and as we mull over the dynamics among competitors, we might see some patterns in their behaviors such as cooperation through strategic alliances. Alternatively, we may conclude that another pattern suggests itself: consolidation through mergers and acquisitions. Pattern recognition is speculative, for it is only a mental construct. It is imposing a certain order or a synthesis on things that occur separately.

Pattern recognition involves the following tasks:

- Isolating the Phenomena: for which we would like to find out if a pattern exists. If, for example, we want to discover if a pattern underlies competitors' behaviors, we start by defining specifically who our competitors are.
- Data Collection: Given a delineation of phenomenon of interest, the next step is to collect as much data as possible about it. In the case of competitors' behavior, we collect every piece of information from the various sources using the techniques of competitive intelligence.
- Analysis: Breaking the phenomenon of interest into the elements or events that constitute it. In our example of competitors' behavior, we can use industry analysis and competitor analysis.

- Categorization: Grouping the elements using some basis. Elements can be grouped based on any of the following criteria:
  — Similarity: Similar or identical elements can be grouped together. For example, acquisitions can be grouped as unfriendly takeovers, if they have been executed without the support of management.
  — Place: Elements can be grouped on the basis of where they occur. The place does not necessarily have to be geographical. It can be a place in the industry such as a certain sub-segment of the industry, e.g., acquisitions among suppliers.
  — Time: Elements can be grouped based on when they occur. For example, if we plot acquisitions by time frame, we might unearth a pattern indicating what happened during a certain stage in the economic cycle. This would help reveal the pattern of economic conditions that were the driving forces here.
  — Sequence: We might wish to group the elements on the basis of their order of appearance. For example, we might find that an industry matures first and then a wave of acquisitions and mergers ensue.
  — Relating Categories/Finding Synthesis: In this step, the various categories of elements are arranged and rearranged to force a pattern to surface. This is like conducting a number of experiments to find out which logical combination (pattern) makes the most sense. This step is analogous to curve fitting. We might have a scatter of data where a number of curves might fit. The challenge is to try a number of curves and see which one best describes the data set on hand.

To continue with the example of competitor behaviour, we might find these categories: industry overall sales leveling off, margins declining, marginal firms suffering cash shortages, firms with economies of scale generating excess cash, acquisitions, and a handful of firms dominating the industry. A pattern suggests itself here. It is as if there is a trend that goes on as follows: as the industry matured, marginal firms weakened, and bigger firms generated more profits, using their cash to acquire the weaker firms in order to dominate the market leading ultimately to an oligopoly.

The concept of strategic groups introduced by Porter (for the purposes of industry analysis) can be used to illustrate pattern recognition. It is illustrated in Exhibit 8.10. Suppose we identify the various firms in our industry and group them based on two criteria: specialization (having a full-line or a narrow line of products); and vertical integration (completely integrated or final assembly).

If we construct each basis as a continuum, we will have a two-dimensional space. If we were to collect data about the degree of specialization and vertical integration for each firm and then plot its combination along the two dimensions, we might end up with four groupings as shown in the exhibit. If we examine the graph carefully, we can discern at least three patterns:

- Individual Players: Who is who in the industry and who flocks with whom in the same orbit. This patterns shows four competitive orbits where similar firms are going head-on against one another.
- Groups: Group 1 (firms A, B, and C) exists by being vertically integrated to offer a full line of products with a commodity type quality, low price, and low service. Group 2 (firms D, E, and F) exists by offering a narrow product line, high automation, low price, and low service. By contrast, group 4 (firms J, K, and L) exists by offering a narrow but high quality line, and operating primarily as an assembler using a high tech process.

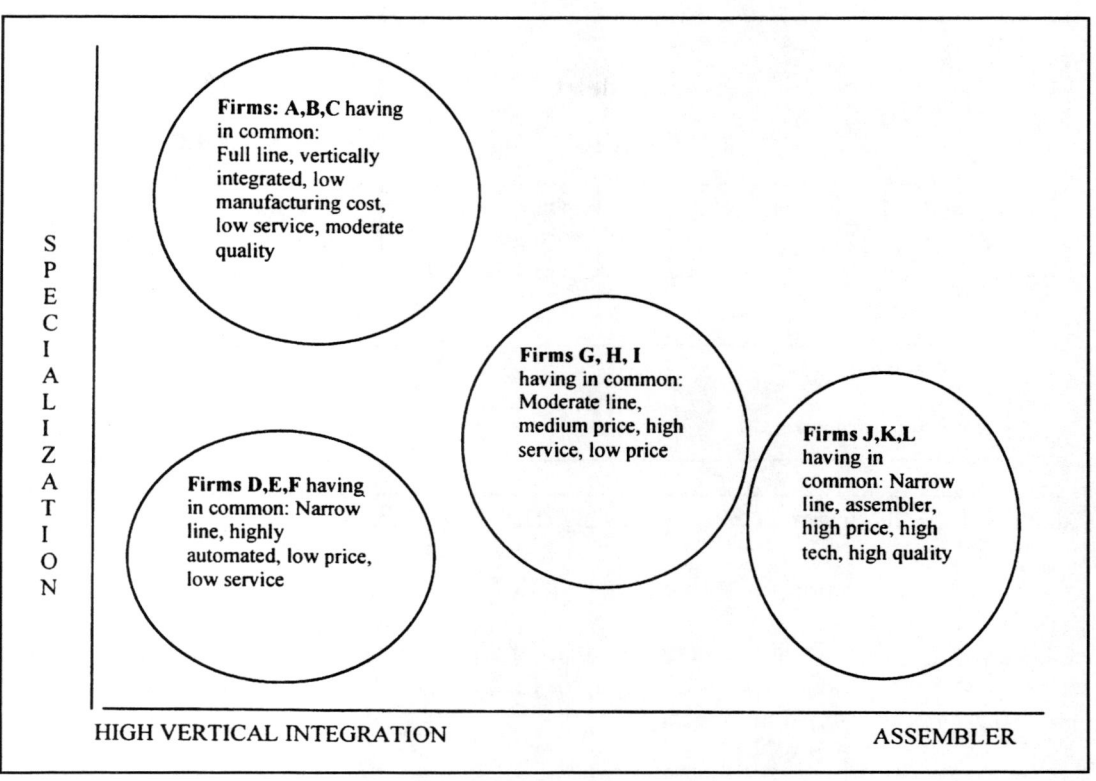

Exhibit 8.10: An Illustration of Pattern Recognition

- Basis of Competition: Firms in this industry compete based on breadth and depth of product line, price, and quality.

# MAPPING

Mapping is the graphing of a blob. If we can think of the blob as a "landscape," mapping then visualizes the lay of the land. To illustrate the use of mapping, take the example of process mapping as practiced at General Electric to come to grips with the chaos of operations. According to a GE document on the topic:

> "Process mapping is a dynamic, simple, and effective method for graphically displaying the various steps, events, and operations that constitute a process. It provides a picture, in the form of a diagram, of what is actually happening when a product is produced or a service is provided."

The document emphasizes that a key benefit of process mapping is "An ability to 'see' the entire process." Process mapping involves five steps as follows:

- Defining the process in general with special attention to its natural beginning and end.
- Identifying and listing the various steps or elements in the process.
- Arranging the steps or elements in their sequence showing the proper relationships, e.g., what precedes what, and what is concurrent with what.
- Revising the process map to arrive at a clearer synthesis or picture of the process.

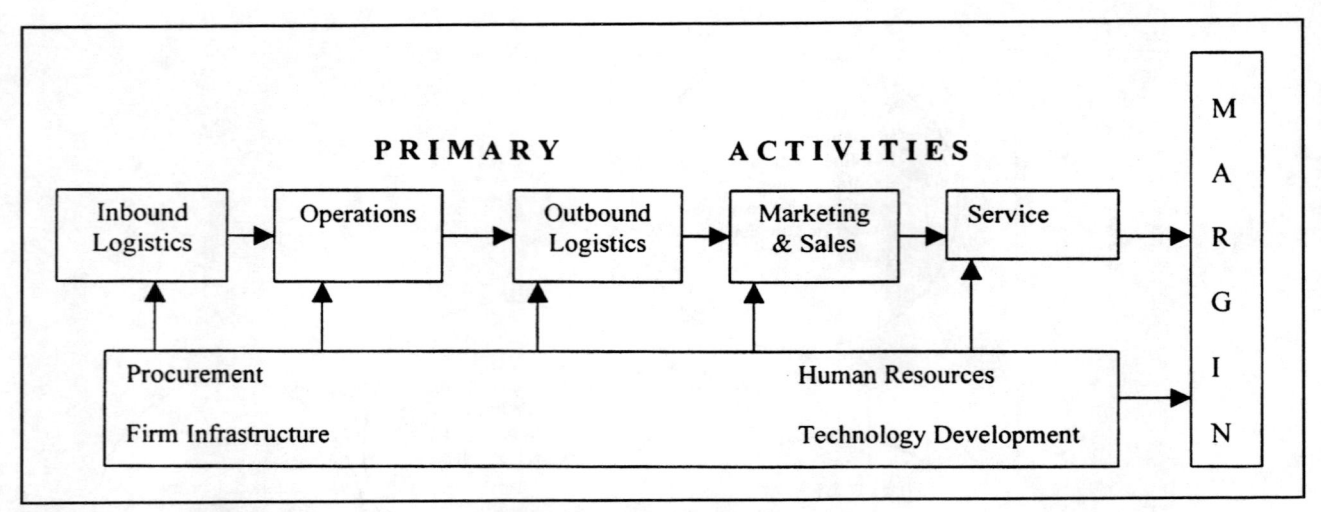

```
┌─────────────────────────────────────────────────────────────────────┬───┐
│                PRIMARY         ACTIVITIES                           │ M │
│ ┌─────────┐  ┌──────────┐ ┌─────────┐ ┌─────────┐ ┌─────────┐       │ A │
│ │Inbound  │→ │Operations│→│Outbound │→│Marketing│→│Service  │─┐     │ R │
│ │Logistics│  │          │ │Logistics│ │& Sales  │ │         │ │     │ G │
│ └─────────┘  └──────────┘ └─────────┘ └─────────┘ └─────────┘ │     │ I │
│      ↑            ↑            ↑           ↑           ↑      │     │   │
│ ┌───────────────────────────────────────────────────────────┐ │     │ N │
│ │ Procurement                       Human Resources         │→┘     │   │
│ │ Firm Infrastructure               Technology Development  │       │   │
│ └───────────────────────────────────────────────────────────┘       │   │
└─────────────────────────────────────────────────────────────────────┴───┘
```

Exhibit 8.11: An Illustration of Process Mapping: The Value Chain

Another example of mapping is Porter's Value Chain concept.[7] In essence, the diagram represents a cognitive map of the process of doing business. Exhibit 8.11 presents an adaptation of Porter's model.

# CONCLUSION

This chapter dealt with the first category of self-organization activities, namely, sensing prevailing turbulence as a prelude to responding to it. Turbulence sensing activities are like constructing a radar system picking up and plotting signals of turbulence on the screen. Three basic methods were presented for constructing this radar screen and for forcing happenings to register on it. These are analysis (environmental, industry, competitor, and the firm itself), pattern recognition, and mapping.

The output of these methods can be categorized as follows:

- Events: An event is a single occurrence. Some events are isolated incidents. They never occur again. Yet, some events might be signals or antecedents of more fundamental changes to occur later.
- Developments: A development is a cluster of or a series of events that have a common thread or a theme occurring within a certain time frame. For example, a series of customer complaints in one month is a development. It begs an explanation.
- Trends: A trend is a series of developments that are consistent over time. For example, several clusters of customer complaints about a certain product over several months form a trend, customer dissatisfaction with the product.

Each of these calls for a response from the firm. Although the response is born out of current turbulence, it will be implemented in the future, perhaps under different turbulence conditions. To be effective, our response must not only reflect impending turbulence, but it also must factor in future turbulence into its planning. Anticipating or sensing future turbulence is the topic of the next chapter.

# ENDNOTES

1. Fahey, L. and R.M. Randall, *The Portable MBA in Strategy*, New York, NY: Wiley & Sons, 1994, pp. 199–200.

2. Porter, M. *Competitive Strategy*, New York, NY: Free Press, 1980.

3. Ibid., p. 49.

4. Halpern, P., J.F. Weston, and E.F. Brigham, *Canadian Managerial Finance*, 4th ed., Harcourt Brace & Company, 1994, p. 122.

5. Ibid., pp. 120–121.

6. Adapted from Pearce, II, J.A. and R.B. Robinson, *Formulation, Implementation, and Control of Competitive Strategy*, Boston, MA: Irwin-McGraw Hill, 2000, p. 204.

7. Porter, M. "Global Strategy: Winning In the Worldwide Marketplace" in Fahey, L. and R.M. Randall, *The Portable MBA in Strategy*, New York, NY: Wiley & Sons, 1994, pp. 108–141.

# CHAPTER 9

# Sensing Future Turbulence

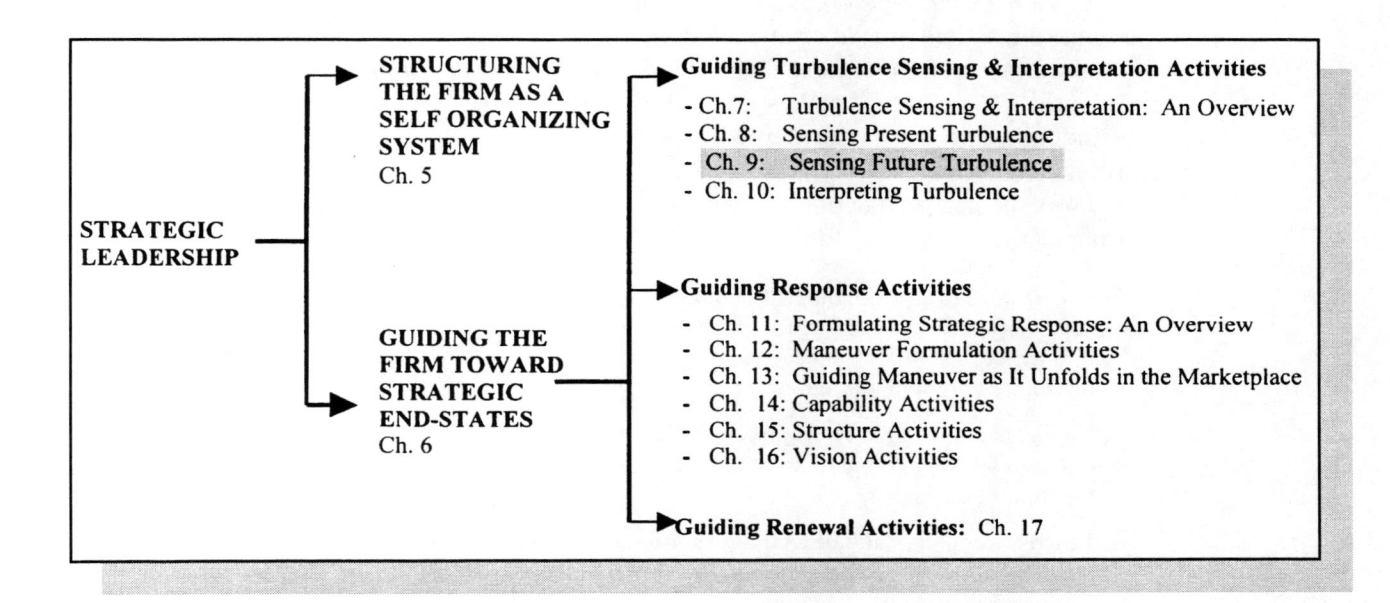

```
STRATEGIC          STRUCTURING              Guiding Turbulence Sensing & Interpretation Activities
LEADERSHIP  ──▶   THE FIRM AS A             - Ch.7:   Turbulence Sensing & Interpretation: An Overview
                  SELF ORGANIZING           - Ch. 8:  Sensing Present Turbulence
                  SYSTEM                    - Ch. 9:  Sensing Future Turbulence
                  Ch. 5                     - Ch. 10: Interpreting Turbulence

                                          ▶ Guiding Response Activities
                  GUIDING THE               - Ch. 11: Formulating Strategic Response: An Overview
                  FIRM TOWARD               - Ch. 12: Maneuver Formulation Activities
            ──▶   STRATEGIC                 - Ch. 13: Guiding Maneuver as It Unfolds in the Marketplace
                  END-STATES                - Ch. 14: Capability Activities
                  Ch. 6                     - Ch. 15: Structure Activities
                                            - Ch. 16: Vision Activities

                                          ▶ Guiding Renewal Activities: Ch. 17
```

Sensing current turbulence is essential. It is crucial for identifying the opportunities and threats to which the firm must respond. However, the response will be executed in the future, under a different set of circumstances. A good response, therefore, must satisfy two conditions. First, it must address the current pressing challenges and opportunities. Second, it must incorporate future turbulence into its calculation. This chapter examines the topic of anticipating future turbulence. It begins with a discussion of the viewfinder that guides our search for the future and for defining it. After that, attention shifts to approaches for anticipating the future. Three such approaches will be explored, intuitive methods, forecasting, and constructing alternative scenarios.

# THINKING ABOUT THE FUTURE

Leaders of business organizations have always encountered the problem of predicting the future since time immemorial. However, the problem is becoming more intense and more difficult because of the current rapid, unpredictable, and discontinuous change in the business world. This not only makes the present hard to grasp, but also makes the future even more unknowable and harder to predict. Yet, the problem of anticipating the future must be confronted somehow.

From the perspective of a business leader, the future poses a serious problem. One CEO articulated the problem as follows:

"The future is a puzzlement. Economists disagree about the next three months. Yet we need to plan for the next three years. I believed that my responsibility was to climb up into the corporate crow's nest, peer into the swirling mists of uncertainty, and pronounce the future corporate direction . . .

I struggled to read the future. Even though it was difficult, I knew it was essential if I was going to lead my company to prepare for the future. The time to build a seawall is *before* the high tide comes crashing in.

I tried several crystal ball techniques. I hired futurists, like Alvin Toffler, to talk with us about what he saw. He was fascinating, but my people just couldn't make the connection between his 'global village' and our business. We talked to industry 'experts.' Every industry has a 'guru' and ours was no exception. I was faced with the problem of deciding which 'guru' to believe, if any, because the different 'gurus' gave different predictions. For all I knew, maybe they all were wrong."[1]

An analysis of the concept "future" shows that it is a composite of three elements: essence, scope, and time frame. First, the "future" has an essence or a central idea. The essence of the "future" is a state of affairs, a number of factors that will hang together in a certain way; i.e., there are relationships among them. Thus, when we talk about the future of the economy, we are in essence thinking about its key components that will be there at that future point in time and the interrelationships among them. These components include production, income, investment, business spending, consumer spending, durables, non-durables, services, government spending, and taxes. The future is thus a vision of the would-be state of affairs at the end of a specified time horizon.

Second, the concept future has a spatial scope or a boundary, an arena that encloses certain things and excludes others. Thus, when we think about the future, we should ask the future of "what." The "what" determines the scope of our future vision. In delimiting the "what," one must keep in mind that it does not exist in a vacuum. It is part of an interrelated universe. Hence, to define the future of one phenomenon, e.g., the industry, we might have to broaden the boundary to include others such as the economic sector in which the industry exists, the economy as a whole, and so on. Exhibit 9.1 illustrates the range of entities that might be included in delineating the scope of the future for a business firm.

Third, the concept "future" has a time dimension. The "future" of anything is not foreseeable unless we "anchor" it in time somehow, i.e., delimit the time horizon over which the future takes place. The specification of the time horizon depends on many factors, including the leader and the system's style of viewing the future (short-term oriented versus long-term oriented), visibility of the future (availability of forecasts and foresights), the cost and time it takes to map out the future, time pressure (how soon the picture of the future is needed), futurecasting know-how, availability of qualified persons, and the behavioral complexity of the entities of interest, among others.

# APPROACHES FOR SENSING FUTURE TURBULENCE

There are three main approaches for sensing future turbulence. These are the intuitive approaches, forecasting, and scenario construction. They are examined next.

## I. Intuitive Approaches

Intuitive approaches utilize the "sixth sense" to provide data about the future. They rely mainly on the mind's ability to guess what is going to happen next. The key approaches here are: flash of genius, intuition, experience, expert opinion, and group methods. All of these methods have strengths and weaknesses. Generally, they are inexpensive. They are quick and hence they are helpful in developing a quick response to sudden change. However, they are not scientific. The reliability of their depiction of the future is questionable. They have to be used with great caution.

### Flash of Genius

Flash of genius is common in human thinking. Upon encountering a situation, and immersing oneself in it, somehow a sudden thought comes to mind. There is no explanation or

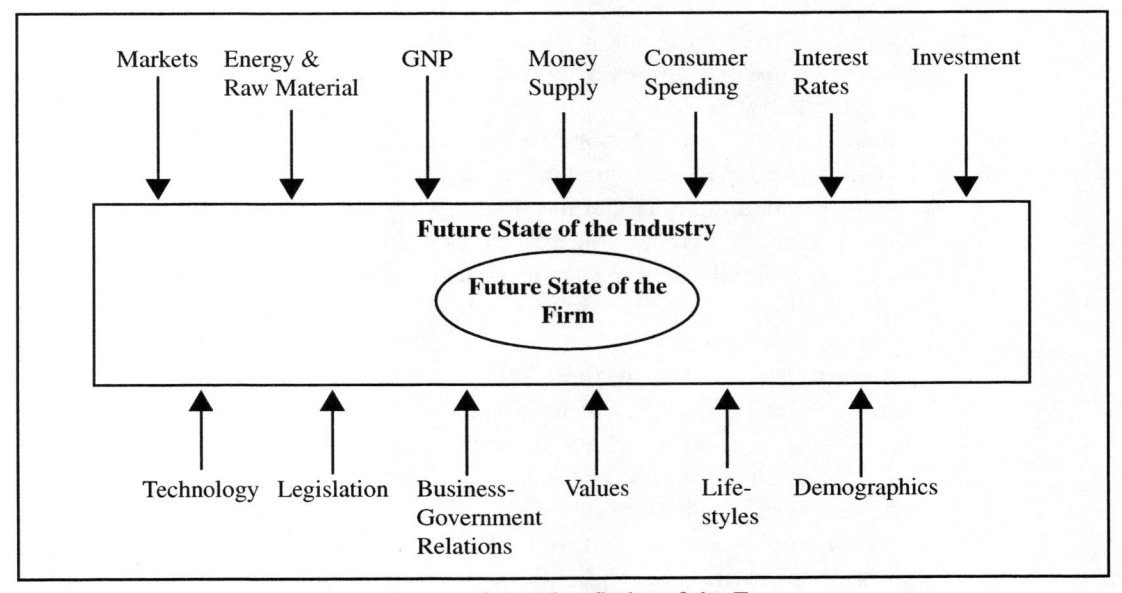

Exhibit 9.1: An Illustration of the Scope of the Viewfinder of the Future

justification. A vision of the future just surfaces as a breakthrough. This is not a "method" for predicting the future. The term "method" implies a systematic sequence of steps. A flash of genius just happens whether as the result of "method" or just random thinking.

A flash of genius is like a "revelation." Only the person proclaiming it can "see" it. Business history is full of examples of flash of genius type visions. Take Henry Ford, for example. As a young mechanic, he saw "America on wheels" at a time when the only means of transportation was the horse and buggy. Cars need roads, highways, gas stations, and the rest of the infrastructure. None of these existed then. Yet, he saw in his mind's eye that America would have the infrastructure some day. Where did this vision come from? It was a flash of genius vision. In the absence of perfect information about the future, who is to say that a flash of genius is an inappropriate prediction? It is like making a bet and like all bets; it has a chance of being right. Because of its subjectivity, no one can quantify the chances of a certain prediction.

## Intuition

Intuition is slightly more systematic than flash of genius. Sensing the future intuitively involves considerable thinking and marshalling of all our inner resources to come up with a picture of the future. After considerable deliberate contemplation, an image emerges. The data for the projected image are internal. The process of synthesizing the data and projecting the future from it is purely subjective. The resulting image of the future is difficult to defend except on inner grounds, only "I just know it is so."

The psychologist, de Bono, provided an explanation of how intuition works.[2] He maintained that the mind acts as a "pattern creating" system. As the mind receives information from all sources, it searches for and discovers patterns (concepts, abstractions, models, etc.) that condense, organize, and give meaning to the incoming data. The problem of anticipating the future is a mental exercise in pattern formation. Once patterns are formed, they are extended into the future. The future is thus seen as a projection of the present. When Jobs and Wozniak developed the first Apple computer, intuitively they could see the size of the market. At that time, computing was the domain of expensive mainframe computers. However, they believed that millions of individuals could use some inexpensive computing power. The two inventors saw this future at that time.

De Bono's research alerts us to two possible dangers in mental pattern development and use. First, the existing patterns serve as filters that weed out inconsistent and conflicting new patterns. This is what is known as "thinking inside the box." The "box" is our present pattern of what we know. We venture in and around the edges of the box, but not outside these boundaries. When Japanese cars entered the American market in the early 1970's, they were quickly dismissed as inferior rust buckets. Domestic auto executives did not project a future in which the Japanese carmakers would be a major factor.

Second, although the mind naturally forms patterns, it finds it unnatural to replace them with new ones when the time comes. Consequently, the mind then cannot forecast the future based on radically new information. The mind is comfortable with the existing knowledge and it easily sees the future in this light. When new information comes, it is molded in terms of the existing pattern, instead of quickly inventing a new pattern. It takes time for a new pattern to evolve. Hence, there is mental inertia when it comes to the mind shifting paradigms. A recent conference held a session humorously titled "Help, my paradigm won't shift"—the typical lament about mental inertia.

Intuition as an approach for visioning the future tends to be discounted by our "scientific" culture. We insist on objectivity, on proof, on quantitative evidence, on being scientific. Yet, the same scientific culture makes it difficult to develop knowledge. Many phenomena do not lend themselves (quickly or economically) to scientific method. Turbulence is certainly one of them.

In essence, the leader and the people are left to their own devices. The CEO quoted above came to this conclusion: "I inevitably fell back on my own 'golden gut' believing that my intuition was the most reliable future predictor."[3] Gut feel has been a popular approach for leaders since time immemorial. When one examines business leaders who transformed the face of industry and the economy, one will find that they followed their intuition as "knowledge" of the future. They called it "vision." They might have verified intuition later through "scientific" research, but the premise was strictly gut feel.

Intuition can be sharpened by undertaking these steps as suggested by Mendell:[4]

- Scrutinizing Obsolete Patterns: Since the mind does not replace old patterns, the leader must deliberately search out and eliminate patterns that no longer hold true. Such patterns often have polarized tendencies (e.g., either-or statements), misplaced moral or legal boundaries (e.g., 'have to,' 'must,' 'ought to,' 'should,' etc.), misplaced temporal boundaries (e.g., the unchallenged 'musts' about 'before,' 'during,' or 'after'), misplaced spatial boundaries (e.g., the unchallenged musts about 'within,' 'inside,' 'outside'), and misplaced reliance on habit (things without a foundation or an explicit justification).
- Empathizing: Putting ourselves in the shoes of the people or in the situations that we are trying to predict.
- Analogizing: Since the future is unfamiliar, we can gain insight into it by examining a situation with which we are familiar. The success of the "McDonald's" way of doing business can be used as an analogy for predicting the future of other lines of food or that of very different industries. Pizza makers could have used the McDonald's analogy to predict the coming of Pizza Hut, Little Caesar's, and Domino's. Producers of PC clones used the success of the IBM desktop computer as an analogy for predicting the market for their computers.
- Playing Mind Games: One can make imagining the future a mental exercise by trying to describe in some detail what a future situation will be like. For example, one can assume that a giant competitor enters the market (long before the competitor does so) and then one writes down what state the company will be in, given the presence of that dominant competitor.
- Browsing for Background Information: The deliberate search for information might reveal newer patterns that can challenge our existing ones. When such patterns are found, they become warning lights that alert us that it is time to question existing patterns. Examples of useful background information include: science fiction (visions of the future), magazines and journals devoted to future studies (e.g., *Futures* and *The Futurist*), publications about trends (e.g., Naisbit's megatrends series), published research, opinion polls, correlation among two dynamics, and the like.

## Experience

Closely related to intuition is experience. While intuition amounts to jumping to conclusions about the future (proclaiming a prediction) without an "objective" basis, the experience approach relies on a more concrete foundation, one's own track record. In this case, experience is projected into the next time horizon and viewed as the future state of affairs. In the process of projection, some assumptions (about the future) may be introduced. A good example of this is the development of *pro forma* financial statements. One takes the existing income statements, and "plugs" in different assumptions about increases (or decreases) in sales and expense figures and arrives at what the income statement will look like in the future. The same approach can be applied in anticipating the behavior of competitors or the environmental variables. Although experience provides a clue into the future, it is not totally reliable. We live in an era of unprecedented "discontinuous" change. Many of these sudden leaps lie outside the conservative assumption that the future flows from the present. Hence, experience must be used with caution, just like intuition.

## Expert Opinion

A popular way of arriving at a picture of the future is to invite the opinion of experts who have training and talent in anticipating the future. As of late, a number of futurists have been able to identify trends that have turned out to be true to some extent, e.g., Alvin Toffler and John Naisbit. There are also management consultants and industry experts who have a "sense" of where the future is going. Such experts can be hired to provide a sophisticated description of the future. A variation of this is the use of a "jury of experts." A number of experts are brought together as a focus group to provide their prognostications. These are then assembled as a picture of the future.

## Group Methods

Group methods can be utilized to arrive at a consensus concerning a picture of the future. Brainstorming is such a method. To apply this approach, the leader can work with people using the help of a moderator who is experienced in brainstorming. During such brainstorming sessions, visions of the future will surface. These are then assembled into a composite that can stand as a picture of the future.

The Delphi method is one of the most popular group methods. Conducting a Delphi comprises ten steps as follows:

1. Define and state the area of interest that is going to be the subject of the Delphi, e.g., to forecast the future of market X, product Z, or industry Y.
2. Translate the area of interest into a questionnaire. A number of specific questions are generated, and then the respondents are asked to anticipate the future level for each of the variables of interest at an established point in the future, e.g., what level will interest rates assume by the year 2003. The responses to the questions can be in the form of checking the right answer in a series of multiple-choice questions or filling in the blanks in open-ended questions.
3. Select a panel of knowledgeable persons, e.g., external experts, experienced members of the organization, or some appropriate group whose members can make the needed judgment. The panel has to be large enough to provide different mental orientations. It also has to be diversified enough to bring in different perspectives.
4. Administer the first round of the Delphi. The questionnaire is sent out (or e-mailed) to panel members with the clear request that the purpose is to arrive at a consensus about the future states of the listed variables. The Delphi is looking for consensus, not creativity. Thus, respondents should be informed that extreme guesses will be discarded and that only the cluster of responses near the average will be utilized.
5. When the completed questionnaires are received, the answers should be tallied, and presented in a graphic form, so those respondents can easily see where the consensus is. The average for each question is calculated.
6. Forward the results to the panel, particularly the graphs for the various questions, without revealing any names so that no one can be influenced by the opinion of someone else, especially if a person is considered "an authority" on the subject.
7. Start the second round. A second questionnaire is sent (the same as the first one). The panel members are asked to complete it in light of the results of the first questionnaire. In an attached memo, respondents are told that they may change their votes, again emphasizing that the purpose is consensus, not creativity.
8. Receive and tabulate the second questionnaire, preparing a report showing a graph that exposes consensus or lack of it. Next, the report is sent to the panel.

9. Start the third round. A third questionnaire is sent (the same as the first one). The request this time is the same as the second time, but the stress is on the search for consensus. When the third round questionnaires are received, they are tabulated in the same manner as before. The third round is usually the final round.
10. Prepare the report. In preparing the Delphi report, extreme answers in the third round are discarded and the central tendency or measures of consensus (e.g., the mode) in the data are extracted and reported. The report should include all the graphs for the three rounds. The graphs should be presented in such a way to show the progression from the first to the third round. The third graphs (or sets thereof) should be labeled as "the final opinion." The final opinion is generally viewed as the estimate of the future.

## II. Forecasting

Forecasting is the process of predicting the future. It has evolved into a field of its own. The field of economic forecasting, for example, is a well-known discipline. Along the same line, the fields of technological forecasting, sociological forecasting, and political forecasting have evolved. Each field has its own methods, tools, and techniques. The thrust of forecasting is to arrive at an estimate for the value of a critical variable, at a specified point in time in the future. For example, economic forecasting will yield a point estimate of the GDP's growth, e.g., two percent. In sociological forecasting, demographics are projected in a similar manner. Age distribution or geographical distribution are stated in quantitative terms. Although the thrust of forecasting tends to be quantitative, there are times when qualitative estimates are forecasted also. This is especially true when the factors forecasted are not quantifiable, such as predicting changes in societal values, life styles, states of technology, and the like.

### The Forecasting Process

The forecasting process comprises six steps as follows:

1. Determining the Purpose of the Forecast: The first step is to determine the reason for undertaking the forecasting effort. Is it simply to be informed about the future? Is it to make a specific decision? Is it to forecast the life of an opportunity (or a threat)? One has to be very clear about why a forecast is needed.
2. Delimiting the Scope of What Is to Be Forecasted: The next step is to "bound" the future to be forecasted. As stated earlier, the future has three dimensions: essence, scope, and time frame. To illustrate, the bounding of the future of competitor behavior can be as follows:

- Essence: state of competitive rivalry.
- Scope: A given industry, the firm's immediate industry.
- Time frame: two years.

3. Selecting Critical Factors: Once the "future" is defined, the next task is to determine and select the variables to be forecasted. To follow through with the above illustration, the critical factors for competition can be established as follows:

- Number of competitors.
- Competitors' strategies.
- Number of expected new entrants.
- Number of buyers and their relative size.
- Technology.
- Number of substitutes.

- Number of potential entrants.
- Economic conditions.

A key problem in forecasting is complexity. There can be several factors entailed in the definition of the future. At some point in time, a decision has to be made as to which factors are to be forecasted. The number will have to be narrowed down because of the cost and time involved. Further, some factors might not lend themselves to forecasting. The following guidelines can be used to reduce the number of factors to be forecasted:

- Only variables that will have a significant and high impact should be included.
- Major disasters can be disregarded.
- Aggregation should be undertaken whenever possible, e.g., an estimate of technology can be formulated in terms of an overall "state of the art," instead of forecasting every detail in basic and applied research.
- Focusing on independent variables. If one variable is a function of another variable, then the latter should be the one to be forecasted instead of forecasting both of them.

4. Selecting Data and Data Sources: In preparation for forecasting, all relevant data must be collected to provide a benchmark for the forecast. Hence, it is essential to survey the various sources of data, evaluate their credibility, and decide which sources to use, and which of their data to use. For example, if one is to forecast innovation, there are many sources of data, e.g., scientific journals, independent research laboratories, university research laboratories, and corporations' R&D units. Which of these is most credible? What kind of data does one collect? Number of projects? Number of discoveries? Number of projects ready for commercialization?

5. Evaluating Forecasting Methods: There are numerous methods of forecasting ranging from the very hard (mathematical and statistical models) to the very soft (judgment). At some point in time, a decision will have to be made as to which method or mix of methods is to be used to forecast which factor. Methods of forecasting will be surveyed in the next section. At this junction, it is important to develop some criteria that can help in screening the various methods and in making a reasonable choice.

Ascher and Overholt suggested seven criteria that can help in the choice process:[5]

- Plausibility: The forecasting method should be plausible on two accounts. First, the logical structure of the method itself should appear to be reasonable, consistent, and effective. Second, the results obtained after applying the method should make sense. If a method fails the plausibility test, it should be used with caution or perhaps rejected.
- Capacity to display counterintuitive implications: To avoid relying on the mental pattern described by de Bono above, a good forecasting method should be able to generate results, or at least implications, that are not necessarily consistent with intuition. Only when it does so will we be able to look at things "outside the box." Consider Laffer's model of supply side economics. It produces counterintuitive results that are very enlightening. In essence, it says that lowering marginal income tax rates can yield equal or even higher government revenues.
- Explicitness: The explicitness of a method separates it from the technical person (the forecaster) applying it. A good method should be a stand-alone entity. Explicitness is important for it allows an objective analysis of the method itself as well as eliminates the bias of the forecaster.
- Comprehensiveness: A method should allow for a large number of factors to be taken into account. Using overly simple methods (ones that leave some factors out

of the analysis) will lead to unpleasant surprises. Such methods only expose the tip of the iceberg.
- Sensitivity to nuances: A good method should be able to take into account the peculiarity of the situation to which it is applied. If it does not, then arbitrary and crude estimates will result. For example, an input-output model might be useful for forecasting a certain economic sector. But, can it be applied to another sector? Will it fail to take into account the nuances of the second industry?
- Capacity to incorporate well-founded theory: A good method should be based on accepted theory, if one exists. A good theory is useful for prediction. If a forecasting method does not use the predictive ability of theory, it is deprived of predictive power.
- Simplicity: A good theory should be simple and straightforward. Simplicity eases understanding and makes the results easy to comprehend. Complicated methods are difficult to apply, thus increasing the cost and chances of errors.

6. Developing and Testing the Forecast

The application of a method should result in an output, the forecast itself. A forecast, however, is at best a "guestimate" of the future. It should be viewed with some skepticism. It has a certain probability of being correct. To minimize the probability of accepting the "wrong" forecast, its validity must be tested. One way of testing validity is to use another method to verify the results obtained by a given method. If the results converge, chances are we have a reliable forecast. If the method utilizes a model, the predictive ability of the model can be tested by plugging in past values for the independent variables for a given year in the past and computing the values of the dependent variables. If the resulting values are identical to the values obtained for that same year, chances are the model is reliable and its forecasts have validity.

## Forecasting Methods

The field of forecasting is rich in methodology. It has an extensive body of methods, tools, and techniques. This section is only a brief overview of the generic approaches utilized in forecasting nowadays. It is based largely on the work by Ascher and Overholt.[6] The methods covered here are: extrapolation, regression, leading indicators, complex models, curve fitting, analogy, and judgment methods.

1. Extrapolation

The essence of extrapolation is projecting a historically based quantitative trend at a constant rate. Extrapolation poses some thorny issues. First, it assumes that a straight line lies at the center of past data. The future is then estimated by simply extending that line into a future period. It is a rare situation when this estimation will be dead on. Second, it assumes that the rate of increase is somewhat constant, another rarity. Arbitrarily, the forecaster arrives at a rate and holds it constant throughout the projection. Nevertheless, extrapolation has its own place as a forecasting approach. It is neat and straightforward. Its thesis is simple: let the numbers speak for themselves. Further, it is explicit. Everyone can see every step in the exercise.

2. Regression

Forecasting through regression is the prediction of one factor based on its relationship with one or more other factors. The approach works as follows. The factor(s) of interest is viewed as a "dependent" or "predicted" variable. An appropriate independent (predictor) variable(s) is found. The correlation between them is established through correlation measures. Once a strong correlation is established, the values of the dependent variable are plotted against the values of the independent variable over a period of time. Through standard regression analysis, an equation is developed that expresses the dependent variable as a function of the independent variable(s).

Regression analysis assigns coefficients (beta weights) or parameters to the independent variables. The weights determine the relationship between the two variables. The relationship is presumed to be linear, in that a change in the predicted variable is directly proportional to a change in the independent variable. To forecast the value of the dependent variable, one plugs in the values of the independent variables and multiplies them by the respective coefficients. The equation can look something like this: [Predicted variable = constant $a$ + (constant $b1$ × independent variable 1) + (constant $b2$ × independent variable 2) +.........+ (constant $bn$ × independent variable n)].

As a forecasting method, regression has some shortcomings. First, the relationship is conditional upon the set of data from which the regression equation is derived. The data set pertains to the past and the present. Whether this relationship will hold in the future is uncertain. Second is the assumption of linearity. Real life relationships are not necessarily linear. Third, the relationship between the predicted and the predictor variables is subject to error. Some data sets will produce spurious relationships, which mislead the forecaster to assume that there is a real relationship between them while none exists.

3. Leading Indicators

In this approach, it is assumed that the factor being forecasted is preceded or signaled by a number of earlier changes in the direction of certain other factors, called "leading indicators." These leading indicators can be identified by examining the time series of numerous indicators and ascertaining the precedence relationship between them and the factor being forecasted. If they behave in a characteristic way prior to changes in the factor of interest, this would be sufficient to establish a leading indicator type of relationship. The underlying assumption here is that there are regularities in sequencing that permit the forecaster to predict a certain trend from its leading indicators.

The use of leading indicators is popular, particularly in economic forecasting. The anticipation of economic cycles relies on leading indicators. In forecasting the economy for the next year or so, economists scrutinize leading indicators such as manufacturers' inventories, capital expenditures, wholesale price index, and the like. It is worth noting that leading indicators do not tell the forecaster how to project a trend. Regression is used to project trends. Further, leading indicators do not predict exact values for the factor they signal. They may indicate levels of intensity but not exact values as in the case of regression or extrapolation.

4. Complex Models

Complex models take into consideration many variables and their dynamics (changing relationships). They combine multiple, interconnected propositions (where outputs of one become inputs of another, or solutions that must satisfy several equations simultaneously) that express feedback mechanisms, mutual causation, balancing effects, and other complicated dynamics.

The two most popular types of complex models are the econometric models and the system's dynamics model. The term "econometric" means economic analysis involving measurement. Econometric models are systems of equations where constants, or parameters, are estimated using regression analysis of existing data. Once these parameters are estimated, the equations are solved simultaneously to estimate the values of the dependent variables that satisfy all of the equations. These models inherit the weaknesses of regression, which is the reliance on historical data at the expense of other relationships that may become important in the future. Past and present data sets do not have these futuristic relationships. Hence, the models often become impotent in forecasting the future. This is often expressed in the humorous line about the definition of an economist: an economist is a person who tells you on Wednesday what you should have done on Monday.

System's dynamics models also involve describing a situation as a large system of equations. However, they do not involve regression analysis. Rather, they employ the calculus of finite difference, a procedure for updating the whole set of equations by one short period at a time. This allows capturing the nearly simultaneous mutual causation in the relationships among variables. Parameters are derived from various sources. Even if the equations cannot be fitted to past patterns, the system dynamics modeler can frequently derive parameters by conducting experimental research, databased estimation, elaborate theory, or just common sense. This frees the models from relying on historical data alone, like econometric models. In turn, this allows the model to incorporate factors that are more diverse, as well as those representing longer-term relationships.

The main weakness of system dynamics models is that they are less testable and more difficult to substantiate. However, they have the advantage of allowing the "what-if" type of forecasting. This allows decision-makers to test the impact of various decisions and policies. Ten years ago, a system's dynamic study examined the effect of welfare government programs in the U.S. over a long period. It predicted that such programs increase the welfare load rather than reduce it. So far, the forecasts of that study appear to be holding.

5. Curve Fitting

Curve fitting involves plotting and analyzing data to discover a pattern that is expressible as a curve (or a cycle) that may be embedded therein. The applications of curve fitting can be found wherever cycle theories exist, e.g., economic cycles, political cycles, and the like. Although this method is essentially equivalent to extrapolation, it allows the forecaster to spot patterns that are more sophisticated than simple extrapolation. The attractiveness of curve fitting is that it assumes that a powerful, simple, consistent dynamic underlies the past and the future pattern of the trend. The premise underlying this method is that there is a microscopic pattern of the trend under study. This microscopic pattern is conditioned by a predetermined pattern that can be described in a straightforward manner as a mathematical equation. This pattern or curve may be a simple one (a straight line), convex, concave, or "S" shaped.

Given the plotting of the curve, the forecaster then has to determine its specific shape or parameters for the trend. This is often done by estimating the parameters using traditional econometric methods, i.e., the parameters that best historical data are selected. The choice of a curve type is a matter of judgment. It can be guided by a theory, if one exists.

6. Forecasting by Analogy

This approach attempts to forecast a factor by finding another factor that, in the past, has behaved like it. The assumption is that the factor under examination will behave like the reference factor. To illustrate, if a new product is introduced in the market, one can find a product (a reference product) in the same class. One can then forecast the future behavior of the new product's sales based on the past behavior of the reference product. If one was trying to forecast the future of the PC industry in the early 1970s, one could have used the analogy of an infant hi-tech industry. Such industries follow a "typical" pattern: initial rapid growth, price reduction, and then market saturation. This is, more or less, the pattern that television sets, microwave ovens, and calculators assumed. They could be used as analogies for forecasting the future development of other hi-tech products.

The main strength of this method lies in its allowing the forecaster to explore virgin territory where no historical data exist. Its main weakness lies in finding an analogue, a variable that behaves in a manner identical to the variable of interest. There is considerable subjectivity involved in discovering the analogue and in pairing its behavior with that of the variable being forecasted.

7. Judgmental Forecasting

Arriving at a point estimate of the future value of a certain factor can be reached by human judgment. In this approach, a human being, usually an expert, is called upon to come up with an estimate of the future value of a given factor. The assumption underlying this approach is that the human mind understands much more about the dynamics of the factors of interest than it can express explicitly. The mind can detect subtleties and complexities that the quantitative approaches cannot capture. A major advantage of judgment forecasting is that it allows the forecaster to assess the probability of a forecast's correctness by expressing a level of confidence in it. Although an element of bias lurks behind the estimate, this can be balanced by the fact that the forecaster is an "expert." There are at least two approaches for applying judgmental forecasting by experts. Both were discussed earlier. The first is the Delphi method utilizing a panel of experts to arrive at the quantitative estimates needed. The second is brainstorming by a panel of knowledgeable people.

## Applications of Forecasting

Economic forecasting is a familiar application. Aside from economic forecasting, there are countless others such as business forecasting, social forecasting, political forecasting, technological forecasting, and the like. The domain of business forecasting is estimating the future values of critical business variables. Examples of business forecasting include sales forecasts, expense projections, cash flow forecasts, financial forecasts, industry trends, competitive trends, as well as some or all of the others mentioned in this section. Business forecasting tends to be quantitative. It always boils down to a number to help forecast the bottom line. Political forecasting attempts to predict the future behavior of political factors, e.g., political leanings, size of government, budgets, tariffs, tax rates, government spending, growth in regulatory bodies, and the like. For companies operating in the global environment, forecasting the politics of foreign countries is crucial. Political risk is a threat to investments in such countries. Many of the methods mentioned above are utilized in political forecasting. However, because of the absence of databases, political forecasting tends to dwell on the softer methods such as judgmental forecasting, forecasting by analogy, and scenarios analysis (which will be taken up in the next section).

Predicting technological trends has always been the subject of interest for members of the business and scientific community. The revolutionary changes in technology have made the field of technological forecasting a crucial endeavor. Technological forecasting utilizes all the methods presented in this section. However, because of the breakthrough nature of technological change, forecasting in this arena tends to rely on human judgment. Brainstorming and the Delphi methods are popular methods in technological forecasting.

## III. SCENARIO CONSTRUCTION: ALTERNATIVE FUTURES

The third approach for anticipating the future is scenario construction. The term "scenario" has many definitions. It was used initially in theatrical arts and later in the motion picture industry where the word "scenario" referred to the sequence of the actions, scenes, and the interplay among characters leading to the plot. In this case, a "scenario" is an outline of the plot, rather than the manuscript itself. It is the "sketch" of the play.

In the field of futures research, the concept of scenarios is a core methodology for mapping the future. To get a tentative understanding of the term, let us survey a sample of definitions:

- A scenario is ". . . an exploration of an alternative future . . . an outline of one conceivable state of affairs given certain assumptions."[7]

- "Scenarios describe how the major economic, social, political, and technological driving forces might plausibly combine to shape the future, based on how those forces have behaved in the past."[8]
- A scenario is ". . . a chronological chain of events leading to a particular end state."[9]
- "A scenario is simply a description of the future."[10]

In articulating the concept, Wilson suggested four essential characteristics of a scenario:[11]

- Scenarios are hypothetical. Scenarios represent knowledge about the future and the future is fundamentally unknown and unknowable. The best that scenarios can do is to explore alternative possible futures. For such an exploration, scenarios are appropriately suited.
- Because scenarios are hypothetical, no scenario will ever materialize exactly as described, conceived, or written.
- A scenario is no more than a sketch, an outline at best. A scenario is essentially an attempt to map out the key branching points of the future, to highlight the major determinants that might make it evolve from one branch instead of another, and to sketch in the primary consequences. Because it is a sketch, Wilson warns that there is considerable "selectivity" in constructing scenarios.
- Scenarios are multifaceted and holistic in their approach to the future. They represent a flow process combining a range of aspects of the environment including (whenever applicable) demographic changes, social trends, political events, economic variables, and technological developments.

## The Concept of "Alternative Futures"

The use of scenarios rests on one fundamental concept, alternative futures. Prior to the use of scenarios, forecasting was the main approach for predicting the future. However, forecasting posed a serious difficulty. Forecasting often provides "a single point estimate" of a variable of interest in the future. For example, interest rates are projected to be a single number. The problem is that the future rarely, if ever, materializes according to this point estimate. Almost invariably, the forecasted value is either above or below the single point estimate, and it sometimes falls outside the chart altogether, as we often see in economic forecasts and weather forecasts.

Common sense tells us that the forecasted state is only one of the many possibilities that the future might assume. Hence, the concept of "alternative futures" evolved. According to this concept, the future (of anything) is a set of alternative pictures or possibilities; each one of them is called a "scenario." Hence, the future as perceived in the present, is a number of alternative scenarios. Clearly, the safer way to anticipate the future is to construct those alternative scenarios and look upon them as the view of the future.

Viewing the future in terms of alternative scenarios requires considerable intellectual elasticity. Some of the scenarios might represent different and even conflicting pictures of the same future. We must be able to live with these variant views of the same thing. Some individuals are uncomfortable with the thought of entertaining multiple possibilities, let alone conflicting ones. However, one must learn to live with such intellectual discomfort. The alternative, a single point estimate, is risky, the hazard of losing, betting on a single point estimate that might not materialize. By contrast, the alternative futures' view reduces risk by allowing the decision-maker the luxury of being mentally prepared (in advance) for a range of possibilities. Finally, a scenario is not identical to a forecast, although they are both visions of the future. To expose the differences between the two concepts, Exhibit 9.2 was prepared by Meristo.[12]

| Forecasts | Scenarios |
|---|---|
| Statistical summary of expert opinion | Mostly verbal description of archetypal futures |
| Sources of uncertainty not specified | Focus on key variables and relationships |
| Efficient, but an impoverished summary of expertise | Information-rich, but inefficient summaries |
| Directly usable as input to decision process. | Require further judgments and translation |
| Can be tested for accuracy (in the long run) | Hard to test, more of a thinking tool |
| Assume it is useful and possible to predict the future | Assume the future cannot be predicted or it is dangerous to do so |

Exhibit 9.2: Forecasts versus Scenarios

## The Nature of Scenarios

In this work, a scenario is defined as a narrative that paints a moving picture of a certain phenomenon (that is beyond the control of the leader and the people) over a defined time interval in the future. We stress the condition that the phenomena are beyond the control of the decision maker. Factors that are under the control of the decision maker do not need scenarios. The decision maker can make them behave any way he/she wishes. To that extent, they are predictable. What is not predictable is what is beyond the decision-maker's powers. Accordingly, we do not construct scenarios for the behavior of our firm for it is under our control.

As a narrative, a scenario is a verbal account of: (1) a possible projection of the behavior of certain driving forces, along with (2) the end state at which the projection of each driving force rests at the end of the time interval. Driving forces are those entities that make up a certain phenomenon and shape its state at a given point in time. For example, an industry is made up of a number of inner factors such as producers (players), suppliers, customers, and technology.

Driving forces are dynamic. They change over time on their own and in response to changes in the behavior of other driving forces. For example, as suppliers seek economies of scale, they merge with and acquire one another. As they do so, they control supply and prices and ultimately producers. Realizing this, producers might merge with and acquire one another to become a major force too. They might even merge with or acquire the suppliers.

As a driving force plays out in the marketplace, its behavior takes the form of "events," e.g., raising the price of a certain item, introducing a new product, acquiring a competitor, and the like. Over a period of time, the behavior of a driving force can be viewed as a stream of events that have a discernible direction and momentum, a trend if you will. Projecting the behavior of a driving force means anticipating the future series of events it might assume. At some point, the projection plateaus and pauses, for a moment, at a certain state. We can call this the "end state" for the variable of interest. In making a projection, we might wish to rely on some or all of the forecasting methods mentioned previously. We might also rely on the softer methods such as intuition, experience, and group methods. If we were to take this stream of events and extend it into the future (fast forwarding in time) and pause at a certain year, we will end up with a "still picture" or an end state of this particular driving force. This is illustrated in Exhibit 9.3 for a single driving force. *It is also possible that we foresee more than one end state.* To simplify the presentation, we are using the case of only one end state throughout this presentation.

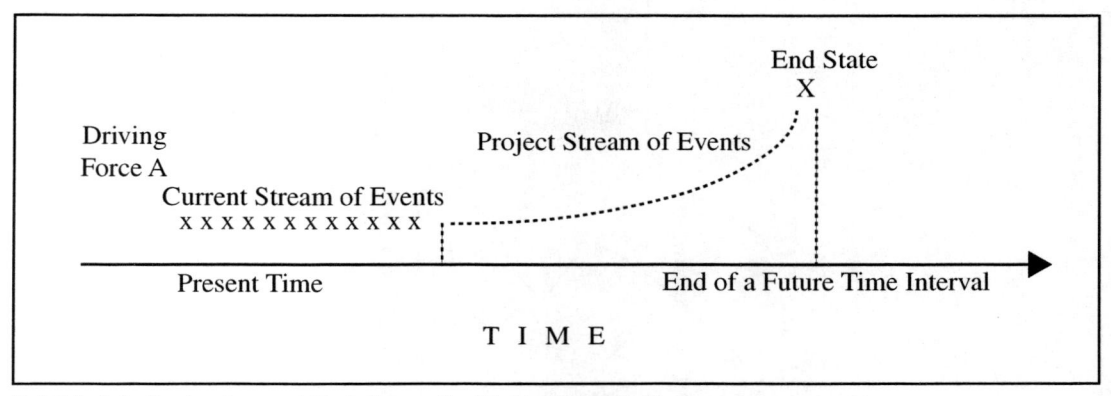

```
                                            End State
                                               X
    Driving              Project Stream of Events  ⋰
    Force A                                     ⋰
              Current Stream of Events       ⋰
              x x x x x x x x x x x x ┊------------⋰      ┊
    ──────────────────────────────────┼─────────────────────┼──────▶
              Present Time                          End of a Future Time Interval
                                    T I M E
```

Exhibit 9.3: Projection and End State of a Single Driving Force

To illustrate the concepts of projections and end-states, let us take the "players" in a certain industry as one of its driving forces. The current stream of events consists of cutthroat competitors set on pursuing a fragmented market through expensive product differentiation. Let us project this behavior into the future, say the next five years. What do we see? We can probably project a future stream of events like this: thinning margins, marginal firms going out of business, more acquisitions, and more mergers. If we pause at year 5, we can see an end state for this stream—this being an industry dominated by five or six players.

The projected stream of events, along with its end state, constitutes a scenario for this one driving force. If we were to do this for every driving force of a given situation, we would then have a scenario for this situation. This can be visualized by adding more driving forces to Exhibit 9.3 in addition to driving force A. This, however, will be only one scenario or one possibility. We still need to generate other scenarios so that we can develop alternative futures. We need to know all or most of the possibilities that the future might assume so that we can gauge it and consequently reduce the uncertainty inherent in anticipating the future. What do we do?

In projecting each driving force's behavior, we generate a number of projections as shown in Exhibit 9.4, which illustrates the idea for just one driving force. Returning to the example of "players," one projection is consolidation leading to an end state of oligopoly. Another projection may anticipate a technology revolution that reduces barriers to entry and brings in many, many new players leading to an end state approximating perfect competition. A third projection may foresee significant demographic change that turns the market upside down, e.g., an aging population. *It should be stressed here that we could generate more than one end state for each projection or trend.*

To recap, three points need to be stressed:

- The scenario approach for anticipating the future instructs us to view the future in terms of the alternative possibilities that it may assume.
- We generate the alternative scenarios by identifying alternative paths for the projections of a given set of driving forces and their respective end states. Thus, we generate one set of projections and their end states and this will constitute one scenario. We generate another set of projections and their end states and this will constitute the second scenario. To generate a third scenario, we plot another set of projections and end states. We repeat this process until we are satisfied that we have covered all the plausible possibilities that the future may take.

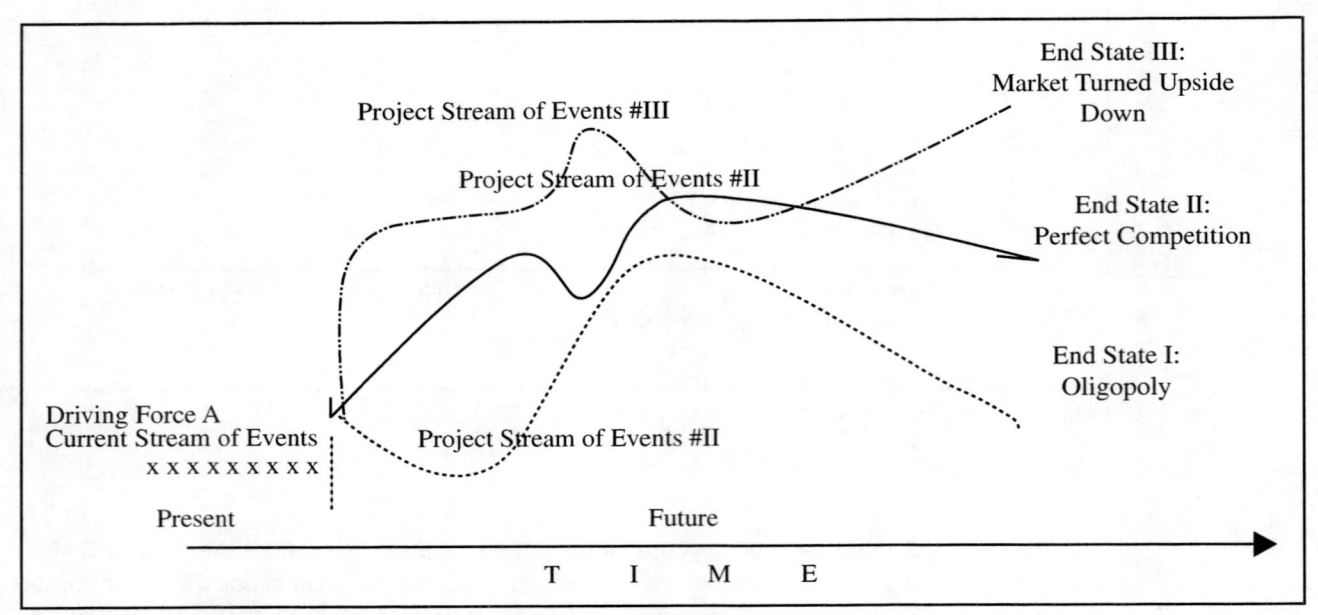

Exhibit 9.4: Alternative Futures (Scenarios) for a Single Driving Force

- Each one of the alternative scenarios is *an array of projections* coupled (matched) with another *array of end states*. When stated in words, the matched arrays of projections and end states form *a narrative that tells a story of how we got from the present to the future* (as represented by the array of end states) via the array of projected streams of events.

## Process of Constructing Scenarios

The field of futures research methodology contains many methods and techniques for constructing scenarios. Some are quantitative, relying heavily on mathematical and statistical models. Others are fairly qualitative and "intuitive." It is worth noting that the scenario construction and forecasting methodologies are not mutually exclusive. Forecasting techniques are utilized in constructing scenarios to generate values for the variables that make up a certain scenario.

One possible scenario construction process is proposed here. It is a "quick and dirty" method, a rearrangement of ideas in the literature. It has the advantage of allowing the decision-maker to survey the future without falling in the trap of "paralysis by analysis." It is inexpensive. It builds on the intuition and experience of the persons attempting to anticipate the future. It consists of five steps as: (1) bounding the future to be mapped; (2) determining the driving forces that shape this phenomenon; (3) constructing the scenario space; (4) composing alternative scenarios and assigning likelihood for each; and (5) writing up the scenarios.

1. Bounding the Scope of the Future

The scenario construction process begins with the delineation of the future horizon that we are trying to anticipate. This requires two decisions:

- Isolating and defining the phenomenon to be projected into the future.
- Establishing the point in the future at which we stop our projection.

The first step in anticipating the future is to answer the question: the future of what. This calls for defining the phenomenon of the future of interest to us. Since phenomena are interrelated (as part of one universe), we must arbitrarily isolate the one phenomenon that pertains most to the decision at hand. In the context of sensing turbulence by a business firm, here are examples of the relevant phenomena depending on the size of the firm: the industry, the economy, population demographics, and societal values. A large firm might go as far as developing scenarios for the future of global trade. A small firm might just stop at the industry level.

Once we isolate the phenomenon the future of which we want to map, the next step is to determine how far in the future we want to foresee. This calls for establishing a specific time frame. For example, we want to know the future of the industry at the end of five years. The selection of a time frame depends primarily on the visibility of the future behavior (availability of data) of the driving forces. If the data are available to make some reasonable projection for three years, we might want to set our sights on three years. If the driving forces are changing quickly and unpredictably, we will have to shorten the time frame since visibility will be limited.

2. Determining the Driving Forces that Shape the Phenomenon of Interest

Given a delineation of the phenomenon the future of which is to be mapped, the next step is to analyze it to determine the driving forces that constitute it. In the previous chapter, the concept of analysis was used to decompose ambiguous entities (blobs) into their primary components, e.g., environmental analysis, industry analysis, competitor analysis, and the like.

If the phenomenon of interest is the firm's industry, the driving forces can be the following: (1) the players or the producers, (2) the suppliers, (3) the customers, (4) new entrants, (5) the producers of substitutes, and (6) technology. If the designated phenomenon is the macro-environment, then the driving forces include the economic system, the social system, the political system, the technological system, the legal system, etc. Each one of these systems, in turn, has a number of driving forces. The social system is driven by forces such as population demographics, social values, employment, etc.

3. Constructing the Scenario Space[13]

In this step, we take *each* of the driving forces and do three things:

- First, we identify each driving force's current stream of events. This will be the point of departure from which we extend our vision into the future.
- Second, we generate the benchmark projection and end state for each driver. This involves projecting from the current stream of events to arrive at a future stream of events (trend) as the driving force moves into the future. This benchmark projection is based on extending the present into the future. In a way, it assumes that what is happening now is most likely to continue in the future. Once this projection is made, we attempt to identify the end state that it will most likely rest at by the end of the established time frame. We might wish to identify more than one end state depending on what we foresee.
- Third, we generate projections and end states for each driving force (each based on a different set of assumptions for its future behavior). We repeat the same process, using a different set of assumptions each time, for all of the drivers that we have identified.

Once we have completed the three tasks above for all the driving forces, we arrange our projections and end states in the form of a matrix like the one shown in Exhibit 9.5 in an abstract form. The horizontal dimension shows the various driving forces. The vertical di-

|  | DRIVING FORCES ||||| 
|---|---|---|---|---|---|
|  | **Driving Force 1** | **Driving Force 2** | **Driving Force 3** | **Driving Force 4** | **Driving Force n** |
| P R O J E C T I O N S  &  E N D  S T A T E S | Projection 1,1: Description of the projected stream of events<br><br>End-State 1, 1: Description of the end-state that the projection will rest at by the end of the established time horizon | Projection 1,2: Description of the projected stream of events<br><br>End-State 1, 2: Description of the end-state that the projection will rest at by the end of the established time horizon | .......... .......... .......... .......... | .......... .......... .......... .......... | Projection 1,n: Description of the projected stream of events<br><br>End-State 1, n: Description of the end-state that the projection will rest at by the end of the established time horizon |
| | Projection 2,1: Description of the projected stream of events<br><br>End-State 2, 1: Description of the end-state that the projection will rest at by the end of the established time horizon | Projection 2,2: Description of the projected stream of events<br><br>End-State 2, 2: Description of the end-state that the projection will rest at by the end of the established time horizon | .......... .......... .......... .......... | .......... .......... .......... .......... | Projection 2,n: Description of the projected stream of events<br><br>End-State 2, n: Description of the end-state that the projection will rest at by the end of the established time horizon |
| | Projection . . .: Description of the projected stream of events<br><br>End-State . . . Description of the end-state that the projection will rest at by the end of the established time horizon | Projection . . .: Description of the projected stream of events<br><br>End-State . . . Description of the end-state that the projection will rest at by the end of the established time horizon | .......... .......... .......... .......... | .......... .......... .......... .......... | Projection . . .: Description of the projected stream of events<br><br>End-State . . . Description of the end-state that the projection will rest at by the end of the established time horizon |
| | Projection m,1: Description of the projected stream of events<br><br>End-State m, 1: Description of the end-state that the projection will rest at by the end of the established time horizon | Projection m,2: Description of the projected stream of events<br><br>End-State m, 2: Description of the end-state that the projection will rest at by the end of the established time horizon | .......... .......... .......... .......... | .......... .......... .......... .......... | Projection m,n: Description of the projected stream of events<br><br>End-State m, n: Description of the end-state that the projection will rest at by the end of the established time horizon |

Exhibit 9.5: An Illustration of the Concept of Scenario Space

mension represents the alternative projection and end states. The cells (the body) of the matrix represent the scenario space. The reason this matrix is called the scenario space is that it contains a whole population of possible scenarios. Each scenario represents a matched set (of projections and end states) of all the driving forces taken together. Every time we want to generate a scenario, we search for a different combination of projections and matching end states (a different end state for each driver, each time).

To demonstrate the concept of scenario space, let us take one phenomenon, an industry. Suppose we decide that there are six driving forces that shape this particular industry: producers, customers, suppliers, substitutes, new entrants, and technology. If we take each force and identify three possible projections and end states, we will have a 3 x 6 matrix comprising 18 cells. These 18 cells then become the scenario space. This is shown in Exhibit 9.6.

Sensing Future Turbulence    135

|   | CUSTOMERS | SUPPLIERS | SUBSTITUTES | NEW ENTRANTS | COMPETITORS/ PRODUCERS | TECHNOLOGY |
|---|---|---|---|---|---|---|
| **PROJECTIONS** | Projection: Demand increases. Customer numbers increase. They remain fragmented. They remain small in size End State: No bargaining power for customers. They don't dictate prices or terms of sale. [1] | Projection Supply remains stable. Number of suppliers increase. They remain small and compete fiercely amongst each other. End State: No bargaining power for suppliers. They don't dictate prices and terms. [4] | Projection: Substitutes remain distant alternatives. End State: Producers of substitutes are no threat. [7] | Projection: The industry becomes very attractive enjoying high margins. New firms form to take advantage of a growing industry. End State: New entrants become real competitors and market structure is rearranged to reflect a fragmented industry. [10] | Projection: The industry grows. Number of players increase due to new business formation and entry of new entrant. There are too many players. End State: Fragmented market structure. [13] | Projection: The players use traditional technology. Minimum innovation in process and minimal investments in R&D. End State: Technology is primitive and fragmented. No effect on cost structure for players. [16] |
| **AND** | Projection: Demand increases. Customer number decreases due to mergers and acquisitions among them. They become big in size. End State: Customers enjoy strong bargaining power. They dictate prices and terms of sale. [2] | Projection: Supply volume remains unchanged. Intense merger activity takes place. Their numbers are reduced. The field is reduced to few key suppliers. End State: Suppliers' bargaining power increases substantially. They dictate cost structure. [5] | Projection: Substitutes gain in popularity. Customers are experimenting. Producers of substitutes are large in numbers and small in size. End State: Producers of substitutes become a real threat. [8] | Projection: The industry becomes attractive enough to attract big players to diversify in it. End State: Market structure is changed dictated by the new big players. [11] | Projection: Growing industry but the number of players decreases due to intense merger and acquisition activity. End State: Market structure becomes an oligopoly with few firms dominating the industry. [14] | Projection: New technology evolves changing process and altering cost structure somewhat for players. End State: Somewhat advanced technology. Efficiency and margin gains. [17] |
| **END STATES** | Projection: Demand decreases. Customers' numbers decrease. They remain small in size and fragmented. End State: Customers have no bargaining power. They don't dictate terms of sale. [3] | Projection: Supply decreases somewhat. Suppliers remain small and fragmented. End State: Suppliers enjoy moderate bargaining power. They affect cost structure to some extent. [6] | Projection: Substitutes become true alternatives. Firms that produce them are large. End State: Producers of substitutes are full fledged competitors to be dealt with like industry competitors. [9] | Projection: The industry is maturing with declining margins. Attraction to new entrants is nil. End State: No threat of new entrants. [12] | Projection: Growth stabilizes. The number of players remains large. They scurry for building defensible positions through product differentiation and market segmentation. End State: Market structure becomes monopolistic competition. [15] | Projection: New discoveries are made. Process and products are reinvented. The industry has changed radically. End State: A technology revolution. Rules of the game have changed. [18] |

DRIVING FORCES

Exhibit 9.6: An Illustration of a Hypothetical Scenario Space for an Industry

4. Composing Alternative Scenarios and Assigning Likelihood

Once the scenario space is developed, the next step is to identify the possible scenarios that represent plausible futures for the phenomenon of interest. Composing scenarios boils down to identifying the possible combinations of the cells in the scenario space matrix. Numbering the cells facilitates this process. For example, if we look at the scenario space matrix in Exhibit 9.6, there are 18 cells. We can start by identifying the benchmark scenario—the one that assumes "business as usual" or simply extends the present into the future. This scenario can be the content of the combination of cells 1, 5, 7, 11, 13, and 16. We then assign likelihood to this scenario. The likelihood is a subjective probability estimate. It can be quantitative, a number between 0.0 and 1.0. It can also be qualitative, e.g., highly likely, or most likely. Since the driving forces of an industry are interdependent (related to one another), the contents of a combination of cells have to be internally consistent. For example, we cannot choose cell #1, which shows an increase in customers, and another cell that shows a projection of the industry declining. *An industry scenario is an internally consistent combination of cells.* If the driving forces are not interdependent, then internal consistency among cells is unnecessary.

Thus, the essentials of a benchmark scenario (as composed from Exhibit 9.6) paint a picture of the future composed of the following combination of projections and end states:

[Demand will increase. Customer numbers will increase. They will remain fragmented. They will remain small in size. There will be no bargaining power for customers. They will not dictate prices or terms of sale (Exhibit 9.6, cell #1),

plus

Supply volume will remain unchanged. Intense merger activity will take place. Their numbers will be reduced. The field will be reduced to few key suppliers. Suppliers' bargaining power will increase substantially. They will dictate cost structure (Exhibit 9.6, cell # 5),

plus

Substitutes will remain distant. Producers of substitutes will not be a threat (Exhibit 9.6, cell #7),

plus

The industry will become attractive enough to cause big players from other industries to diversify by entering it (Exhibit 9.6, cell # 11),

plus

The industry will grow. Number of players will increase due to new business formation and entrants. There will be too many players. Market structure will be fragmented (Exhibit 9.6, cell #13),

plus

New technology will evolve and will alter cost structure. Efficiency will increase (Exhibit 9.6, cell #17)

Having generated the benchmark scenario, we next proceed to generate a second scenario. We can do so by choosing the combination of cells 3, 5, 8, 12, 15, and 17. We then assign a subjective probability estimate for it. We might decide that the scenario has a low probability of occurring. Although it is highly unlikely to occur, it still has a certain chance of happening. We must become aware of this possibility. The mere awareness of such a scenario prepares us emotionally for the future. In a way, we have been forewarned. We might wish to call it the surprise scenario for example. To generate other scenarios, we proceed to experiment with the various combinations of cells as long as they are internally consistent and make sense in light of experience and common sense. We can generate as many scenarios as needed to appease the anxiety about the uncertainty of the future.

5. Writing up the Scenarios

Once all alternative scenarios are composed in an abstract form (like the benchmark scenario illustration mentioned above), we take each combination of cells and write it up in prose to paint a picture of each future. A separate write up is needed for each alternative scenario. Each scenario can be given a name that captures the essence of the scenario, e.g., status quo, smooth sailing, or hard times ahead. Here is an example of the writing of one scenario for the future of society:

> "The future society will be independent in its political alignment, possibly resulting in a new type of federalism. People will have traditional social values but with some modification—unlike the past. Institutions will be undergoing evolutionary change with more concentration as opposed to proliferation. The economy will be marked by business-government partnerships rather than adversarial relationships. Attitudes towards work will be different with a new motivation for work—not the traditional forms. The rapid rate of technology will shift society's concern toward the ecology in an attempt to protect the health of the planet."[14]

## Using Scenarios

The scenario construction process yields a number of scenarios that represent alternative futures of the firm's environment. Each scenario has a certain likelihood of occurring, albeit it a subjective estimate. We might end up with three or more scenarios; the most likely scenario plus two or more other scenarios with lesser probability of occurring. The question now is what do we do with these alternate scenarios. There are several uses as follows:

1. The most immediate use of the resulting scenarios is to extract a number of future events, developments and trends. In a way, each scenario is like a radar screen with a number of specs on it. Each spec if a possible event, development, or a trend to be inputted in the issues analysis process discussed in Chapter 10.
2. The most likely scenario is the picture of the future upon which the strategic response will be based. At the other end of the continuum, there is the least likely or the surprise scenario where we expect the unexpected. This will be the basis of our contingency planning (Chapter 11).
3. The range of variation among scenarios is a depiction of the uncertainty facing the firm. In a way, the scenarios help us assess risk because they show the possibilities of what can happen. Knowing these possibilities reduces the hazard of losing due to surprise. If we are thorough enough and expose all possible scenarios, surprise will be minimized.

# CONCLUSION

This chapter and the preceding one dealt with the system's activities in sensing current turbulence and anticipating future happenings. Sensing present and future turbulence is like constructing a radar screen where happenings (present and future) in the firm's environment register. They appear as specs on the screen. The specs represent events, developments, and trends. These are then carried forth to the next phase, interpreting turbulence, where they will be inputted in the issues analysis process. They form the pool of issues to which the firm must respond. This is the topic of the next chapter.

# ENDNOTES

1. Belasco, J.A. and R.C. Stayer, *Flight of the Buffalo: Soaring To Excellence, Learning To Let Employees Lead*, New York, NY: Warner Books, 1993, pp. 125–126.

2. de Bono, E., *Lateral Thinking For Management*, New York, NY: American Management Association, 1971.

3. Ibid., p. 126.

4. Mendell, J.S., "The Practice of Intuition," in J. Fowles (ed.), *Handbook of Futures Research*, Westport, CT: Greenwood Press, 1978, pp. 149–161.

5. Ascher, W. and W.H. Overholt, *Strategic Planning and Forecasting: Political Risk and Economic Opportunity*, New York, NY: John Wiley & Sons, 1983.

6. Ibid.

7. Wilson, I.H., "Scenarios" in J. Fowles (ed.), *Handbook of Futures Research*, Westport, CT: Greenwood Press, 1978, p. 225.

8. Schwartz, P., "Composing a Plot for Your Scenario," *Planning Review*, May/June, 1992, p. 5.

9. Mason, D.H. and R.G. Wilson, "Future Mapping: A New Approach To Managing Strategic Uncertainty," *Planning Review*, May/June 1987, p. 29.

10. Meristo, T., "Not Forecasts But Multiple Scenarios When Coping With Uncertainties In the Competitive Environment," *European Journal Of Operational Research*, vol. 38, 1989, pp. 350–357.

11. Wilson, I.H., op. cit., p. 226.

12. Meristo, op. cit., p. 351.

13. Adapted from I.H. Wilson, "Scenarios," in J. Foles, ed., *Handbook of Futures*, Westport, CT: Greenwood Press, 1978.

14. Wilson, I.H., op. cit., p. 226.

CHAPTER
# 10

# Interpreting Turbulence

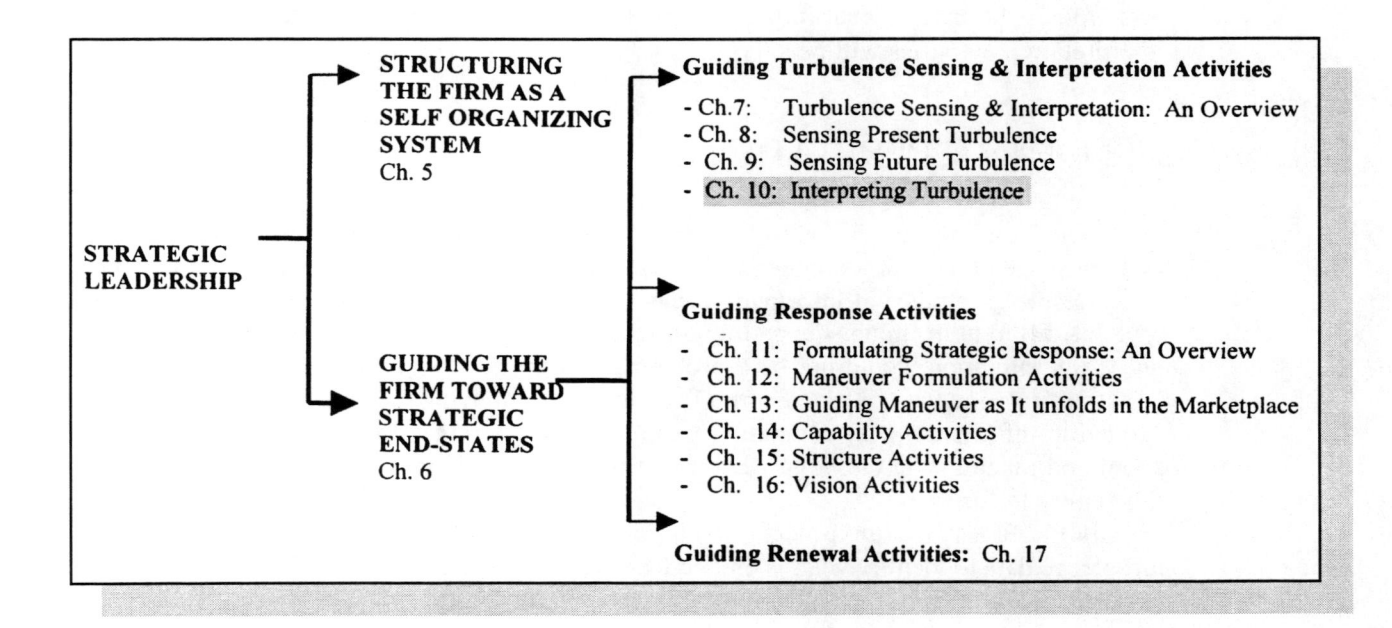

**Guiding Turbulence Sensing & Interpretation Activities**
- Ch.7: Turbulence Sensing & Interpretation: An Overview
- Ch. 8: Sensing Present Turbulence
- Ch. 9: Sensing Future Turbulence
- Ch. 10: Interpreting Turbulence

**STRUCTURING THE FIRM AS A SELF ORGANIZING SYSTEM**
Ch. 5

**STRATEGIC LEADERSHIP**

**GUIDING THE FIRM TOWARD STRATEGIC END-STATES**
Ch. 6

**Guiding Response Activities**
- Ch. 11: Formulating Strategic Response: An Overview
- Ch. 12: Maneuver Formulation Activities
- Ch. 13: Guiding Maneuver as It unfolds in the Marketplace
- Ch. 14: Capability Activities
- Ch. 15: Structure Activities
- Ch. 16: Vision Activities

**Guiding Renewal Activities:** Ch. 17

Turbulence *per se* is not cause for alarm. It is the "normal" state of affairs in the business world. However, turbulence becomes important only when it has serious implications for the firm. In Chapters 8 and 9, we explored how the self-organizing system gathers data about turbulence. These data take the form of change in the environment. This change can assume the form of events, developments, and trends. Once the system registers such change, the next step is to make sense of it; in other words, interpret it. Interpretation here means contemplating the implications of turbulence for the firm; whether the change is an opportunity, a threat, or simply a non-issue. Clearly, interpretation yields premises for the firm's response to turbulence. Interpretation paints a picture of the situation facing the firm. Based on this picture, response decisions are made, namely, formulating and implementing a strategy that embodies the firm's response. An inappropriate interpretation will produce the wrong response. A wrong response means wasted investments and time that could have been spent getting ahead.

This chapter explores the self-organizing system's activities in interpreting turbulence. It begins with an exploration of the concept of interpretation and what is involved in it. Next, it examines the barriers that impede or inhibit proper interpretation. After that, turbulence interpretation activities will be surveyed.

## THE NATURE OF INTERPRETATION

The term "interpretation" refers to a set of mental activities that are concerned with making sense of a set of ambiguous data. The term ambiguous suggests that a certain object of interest (e.g., a piece of information) can mean different things to different people or that it yields different meanings depending on which angle one looks at it. Were it not for ambiguity, interpretation would not be a problematic task. For the purposes of this work, interpretation is defined as the process of: (1) deducing or inferring the "reality" that may be embedded in information; (2) explaining this reality by relating it to the forces that brought it about and placing it in the larger scheme of things; and, (3) identifying the implications of this reality to the firm.

In the first place, the process of interpretation *begins* with the task of sifting through turbulence data to identify what is embedded in such data. We should be interested in extracting three main things:

- Events: An event is a one-time occurrence created by the action of a driving force such as competitors, suppliers, customers, the government, and the like. An event can be an isolated incident. It can be the antecedent of another event, e.g., a price reduction as the first move in a price war planned by a competitor. It can also be the consequence of another event.
- Developments: A development is a cluster of events that have a common thread among them and spans a definable time interval. For example, the bankruptcy of several firms in a certain industry over a short span of time is a development. A number of mergers or acquisitions in a certain industry happening in rapid succession during a short period is another example of a development.
- Trends: A trend is a cluster or a series of developments that have a common thread among them and spans a longer time horizon (longer than a development). An example of a trend is the steady increase in the computing power of the desktop computer. Other trends include continued globalization of business and the increasing popularity of the Internet.

Once the events, developments, and trends are isolated, the next step is to identify the forces or the causes that drive them. If an event is taking place, interpretation continues by raising questions: Why is it happening? What are the causes? How strong are these causes? For example, take a price reduction by a competitor. What fuels it? A promotional campaign? If yes, then the price reduction is a short-term occurrence. What if the price reduction was an attempt by a competitor to drive our firm out of business? If the competitor wants to drive others out of business, what drives this determination? Is it that the competitor has deep pockets or excess cash flows? Does it enjoy enormous economies of scale or a proprietary, revolutionary technology? These questions are crucial in interpretation. Interpretation goes as far as finding the why's behind the why's and the what's behind the what's. Our answers to these questions would help us conclude whether an incident is an isolated event or a tracer of many things to come. Our diagnosis will affect the strength and the scope of our response to the incident. The same process applies to the interpretation of developments and trends. Identifying events, developments, and trends is not useful unless we decide what they *mean* to the firm. An event, development, or trend means something if it has strategic implications for the firm. A strategic implication is a strong negative or positive impact on the firm in its entirety. The term "strategic" signifies that the impact is a matter of life and death, i.e., it can make or break the firm.

Clearly, interpretation is a thorny process, tentative and speculative. Because the firm's situation is part of a complex system (the universe) that is impossible to understand thoroughly, we can only guess when we try to make sense of a singular event or development. The outcome of interpretation is uncertain, as there can be many interpretations of the same set of data. Sometimes, we make the right interpretation. Other times, we arrive at the wrong conclusions. The main reason for this predicament is that the data are laced with complicating factors, namely ambiguity, complexity, and uncertainty. We deal with this topic next.

## FACTORS COMPLICATING THE INTERPRETATION PROCESS

Turbulence does not easily lend itself to interpretation. It embodies three main conditions that make it defy precise interpretation. These are uncertainty, ambiguity, and complexity. Uncertainty results from the erratic behavior of turbulence phenomena such as sudden leaps, sudden reversals, rapidity, and the like. From moment to moment, we are not sure just what exactly is going on. Ambiguity is the lack of data about turbulence variables because of the inherent uncertainty. Complexity results from the multitudes of factors that create turbulence and this complicates the task of knowing what is going on and where it is coming from.

The offshoot of uncertainty, ambiguity, and complexity is that they create a fog-like condition where it is difficult to discern what is taking place in a given situation. As a result, our interpretations are always shaky. We often end up with an interpretation that falls into one of four categories:

- Head-on: Our interpretation is a precise perception of the reality out there.
- Overstatement: Our interpretation deviates from reality on the upside.
- Understatement: Our interpretation deviates from reality on the downside.
- Totally Irrelevant: Our interpretation missed the reality altogether.

To minimize the above risks, it is crucial to examine the impeding factors of ambiguity, complexity, and uncertainty. The topic of uncertainty was discussed earlier in connection with the topic of sensing future turbulence. The remedy for dealing with uncertainty is to construct alternative scenarios. Once we develop the full range of scenarios, we have in essence reduced the uncertainty. We will have a quasi distribution for the states of the future, which can range from most likely to least likely. This does not eliminate uncertainty altogether, but it is better than having no idea at all. The hope is that the future will turn out to be one of the scenarios that we prepared in advance. We focus here on ambiguity and complexity.

## AMBIGUITY

### Nature of Ambiguity

Ambiguity is a lack of information. It results from the swirls and swirls of motion (rapid, erratic, surpriseful change) inherent in turbulence. These swirls render the human mind unable to grasp what is going on and make sense of it. It creates a fog-like condition where visibility is severely impaired. For example, no CEO knows for sure what customers really want. Take, for example, the case of a newly appointed CEO at a large corporation. One of the first things he or she will need to do is to assess the situation of the corporation. He or she will need considerable data to make this assessment. However, getting all the facts about all of the variables is an impossible task. Sometimes the data are not even collectable (e.g., competitors' strategic intentions and plans). Even if the data are available, it might take a long time to gather; time that turbulence might not allow us to have. Sometimes, the cost of obtaining some or all the information is prohibitive. Even after we obtain all the data, there is the question of how reliable and valid they may be especially if we allow for human error, misinterpretation, organizational politics, etc.

Ambiguity is experienced by the firm in three forms:

- A "Blob": The blob is an irregular, indefinable shape. It can be seen somehow, but it is difficult to ascertain what it is for sure. Take the case of a radically new product. Does it have a market? If so, what are the characteristics of such a market? How big is it? To illustrate, imagine the questions that went through the minds of Steve Jobs and Steve Wozniak while developing the first Apple computer. Could they answer the previous questions? They could not. They only made assumptions (educated guesses) about the market.
- A "Weak Signal": An event might be reported as a happening, but there are only unconfirmed rumors about it. Such is the case when a competitor is plotting to surprise another competitor. The competitor at the receiving end will get strands of news here and there, but it is difficult to "piece them together" into a picture of what the other competitor is up to. Another example is the case of IBM. In the early stages of the spread of Local Area Networks (LANs) of desktop computers, IBM could not tell whether the main frame or the LANs would be the main state of affairs in the marketplace.
- "Mixed Signals": Events produced by turbulence often produce a wide range of conflicting signals that make it hard to determine which state of affairs is prevailing. A competitor, for example, planning to do one thing might decide to leak rumors about something else altogether. Paradoxes are examples of mixed signals. In a paradox, two opposite views appear to be "right" at the same time, which is hard for the mind to reconcile.

### Approaches for Tackling Ambiguity

Ambiguity cannot be eliminated, but it can be clarified. There are some ways of dealing with ambiguity during the interpretation process. A sampling of these approaches is presented next.

## Analysis

Analysis is the dissection of a blob in order to learn more about it. It involves breaking down something to the elements that constitute it. When such dissection is done, it generates new information, mainly details about elements and their interrelationships. This new information helps us to develop a clearer picture of the entity embedded in the respective blob. Analysis is used intensively in the business world. With respect to strategic leadership, many applications of analysis have assumed prominence in the literature. The applications of analysis were presented earlier. These include environmental analysis, industry analysis, SWOT analysis, vulnerability analysis, financial analysis, and issue analysis.

## Pattern Recognition

Pattern recognition is a method for helping us make sense of a series of isolated events or confusing signals. For example, a competitor in the fast food business buying one piece of real estate is a weak signal. What does it mean? However, if the competitor purchased twenty parcels of real estate, a pattern suggests itself, namely, the competitor is getting ready for a preemptive strike.

Pattern recognition involves four steps: identifying signals, plotting signals, categorizing signals, and relating categories to one another. Identifying signals refers to the process of scanning, gathering data, analyzing data, and extracting events contained therein. Plotting involves anchoring a signal to one or more important dimensions, e.g., time and/or space. For example, if the twenty locations purchased by that fast food competitor are plotted on a map and they all fall into one part of the region, the signal becomes clearer, an intent to corner this particular part of the region. If they are scattered, the signal becomes clearer, perhaps indicating intent to encircle an existing competitor. Plotting thus makes a pattern surface.

Categorization refers to the grouping of signals based on some similarity in order to expose the presence of a pattern. A number of signals that are similar with respect to one or more characteristics may form a pattern. For example, one plant shutdown in one area is a signal. However, if several plants in one area are shut down, there might be a pattern there. What do all these shutdowns have in common? When a pattern is extracted, ambiguity has been clarified.

The final step in pattern recognition is relating categories to one another in order to come up with a composite of the total picture that is taking place out there. For example, take "insolvency." Insolvency is a pattern that comprises a number of categories coalescing to create it. The categories (with patterns of their own) are: inventory (declining turnover), receivables (increasing and aging), expenses (increasing, out of line), sales (declining), and losses (increasing). As these factors "hang together," they create a general pattern, an inability to meet current obligations or insolvency.

## Mapping

Mapping is a useful approach for clarifying ambiguity. Mapping enables the interpreter to "see" an entire turbulent situation: the elements that constitute it and how they hang together to make up the situation. Mapping was discussed in Chapter 8.

## Analogy

Ambiguity stems from the fact that a certain entity or object of interest cannot be "seen" directly. One way of making an object "seeable" is to find a known, similar object. Our knowledge of the known object can be transferred to the unknown one, thus increasing our understanding of it. Throughout this work, analogies have been used extensively. Porter's concept of value chain is an example of analogy. In this case, the concept "chain" is used as an analogue to represent the interconnectedness among the activities of the business firm.

Business executives utilize analogy as a way of understanding and communicating concepts. In Chapter 2, we saw Stayer using "a herd of buffalo" as an analogy for the CEO-led organization. His concept of the organization is built around the analogy of the employee-led organization as "a flock of geese." He used each analogy to represent a different type of organizational reality. The analogies helped us understand each type of organization.

Analogies also help in clarifying "what-if" questions. A balance sheet is an analogue of the firm. One can make decisions, by manipulating the analogue, i.e., by changing various variables on the balance sheet to find out what the consequences might be. The financial positions resulting from implementing all of these manipulations would clarify the issue of what would become of the firm if certain actions were carried out.

## Modeling and Simulation

A model is a representation of a certain reality. "Reality" is always invisible to us. If we can represent it in a visual manner, we will be able to "see" this reality and ambiguity will be clarified. A model, in its crudest form, is a number of elements that are thought to exist in a certain situation and how they hang together to make up the phenomenon of interest. Models are commonplace in the business world. An income statement is a model of a firm's performance. A balance sheet is a model of the firm's financial position. Econometric models are applied widely to macroeconomics as a way of understanding the dynamics of the economy. Statistical models are applied to quality and process control. Porter's portrayal of the dynamics of an industry and the value chain analysis are applications of modeling.

Models can be constructed in three ways. Quantitative models utilize mathematics and statistics in model building. They describe relationships in the form of tested equations. Qualitative models describe the elements and how they hang together in descriptive, verbal terms. Diagramming can be used to construct visual models. A diagram of a process is a model.

Once a model is constructed, it can be used to clarify further ambiguities with respect to the possible behavior of the elements of the model. This is accomplished by means of simulation. To use an analogy, simulation is like test-driving the model. By changing assumptions and parameters of relationships, one can observe what may happen. "Financial scenarios" are examples of simulation. By changing assumptions about revenues and expenses, one can find out what the income statement and the balance sheet would be like under different sets of assumptions. Thus, if one enters the pessimistic estimates of revenues and expenses, the resulting income statement and balance sheet will reflect the worst-case scenario. By entering optimistic assumptions, the resulting financial statements will represent the best-case scenario. By examining several possibilities, a simulation allows us to plot a range of concepts of the reality "out there." It is somewhere in this range. Knowing this is a considerable improvement over taking a stab in the dark.

## Consensus Methods

Consensus is another approach for clarifying ambiguities. If a number of knowledgeable persons examine a certain fuzzy situation, each will view it from a different perspective. When these perspectives are put together, a composite may emerge. The composite will be a better or clearer picture than the initial one. That is how consensus clarifies ambiguity. Brainstorming is a technique for teasing out the dimensions of an ambiguous entity. Discussion, with a moderator, is another way of bringing about consensus and clarification. A well-known consensus seeking technique is the "Delphi Method" described in the previous chapter.

# COMPLEXITY

## Nature of Complexity

The second obstacle in interpreting turbulence is the problem of complexity. Complexity occurs in two ways. First, the forces of turbulence behave in complex ways, e.g., continuously branching out in a manner that defies tracking them to get the total picture. Second, the forces of turbulence are also part of a bigger set of variables that are part of a larger set of variables and so on indefinitely because the universe defies bounding. The mind cannot come to grips with this multitude of factors that defy definition; hence complexity. This interconnection of everything with everything else overwhelms the human mind. Nothing is as simple as it seems. Exhibit 10.1 presents an analysis of the concept "complexity" showing its various aspects.

1. Behavioral Complexity:

   The factors that drive turbulence behave in the form of swirls and swirls of motion. These factors behave in chaotic manners. We have one blip after another, up and down in an irregular fashion. Look, for example, at a chart of the stock prices over a period of ten years, the ups and downs and the reversals. Behavioral complexity can be reduced by some of the approaches mentioned above in connection with clarifying ambiguity. Examples of such methods include:

   - Mapping: Charting and plotting are useful for visualizing behavioral complexity. It makes complexity understandable.
   - Modeling: Statistical models such as multiple regression are useful for cutting through behavioral complexity, e.g., curve fitting.

2. Multi-Factor Complexity:

   The source of complexity comes from the interconnectedness of everything in the universe. As it organizes some perception of what is going on around it, thousands of factors come into play. A strike by a major trucking company will shut down supermarkets, factories, retail chains, which in turn will cause shutdowns among their suppliers, and the suppliers of those suppliers and so on in an endless chain of events.

   Because of this interconnectedness, there is always a large number of factors in any situation. This creates two further aspects of multiple-factor complexity:

   - The "Too Many Factors" Problem. In some situations, the number of factors involved can be accounted for, but they are too numerous to accommodate in one

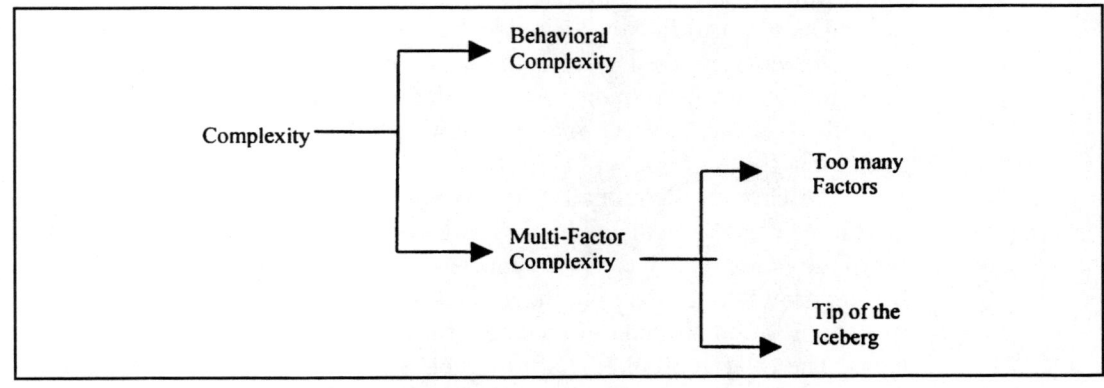

Exhibit 10.1: The Concept of Complexity

coherent perception. Imagine reading an inventory list of a department store or supermarket. There are over 300,000 items coupled with the behavior of their individual sales inventories. Along the same line, consider the problem of the CEO of a diversified conglomerate that has 30 or 40 strategic business units (SBU's). Each SBU has a number of factors that describe its performance, from market share to financial performance indicators. Looking at a printout of all these units, how can the mind come up with a total picture of the company's position as a whole? It is overwhelming.

- The "Tip of the Iceberg" Problem. In other situations, the large number of factors involved may be too numerous to comprehend. Consequently, we are only able to account for a few of them and the rest lurk in our "ignorance zone," and often surprise us. The danger here is that we see only the "tip of the iceberg." At any moment, the firm is bound to collide with the rest of the iceberg.

We will focus here on the multi-factor aspect of complexity. Multi-factor complexity is the more serious issue since it leads to paralysis and surprises.

## Reduction: An Approach for Tackling the "Too Many Factors" Complexity

The main approach for dealing with multi-factor complexity is reduction. Reduction approaches are commonplace in business life. The following is a quick survey of three of the popular reduction approaches, namely, cataloguing, exposing underpinnings, and modeling.

### Cataloguing/Categorization

When faced with a large number of factors, one can examine them singularly and then group them based on some similarity into categories. Immediately, the number of categories is much smaller than the total number of items. Complexity has thus been reduced. We are all familiar with the applications of categorization, e.g., categories of accounts in the balance sheet. Accounts are grouped into the groups called cash, inventory, and receivables. These are then further grouped into one category, current assets. As another illustration, consider the concept of strategic groups. A "Strategic Groups Map" is a straightforward application of reduction, using cataloging and categorization.[1] The strategic group map idea was discussed in Chapter 8.

Multi-business companies pose a complexity problem that has been dealt with through reduction. A firm might have 30 or 40 strategic business units. Each unit has a large number of characteristics. To hold the reign on all these businesses, the leader needs to reduce all the details into a manageable number that allows him or her to deal with each SBU as well as the firm as a whole. Reduction was applied to solve this problem. First, the SBUs were viewed as a "portfolio" of businesses rather than a large number of singular units. Second, a portfolio was perceived as a two-dimensional matrix (2x2 or 3x3) with each dimension representing a relevant property. One of the most well-known portfolio models is the Boston Consulting Group's (BCG) matrix, known simply as the growth-share matrix. It is illustrated in Exhibit 10.2.

The Growth-Share matrix has two dimensions. The x-axis represents the relative market share. This is calculated by dividing our firm's sales by the sales of the leading competitor in the industry. It has two categories: high (more than one), and low (less than one). The market growth rate is simply the annual percent of increase in the overall sales of the industry. This is often plotted in two categories: high (more than 10%) and low (less than 10 percent). The relative market share of each SBU and its market's growth rates are then computed. Each SBU will then have a pair of ratings. The pair of ratings is then entered in the

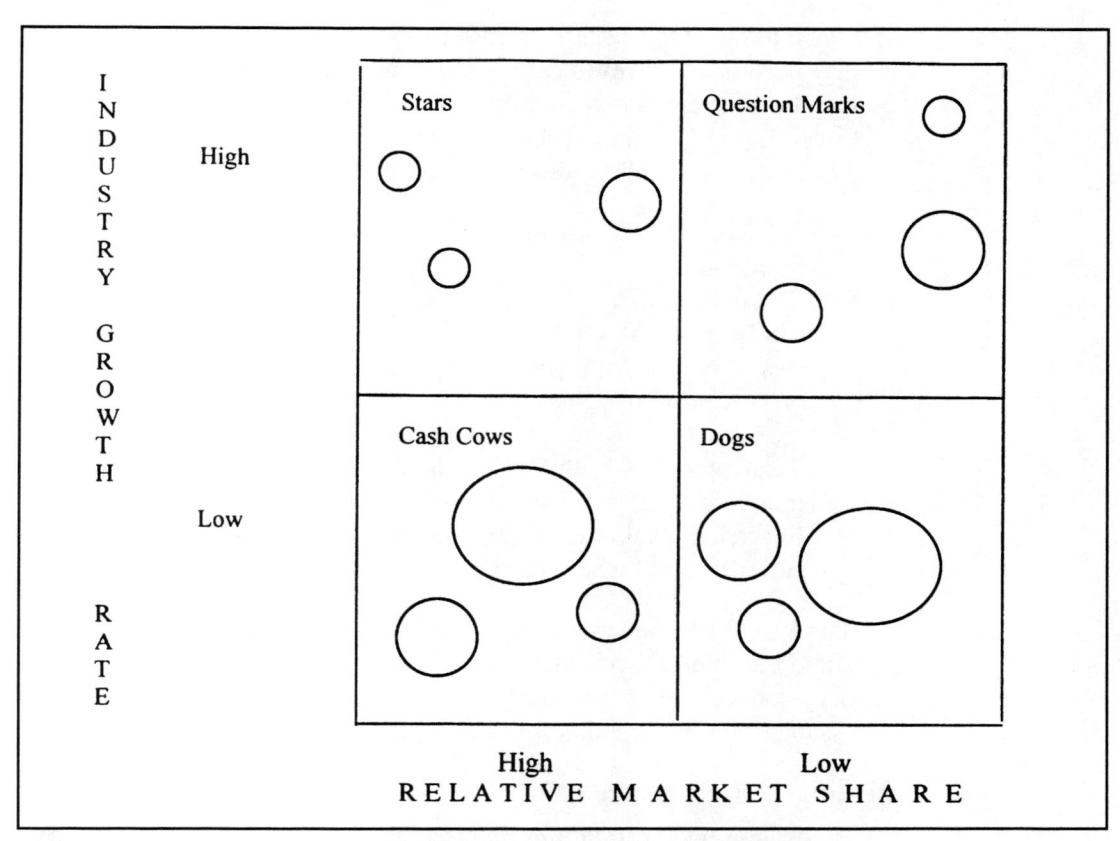

Exhibit 10.2: The BCG Growth-Share Matrix: An Application of Reduction

BCG chart. However, rather than entering the pair as one point, it is entered as a circle representing the sales volume of the SBU.

The matrix comprises four quadrants. The content of each is then characterized as follows:

- High growth, high relative market share: SBU's in this quadrant are labeled "stars." This combination has certain "cash generation" connotations: the SBU is neither a pure user nor a generator of cash.
- Low growth, high relative market share: An SBU here has a high market share in a declining industry. The firm has somewhat of a monopoly that translates into "cash generation." Therefore, SBUs in this quadrant are labeled "cash cows."
- High growth, low relative market share: An SBU in this quadrant exist in a promising industry but it is weak judging by market share. It is a cash generator. The market is yet to materialize. It can be in an industry that is in the early growth stages. That is why SBUs in this category are labeled "problem children or question marks." These are "tomorrow's businesses."
- Low growth, low relative market share: SBUs here are weak and exist in a declining industry. They are cash users. Hence, they are labeled "dogs."

The vast data about the multitude of SBUs have now been reduced to four groups with a few, but critical, common characteristics. This, in turn, facilitates decision making about each SBU and the portfolio as a whole. Because of the cash use/cash generation patterns, the matrix has implications for bringing about a satisfactory portfolio. Theoretically, the leader is expected to move the cash from cash cows to stars (in order to finance their growth so that they may become tomorrow's cash cows), and to question marks (to fund their growth so that they may become tomorrow's stars). "Dogs" are to be divested since they do not contribute to the overall cash position of the conglomerate.

Further, the portfolio now can be described as a structure composed of the following:

- Number: This is the number of SBUs in the portfolio and the number of SBUs in each quadrant.
- Diversity: the distribution of the SBUs over a number of industries. The diversity can be minimal when the SBUs are related to one another according to some common denominator (synergy) such as ultimate customer, technology, process, and so on. It can be maximal as in the case of unrelated diversification where the SBUs are in totally different, unconnected industries.
- Relative size of each SBU in the four quadrants. A large relative size of cash users indicates the portfolio as a whole will be a cash user.
- Interrelationships among the SBUs in the quadrants. A central relationship is "cross subsidization" where cash cows subsidize question marks and stars.

The BCG matrix is not the only model. There are other matrices like the GE/McKenzie matrix and the Shell Directional Policy matrix. They use different dimensions and different categories for each. However, the idea is the same: to reduce the masses of data about SBUs into a manageable picture that facilitates perception at a glance.

### Exposing Underpinnings

By examining several items and relating them to one another (i.e., exposing their association), we might discover that one factor is common to all of them. It underlies them. It drives them. In this case, we need to deal with this one factor instead of many. Statistical techniques such as regression analysis and correlation help us in weeding out factors that do not affect the dependent variable. Factor analysis and cluster analysis use association among variables to reduce them to a small number of factors or clusters respectively.

### Model Building

Modeling is a popular approach for reducing complexity. A model is an abstraction (a reduction) derived from considerable detail. We have already seen some of the applications of modeling in reducing complexity, e.g., Porter's model of industry structure (industry analysis), Porter's strategic groups map, and the BCG Growth-Share matrix. Quantitative models are well known for the use of mathematics as shorthand that reduces complicated phenomena to a few equations.

## Approaches for Dealing with "Tip-of-the-Iceberg" Complexity

As defined earlier, the problem is that there are too many factors, and many of them remain concealed by turbulence. There are three approaches for dealing with this type of complexity: analysis, causal analysis, and group methods. Each will be described briefly below since some of their applications have been introduced earlier.

### Analysis

Analysis means dissection. Dissection begins by breaking an entity into the main parts that constitute it. The main parts are then dissected into "minor" parts. The minor parts are then dissected into more minute parts. If the process is repeated, then we will end up with considerable detail. At this point, the rest of the iceberg will become apparent. Environmental analysis is an application of analysis that exposes the rest of the iceberg. By dissecting the concept "environment" into several spheres around the firm (economic, social, political, etc.), and then dissecting each sphere further, a multitude of factors becomes apparent.

### Causal Analysis

A useful application of analysis in this context is "causal analysis." In causal analysis, we begin with whatever developments we are encountering, but then view them as "symptoms." We next ask what caused the symptoms. We will have some other developments that caused the symptoms. Then again, what caused these "causes"? We repeat the process until we can no longer find any further cause. These will be the "root" causes. The set of "root causes" is the hidden part of the iceberg.

### Group Approaches

Some of the group approaches mentioned in connection with clarifying ambiguity can also be used for teasing out a situation to expose the remainder of the iceberg. Brainstorming is particularly helpful. When a number of individuals look at a situation, each will have a different interpretation of it. When all these interpretations are put together, more dimensions of the situation will surface, including the hidden parts.

The Delphi method can also be applied here. However, the rounds can focus on interpretation (what is happening and why is it happening). The final round often reveals some stability in interpretations. A consensus might emerge. This is the point where the hidden part of the iceberg is exposed.

# A FRAMEWORK FOR TURBULENCE INTERPRETATION: ISSUES ANALYSIS

To overcome the above barriers, we propose issues analysis as a framework for organizing and integrating the turbulence interpretation activities. Although it is time consuming, it is worth the effort. The alternative to issues analysis is to jump to conclusions intuitively. The risk in jumping to conclusions is seeing *only* the tip of the iceberg and missing the rest of it. Our perception of the situation will be distorted and our response will address only the surface issues. Issue analysis forces us to examine the whole iceberg. The unit of issue analysis is the "issue." We begin by exploring this concept.

## THE CONCEPT OF ISSUES

According to Brown: "An issue is a condition or pressure, either internal or external to an organization, that, if it continues, will have a significant effect on the functioning of the organization or its future interests."[2] Brown further distinguishes between an issue and a trend: "A trend is an environmental force that may or may not germinate into an issue."[3] We build on Brown's definition to develop the following definition of the term issue: *An issue is the implication(s) of a relevant event, development, or a trend*. Some definition of terms is in order. The critical term here is "implications." An implication is a strategic impact, something that will alter the firm in a significant manner, negatively or positively. An impact can be negative or adverse amounting to a loss of some sort. Alternatively, it can be positive, i.e., an improvement in the bottom line signaling the presence of a major opportunity for the firm. If an event, development, or trend has no implications for the firm, then it does not pose an issue. For example, the entry of a large competitor in the firm's market might be an issue or a non-issue depending on its implications. If the large competitor is more powerful, it will likely take away the firm's market share. Clearly, this event will have implications for or impacts on the firm, i.e., negative change in sales and profits. However, if our firm's position is invincible (e.g., protected by patents or highly sophisticated competencies), then the entry of the competitor is a "non-issue." If the competitor is big enough and is in the habit of aggressive advertising, the entry might be a good thing, an opportunity. This is how Apple Computer viewed IBM's entry in the PC market in the 1980s. IBM's investment and weight were bound to expand the desktop computer market for everyone, including Apple.

## Anatomy of an Issue

If we analyze this thing called "issue" we will find that it has eight elements: source, content, location on the cause-and-effect chain, timing, duration, focus of impact, magnitude of impact, and likelihood of impact.[4] These are defined next.

1. Source or Driving Force: Every issue has a source or a driving force, the behavior of which created the event, development, or trend that became an issue.
2. Content or Inherent Character: Every issue has a content or character in terms of its implications for the firm. The content of an issue may fall into one of these five categories:

- Problem: The implication (of a given event, development, or trend) is negative or devastating to the firm, e.g., an obstruction such as a restrictive law might make it illegal for the firm to do business.
- Opportunity: The implication (of a given event, development, or trend) is positive for the firm, i.e., the firm has a strong chance to increase its sales volume, market share, and profitability. For example, the emergence of a new market segment (Internet shoppers) promises more sales for small retailers. The development of a new technology might present an opportunity in the form of cost reduction or introducing new superior products. Generally speaking, an opportunity pertains to a vacuum(s) or pockets of demand in the marketplace.
- Threat: This is a potential negative impact of a particular future event, development, or trend. The impact is not here now but will most likely occur in the visible future. For example, the entry of a new substitute for our product is a threat. Threats will become problems in the future if they are not acted upon now.
- Strength: A strength is the positive implication of an internal development inside the firm that enables the firm to increase sales, market share and profits. This development results in the firm possessing a weapon-like item that it can use to exploit opportunities or evade threats. For example, if a specialized competence evolves inside the firm, it can be used as a competitive advantage in the marketplace, e.g., a pharmaceutical company having an R&D process that consistently results in discovering drugs with wide market appeal. A firm that has a leverage that it can exploit to constrain its competitor has a strength in the form of this leverage, e.g., Microsoft using WINDOWS as a leverage against competing software firms.
- Weakness: A weakness is the negative impact of an internal development or condition that weakens the firm's market position and causes it to lose sales, market share, and profits. Furthermore, a weakness inhibits and obstructs the firm's effort in responding fruitfully to turbulence. It is worth noting that a weakness, if not addressed, is a problem in waiting. Examples of weaknesses include management inability to provide effective leadership to the people, obsolete equipment, ineffectiveness, and operational inefficiency.

3. Location on the Cause-Effect Chain: An issue does not exist in a vacuum. It is part of a chain of issues. Some issues cause other issues. Take the case of shortage of working capi-

tal, which leads to another issue, "insolvency." In this case, insolvency is a symptom of working capital shortage. However, is working capital shortage a symptom or an effect of something else? Changes in market demographics? Changes in the firm's operational system or equipment? Poor management?

4. Timing or Stage: At any given point in time, an issue can be in one of three stages:

- Current: The issue is taking place at the present.
- Emerging: The issue is in the earliest stages of its existence, perhaps appearing as a weak signal that is expected to gather momentum in the near future and become a full-fledged issue. For example, sporadic shortages of cash represent an emerging issue, e.g., insolvency.
- Future: The issue is anchored to a future event, a development, or a trend and hence it will materialize in the near or distant future. For example, we might not have a shortage of working capital now, but if we are expecting to land a large order that will call for huge outlays, it goes without saying that capital shortage will be an issue that we will face at the time of manufacturing and delivering this order.

5. Duration: Every issue has duration. Some have a short life span, e.g., sporadic cash flow shortages. Others persist for a long time, e.g., the maturation of an industry or issues stemming from damaging the environment for chemical firms.

6. Magnitude of Impact: Every issue has an impact that varies in degree. Some might have a negligible impact, e.g. effects of tobacco on lung cancer for automobile manufacturers. Some have a massive impact, e.g., concern for the environment for automakers. Impact is crucial for pinpointing issues. Clearly, an event or a development with a negligible impact on the firm is not an issue for its decision makers. However, if the impact is massive, then we have an issue on our hands.

7. Locus of Impact: An issue's impact has a point where it hits. The important question here is the scope of the impact. If the issue affects only one area of the business, then it has a limited impact. Another issue might have a "global" impact in that it impacts on the firm in its entirety and these are the ones that concern the CEO. The "local" ones are referred to the appropriate unit in the firm.

8. Likelihood of Impact: The fact that an issue has an impact, even if it is serious, does not make it a full-fledged issue. The likelihood of impact derives from the likelihood of the respective event or development itself. Thus, if a development has a great impact, but it is unlikely to happen, then there is no issue in this case.

## What Makes an Issue Strategic?

Not all issues are strategic. A crucial task in interpreting turbulence is to determine and segregate strategic from non-strategic issues. An issue is strategic if it meets all the following conditions:

- It should cause or drive other issues.
- It has a highly likely, major impact on all or most aspects of the firm.
- The impact will last over a number of time horizons—a long run impact.
- Responding to the issue calls for a major change in the company's pattern of existence (most or all of its sub-patterns).
- Responding to the issue calls for a major allocation of resources in an irreversible manner (i.e., once committed the resources cannot be recovered and redeployed back to cash in the short term).

An issue that does not meet all the above criteria, even if it is important, will not be deemed strategic. As such, it is not in the domain of strategic leadership because it does not involve the firm in its entirety. Perhaps it affects one or more parts (e.g., marketing, finance, or production) of the firm. In this case, it is referred to the respective part(s) to deal with it.

### Writing up an Issue Statement

Issues are abstract thoughts. They need to be written up in business English. An issue statement has two components: (1) a description of *the event, development, or trend* itself, and (2) a *specific description of its implication*(s) for the firm. One needs to be very specific about each of these descriptions. In writing up the issue statement, one must incorporate the eight elements mentioned above. Here is an example:

> *"Company X announced its intention to enter our market this fall. Company X is a giant in its field with assets of $x billions and a dominant market share (60%). It has excess cash flows estimated to be $x billion. Our company is much smaller. When Company X enters the market, it plans to offer the customer a much superior product (with such and such specifications) at a price 20% below ours. X% of our customers are expected to switch. Our gross sales will decline by 30%. Our margins will decline by about 50%. Our net profit will decline by 40%. Our product-market position stands to be wiped out. In the span of three years, we might eventually be squeezed out of the market."*

As stated above, the activities involved in interpreting data centered around the extraction and definition of strategic issues. Below is a methodology for extracting strategic issues. It can be used as a framework for organizing the self-organizing system's turbulence interpretation pattern.

## ISSUES ANALYSIS METHODOLOGY

A model of extracting strategic issues (from turbulence data, present and future) is presented in Exhibit 10.3. It comprises three main phases: (1) developing an issues pool; (2) extracting strategic issues through impact analysis; and (3) prioritization and diagnosis.

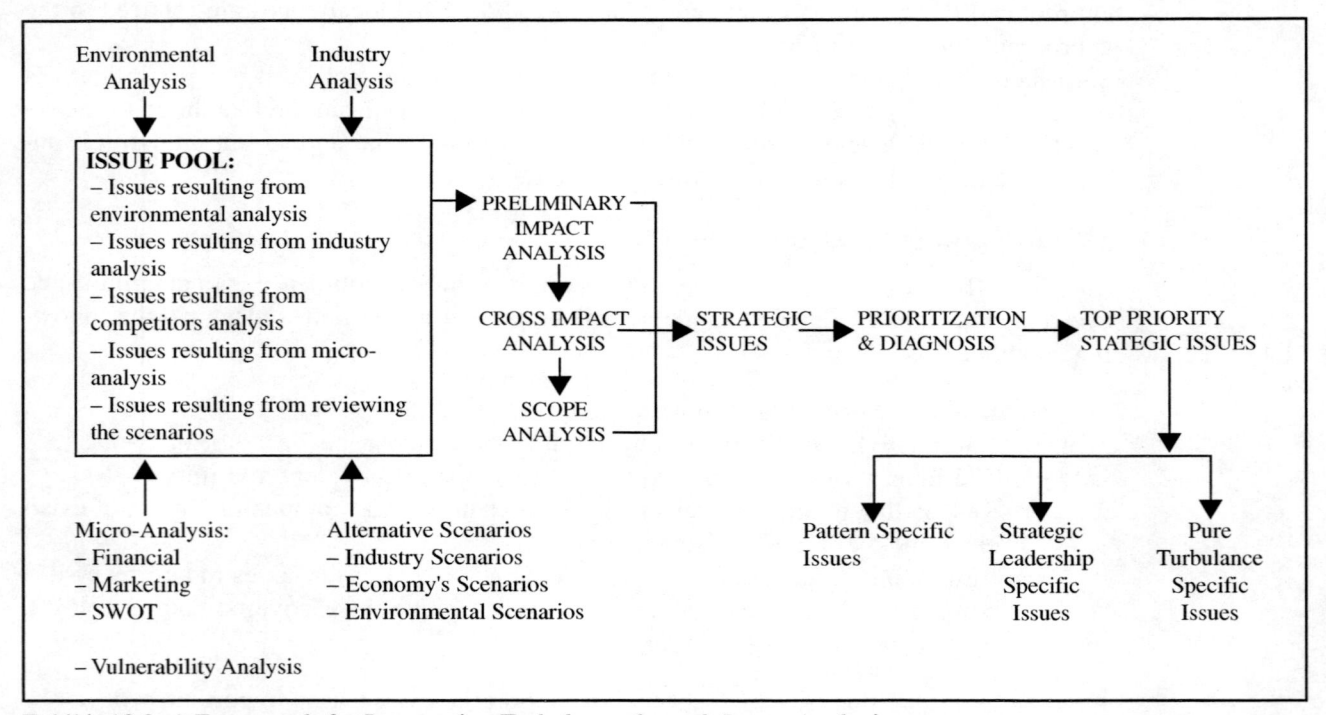

Exhibit 10.3: A Framework for Interpreting Turbulence through Issues Analysis

## Phase I: Developing the Issue Pool

The outputs of sensing present and future turbulence are sets of data (environmental analysis, industry analysis, firm or internal analysis, and alternate scenarios). These sets contain events, developments, and trends that are prevailing now and those that are most likely to take hold in the future. The first step in issue analysis is to identify the issues by constructing an issue pool as shown in Exhibit 10.4. This is accomplished by taking each event, development, or trend and then identifying its impact (if any) on the firm. Events, developments, or trends that have an impact will go into the issue pool. The rest will be thrown out of the analysis. In constructing the issue pool, we will be guided by this model:

> **An issue = [an event, development, or trend + its implications for the firm]**

The issue pool at this point will be brimming with various issues that take the form of problems, opportunities, threats, strengths, and weaknesses. The issue pool would comprise issues coming from many sources as follows:

- Issues that resulted from conducting a macro-environmental analysis.
- Issues that resulted from doing an industry analysis and competitor analysis.
- Issues resulting from performing an internal analysis of the firm, including SWOT analysis, financial analysis, vulnerability analysis, etc.
- Issues that the scenarios for the future suggest, especially the industry scenarios.

To develop an issue pool, the worksheet in Exhibit 10.4 was prepared. Column 1 is reserved for descriptions of the identified events, developments, and trends and their source (environmental analysis, industry analysis, internal analysis, and scenarios). Column 2 is reserved for identifying the impacts of each event, development, or trend. The impact must be described in clear terms with continuous reference to the bottom line. If an event, development, or a trend has a clearly identifiable impact on the firm's bottom line, it will be easy to decide whether it is an issue or not. In column 3, the event, development, or trend *along with* its impact is categorized in one of five categories, "problem," "threat," "opportunity," "strength," or "weakness." Column 4 is reserved for the decision whether the event development or trend along with its impacts are accepted as an issue (column 4.a) or a non-issue (4.b) from a "corporate" point of view. In the final analysis, the *issues in column 4.a are the ones that constitute the issue pool.* They will be carried forward to the next stage in issue analysis. Non-issues will be sent to the appropriate department to address them or even ignored altogether depending on the situation.

The issue pool (column 4.a.) might turn out to be a long one. Given time and resource limitations, the leadership cannot respond to all of them. They must be scrutinized further and reduced in an effort to identify the strategic ones. This is the subject of the next phase.

## Phase II: Impact Analysis

Once the issues pool is compiled, the next step is to sift through it to extract the "strategic" issues. The issues in the pool are then subjected to further reduction through impact analysis. Impact analysis takes three successive phases: (1) preliminary impact analysis, (2) cross-impact analysis, and (3) scope analysis.

### 1. Preliminary Impact Analysis

Preliminary impact analysis is a procedure for sorting issues by magnitude of impact and likelihood of impact. The procedure is illustrated in Exhibit 10.5. The purpose here is to

| Description of Event, Development, or Trend (1) | Description of Implications for the Firm (2) | Categorization (3) ||||| Decision (4) ||
|---|---|---|---|---|---|---|---|---|
| | | Problem. (3.a) | Oppty. (3.b) | Threat (3.c) | Strgth (3.d) | Weakness (3.e) | Issue (4.a) | Non-issue (4.b) |
| **From Environmental Analysis** (Ch. 8)<br>• xxx<br>• xxx<br>• xxx.<br>• Etc. | • xxxxxxxxxx<br>• xxxxxxxxxx<br>• xxxxxxxxxx<br>• xxxxxxxxx | X | X | X | | X | X | X<br>X |
| **From Industry Analysis** (Ch. 8)<br>• yyy<br>• yyy<br>• yyy<br>• Etc. | • yyyyyyy<br>• yyyyyyy<br>• yyyyyyy<br>• yyyyyyy | X<br>X | | X<br>X | | | X<br>X<br>X | X |
| **From Micro-Analysis** (Ch. 8)<br>• zzz<br>• zzz<br>• zzz<br>• Etc. | • zzzzzzzz<br>• zzzzzzzzz<br>• zzzzzzzz<br>• zzzzzzzz | | | | X<br>X | X<br><br><br>X | X<br>X<br><br>X | X |
| **From Scenarios** (Ch. 9)<br>• www<br>• www<br>• www<br>• Etc. | • wwwwww<br>• wwwwww<br>• wwwwwww<br>• wwwwwww | X<br><br><br>X | X<br>X | | | | <br><br>X<br>X | X<br>X |

Exhibit 10.4: An Illustration of the Construction of an Issue Pool

isolate the high impact/high likelihood issues so that they may be addressed adequately and on time. No firm has all the needed resources to address every issue. We need to focus our resources on the truly critical issues.

The first column in Exhibit 10.5 is a listing of all the issue statements (positive and negative) in the issue pool. The second column is a subjective quantification of the magnitude of the impact of the issue on a scale from 1 to 10, where "1" represents minimum impact and "10" represents maximum impact. We can use + or – to indicate the direction of the impact, whether positive or negative respectively. As we rate the magnitude of impact, we should consider it from the perspective of the total company. We are interested in issues that impact the company in its entirety. Such issues are in the domain of strategic leadership. Lesser issues might belong to a different level in the organization, the unit level, for example.

The third column is a subjective estimate of the likelihood of the rated magnitude. This can range from "0" (no chance it will happen) to "1" (will happen for sure). Fractions reflect likelihood ratings that are in between. These estimates reflect individual interpretations of the data. The scoring should be a group exercise to reflect many different perspectives. When done in a group, the relevant average here is the mode, not the arithmetic mean. The mode is a better measure of consensus. The mode for the group for each issue is then entered in the matrix.

The fourth column is the product of multiplying column two by column three. This score becomes the combined index of the importance of the issue. It is used for ranking the issues so that the unimportant ones can be weeded out. Issues that have a high score, whether

| Issue | (1) Impact [Scale: 1–10] | (2) Probability of Occurrence [Scale: 0.0–1.0] | (3) Impact Index [Impact × Probability] | (4) Ranking (Using a cut-off score of 4) |
|---|---|---|---|---|
| ABC | −8.8 | 0.3 | −2.64 | 5 |
| DEF | +6.7 | 0.7 | +4.69 | 3 |
| GHI | −4.4 | 0.9 | −3.96 | 4 |
| JKL | +9.0 | 0.8 | +7.2 | 1 |
| MNO | −8 | 0.8 | −6.4 | 2 |

Exhibit 10.5: Illustration of Preliminary Impact Analysis

positive or negative, are viewed as important. The question here is how high should a score be in order for an issue to qualify as having a high impact and a high likelihood. It is useful here to use a cut-off score to reflect what is considered high or low. If one uses a cut-off score of four, then the issues above this score are accepted as important issues. They are then transferred to the next step in issue analysis, i.e., to cross impact analysis. Issues with scores below the cut-off score are dealt with differently depending on their nature. If they have the potential of being important, we can keep them in a certain list, issues to watch. They can also be referred to the appropriate unit in the company to deal with. Alternatively, we might decide to ignore them altogether. The result of sorting various issues based on their individual impacts and likelihood is a matrix like the one shown in Exhibit 10.6.

## 2. Cross Impact Analysis

The previous step singled out the issues that have a high impact/high likelihood combination and ranked them in a descending order. In this step, we take the issues that lie above the cut-off score and subject them to cross impact analysis. To do so, we first array them as rows in a matrix. Next, we array them as the columns in the same matrix. This is shown in Exhibit 10.7. We then take each row issue and consider its impact on the column issue. We assign a value to this impact as a number on a scale ranging from 1–10. We can still attach a sign + or − to indicate the direction of the impact. To illustrate, suppose the row issue was shortage of working capital and the column issue was declining sales. What impact does the

|  |  | MAGNITUDE OF IMPACT | |
|---|---|---|---|
|  |  | High | Low |
| LIKELIHOOD OF IMPACT | High | Issue x / Issue y | Issue / Issue |
|  | Low | Issue / Issue | Issue / Issue |

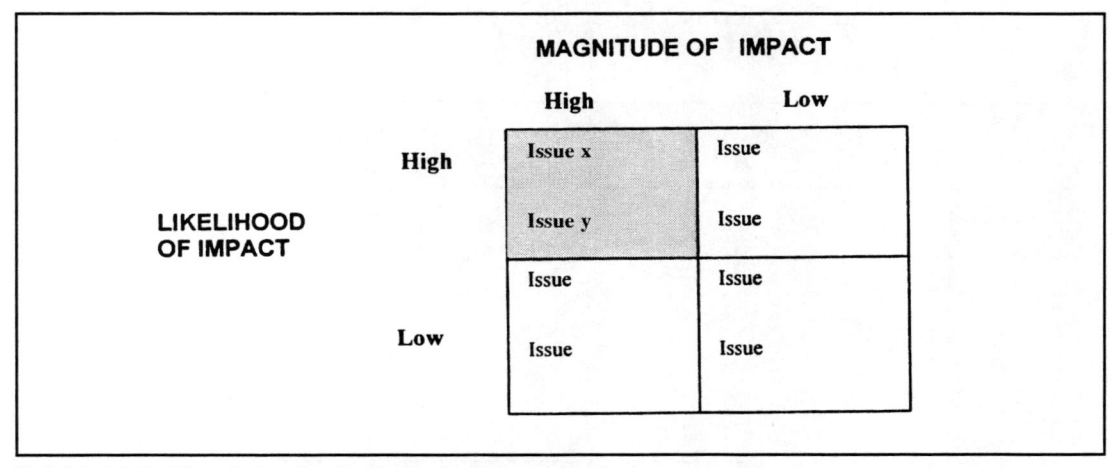

Exhibit 10.6: Visualizing the Preliminary Impact Analysis

shortage of working capital have on the declining sales? We might decide that the impact is very high and negative, since shortage of working capital inhibits spending on advertising on sales promotion; and this leads to a further decline in sales. We can then give such an impact a rating of –8, or even –10. Rating the issues can be done individually or by a group of knowledgeable persons. The average for the group for each issue is entered in the matrix. The mode is a better average than the arithmetic mean because it is a good measure of consensus. Again, a cut-off score must be determined by the group doing the analysis in order to establish what a strong impact is. For example, is a score of 5 acceptable as a strong impact? Some people might insist on at least 7.

The purpose of this kind of analysis is to identify the issues that impact on other issues. If a certain row issue impacts heavily on a number of column issues, this raises the possibility of an association among them. If they are closely associated, chances are they have a more fundamental issue that drives them. What can this root issue be? Knowing the root issue is important. It is new information about the rest of the iceberg. It helps in diagnosis. The row and column issues are symptoms; the root issue is the disease. This finding is very important. If we are to stop the symptoms from recurring, we must tackle this disease. This will point our decision-making (and eventually our strategic response) in the right direction. For example, if the shortage of working capital (column issue) is the effect of a poor cash budgeting system (row issue), then we must fix this system if we are to avoid the recurrence of working capital shortages in the future. The separation of the root issues from their surface issues has significant implications for planning our response to them. Our response will have to be a two-pronged plan of action that contains two concurrent tracks. The first is the *short-term* response track and it addresses the symptom issues. The second is the *long-term* response track and it deals with the root issues. It is more economical to manipulate the root issue. Tackling this one issue means dealing with all the surface ones at the same time, since they are derivatives of it.

To help extract root issues, we form clusters from the interrelated issues. Thus, each row issue and the column issues that are highly associated with it form a cluster. Once we isolate cluster, we begin the search for a root issue. It is possible that we will find none. In this case, all the issues are stand-alone, so to speak. It is possible that we find one or more. There can be more than one root issue. When we find a root issue(s), we add it to the list of issues and carry all of them to the next step in the analysis, scope analysis.

The challenge here is pinpointing clusters and interpreting them. To identify clusters, we scan the rows in the matrix of Exhibit 10.7. In each row, the presence of high ratings indicates a cluster. For example, in the first row, we observe the ratings 8.8 (for column issue Def), 9.0 (for column issue Jkl), and 7.8 (for column issue Nnn). Clearly, issues Abc, Def, Jkl, and Nnn form a cluster. The high ratings indicate that they are closely related somehow.

| Issue | Abc | Def | Ghi | Issue Jkl | ... | ... | Nnn |
|---|---|---|---|---|---|---|---|
| *Abc* | — | 8.8 | 1.2 | 9.0 | ... | ... | 7.8 |
| *Def* |  | — | 7.3 | 3.4 | ... | ... | 8.9 |
| *Ghi* |  |  | — | 7.6 | ... | ... | 1.9 |
| *Jkl* |  |  |  | — | ..... | ... | 9.2 |
| ... |  |  |  |  | — |  | ... |
| ... |  |  |  |  |  | — | .... |
| *Nnn* |  |  |  |  |  |  | — |

Exhibit 10.7: Illustration of Cross-Impact Analysis

Next, what do we make of this? To interpret this information, we eyeball the four issues to see if the row issue Abc is the one that drives them. If this is the case, then Abc is the cause or the root issue. If we cannot determine that issue Abc is the cause, then we take all four of them together and see if they are driven by another factor that is not in our analysis so far. In this case, we try to discover what this new cause might be. This new factor must be added to our analysis as a new issue to be carried to the next step. To illustrate, suppose a row issue like working capital shortage impacts heavily on the column issues of "declining sales," "bulging finished goods inventory," "soaring short term debt," and "chronic budget overruns." Clearly all four issues form a cluster. We next ask the question: what can be causing or driving all of them? What is the common thread? We might infer that our budgetary system is the culprit. In this case, we now add a new issue to the analysis, the budgetary system as a root issue. What about row issues that do not have an impact on other issues? Dealing with such issues calls for considerable judgment. Since such issues have a highly likely significant impact, we cannot ignore them. We treat them as stand-alone issues and transfer them to the next step, scope analysis.

The output of the cross impact analysis will be as follows:

- A number of clusters where the row issue is the root one.
- A number of clusters that do not have row issues as their roots, but they have root issues that we inferred.
- A number of stand alone issues, the ones for which we could not identify root issues.

## 3. Scope Analysis

In this analysis, we take the issues that resulted from the cross impact analysis and assess the extent or scope of their impact on the firm in its entirety. The purpose here is to identify issues that impact the firm in its entirety for they are what we call strategic issues. The sufficient and necessary condition for an issue to be strategic is that it must affect the firm in its entirety (given that it has a high impact, high likelihood, and its impact affects other issues). Issues that have a limited scope are important, but not strategic. They are referred to the appropriate area or department in the firm to deal with them.

The typical firm consists of a number of functions that constitute its business activities, e.g., the component of the value chain in Porter's model presented in Chapter 8. Examples of the functions include: marketing (sales, pricing, promotion, distribution, and so on), production (operations planning, equipment, quality control, and so on), human resources (hiring, structure, morale, etc.), and financing (raising capital, capital allocation, working capital management, and the like). Other aspects of the company can be added as well, including strategic position, supplier relations, financial position, and so on.

In conducting a scope analysis, we construct a two dimensional matrix (Exhibit 10.8). On the y-axis (rows), the issues that made it through the cross impact analysis are listed. On the x-axis (columns), the various facets or aspects of the firm's operations and organization are listed. Each major facet column can be further subdivided into sub-columns, one for each of the sub-areas under the main area. For example, the column for the major aspect marketing can be split into sub-aspects, one for each of customers, product-market scope, channel relations, distribution system, pricing, and the like.

In the cells, we enter the rating of the impact of each row issue on each of the facet columns. The rating is a number ranging from plus/minus 1–10, depending on the direction of the impact. If the row issue does not impact the facet column at all, we assign it a rating of zero. The sign + or – is used only to indicate the direction of the impact. However, the signs will not be factored in our calculations. They are only included to show how the issue impacts on a given aspect of the firm. The ratings can be done individually or by a group of

| If this issue materializes, | It will have | Impacts | On These | Aspects | Total (not an algebraic addition) | Rank |
|---|---|---|---|---|---|---|
| | Marketing (1) | Production (2) | Etc. (3) | Etc. (4) | | |
| **Cluster # 1** | | | | | | |
| —Issue | −8 | −9 | −9 | −5 | 28 | 3 |
| —Issue | +9 | −3 | +1 | 0 | 13 | 4 |
| —Plus: *Inferred Root Issue* (*if applicable*) | +8 | +8 | +9 | +5 | 30 | 2 |
| **Cluster # 2** | | | | | | |
| —Issue # 1 | ... | .... | .... | .... | .... | |
| —Issue # 2 | | | | | | |
| —Plus: *Inferred Root Issue* (*if applicable*) | | | | | | |
| —Stand alone issue | −8 | −9 | −8 | −7 | 32 | 1 |
| —Stand alone issue | | | | | | |

Exhibit 10.8: Illustration of Scope Analysis

knowledgeable people and then the average for the group for each issue is entered in the matrix. The mode is a better average than the arithmetic mean because it is a good measure of consensus. Once these ratings are entered in the matrix, they are then added (ignoring the algebraic signs) horizontally and a total score using absolute values only is calculated for each issue. The higher the total score, the more encompassing the impact of an issue is. We can then use a cut-off score to separate issues with broadest impact from those that have limited impact. We can then rank the issues based on the comprehensiveness of their impacts. The ones with the broadest impact are then viewed as the strategic issues facing the firm. The ones with limited or local impact are referred to the appropriate unit to deal with them.

Scope analysis is a useful approach for exposing the rest of the iceberg. Some issues might appear initially (or intuitively) as limited in impact. However, when an issue is subjected to this kind of analysis, it might reveal that the issue cuts across many aspects of the company. What looked like a small issue has become now a major one (the rest of the iceberg). On the other hand, an issue might appear compelling. Yet, its impact on the firm does not penetrate all aspects of the firm. It might be crucial for only one area or unit of the firm. Such an issue is not a truly strategic one since it does not impact the firm in its entirety. In this case, the issue is often referred to the respective unit of the firm to deal with it. The issues with the broadest cross impact are carried to the next phase.

The output of the scope analysis step is *the strategic issues*. In a way, strategic issues describe the turbulence facing the firm. Turbulence data have been distilled and the strategic issues are the net results. Genuine strategic issues have the following characteristics:

- They have high-impact, high-likelihood (high scores in column 3 of Exhibit 10.6).
- Their impact envelops most or all facets of the firm; high average scores in column 7 in the matrix (Exhibit 10.8).
- Some of them are root issues (Exhibit 10.7) that cause others to surface and impact the firm in its entirety. They become the focus of our response.
- Some of them are symptoms, but they affect the firm in its entirety and they are very pressing. These must be dealt with immediately regardless of their cause (e.g.,

negative working capital). Although we must tackle them immediately, we must at the same time deal with their root issues in order to keep the symptoms from reappearing.

## Phase III: Prioritization and Diagnosis

The strategic issues that emerged thus far are taken to two further stages. The first is prioritizing, i.e., arranging the issues in an order that reflects the urgency of the situation; first things first. The second is diagnosis, viewing the strategic issues themselves as symptoms of deeper causes or roots. The theory here is that the issues are symptoms of factors that lie under the surface. The function of diagnosis is to make these factors surface so that they can be dealt with.

## 1. Prioritization

First, the strategic issues must be prioritized since we cannot respond to all of them at the same time. There are constraints. To begin with, the organization may not have all the *resources* to tackle all the issues at once. Some issues will be dealt with now, the others will have to be tackled later. Furthermore, the time window available may not permit us to deal with all of these issues. Again, most pressing issues will be tackled first. The others will be in the next order of priority.

Finally, the strategic issues may be interconnected somehow, in a pattern that forces an order of priority in tackling them. Some issues may have a cause-and-effect pattern among them. In this case, symptoms are attacked first, but the disease still has to be dealt with once the situation is stabilized. Some issues display "precedence" patterns. For example, one cannot solve a delay in product delivery before dealing with poor production scheduling and control problem first.

To sum up, there are three rules for sorting out strategic issues with respect to priority. The application of these rules will force a ranking of the issues. This ranking will provide the leader and the organization with a sense of mission and sense of urgency. The three rules are:

- Time Pressure Rule: Issues that must be dealt with *in real time* (as the respective event or trend takes place) shall be tackled first. If the firm is insolvent, and the bank is calling a note payable, paying the note must take precedence even at the expense of other priorities on cash. The bank can force the company to go into receivership.
- Precedence Relationship Rule: Issues that require other issues to be resolved beforehand should be assigned a second order of priority; first things first.
- Cause-and-Effect Rule: Root or causal issues should be tackled first or at the same time as dealing with the issues stemming from them.

## 2. Diagnosis: Tracing Issues to Their Underlying Causes

The final step in issue analysis is diagnosis. Diagnosis is simply tracing and attributing the strategic issues to the factors that caused them. *Three* factors often account for the strategic issues that a firm faces: *turbulence*, the *system's activities* themselves, and *strategic leadership practices*.

First, turbulence is often the general cause of whatever issues the firm faces. It is thus crucial to identify the issues that appeared purely because of turbulence, not because of strategic leadership practices or the system's ways of doing things (patterns). We will call these "turbulence-specific issues."

The second cause of strategic issues is the system's activities themselves. The relevant ones here are turbulence sensing and interpretation (chapters 8, 9, and 10), and, response (maneuver, structure, capability, and vision, as Chapters 12–16). If these activities are ill-conceived or obsolete, the firm is bound to respond to turbulence in ineffective ways. When these activities are not constructive, some undesirable consequences surface, namely problem, threat, and weaknesses-type of issues. When they are well conceived, planned, and executed properly, opportunity and strengths-type of issues materialize. Therefore, it is crucial to determine whether the issues are attributable to them not. If they are, then the response to the issues lies in changing them. We will call these system's activities-specific issues.

The third factor that could have caused the strategic issues is the nature, constitution, structure, and style of strategic leadership in the firm. Strategic leadership is ultimately responsible for all issues. Strategic leadership was supposed to steer the firm through turbulence. Furthermore, the job of strategic leadership is to corral and steer people's activities. In other words, issues are the results of strategic leadership practices in the firm. The crux of diagnosis is to pinpoint the strategic leadership practices that could have produced these issues. As introduced in Chapter 4, strategic leadership comprises two main streams of activities: structuring the firm as a self-organizing system and then guiding the system's activities. If the leadership, through ill-conceived philosophies, has not structured the firm as a genuine self-organizing system, or has not corralled and steered its activities in an intelligent manner, this can also create issues, e.g., the firm is misinterpreting turbulence, pursuing the wrong maneuver (or vision), or possessing an obsolete capability (or structure).

The challenge in diagnosis is making a determination as to what extent each of the above three sources could have caused each of the strategic issues. If we decide that the issues stem purely from the turbulence and not due to a fault of our own, we proceed next to develop a response (guided by the concepts of Chapters 12–16). If, on the other hand, we determined that (1) the system's activities, and/or (2) strategic leadership practices are the culprits, then we pinpoint the specifics in each of these two areas. It should be stressed here that the diagnoses are then treated as strategic issues too. In fact, they should be treated as root issues since they caused the other strategic issues to take place. Our focus here is not just pinpointing what is "wrong" or improper. We are also interested in what is "right" (best practices) so that we may capitalize on it.

In the final analysis, interpreting turbulence boils down to the following

- Extracting *a list of prioritized genuine strategic issues.*
- *Attributing these issues to their driving forces*, namely:
  —The strategic issues due to *turbulence* alone: Issues that occurred because of reasons beyond the control of the firm
  —The strategic issues that resulted from *the way the firm conducts itself*, i.e., how it senses and interprets turbulence and how it responds to it (the particulars of its maneuver, capability, structure, and vision configurations).
  —The strategic issues that resulted from *the particulars of strategic leadership* in the firm, i.e., the personalities of the CEO and senior management, their designs for structuring the firm and for guiding it towards strategic end-states.

# CONCLUSION

Interpreting turbulence means reducing it to a set of top priority strategic issues. At this point, the leader and the self-organizing system have before them a list of strategic issues. They are the top priorities for the organization. Henceforth, they will become the focus of responding to turbulence. The list of strategic issues will encompass a compelling mix of positive strategic issues (strategic opportunities and strengths) and negative strategic issues (problems, threats, and weaknesses). Furthermore, the leader and the people will have before them a candid assessment of the strengths and weaknesses of the firm's patterns of conducting business as well as the strategic leadership practices that could have contributed to the emergence of the strategic issues. Given an interpretation of turbulence, the firm proceeds to make a strategic response it. This is the subject of the next six chapters.

# ENDNOTES

1. Porter, M., *Competitive Strategy*, New York, NY: Free Press, 1980, p. 131.
2. Brown, K., *Guidelines For Managing Corporate Issues Programs*, Report No. 795, New York, NY: The Conference Board, 1981, p. 1.
3. Ibid., p. 1.
4. Ibid., p. 4. This section is an adaptation of Brown's classification scheme for environments, trends, and issues.

CHAPTER
# 11

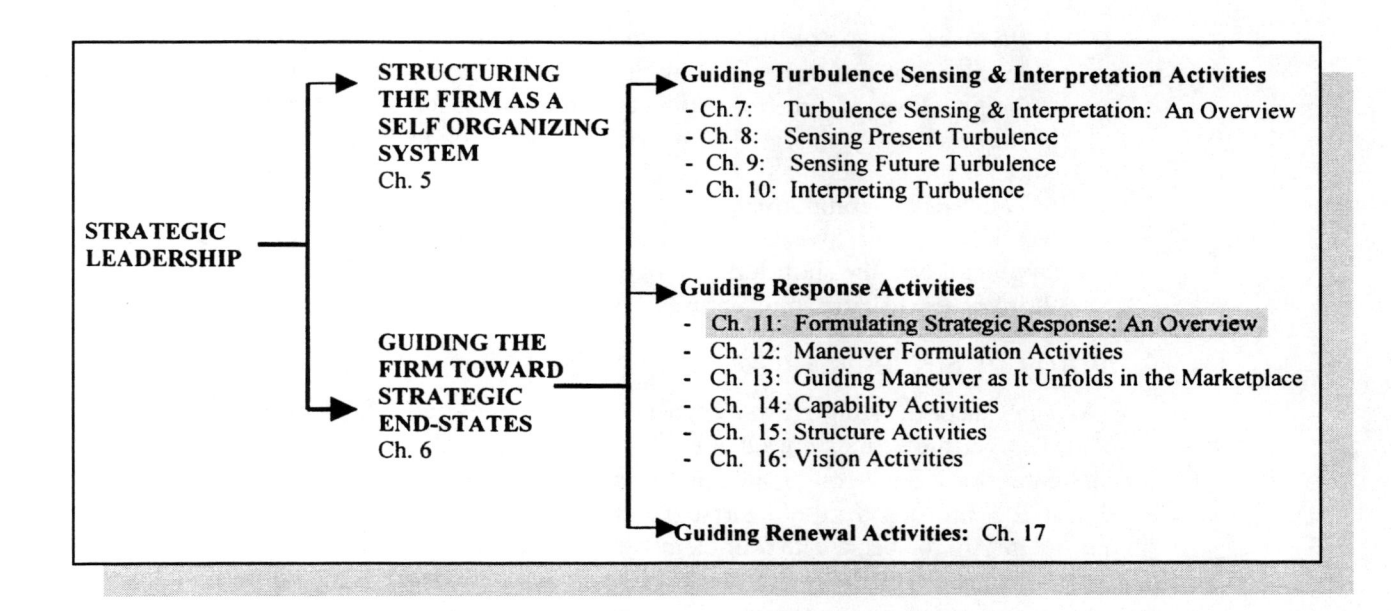

# Formulating Strategic Response: An Overview

```
STRATEGIC          STRUCTURING          Guiding Turbulence Sensing & Interpretation Activities
LEADERSHIP         THE FIRM AS A          - Ch.7:   Turbulence Sensing & Interpretation: An Overview
                   SELF ORGANIZING        - Ch. 8:  Sensing Present Turbulence
                   SYSTEM                 - Ch. 9:  Sensing Future Turbulence
                   Ch. 5                  - Ch. 10: Interpreting Turbulence

                                         Guiding Response Activities
                   GUIDING THE            - Ch. 11: Formulating Strategic Response: An Overview
                   FIRM TOWARD            - Ch. 12: Maneuver Formulation Activities
                   STRATEGIC              - Ch. 13: Guiding Maneuver as It Unfolds in the Marketplace
                   END-STATES             - Ch. 14: Capability Activities
                   Ch. 6                  - Ch. 15: Structure Activities
                                          - Ch. 16: Vision Activities

                                         Guiding Renewal Activities: Ch. 17
```

As it conducts itself in a self-organizing manner, the firm engages in three broad sets of activities: turbulence sensing and interpretation; responding to turbulence; and, renewal. Previously, we explored the first set. We now turn to the second, making a strategic response to the issues posed by turbulence. This will be the subject of the next six chapters. In this chapter, we begin by examining the nature and extent of a strategic response. We next examine a methodology for generating a strategic response, scenario planning. Scenario planning has further applications such as experimenting with proposed strategies or preparing for a particular future.

# A CONCEPT OF STRATEGIC RESPONSE

Turbulence envelops the firm in its entirety. As an episode of turbulence sets in, it poses strategic issues for the firm. In order to survive the firm must respond at some point in time. This response is labeled "strategic" because it has definite characteristics that can be outlined as follows:

- It involves matters of life and death for the firm.
- It involves intense strategic thinking and it represents strategic behavior. It is a calculating, clever scheme for getting to opportunities unimpeded by the hostile forces of turbulence. At the heart of every successful action, there is a strategy of some sort.
- It calls for the commitment of a significant amount of scarce resources in an irreversible manner. Investments cannot be converted into cash or switched to another application in the short term.
- It involves the firm in its entirety.

## Anatomy of Strategic Response

An analysis of the strategic moves that constituted the strategic response of a large number of firms over the years shows that such moves tend to fall into four concurrent, interdependent categories. This composite can be labeled as the firm's "strategy." It is shown in Exhibit 11.1. A full statement of a strategy has to include statements of the four components "in one breath" so to speak. The four elements are so intermeshed with one another, it is difficult to isolate each one. However, they are separated here only for the purpose of analysis and understanding. The four aspects of strategy are:

- A certain destination (vision) leading to a strategic end-state.
- A well-chosen dynamic path to this end-state (maneuver).
- A certain configuration of resources or capability to enable the firm to travel up the chosen route.
- A particular organizational structure or arrangement of people that enables the firm to utilize capability to actually travel the chosen path to the end-state.

1. Destination: This is a concept of a profitable, defensible position for the firm in the marketplace that pleases its stakeholders. As an aspiration, it is expected to remain constant in the short-run. However, it is possible that during a certain time horizon, that turbulence will render it obsolete or even undesirable. In this case, another one is chosen, *en route*. This might be repeated as often as turbulence necessitates. Thus, a destination is not necessarily permanent. It is a transient; a changing entity. We label this element as *vision*. The destination/vision embodies a desired strategic end-state for the firm to reach.

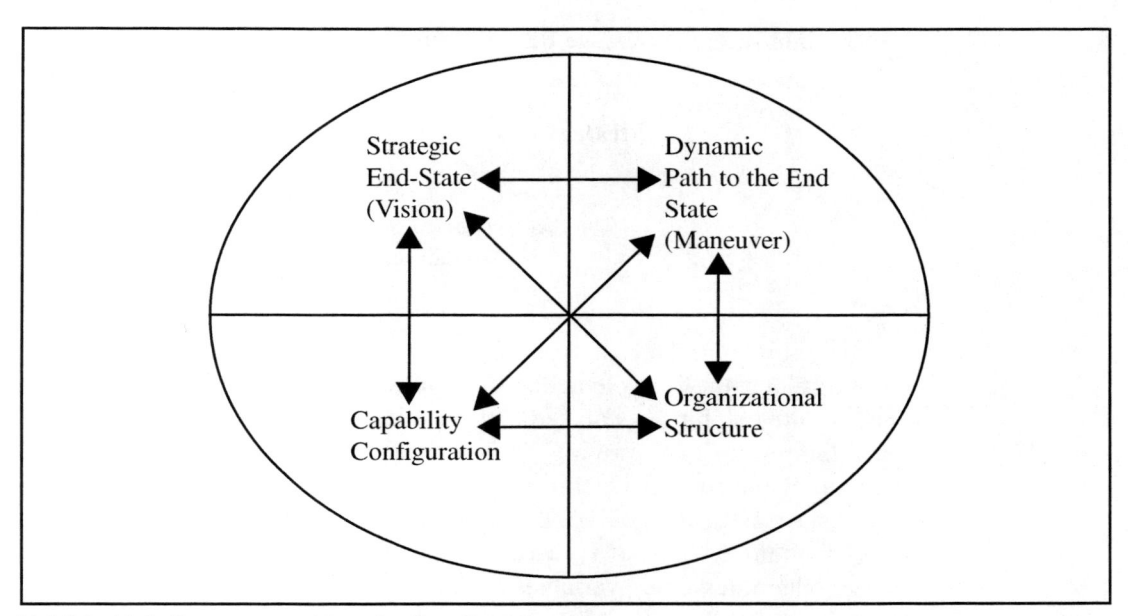

Exhibit 11.1: Strategy as a Four-in-One Concept

2. Path to the Destination: This is a dynamic, well-calculated path to the desired destination. The dynamics of turbulence call for shrewdness in designing this path. Intense outmaneuvering is needed here so that the firm may proceed to the end-state unimpeded by the non-controllable forces of turbulence. That is why we label this path as *maneuver*. Although maneuver is about path, it might also involve the choice of an end-state particularly if the pre-established destination is deemed undesirable *en route*. Maneuver is the dominant component of strategy for several reasons. First, when a firm confronts turbulence, it responds to it in real time through maneuver in the form of immediate strategic and tactical moves. Second, maneuver might involve the choice of a destination as mentioned above, not just the path to it. Third, maneuver and capability determine one another. On one hand, maneuver activities consume the resources that constitute capability. On the other, maneuver affects the building of capability since bits and pieces of resources are acquired in order to enable the various moves. Fourth, maneuver is a strong determinant of the results of the firm's efforts, particularly financial and market achievements, as well as the end-state to which the firm arrives. In view of these considerations, we start the discussion of strategic response with the topic of maneuver.
3. Capability: If maneuver is the path or route to the destination, capability is the vehicle that will take the firm there. The vehicle has to be aligned not only with the particulars of the path, but also with road conditions (the surrounding turbulence). Capability is the mix of resources, processes, and skills that the firm utilizes to deliver the moves called for by maneuver.
4. Structure: In a business firm, all activities, whether they may pertain to maneuver, vision, or capability, are carried out by people (employees). To allow them to function in an organized manner, a structure is needed. The structure determines who is to do what, when, how much, and how, among others. The choice of structure is crucial and strategic. Depending on structure, things (e.g., maneuver moves) will be done or left out. In Chapter 5, we saw how the command-and-control structure made the firm like a herd of buffalo (as Stayer, CEO of Johnsonville suggested in Chapter 3). Other structures, like the self-organizing system, empower people to act. When people are empowered, they will respond quickly to changes in the marketplace.

In light of the above, we define strategy as follows:

> **Strategy =**
> **vision +**
> corresponding **maneuver** configuration +
> corresponding **capability** configuration +
> corresponding architecture of **structure**

To show how the four components of strategy hang together, Exhibit 11.2 was developed. It relates the four elements of strategy to the prevailing external environment turbulence. In the exhibit, we can see that turbulence forces the firm to choose an end-state (albeit a temporary or a moving one). Logically, the end-state comes to mind first as the direction of the firm. It becomes the impetus or the motivation for maneuver. At the same time, it stays as an end goal for the maneuver. That is why the element "vision" appears twice in the diagram. Maneuver is the effort directed at customers. However, on the way to customers, other intervening variables exist, e.g., competitors, obstacles, factors beyond our control, and unfriendly states of affairs (such as a recession or a decline). In interfacing with the marketplace, maneuver is supported by two underpinnings, capability and structure.

In a firm structured as a self-organizing system operating in an edge-of-chaos world, strategy evolves (under the influence of vigilant strategic leadership) as a semicoherent direction, out of the initiatives of empowered employees. As they work to improve the firm's position in the marketplace, empowered employees undertake many initiatives, e.g., planning and executing many actions, acquiring and modifying capability, and rearranging organizational structure. They might even go as far as redefining the firm's vision. In such an environment, strategy emerges in bottom-up fashion. The leadership is watching a sea of initiatives to identify any directions that may suggest themselves, formulates a strategy out of them, and pronounces it as "the" strategy.

When strategy evolves as a semicoherent direction, it displays certain properties that are worth stressing at this point. These are:[1]

- A semicoherent direction is unpredictable because it changes with an unpredictable environment. It involves making some moves, observing what happens, and continuing with whatever seems to work.
- A semicoherent direction is uncontrolled, too much is going on in an edge of chaos environment. Many empowered employees make many moves on their own.
- A semicoherent direction is inefficient. In an edge of chaos environment stumbling into the wrong markets, making mistakes, bouncing back, and falling into the right ones seem to be unavoidable. Eventually, the right ones graduate to become a semicoherent strategic direction. Duplication, misfit, and error cause it to be an inefficient process.
- It is proactive, i.e., based on anticipating the future and being early in the market is part of the course.
- A semicoherent direction is continuous, i.e., a pattern of moves over time, repeated, relentless change that becomes endemic to the firm.
- Finally, a semicoherent direction is diverse as it encompasses a variety of moves with varying scale and risk.

Once a semi-coherent direction or pattern evolves, it becomes the strategy of the firm for a short while. Strategy has a short life for two reasons. First, there is constant creativity and restlessness in the organization as empowered people keep trying different things.

```
┌─────────────────────────────────────────────────────────────────────────┐
│ THE MARKETPLACE                                                         │
│        ┌─────────────────────────────────────────────┐                  │
│        │ C   U   S   T   O   M   E   R   S           │                  │
│        └─────────────────────────────────────────────┘                  │
│            ┌───────────────────────────────────────┐                    │
│            │ Competitors, Obstacles, Non-Controllables, Unfriendly │    │
│            └───────────────────────────────────────┘                    │
└─────────────────────────────────────────────────────────────────────────┘
```

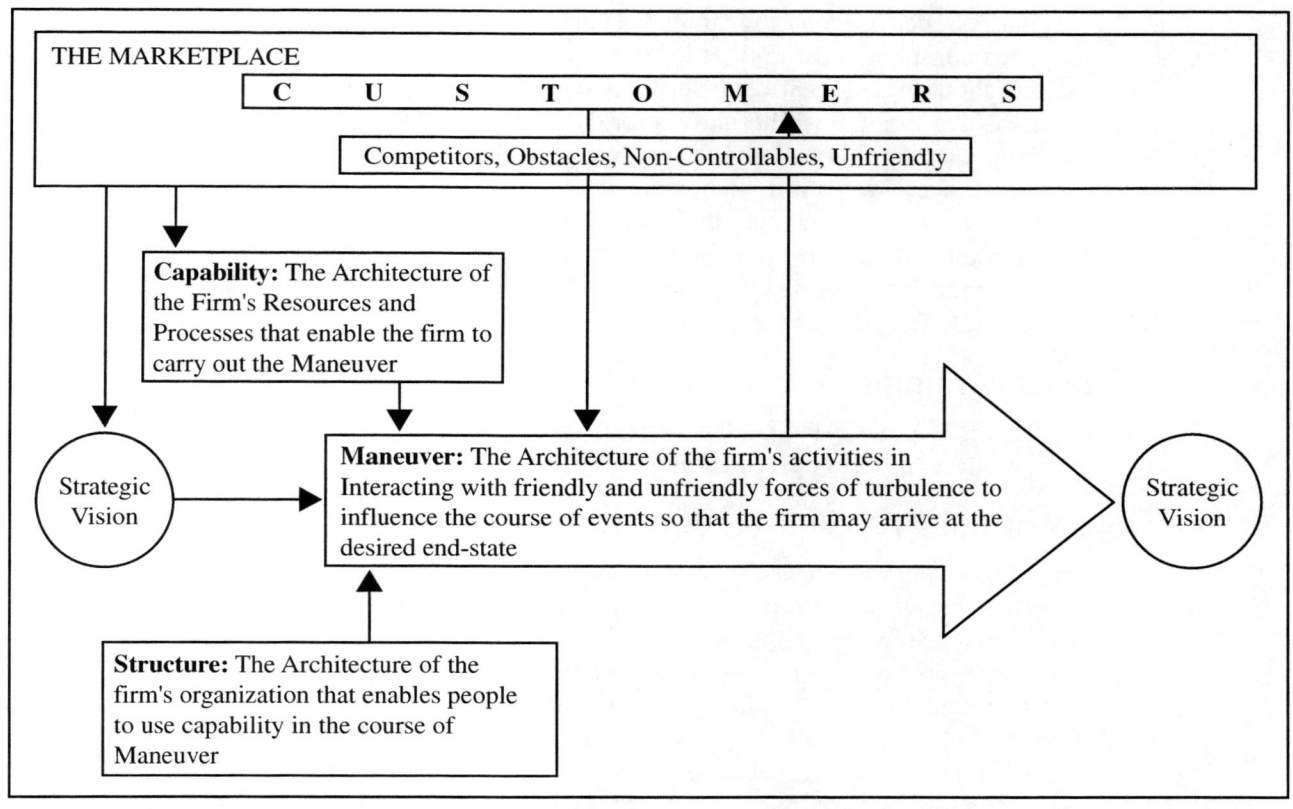

Capability: The Architecture of the Firm's Resources and Processes that enable the firm to carry out the Maneuver

Strategic Vision → Maneuver: The Architecture of the firm's activities in Interacting with friendly and unfriendly forces of turbulence to influence the course of events so that the firm may arrive at the desired end-state → Strategic Vision

Structure: The Architecture of the firm's organization that enables people to use capability in the course of Maneuver

Exhibit 11.2: How the Elements of Strategy Hang Together

Second, the upheavals in the environment are frequent. They will prompt people to respond in creative ways. As they do so, strategy becomes as uncertain as the business environment itself. In fact, *strategy is a continuously changing response to a continuously changing situation.*

To sum up, it seems that, in responding to turbulence, a self-organizing firm engages in four basic sets of activities, namely, formulating maneuver, building capability, structuring the organization, and visioning. The next five chapters will explore each of the four subsets and the work of the CEO in guiding them. Now that we have a general idea about what is involved in responding to turbulence, we turn our attention to the question of how to generate a good response.

## SCENARIO PLANNING

Formulating a strategic response then amounts to formulating and implementing a four-pronged strategy as defined above. Making a strategic response involves considerable calculation. We have to factor in many unknowns, namely, the various forces that turbulence embodies and their dynamics (as shown in Chapter 7). Not only do we have to take present turbulence now, but we also must include the future as well, since our response will be implemented in the future. We have to consider our constraints and capabilities. We have to think of our own plans and how they may pan out as turbulence unfolds. Will we win? Will we lose? What will the outcomes be? A good approach for making all these computations is scenario planning. Scenario planning is a strategic planning technique.

The essence of scenario planning is conceiving courses of actions in light of future scenarios (as constructed using the framework of Chapter 9) and simulating their implementation in light of these scenarios. It serves two purposes. First, it is a framework for organizing the process of generating alternatives for dealing with the situation facing the firm. Second, it is a framework for organizing the process of evaluating these alternatives in order to make a sound choice. Evaluation is accomplished by test-driving the various alternatives under future conditions, or simulating their implementation on paper. This saves considerable costs. The alternative to scenario planning is to actually implement a strategy to find if it works or not, an expensive way of doing business. The process of scenario planning is outlined in Exhibit 11.3. The steps are as follows:

## 1. Determining Strategic Issues

In this step, we establish the strategic issues. We can do so by following the process of issues analysis process described in Chapter 10.

## 2. Formulating Alternative Responses to Each Issue

In this step, we take each issue separately and attempt to formulate alternative responses to it. To do so, we need to construct a corporate model, a representation of the firm as it stands now. In essence, we are going to be manipulating (playing with) the elements of this model (rearranging its parts) in the course of formulating a strategic response. As a minimum, this corporate model should contain two main items: (1) the latest end-state to which the firm has arrived, particularly its market position and financial position; and (2) its current strategy, namely, intended vision, maneuver being implemented, existing capability, and the organization structure in force. We should keep in mind that the end-state is also a function of the turbulent situation that the firm has been facing. However, we cannot do much to change it. It is a non-controllable. We can only play with the other components. The corporate model is visualized in Exhibit 11.4.

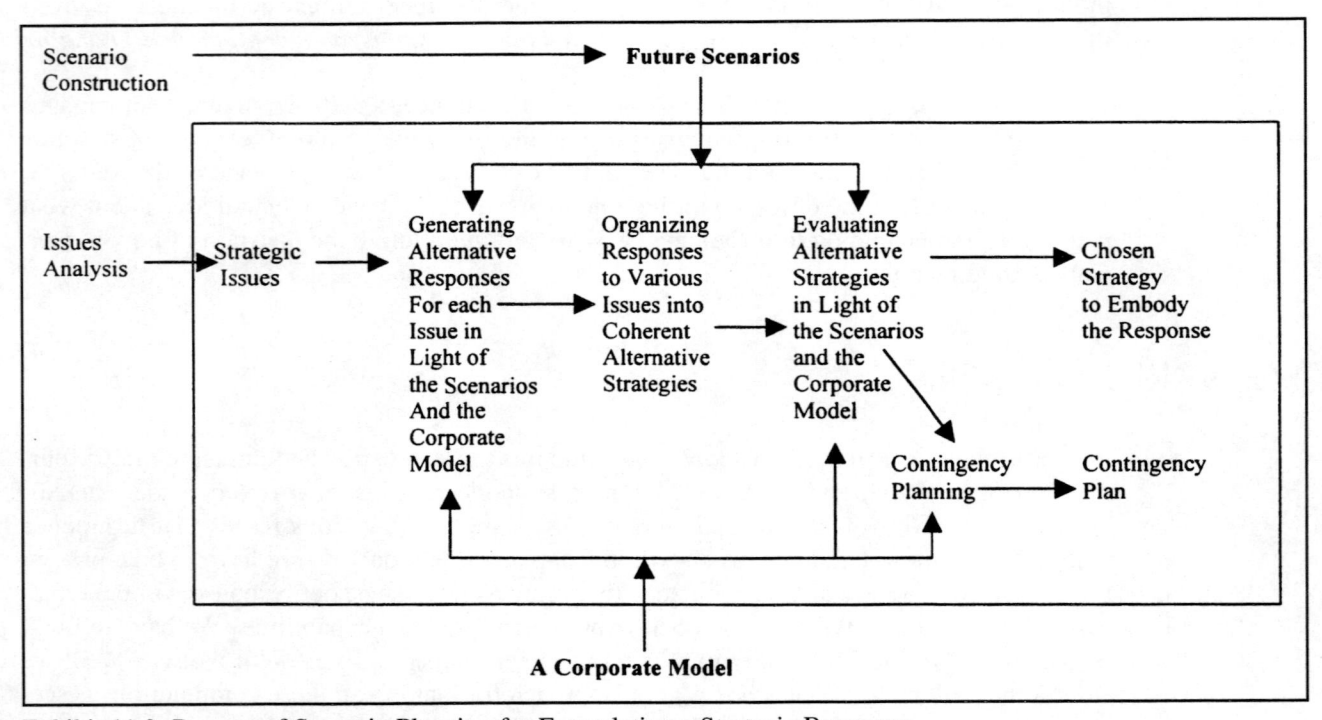

Exhibit 11.3: Process of Scenario Planning for Formulating a Strategic Response

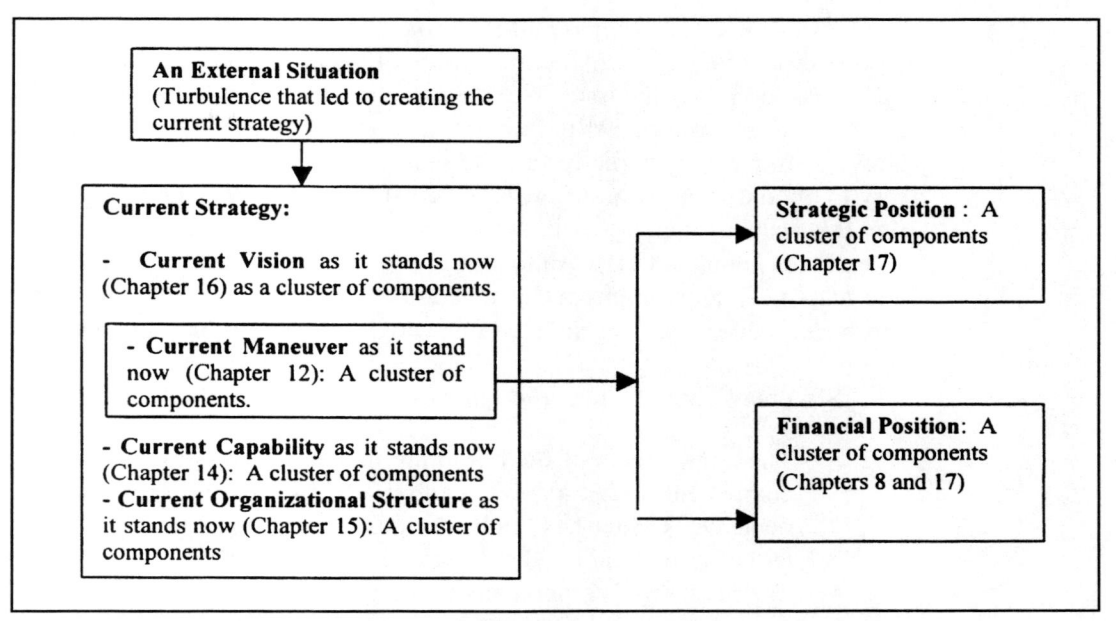

```
┌─────────────────────────────────────────────────────────────────────────┐
│                   ┌─────────────────────────────┐                       │
│                   │   An External Situation     │                       │
│                   │ (Turbulence that led to     │                       │
│                   │  creating the current       │                       │
│                   │  strategy)                  │                       │
│                   └──────────────┬──────────────┘                       │
│                                  ▼                                      │
│  ┌──────────────────────────────────────────┐                           │
│  │ Current Strategy:                        │    ┌──────────────────┐   │
│  │                                          │───▶│ Strategic Position│  │
│  │ - Current Vision as it stands now        │    │ : A cluster of   │   │
│  │   (Chapter 16) as a cluster of           │    │ components       │   │
│  │   components.                            │    │ (Chapter 17)     │   │
│  │   ┌────────────────────────────────┐     │    └──────────────────┘   │
│  │   │ - Current Maneuver as it stand │─────┼──▶                        │
│  │   │   now (Chapter 12): A cluster  │     │                           │
│  │   │   of components.               │     │    ┌──────────────────┐   │
│  │   └────────────────────────────────┘     │    │ Financial Position│  │
│  │ - Current Capability as it stands now    │───▶│ : A cluster of   │   │
│  │   (Chapter 14): A cluster of components  │    │ components       │   │
│  │ - Current Organizational Structure as    │    │ (Chapters 8 and  │   │
│  │   it stands now (Chapter 15): A cluster  │    │  17)             │   │
│  │   of components                          │    └──────────────────┘   │
│  └──────────────────────────────────────────┘                           │
└─────────────────────────────────────────────────────────────────────────┘
```

Exhibit 11.4: Visualization of the Corporate Model

The process of generating a response goes like this. Given a certain issue, we determine which element(s) of the corporate model must be changed in order to respond to this issue, and how such element(s) should be changed. To illustrate, let us use the analogy of the cockpit of an airplane where there is a number of knobs. Each knob represents an aspect of the aircraft. Each knob also has a number of positions. The particular combination of knobs' positions at a given point in time is a corporate model of the aircraft. Each combination of selections sends the aircraft in one direction or another. If we want to redirect the aircraft in response to certain developments, we simply reset the appropriate knobs and the appropriate position for each knob.

Along the same lines, the corporate model of a business firm is a set of knobs (vision knobs, maneuver knobs, capability knobs, and structure knobs (as shown in Chapters, 12, 14, 15, and 16) set at a certain combination of positions, the way we do business now. Given the issue on hand, the response to it boils down to selecting a number of relevant knobs, and formulating a combination of their respective positions. It should be stressed that each position is also a business move or action. Setting the price knob at the low position designates a certain business move, "reduce price." The positions of the various knobs are mutually exclusive. A knob cannot be set at two positions at the same time.

Let us take an example. Consider an issue like insolvency (negative working capital). We start by identifying the appropriate knobs and their possible positions. Suppose the relevant knobs here are the components of working capital, i.e., inventory, receivables, and cash. Each of them has a number of positions. The inventory knob can have two possible positions such as stocking inventory in anticipation of demand (a large inventory) and stocking to demand, just-in-time order filling (zero inventory). The receivable knob can have three possible positions: collecting in 30 days, collecting in 7 days, and zero receivables. The cash knob can have positions represented by ratios of cash to current liabilities, e.g., 1:1, 0.5:1, and 0.8:1. If we want to address insolvency, we might select these three knobs. We might then set the inventory knob at the position "zero inventory," the receivables' knob to the position "zero receivables," and the cash ratio of 0.8:1. The response to the issue of insolvency can then be described as follows: liquidate and carry no inventory; collect or factor receivables immediately and sell for cash; and, raise the acid test ratio to 0.8:1.

At this point, it is important to define the concept of an alternative response. An alternative response is a particular combination of knobs' positions or settings. We first determine the knobs in light of the issue. Next, we determine the possible positions for each knob. Every time we set the number of knobs at a certain position, we generate an alternative. In the above example, the alternative was a combination consisting of: zero position for the inventory knob and zero position for the receivables' knob. We can generate a second combination (alternative) such as stocking to demand in the inventory knob, 7 days collection for the receivables knob, and 1:1 cash to current liabilities ratio. We can go on to formulate a third alternative, namely minimum (for inventory), 30 days (for receivables) and 0.5:1 cash ratio. More alternatives can be generated this way just by experimenting with the possible combinations.

Six points should be kept in mind as we generate alternatives:

- The components of the corporate model are complex entities. Each one of these components is not just one knob. Rather, it is a cluster of knobs. For example, the maneuver cluster has knobs such as strategic thrust, business model, and the system of moves, as will be discussed in Chapter 12.
- The number of components (clusters of knobs) to be manipulated depends on the issue. For example, the entry of a major competitor might call for manipulating our maneuver cluster of knobs, our capability cluster, and maybe our vision cluster of knobs.
- Generating alternatives at this stage is done on an issue-by-issue basis. Each issue is taken separately and a response is formulated especially for it by manipulating the relevant knobs.
- The various knobs and their positions are determined in light of the firm's capability. If a certain position for a knob exceeds the limits of our capability, it is not a possible one. For example, if the firm is insolvent, then the acquisition knob (along with its positions) does not exist. An insolvent firm does not have the financing needed to acquire another company. Although capability is a constraint, we should always treat it as a flexible one since additions to capability can be made *en route*.
- As we generate alternatives, it is crucial to keep the scenarios for the future in mind. There is no point in selecting a knob's position that will be irrelevant by the time of its implementation.
- The combination of knobs' positions that form a certain alternative must be coherent or internally consistent. No position should cancel out another. For example, we do not set the product positioning knob at the premium position, and the price knob at the bargain basement position. A premium product positioning requires a premium price.

To help the process of generating alternatives for a set of strategic issues, the table in Exhibit 11.5 was constructed. In the Exhibit, column (1) is reserved for the statements of the strategic issues. In column (2), we identify the knobs that we need to manipulate to address each row issue. It is possible that the same knob will appear a number of times if it has to be manipulated in the course of responding to several issues. The price knob, for example, might need to be reset when dealing with product issues, pricing issues, positioning issues, or competitors' issues. We use letters here as symbols to stand for the various knobs. In column (3), we determine the possible positions for each knob. Again, we use alphanumeric symbols to label the positions. In column 4, we enter the first combination of knobs' positions (first alternative) for the row issue. In Column 5, we enter the second combination. In Column 6, we enter the nth combination, and so on.

It is worth emphasizing that the knobs in column (2) might fall into one or more of the categories of the firm's current strategy. In all likelihood, most of them will pertain to maneuver since it is the immediate form of responding to issues. However, changing one or more of the maneuver knobs (Chapter 12), might necessitate altering one or more of the capability knobs (Chapter 14), one or more of the structure knobs (Chapter 15), or even the vision knobs (Chapter 16) if necessary. For example, Sears (in responding to the spread of e-business) decided to enter the e-tailing marketplace. Sears had to change capability (added an e-business unit). It also changed its structure (set the e-business unit outside its traditional organizational structures). This probably called for a change in vision. Sears perhaps sees itself as a bricks-and-clicks retailer rather than a purely brick-and-mortar one. In general, the vision is expected to remain more or less constant in the short term. However, a certain strategic issue might call for a change in vision. Hence, vision knobs (Chapter 16) might be involved here as well. Accordingly, each combination of knobs for any issue might cut across one, two, three, or all of the components of strategy. It all depends on what the issues require.

### 3. Formulating Alternative Complete Strategies to Address the Situation in its Totality

This step involves taking the individual alternative responses for each issue developed above and organizing them into sets of alternative strategies that are complete, i.e., each strategy is a complete response to the situation facing the firm in its totality. If we examine Exhibit 11.5, we can see that each issue has a number of alternative combinations of knobs' positions for a number of issues. They are too scattered and possibly confusing. To make sense of them, they need to be integrated in one master configuration, a strategy. To do so, we take the contents of each of columns (4), (5), and (6) for all the rows and organize them into a coherent strategy. If we scan each of these columns vertically, we can see that it will have a number of knobs' positions that involve one or more of the components of the firm's strategy, i.e., maneuver, capability, structure, and vision. So, we take the elements in the column, examine them to eliminate redundancy (same knob position mentioned in several rows), and assemble them into one strategy. Most of the time, we will see three components, namely maneuver and the commensurate changes in capability and/or structure to align them with it. In a few occasions, we might see a fourth element, the vision.

If we look then at the contents of each of columns (4), (5), and (6), they will form three alternative strategies. Each alternative strategy will look like this:

> **A Strategy Alternative** = [**maneuver** moves (positions of some of maneuver knobs) + corresponding **capability** moves (positions of the capability knobs) *if necessary* to align capability with maneuver + corresponding **structure** moves (structure knobs' positions) *if necessary,* to align structure with maneuver and capability + **vision** moves (positions of vision knobs) *if needed, to align maneuver, capability and structure with it*]

At the end of this step, we will have a number of alternative strategies for responding to the strategic issues facing the firm. The challenge now is to choose one that will become the firm's strategy for the next time horizon.

### 4. Evaluating Alternative Strategies

With a number of alternative strategies generated in step 3, we now evaluate these alternatives in order to choose one that will become the firm's official strategic response or

| Strategic Issue (1) | Knobs Relevant to the Row Strategic Issue (2) | Possible Positions for Each Knob (3) | Generating Alternatives: Combinations of Knobs' Positions |||
|---|---|---|---|---|---|
| | | | Combination #1 (4) | Combination #2 (5) | Combination #n (6) |
| Issue # 1 | A | A1, A2, A3 | A1 + B1 + C1 + D1 | A2 + B2 + C2 + D2 | A1 + B3 + C2 + D4 |
| | B | B1, B2, B3 | | | |
| | C | C1, C2 | | | |
| | D | D1, D2, D3, D4 | | | |
| Issue # 2 | B | B1, B2, B3 | B1 + F1 + G1 + H1 | B2 + F3 + G4 + H2 | B1 + F2 + G2 + H3 |
| | F | F1, F2, F3 | | | |
| | G | G1, G2, G3, G4 | | | |
| | H | H1, H2, H3 | | | |
| Issue # n | I | I1, I2, I3 | I1 + J2 + A1 | I2 + J2 + A2 | I1 + J1 + A1 |
| | J | J1, J2 | | | |
| | A | A1, A2, A3 | | | |
| | | | All Combinations in this column should be organized as Coherent Alternative Strategy # 1 | All Combinations in this column should be organized as Coherent Alternative Strategy # 2 | All Combinations in this column should be organized as Coherent Alternative Strategy # n |

Exhibit 11.5: A Worksheet for Generating Alternative Responses to Strategic Issues

strategy. The evaluation here consists of two steps. First, we test-drive each alternative strategy under future conditions. Future conditions are represented by the scenarios that we constructed (using the process outlined in Chapter 9). As we consider each strategy in light of the scenarios, we will find that it will produce certain outcomes or impacts on the firm, mainly on its market position and financial position. The second step, therefore, is to assess these impacts. We assess them in light of stakeholders' expectations. Such expectations are often stated as a set of strategic and financial objectives (Chapter 12). If the outcomes of a given strategy meet these objectives, then the strategy is a good one since there is no gap between what the firm wanted and what the strategy will deliver. By contrast, if the outcomes fall short, then we will have a gap, a negative one. For example, if one financial objective called for a 15% ROI and a particular alternative strategy will produce only a 5% ROI, then we have a negative gap of [−10%]. On some occasions, the outcomes exceed the expectations. In the case, we will have a positive gap.

To facilitate the testing process, the worksheet in Exhibit 11.6 was developed. In the first column of Exhibit 11.6, a summary of the alternative is entered. The next set of columns are reserved for a summary of each of the scenarios developed. The key highlights of each scenario should be entered in the top part of the column as a way of keeping scenarios in the forefront of our thinking. Each scenario column is split further into two main sub-columns. In the first sub-column, the outcomes of the row strategy are entered. In the second sub-column, we enter the gaps associated with these outcomes.

## 5. Choosing from among Alternative Strategies

Given the information in Exhibit 11.6, we are now in a position to choose the best strategy. To make a choice, we start by scanning horizontally to ascertain the outcomes and the gaps associated with each row strategy across all the scenarios. When we do so for each alternative, we will find these possibilities:

- Some alternative strategies may have positive or zero gaps regardless of scenario. These are the robust ones. Choosing any of them for implementation is acceptable.
- Some strategies will have negative gaps regardless of scenarios. These should be discarded.
- Some alternatives, and this is the most likely case, will fare well under some scenarios, but poorly under others. In this case, we do the following:
  —Choose the alternative strategy that will have zero and/or positive gaps under the most likely scenario.
  —Since this strategy will fare well under the most likely scenario, but not under the other scenarios, it will leave the firm exposed should one of them materialize. To minimize this exposures, we will have to develop a contingency plan to be invoked should a scenario other than the most likely one happen.

| If this strategy is implemented, ⟶ | and | | this | scenario | materializes | |
|---|---|---|---|---|---|---|
| | Enter here a summary of the most likely scenario. | | Enter here a summary of the second scenario. | | Enter here a summary of the third or nth scenario. | |
| ↓ | What are the **Outcomes** of implementing this strategy under the most likely scenario? | What are the **Gaps** associated with these outcomes? | What are the **Outcomes** of implementing this strategy under this scenario? | What are the **Gaps** associated with these outcomes? | What are the **Outcomes** of implementing this strategy under this scenario? | What are the **Gaps** associated with these outcomes? |
| Enter summary of alternative strategy # 1 | List the outcomes here | List the gaps associated with them here | List the outcomes here | List the gaps associated with them here | List the outcomes here | List the gaps associated with them here |
| Enter summary of alternative strategy # 2 | List the outcomes here | List the gaps associated with them here | List the outcomes here | List the gaps associated with them here | List the outcomes here | List the gaps associated with them here |
| Enter summary of alternative strategy # 3 | List the outcomes here | List the gaps associated with them here | List the outcomes here | List the gaps associated with them here | List the outcomes here | List the gaps associated with them here |

Exhibit 11.6: Worksheet for Evaluating Alternative Strategies

In this case, we will end up with two strategies: one to be implemented if the most likely scenario happens, the second strategy, the contingencies plan itself to be applied if the least likely scenario (or surprise) occurs. We explore the process of contingency planning next.

## Contingency Planning

As stated above, a robust strategy is a rare phenomenon. Most of the time, we will be able to find a strategy that will perform well under the most likely scenario, but poorly under one or more of the other scenarios. What if one of these other scenarios materializes? To guard against this possibility, we develop a contingency plan.

O'Connor defined contingency planning as follows:

"Simply stated, contingency planning is the preparation, in advance, of a course of action to meet a situation that is not expected, but that, if it transpires, will have a significant impact on the firm. A contingency plan has also been defined as one that is devised or put into effect when an unforeseen event actually occurs."[2]

The purpose of contingency planning is to minimize the panic of surprise. The first step in minimizing surprise is to develop an exhaustive set of alternative scenarios to cover all the possibilities that the future might assume, if they are foreseeable. If we have an exhaustive set of scenarios, it is highly unlikely that the future will assume a state that we have not considered. However, no amount of scenario generation can anticipate the future precisely. There will always be surprises. Again, O'Connor states:

"Contingency planning attempts to avoid surprise—the hobgoblin of planning. When crises and emergencies do arise, when swift decisions and actions are demanded, a plan prepared in advance—when time is not critical—eliminates scrambling for response. . . . (it) reduces the expense and confusion of 'turning on a dime', thereby affording a clearer idea of risks and possible losses."[3]

One executive eloquently stated the contingency planning imperative:

"There is never enough time for a manager to be completely rational. The executive is like a chess player in a 60-second-per-move game. He *must* move. Deadlines must be met whether or not he has what he considers enough information to make a decision. Contingency planning permits more rational decisions because they are made in advance and in a more leisurely fashion."[4]

### The Process of Contingency Planning

After researching contingency planning practices, O'Connor reduced them to a model. An adaptation of this model is presented in Exhibit 11.7. To develop a contingency plan, there are three steps to follow: (1) identifying the contingent event; (2) establishing the trigger points; and, (3) developing a strategic response and its implementation tactics.

1. Identifying the Contingent Event

The first step in contingency planning is to identify the scenario(s), which will cause the most disruption for the firm. This often is a surprise scenario, when the unexpected happens. Moderation (in terms of the number of contingency scenarios) is required here because of the cost of contingency planning. The events in these scenarios must be "critically significant," not merely troublesome. Troublesome ones are "part of the course."

Once a contingent event is identified as critical, it has to be analyzed carefully. This analysis includes estimating the impact that it will have on the company in qualitative and quantitative terms especially impacts on the financial statements. The effect of the response and the cost of the response must be expressed in financial terms.

2. Establishing Triggers

Now that we know the contingencies (events), they should be monitored so that we may be informed about them in case they take place. This can be accomplished by following this procedure:

- Developing the information needed to track the event or scenario. If the contingency is a strike at our supplier's plant, the information here can be frequency of grievance, morale, walkouts, expiry of collective agreements, accord (or discord) between management and the union, and so on. In essence, these bits and pieces of information are the "leading indicators" of a strike.
- Tracking the scenario or event by continuously gathering data about its leading indicators. This will help us to keep informed about the event and to assess the likelihood of its occurrence as it progresses.

| STEP | CONCERN | CONTINGENCY PLANNING ACTION |
|---|---|---|
| **Step 1: Identifying Contingency Events** | What if? | Identifying and listing the events that may occur in the future that have a critical significance for the company—from the scenarios where our best alternative fails. |
| | What impact will it have on the firm? | Evaluating and selecting the major contingencies by the impact they would have on the company's operations and plans. |
| | How probable is it? | Estimating the likelihood of occurrence—part of the likelihood of the scenario that includes it. |
| | How will we know the contingency event is about to happen? | Identifying and listing the leading indicators that show the respective scenario is about to take place. |
| **Step 2: Establishing the Trigger Point** | Who will alert us? | Identifying and designating the responsibility for tracking the indicators and sounding the alarm that the contingent event is about to occur in the near future. |
| | What will we do when we are alerted? | Invoke the contingency plan, or improvise new strategic action that minimizes the impact of the contingency and preferably turn it to our advantage. |
| **Step 3: Assessing Effectiveness of Strategic Response and Developing Implementation Tactics** | What effect will our strategic response have on the event? | Estimating the financial impact of the strategic response and how it will affect the original plan? |
| | How will we accomplish our response? | Developing the tactics to implement the response including the specifics of the actions to be taken, their timing, and individual responsibilities. |

Exhibit 11.7: Elements of Contingency Planning

### Implementation Planning

Now that a master strategy and a contingency plan is in place, the next step is to think about the details of implementation. The implementation plan comprises four main items:

- Operational Plans: The operational plan contains the steps needed to implement each of the sub-strategies in the master one. For example, if a move in one alternative calls for selling direct to customers, then we need to develop a plan to show the detailed operations entailed in selling direct.
- Required Resources: To make the master strategy a reality, certain resources will be needed. They have to be specified at this point, particularly their types (physical, human, etc.), quantities, and quality.
- Financial Plan: A financial plan is needed to provide the necessary funds not only to acquire the needed resources but also to fund the activities called for by the chosen strategy. A financial strategy is needed to underlie this financial plan since the firm will have to outmaneuver other funds seeker and funds owners in order to obtain the needed funds while minimizing the cost of capital.
- Time Table: The timing of the various moves in the master strategy is crucial for success. Being too early or too late can be costly. Accordingly, a timetable must be formulated to show when each major move will be undertaken.

## FURTHER APPLICATIONS OF SCENARIO PLANNING

Besides formulating a strategic response to a given set of strategic issues, scenario planning has three important applications that are part of strategic planning for an uncertain future. These are:

1. Scenario Planning for an Overarching Goal: There are times when the leadership challenges the organization to a higher level of achievement by establishing an overarching objective that represents considerable stretch. Scenario planning can be used to formulate strategy to achieve this goal.
2. Scenario Planning for a Particular Future: The future is always uncertain. Sometimes, there are certain types of futures that are a source of concern for the leadership if they happen. For example, a dooms-day scenario is a kind of dreaded future. Alternatively, a rosy scenario, full of opportunities, is also a source of concern about how to take advantage of it. Scenario planning is undertaken here to help the firm prepare a plan.
3. Strategy Experimentation: Dynamic firms are always looking for new and different strategies, even if the current strategy is acceptable. The saying, "If it ain't broke, don't fix it" does not apply nowadays. Even successful strategies have a short shelf life in a turbulent world. Scenario planning is a useful technique for generating new strategies and testing them to ascertain if they need significant improvements.

A large number of exhibits have been developed to map the process involved in each of the three applications. To avoid interrupting the flow of the presentation, all exhibits will be presented at the end of the chapter.

## Scenario Planning for an Overarching Goal

The main feature of goal-driven scenario planning is the generation of a number of alternative strategies to achieve the overarching goal. The goal in this case is a lofty one that represents stretch for the organization. It involves raising the bar significantly. For example, Patrick Kelly (PSS/World Medical, Chapter 3) challenged his firm to become a $500 million dollar company. When it became a $500 million dollar company, he challenged it again to become a billion dollar company. When this was accomplished, he challenged it to become a global corporation. An overarching goal is futuristic, visionary. It is not motivated by present conditions. Rather it is driven by ambition. The scenario planning process here flows according to Exhibit 11.8.

The scenario planning process begins with a description of the goal itself. The next step is to formulate a strategy to achieve it. Formulating this strategy begins with the formulation of a vision of the firm in light of this goal. This calls for generating alternative visions and then testing them to choose the most appropriate ones. Exhibits 11.9 and 11.10 show how this is done. Given a chosen vision, we proceed to formulate a maneuver to achieve the goal and the vision that stems from it. This involves generating alternative maneuvers and testing them in order to identify the one that will maximize the attainment of the goal. This process is outlined in Exhibits 11.11 and 11.12. Now that we have a maneuver chosen as the plan to achieve the goal, the next step is to align the firm's capability with it. This will require changes in capability. They can be radical depending on how audacious the aspired goal is. Now that we have a maneuver and capability, we align the firm's organizational structure with them. Taken together, the four components will then be the strategy for achieving the goal.

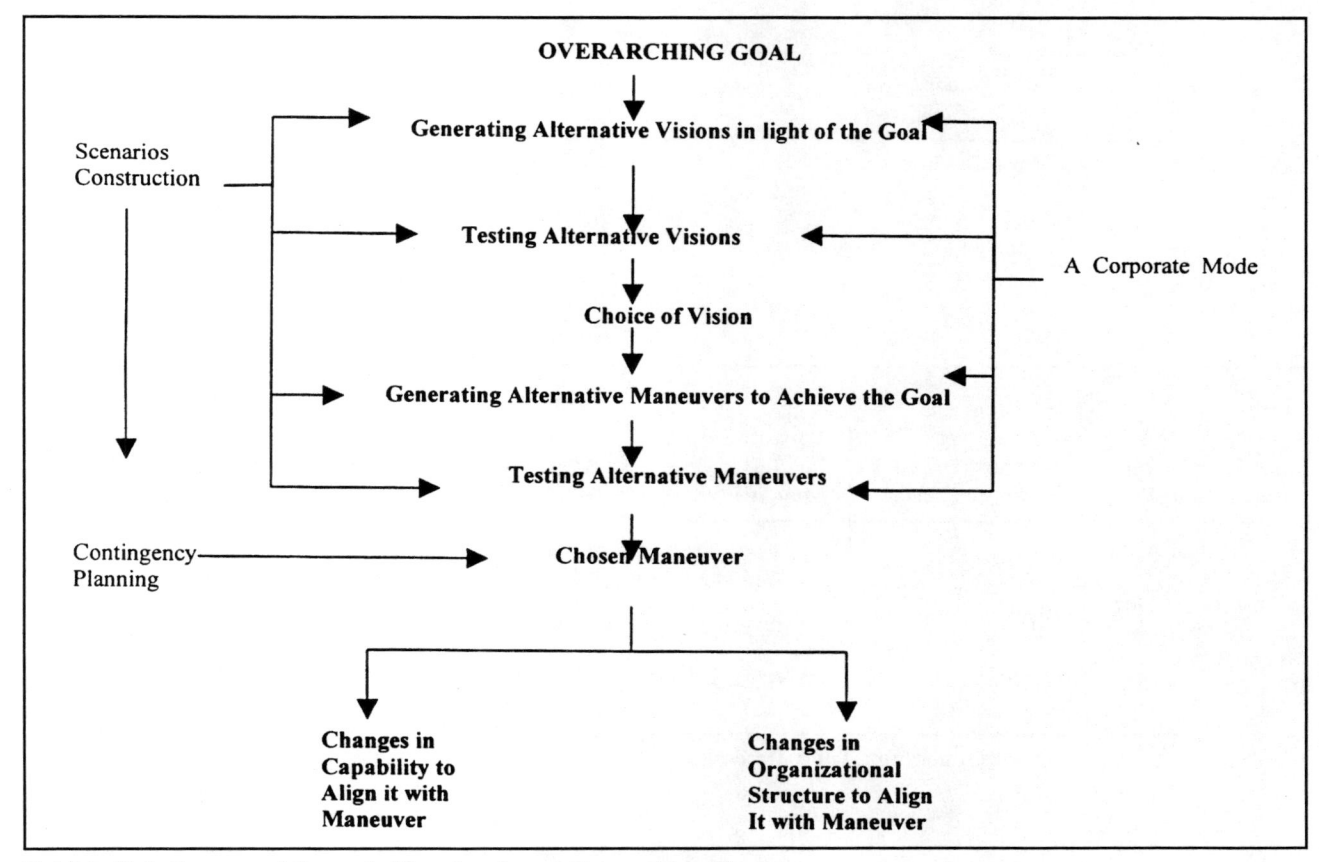

Exhibit 11.8: Process of Scenario Planning for an Overarching Goal

178  Chapter 11

| Statement of the Overarching Goal | Relevant Vision Knobs (from Chapter 16) | Possible Settings for the Vision Knobs | Generating Alternative Visions |||
|---|---|---|---|---|---|
| | | | Alternative Vision I | Alternative Vision II | Alternative Vision n |
| Description of the goal and what it entails | A<br>B<br>C | A1, A2, An<br>B1, B2, Bn<br>C1, C2, Cn | A1 + B2 + Cn | A2 + B1 + C1 | An + B1 + C2 |

Exhibit 11.9: Worksheet for Generating Alternative Visions Given the Choice of an Overarching Goal

| If the Vision below is Adopted, | What are the outcomes of having a vision in light of the Overarching Goal? | What are the gaps associated with these outcomes in light of the Overarching Goal? |
|---|---|---|
| Enter here a summary of alternative Vision # 1 | List the outcomes here In relation to the goal | List the gaps associated with them here |
| Enter here a summary of alternative Vision # 2 | List the outcomes here | List the gaps |
| Enter here a summary of alternative Vision # 3 | List the outcomes here | List the gaps |

Exhibit 11.10: Worksheet for Testing Alternative Visions Given an Overarching Goal

| Statement of the Overarching Goal | Relevant Maneuver Knobs (from Chapter 12) | Possible Settings for the Maneuver Knobs | Generating Alternative Maneuvers in light of the Overarching Goal and the Chosen Vision |||
|---|---|---|---|---|---|
| | | | Alternative Maneuver I | Alternative Maneuver II | Alternative Maneuver n |
| Description of the goal and what it entails | A<br>B<br>C | A1, A2, An<br>B1, B2, Bn<br>C1, C2, Cn | A1 + B2 + Cn | A2 + B1 + C1 | An + B1 + C2 |

Exhibit 11.11: Worksheet for Generating Alternative Maneuvers to Achieve an Overarching Goal

| If the Maneuver below is Adopted, | What are the outcomes of having this Maneuver in light of the Overarching Goal? | What are the gaps associated with these outcomes in light of the Overarching Goal? |
|---|---|---|
| Enter here a summary of alternative Maneuver # 1 | List the outcomes here in relation to the goal | List the gaps associated with them here |
| Enter here a summary of alternative Maneuver # 2 | List the outcomes here | List the gaps |
| Enter here a summary of alternative Maneuver # 3 | List the outcomes here | List the gaps |

Exhibit 11.12: Worksheet for Testing Alternative Maneuvers to Achieve an Overarching Goal

## SCENARIO PLANNING FOR A PARTICULAR FUTURE

Scenario planning here is undertaken to plan a strategy to deal with a particular future. The leadership might perceive a certain future (scenario) for the industry or the environment. That future is a major source of concern for the firm. Sometimes, this type of future can be a bleak one, e.g., dooms day scenarios. The firm wants to guard against its negative impacts. Sometimes, the particular future can be a positive one, e.g., the emergence of a certain technology that brings considerable opportunities with it. For example, some traditional retailers are planning for a future where retailing is dominated by the Internet. Sometimes, the particular future can be a source of great uncertainty, e.g., a future where a major competitor withdraws from the market, or is acquired by a bigger firm. In this case, the firm will want to know what to do when such a future materializes. The scenario planning process here flows according to Exhibit 11.13.

Given a full picture of the particular future, the planning process starts with the formulation of a vision for the firm under these circumstances. This requires the generation of alternative visions and evaluating them in light of this future. The process of generating an alternative vision in this case is illustrated in Exhibit 11.14. Testing or evaluating the alternative visions can be done according to the process outlined in Exhibit 11.15. Once the vision is chosen, the next step is to generate alternative maneuvers that the firm can undertake to deal with the particular future. The process for doing so is outlined in Exhibit 11.16. Given a number of alternative maneuvers, the next step is to evaluate the alternative maneuvers as shown in Exhibit 11.17. Once the maneuver is chosen, then the firm's capability and structure need to be aligned with it.

## DESCRIPTION OF THE PARTICULAR FUTURE

↓

**Generating Alternative Visions in light of The Particular Future**

↓

**Testing Alternative Visions In light of the Particular Future** ← A Corporate Model

↓

**Choice of Vision**

↓

**Generating Alternative Maneuvers Given the Particular Future**

↓

**Testing Alternative Maneuvers** ←

↓

**Chosen Maneuver**

↓

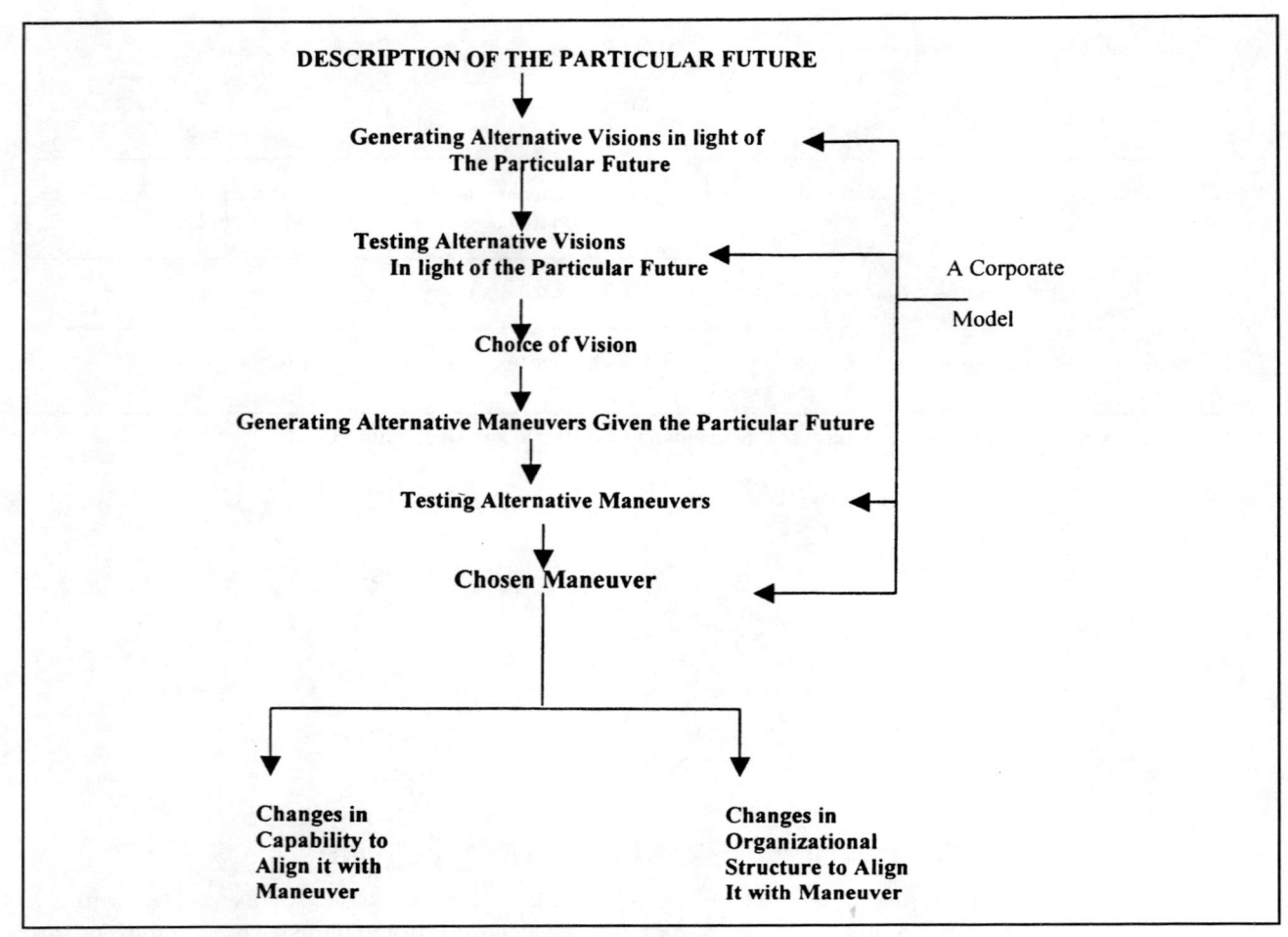

- **Changes in Capability to Align it with Maneuver**
- **Changes in Organizational Structure to Align It with Maneuver**

Exhibit 11.13: Process of Scenario Planning for a Particular Future

| Statement of the Particular Future | Relevant Vision Knobs (from Chapter 16) | Possible Settings for the Vision Knobs | Generating Alternative Visions |||
|---|---|---|---|---|---|
| | | | Alternative Vision I | Alternative Vision II | Alternative Vision n |
| Description of the particular future that is a source of concern for the firm | A  B  C | A1, A2, An  B1, B2, Bn  C1, C2, Cn | A1 + B2 + Cn | A2 + B1 + C1 | An + B1 + C2 |

Exhibit 11.14: Worksheet for Generating Alternative Visions Given a Particular Future

| If the Vision below is Adopted, | What are the outcomes of having a vision in light of the Particular Future? | What are the gaps associated with these outcomes in light of the Particular Future? |
|---|---|---|
| Enter here a summary of alternative Vision # 1 | List the outcomes here in relation to the goal | List the gaps associated with them here |
| Enter here a summary of alternative Vision # 2 | List the outcomes here | List the gaps |
| Enter here a summary of alternative Vision # 3 | List the outcomes here | List the gaps |

Exhibit 11.15: Worksheet for Testing Alternative Visions Given a Particular Future

| Statement of the Particular Future | Statement of the Chosen Vision | Maneuver Knobs (from Chapter 12) Relevant to the Goal and Chosen Vision | Possible Positions for Each Knob | Alternative Maneuvers |||
|---|---|---|---|---|---|---|
| | | | | Alternative Maneuver I | Alternative Maneuver II | Alternative Maneuver n |
| Description of the particular future that is a source of concern for the firm | Description of the chosen vision | A<br>B<br>C | A1, A2, A3<br>B1, B2, B3<br>C1, C2, C3 | A1+B1+C3 | A2+B2+C1 | A3+B2+C2 |

Exhibit 11.16: Worksheet for Generating Alternative Maneuvers for Generated Visions Given the Particular Future

| If the Maneuver below is Adopted, | What are the outcomes of having this Maneuver in light of the Particular Future? | What are the gaps associated with these outcomes in light of the Particular Future? |
|---|---|---|
| Enter here a summary of alternative Maneuver # 1 | List the outcomes here in relation to the goal | List the gaps associated with them here |
| Enter here a summary of alternative Maneuver # 2 | List the outcomes here | List the gaps |
| Enter here a summary of alternative Maneuver # 3 | List the outcomes here | List the gaps |

Exhibit 11.17: Worksheet for Evaluating Alternative Maneuvers Given a Particular Future

## SCENARIO PLANNING FOR STRATEGY EXPERIMENTATION

In a turbulent world, there is always need for change. The best time to change is before turbulence forces it on the firm. As Jack Welch always advised, "Change before you have to." In order to do this, the leadership and the firm have to search for new strategies constantly. Scenario planning is very useful for generating new strategies and testing them.

Experimentation with strategy occurs in two stages. First, we must generate a number of alternative strategies. Second, we test them to establish which one(s) will perform better for the firm under the expected futures. There are four avenues for creating alternative strategies as follows:

1. Flash of Genius: A new strategy sometimes appears as a flash of genius or a breakthrough idea in the mind of one or more members of the organization. The breakthrough idea is then articulated and expanded to form a strategy by defining the components of vision, maneuver, capability, and structure. Creativity is a critical source of new strategic thoughts. Scenario planning is ideal for testing this strategy to establish its viability. The worksheet in Exhibit 11.18 facilitates the testing process. The determination of the outcomes and the gaps should help decide whether this strategy is viable or not.

2. Suggestion by Current Initiatives: A new strategy may suggest itself out of the numerous initiatives in the firm as a semicoherent direction. The semicoherent direction can then be articulated to become a full strategy, i.e., vision + maneuver + capability + structure. The strategy is then tested using the scenario planning process as shown in Exhibit 11.18.

3. Inspiration: In many cases, new strategies come through inspiration. A successful strategy of another company might inspire a certain firm to pattern its own strategy after that company. McDonald's business strategy (speed, standardization, pre-assembled inputs to be staged just before delivery to customers, location convenience, etc.) inspired the strategies of many companies inside and outside the fast food industry. In this case scenario planning is a good tool for testing the borrowed strategy to ascertain whether it will work for the firm or not. Given a strategy model (vision + maneuver + capability + structure), we test it using the process outlined in Exhibit 11.18.

| If this strategy is implemented, | and | | this | | scenario | materializes |
|---|---|---|---|---|---|---|
| | Enter here a summary of the most likely scenario. | | Enter here a summary of the second scenario. | | Enter here a summary of the third or nth scenario. | |
| | What are the outcomes of implementing this strategy under the most likely scenario? | What are the gaps associated with these outcomes | What are the outcomes of implementing this strategy under this scenario? | What are the gaps associated with these outcomes? | What are the outcomes of implementing this strategy under this scenario? | What are the gaps associated with these outcomes? |
| Enter here summary of the proposed strategy as a combination of vision, maneuver, capability, and structure | List the outcomes here | List the gaps associated with them here | List the outcomes here | List the gaps associated with them here | List the outcomes here | List the gaps associated with them here |

Exhibit 11.18: Worksheet for Testing a Possible Strategy

4. Deliberate Creation of Strategy: Finally, a new strategy can be generated systematically by attempting to rearrange the components of the firm's strategy. In this case, the purpose is to experiment with the various components of strategy to generate a number of viable arrangements. Each arrangement will be a strategy. Once several strategies are generated, we test them using the scenario planning process.

The knobs' concept mentioned earlier is useful in this regard. Each component of strategy is a cluster of knobs, e.g., vision knobs (Chapter 16), maneuver knobs (Chapter 12), capability knobs (Chapter 14), and structure knobs (Chapter 15). Each one of the knobs in any cluster can be thought of as having a number of positions. Every time we formulate a combination of knobs' positions, we generate a strategy. With so many knobs and positions, the process of developing a combination becomes rather complicated. To simplify the process, we can start with the formulation of a vision in light of the most likely scenario for the future. To do so, we generate a number of visions. We then test these visions and choose the two or three most appropriate ones. With few visions on hand, we next proceed to generate alternative maneuvers for each one. We then test these maneuvers and choose the appropriate maneuver for it. We now have two or three acceptable visions and two or three matching maneuvers. For each of these maneuvers, we develop the kind of capability that is most suitable for it. For each matching maneuver and capability, we develop the appropriate organizational structure for it. This process is visualized in Exhibit 11.19

Two processes in Exhibit 11.19 need to be highlighted at this point. The first pertains to generating and testing alternative visions. The second involves the generation and testing of maneuvers given a choice of vision. Exhibit 11.20 is a worksheet to facilitate the generation of alternative visions given the most likely scenario. Exhibit 11.21 is a worksheet for testing these alternative visions in order to reduce them to a smaller number. Along the same lines, Exhibit 11.22 represents a worksheet for generating alternative maneuvers, given a certain vision and the most likely scenario. Exhibit 11.23 is a worksheet for testing these maneuvers in light of the anticipated scenarios for the future.

At this point, we will have two or three visions, two or three matching maneuvers, two or three capability configurations matched to each maneuver, and two or three organizational structures matched to each maneuver-capability pair. In other words, we will have two or three strategies, each comprising a vision, a maneuver, a capability configuration, and an organizational structure. We next proceed to test these alternative strategies, along with our present strategy, to see how each fares in light of the scenarios for the future. The worksheet in Exhibit 11.24 facilitates the testing process. The object of the exercise at this point is to discover if one of the proposed strategies produces better outcomes and acceptable gaps (exceeding expectations) than our present strategy at least under the most likely scenario. If one of them performs better than our current strategy under all scenarios, then it is more robust than our current one. The firm should switch to it. If one of the generated strategies greatly exceeds our current one under the most likely scenario, switching to it should be considered, provided that a suitable contingency plan is developed to guard against surprises.

# Chapter 11

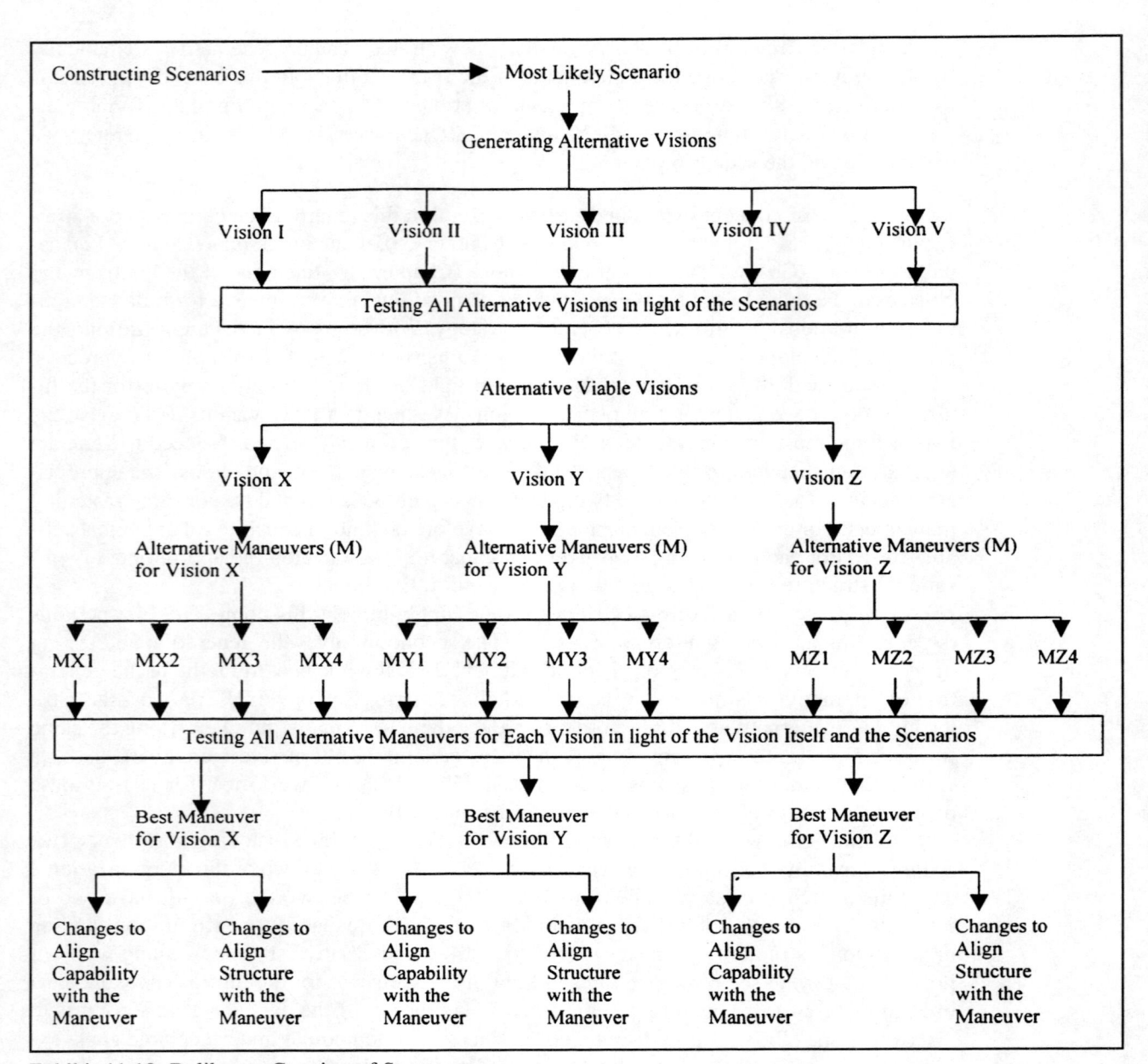

```
Constructing Scenarios ──────────▶ Most Likely Scenario
                                           │
                                           ▼
                              Generating Alternative Visions
                   ┌───────────┬───────────┼───────────┬───────────┐
                   ▼           ▼           ▼           ▼           ▼
                Vision I   Vision II  Vision III   Vision IV   Vision V
                   │           │           │           │           │
                   ▼           ▼           ▼           ▼           ▼
        ┌─────────────────────────────────────────────────────────────────┐
        │   Testing All Alternative Visions in light of the Scenarios     │
        └─────────────────────────────────────────────────────────────────┘
                                           │
                                           ▼
                              Alternative Viable Visions
                ┌──────────────────────────┼──────────────────────────┐
                ▼                          ▼                          ▼
             Vision X                   Vision Y                   Vision Z
                │                          │                          │
                ▼                          ▼                          ▼
       Alternative Maneuvers (M)  Alternative Maneuvers (M)  Alternative Maneuvers (M)
            for Vision X                for Vision Y                for Vision Z
        ┌────┬────┬────┐           ┌────┬────┬────┐           ┌────┬────┬────┐
        ▼    ▼    ▼    ▼           ▼    ▼    ▼    ▼           ▼    ▼    ▼    ▼
       MX1  MX2  MX3  MX4         MY1  MY2  MY3  MY4         MZ1  MZ2  MZ3  MZ4
        │    │    │    │           │    │    │    │           │    │    │    │
        ▼    ▼    ▼    ▼           ▼    ▼    ▼    ▼           ▼    ▼    ▼    ▼
   ┌──────────────────────────────────────────────────────────────────────────────┐
   │ Testing All Alternative Maneuvers for Each Vision in light of the Vision     │
   │                     Itself and the Scenarios                                 │
   └──────────────────────────────────────────────────────────────────────────────┘
                │                          │                          │
                ▼                          ▼                          ▼
         Best Maneuver              Best Maneuver              Best Maneuver
          for Vision X               for Vision Y               for Vision Z
          ┌─────┴─────┐              ┌─────┴─────┐              ┌─────┴─────┐
          ▼           ▼              ▼           ▼              ▼           ▼
      Changes to  Changes to     Changes to  Changes to     Changes to  Changes to
      Align       Align          Align       Align          Align       Align
      Capability  Structure      Capability  Structure      Capability  Structure
      with the    with the       with the    with the       with the    with the
      Maneuver    Maneuver       Maneuver    Maneuver       Maneuver    Maneuver
```

Exhibit 11.19: Deliberate Creation of Strategy

| Vision Knobs (Ch. 16) | Possible Positions for Each Vision Knob | Summary of the Most Likely Scenario ||||||
| | | Generating Alternative Visions in Light of the Most Likely Scenario |||||
| | | Alternative Vision I | Alternative Vision II | Alternative Vision III | Alternative Vision IV | Alternative Vision N |
| A | A1, A2, A3, etc. | A1+B1+C2 +D1+E2 | A2+B3+C1 + D2+E3 | A3+B1+C3 +D1+E1 | A1+B3+C3 +D3+E3 | A2+B1+C2 +D1+E2 |
| B | B1, B2, B3, etc. | | | | | |
| C | C1, C2, C3, etc. | | | | | |
| D | D1, D2, D3, etc. | | | | | |
| E | E1, E2, E3, etc. | | | | | |

Exhibit 11.20: Worksheet of Generating Alternative Visions Given a Most Likely Scenario

| Alternate Visions | Summary of the Most Likely Scenarios ||
| | What are the **outcomes** of pursuing this vision given the most likely scenario? | What are the **gaps** associated with these outcomes? |
| Enter here a statement of Alternative Vision I | List the outcomes here | List the gaps associated with them here |
| Enter here a statement of Alternative Vision N | List the outcomes here | List the gaps associated with them here |
| Enter here a statement of our current Vision | List the outcomes here | List the gaps associated with them here |

Exhibit 11.21: Worksheet for Testing Alternative Visions Given the Most Likely Scenario

| Acceptable Alternative Visions | Relevant Maneuver Knobs in light of this vision given the most likely scenario (Ch. 12) | Possible Positions for Each Maneuver Knob | Enter here a Summary of the Most Likely Scenario ||||
|---|---|---|---|---|---|---|
| ||| Generating Alternative Maneuvers in Light of the Most Likely Scenario and a Given Row Vision |||||
| ||| Alternative Maneuver I | Alternative Maneuver II | ...... | ..... | Alternative Maneuver N |
| Enter here a statement of Alternative Vision X | A<br>B<br>C | A1, A2, A3, etc.<br>B1, B2, B3, etc.<br>C1, C2, C3, etc. | A1+B1+C1 | A2+B3+C3 | | | A3+B1+C2 |
| Enter here a statement of Alternative Vision Y | A<br>D<br>F | A1, A2, A3, etc.<br>D1, D2, D3, etc.<br>F1, F2, F3, etc. | A1+D3+F1 | A3+D2+F3 | | | A2+D1+F2 |
| Enter here a statement of Alternative Vision Z | B<br>F<br>H | B1, B2, B3, etc.<br>F1, F2, F3, etc.<br>H1, H2, H3, etc. | B3+F3+H1 | B1+F1+H1 | | | B2+F3+H2 |

Exhibit 11.22: Worksheet for Generating Alternative Maneuvers Given a Most Likely Scenario and a Choice of Vision

| Alternate Maneuvers | Enter here a Summary of the Most Likely Scenario ||
|---|---|---|
| | What are the **outcomes** of implementing this maneuver under the most likely scenario? | What are the **gaps** associated with these outcomes |
| Enter here a statement of Alternative Maneuver I | List the outcomes here | List the gaps associated with them here |
| Enter here astatement of Alternative Maneuver n | List the outcomes here | List the gaps associated with them here |
| Enter here a statement of Our Current Maneuver | List the outcomes here | List the gaps associated with them here |

Exhibit 11.23: Worksheet for Testing Alternative Maneuvers in Light of a Chosen Vision and a Most Likely Scenario

| If this strategy is implemented, | and | | this | | scenario | materializes |
|---|---|---|---|---|---|---|
| | Enter a summary of the most likely scenario (e.g., most likely scenario). | | Enter here a summary of the second scenario. | | Enter a summary of the third or nth scenario. | |
| | What are the outcomes of implementing this strategy under the most likely scenario? | What are the gaps associated with these outcomes? | What are the outcomes of implementing this strategy under this scenario? | What are the gaps associated with these outcomes? | What are the outcomes of implementing this strategy under this scenario? | What are the gaps associated with these outcomes? |
| Enter here a summary of Generated strategy # 1 | List the outcomes here | List the gaps associated with them here | List the outcomes here | List the gaps associated with them here | List the outcomes here | List the gaps associated with them here |
| Enter here a summary of Generated strategy # 2 | List the outcomes here | List the gaps associated with them here | List the outcomes here | List the gaps associated with them here | List the outcomes here | List the gaps associated with them here |
| Enter here a summary of our Current Strategy | List the outcomes here | List the gaps associated with them here | List the outcomes here | List the gaps associated with them here | List the outcomes here | List the gaps associated with them here |

Exhibit 11.24: Worksheet for Testing Deliberately Generated Strategies

# CONCLUSION

This chapter presented scenario planning as a framework for formulating a strategic response. The philosophy of scenario planning calls for factoring the future into our thinking in the present. All contemplated strategies for responding to turbulence have to be "test-driven" into the future before they are undertaken. In doing so, we ensure that our response would be workable at time of implementation (in the future). Scenario planning is a continuous process because the firm is always responding to turbulence that never ceases. The methodology presented here was described in general terms. It has to be applied to each of the four aspects of business strategy, maneuver, capability, structure, and vision. Thus, whenever we need to reconfigure each of these four prongs of strategy, scenario planning is a good approach.

# ENDNOTES

1. Brown, S.L. and K.M. Eisenhardt, *Competing On the Edge: Strategy As Structured Chaos*, Boston, MA: Harvard Business School Press, 1998.

2. O'Connor, R., *Planning Under Uncertainty: Multiple Scenarios and Contingency Planning*, A Research Report from the Conference Board, New York: The Conference Board, 1978, p. 13.

3. Ibid., p. 13.

4. Ibid., p. 13.

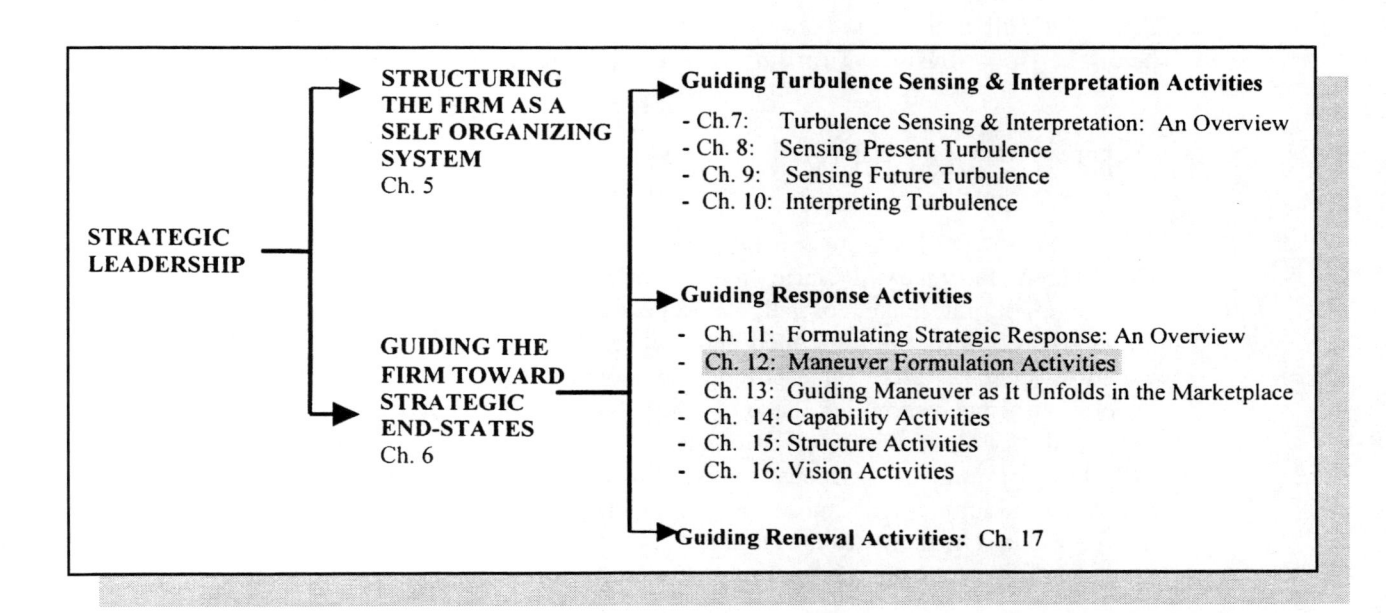

CHAPTER
# 12

# Maneuver Formulation Activities

**STRATEGIC LEADERSHIP**

**STRUCTURING THE FIRM AS A SELF ORGANIZING SYSTEM**
Ch. 5

**GUIDING THE FIRM TOWARD STRATEGIC END-STATES**
Ch. 6

**Guiding Turbulence Sensing & Interpretation Activities**
- Ch. 7: Turbulence Sensing & Interpretation: An Overview
- Ch. 8: Sensing Present Turbulence
- Ch. 9: Sensing Future Turbulence
- Ch. 10: Interpreting Turbulence

**Guiding Response Activities**
- Ch. 11: Formulating Strategic Response: An Overview
- Ch. 12: Maneuver Formulation Activities
- Ch. 13: Guiding Maneuver as It Unfolds in the Marketplace
- Ch. 14: Capability Activities
- Ch. 15: Structure Activities
- Ch. 16: Vision Activities

**Guiding Renewal Activities:** Ch. 17

Responding to turbulence involves formulating a well-conceived four-pronged strategy and implementing it. The first and foremost aspect of strategy is maneuver. It is the core of strategy. A firm's strategic response consists mainly of choosing a destination and a way to get there. The focus of maneuver is the formulation of a well-calculated path to a desired destination such that the firm may proceed to it unimpeded by the non-controllable forces of turbulence. Although maneuver is mainly concerned with how to get to the end-state, it might also involve finding and targeting a desirable end-state. The firm might start with a certain destination in mind, but then the forces of turbulence might derail it *en route*. Sometimes, a destination might vanish or erode before the firm can arrive at it, e.g., when the window of opportunity closes. Such is the nature of operating in a turbulent environment.

This chapter focuses on the firm's activities in formulating intelligent maneuver. It begins with an exploration of the concept of maneuver in general. Next, it presents a conceptual framework that shows all the elements of maneuver and how they hang together. This should shed light on the scope of activities involved in maneuver formulation. The chapter concludes with a discussion of how the CEO guides maneuver activities. Our focus here will be on the single-business firm since it is the most prevalent case in the business world.

## THE CONCEPT OF MANEUVER

The concept of maneuver is borrowed from military literature. According to the Webster Unabridged Dictionary, the term "maneuver" is both a verb and a noun. As a verb, it means, "to move, get, put, make, compel, etc. (a person or thing) by some stratagem or scheme." As a noun, it refers to: (1) a planned and controlled tactical or strategic movement of troops, warships, etc.; (2) large scale practice of movement or exercise of troops, warships, etc., under conditions resembling those of combat; and (3) any movement or procedure intended as a skillful or shrewd step toward some objective, stratagem, artifice, or scheme.

The importance of maneuver was stressed by Winston Churchill when he said, "Battles are won by slaughter and maneuver. The greater the general, the more he contributes in maneuver, the less he demands in slaughter."[1] He further identified its essence as unfolding with the unfolding circumstances by being alive to opportunity:

> "We do not think logic and clear-cut principles are necessarily the sole keys to what ought to be done in swiftly changing and indefinable situations... [We] assign a larger importance to opportunism and improvisation, seeking to live and conquer in accordance with the unfolding event than to aspire to dominate it often by fundamental decisions."[2]

An excellent insight into the nature of maneuver was provided by General Beaufre:[3]

> "Taking fencing as an analogy, it is clear that there are a number of possible forms of action and reaction: offensively there are eight postures—'attack' which may be preceded or followed by 'threat,' 'surprise,' 'feint,' 'deceive,' 'thrust,' 'wear down,' 'follow-up.' Defensively there are six postures—'on guard,' 'parry,' 'riposte,' 'disengage,' 'retire,' 'break-off.'"[4]

The essence of maneuver is choosing what precedes and what follows what opponents do or do not do, the moves and counter moves in the *counterplay* between two opposing forces. General Beaufre stressed that the moves in maneuver "... are aimed ultimately at freedom of action, the object being either to gain it, regain it, or deprive the enemy of it. It will also be clear that to ensure freedom of action it is essential to retain the initiative which is a fundamental factor in maneuver."[5] Freedom of action permits us to undertake initiatives to bring about desired outcomes, i.e., the ability to drive turbulence, to put opponents on the defensive, or to make them play on our terms instead of theirs. We then become the rule maker.

General Beaufre stressed some key principles (doctrines) of maneuver. Two are worth stressing here. The first is the "rational application of force." In business terms, this principle calls for applying or deploying resources at the point(s) where they can accomplish *disproportionate* results, i.e., the beneficial outcomes by far outweigh the cost. In the 1990s, Bill Gates, for example, chose to focus Microsoft's resources on the systems (MS-DOS, and Windows). By doing so, Microsoft has become the gatekeeper and the rule maker. The second doctrine, according to General Beaufre, is that of "guile," "The solution chosen should be the one that is best calculated to throw the enemy off balance, disorientate him and deceive him. . . . The object will be to gain victory by acting in strength against the enemy's weak points. . ."[6] In a business setting, the doctrine needs some adaptation. We can use the doctrine of guile to mean "outwitting" or "outsmarting" *the non-controllable factors in a business situation* instead of taking them head-on and losing resources in a collision with them. Evasive action is preferred over confrontation. Bill Gates displayed the use of guile when he raced before anybody else to control the interface between the user and the PC through WINDOWS. By doing so, he outmaneuvered software and hardware firms to become the rule maker and the standard setter.

## MANEUVER: THE FOCAL ELEMENT OF BUSINESS STRATEGY

The concept of maneuver has special importance in business strategy. The forces of turbulence will overpower any company regardless of how big and formidable it may be. The crises that GM and IBM experienced during the turbulence of the 1990s attest to the fact that no firm is invincible. No firm has the resources to confront the forces of turbulence head-on, and win using brutal force. By necessity, the business firm will have to resort to the element of maneuver to navigate its way through turbulence. Maneuver is needed in order to avoid losing scarce resources in a head-on collision. It is required in order to evade threats and to negotiate obstacles. Maneuver is essential for blocking and tackling opposing forces while the firm exploits strategic opportunities along the way to its desired strategic end-states. As it entered the bookselling business, Amazon.com carved a niche for itself through maneuver, not through direct collision with traditional booksellers. Had Amazon followed a collision course with traditional booksellers, it would have had to build one major brick-and-mortar bookstore after another and sink millions of dollars in the process.

It is for these reasons that maneuver is the centerpiece of the firm's strategic response to turbulence. Maneuver is the core of the strategy. It embodies the firm's response. The term maneuver is used here for three reasons. First, it conveys that a firm's response to turbulence is a dynamic one, alive to change. It is a continuously changing response to a continuously changing situation. Second, it underscores a certain principle for dealing with non-controllables, namely "evasive action," "outthinking," "outsmarting," and "outwitting" instead of head-on confrontation. Third, the word further conveys the idea of scheming or cunning, i.e., using a clever ploy to help us get what we want unimpeded by opponents.

The essence of maneuver is the skillful, dynamic, anticipative choice of what to do given a scenario for the behavior of hostile and friendly forces of turbulence. We should keep in mind that the forces of turbulence come in a variety of shapes as follows:

- Customers: When they change, their buying behavior changes too. This might create opportunities or threats especially if it means a decline in demand for the firm's product.

- Competitors: When they perceive the situation as a zero-sum game, they attack to gain market share. They retaliate to defend market share. In either case, they distract the firm from its path toward its desired strategic end-state.
- Suppliers: Changes in their behavior creates challenges or opportunities for the firm. Their behavior affects the firm's ability to design products, produce them, and price them competitively.
- Organizations that are against the firm's business practices, e.g., the antismoking lobby versus a tobacco company, or animal rights groups versus a fur manufacturer, and so on.
- Societal institutions that represent obstacles to the firm's business activities, e.g., values that inhibit or limit the firm's market expansion and business practices such as refusal to go in debt to buy products.
- Macro external conditions that impact negatively on the firm, such as a recession or an industry structure characterized by a monopoly or an oligopoly.

The type and intensity of the forces of turbulence affects the shape and content of maneuver. Here are some examples:

- With respect to competitors, maneuver centers on a certain ploy or stratagem to block and tackle them.
- With regard to societal organizations, maneuver takes the form of evasive action. For example, when tobacco companies were prohibited from using television to advertise cigarettes, they turned to billboards and sponsoring sports events where their brand names were displayed prominently.
- In dealing with societal institutions, maneuver takes the form of patient, long term offering of incentives for society to change its ways. Once upon a time, buying on credit was frowned upon. However, with continuous, persistent incentives and promotion of the principle of "buy now and pay later," many firms were able to reorient society's thinking. Currently, going in debt is a common buying behavior.
- A macro condition can be outmaneuvered in many ways. The firm can evade it through proactive action, e.g., retrenching in anticipation of a recession. Alternatively, it might decide to drive the condition. For example, Dell changed the way computers are sold. Amazon.com changed the way books are sold.

In the final analysis, maneuver is a system of integrated, internally consistent moves to be played out against the forces of turbulence. At the core of this system of moves is a certain scheme, stratagem, or ploy that sets the tone for the whole system. The system of moves must have built-in provisions for change with the changing, unpredictable behavior of the unfriendly forces. For example, competitors will not just sit idle for us to block and tackle them. They will retaliate. We must anticipate their retaliation and be prepared with another round of action to neutralize such retaliation and so on. In this regard, maneuver has to project rounds and rounds of behavior on the part of these forces and rounds and rounds of plotting to neutralize them. It is not enough to outmaneuver them once or twice. It has to go on indefinitely. It is a race without a finish line.

To recap, maneuver has some characteristics that must be stressed at this point:

- Maneuver is circumstantial. It is a "contingent" action. It is an "if-then" proposition. Even though it is driven by a strategic objective, it is born out of the prevailing circumstances reflecting their peculiarities more so than the objective itself.
- It involves making choices, not just about the "then's" but also about the "if's." Part of the essence of maneuver is *picking and choosing* the terms of engagement. To

compete with IBM, Apple, Compaq (and other PC makers), Michael Dell chose to create his own brand and by selling direct to customers. IBM and the others were utilizing the traditional wholesale-retail channel of distribution. Along the same lines, Jeff Bezos (CEO, Amazon.com) chose to sell books on the Internet instead of the traditional brick-and-mortar strategy.
- It is "multi-track" in that it comprises a network of maneuvers on several fronts simultaneously including production, purchasing, marketing, financing, human resources management, etc.
- Maneuver is a continuous activity; as continuous as turbulence itself. It is a continuously changing response to a continuously changing situation.
- Maneuver is the path to a desired strategic end-state. However, it might expand to include the search for and the choice of an end-state as well, especially when turbulence renders a pre-established end-state as undesirable.
- It is financially oriented, with costs and returns continuously computed.
- The unit of maneuver is the business move. A maneuver is a system of moves, a coherent, interdependent set of actions built around a ploy that outwits or outmaneuvers the unfriendly forces. The concept "move" will be explored further in Chapter 15 in connection with the topic of capability since capability is the inventory of moves that the firm draws from to maneuver its way in the marketplace.
- To be effective, a maneuver must meet two criteria. First, it has to be "robust," i.e., produces satisfactory outcomes under a wide range of scenarios. Second, it has to have intelligence, i.e., it has built into it a wide range of adaptive actions to suit a range of circumstances (that may emerge in the future). It changes with the changing circumstances themselves. A good maneuver thus has to be "fluid."
- The architecture of maneuver evolves as a semicoherent direction that suggests itself out of the many initiatives of empowered employees operating as frontline entrepreneurs.

As a business phenomenon, maneuver seems to take place in two stages. In the first stage, maneuver is formulated as a plan of attack on paper. This is part of the strategic planning process. This stage is carried through scenario planning as explained in Chapter 11. We call this stage "maneuvering at the thinking plane." This is analogical to what military planners call "war-on-map." In the second stage, the plan is acted out in the marketplace and business facts are actually created. We call this stage "maneuvering at the acting plane." This also is analogical to what military planners call "war-in-the field."

As in military thought, business maneuver has doctrines too. Consider the following principles that Yoffie and Cusumano discovered after studying the strategic behavior of e-business firms.[7] These are presented in Exhibit 12.1. The work of Yoffie and Cusumano shows that it is possible to develop principles that can be used in formulating maneuver for a business firm. It is part of strategic leadership to uncover such principles and spread them throughout the organization so that sound maneuvers can be formulated.

## BUSINESS MANEUVER: A CONCEPTUAL FRAMEWORK

### Establishing Corporate Objectives

Before formulating maneuver, it is crucial to establish a set of corporate objectives. Maneuver is essentially wheeling and dealing in the marketplace. It has to be purposive and focused. Establishing corporate objectives sets boundaries for this focus. Corporate objectives

> **Principle #1: Move rapidly to uncontested ground to avoid head-to-head conflict.**
> - Move to new products that redefine the competitive space.
> - Move to new pricing models that competitors are unable to emulate.
> - Move to new testing and distribution models that avoid competitors' strength.
> - Constant movement is not always possible or desirable.
> - Do not allow excessive movement to destroy your focus and weaken your credibility.
> - Rapid movement is not a substitute for long-term vision.
> - Speed and time-to-market are not substitutes for quality to customers.
>
> **Principle #2: Be flexible and give way when attacked direct by superior force.**
> - Avoid sumo matches unless you are bigger and stronger than your opponent.
> - Embrace and extend rivals' smart moves.
> - Mesh flexibility and tactical adjustments with a long-term strategic plan.
> - Avoid escalating unwinnable wars.
> - Cannibalize your own products if you need or have to.
>
> **Principles #3: Exploit leverage that uses the weight and strength of opponents against them.**
> - Turn your opponent's strategic commitments and investments to your advantage.
> - Cooperate with others who are threatened by your opponent's success.
> - The greater your success, the more that leverage can be used against you.

Exhibit 12.1: Doctrines of Maneuver in the E-Business Marketplace

involve the firm in its entirety. They are formulated as derivatives of the expected outcomes established as part of the firm's vision (Chapter 16).

Objectives are different from the expected visionary outcomes. The envisioned outcomes are long-term since they pertain to the desired strategic end-state. This end-state is not arrived at in the immediate term. It takes a few time horizons to reach it. Along the way to the end-state, the organization needs a number of guideposts or landmarks. These landmarks are the corporate objectives. When corporate objectives are attained at the end of a given time horizon, then the firm would be a step closer to its strategic end-state. For the next time horizon, new objectives are established. When these are attained, then the firm would be another step closer to its desired end-state. This process is repeated until the firm arrives at the desired end-state. In a turbulent environment, the time horizons for objectives become rather short. No matter how short the time horizon becomes, the organization needs to focus on a few important objectives to achieve.

Corporate objectives have definite characteristics as follows:

- They are shorter in time horizon than the envisioned outcomes in the firm's vision, the desired end-state.
- While the envisioned outcomes are stated in general terms (as ambitions), objectives are framed in specific terms as performance levels to be achieved, e.g., increase market share or distribute a certain level of dividend payment.
- A statement of an objective has four crucial components:[8]
  —A certain attribute being sought, e.g., market standing, financial structure, etc.
  —A certain index for measuring the attribute, e.g., a percent, a ratio, a rate of increase, or an absolute value.
  —A certain level of achievement as a target or a hurdle, e.g., 30% market share instead of 50% or 10%.

—A time frame or a deadline for achieving the objective, e.g., 30% market share by the third year.

Two types of objectives need to be formulated before maneuver is designed. These are strategic objectives and financial objectives.

## Strategic Objectives

Strategic objectives cover a wide range of areas. A study of corporate annual reports can quickly show the variety of such objectives. Here are some examples:

- Achieving a certain market share, e.g., like 30% or 40%.
- Achieving a certain market, e.g., establishing and maintaining a dominant leadership position in the international market, or to be number one in the industry.
- Achieving a certain sales penetration rate that would assure the firm of a certain position in a certain product-market segment, e.g., achieving a net sales growth rate of 10% per year.
- Innovation, e.g., having 30% of its annual sales coming from products that are four years old or less.
- Achieving a certain size, e.g., Patrick Kelly's (Chapter 3) goal of making PSS/ World Medical a $500 million company and then a billion dollar company.
- Achieving a certain level of customer satisfaction, e.g., 100% total customer satisfaction every day for every customer.

## Financial Objectives

Premised on the strategic objectives, the financial objectives specify the financial results of the firm's operation. Financial objectives tend to cluster around themes like earning growth, stock prices, dividend payments, financial structure (debt to equity balance), and the like. Here are some examples of financial objectives from past corporate annual reports:

- A double-digit annual earnings per share.
- Dividend payments consistent with earning growth.
- Quality earnings and cash flow returns.
- 20% return on equity.
- 15% average growth rate in earnings per share.
- 40% or less total debt to capital ratio.
- Pay out 25% to 35% of net income in dividends.

## STRUCTURE OF MANEUVER

Given the vision of the firm translated as a set of corporate objectives, maneuver comprises a number of elements as shown in Exhibit 12.2. It is worth stressing that the firm's capability and organization structure also influence the maneuver. They are all aspects of one entity, the firm's strategy that embodies a strategic response to turbulence.

Exhibit 12.2 reads as follows. In light of the established strategic and financial objectives (as well as the vision, capability, and structure), the first element of maneuver is a set of strategic issues chosen to be addressed, e.g., certain compelling opportunities to exploit and/or critical challenges to be faced. This element also might include the choice of a strategic end-state should there be the need for one as stated above. Given a set of strategic issues (and possibly an end-state), the next element is the choice of the strategic thrust, the decisive broad action that serves as the direction for the path toward the end-state. Given the strategic thrust, the next element expands it into a business model, a way of doing business and making profits. Now that we have a business model, the next element is a translation of the

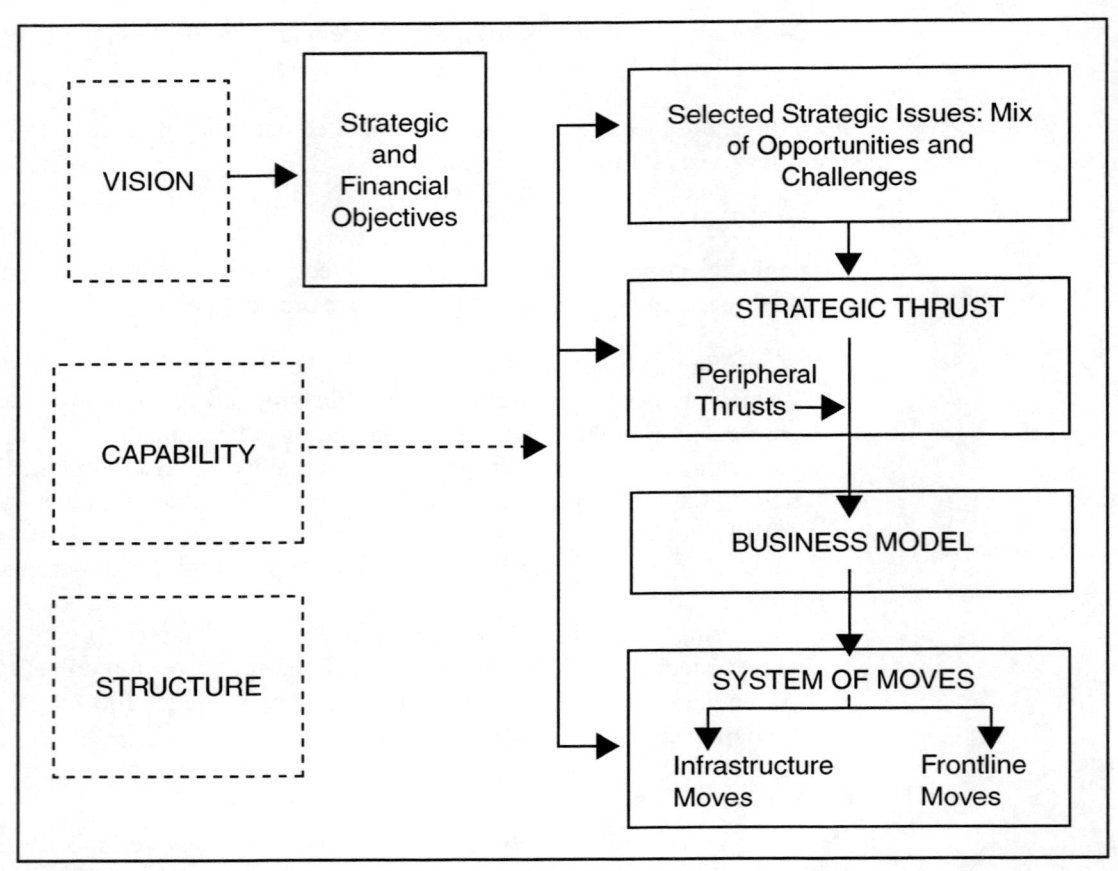

Exhibit 12.2: Structure of Maneuver

business model into a system of moves to be executed in the marketplace. When these moves are carried out, the strategic issues would have been addressed, the firm would be a step closer to the desired end-state, and the non-controllable forces of turbulence would have been tackled somehow. In the pages to follow, each one of these elements will be explored in more depth.

## I. Opportunities and Challenges/New Strategic End-State

This element depends on whether we are pursuing a viable strategic end-state or not. If we are pursuing a promising end-state, then the first step is to identify matters that enhance or block the path towards it. Strategic opportunities and strengths enhance the path. Crippling problems, weaknesses, and threats block the path. It is crucial then that we start by selecting certain opportunities and strengths to exploit; and certain problems, weaknesses, and threats to address or evade. We need to narrow down the selection in order to focus our resources. We cannot address all of them due to limited resources. Maneuver is a focused effort and this is the beginning of the focusing process. The application of the issues analysis methodology of Chapter 10 can help unearth these issues. The choice of what issues to focus on and what to leave out is an act of maneuver by itself. It is a way of zigging and zagging around whatever turbulence poses for us.

By contrast, if turbulence has rendered our envisioned end-state undesirable, then maneuver also includes the choice of a new end-state. If we apply the issues analysis methodology, the resulting strategic issues will help us decide whether the currently pursued end-state has become questionable or not. If it has become undesirable, then we need to search for and designate a new end-state at this point, and then design a path towards it as part of this step.

It is worth noting that the strategic issues fall into three major categories as follows:

- Situation-Specific Strategic Issues: These are the issues inherent in turbulence (that were extracted through issues analysis methodology) and they fall generally into one of these three categories:
  —Problems Type Issues: Events, developments, and trends that *currently* impact negatively on the firm. These are addressed by tackling them. These are viewed as *challenges*.
  —Opportunities Type Issues: Events, developments, and trends the impact of which is positive now, or can be positive with high likelihood in the future. These are addressed by exploiting them. Obviously, these are viewed as *opportunities*.
  —Threats Type Issues: These are the events, developments, and trends that impact negatively on the firm. These are addressed by evading them or responding to them proactively (by having a response prepared in advance to be invoked if they materialize). Threats are treated as *challenges*.

- System's Activities Issues: These are inherent in the system's activities. They could have contributed to or exacerbated the situation specific issues. There are two categories:
  —Strengths' Issues: These refer to characteristics inherent in the system's activities. They may translate into opportunities for the firm. For example, if the firm has an ingenious maneuver or an advanced, unique capability. Strengths are generally viewed as *opportunities* because they can be used to enhance existing opportunities or create new ones.
  —Weaknesses' Issues: These are inherent in the system's activities that could have created problems for the firm, or increased its exposure to threats. For example, if the firm has an ineffective maneuver, an obsolete capability, or a stifling structure. Weaknesses are treated as *challenges*. They are hurdles to be overcome.

- Strategic Leadership Issues: These are inherent in the way the leadership corrals and steers the system's activities. For example, if the leadership philosophies pertain to the command and control paradigm, this may contribute to the situation specific issues as well as the system's activities issues.

## II. The Strategic Thrust

Given a choice of corporate objectives and a set of strategic issues (or a new end-state), the next act of maneuver is the design of a path towards the designated strategic end state. The design of a path begins with the choice of a direction or a decisive focus for the firm's effort. At this decisive focus, the bulk of the firm's resources will be poured in order to achieve maximum impact. The choice of a focus is a masterstroke that seems to have the power to address the strategic issues, exploit opportunities, evade threats, and achieve the strategic and financial objectives. Such is the compelling nature of a focus. This focus is what we call here "the strategic thrust." The choice of a central focus does not preclude other crucial pursuits. There can be a focus and other pursuits, but they are peripheral to the central one. These are secondary strategic thrusts and they will be discussed in the next section. The strategic thrust is an abstract thought that singles out a decisive point or a focus for the firm. It is not a plan. It is not a move.

The strategic thrust is thus a very powerful idea, so compelling that it justifies the commitment of the firm's resources to it *en mass*. Its power lies in its ability to enable the firm to exploit sizeable opportunities (critical for achieving the desired strategic end-state) and at the same time, it disables competitors such that they do not impede the firm's effort. It does have an element of ploy. To illustrate, consider the case of Jeff Bezos, CEO and founder of Amazon.com. He wanted to get in the book selling business. The traditional business model (brick-and-mortar in numerous locations) posed serious problems: high cost of entry, investment in stores, not to mention the dominance of large competitors (e.g., Barnes & Noble, Borders, etc.). Yet, Bezos wanted to get in the business and at the same time wanted to evade these obstacles. To outmaneuver them, a breakthrough idea emerged: why not sell books on the Internet? Selling books on the Internet became the strategic thrust for Amazon.com.\

Here are some examples of powerful ideas that served as strategic thrusts for well-known companies.[9] Exhibit 12.3 provides more examples.

| COMPANY | BUSINESS | STRATEGIC THRUST |
|---|---|---|
| Intel | Semiconductor manufacturer | Focus on developing tools to enable OEM's to write application programs. |
| Loblaws | Supermarket chain | Reinventing an existing industry by popularizing the no-name grocery products and acting as a consultant to other chains in implementing the no-name concept. |
| Nucor | Steel manufacturer | Reinventing the way business is done. Building a geographic network of mini mills located near customers to service them quicker and better. |
| United Health Care | Managed health care provider | Developing and expanding HMO business. |
| Brinker International | Casual restaurant chain operator | Rapid expansion and introduction of new restaurant concepts. |
| Sysco Foods | Foodservice distributor | Becoming the first national foodservice distributor. |
| Gap Stores | Specialty clothing retailer | Rapid expansion and introduction of child and adult category stores. |
| MCI Communications | Long distance service provider | Becoming the first nationwide, long-distance competitor to AT&T. |
| The Body Shop | Cosmetics | Reinventing exiting industries. Selling ideology and social conscience—developing and marketing products that make customers feel that they helped make the world a better place. |
| Apple Computers | Computers | Inventing a brand new industry—starting from scratch. |
| Swatch | Watch manufacturer | Reinventing an existing industry—reinventing the very concept and functionality of the watch itself by making it a fashion accessory. |
| Dell Computers | Computer marketing | Reinventing the way business is done. Marketing and distributing computer hardware through mail order operations. |
| Benetton (of Italy) | Fashion | Reinventing the way business is done by going "virtual." Creating a virtual network of manufacturers and marketers while focusing on design. |
| Microsoft | Software | Setting new industry standards—making the DNA for all PC software. |
| General Magic | Software | Setting new industry standards. Created and imposed multi-media technology standards for fiber optics and wireless communication software. |

Exhibit 12.3: Examples of Strategic Thrust[10]

- Power retailing, as in the cases of Home Depot, Circuit City, Future Shop, Chapters, Barnes & Noble, and Wal-Mart.
- Bypassing one or more steps in the value chain as in the cases of Dell Computer, Frito-Lay, and Amazon.com.
- Standardizing and simplifying business processes, as in the cases of McDonald's (and business format franchises) and Nucor (in the steel industry).
- Mega branding, as in the case of Disney and IBM as well as other firms that extend their brand to a wide range of products and services.

## The Necessity of Having a Strategic Thrust

Now, why is it necessary to have a strategic thrust? Is it not better (and less risky) to pursue several thrusts at the same time? The reason is this: to maximize the effectiveness of limited resources. No firm has an infinite supply of resources. To get the most of limited resources, they must be focused on a single task. A good analogy here is the convex lens burning a hole in a sheet of paper. On a sunny day, if we hold a convex lens (a couple of inches away from a sheet of paper) for a few minutes, a hole will be burned in the paper. The lens assembles the individual sunrays and focuses them on the particular spot on the paper. As the rays are assembled, they (as a group) generate enough heat to burn a hole. Without the lens (assembling and focusing them), the various rays were spread all over the surface of the sheet of paper. They do not have to burn a hole. The lesson here is that when resources are focused (i.e., assembled and applied at a single point), they make an impact. Without a focus, they will be applied to many things. They will be spread too thin with a negligible impact in each area of application. Many CEOs caution against the temptation "to be all things to all people." In other words, they advise us not to undertake many ventures simultaneously with a limited set of resources. Focusing is a direct application of the doctrine of the rational application of force suggested by General Beaufre as stated earlier in this chapter.

Now, does the choice of a strategic thrust preclude other important and promising thrusts? This is not suggested here. The firm can pursue several thrusts simultaneously. However, only one strategic thrust will be the focus. It will get the majority of resources. The other thrusts will be treated as sidelines or peripheral thrusts. They will be carried out but they will not consume the bulk of resources. Experimentation with sidelines on the peripheries is important. Such experimentation might lead to the discovery of a greater strategic thrust. For example, Amazon.com's initial thrust focused on books. However, the presence of lateral opportunities attracted it to go into toys, electronics, and other products.

What about companies that do business in different industries? Such firms are multi-business firms. A multi-business firm is a conglomeration of smaller units, a portfolio of single business units (SBU's). Each SBU will have a singular strategic thrust. The conglomeration itself has a different strategic thrust, mainly a directive for building its portfolio of businesses. This type of firm will be discussed later on in this chapter.

It should be stressed here that the strategic thrust can change over time. It is part of the firm's effort to respond continuously to a continuously changing situation (turbulence in the business world). Depending on market dynamics, the firm can pursue a thrust for a period and then when the market changes, it would switch thrusts. Take the case of Amazon.com again. At the outset, its strategic thrust was to sell books over the Internet. Then the thought came to the founder that the firm is a broker between customers who have a need and suppliers with products that can fill this need. He discovered that Amazon.com could be a conduit for any consumer product. The firm's strategic thrust was changed from selling books to selling consumer products over the Internet. Since then, Amazon.com branched out into other products such as toys and electronics among others. The new thrust appears to be the Wal-Mart of the Internet.

## Strategic Thrust, Strategic Intent, and Mission: Resolving the Terminology Confusion

As the focal task for the firm to achieve, the strategic thrust is the *mission* of the firm. The term mission deserves some clarification here since it has different meanings in the literature. Quigly, for example states that the term mission is the answer to the question: "What are we today? What are our aspirations for the future?"[11] Other writers define mission as the reason for being, "why does the firm exist?" In corporate practice, the firm's mission is often stated in generic terms that are too ambiguous to accomplish, e.g., "to be the best," or "to serve customers." Such statements seem to be an expression of ambition rather than a mission. We should recall, however, the term mission was borrowed from the military. For the military leader, the term refers to a specific task assigned to a military unit to achieve. This task is often well defined, specific, and anchored in time, e.g., capture the xyz strategic point (e.g., hill, bridge, road, access, etc.) by a certain hour or day. There is a reason why the military leaders define the mission clearly. They have discovered that a precise definition of a mission or a thrust leads to its achievement, as the troops will be focused on this one task to accomplish. They often do it—unless the enemy outmaneuvers them. We suggest the use of the military definition of the term mission. Hence, the terms "mission" and "strategic thrust" are equivalent.

### Anatomy of the Strategic Thrust

A strategic thrust is a *thought* that is captured in one phrase, a sentence, or a few sentences. Yet, this thought is a complex one. It has a number of fundamental elements built into it. If we decompose this thought, we will find five components as shown in Exhibit 12.4. The five elements are not stated separately. They are designed individually, but they are collapsed into one sentence or two. We separate only for the purposes of analysis and deeper understanding.

Here is a brief description of each of the five elements of the strategic thrust:

### 1. Perspective

The heart of the strategic thrust is the focal task itself, e.g., selling books on the Internet. However, this task derives out of a certain perspective, predisposition, or attitude towards the world we live in. For example, some persons might be predisposed to the philosophy that "offense is the best defense." Others might be inclined toward the idea that "he who runs away shall live to fight another day."

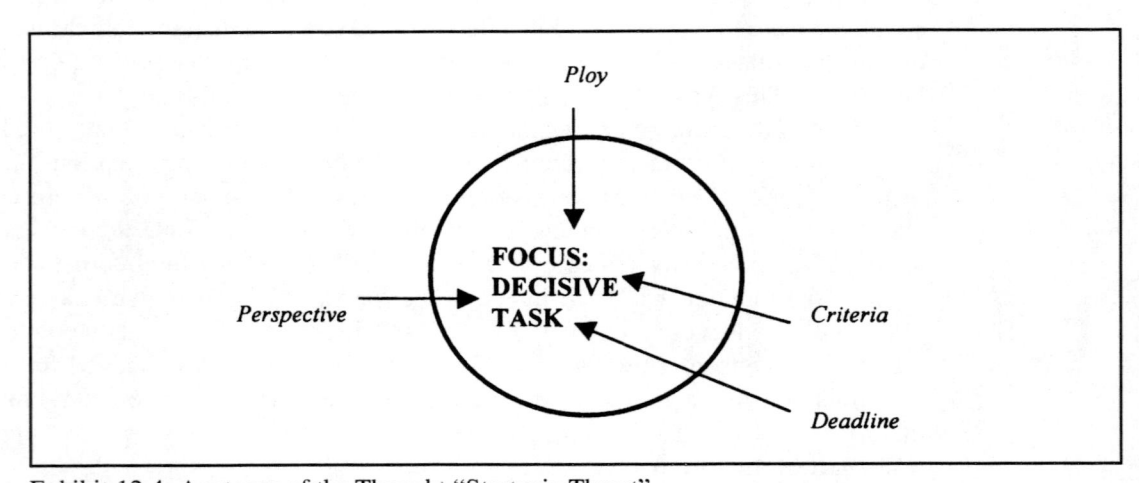

Exhibit 12.4: Anatomy of the Thought "Strategic Thrust"

In the business world, turbulence is the "enemy." Predispositions towards turbulence appear to fall into three categories: *driving* it, *adapting* to it, or *ignoring* it.

1.1. Driving Turbulence: This is an aggressive stance. It calls for creating turbulence that would benefit the firm. This can be one of two postures:

- Offensive: Driving turbulence by undertaking new initiatives that may put others on the defensive by attacking their core market, e.g., Lexus' Division of Toyota's thrust "Get Mercedes."
- Encircling, Enveloping: A variation on the main theme of driving turbulence by attacking from the peripheries and avoiding a strong competitor's "core" market, e.g., Komatsu's thrust: "encircle CAT" (Caterpillar Corporation).

1.2. Adapting To Turbulence: This is a defensive perspective. It calls for accommodating or absorbing turbulence. It can be one of four postures as follows:

- Defensive: Taking action to neutralize or to adjust to the initiative of others.
- Branching out: Entering into other sub-arenas and pursuing other opportunities to reduce the risk of dependence on one opportunity that is threatened now or will be in the future.
- Retrenchment: Retreating from peripheries, regrouping, and defending the core opportunity.
- Withdrawal: Vacating the field altogether including divestment or liquidation.

## 2. The Decisive Task: The Mission

The backbone of the strategic thrust is the decisive task that becomes the central focus of the firm's activities to which the bulk of its resources will be committed. This task is then the mission that the firm must accomplish. Let us consider some examples of decisive tasks that served as the core of the strategic thrusts of well-known companies:[12]

- Amazon.com: Sell books on the Internet (the early thrust). The thinking goes something like this: If this task was accomplished, it would enable the firm to exploit opportunity in the book market in a way (the Internet) that would outmaneuver traditional brick-and-mortar bookseller chains (who did not have or believe in the Internet at that time).
- Komatsu: "Encircle CAT." This was its thrust for years. The act of encircling was believed to be important in enabling Komatsu to exploit the opportunity in the earth moving equipment market by slowly taking away segments at the peripheries so that the giant CAT does not wake up to retaliate.
- Starbucks: Sell coffee by the cup in a certain ambiance, the coffee bar. This was crucial for exploiting the opportunity in coffee drinking by going around traditional retailers and restaurants.
- Boeing: The Company "bet the pot" on the B-17, the 707, and 747 aircraft.
- IBM: Commit $5 billion gambling on the mainframe 360 computer to meet the emerging demand for electronic data processing in the 1970s.
- Motorola: Invent a way to sell 100,000 TV's at $179.95; attain six-sigma quality; win the Baldridge Award.
- Philip Morris: Slay Goliath and become the front-runner in the tobacco industry despite the social forces against smoking.
- Sony: Change the worldwide image of Japanese products as poor quality; create a pocketable transistor radio.

- Disney: Build Disneyland and build it in our image, not industry standards.
- Merck: Become the preeminent drug maker worldwide via massive R&D and new products that cure disease.

A decisive task has to meet certain criteria. Here is the minimum:

- It has to be *clear*, requiring little or no explanation.
- It has to be *compelling*, i.e., promising the exploitation of a great opportunity (life and death opportunity) and/or evasion of a life threatening problem, obstruction or a threat. A strategic thrust has to be compelling enough to serve as a rallying cry for motivating the organization.
- It has to fall well outside the firm's comfort zone. It should represent a *stretch* beyond the usual expectations.
- It has to demonstrate marked genius, i.e., considerable creativity and possible breakthrough thinking.
- It has to be *bold* and *exciting* in its own right, potent in enlisting people's enthusiasm and commitment.
- It has to be consistent with the company's vision and core ideology, especially if they are not outdated by turbulence.

## A Typology of Focal Tasks

A survey of the strategic thrusts of a number of companies suggested ten categories of focal tasks. These categories serve as a typology for focal tasks. These are:

- Focusing on a Certain Customer Segment: Thrusts here tend to target a certain market segment as the focus for the firm's efforts and resources on satisfying a wide range of needs for this segment. Consider Home Depot or Canadian Tire's focus on the do-it-yourself market segment. Both these firms focus on providing a full line of products and services for this segment.
- Focus on a Certain Market Need Regardless of Segment: Thrusts here take the form of a certain customer need and the firm's efforts and resources will be focused on satisfying it for all market segments. Management consulting firms focus on the need for guidance. Accounting firms concentrate on financial information. Brokerage firms fall in this category as well.
- Focusing on a Certain Process: Thrusts in this category pertain to a particular process of doing business where all the firm's resources will be focused on it. Examples here include Dell's thrust of selling direct, or Amazon.com's current emphasis on the e-business process.
- Focusing on a Certain Product/Service Concept: This type of thrust relates to a particular product design such as Apple Computer's user-friendly computer in the early days and the fashion computer in the 2000s (the I-Mac). Amazon.com's focus on books in the early days is another example.
- Focusing on a Certain Role in the Industry: Thrusts here pertain to a certain role to play in a certain market landscape. Virtual corporations tend to focus on the role of brokering between customers, producers, and distributors of a certain product. They build networks of suppliers and marketers to get the product to the market.
- Focusing on a Certain Business Concept: Thrusts here pertain to a certain interpretation or understanding of the business. Nucor, for example, developed a specific concept of the steel business: mills geared to special applications located near customers who need them. Rolls Royce thrived on a particular concept of the auto business: the automobile as an extension of the aristocracy (large, comfortable leather

seats, traveling quietly in an ambiance of understated elegance). BMW has its own concept of the auto business too, the ultimate in engineering.

- Focusing on Innovation: Thrusts in this category tend to assume the form of continuous innovation to drive change in the marketplace. The firm in this case commits the bulk of resources to a continuous stream of innovation not just in its product but also in its business processes as well. Strategic thrusts of electronic products' manufacturers tend to fall in this category. Sony is a good example. Intel commits to innovation as its way of driving the computer industry.

- Focusing on a Certain Opportunity: The thrust in this case is a certain opportunity to be pursued in a single-minded manner. The firm is not tied to a particular product, market, or process. It commits to a specific opportunity. Once the opportunity is exploited, the firm moves to another one and so on. Investment bankers operate in this fashion where a particular deal will be the thrust until it is completed and then it moves to the next one and so on. Many of the Dot-Com's fall in this category. Even a casual surfing of the Internet can show the impressive variety of these companies and the opportunities on which they focus.

- Focusing on Creating the Brand: In today's world, intrinsic product differentiation is difficult to maintain. Competitors tend to imitate one another and compete on price. The result is that a differentiated product can quickly become a commodity where the customer cannot distinguish between one competitor's product and another. Hence, the pressure is on creating the brand, i.e., engraving the brand name in the customers' minds such that they trust and seek out only this particular brand. In the dot.com age, creating the brand is crucial since the firms exist in cyberspace, with no bricks-and-mortar edifice to identify with.

- Focusing on Value to the Customer: In the brick-and-mortar, big business era, overhead expenses dominated the firm's cost structure. In many cases, what the customer actually got (the cost of goods sold) was an unduly small percent of the price he/she paid. The rest of the price went for selling and administrative expenses, depreciation, etc. Some of these expenses pertain to activities that create value, e.g., transforming inputs into finished products, purchasing, marketing, etc. However, many do not add value, e.g., unduly large hierarchies and bureaucracy. As a result, many firms capitalized on this weakness. They focused on increasing the ratio of what the customer gets. They called this creating value for the customer. They competed on value. Their strategic thrust focused on value creation. Most of the dot.com firms compete with traditional brick-and-mortar companies based on value. They have little overhead and as a result they are able to increase what the customer gets to what the customer pays ratio.

## 3. Ploy

Embedded in the decisive task is a scheme or a ploy for winning customers and neutralizing (blocking and tackling) opposition. The ploy is not separable from the task itself. The reason is this: we formulate a strategic thrust as a masterstroke to win customers and outmaneuver the opposition. Hence, the decisive task has a "built-in" ploy for doing so. In the examples of the decisive tasks mentioned above, the ploy was loud and clear. Amazon.com's ploy was to leave out the brick-and-mortar arena and sell books using a novel, radically different approach, the Internet. Hopefully, by the time the traditional booksellers realize what is going on, Amazon.com would have become a major bookseller. For Komatsu, "encircling" desensitized CAT. Through incremental encircling, CAT did not see Komatsu as a formidable opponent to be wiped out. For Starbucks, the use of a novel concept and spreading the locations very quickly not only outmaneuvered traditional coffee sellers, but it also discouraged others from entering the coffee bar business. Exhibit 12.5 contains five possi-

| Type of Ploy | Description |
|---|---|
| **Rule Making:** | The thrust here is to mold and "socialize" the whole industry to play by the firm's rules. The firm sets the standards and the rules of the game. Good cases in mind are Microsoft and Intel. |
| **Rule Breaking:** | The thrust in this case focuses on destabilizing an entrenched industry and pioneering the new trend. Firms that followed this thrust include Apple Computer, Club Med, MCI, and Honda. |
| **Playing the Game:** | This thrust is most suitable for companies in growing industries. The thrust is to push the product taking advantage of the order established by the rule makers. Companies in this category include Pepsi, Xerox, Boston Market, and Starbucks. |
| **Specializing**: | The thrust here is to create a market niche outside a mass market. Midwest Express, Exxon, and Nordic Track follow this type of thrust. |
| **Improvising:** | This is most suitable when the industry is in a state of upheaval and the rules of the game are up in the air. The thrust is to live the moment and concentrate on immediate goals. Current followers of this thrust include: Baby Bells, GM, Digital Equipment, IBM, and Kodak. |

Exhibit 12.5: Five Generic Ploys

ble types of ploys that can be embedded in a chosen focal task.[13] Exhibit 12.6 (adapted from Lele[14]) suggests further ploys, taking into consideration the competitive situation, the industry's market structure, and the industry's stage of development.

In Exhibit 12.6, the table has three dimensions: competitive situation, industry structure, and stage of industry development. The ploy recommended for each competitor is entered in the cells. For example, in a growing industry where the situation is win-win, the best ploy for the leader of the pack is to "define the game," i.e., set the rules, so to speak, and let the others adapt to it. For the number 2 and 3 competitors, the recommended ploy is to "define or modify the game." For those below that echelon (followers), the recommended ploy is to learn the game or anticipate the rules.

Other combinations of situation, structure, and industry's stage of development call for different ploys. For example, in a lose-lose situation (an industry in the decline stage), the leader can follow the ploy of changing the game. For the others, there is nothing to do. It is

| Competitive Situation | Industry Structure ||||  Industry's Stage of Development |
|---|---|---|---|---|---|
|  | Leader | # 2 or # 3 | Follower | Entrant |  |
| Win-Win | • Define the game | • Define/Modify the game | • Learn the game<br>• Anticipate the rules | • Exploit the game<br>• Become #1 or #2 | Emerging/Growing |
| Limited Warfare | • Set, enforce the rules | Exploit the rules Nibble | • Raise the barricades higher | • Change the rules<br>• Change the game | Early Maturity |
| Win-Lose | • Force Consolidation | • Change the rules: "saw the floor" | • Exit | • Do not enter the game | Late Maturity |
| Lose-Lose | • Change the game | • Exit | • Exit | • Do not consider the game | Decline |

Exhibit 12.6: Possible Ploys to Underlie the Business Model

better to quit the game altogether. In a win-lose situation (an industry in the late maturity stage), the no. 2 and 3 competitors can change the rules or "saw the floor" as Lele suggested. The recommendations explore the entire range of available ploys.

Exhibit 12.7 presents further ploys that were derived from an analysis of the strategic behavior of many firms over the years. Some of them are already implied in the ploys suggested in Exhibits 12.5 and 12.6.

## 4. Criteria

The wording of the decisive task and the ploy should contain some indicators that signal when the thrust is accomplished. Without such criteria, the organization will never be in a position to declare that it has accomplished its mission. For example, Komatsu's thrust, encircle CAT, has an implicit criterion that would tell the firm that its thrust has been realized. The criterion is in the word "encircle." In essence, it says that Komatsu must encircle CAT. The term encircle can be translated into many indicators such as:

- Product encirclement, i.e., Komatsu will have a product that shadows every CAT product.
- Market encirclement, i.e., Komatsu is present in every market segment that CAT serves.
- Geographical encirclement, i.e., Komatsu will be in every country where CAT operates.

## 5. Deadline/Timing

A deadline is crucial to any strategic thrust. In business, timing is crucial. Before their time, thrusts do not succeed. Delayed thrusts might be too obsolete. Furthermore, a deadline establishes accountability for achieving the task. It reduces the danger of taking forever to implement the strategic thrust. This way, the firm avoids the risk of being trapped in the pursuit of one thrust in a changing world. When the deadline arrives and the thrust is accomplished, it is time to move on to the next one. If it is not, then it is time to investigate the

| Ploy | Description |
| --- | --- |
| The breakthrough breakout | A totally radical business concept or process that no one else has |
| Innovation | Focus on what is new |
| Brutal Force/ Doing the Impossible | Outdoing competitors knowing that they do not have the resources to catch up. |
| Focusing on the customers/ Ignoring the competition | Concentrating resources on the customer only without wasting resources matching the competitors' moves. |
| Time Leap | Being several steps ahead of the competition, thus neutralizing their action even before it takes place. |
| Guile | Misleading competitors so that they may think we will undertake a certain action while we are focusing on a different task altogether. |
| Surprise | Staying secretive and surprising competitors where they least expect to be attacked. |
| Cooperation | Building alliances with competitors at some level (e.g., R&D, market development), but then competing at another level, the customer level. |

Exhibit 12.7: Eight Generic Ploys

reasons why. Is the thrust beyond reach? Is the organization inept? Furthermore, when the task is achieved by the deadline, it is a cause for celebration; the firm has won a victory. The sense of victory reinforces the spirit of achievement in the firm. It positions the organization for the next task, which is often a more daring task.

## Composing the Mission/Thrust Statement

All the preceding thoughts (perspective, decisive task, ploy, criteria, deadline) are encoded in a verbal statement. This statement might be one sentence, or a paragraph. Once written, it becomes the mission statement of the firm. From this point onward, the rest of the firm's maneuver is conceived in light of it. It also serves as the key leadership instrument. It is the war cry for rallying the troops.

## Strategic Thrust Formulation

The strategic thrust appears in someone's mind (CEO, a member of the organization, or a team) as a flash of genius or as breakthrough thinking sparked by a certain situation or event. It can be generated in at least seven ways as shown below.

### 1. Market Experience and Experimentation in the Marketplace

Ideally, the strategic thought should come from numerous experimentations by members of the firm. It sometimes suggests itself out of the numerous initiatives of people in an organization particularly if it was a self-organizing one. In a self-organizing system's culture, people often feel empowered to engage in various experiments in an effort to help the organization survive. Consequently, there will be a pool of diverse initiatives and visions. Often the strategic thrust suggests itself as a semicoherent direction or a promising focus for the organization as a whole. Once this thought is picked up, articulated, and assessed, it is chosen as the strategic thrust of the firm. For example, Microsoft started as a supplier of the disk operating system known as MS-DOS. After engaging in this for a while, a discovery was made that the future of the company lies in becoming the controller of the interface between the desktop computer and the user. From that point on, the company's focus was on products to control this interface and to place Microsoft as the dominant force in this interface. This led to the development of WINDOWS and the products that followed. This strategic thrust dominated the company so much so that Bill Gates once said that Microsoft's strategy can be summed up in one word "WINDOWS."

### 2. The Vision as a Source of Strategic Thrust Thoughts

The vision is the desired strategic end-state. As we will see in Chapter 16, the vision includes factors that influence the formulation of the strategic thrust. For example, a vision might specify a specific opportunity arena. This can become the strategic thrust. It might also involve a certain business concept or a business model that suggest the strategic thrust. In such cases, the strategic thrust is a direct application of the firm's vision (Chapter 16). If the firm has an established vision and it is adhering to it, the strategic thrust derives from the firm's concept of business. After success with selling books on the Internet, Amazon.com started seeing itself (vision) as a broker between suppliers of a product and its buyers. This became its concept of business. Out of this vision came several thrusts, including selling toys, electronics, tools, and many others.

### 3. A Particular Event or Personal Experience

Sometimes, the thought comes from an experience that leads to a flash of genius, the discovery of a strategic thrust. Here is an example of how the thought of a strategic thrust struck a CEO, Howard Schultz of Starbucks Coffee. Originally, Starbucks was a retailer of coffees from around the world that sold coffee for customers to brew and serve at home. He described the strategic thrust thought-provoking experience as follows:

> "After I had been at Starbucks for a year, I had an experience that changed my life. I went to Milan to attend an international housewares show. On my first morning, I noticed a little espresso bar. Behind the counter a tall, thin man was cheerfully greeting customers.
>
> 'Espresso?' he asked, holding out a cup. After three sips it was gone, but I could still feel its warmth and energy.
>
> That day I discovered the romance and ritual of coffee bars in Italy. My mind started churning. My company's connection to coffee lovers did not have to limited to their homes, where they ground and brewed out coffee. What we should do was sell coffee by the cup, in coffee bars."[15]

From that point on, Shultz bet the farm on the coffee bar concept. He left Starbucks to start his own firm, Il Gionale, which had the coffee bar concept as its strategic thrust. Later on, Il Gionale acquired the old Starbucks stores and transformed them into a national chain with the coffee bar concept as its strategic thrust.

### 4. The Successes of Other Companies and Other Business Models

In many cases, the strategic thrust can be triggered by an inspiration from the experience of other companies in the same field or other fields. For example, Ray Kroc's thrust for McDonald's (fast, low cost menu in a standardized clean restaurant concept replicated nationally through franchising) inspired Burger King and Wendy's and many others in the fast food business. His thrust became a business model for firms outside fast food such as Midas Muffler. To do so, one needs to survey a number of thrusts like the examples mentioned in this section.

### 5. The Application of Generic Models

To get additional inspiration for a strategic thrust thought, one can use generic models to start the process. If one examines corporate strategic thrusts and catalogues them, it is possible to identify some generic ones like the ones that Tomasko identified in Exhibit 12.5. Porter also suggested a number of thrusts for the single business firm, what he called generic strategies.[16] These are known as overall cost leadership, differentiation, and focus. The low cost thrust involves becoming the lowest cost producer in order to win market share. Differentiation, as the name implies, means creating unique products that are clearly different from those of competitors. This uniqueness would help the firm attain a superior position in the marketplace. Amazon.com, for example, differentiated itself by selling on the Internet. The third thrust is focus and this calls for choosing one or more market segments and focusing on them exclusively, such as Rolls Royce for example.

### 6. The Particulars of the Firm Itself

In many cases, the particulars of the situation facing the firm might suggest a strategic thrust. For example, if one plots the issues facing the firm on a graph like the one shown in Exhibit 12.8, the clustering of the issues might suggest a thrust. There are certain quadrants depending on the mix of opportunities, threats, strengths, and weaknesses confronting the firm. If the mix is more threats and weaknesses, the thrust that suggests itself is that the firm ought to be on the defensive. If, on the other hand, it has more strengths and opportunities, the thrust here should be to go on the offensive. Alternatively, if there are more strengths but the threats are just as compelling, perhaps the thrust should be to diversify.

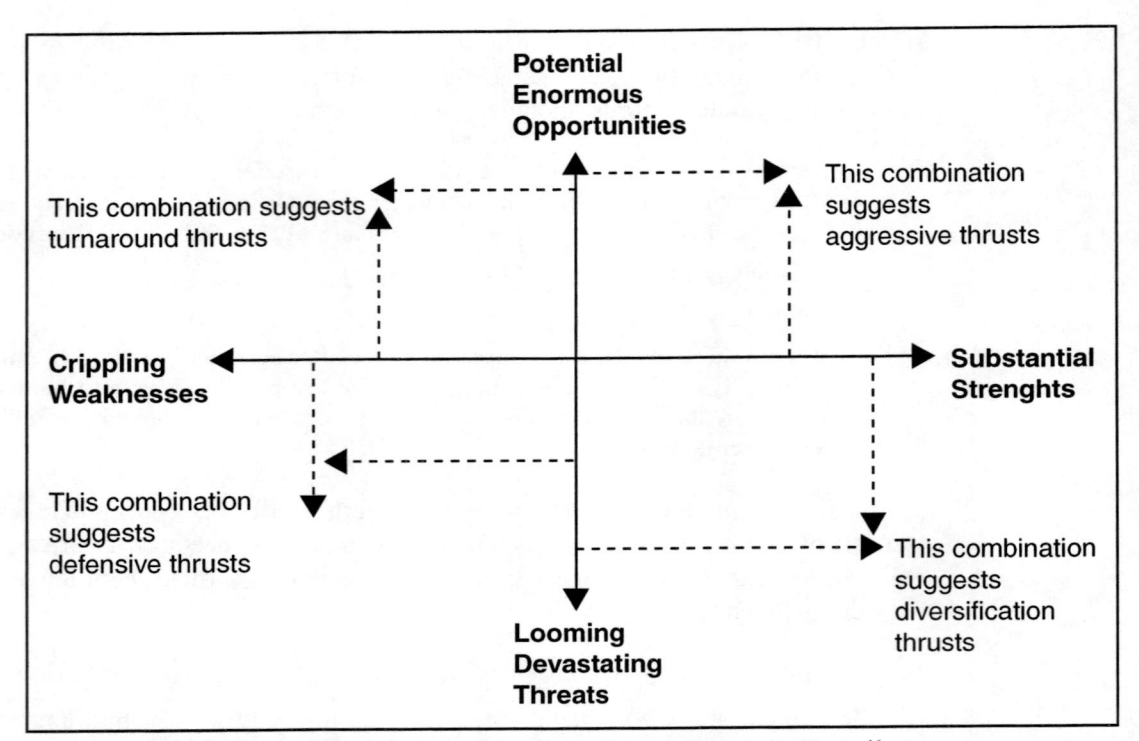

```
                    Potential
                    Enormous
                    Opportunities
                         ▲
This combination suggests      This combination
turnaround thrusts             suggests
                               aggressive thrusts

Crippling  ◄─────────────────►  Substantial
Weaknesses                      Strenghts

This combination
suggests                       This combination
defensive thrusts              suggests
                               diversification
                               thrusts
                    ▼
                    Looming
                    Devastating
                    Threats
```

Exhibit 12.8: The Firm's Particulars and How They Suggest Strategic Thrust[16]

## 7. Deliberate, Systematic Formulation

The strategic thrust can be formulated in a systematic, deliberate manner by using the scenario planning process outlined in Chapter 11. The strategic thrust can be viewed as a set of knobs as shown in Exhibit 12.4. Three knobs are relevant here. These are: (1) the perspective, (2) the ploy, and (3) the central task or mission. Keeping the strategic issues, future scenarios, and capability in mind, we can start by identifying the possible settings for each knob. If we view the element "perspective" as a knob, we can see that it can have positions or settings such as offensive, defensive, withdrawal, etc. Along the same lines, the ploy knob can be set to many positions as Exhibits 12.5, 12.6, and 12.7 show. Alternatively, we can create any ploy through imagination and inspiration. The decisive task knob can have many positions depending on the alternative tasks that we can formulate. We next develop alternative combinations of the knobs' settings or positions. Each combination would represent a strategic thrust. Now that we have formulated a number of alternative strategic thrusts, we test drive them in the future (i.e., under the different scenarios), and identify their consequences and the gaps associated with each. We can then choose the thrust that is clearly robust, or at least one that would function well under the most likely scenario.

There is another term that is worth considering here, "strategic intent." As articulated by Hamel and Pralhald, *strategic intent* is "The dream that energizes a company."[17] It conveys a "sense of direction," "a differentiated, competitively unique point of view about the future."[18] It further conveys a "sense of discovery" for it "holds out the promise of exploring a new competitive territory."[19] It also implies a "sense of destiny" and has "an emotional edge to it in that people in the organization believe in it as a worthwhile goal."[20] Clearly, this definition of intent describes the concept of strategic thrust presented here. In sum then, throughout this work, the terms "strategic thrust," "mission," and "strategic intent" are viewed as equivalent expressions.

## III. Peripheral Strategic Thrusts

As defined earlier, the strategic thrust is like the basket in which we will put our eggs. This is risky, but is part of the business gamble. However, there will be pressure to reduce this risk by pursuing other strategic thrusts simultaneously. Having several strategic thrusts spreads the resources too thin. The way out of this problem is to designate the strategic thrust as the focus of the firm's effort and the other thrusts as peripheral to this focus. They are pursued at the same time but they are placed in the proper perspective relative to the strategic thrust. This will be demonstrated by allocating resources according to this perspective. There are two types of peripheral thrusts: parallel thrusts and enabling thrusts.

### Parallel Thrusts

Besides the central strategic thrust, the typical firm pursues other thrusts concurrently. Although these parallel thrusts are important, they will not be treated as focal in terms of resource allocation. Resources will still be focused on the central thrust. Lateral opportunities are important to pursue as peripheral thrusts because they offer the firm many advantages. First, the firm might be able to leverage its resources to exploit them in a low cost manner as in the case of synergies where fixed assets can be used to make a different product or service, e.g., Amazon.com adding toys to its line of books. In this case, they generate more cash that can be used to bolster the main thrust. Second, the lateral opportunities might prove so successful that they might become tomorrow's focal thrust for the firm. For example, traditional retailers like Sears & Roebuck are pursuing e-business opportunities at the moment. It is possible that the e-business unit will be so successful that Sears might eventually be an e-tailer. Third, experimentation with lateral opportunities might lead to the emergence of a strategic thrust that the firm might adopt as its focal one. In such a case, the main strategic thrust is discovered or it surfaces out of experimenting with sidelines.

### Enabling Thrusts

In many cases, the strategic thrust may require further major derivative commitments from the firm to help it materialize. An example can clarify this concept. Dell's strategic thrust was selling computers by mail. However, for this thrust to succeed, Dell would have to overcome buyers' resistance. PC buyers might not feel comfortable buying a computer sight unseen by mail. To overcome this fear, Dell would have to offer them a high quality and highly reliable computer. Therefore, having a steady supply of this type of computer was essential for the strategic thrust to materialize. It became the secondary thrust. Furthermore, Dell would have to persuade customers to switch to buying computers by mail. Intensive advertising immediately became another secondary thrust. Clearly, selling computers by mail would have never succeeded without a good product and massive advertising.

In the case of Amazon.com, the strategic thrust, selling books over the Internet, called for two more fundamental secondary thrusts: investing in software and system's development to create a storefront on the Internet; and investing in advertising to create the brand, i.e., to make the words Amazon.com a household name. Secondary thrusts thus play a major role in maneuver. They amplify the strategic thrust as the focus of the firm's maneuver response.

## IV. The Business Model

The strategic thrust points the way. It is an abstract thought that sets a direction or a focus for the path toward the desired end-state. It cannot be implemented in this abstract form. It has to be amplified into a more detailed concept. For example, Amazon.com's initial strategic thrust was to sell books on the Internet. This thought was a breakthrough, but it needed to be translated into a business system, a design for doing business. We call this system the business model. The business model is a specification of how we do business.

In the context of maneuver, the business model is an application of the firm's general business model described in its vision. As we will see in Chapter 16, a central element of the firm's vision is an abstract business model, its envisioned way of doing business. This general model is interpreted in light of the prevailing circumstances and is then applied as a way of responding to a particular situation. At the core of its vision, Amazon.com has a general business model, essentially brokering between producers and customers.[21] However, this model is often interpreted and applied in the course of its maneuvering in the marketplace. As a result of interpretation and application, the firm was able to make moves in electronics, toys, and many others. The abstract model has given rise to a business model.

The specification of a business model has become very important in business strategy nowadays. Firms in the digital economy compete based on business models. Amazon.com built its book selling business using a different business model than the traditional brick-and-mortar booksellers. As one observer put it, "We used to ask, 'What business are you in?' Now we find ourselves asking, 'what is your business model?'"[22]

Is it possible for a firm to have more than one business model? This depends on the number of distinctive basic products it has and separate market segments it serves. A firm might have a basic product for the consumer market and another one for the industrial market. Such a firm will have two business models, one for each type of customer since they are two separate markets. Along the same lines, if the basic products are different (by virtue of process, production, and customer), then it will need a different business model for each.

To clarify the concept of a business model, let us consider a couple of examples.[23] Southwest Airlines' business model can be summed up as follows:

- Market segmentation and selection; "cherry picking" of high volume pairs of cities rather than the "hub and spoke" design that all other airlines have.
- High asset management and utilization by avoiding the expensive hub and spoke system, one type of aircraft, and a unique approach that emphasizes doing more for less.
- No frills; no reservations, no expensive printed tickets, no meals on board, and so on.
- Low price using ground transportation as a benchmark.

Wal-Mart's business model can be outlined as follows:

- Market and site selection: singling out on second and third tier smaller markets.
- Procurement and distribution: a network of suppliers and local distribution networks operating on a just-in-time basis.
- Information management: speed and comprehensiveness in capturing and tracking product position on a department by department and store by store basis throughout the continent every working day.
- Customer service and employee motivation: the ultimate in customer service delivered by highly motivated employees who operate under a structure that connects customer service with the store's financial performance.
- Low every day prices; no sales.

A business model comprises a number of components as shown in Exhibit 12.9. A business model comprises a business concept, business processes, an economic model, and a value proposition all targeted to a certain set of customers.[24] These are explained next.

```
┌─────────────────────────────────────────────────────────┐
│           ┌─────────────────────────────────┐           │
│           │   A TARGETED SET OF CUSTOMERS   │           │
│           └─────────────────────────────────┘           │
│                    │           │                        │
│                    │           ▼                        │
│                    │      ┌──────────┐                  │
│                    │      │ BUSINESS │───┐              │
│                    │      │ CONCEPT  │   │              │
│                    │      └──────────┘   │              │
│                    ▼                     │  ┌──────────┐│
│           ┌─────────────────────┐        └─▶│COMPELLING││
│           │  BUSINESS PROCESSES │──────────▶│  VALUE   ││
│           └─────────────────────┘        ┌─▶│PROPOSITION││
│              ┌────────────┐              │  └──────────┘│
│              │AN ECONOMIC │──────────────┘              │
│              │   MODEL    │                             │
│              └────────────┘                             │
└─────────────────────────────────────────────────────────┘
```

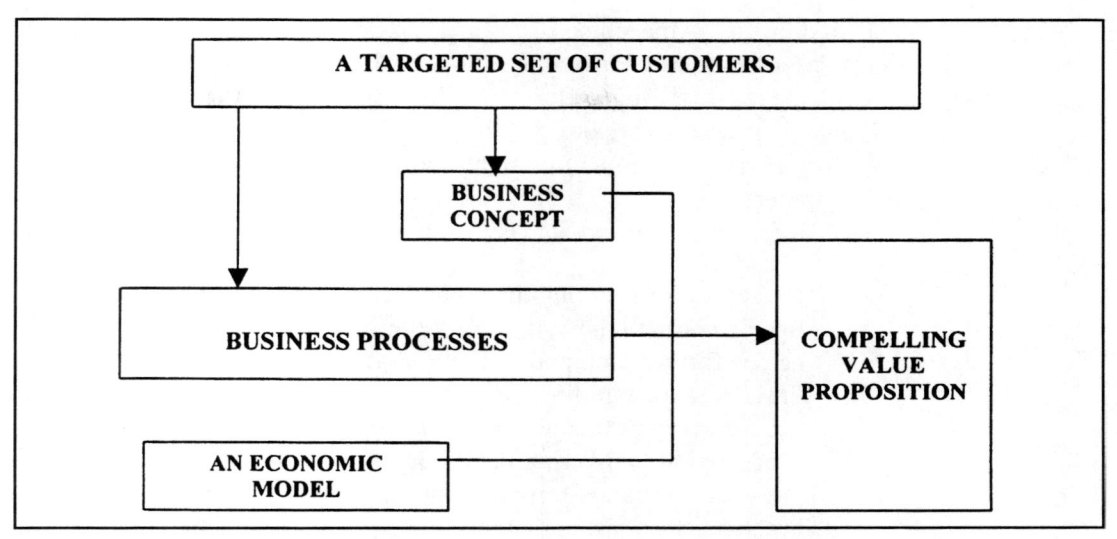

Exhibit 12.9: The Business Model

### Targeted Set of Customers

The first element in a firm's business model is a targeted set of customers. This is a well-defined market segment with certain characteristics, demographic, life style, and the like. It is derived from the opportunity arena that the firm stakes for itself. The targeting of this customer segment sets the tone for the whole business model. All the components are conceived with the particulars of this set in mind. Take, for example, the customer set for Amazon.com. They have certain characteristics. They have a certain demographic profile, age, income, and location wise. They have a certain life style, busy persons who are computer literate, and they prefer clicking to actually going to a shopping mall to touch the product before buying it.

### Business Concept

Given a targeted set of customers, the next element in a business model is a certain business concept. This is an interpretation of what the customer set needs and what it will take to satisfy this need in a superior way. The business concept has to be clear, definable, and distinctive. It has to differentiate the firm from other competitors. It has to represent a significant competitive advantage that will warrant investing the firm's resources in it. Let us consider some examples:

- Amazon.com: a wide selection of books at prices significantly below retail, accessible at a click.
- McDonald's: consistent good food at low prices everywhere.
- Wal-Mart: to be the one-stop shopping for rural areas, relatively distant from large cities.
- Southwest Airlines: no frills short distance travel at low fares (competitive with ground transportation).

### Business Processes

The business processes are designs for creating a product or a service and delivering it to the targeted set of customers. They need to be well conceived so that they deliver what the firm promises. Amazon.com's business processes include the sourcing of books from publishers, building a virtual inventory of books, building the virtual storefront (conducting business on the web, filling orders speedily, and the delivery of the books to customers. McDonald's processes are designs that enable unskilled workers to deliver the same meal to customers everywhere in a consistent manner and partnerships with suppliers of both food and equipment.

Business processes encompass the basic designs for the following:

- Processes for sourcing the inputs needed to make the product/service and the logistics of continuously supplying the firm with them. Nowadays, this includes processes for building and utilizing a network of partnerships with suppliers.
- Processes for building the product/service; transforming the inputs into the products or services that actualize the business concept.
- Processes for delivering the product/service to the targeted set of customers, including sales, service, promotion, pricing, all to ensure customer satisfaction.
- Processes that ensure that the above processes function properly such as R&D, technology development, recruiting and training people, and so on.

### Economic Model

Underlying the business processes is an economic model, a design for allowing the firm to generate profits for itself. The economic model is a configuration for the relationship between cost, volume, price, and profits, as illustrated by breakeven analysis. An economic model has to be configured in such a way that the firm's processes will generate a strong cost advantage. With this advantage, the firm's prices become low enough to maintain its current customer base and to attract new ones as well. It should be stressed here that the economic advantage lies in the ingenuity of the business processes and not necessarily in scale. Profits can be made at a small scale as long as the process embodies a good economic model. For example, Dell computer is a profitable firm despite a small scale relative to IBM. For another example, consider Southwest Airlines. It operates point-to-point, no frills travel using fewer planes and minimal overhead. This allows it to fly full planes thus reducing the cost per air mile. This enables it to lower airfares to attract more customers. In this case, we have small scale, but profitable volume.

In this digital age of ours, e-business processes are mostly virtual. The e-business firm does not have to invest millions in real estate, buildings, several warehouses, truck fleets, management ranks, and an army of employees. Instead, a small office and a warehouse will suffice. Its biggest investment is in information technology so that it may run the business digitally. The elimination of this overhead allows an e-business to lower its costs significantly. Meanwhile, its inventory is virtual, not costing much to acquire and maintain. All these reductions in overhead allow the firm to cut its prices. The convenience of the web and low prices attract a large volume of customers. This economic model gives the firm a large volume, minimum overhead cost, and minimum variable costs. This is a recipe for profitability.

### Value Proposition

The business concept, business processes, and the economic model combine to allow the firm to make a value proposition to the customers. The value proposition is a concrete statement of what the customer will get for the price of the product or service. The value propositions should be so compelling that the customer will choose our firm over all others. It has to convey the strong competitive advantage the firm has. Consider Amazon.com's value proposition: low price, huge inventory (over 2 million titles), convenience of ordering anywhere anytime, reliability, and a range of services (e.g., book reviews, recommendations for other relevant books on the topic, new release alerts, and the like). The value proposition for McDonald's consists of the following: consistent quality, good food, prices, speed, convenient locations, and clean facilities. The value proposition for Southwest Airlines emphasizes the following: air fares priced to compete with ground transportation, no-frills but fun in-flight service, and frequent schedules from city to city.

A value proposition, in essence, is an inequality: [price is less than (core + supporting components)]. Mariotti, a CEO, calls it the value architecture, the skillful arrangement of six components.[25] These are: (1) *core,* the part of the product or service that goes to satisfying the respective need; (2) *quality,* product/service attributes better than the alternatives in the marketplace; (3) *service,* having what the customers want, where and when they want it, "their own way"; (4) *speed,* delivering fast and on-time; (5) *cost,* low price stemming from the low-cost advantage accorded by the economic model, and (6) *innovation,* newness, uniqueness.

## V. System of Moves

The business model is a design. It is still an abstract concept. It has to be translated into a system of moves in the marketplace. The concept of moves will be discussed further in Chapter 14 in more depth. Suffice it to say at this point that a move is a complex structure that has a specific action as its core, but this action has a number of descriptors or qualifiers such as scale, speed, reach, duration, and novelty. For example, a price move has at its core a certain increase or decrease in price level. In addition, we must specify the scale of price change (minor or big), reach (how many market segments will be affected), duration (how long to hold it), speed (how quickly do we cut the price), and novelty (imaginative price structure and discounts).

The business model dictates the nature and the extent of the system of moves needed to translate the model into action in the marketplace. There are two sets of interdependent moves that make up the system. First, there are the frontline moves. The frontline moves rely on a second line of moves to support and enable them. Exhibit 12.10 provides a visual illustration of a system of moves for an Internet firm.[26]

### Frontline Moves

These are specific actions designed to: (1) achieve the strategic and financial objectives; and, (2) deal with the selected strategic issues—all while blocking and tackling the non-controllable forces of turbulence, e.g., competitors, opponents, macroeconomic conditions, and the like. Frontline moves are the moves that are aimed at the customers and competitors. On one hand, they help us to maintain our customer base and attract new ones. On the other hand, they are supposed to keep the competitors and other hostile forces at bay while we win our desired share of customers. Here are examples of frontline moves:

- Product Line Moves: the addition of new products, the deletion of others, the improvement of others, product specifications (e.g., quality and reliability standards) and so on.
- Pricing Moves: price levels, discount structure, price changes, and the like.
- Selling Moves: approach to customers whether to sell direct or through channels; whether to be brick-and-mortar, clicks only, or brick-and-click.
- Sales Promotion Moves: especially the use of advertising and other promotional actions to create the brand and entrench the value proposition in the marketplace. They generally achieve a certain positioning for the firm and its product or service in the customer's mind.
- Service Moves: especially before and after sale service.

| Support Moves | Financing, Legal, Accounting | | | | | |
|---|---|---|---|---|---|---|
| Human Resources Moves | Recruiting, Training, Incentive Systems, Employee Feedback | | | | | Infrastructure Moves |
| Technology Development Process | Inventory System | Site Software | Pick & Pack Procedures | Site Look and Feel<br><br>Customer Research | Return Procedure | |
| Procurement Processes | CDs Shipping | Computers Telecom Lines | Shipping Services | Media | | |
| | Inbound shipment of top titles<br><br>Warehousing | Server Operations<br><br>Billing<br><br>Collections | Picking and shipment of top titles from warehouse<br><br>Shipment of other titles from 3rd party distributors | Pricing Promotion Advertising Brochures Affiliations with other Web sites | Refund<br><br>Returns<br><br>Customer feedback | Frontline Moves |
| | Inbound Logistics Processes | Production Processes | Outbound Logistics Processes | Marketing and Sales Processes | Service Processes | |

Exhibit 12.10: An Illustration of a System of Moves for an Internet Firm

- Distribution Moves: particularly the designation of channels when we do not sell direct, and if we do not, then the use of other means of delivering the product or service to customers.

## Infrastructure Moves

Frontline moves cannot happen unless a number of other moves are in place. For example, a price reduction move is often supported by a set of moves involving the firm's cost structure, e.g., the acquisition of a new technology, adding new capability, or rearranging of supply sources and logistics. Here are examples of support moves:

- Production/Operations Moves: These pertain to the process of making the product or service including the choice of equipment, plant layout, order processing, the design of the operations involved in making the product or service, production schedule, quality assurance, and the like. Without these moves, there will be no product or service available to the frontline moves with which to work.
- Physical Positioning of Facilities: especially whether to centralize or decentralize the various locations in relation to the location of customers.
- Technology Moves: These involve the choice of technology to underlie for the production/operations moves as well as all the other business processes such as order taking, order filling, collecting from customers, and so on.
- Human Resources Moves: These include recruitment, training, and motivating the employees so that they execute all the moves whether frontline or supporting.
- Organizational Structure Moves: These involve the structuring of the organization so that employees may have the decision-making power and resources to execute all moves.

- Acquisition of Resources/Capability Building Moves: These relate to acquiring physical resources for the firm so that all the moves can be carried out.
- Financing Moves: These generate the funds necessary to finance all the above moves and structures. They involve the determination of funding requirements, locating sources of funds, sourcing the funds, and then allocating them to the various moves.

## Formulating Maneuver in the Single Business Firm

Now that we know what the element of maneuver entails, we can tackle the issue of how to formulate a maneuver. Scenario planning is a very useful technique in this regard. First, it can be used to generate some of the key components of maneuver in order to generate alternatives. Generating alternatives gives the firm the chance to choose from several maneuvers. Second, scenario planning is useful for testing the alternative maneuvers in order to choose the most appropriate one. The principles of scenario planning were discussed in Chapter 11. They are revisited here briefly.

The process of formulating maneuver consists of five steps, as follows:

### 1. Preparation

In preparation for planning a maneuver, the following items must be in place:
1.1. Establishing a time frame for the maneuvering effort in years or months depending on the rapidity of change in the marketplace.
1.2. Revisiting the firm's vision statement (Chapter 16) in light of the selected time frame. If the vision is viable, then a set of corporate strategic and financial objectives is established as installments to be achieved (in the selected time horizon) toward this vision. If the vision is questionable, then objectives are set and a visioning process should be triggered (Chapter 16).
1.3. Constructing alternative scenarios for the chosen time frame (Chapter 9).
1.4. Conducting an issues analysis to extract the important strategic issues (Chapters 10, 9, and 8).
1.5. Constructing a corporate model: The corporate model is a representation (a snapshot) of the firm's current strategic and financial positions as a function of its strategy (vision + maneuver + capability + structure); and, its situation (environment and the dynamics of turbulence in it). These items can be illustrated visually as knobs, set at certain positions, as discussed in Chapter 11.
1.6. Mapping the firm's capability, particularly the portfolio of moves or the range of *doable* things (Chapter 14).

### 2. Selecting the Mix of Opportunities and Challenges to Address in the Next Time Frame

As defined above, these are the specific issues to be dealt with specifically in the set time frame. Along with corporate objectives, they should be kept in mind at all times.

### 3. Formulating a Strategic Thrust (or the firm's mission) for the Selected Time Frame

There are two possibilities here. If our current thrust is working well (helping in achieving the strategic and financial objectives), then it is kept as the thrust for the next time frame. If it is not, then we need to formulate a new one and this occurs in two phases. First, we must generate alternative thrusts. Second, we must test these thrusts using scenario planning. A thrust can be generated using some or all of the approaches mentioned in this chapter. Alternative thrusts can be generated systematically by manipulating the elements of the thrust of perspective, task, and ploy. As was suggested in Chapter 11, they can be viewed as knobs that can be set to a number of positions. Each combination of knobs' positions is a possible strategic thrust. This process is illustrated in Exhibit 12.11.

Now that we have three alternative thrusts, we can proceed to test them using scenario planning to ascertain which thrust will perform well for the firm, given the scenarios for the future. Exhibit 12.12 is a worksheet for the testing process. To provide a benchmark, the outcomes of the generated alternatives are compared with the projected performance of our current thrust. If they do not perform better than our current thrust, then the generation process is back to the drawing board. As stated in Chapter 11, the best alternative will be the one that performs well under all scenarios or at least under the most likely scenario.

### 4. Formulating the Business Model

Given a strategic thrust, the next step is to amplify or expand it to become a business model. If our current business model is consistent with the new thrust, then we continue with it. If it is not, then we will need to generate alternative business models and test them. As we did with the strategic thrust, we can view the components of the business model (targeted customer segment, business concept, business process, value proposition, and economic model) as knobs and identify the possible positions for these knobs (in light of our capability or portfolio of possible and potential moves). We can then use a worksheet like the one in Exhibit 12.11 (after adapting it to suit the business model knobs and their positions) to generate alternative business models. It is also possible that we can generate a business model by adopting a model that is already in existence ("borrowing" a model from a firm in the same or a different industry). Once the alternative business models are generated, then we test them, using a worksheet like the one in Exhibit 12.12 (after due adaptation).

| Knobs of Strategic Thrust | *Enter here a Summary of the Most Likely Scenario* | *Enter here a Summary of Chosen Opportunities and Challenges* | *Enter here a Summary of Corporate Strategic and Financial Objectives* |
|---|---|---|---|
| | **Possible Positions for the Knob** | **Generating Alternative Strategic Thrusts** | |
| | | Alternative Thrust #1 | Alternative Thrust #2 | Alternative Thrust #3 |
| **Perspective** | P1: Offensive<br>P2: Encircling<br>P3: Defensive<br>P4: Branching out<br>P5: Retrenchment<br>P6: Withdrawal | P1 | P2 | P5 |
| **Decisive Task** | T1: Decisive Task X<br>T2: Decisive Task Y<br>T3: Decisive Task Z | X | Y | Z |
| **Ploy** | O1: Rule Making<br>O2: Rule Breaking<br>O3: Playing the Game<br>O4: Specializing<br>O5: Improvising | O2 | O3 | O4 |
| | | **Thrust # 1 = P1 + X + O2** | **Thrust # 2 = P2 + Y + O3** | **Thrust # 3 = P5 + Z + O4** |

Exhibit 12.11: Deliberate Generation of Alternative Strategic Thrusts

### 5. Formulating the System of Moves

With the business model in mind, the next step is to formulate the system of moves in order to implement this model. At this point, we must revisit our capability and structure. Capability is a portfolio or an inventory of moves embedded in the firm's resources. It is crucial to ascertain this portfolio in order to generate the moves needed to carry out the business model. The system of moves is drawn from this portfolio of moves. At the same time, we must consider the firm's organizational structure because it might inhibit or encourage certain moves. In light of our capability and structure, we then generate the front-line and infrastructure moves. If capability and structure turn out to be constraints, then these constraints must be relaxed somehow or perhaps removed. It is possible then that our system of moves will include moves to add (or alter capability) and change the organizational structure.

To visualize the above process, Exhibit 12.13 was formulated to show the flow of activities in formulating a maneuver.

## Maneuver in the Context of the Multi-Business Firm

The presentation thus far focused on a model of maneuver for the single business firm. The case of the multi-business firm requires a different treatment. A multi-business firm is a constellation of single businesses that are often referred to as strategic business units (SBUs). It operates on two levels: the level of the SBU where each is treated as a single business firm and the above model applies; and the "corporate" level where the head office functions as the unit holding the center of the firm. At the head office level, there is a different kind of

| If this Thrust is implemented, | and this scenario materializes ||||||
|---|---|---|---|---|---|---|
| | Enter here a summary of the most likely scenario (e.g., most likely scenario). || Enter here a summary of the second scenario. || Enter here a summary of the third or nth Scenario. ||
| | What are the **outcomes** of implementing this strategy under the most likely scenario? | What are the **gaps** associated with these outcomes?—in light of the strategic and financial objectives? | What are the **outcomes** of implementing this strategy under this scenario? | What are the **gaps** associated with these outcomes?—in light of the strategic and financial objectives? | What are the **outcomes** of implementing this strategy under this scenario? | What are the **gaps** associated with these outcomes?—in light of the strategic and financial objectives? |
| **Strategic Thrust # 1 (from Exhibit 12.11)** | List the outcomes here | List the gaps associated with them here | List the outcomes here | List the gaps associated with them here | List the outcomes here | List the gaps associated with them here |
| **Strategic Thrust # 2** | List the outcomes here | List the gaps associated with them here | List the outcomes here | List the gaps associated with them here | List the outcomes here | List the gaps associated with them here |
| **Strategic Thrust # 3** | List the outcomes here | List the gaps associated with them here | List the outcomes here | List the gaps associated with them here | List the outcomes here | List the gaps associated with them here |
| **Our Current Strategic Thrust** | List the outcomes here | List the gaps associated with them here | List the outcomes here | List the gaps associated with them here | List the outcomes here | List the gaps associated with them here |

Exhibit 12.12: Testing Alternative Strategic Thrusts

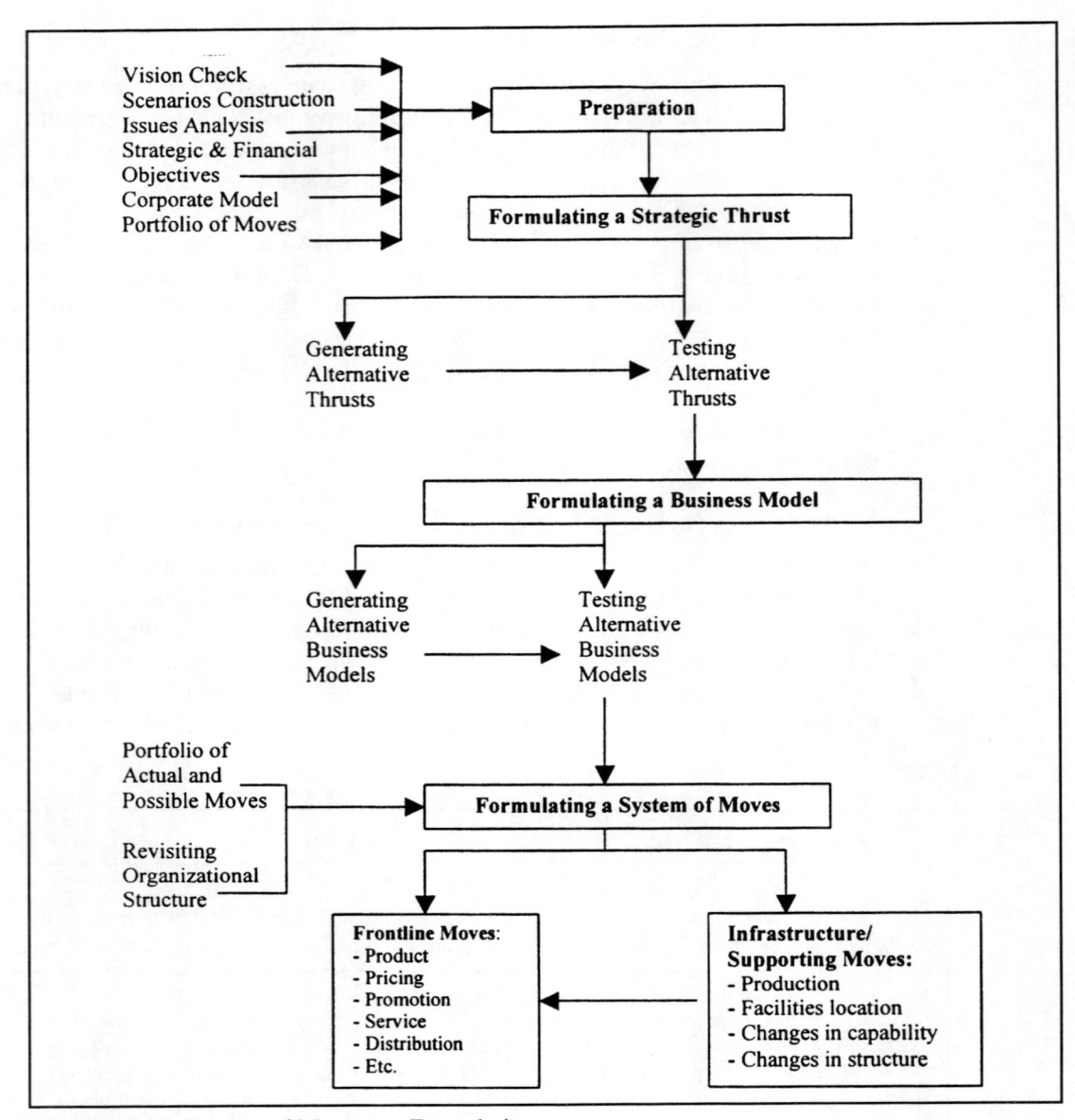

Exhibit 12.13: Process of Maneuver Formulation

maneuver. It is different because the perspective is different (a multi-industry view since the firm exists in several industries) and the levers to be manipulated in maneuver are different.

The most fundamental maneuver question for this type of firm is: what mix of businesses to be in? The business model for the multi-business firm is that of a portfolio of businesses. The concept of a portfolio of businesses was introduced in an earlier chapter. It is reviewed briefly below. Exhibit 12.13 presents a visual of what a portfolio configuration looks like based on the Boston Consulting Group growth-share matrix. The area of the circle for each SBU represents its respective sales volume. The portfolio consists of four main abstract building blocks:

- Numbers—of the SBUs in the portfolio.
- Diversity—the distribution of the SBUs over a number of industries.
- Relative sizes of each SBU in terms of sales volume.

- Interrelationships among the SBUs such as synergy, complimenting one another, subsidizing one another, and so on.

The SBUs are distributed over four quadrants. The position of each SBU in a given quadrant is a combination of two readings: its relative market share (its sales divided by the sales volume of its next biggest competitor) and the growth rate in its market. This combination also sheds light on the financial health of the SBU, i.e., whether it is a cash user or a cash generator. An SBU that has a small market share in a declining market is a cash user (labeled as a "dog") and hence unhealthy. It takes more cash to keep it operating than the cash it generates, because the market is declining and the unit's position in it is weak. The ratio of cash generators to cash users determines the overall financial health of the portfolio. If the portfolio is composed of cash users, the firm will be a cash user too. Accordingly, it is useful to plot the portfolio along the two dimensions of cash use and cash generation, as shown in Exhibit 12.14. This is especially important when relative market share and growth data are hard to ascertain because data are not available.

An SBU that has a small market share in a growing market is a promising one (a question mark). It is a cash user, but it operates in an industry in the early growth stages and hence it is worth holding. It requires considerable cash to invest in it in order to develop a sizeable market share in a potential growth industry. An SBU that has a large market share in a maturing or declining industry (cash cow) generates cash because the firm has a dominant market share. The SBU does not require huge investments to maintain it. Such SBUs are managed for cash. Finally, an SBU that has a large market share in a growing industry (star) might not be generating cash because we need to invest in it to expand and/or maintain market share in a competitive environment. Such a unit is not a cash user, but it is not much of a cash generator either. When its market growth slows down, a star will be a cash cow. Maneuver in the multi-business firm focuses mainly on arranging and rearranging the position of the various SBUs as well as on shaping the portfolio itself.

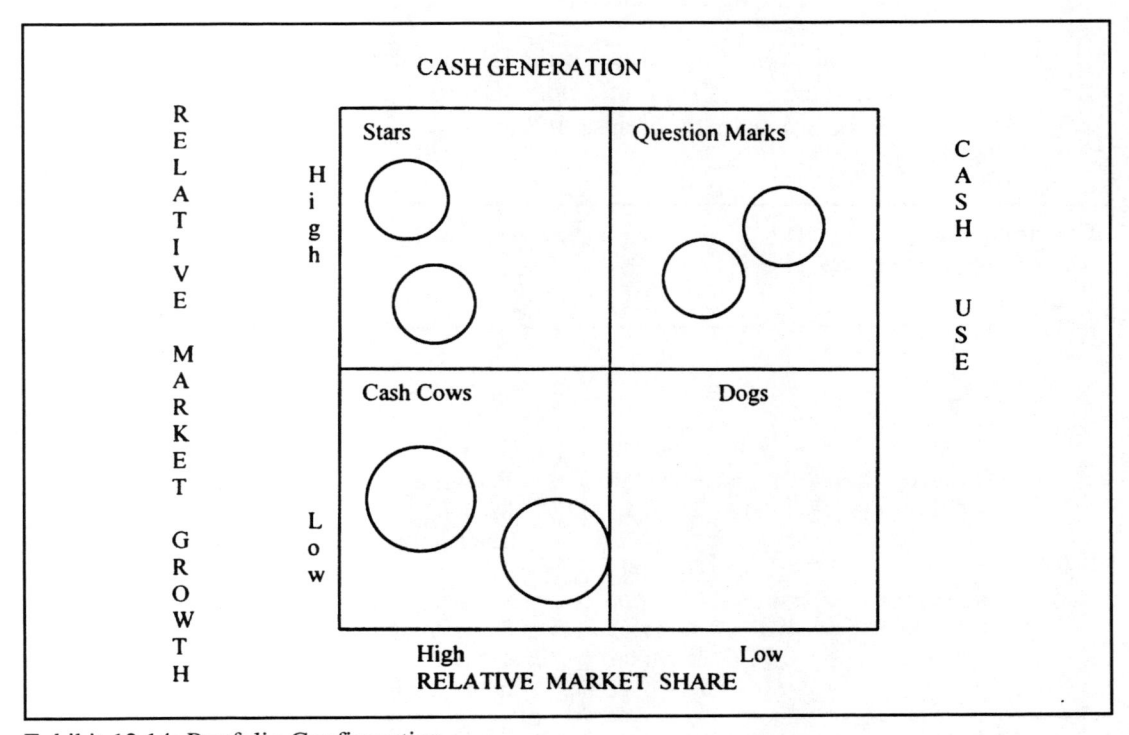

Exhibit 12.14: Portfolio Configuration

For the multi-business firm, maneuver formulation can be modeled as shown in Exhibit 12.15. The elements in the model are (1) the mix of opportunities and challenges, (2) strategic thrust, (3) portfolio configuration, and (4) repositioning the SBUs. They are influenced by the firm's corporate objectives, capability, and structure.

1. The mix of opportunities and challenges is also a subset of the strategic issues facing the corporation as a whole, rather than individual SBUs. The multi-business firm operates in a number of industries and hence its issues stem from the whole economy. The marketplace of the multi-business firm is the economy, not an industry as in the case of the single business firm. Hence, the emphasis here is on the macro-environmental analysis as well as the conglomeration itself. The process of extracting the issues is still the issues analysis methodology presented before. Once the strategic issues are extracted, the next step is to isolate the subset to work on—the mix of opportunities and challenges. They will pertain mainly to the conditions of the portfolio of businesses that form the conglomeration, e.g., whether the portfolio is producing adequate returns or not, whether the portfolio is financially healthy (i.e., made up of strong SBUs), or whether the portfolio is in maturing or growth industries, and the like.

2. The strategic thrust here is the general tendency chosen for the portfolio to tackle the strategic issues. Examples of such strategic thrusts include:

- Expanding the portfolio: Adding more SBUs.
- Growing the portfolio: Increasing the relative sizes of the SBUs in the portfolio.
- Streamlining the portfolio: Getting rid of SBUs that do not contribute to the financial health of the conglomeration.
- Contracting the portfolio: Reducing the number of SBUs to the ones that represent the old "core" business of the firm.
- Having a portfolio with SBUs concentrated in one particular quadrant or two.
- Having a balanced portfolio, e.g., distributed intelligently over the four quadrants.

The strategic thrust, as a thought, needs to be amplified to make it happen. The amplification takes the form of a *portfolio configuration*. A portfolio configuration refers to the specific arrangement of the SBUs in the portfolio, namely, how many, their relative sizes, and

```
Corporate Strategic              Financial Capability              Organizational Capability
and Financial Objectives
         |                                |                                    |
         v                                v                                    v

    Opportunities         Strategic         Mix of              Repositioning the SBUs:
    & Challenges:         Thrust:           Portfolio           Moving the SBUs
    Strengths &           The               Model:              in and out and around
    Weaknesses            General           The numbers         in the Portfolio
    In the firm's         Direction         Relative
    Portfolio of          of the            Sizes and
    Businesses            Portfolio         Distribution
                                            of the SBUs
                                            In the Portfolio.
```

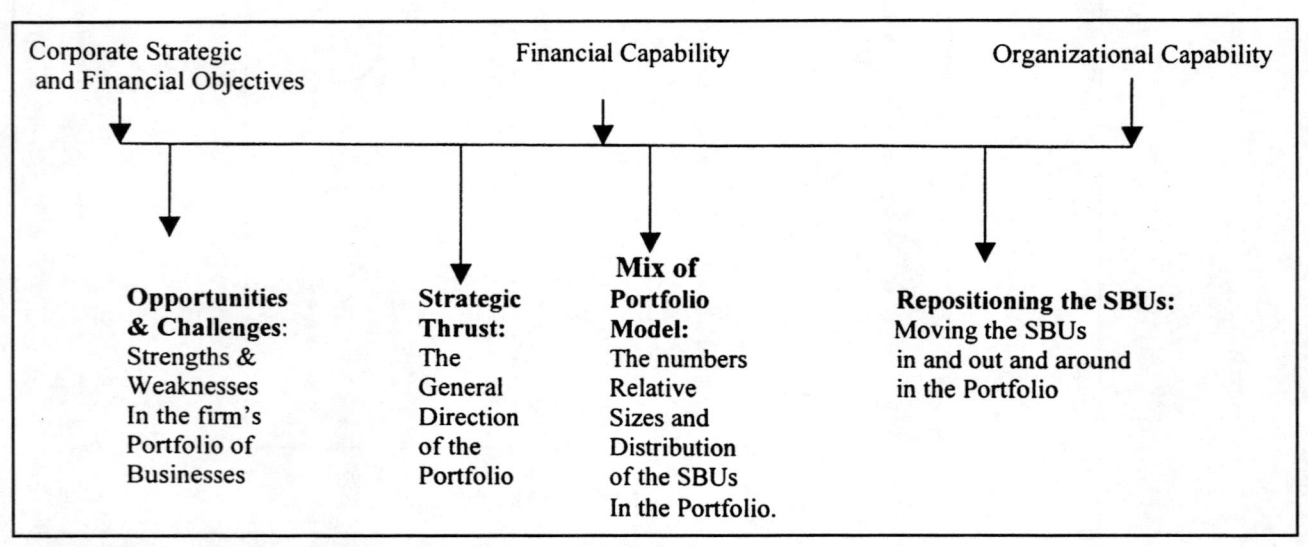

Exhibit 12.15: Maneuver Formulation in the Multi-Business Firm

where they fall in the quadrants. Take, for example, Jack Welch's configuration of GE's portfolio. His strategic thrust appears to be "to build a portfolio of high growth, futuristic, profitable businesses." The configuration he chose to implement this thrust is that all SBUs are to be in one quadrant, (stars)—to be #1 or #2 in their industries. Cash users are not tolerated. Other CEOs prefer a balanced configuration where there is: (1) a number of large size cash cows (to subsidize important cash users such as tomorrow's businesses that are question marks today), (2) a number of large size stars (to be tomorrow's inventory of cash cows), and (3) a good number of small size promising question marks. Some firms include a small number of small size "dogs." Sometimes, dogs are needed to complete a product line, to satisfy certain large customers, or even to attack the stars and cash cows of the competition (especially when subsidized by a number of large cash cows).

Given a configuration of the portfolio, the last element in maneuver for the multi-business firm is the actual *repositioning of the SBUs*. The SBUs will be in a certain position in a particular quadrant. Now, they need to be repositioned according to the new configuration. The repositioning may include some or all of the following:

- Growing an SBU, e.g., investing cash in an SBU, e.g., a question mark to increase its market share or a star to give it a dominant position so that it may become tomorrow's cash cow.
- Maintaining: Investing just enough in an SBU to hold its position in the marketplace and in the quadrant. This is especially true of stars.
- Harvesting: Taking cash from an SBU (a cash cow) perhaps to subsidize a question mark.
- Divesting: Liquidating an SBU; removing it from the portfolio altogether.
- Investing: Creating a new entry in the portfolio, e.g., the acquisition of another business firm to be entered in the portfolio as a question mark, or internal development of a new SBU in the question mark quadrant.

# GUIDING MANEUVER FORMULATION

Maneuver formulation is also known as strategy formulation. The task is considered a prerogative of the CEO and top management who gather together in strategic planning sessions to arrive at the important decisions such as the strategic thrust, business model configuration, and the broad frontline moves. However, in a self-organization firm, maneuver formulation follows a different course. In the first place, it is transferred to the organization as part of self-organization activities. The organization is charged with the responsibility of formulating maneuvering plans. This may seem odd, but the nature of turbulence calls for it. As we argued before, top management cannot stay on top of developments in a changing market. Such developments might call for change in maneuver and tactics on a moment-by-moment basis. Frontline entrepreneurs are in a better position to do so. Furthermore, in a firm structured as a self-organizing system, employees will be genuinely involved. They will be undertaking numerous initiatives depending on their visions and actions to help the firm negotiate obstacles posed by competition. This capitalizes on the intelligence and creativity of many employees and thus enriches the range of maneuver ideas for the firm.

The sagacious CEO focuses on two essential measures:

- Discovering Semi-Coherent Directions in the Diverse Initiatives that People Undertake: A semicoherent direction in this case is a strategic thrust. Some semicoherent directions will appear more promising than others. Scenario planning can be utilized

to test them until one suggests itself as a promising maneuver or strategy for the firm. Once such a semicoherent direction is spotted, the CEO then, in consultation with the various groups, legitimizes it by acknowledging and affirming it as the strategic thrust of the firm.
- Inducing and Orchestrating Strategic Collaboration: The focus of collaboration here will be on refining the chosen thrust, detailing it, translating it into a business model, and transforming it into a system of moves. The topic of stimulating strategic collaboration was examined in Chapter 6. We visit it briefly here.

## Creating an Environment Conducive to Collaboration

1. Cultivating Paradigms: The doctrines of maneuver must be part of every employee's mindset, particularly winning by outwitting competitors, not through direct confrontation. Important seminal thoughts here include competing on creating value for customers, on being several steps ahead of the competition, and on being agile and nimble.

2. Building Shared Goals: The work of the CEO here involves persuading all diverse groups to adopt creating value to customers as the goal. If they all adopt this overall goal, chances are they will collaborate to do so. Then, the firm as a whole will exceed competitors in creating value to customers. Exceeding competitors in value creation is the key to success in today's economy.

3. Defining Boundaryless Roles: As we saw, a business model defines roles for various units. It is important to have these specialized roles so that each unit can contribute to the whole model. However, no unit should be allowed to focus on its specialty while ignoring the rest. Integrated in each of these specialized roles is a part that calls for pulling together with the other units to maximize the value created for the customer. Roles pertaining to maintaining agility and nimbleness must be included in the mix too.

4. Networking: Making all information available to all units is a crucial element in getting all units to pool their ideas and visions together to create maneuver plans for the firm.

5. Orchestrating Shared Workspace: The workspace can be configured to allow all units to interact freely so that they may update the business model to keep up with customers and to exceed the competition.

6. Charging Emotions: Maneuver formulation can be viewed as preparation for war against competitors and other hostile forces of turbulence. It is a good opportunity for getting all units to rally together to do battle.

## Inducing and Stimulating Conversation on Maneuver

The usual vehicle for stimulating conversation about maneuver formulation is strategic planning sessions. In such sessions, people from different units assemble to contemplate how to outmaneuver competitors, in order to get the firm to the desired strategic end-state. In strategic planning sessions, these individuals review the results of turbulence sensing and interpretation, and then exchange views on the strategic issues, and the kinds of strategic thrusts that are open to the firm and ways to make them happen.

## Marshalling Strategic Conversation to Strategic Action

The role of the CEO here is to move strategic planning conversation into actual strategic plans and strategic action. This involves the steps listed below:

1. Developing and Cultivating Frameworks for Action: The key frameworks here are scenario planning and the structure of maneuver itself as shown in Exhibits 12.2 and 12.3. Following such frameworks systematizes the search for maneuvering thoughts.

2. Keeping the Vision: Maneuver thoughts must be aligned with the firm's vision as its desired end-state. It has to be kept front and center during all strategic planning sessions. However, it should be stressed here that there will be times when the vision itself is changed in the course of maneuver formulation. Even though the focus of maneuver is on how to get to the desired end state, the vision is not an end in itself. Broadly interpreted, the choice of an end-state is an act of maneuver in its own right. If a certain end-state will bring the firm to a collision with a stronger force (a larger competitor for example), then a different end-state is chosen to evade this force.

3. Building Collaborative Networks: Building networks is essential for two reasons. First, they bring different points of view and this enriches the supply of creative maneuver ideas. Second, the presence of networks ensures that maneuver plans will be carried out properly by all concerned.

4. Staffing Critical Positions: The CEO can help guide strategic planning by assigning it to certain leaders who champion the cause and ensure that it is done properly. They can also be charged with the responsibility of ensuring that plans are updated on a moment-by-moment basis.

5. Allocating Resources: Maneuver formulation calls for committing the firm's resources. After all, the strategic thrust is the basket where the firm will put its eggs. The business model will call for major investments. Frontline moves are where the firm's working capital is spent. Resource allocation is a potent weapon in the hands of the CEO. By approving funds, the CEO firms up the strategic plan.

## Affirming Accountability and Governance

Maneuver formulation is a central task in the firm. Without it, the maneuvering effort will be haphazard. Every unit must be held accountable for doing the necessary planning, for doing it right, for doing it on time. Timeliness is critical in a rapidly changing marketplace. The CEO has an arsenal of tools here including periodic audits of collaboration on planning, tracking strategic plans, and challenging the assumptions underlying them.

## Exercising Personal Influence

The role of the CEO's personal influence in guiding maneuver formulation cannot be exaggerated. In a self-organizing system, influence replaces unilateral dictation. It is thus important for the CEO to be personally involved in finalizing maneuver decisions. The CEO is the one ultimately responsible for the soundness of these plans. There are many tools at his/her disposal including participation in planning sessions, facilitating meetings, concurring with certain thoughts, approving plans, and issuing directives that proclaim such plans as the firm's official maneuver.

# CONCLUSION

This chapter dealt with the first and foremost element of a firm's strategic response, the element of maneuver. A conceptual framework for maneuver in business was presented. This framework specifies the various self-organization activities involved in outmaneuvering turbulence in the firm's marketplace.

Maneuver is all about the charting of a dynamic path to the firm's desired strategic end-state. If the end-state proves unattainable or unworkable, then maneuver is broadened to include the search and the designation of a new end-state. This is especially true in severely turbulent industries where visibility is so poor that the firm cannot select a target end-state or stay with an existing one for a long time.

Maneuver is viewed as a complex structure, a composite of four layers of zigging and zagging action by the firm in the course of interfacing with turbulence. It starts with the choice of what stimuli or issues to respond to. Next is the choice of strategic thrust to set the tone for the firm's path to its strategic end-state. The strategic thrust is then amplified in the form of a business model that becomes the firm's platform for doing business. Finally, the business model is translated into a set of physical moves that are carried out in the marketplace. From that point onward, the battle begins. Competitors respond, retaliate, or may even ignore the firm. Customers are won and lost. Turbulence pulls the firm in many directions. The maneuver is unfolding. As the maneuver unfolds in the marketplace, the CEO's tasks shift to a different gear and assume a new scope. This is examined next in the next chapter.

# ENDNOTES

1. As quoted in Humes, J.C., *The Wit & Wisdom of Winston Churchill*, New York, NY: Harper Perennial, 1994, p. 40.

2. As quoted in Humes, op. cit., p. 75.

3. Baufre, A., *An Introduction To Strategy With Practical Reference To Defense, Politics, and Diplomacy In the Nuclear Age*, Translated by R.H. Barry, New York, NY: Frederic A. Praeger, Publishers, 1965.

4. Ibid., p. 36.

5. Ibid., p. 36.

6. Ibid., p. 42.

7. Yoffie, D.B., and M.A. Cusumano, "Judo Strategy: The Competitive Dynamics of Internet Time," *Harvard Business Review*, January–February, 1999, pp. 71–81.

8. Higgins, J.M. and J.W. Vincze, *Strategic Management, Text and Cases*, 3rd ed., Fort Worth, Texas: The Dryden Press, 1993, p. 71.

9. Lucier, C.E. and J.D. Trosiliere, "The Trillion-Dollar Racer to 'E'," *Strategy & Business*, First Quarter, 2000, pp. 6–14.

10. Compiled from the works of Goldstein, S., "Exploit Discontinuities To Grow," *Strategy & Leadership*, September/October, 1996, p. 14; and, Kiernan, M. J., *Get Innovative or Get Dead: Building Competitive Companies for the 21st Century*, Vancouver, B.C.:, Douglas & McIntyre, 1995, Ch. 1.

11. Quigly, J.V., *Vision: How Leaders Develop It, Share It & Sustain It*, New York, NY: McGraw-Hill, Inc., 1993, p. 25.

12. This and the next six examples are taken from Collins, J.C, and J.I. Porras, *Built To Last: Successful Habits of Visionary Companies*, New York, NY: Harper Business, 1994.

13. Robert Tomasko, a keynote address to the International Strategic Leadership Conference, Strategic Leadership Forum, Atlanta, GA, 1996.

14. Lele, M.M., "Selecting Strategies That Exploit Leverage," *Planning Review*, January–February, 1992, pp. 15–21.

15. Schultz, H. and D.J. Yang, *Pour Your Heart Into It: How Starbucks Built a Company One Cup at Time*, New York, NY: Hyperion, 1997—quoted from Howard Schultz and Dori Yang, "Birth of the Coffee Bar: How a Simple Idea Became a Huge Business," *Reader's Digest*, May 1998, pp. 107–108.

16. Porter, M., *Competitive Strategy: Techniques for Analyzing Industries and Competitors*, New York, NY: The Free Press, 1980.

17. Adapted from Pearce II, J.A. and Robinson, R.B., *Formulation, Implementation, and Control of Competitive Strategy*, Boston, MA: Irwin-McGraw-Hill, 2000, p. 204.

18. Hamel, G. and C.K. Prahalad, *Competing For The Future*, Boston, Mass: Harvard Business School Press, 1994, p. 129.

19. Hamel and Prahalad, op. cit.
20. Hamel and Prahalad, op. cit.
21. Hamel and Prahalad, op. cit.
22. "Leadership Online: Barnes & Noble versus Amazon.Com (A), case study in Ghemawat, P., *Strategy and the Business Landscape: Text and Cases*, Reading, MA: Addison-Wesley, 1999, pp. 9-1 to 9-26.
23. Rothenberg, R., "An Interview with Lynda Applegate," *Strategy & Business*, First Quarter, 2000, p. 145.
24. Furey, T.R. and S.G. Diorio, "Making Reengineering Strategic," *Planning Review*, July–August, 1994, pp. 7–11.
25. Lucier, C.E. and J.D. Trosiliere, "The Trillion-Dollar Racer to 'E'," *Strategy & Business*, First Quarter, 2000, pp. 6–14.
26. Mariotti, J.L., The Shape Shifters: Continuous Change for Competitive Advantage, New York, NY: Van Nostrand Reinhold, 1998, p.18.
27. Adapted from a display by Ghemwat, P., *Strategy and the Business Landscape: Text and Cases*, Reading, MA: Addison-Wesley, 1999, p. 55.

CHAPTER
# 13

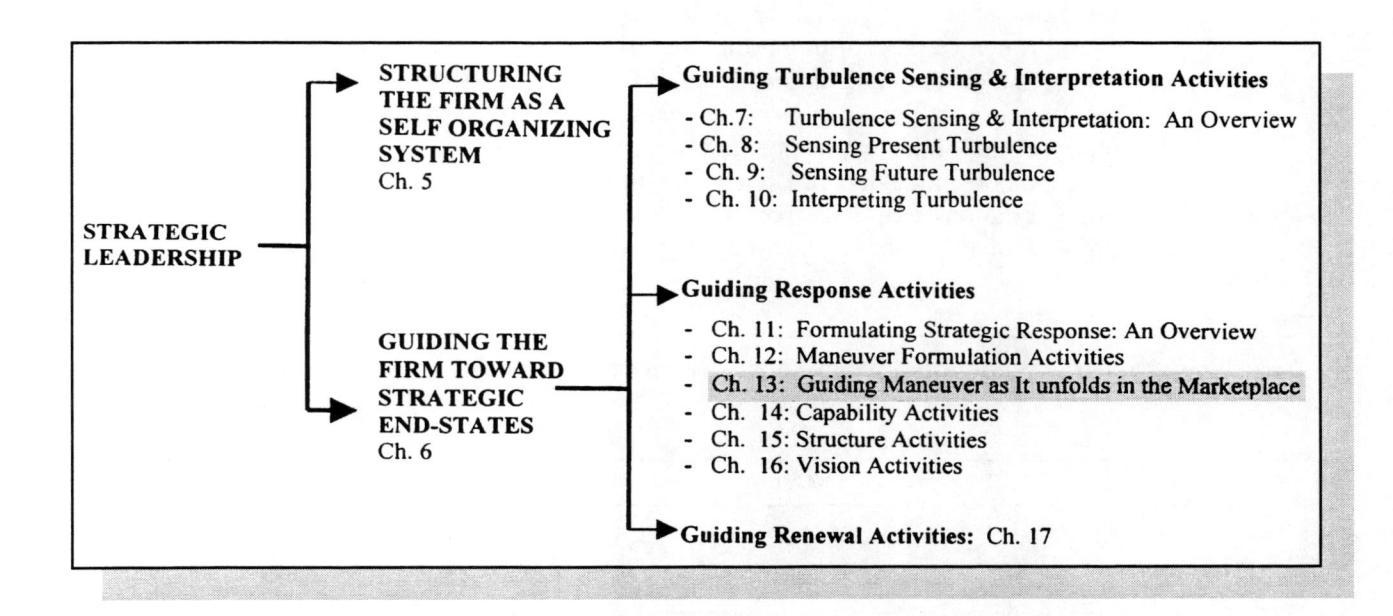

# Guiding Maneuver as It Unfolds in the Marketplace

```
STRATEGIC          STRUCTURING         Guiding Turbulence Sensing & Interpretation Activities
LEADERSHIP     →   THE FIRM AS A
                   SELF ORGANIZING       - Ch. 7:  Turbulence Sensing & Interpretation: An Overview
                   SYSTEM                - Ch. 8:  Sensing Present Turbulence
                   Ch. 5                 - Ch. 9:  Sensing Future Turbulence
                                         - Ch. 10: Interpreting Turbulence

                                       Guiding Response Activities

                   GUIDING THE           - Ch. 11: Formulating Strategic Response: An Overview
                   FIRM TOWARD           - Ch. 12: Maneuver Formulation Activities
               →   STRATEGIC             - Ch. 13: Guiding Maneuver as It unfolds in the Marketplace
                   END-STATES            - Ch. 14: Capability Activities
                   Ch. 6                 - Ch. 15: Structure Activities
                                         - Ch. 16: Vision Activities

                                       Guiding Renewal Activities: Ch. 17
```

**228** Chapter 13

Maneuver occurs at two planes: the thinking plane and the acting plane. At the thinking plane, it is a set of strategic thoughts formulated through scenario planning, a strategic plan. At the acting plane, the plan is translated into action. The focus of this chapter is on the various tasks of the CEO during the implementation phase. To place the role of the chief executive in perspective, the chapter begins by depicting a picture of the implementation phase. What do things inside the firm look and feel like as the strategic plan moves from thought to action? Next, it surveys the various tasks of the CEO in guiding implementation activities.

## REALITIES OF IMPLEMENTATION

The dynamics of implementing a maneuver are captured in Exhibit 13.1. There are numerous projects to implement the moves and the maneuvers. Project teams are working (engaging turbulence) on numerous fronts. They are progressing at different rates, deploying various aspects of the firm's capability. The hostile non-controllable forces of turbulence (competitors, obstructions, etc.) are pulling them in many directions every hour of the day. Internal turbulence is also impinging upon the teams in various ways. Politics, misunderstandings, and miscommunication affect performance. Interpersonal and inter-group dynamics (conflict and cooperation) sway the teams in one direction or another. This brings about a wide spectrum of accomplishments, successes, and failures.

One major source of confusion is that the formulated maneuver (as a strategic plan) was based on certain assumptions (scenarios) about the future. Now that the future has become the present, many of these assumptions might not be holding. Some are turning out to be

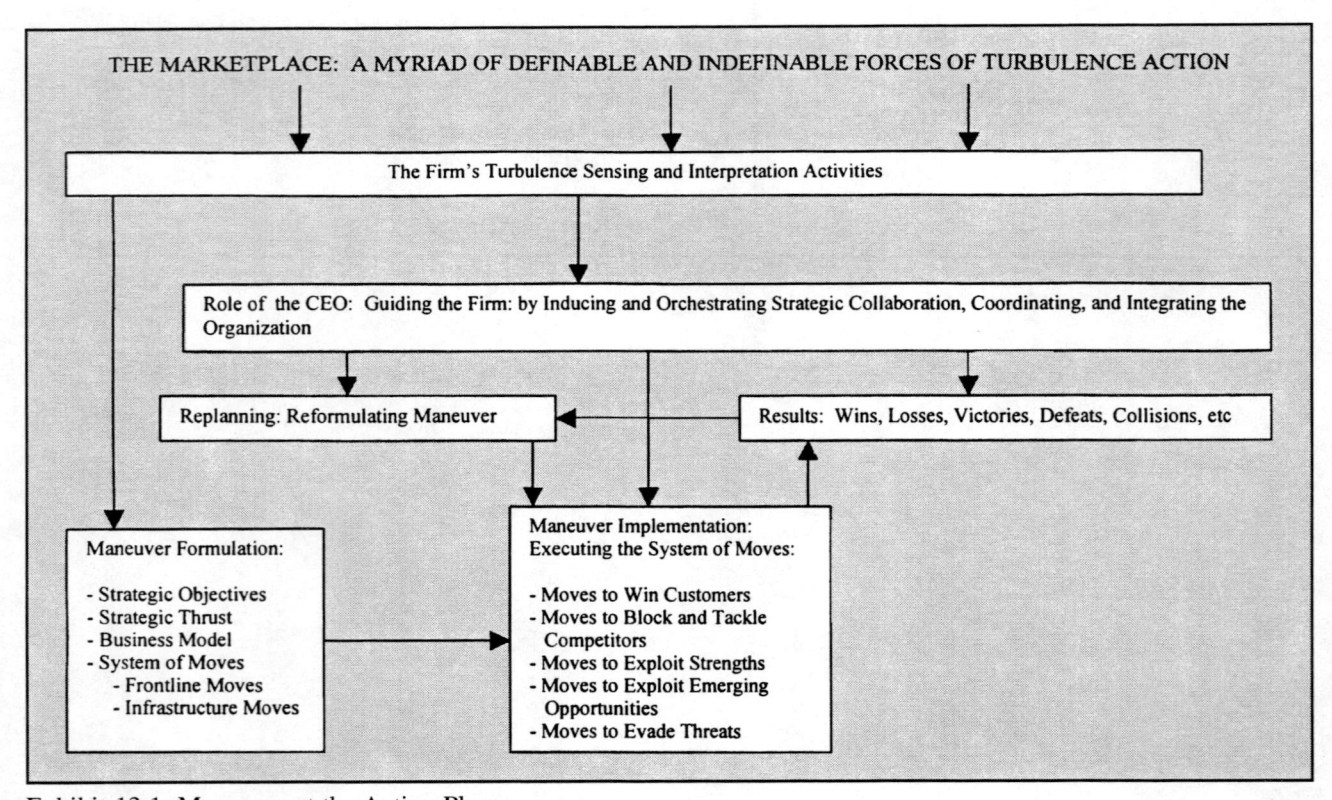

Exhibit 13.1: Maneuver at the Acting Plane

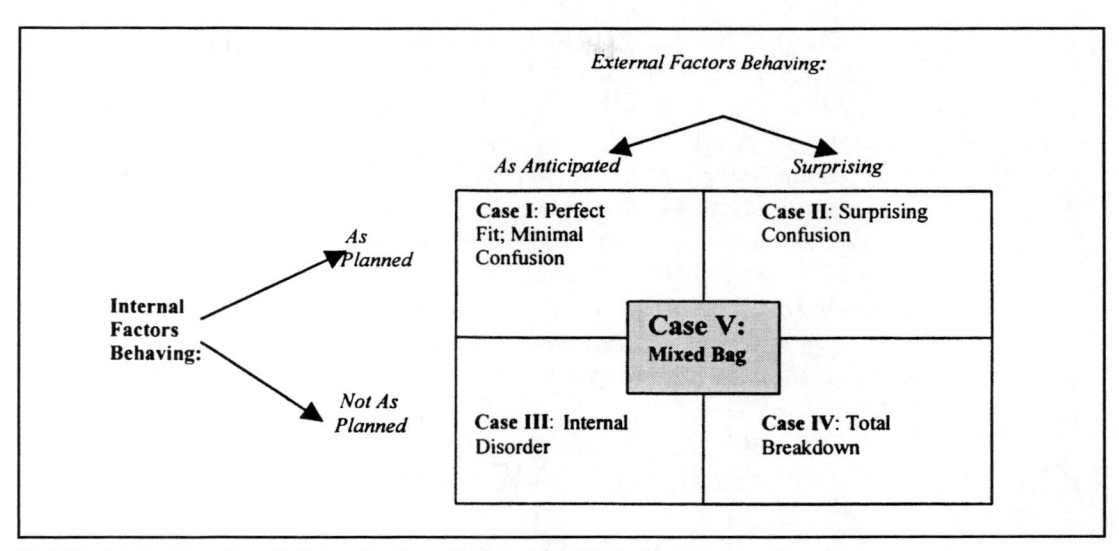

Exhibit 13.2: Five Possibilities for Interfacing with Turbulence

overestimates or underestimates. Almost invariably, the marketplace unfolds, but not according to the scenarios we constructed for it. Accordingly, considerable confusion ensues.

To show the confusion at the acting plane, let us consider the possible matches between the firm and its environment. As the firm interacts with its environment, five possibilities can occur, as shown in Exhibit 13.2. The vertical axis represents the behavior of the factors inside the firm, e.g., group dynamics, following plans, people acting in a self-organizing manner, and the like. There are two intervals in this axis: internal factors behaving according to plans or they are not. The horizontal axis represents the behavior of the external factors. There are two intervals here. Either they are behaving as anticipated (i.e., according to the scenarios we constructed), or they are behaving in a manner that is surprising to us.

As shown in Exhibit 13.2, the interaction between these two sets of factors reveals five possible states that implementation may assume: perfect fit, internal disorder, surprising confusion, total breakdown, and a mixture of these four states.

Case I: Perfect Fit: In this state, internal factors are acting as prescribed and the external world is materializing as we envisioned. This is perfect implementation. Confusion is perhaps minimal or absent. This, however, is a rare occurrence. It requires considerable luck and a predictable marketplace for it to happen.

Case II: Surprising Confusion: This is the case where the internal forces implement the maneuvers as prescribed, but the real world surprises the firm by unfolding in an unexpected manner. In this case, there is considerable confusion. If contingency plans are inapplicable, panic decisions are being made. This case is not rare. It is often encountered in the business world due to the inherent uncertainty in it.

Case III: Internal Disorder: Here the internal factors are not behaving as planned although the real world is behaving as anticipated. Something is wrong internally. The organization is not able to function as a self-organizing system. There is a high degree of confusion, but its source is the internal workings of the company. Internal turbulence has taken over. This case is not rare in the business world.

Case IV: Total Breakdown: In this case, both the internal factors and the external world are not unfolding as we hoped. Everything is going wrong. The confusion is at maximum. This situation is rather rare. At this level of confusion, the maneuver at the acting plane is in a state of disarray.

Case V: Mixed Bag: In this case, parts of the firm achieve various degrees of successes and failure in their respective spheres. Some units experience Case I or II. Others experience Case III or even IV. This is perhaps the most common case. Viewing the company as a whole, there will be a little bit of every case.

At the acting plane, maneuver is fraught with confusion. Military leaders have long been aware of this fact of life so much so that they defined the role of the commander as "managing confusion at a distance." Business leaders can benefit from this perspective. The bulk of the CEO's work involves managing confusion at a distance since he/she cannot be everywhere to fix all problems. Clearly, structuring the firm as a self-organizing system helps significantly in this regard. Since the firm is self-managing, it is in a position to deal with turbulence on its own without waiting for the CEO to clarify confusion and tell it what to do.

# GUIDING MANEUVER IMPLEMENTATION

The CEO's work in guiding physical maneuvering activities focuses on inducing and orchestrating strategic collaboration as discussed in Chapter 6. Aside from managing strategic collaboration, progressive CEOs engage in hands-on activities to corral and steer the frontline and infrastructure moves in order to make the strategic thrust and the business model become a reality. Their activities in this regard span five categories as shown in Exhibit 13.3.

## COORDINATION AND INTEGRATION

A self-organizing system has the attribute of distributed being, i.e., it exists as a collection of autonomous units. Because the units act autonomously (responding to the pressures and confusion in their own spheres), they need the semblance of a center. The units are somewhat "free" but there is a coordinating center. The role of the center is *not* to command and to control, but rather to nurture and support; or simply to guide.

Coordination and integration is a category that includes five items as follows:

- Assurance of a continuous supply of resources.
- Keeping the vision.
- Upholding values and beliefs.

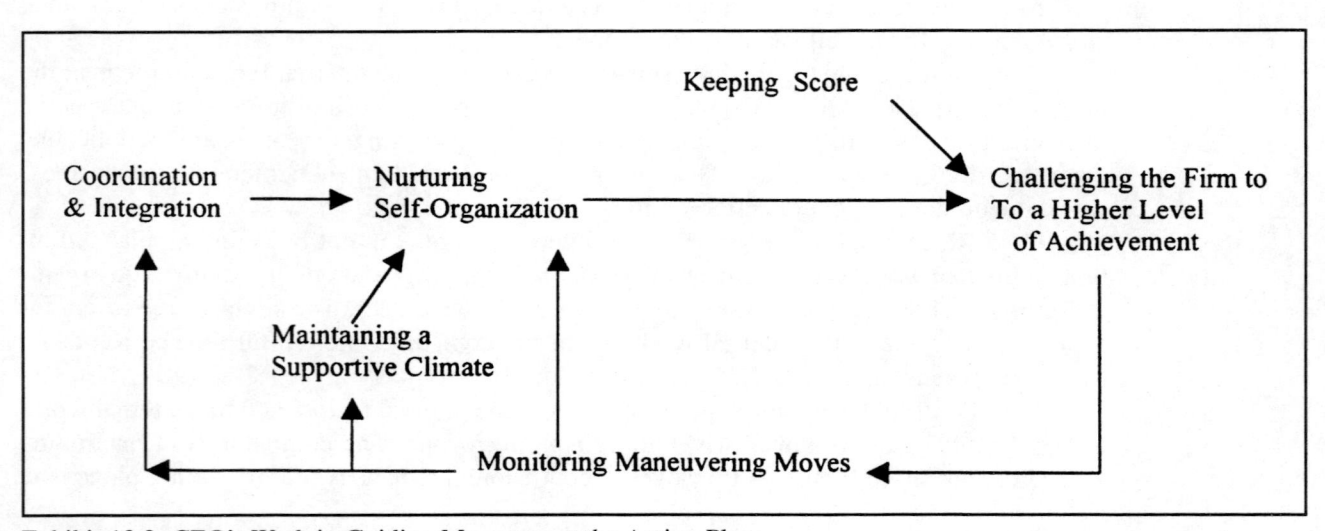

Exhibit 13.3: CEO's Work in Guiding Maneuver at the Acting Plane

- Powering the information network.
- Spreading best practices

## 1. Assurance of a Continuous Supply of Resources

An essential CEO activity is the maintenance of the firm's pool of resources and the allocation of this pie to the various modules. It is the job of strategic leadership to raise the funds necessary from financial markets in order to secure the resources needed to mount the kind of maneuver called for by the unfolding turbulence. When the acquisition of funds is not feasible (e.g., at times of insolvency or tight money markets, and high interest rates), strategic leadership resorts to alternative approaches such as stretch, leverage, and improvisation (Chapter 14). These three approaches can create "more" resources, in the form of doing more with less.

## 2. Keeping the Vision

In the heat of interfacing with turbulence, people sometimes lose sight of the ultimate destination. Imagine a firm with many employees working on different fronts with different mandates responding to things happening around them every hour. The orchestration of all this is a massive undertaking. People drown in detail. There is a need for the leader to move around the various positions on all fronts to remind everyone of "the big picture," the vision.

Effective leaders have long realized this simple fact and worked with it. Take the example of Jack Welch of General Electric:

> "Good business leaders create a vision. They articulate the vision, passionately own the vision, and relentlessly drive it to completion. Above all else, good leaders are open. They go up, down, and around their organization to reach people. They don't stick to established channels. They're informal. They're straight with people. They make a religion out of being accessible. They never get bored telling their story.
>
> Real communication takes countless hours of eyeball to eyeball, back and forth. It means more listening than talking. It is not pronouncement on a videotape; it's not announcements in a newspaper. It is human beings coming to see and accept things through a constant interactive process aimed at consensus. And it must be absolutely relentless."[1]

As part of his activities in keeping the vision, Welch spent considerable time interacting with GE employees face to face. Such meetings were not the run of the mill CEO posing for photo ops with employee orchestrated by the Company's public relations department. They were frank, blunt, candid exchanges with intense give and take. The theme of his talks captured and reiterated the main themes of his vision, as follows:[2]

- Competitiveness: "Be number one or a strong number two in your business or get out."
- Realism: "Don't finesse the numbers, tell it like it is, address the harsh realities of your situation."
- Excellence: "We must be the best at what we do."
- Entrepreneurship: "Take a swing, take risks, we will not punish a well-reasoned and well-executed failure."

Keeping the vision is a continuous activity. Preaching the vision does not mean that it will be automatically internalized and acted out by people. There is always a difference between what is intended and what actually takes place. Consider this statement by a former GE executive who lived through Welch's preaching of the vision:

> "What I found was everything that Jack abhors. Instead of decisions being made by a liberated and empowered middle management, all decisions—save an individual's preference for lunch—were made by the unit's CEO. The spirited repartee in which Welch engages his executives to advantage by pushing the boundaries of their knowledge of, and commitment to, a project were instead viewed as personal affronts to authority.
>
> In my own business unit, attempts to ignite productivity by clearing the decks of mediocre performers were met with resistance at the top. Despite what was happening at Corporate, at GECC (General Electric Capital Corporation) change was not really viewed as either necessary or positive."[3]

### 3. Mobilizing Values and Belief Systems

A crucial activity in coordination and integration is ensuring that values and beliefs are put into practice (attitudes and behaviors) minute by minute. Values and beliefs are intended to be practiced and internalized by everyone. They keep the people focused on what is important. Like keeping the vision, upholding values and beliefs needs support systems. To uphold GE's values on empowerment, boundarylessness, and productivity, Welch instituted a process called "Work-Out." Work-Out is a well planned exchange among members (cutting across vertical and horizontal lines) of a unit. Facilitated by an outside consultant, work-out sessions examine a range of concerns from productivity blocks to outdated work practices to specific and general issues facing the unit. In explaining the concept of Work-Out, Welch said:[4]

> "Work-Out is absolutely fundamental to our becoming the kind of company we must become. . . We're not going to succeed if people end up doing the same work they've always done, if they don't feel any psychic or financial impact from the way the organization is changing. The ultimate objective of Work-Out is so clear. We want 300,000 people with different career objectives, different family aspirations, different financial goals, to share directly in this company's vision, the infuriation, the decision-making process, and the rewards. We want to build a more stimulating environment, a more creative environment, a freer work atmosphere, with incentives tied directly to what people do.
>
> Work-Out has a practical and an intellectual goal. The practical objective is to get rid of thousands of bad habits accumulated since the creation of General Electric. . . . We want to flush them out, . . . to begin the whole game again.
>
> The second thing we want to achieve, the intellectual part, begins by putting the leaders of each business in front of a hundred or so of their people, eight to ten times a year, to let them hear what their people think about the company, what they like and don't like about their work, about how they're evaluated, about how they spend their time. Work-Out will expose the leaders to the vibrations of their business—opinions, feeling, emotions, resentments, not abstract theories of organization and management
>
> Ultimately, we're talking about redefining the relationship between boss and subordinate. I want to get to a point where people challenge their bosses every day: 'Why do you require me to do these wasteful things? Why don't you let me do the things you shouldn't be doing so you can move on and create? That is the job of a leader—to create, not to control. Trust me to do my job, and don't make me waste all my time trying to deal with you on the control issue.'
>
> Now, how do you get people communicating with each other with that much candor? You put them together in a room and make them thrash it out. These Work-Out sessions . . .

---

Reprinted by permission of Harvard Business Review. From "Speed, Simplicity, Self Confidence" by Noel Tichy and R. Charum, *Harvard Business Review*, Sept.–Oct., 1989. Copyright © 1989 by the Presidents and Fellows of Harvard College; all rights reserved.

create all kinds of personal dynamics. Some people go and hide. Some don't like the dinner in the evening because they can't get along with the other people. Some emerge as forceful advocates. As people meet over and over, though, more of them will develop the courage to speak out. The norm will become the person who says, 'Dammit, we're not doing it. Let's get on with doing it.' Today the norm in most companies, not just GE, is not to bring up critical issues with a boss, certainly not in a public setting, and certainly not in an atmosphere where self-confidence has not been developed. This process will create more fulfilling and rewarding jobs. The quality of work life will improve dramatically."

### 4. Powering the Information Network

Self-organization occurs when all the units of the firm are networked. Being networked is necessary for the "invisible hand" to emerge. Being networked also means that everyone should have access to all the information. This requires the gathering and circulating information in real time to all concerned. This is a logical function to be performed at the center simply because the center "sees the total picture."

In the information age, this is easy to dispense with. The Digital Age is here and the Digital Organization is here. Wal-Mart invested heavily to keep everyone "networked"—including satellite communications stations, electronic data interchange, and a fleet of corporate jets that takes managers from location to location to exchange information and experiences. By the time the last store closes on the west coast, all the figures from every store in the continent is assembled, analyzed, reviewed, and redistributed.

Some CEOs are afraid to circulate information for competitive purposes. Enlightened leaders however accept the risk of exposure to competition. Lars Kolind (CEO of Oticon), for example instituted the principle of "transparency" which he defines as follows:

> "The principle of transparency means that every piece of information, with very few exceptions, is available to everybody. Anyone can click on our strategic plan and see what we intend to do to beat Siemens. If people know what we're doing and why we're doing it, they know exactly which project to work on."[5]

In Kolind's view, the increased agility and integration of the organization, achieved by openness, outweighs the danger of exposure to competitors getting sensitive information. Further, having information is a measure and proof of trust in employees. This, in turn, breeds trust on their part. Finally, information is power. Sharing information is sharing power. It is an effective form of empowerment, which is needed to enable people to act quickly in a changing marketplace.

### 5. Spreading Best Practices

The maneuvers of the various units will vary. Some will be more inventive than others. Some will discover short cuts and improvisations. People in the various units might be too busy to pass on the experiences to others. The role of the center is to gather these successful practices and spread them around so that every unit can benefit from them. This way all units will be performing at a higher level. There will be no need to reinvent the wheel. By tracking the experiences of the various units, the center is in a position to identify the most effective and efficient ways of dealing with problems and obstacles. By virtue of being the center, it has some moral authority to give legitimacy and validity to best practices. This would help in gaining acceptance for such practices by the other units.

## NURTURING SELF-ORGANIZATION

One of the fundamental premises underlying this book is that the firm is structured as a self-organizing system. However, having the structure is one thing, actually becoming a genuine self-organizing system is a different matter altogether. Self-organization needs to be practiced and reinforced so that it might become a reality rather than an abstract organizational concept. A critical function of the CEO is to continuously reinforce self-organization and "make it stick." Nurturing self-organization comprises five tasks: (1) assuring individual autonomy, (2) managing contention, (3) rewarding, (4) practicing deliberate ambiguity, and (5) enabling.

## 1. Assuring Individual Autonomy

For the firm to become a true self-organizing system, the individual has to be a self-managing, individuals have to have the freedom and the authority to respond to whatever challenges as they appear from moment to moment. An essential function of strategic leadership (at time of implementation) is to ensure that individual autonomy is not forgotten in the heat of the battle and the pressure for results.

Developing and enforcing systems and procedures (bureaucracy) is a strong temptation for leaders. They are top-down tools to control people, to ensure order, control, and stability. However, they inhibit people from functioning as a self-organizing system. Progressive leaders always made a strong point of abolishing bureaucracy. Jack Welch invented the term "debureaucratization" and "boundarylessness" to destroy traditional bureaucracy. His objective was to make the company agile and nimble. Stayer's program called for removing the obstacles that prevent great performance. The main obstacles, in his view, were systems and procedures. Kollind worked hard to create what he called the "spaghetti organization" that has fluid and elastic three dimensional existence emphasizing informal communication and minimizing paper work.

As an illustration, consider the following practices by Dentsu, one of Japan's largest advertising agencies. As Pascale reported, the agency focuses on what is called the "Dentsu person."[6] To entrench individual autonomy, Dentsu's first chairman, Hideo Yoshida, institutionalized ten important practices that he called "The Ten Rules of the Demon."[7] They are shown in Exhibit 13.4.

Ralph Stayer (Johnsonville Foods) reinforces autonomy by "transferring ownership" of the respective decision and the commensurate responsibility to employees. He refuses to deal with them himself in order to demonstrate the principle of autonomy unequivocally. Consider the following incident:

---

**The Ten Rules of the Demon**

- Initiate projects on your own instead of waiting for work to be assigned.
- Take an active role in all your endeavors, not a passive one.
- Search for large and complex challenges.
- Welcome difficult assignments. Progress lies in accomplishing difficult work.
- Once you begin a task, complete it. Never give up.
- Lead and set an example for your fellow workers.
- Set goals for yourself to ensure a constant sense of purpose. This will give you perseverance, purposefulness, and hope.
- Move with confidence. It gives your work focus and substance.
- At all times, challenge yourself to think creatively and find new solutions.
- When confrontation is necessary, don't shy away from it. Confrontation is the mother of progress and the fertilizer of an aggressive enterprise. If you fear conflict, it will make you timid and irresolute.

---

Exhibit 13.4: Dentsu's Practices for Assuring Individual Autonomy

"I encountered a quality problem in one of my plants. Vowing to avoid taking responsibility for the problem, I called a meeting of the employees involved and asked them for their input on fixing the problem. This time, however, I insisted that they had to be responsible for implementing any solutions they suggested. The discussion took a very different tack.

The first suggestion was to change the equipment. When I revealed to the people that the cost of that change would be $1.5 million, they were shocked. Next, they suggested that I talk the customer into taking a lesser quality product. I arranged for a group of them to visit the customer and discuss it face-to-face with him. The group returned from the visit with higher quality standards not a lower one. 'Whew,' one of the group told me, 'this is hard work.' "[8]

## 2. Managing Contention

Conflict is a human phenomenon. It is unavoidable in human organization because of the diversity among people. This is more so in the context of the self-organizing system where empowering people leads to constructive anarchy. Diversity takes many forms: different backgrounds, different educational levels, different motivations, and different perspectives. Sagacious CEOs devote considerable effort to ensure collaboration while allowing a degree of conflict to encourage creative competition among the units. Collaboration is crucial, but so is contention. Pascale's views are worth considering here. He described contention as follows:

"Contend. Draw attention to the presence of and value of constructive conflict. There are some tensions in organizations that should never be resolved once and for all (such as between cost control and quality, or between manufacturing efficiency and customer service). The functional disciplines that advocate these points of view rub up against one another and generate debate. Contention across these boundaries is inescapable. Moreover, it can be productive. We are almost always better served when conflict is surfaced and channeled, not suppressed."[9]

According to Pascale, the opposite of conflict is "fit," where there is considerable harmony among parts of the organization. He presented the case of Honda where the founders were concerned that there was too much fit. They broke the company apart in a radical fashion in order to create some constructive contention. R&D and Engineering were split as separate companies. Although Honda continued to be their primary customer, each of the three firms has its own distinct identity and character. As Pascale noted, "The tension between these three companies, each highly independent, yet each interdependent, was the best way to arrest decay."[10]

In explaining Honda's approach to contention, Pascale further states:

"Not surprisingly, Honda's extraordinary degree of decentralization generates a lot of internal heat. To cope with conflict, Honda dedicated itself to explicitly surfacing and managing contention in a constructive way. Honda simmers with contention by holding sessions in which subordinates can openly (but politely) question bosses and challenge the status quo. This is not an empty ritual but a vital force in keeping Honda on its toes. It sustains a restless, self-questioning atmosphere that one expects to see in new ventures—yet Honda is into its fourth generation of management. Its founders retired in 1970."

Genuine leaders are comfortable with constructive discord and contention. In interviews with Pascale, the co-founder of Honda, Takeo Fujisawa provided an excellent insight:

"My taste in classical music has changed from Wagner and Mozart to Stravinsky and Bartok. Modern music sounds discordant at first—the instruments seem to be playing independently. But you can hear a harmonious formulation if you listen carefully. This is an important lesson for managing contemporary organizations.

> I like Bartok and Stravinsky's music. It's discordant sound—and there are discordant sounds inside a company. As president, you must orchestrate the discordant sounds into a kind of harmony. But you never want too much harmony. One must cultivate a taste for finding harmony within discord, or you will drift away from the forces that keep a company alive."[11]

Welch took pains to stimulate contention and constructive conflict. The *Wall Street Journal* referred to this practice as Welch's "hazing-shouting-match approach that requires managers to argue strenuously with (Welch) even if they agree." A replaced top executive complained to the Journal: "You can't even say hello to Jack without him being confrontational. If you don't want to step up to Jack toe-to-toe, belly-to-belly, and argue your point, he doesn't have any use for you."[12]

## 3. Rewarding

To be a self-organizing system, requires intensive effort and significant sacrifices from people. Although they gain self-actualization and control over their destiny, the work, however, goes beyond a fair day's work for a fair day's wage. There are sacrifices in terms of assuming personal responsibility, personal involvement, foregoing social and family life, working long hours, and participating in weekend meetings, and the like. Stretch and improvisation (doing more with less) tax employees. Unless these sacrifices are rewarded generously, there is no incentive for people to go the extra mile.

As CEO of Johnsonville Sausage, Stayer struggled continuously with the issue of rewards. He suggested that rewards should be tied to performance and that performance should be linked to customers. Given a concrete statement of the vision, mission, and objectives of the firm, Stayer recommends that standards must be set between performers and customers:

> "We need to ensure that standards are set between performers and their customers. Each performer must meet with his or her customers to agree on standards of great performance. Then the performer must meet with other performers to coordinate activities with them. The leadership job is to make certain that this standard setting and coordination take place on a regular basis."[13]

Stayer further suggests that the standard should be reduced to a specific measurable number. He asserts: "People love to be measured. But measure the 'right' stuff. The right stuff is what creates great performance for customers."[14] He then goes on to tie rewards to performance:

> "Performance must have consequences. . . . It must be clear that 'them that do it get it, and them that don't do it don't get it' or get significantly different and much less desirable outcomes.

> F for effort. A for accomplishments. Pay for results, not effort. I learned the hard way that throwing water uphill for sixteen hours a day will only result in standing knee-deep in mud. Get clear on what great performance you want to accomplish. Then be certain that the performer has measures so that he/she knows when he/she does it. Only then can you reward those who achieve great performance. Too many people are rewarded for working hard rather than getting the 'right' things done."[15]

Finally, Stayer advises that monetary rewards should be blended with non-monetary ones. Thus, monetary rewards such as gain sharing, profit sharing, onetime bonuses, and merit increases can be combined with non-monetary ones such as recognition, promotions, job assignments, and autonomy. To be effective, Stayer suggests that the reward system be developed by the performers not by the leadership. The system will be fair, equitable, and motivating. Furthermore, it is part of self-organization, learning to administer things such as the reward system.

## 4. Practicing Deliberate Ambiguity

People are culturally conditioned to come to an authority figure for direction. When they do so, they are stating implicitly that they do not own the problem. Stayer used the metaphor of the buffalo herd to explain the phenomenon:

> "I saw my organization functioning like a herd of buffalo. Buffalo are absolutely loyal followers of one leader. They do whatever the leader wants them to do, go wherever the leader wants them to go. In my company, I was the head buffalo.
>
> Originally, I liked that arrangement in my organization. After all, my brilliance built the organization. I wanted people to do exactly what I told them, to be loyal and committed. I loved being the center of power, and I believed that that was the leader's job.
>
> I realized eventually that my organization didn't work as well as I'd like, because buffalo are loyal to one leader, they stand around and wait for the leader to show them what to do. When the leader isn't around, they wait for him to show up. . . .
>
> I found a lot of 'waiting around in my buffalo-like organization. Worse, people did only what I told them to do, nothing more, and then they 'waited around' for my next set of instructions."[16]

During the confusion of maneuver at the acting plane, there will be the temptation for the subordinates to come for direction (i.e., wait around for them) and for leaders to think they are the only ones who can direct the battle. Japanese management developed an approach for tackling this problem. It is the principle of deliberate ambiguity. The leaders outline general themes or boundaries, but leave the rest of the field ambiguous on purpose in order to encourage people to think for themselves; and find better ways in the process. A Japanese manufacturer told a team of employees to go and design a "better electric coffee pot." When the engineers asked for instructions, none were given. The engineers were not even given parameters for the project. The project produced one of the best selling electric coffee pots in Japan.

Deliberate ambiguity is simply sending the problem back to the employees, so that they are forced to act as a self-organizing system. Here is another incident in the experience of Ralph Stayer. A group of employees with a problem the ownership of which he transferred to them. When they complained about how hard the job was, he asked them if they prefer if he made the decision. Then he said: "Haven't I been making all the decisions? Do you really think it's working out better?" After four days, the group came back with a plan to redo several procedures and learn a new process. Then, he continues:

> "The group tried one last time to hand me over the problem. 'Here it is,' they proudly said. 'Now you go get it fixed.' 'Whoa,' I said, 'that wasn't the deal. How are you going to make it work?' The sheepish grins told me I had successfully transferred the responsibility. 'Here's the plan,' they said. 'We're ready to roll.' 'Go for it,' I said without looking at the papers thrust in front of me.
>
> It took a lot of restraint on my part not to respond to my old leadership instincts and rush to 'help'. . . . It took maximum control to keep from reading their proposal and 'improving' it. My restraint paid big dividends. Their execution of their own plan was flawless. The problem was solved and never came back."[17]

Another example of deliberate ambiguity is Kolind's practices at Oticon.[18] Jobs were reconfigured into fluid combinations of projects. Employees choose the projects to work on and determine their own training needs. An employee who consistently fails to seek out project assignments is dismissed. Employees are more or less on their own to make themselves productive.

## 5. Enabling

Self-organization materializes when two conditions are met. First, employees are capable of handling the awesome responsibility of leading the organization and managing things. Second, they must be motivated to undertake this responsibility. The rewarding system should provide the motivation to do so. However, motivation is not enough. People must have the ability and competence. As one CEO put it: ". . . one of my skills is making heroes of other people."[19]

Enabling involves a number of leadership practices as follows:

- Acquiring Expertise: For people to be truly self-organizing, they must have the competence necessary to participate in the system. Competence is acquired through intensive, continuous training. Retraining is also essential since turbulence renders skill obsolete all the time.
- Developing an Organizational Perspective: People are able to do more things and do them right when they know the total picture (as opposed to being locked into the confining box, the job). This calls for cross training, i.e., training in other functions beyond what the person declares as his or her specialty. By training in other units, a broader perspective evolves which translates into being able to accomplish the assignment more competently.
- Developing Competence: This can be fostered through practices such as:
  —Giving power away: the CEO focuses on being an accountability giver.
  —Allocating resources, so that people can do what is expected of them.
  —Sharing information: part of competence is having access to critical information to allow informed decisions and actions.
  —Cultivating a "peer support" culture: people experience competence when they know that their peers view them as such.

## MAINTAINING A SUPPORTIVE CLIMATE

Self-organization flourishes in a supportive environment. Such an environment has to be permeated by a climate that sustains and reinforces self-organizing behavior. The activities of the CEO in this regard include three main tasks: (1) maintaining visibility and example setting, (2) building trust, and (3) keeping morale high.

## 1. Maintaining Visibility[20]

Strategic leadership, as presented in this work, is the practice of virtual leadership, i.e., leadership that appears to exist, but in reality does not. Leadership is distributed since the CEO lets the employees lead. Despite the fact that leadership is expected to be virtual, the appearance of leadership must exist. In a business firm, the CEO is the legal head of the corporation, with all the vested power and authority. Distributing leadership (through delegation) does not diminish the CEO's image as the head of the organization. In this capacity, the role of the CEO, among others, is to represent and convey symbols that remind all members of the organization what the company is all about including its strategies, values, and beliefs.

Symbols communicate meanings, feelings, and emotions. The CEO's actions symbolize these meanings, feelings, and emotions. If the CEO wants the organization to have certain meanings, feelings, and emotions, then he/she must serve as the symbol that communicates them. Symbols must be visible to all. They do this in two ways: (1) being personally visible, and (2) displaying visible actions. First, a CEO can be personally visible through visits to various locations and groups. Military generals always make a point of visiting and addressing the troops in the field. Effective business leaders do this too. Kelleher of Southwest Airlines makes himself visible by "working" regularly on flights, doing things such as baggage handling or handing out "filet of peanuts" to passengers. Second, besides personal presence, CEOs practice visibility through concrete actions, especially "going first."[21] If the CEO and senior management are not the first to do what they are asking of the employees, the message is obvious, these top managers do not believe in what they are saying. For example, if top management advocates a pay cut, then the CEO and top management should be the first to take a salary reduction.

## 2. Building Trust

The history of management-employees relations is characterized by lack of trust. Labor and management often view themselves as adversaries. Yet, trust is central to self-organization. In a self-organizing system, the leader "trusts" people. Similarly, the people trust that the leader will lead them to a better future. Napoleon Bonaparte, once observed: "a leader is a dealer in hope."

Kouzes and Porras defined the conditions for trust as follows:

"Trust is built when we make ourselves vulnerable to others whose subsequent behavior we can't control." If neither person in a relationship takes the risk of trusting at least a little, the relationship is inhibited by caution and suspicion. If leaders want the higher levels of performance that come with trust and collaboration, they must demonstrate their trust in others before asking for trust *from* others. Leaders go *first*, as the word implies. That includes going first in the area of trust; it means willingness to risk trusting others."[22]

In a self-organizing firm, employees are expected to take ownership of the maneuver, from planning to execution. They are "trusted" to decide what needs to be done and how to do it. Trust is especially crucial at time of implementation. Japanese automakers, for example, "trusted" the assembly line workers to stop the assembly line—on their own—if they judged that there is a quality problem.

## 3. Keeping Morale High

The time of implementing a maneuver, like a time of war, is a time of adversities and challenges. People, on behalf of the company, are fighting the world. They are trying to carry out plans but, there is an earthquake (turbulence) under their feet and competitors are out to thwart their efforts. Two conditions often emerge at this point:

- People on the firing line lose perspective. Every now and then, they lose sight of light at the end of the tunnel. Their fighting spirit sags in a world of endless detail and conflicting demands.
- People on the firing line experience victory and defeat. Victories raise their morale. Defeats deflate it.

A crucial task of strategic leadership is elevating morale at all times. Keeping morale high is not "entertaining the troops." It is providing people with the opportunity to experience self-actualization and a sense of accomplishment. There are several approaches available to the leader for elevating morale and maintaining it at a high level. These include: (1) inducing small wins, and (2) celebration.

## Inducing Small Wins

A small win is an event where the people carried out a move and achieved a goal despite turbulence. It is not winning a battle or the war. It is a small accomplishment, but it is an accomplishment nonetheless. Small wins are leveraged several times their "morale weight" because of their psychological impact on people:

- Small wins generate a sense of accomplishment. It makes people feel good about themselves and about the world.
- Small wins generate self-confidence, a motivating power that makes people go forward sure footed.
- Small wins rejuvenate people's span of attention. Each win generates excitement and exhilaration. If before it wanes, another small win is made, the momentum of exhilaration will continue.

How does a CEO go about inducing small wins? Perhaps the most effective tool is the *project concept*. Komatsu's leaders mastered the art of projects to generate small wins in order to trigger and fuel its growth momentum to become a dominant force in the earth moving industry today. In the early 1960s, its main products, small and medium size bulldozers, were suffering from low quality and low market share. Komatsu's management launched "Project A" in 1964 which crystallized the organization on upgrading the quality of the bulldozer line. The CEO told people to ignore costs, disregard Japanese Industrial Standards, and build the best products. Project A had "spectacular results," a small win that was celebrated and gave people the strength and pride to be ready for the next step up. To conquer foreign markets, the leadership launched "Project B" in 1972 to develop the company's overseas markets. Project B resulted in the company having a strong position in the less developed countries (another small win).

Kouzes and Porras suggested a three-pronged strategy for inducing small wins as follows:[23]

- Experimenting continuously.
- Reducing missions, moves, goals and the like to their essence. When they are reduced to their essence, they become clear and conquerable and thus a small win takes place.
- Acting with a sense of urgency. Waiting for permission kills the zest for action.

Peters reported a number of useful strategies for orchestrating small wins. These include:[24]

- Investing in application oriented small starts.
- Pursuing team product/service development.
- Encouraging pilots of everything.
- Supporting fast (smaller doses of quick experiments) failures. This is needed to stimulate the interest to take initiatives and experiment. Experimentation boils down to hitting and missing. Hitting is a small win. Missing is fine for it is a step towards a hit or a small win.

Collins and Porras came across a number of practices at 3M that are designed to give employees a sense of small wins and simultaneously contribute to the progress of the firm. These are presented in Exhibit 13.5.

| Practice | Purpose |
|---|---|
| • 15% rule—people are encouraged to spend up to 15% of their time on projects of their own choosing and initiative. | • To stimulate unplanned experimentation and variation that might turn into successful, albeit unexpected innovation. |
| • 25% rule—each division is expected to generate 25% of annual sales from new products and services introduced in the last 5 years. | • To stimulate continuous new product development. |
| • Golden Step Award—granted to those responsible for successful new business ventures originated within 3M. | • To stimulate internal Entrepreneurship and risk taking. |
| • Genesis Grants—internal venture capital fund that distributes grants of up to $50,000 for researchers to develop prototypes and market tests. | • To support internal Entrepreneurship and testing of new ideas. |
| • Technology sharing awards—granted to those who develop a new technology and successfully share it with other divisions. | • To stimulate internal dissemination of technology and ideas. |
| • "Own business"—those who champion a new product get the opportunity to run it as their own project, department, or division subject to sales volume. | • To stimulate internal Entrepreneurship. |
| • High Impact programs—each division selects 1–3 products to get to market within a short specified time frame. | • To speed up product development and market introduction cycles. |
| • Small autonomous divisions and units. | • To stimulate individual initiative by promoting a small company within a big company feel. |
| • Problem solving missions—small hit teams sent out to customer sites in response to specific customer problems. | • To stimulate innovation via customer problems. These are the seeds of new opportunities. |
| • Profit sharing. | • To stimulate a sense of individual investment in the overall financial success of the company. |

Exhibit 13.5: Practices to Induce Progress at 3M

### Celebration

Celebration by itself elevates morale. It is also a form of recognition, psychic rewards. Leaders and researchers alike have recognized the importance of celebration as a business practice. Celebration is not a child like approach to make people feel good. Peters found a range of celebration processes.[25] He found many practices ranging from donuts and coffee to large-scale recognition ceremonies. Here are some examples:

- Picking up two dozen doughnuts from a bakery to "award" coffee breaks to a project team that just passed a minor milestone on time.
- Having a special meal at the distribution center cafeteria to celebrate ninety days of meeting the promise "95 percent fulfillment within 24 hours of receiving the order." Hamburgers can be made of top sirloin, cooked, and served by management.
- Sending thank you cards; e.g., a hotel manager makes it a habit to send out at least 100 thank-you notes a month to his staff for jobs well done.
- Trinkets that symbolize recognition of a certain accomplishment, e.g., mugs, belt buckles, etc.

Kozes and Posner posit celebration as a key task of leadership.[26] They suggested the following parameters for celebration:

- Tying celebration to what is important: A critical decision in celebration is what to celebrate. What is to be celebrated is the behavior that fulfills the aspirations and values of the company. If the aspiration is "zero defects," then every time a person or unit meets the "zero defects" goal, celebration should ensue automatically and instantly.
- Making the ceremony public: Celebration is best appreciated by the people being recognized when it is done in public particularly in view of peers and others from related areas especially if they contributed to the cause of celebration.
- Personal involvement of the leaders: Celebration is most effective when it is organized and delivered by the leader. People on the firing line need to feel appreciated by the "higher ups" in the organization. They want to know that their good work is being noted and recognized by those at the top.
- Scheduling celebrations: An effective way to ensure celebrations is to schedule them just like national holidays in celebrating historical figures and events. Similarly, persons can be celebrated, e.g., top 5% of performers in whatever field of endeavour they may be in. Events can be celebrated too, such as stages of organizational change (expansion, reorganization, mergers, introduction of a new technology, etc.), success (e.g., meeting profit targets, promotions), loss (of old procedures, financial opportunities, contracts, a job, status, a failed experiment, etc.), and historical landmarks (e.g., company's anniversary, opening day, or the articulation of company's vision).

An interesting practice of celebration is that of Southwest Airlines. Freiberg and Freiberg noted that the company adhered to the following guidelines:[27]

- The celebration must be authentic, i.e., coming from the heart, emerging out of a genuine appreciation for people. The leadership honestly believes that the company's success could have never been achieved without the employees' dedication, commitment, and creativity.
- The celebration must raise people's dignity and self-confidence. It is never conducted with intent to harm or ridicule anyone for any reason.
- The celebration must be done right. The leadership takes time to ensure that any celebration is well planned, well timed, and flawlessly executed. Three roles are played to ensure the success of a celebration. First, the "imagineer" envisions and engineers the celebration. Second, the "artist" translates the imagineer's concept to reality, i.e., transforming words into songs, pictures into a story, and visuals into balloons and other spectacular visual effects. Finally, there is "evocators," the catalysts who draw people into a spirit of celebration and invite them to act out their own creations. The company's Chairman, Kelleher, is among the chief evocators in the company who has a way of turning a potentially boring business meeting into a celebratory event. By his very example, he arouses the spirit of the company and summons the spirit of cheering and celebrating.
- The celebration must appeal to all senses. The company has mastered the "art of balloonery." Its celebration activities can keep the balloon industry afloat. There are also banners, flags, floats, costumes, posters, photographs, film clips, videos, and music, among others depending on the creativity of the moment.
- The celebration must be seen as an investment. The company does not view celebrations as a cost. They represent one way to raise employee morale, job satisfaction, productivity, and the spirit of the people. Celebration has an excellent return on the investment.

- The celebration must be cost-effective. The company is a low-cost operation and this spreads to its celebrations too. Leaders must find the least expensive way to do a celebration right. This is accomplished by capitalizing on the talents of its employees rather than hiring outsiders to do the work. Even if it has to contract out to a vendor, it tries to barter the work for flight passes for example.

## Monitoring the Unfolding Maneuver

In the confusion of implementation and struggling with turbulence, the actual activities in the field tend to deviate from the planned maneuver. We can, and often do, end up with a maneuver that is different from the intended one. There are more tasks for the CEO in this regard. First, it is crucial that the actual activities be pieced together to identify the emerging actual maneuver. Next, it must be assessed. One way of doing this is to place it in the proper quadrant of Exhibit 13.2. Next, the emerging maneuver must be challenged along with the paradigms underlying it. Finally, the CEO must ascertain that people are acting as a true self-organizing system.

### 1. Piecing Together the Emerging Maneuver

In piecing together the emerging maneuver, the leadership assembles the firm's wheeling and dealing activities in the marketplace and plot them to discern the pattern embedded in them. The process begins with identifying the major moves in the marketplace and working backward to infer the actual thrust and business model that underlies them. It is possible that the thrust and the business model were not implemented as envisioned. If this is the case, then questions should be raised. What is the reason? Poor plans? Poor execution? Surprises?

Once a pattern is pieced together, the next step is to assess it. A quick and dirty way of doing so is to place in one of the cells of Exhibit 13.2. The mere locating of the emerging maneuver in one of the cells is enough to stimulate the invisible hand mechanism. If it is characterized as Case III or IV, this is a major source of alarm. People will mobilize to find out what went wrong and take corrective action. If it is a Case I, or II, this is a reason to celebrate, a win, that emboldens them to shoot higher in the next episode of interfacing with turbulence.

### 2. Challenging Results

No matter how the CEO characterizes the emerging maneuver pattern, he/she has to challenge the organization to a higher and better one immediately even if it is a case I or II. In a turbulent environment, today's accomplishments are history. Challenging results takes the form of questioning and raising the bar. Here are examples of the kinds of questions that prompt a higher level of attainment next time:

- How effective is the maneuver? Did we win our share of customers? Can we win a bigger share? Did we outmaneuver competitors and other opponents? If they retaliate, will we be able to beat them in the next round? Is our business model superior enough to give us the edge we need?
- Is the maneuver futuristic? Will it position the firm favorably in the long term? Will it win the battle but then lose the war?
- How much stretching is there in the system of moves? Is it pushing the envelope or remaining below organizational capability? Is capability utilized fully?
- Is the maneuver consistent with the vision and capability? If not which needs to be changed? The vision? The capability? The maneuvers?
- Is the planning process sound? Does it yield sound maneuvers?

- Does everyone own into maneuver formulation and implementation?
- Is the system of moves updated continually in light of the information flowing from the field? Is there a continuously changing response to a continuously changing marketplace?
- Did the implementation of the maneuver bring about constructive strategic and financial positions?

### 3. Challenging Paradigms

Maneuver is a function of the paradigms of the people planning and implementing it. In challenging results and upping the ante, the leader must make these paradigms surface so that people can find out what truly makes them think and act the way they do. Here are examples of paradigms:

- Assumptions about customers, competitors, the industry, and attitudes towards rules of the game (e.g., rule making or rule breaking).
- Assumptions about the efficacy of avoidance versus confrontation.
- Assumptions about what is "doable" and what is not in light of the firm's capability, structure, and vision.

Central to the monitoring process is ascertaining whether people are acting and behaving as a true self-organizing system. The acid test here comprises the following:

- Do they undertake maneuver action on their own, without being told by the higher ups?
- Do they update the maneuvers in real time on their own?

## CONCLUSION

This chapter concludes our discussion of maneuver as the dominant aspect of the firm's strategic response to turbulence. Maneuver appears to occur in two stages: at the thinking plane and at the acting plane. During the implementation phase, the CEO works hard to corral and steer the various maneuver activities, realizing fully that confusion will set in. To manage this confusion, he/she undertakes the activities discussed in this chapter. As stated earlier maneuver is the bulk of the firm's business activities. However, maneuver is still one aspect of the firm's response strategy. It rests on three pillars, capability, structure, and vision. These will be the topics of the next three chapters

## ENDNOTES

1. Tichy, N. and R. Charan, "Speed, Simplicity, and Self-Confidence," *Harvard Business Review*, September–October, 1989, p. 113.
2. Ibid.
3. Kantz, P.C., a letter to the editor, *Fortune*, April 24, 1988, p. 338.
4. Tichy and Charan, op. cit.
5. LaBarre, P., "The Dis-Organization of Oticon," *Industry Week*, July 18, 1994, p. 26.
6. Pascale, R.T., *Managing On the Edge: How the Smartest Companies Use Conflict to Stay Ahead*, New York, NY: Simon and Schuster, 1990, p. 79.

7. Ibid.

8. Belasco, J.A. and R.C. Stayer, *Flight of the Buffalo: Soaring To Excellence, Learning To Let Employees Lead*, New York, NY: Warner Books, 1993, p. 61.

9. Ibid., p. 24.

10. Ibid., p. 26.

11. Ibid., p. 256.

12. Tichy, N.M., and S. Sherman, *Control Your Destiny Or Someone Else Will: How Jack Welch Is Making General Electric The World's Most Competitive Company*, New York, NY: Doubleday, 1993, p. 154.

13. Belasco and Stayer, op. cit., p. 203.

14. Ibid., p. 204.

15. Ibid., p. 206.

16. Belasco and Stayer, op. cit., p. 17.

17. Ibid., pl 62–63.

18. LaBarre, op. cit., p. 24.

19. Kouzes, J.M. and B.Z. Posner, *The Leadership Challenge: How To Keep Getting Extraordinary Things Done in Organizations*, San Francisco, CA: Jossey-Bass, 1995, p. 204.

20. Ibid.

21. Ibid.

22. Ibid., p. 167.

23. Ibid., pp. 249–252.

24. Peters, T., *Thriving On Chaos: Handbook For A Management Revolution*, New York, NY: Harper & Row, 1987.

25. Peters, op. cit., pp. 371–374.

26. Kouzes and Porras, op. cit., pp. 292–313.

27. Freiberg, K. and J. Freiberg, *Nuts: Southwest Airlines' Crazy Recipe for Business and Personal Success*, Austin, Texas: Bard Press, 1996, pp. 198–201.

CHAPTER
# 14

# Strategic Response: Capability

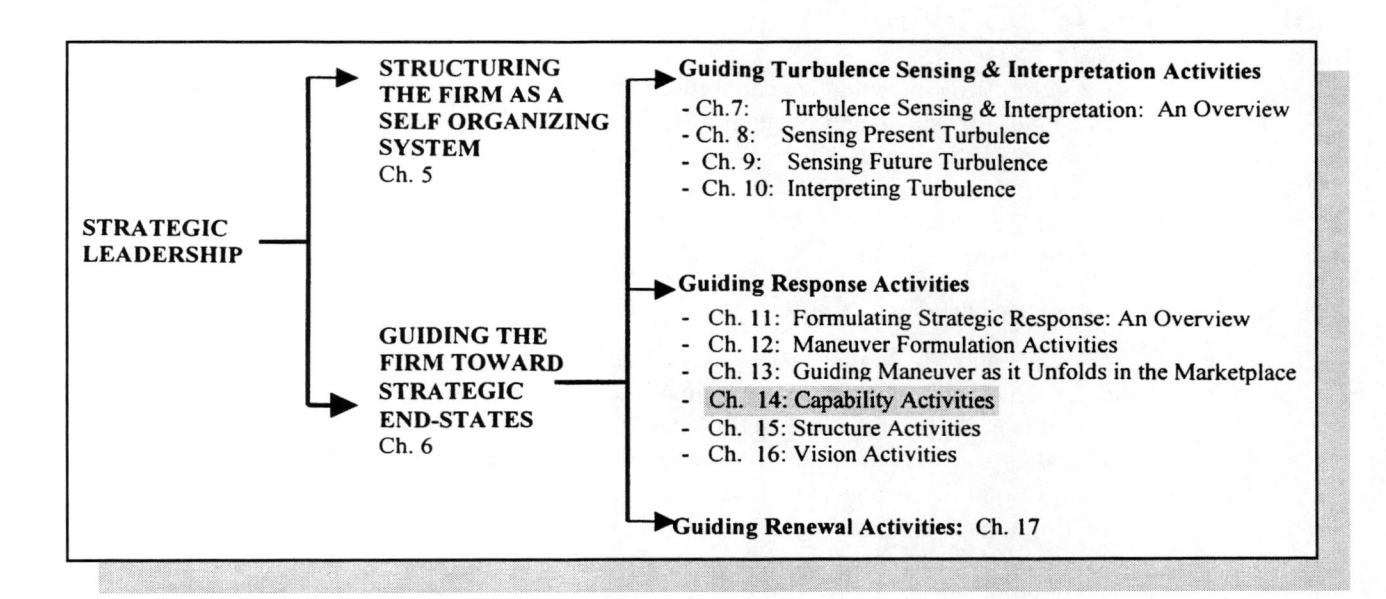

```
STRATEGIC         STRUCTURING           Guiding Turbulence Sensing & Interpretation Activities
LEADERSHIP        THE FIRM AS A
                  SELF ORGANIZING         - Ch.7:   Turbulence Sensing & Interpretation: An Overview
                  SYSTEM                  - Ch. 8:  Sensing Present Turbulence
                  Ch. 5                   - Ch. 9:  Sensing Future Turbulence
                                          - Ch. 10: Interpreting Turbulence

                                        Guiding Response Activities
                                          - Ch. 11: Formulating Strategic Response: An Overview
                  GUIDING THE             - Ch. 12: Maneuver Formulation Activities
                  FIRM TOWARD             - Ch. 13: Guiding Maneuver as it Unfolds in the Marketplace
                  STRATEGIC               - Ch. 14: Capability Activities
                  END-STATES              - Ch. 15: Structure Activities
                  Ch. 6                   - Ch. 16: Vision Activities

                                        Guiding Renewal Activities: Ch. 17
```

247

Responding to turbulence involves the formulation and implementation of a four-pronged strategy, consisting of a maneuver design, a capability configuration, an architecture of the organization, and a vision. The preceding two chapters covered maneuver. This chapter focuses on capability activities. It begins with a review of the literature on the concept of capability. Next, it presents a framework for understanding capability. After that, the various capability activities are surveyed. The chapter concludes with an overview of the role of the CEO in guiding the firm's activities with regard to capability.

In thinking about capability, it should be kept in mind that the concept varies by the complexity of the firm. The content of capability depends on whether the firm is a single-business firm or a multi-business firm. The single business-firm is the most frequent type and hence our discussion will focus on it. The case of the multi-business firm will be presented briefly at the end of the chapter.

# THE NATURE OF CAPABILITY

Attempts to conceptualize capability appear to fall in *four* schools of thought. The first views capability as managerial capability.[1] The second defines it as a "process," i.e., activity designs that create a competitive advantage in the marketplace.[2] The third conceptualizes capability as the "capacity" to undertake or to do things.[3] The fourth presents it as "competencies" or aptitudes and skills that produce a competitive advantage in the marketplace.[4] These are surveyed briefly below.

## Managerial/Organizational Capability

Ansoff and McDonnell defined capability as ". . . propensity and ability to engage in behavior which will optimize attainment of the firm's near and long term objectives".[5] In detailing their concept, they analyzed capability in terms of three elements: climate, competence, and capacity. These pertain to two aspects of the firm, general managers and the organization. Capability is conceptualized as a 3x2 matrix as shown in Exhibit 14.1.

Climate is the propensity to respond in a particular way, e.g., welcoming, controlling, or even rejecting change. Competence is the ability to respond; including ability to anticipate change. Capacity is the volume of work that can be handled. With respect to the general managers, climate is determined by mentality (predisposition) and the balance of power between general management and the rest of the organization. For this group, competence is determined by their talent, skills, and knowledge. By contrast, competence for the organization is determined by the structures and systems that mold people's behaviors along with the amount of shared knowledge and values. Finally, capacity for general managers depends on the individual stamina. For the organization, capacity depends on how the firm is organized to handle the work involved in responding to turbulence.

## Process Capability

Stalk, Evans, and Shulman introduced a new perspective on capability.[6] They view capability as ". . . a set of business processes strategically understood." They maintained that the *core of capability is process*. To illustrate, they discussed the case of Wal-Mart. Its corporate goals called for:

- Providing customers access to quality goods.
- Maximizing their availability in time and space according to customers' wants.
- Developing a cost structure conducive to competitive pricing.
- Building and maintaining a reputation of total trust by the consumer.

| ELEMENTS OF CAPABILITY | ASPECT OF THE FIRM ||
|---|---|---|
| | General Managers | The Organization |
| Climate: willingness to respond | Power Position | Culture |
| Competence: ability to respond | Talents<br>Skills<br>Knowledge | Power position<br>Structures<br>Systems<br>Shared knowledge |
| Capacity: volume of response | Personal | Organizational |

Exhibit 14.1: Ansoff and McDonnel's Concept of Capability

Stalk *et al.* stated that ". . . The key to achieving these goals was the way the company replenished inventory, the centerpiece of its competitive strategy. . ."[7] The emphasis here is on *"the way"* the company replenished inventory, which is called "cross-docking," a largely invisible logistics technique whereby goods are delivered on a continuous basis to the company's warehouses where they are selected, repacked, and then dispatched to Wal-Mart stores without storage. The products just cross from one loading dock to another in 48 hours or less. Clearly, this design enables speed and lowers cost especially inventory cost. They further point to the emergence of "a new logic of integration" as the principle of designing effective process. For this integration to take place, investment in the infrastructure is required. In the case of Wal-Mart, to make cross-docking work, the company made strategic investments in a variety of interlocking support systems (without regard to the immediate return on the investment expectations). Such investments included:

- An elaborate private satellite-communication system that allows continuous contact among all distribution centers, thousands of suppliers, and every store to ensure that orders can flow in and be consolidated in hours.
- A logistics infrastructure of 19 distribution centers serviced by a 2000 truck fleet that allows shipment from warehouse to store in less than 48 hours (compared to two weeks for the industry).

Another element of the infrastructure is the elaborate decentralized control system that allows informal cooperation among stores, warehouses, and suppliers to provide just-in-time delivery based on customer needs. This required the creation of an environment in which individual store managers learn from the market and from each other. While the information system provides video links connecting all stores to each other and to the head office (continuously showing detailed information about customer behavior), the corporate fleet of airplanes regularly shuttles store managers to headquarters for meetings on market trends and merchandising. Then, there is the manner in which the various functions are arranged in the process. Stalk *et al.* stress that cross-functionality is the best way to arrange such functions. They remind us, "capability is everywhere and nowhere." It is everyone's business. Capability thus requires a high degree of integration across all functions. Functional integration is needed to ensure coordination and speed the flow of activities in the process itself.

Finally, for a capability to be truly "strategic," the process must be transformed into superior value for the customer that translates into a superior competitive advantage in the marketplace. Stalk *et al.* stressed the strategic nature of capability when they said "A capability is a set of business processes strategically understood." By "strategically understood" they meant "thinking of the processes as the primary object of competitive strategy," i.e., identifying them, managing them centrally, and investing in them heavily with a view to long term payback and above all connecting them to real customer needs. "A capability is strategic only when it begins and ends with the customer." In the case of Wal-Mart, cross-docking and the accompanying infrastructure generate enormous economies in cost and time that allows the company to maintain superior cost and time advantages in servicing the customer. These economies come from minimum inventories, economies of scale, and considerable timesaving through speed (by shortening the time needed for any operation).

## Capability as Capacity for Action

Another school of thought advocates a different view of capability. First, it makes a distinction between resources and capability. Resources are defined as ". . . stocks of available factors that are owned or controlled by the firm. . . These resources consist, *inter alia*, of know-how that can be traded (e.g., patents and licenses), financial or physical assets (e.g., property and equipment), human capital, etc."[8] By contrast, capability, refers to ". . . a firm's capacity to deploy resources, usually in combination, using organizational processes, to effect a desired end. They are information-based, tangible or intangible processes that are firm-specific and are developed over time through complex interactions among the firm's resources."[9] As a representative of this school, Grant defines capability as ". . . a firms capacity for undertaking a particular activity."[10] He further notes that ". . . capabilities are formed from teams of resources working together."

## Capability as Competencies

Hamel and Prahalad's concept of core competencies. It has important implications for understanding capability.[11] A core competence is ". . . a bundle of skills and technologies that enable a company to provide a particular benefit to customers." They stressed that a competence is ". . . a bundle of skills and technologies rather than a single discrete skill or technology."[12] They further note that "A core competence is just what the name implies, an aptitude, or a skill that translates into a benefit for the customer. To illustrate, they presented Sony and Motorola as examples. Sony's core competence is miniaturization, which provides the "pocketability. Motorola's competence is in fast cycle-time production (minimizing the time between an order and the fulfillment of that order) rests on a broad range of underlying skills, including design disciplines that maximize commonality across a product line, flexible manufacturing, sophisticated order-entry systems, inventory management, and supplier management."[13]

Some conclusions about capability suggest themselves at this point:

- Capability is more than mere resources. Honda is a fraction of the size of GM. Yet, Honda has successfully challenged GM for the leadership position in the North American market. Honda was able to build and defend a strong market share, develop new products, lower its cost structure, and achieve a greater degree of customer satisfaction.
- Capability is more than just a process. A process by itself does not constitute capability. A process cannot take place without resources. It seems logical to view resources as part of "capability."
- Capability is more than core competencies. Competencies appear to be "extrapolations" from capability. They are consequences of the way people use resources.
- Capability is more than a propensity to act. Propensity does not create market and financial facts. Capability is "action" not just the predisposition for it.

Thus far, we have four views of capability. This begs the question: which one of them is capability? One has to be reminded that capability is a construct, i.e., a concept invented especially to refer to a phenomenon of interest. Because of the subjectivity of constructs, they vary from person to person. Clearly, each one of the above schools of thought viewed capability from only one angle. We need a construct that pulls together all these different viewpoints and integrates them in a complete whole. We attempt to develop such a concept next.

# A PROPOSED CONCEPT OF CAPABILITY FOR THE SINGLE BUSINESS FIRM

The most visible part of capability is capacity for action, i.e., what the firm *can* actually do at a given point in time or in a given situation. In this sense, capacity for action represents capability. However, to have a better understanding of capability, we must consider properties beyond capacity for action. Capacity for action has a number of underpinnings as shown in Exhibit 14.2. These include resources, processes, and functions; manner of using resources; and, competencies. Taken together all of them form this thing called capability. They are examined next.

## Capacity for Action

A firm's capacity for action is defined as the range and types of moves that it can actually execute in the marketplace at a given point in time. This range can best be viewed as a

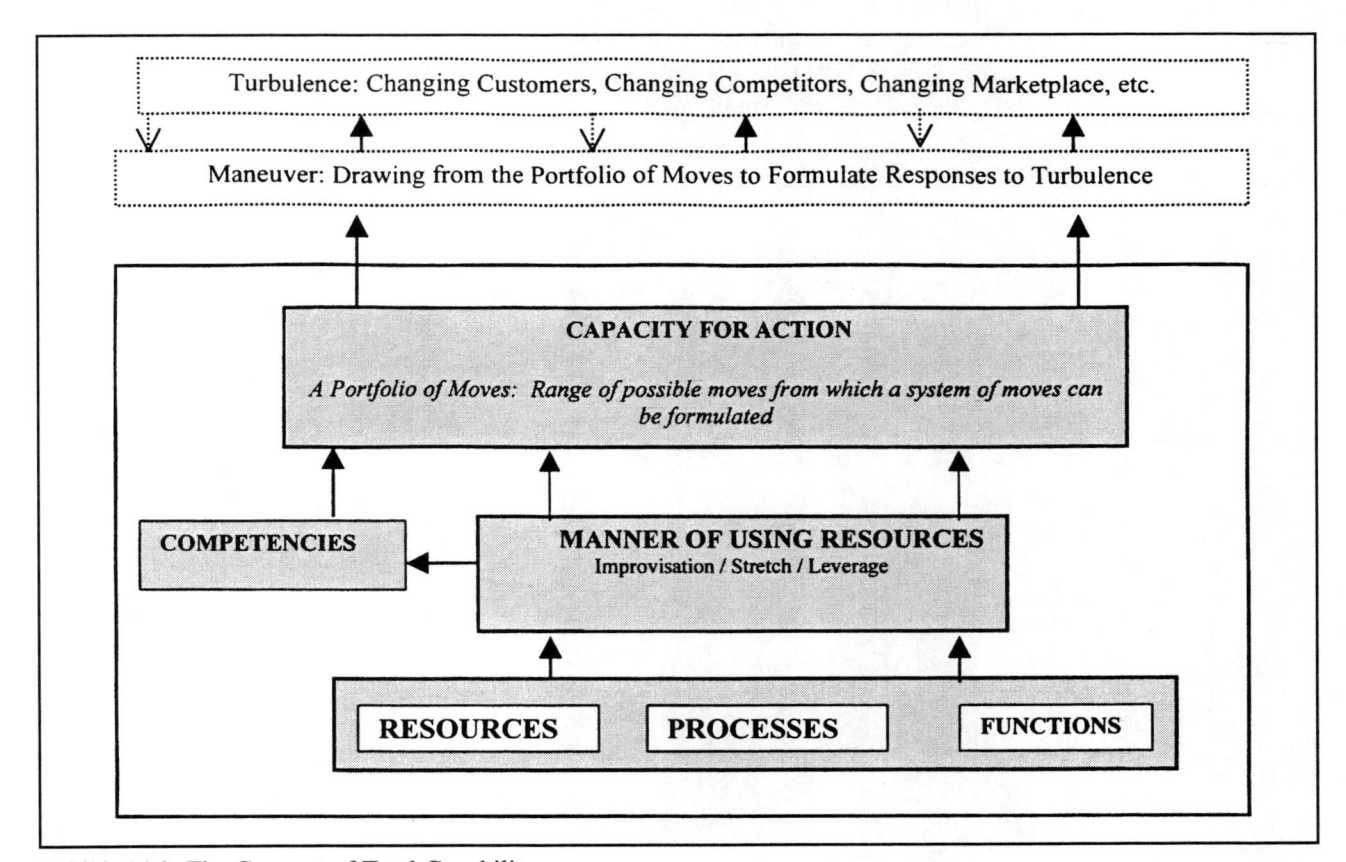

Exhibit 14.2: The Concept of Total Capability

*portfolio of moves*; an inventory of varied moves from which the maneuver's system of moves can be drawn. To have a good capability, a firm's portfolio must be rich enough so that many systems of moves can be formulated. This will enable the firm a repertory of maneuvers that it can actualize depending on the turbulence it encounters. Because the concept "move" is pivotal (to maneuver and to capability), we pause to examine it at the outset.

A move is a singular business action. As such, it is a part of a larger scheme or plan (maneuver). If we put the concept "move" under the microscope, we can discern seven elements as shown in Exhibit 14.3. The core of a move is an abstract idea; a concept of an action to be taken, e.g., raise price or introduce a new product model. This abstract idea is fleshed out by translating it into a number of concrete properties, as described below:

1. Scale: This is a specification of how massive the action is to be. The action can be as small as a symbolic gesture, e.g., matching minor price reductions by a competitor. On the other hand, the action can be an all-out war on all fronts. Consider the scale involved in Amazon.com's action to expand its product line beyond books to toys, consumer electronics, and others.

2. Impact: This is a specification of the degree to which the intended move is to rearrange the situation facing the company. It can be internal and/or external. For example, Dell's move to sell computers direct did alter the marketing of computers not only for Dell but for the other competitors as well. Microsoft's move to introduce WINDOWS had an enormous impact on the computer business. By contrast, some moves may not have much of an impact, e.g., moves designed to maintain the status-quo such as price cuts to match competitors' price reductions.

3. Speed: Speed pertains to how quickly a move is to be executed. In a turbulent environment, time is of the essence; the quicker the response, the higher the chances of coping with turbulence. Some moves are swift, especially when we want to surprise a competitor. Others might be intended to be slow on purpose to achieve stealth because we do not want to wake up the competition.

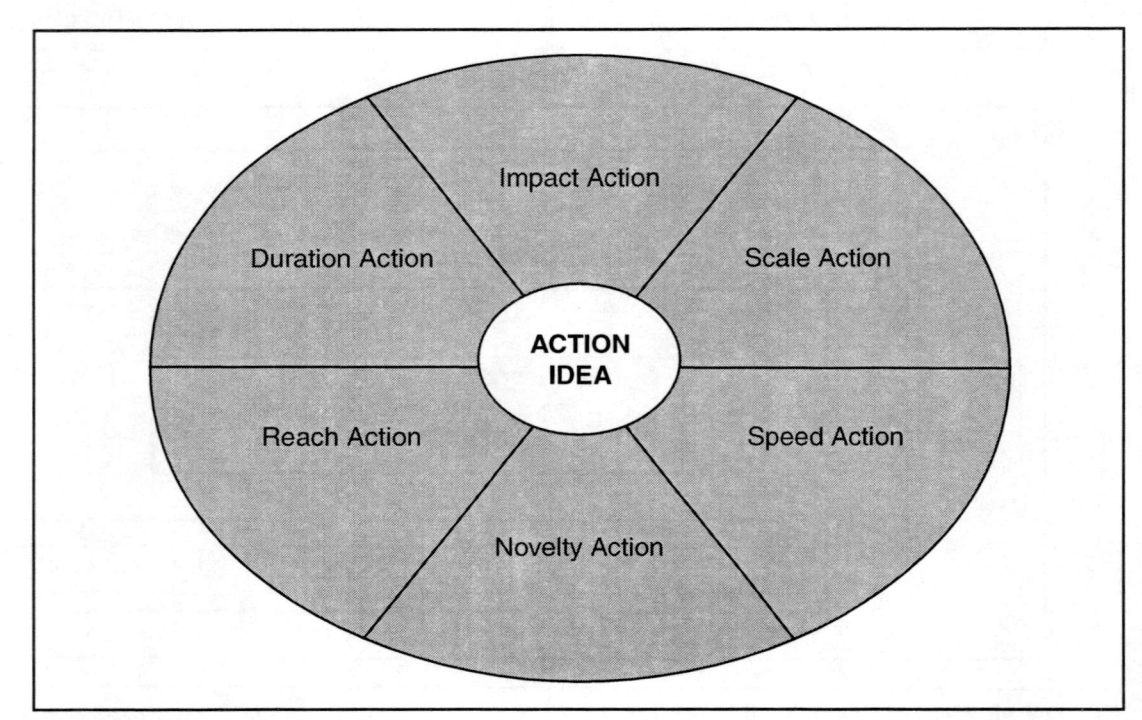

Exhibit 14.3: Anatomy of a Move

4. Reach: This pertains to how far and wide a move is to be. Some moves have a limited reach, i.e., they are focused on a certain segment or a sub-segment of the market, e.g., the introduction or pricing of specialty products. Some moves have wider reach, e.g., the introduction of WINDOWS 95—a move that covered the globe.
5. Duration: This pertains to how long a move is to last, externally and/or internally. Some moves have a short life span, e.g., price moves. Others have a longer life, e.g., positioning moves since it takes a long time to change customers' perception of the product or the company.
6. Novelty: Novelty action specifies how far a move departs from the familiar. Some moves are radical departures, e.g., Dell selling computers by mail or Amazon.com selling books on the Internet. By contrast, annual model changes by automakers represent a minimal degree of novelty. Novelty can also be internal when it reflects innovations in the way we do things in the firm.

Returning to the concept of capacity for action as a portfolio of moves, it can be visualized in the form of a matrix as shown in Exhibit 14.4. The rows are the components of the system of moves. The columns are the elements of a move. In the body of the table, we take each element of the system of moves (e.g., frontline and infrastructure various types of moves), and then we specify the action that can be undertaken along with its properties, i.e., scale, impact, reach, etc. If we fill the cells, we will have an inventory of what the firm can actually do at a given point in time. All the entries in the cells form a population of moves from which individual maneuvers can be formulated by mixing and matching the possibilities in the various cells. It is worth stressing that the inventory sheet of Exhibit 14.4 is an "accounting" of what we can do as of now with whatever resources we currently have. This should not be viewed as a rigid constraint. Constrains can be relaxed while the maneuver is underway. We might then wish to add resources and processing.

## Resources, Processes, and Functions

### Resources

The term "resources" refers to both the *tangible* and *intangible* types. *Tangible resources* include four main categories: physical, human, technological, and financial. Physical resources include machinery and equipment, real estate, buildings, and any other physical asset. Human resources are the people (employees, management, specialists, etc.) in the organization. Technological resources include the technical know-how acquired or possessed by the firm such as process technology. Financial resources include the various types of capital invested in the firm including fixed capital, working capital, cash flows, and excess cash.

Intangible resources include leverages, technology and innovation skills, intellectual property, special relationships, image, and reputation. Leverages are those special features of its operations that give it a disproportionate influence over the industry or the environment, e.g. Intel's and Microsoft's leverages that accord them influence over the desktop computer industry. Technology and innovation skills exist in forms such as proprietary technologies, trade secrets, and the skill and know-how required for its successful application. Intellectual property refers to intangible assets such as patents, trademarks, copyrights, and brand names. Relationships are crucial resources because they can be translated into market power. Relationships with suppliers are critical nowadays where the firm and its suppliers develop partnerships that can create considerable savings. The economies of Just-in-Time (JIT) are only possible through strong buyer-supplier relationships. Such economies include minimum inventory, product availability on demand, and joint product and process development. Similarly, relationships with distributors and other customers are important resources. Strong relationships with distributors ensure prime shelf space for the firm's product, friendlier terms

|                                                                                   | Possible Moves                                                                                                                  |                                                          |                                                           |                                                         |                                                                  |                                                                    |                                                         |
| --------------------------------------------------------------------------------- | ------------------------------------------------------------------------------------------------------------------------------- | -------------------------------------------------------- | --------------------------------------------------------- | ------------------------------------------------------- | ---------------------------------------------------------------- | ------------------------------------------------------------------ | ------------------------------------------------------- |
| **Aspects of Maneuver**                                                           | Possible Ideas for Moves                                                                                                        | Possible **Scales** for each Move                        | Possible **Impacts** for each Move                        | Possible **Reachs** for each Move                       | Possible **Durations** for each Move                             | Possible **Novelty** for each Move                                 | Possible **Speeds** for each Move                       |
| **Frontline Moves:** <br>—Product <br>—Pricing <br>—Selling <br>—Etc.             | List of all possible ideas for frontline actions in each type of move, e.g., product, selling, etc.                             | Specification of the possible scales for each move       | Specification of the possible impacts for each move       | Specification of the possible reachs for each move      | Specification of the possible durations for each move            | Specification of the possible innovations for each move            | Specification of the possible speeds for each move      |
| **Infrastructure Moves** <br>—Production <br>—H.R. <br>—Financing <br>—Etc.       | List of all possible ideas for infra-structure actions in each type of move, e.g., financing, H.R. etc.                         | Specification of the possible scales for each move       | Specification of the possible impacts for each move       | Specification of the possible reachs for each move      | Specification of the possible durations for each move            | Specification of the possible innovations for each move            | Specification of the possible speeds for each move      |

Exhibit 14.4: The Concept of Portfolio of Moves as the Firm's Capacity for Action

of payment, pushing the product through the channel, joint promotions and so on. Such relationships translate into considerable savings and increases in sales and profitability.

Finally, image and reputation represent another important asset that often translates into more volume and more savings. When IBM adopted the MS-DOS as the disk operating system for the PC, it became the standard of the industry. IBM's image and reputation—among others—enabled it to achieve a high market share at the expense of the entrenched companies such as Apple and Tandy Computers. Not only did IBM's image and reputation influence the computer buyers and competitors, it also influenced the supply side. Many firms were competing to become OEM (original equipment manufacturers) suppliers for IBM computers on IBM terms.

### Processes

Resources are utilized by means of processes. These processes are specified as part of the business model as presented in Chapter 12. These often fall in areas such as these:

- Processes for sourcing the inputs needed to make the product/service and the logistics of continuously supplying the firm with them. Nowadays, this includes processes for building and utilizing a network of partnerships with suppliers.
- Processes for building the product/service; transforming the inputs into the products or services that actualizes the business concept.
- Processes for delivering the product/service to the targeted set of customers, including sales, service, promotion, pricing, all to ensure customer satisfaction.
- Processes that ensue that the above processes to function properly such as R&D, technology development, recruiting and training people, and so on.

## Functions

Processes are the sequenced activities involved in transforming some input into an output. The term "function" refers to one cluster of process activities that is assigned to a unit of the organization (an individual, a team, or a department) and it becomes its job, or specialization (or function). Examples of functions include selling, public relations, credit and collection, engineering, production control, field service, and the like. A quick way to identify functions is to examine a firm's organization chart. The organization chart (and the firm's organization manual) identifies, codifies, and labels the various functions.

## Manner of Using Resources

Resources, processes, and functions are passive entities. By themselves, they do not "make" actions or moves in the marketplace. The extent to which moves are created from them depends on the "way" people use these resources, especially their creativity and ingenuity. Hamel and Prahalad[14] alluded to this aspect of capability in discussing their concept of "resourcefulness." They observed that:

- All firms have more or less the same generic capability comprising resources and organizational units.
- Resource constraints do not inhibit firms from achieving even global leadership. Abundance of resources does *not* guarantee such a position.
- Firms achieve entirely different impacts in the marketplace with a given amount of resources.

To illustrate, they mentioned the examples of Honda vs. GM, and Cannon vs. Xerox. Here, we have two firms with much smaller resources but were able to challenge the entrenched leaders. Interestingly enough, the smaller firms succeeded and in some instances, exceeded the market leaders. This success is attributed to the "manner" in which these firms utilized their resources, processes, functions, and competencies.

An analysis of the concept of "manner of using resources" reveals that it can be broken further into three elements: "stretching," "leveraging," and "improvising." They are used concurrently to maximize the output of resources. Each one is described briefly next.

## Stretching

The notion of stretch was introduced by Hamel and Prahalad.[15] The term refers to managing things in such a way that ambition forever outpaces resources. It is assigning resources tasks beyond their normal capacity. As Hamel and Prahalad observed, conventional wisdom requires managers ". . . to be realistic". They note, however that "if JVC engineers had been 'realistic' in the early 1960s, they would have never developed home videocassette recorders. . . If Torakuso Yamaha had been realistic, he never would have dreamed of turning Yamaha into the world's leading manufacturer of grand pianos and other musical instruments." They also mention the case of Komatsu. Komatsu was a small manufacturer of earth moving equipment. Yet, it dared to view itself as a competitor of the world leader, Caterpillar—an unthinkable position at the time.

## Leveraging

Leverage means using a small weight to counterbalance a much heavier force. In business terms, a small amount of resources is applied in such a way that it produces disproportionately larger results. In leveraging, imagination and creativity are applied to find ways to augment the power of the limited resources currently controlled. Leasing is a form of leverage. It allows the possession and use of the asset by paying a fraction of its price periodically. Forming strategic alliances is a form of leverage. By contributing a small share to a pool of resources, the firm will have the benefit of the whole pool—something that it could not afford in the first place.

Leverage also pertains to using a particular strength or an asset to gain a disproportionate advantages over others. A firm that is the only owner of a highly sought after proprietary technology will have leverage (disproportionate power) if its competitors have to buy this technology from it. A firm's image and reputation can be used create more substantial results. IBM used its leverage to enter and dominate the personal computer business. It assembled a team of suppliers who invested their own resources to make the parts and assemble the computer for it. Again, by virtue of its name, IBM's specs for its PC, they became the standard of the industry. Brand name extension is another example of leveraging. A firm with a trusted and respected brand name, can extend it to new products. These new products often sell well in the marketplace. The mere presence of the name IBM on the PC made it a successful brand.

Toyota induced its suppliers to locate in the same proximity and influenced their operations and investments in an effort to integrate them with Toyota. As a result, Toyota multiplied its capacity for parts production without a commensurate investment and enormous administrative burden in its infrastructure (compared to Ford or GM). At the same time, parts are delivered at the right moment, and with minimal parts inventory.

The strategic use of leverage has been demonstrated by researchers such as Hamel and Prahalad. They provided these examples: Chrysler developed the small car "Neon" using a fraction of the resources that GM spent in developing and producing the "Saturn." Honda attained a leadership position in engines and power trains for cars utilizing an R&D budget that is a fraction of GM's. NEC successfully challenged Siemens (in telecommunications equipment), Texas Instruments (in semiconductors), and IBM (in computers), although NEC historically had a much smaller R&D expenditure than these competitors. CNN was able to achieve around-the-clock news coverage with a budget that is estimated to be one fifth of CBS News. All these are applications of leverage: using a small amount of resources to produce disproportionate results.

### Improvising

The third element is the manner of utilizing resources is "improvising." It is the art of creating something out of nothing. This is often attained by getting resources to do things they were not originally intended to do. To illustrate, take a sheet of paper. For most persons, it has only one use, to write on it. However, with improvisation, it can have several applications such as: a toy (a boat or a plane), a fan for cooling on hot days, a "funnel" (when rolled) for pouring liquids, and other uses limited only by imagination.

The spirit of improvisation is captured in the old saying about military strategy: "Strategy is keeping on firing after you have run out of ammunition." Improvising requires creativity and imaginativeness in making a smaller amount of resources behave like a much larger sum. Jack Stack (Springfield Remanufacturing, Chapter 2) once described how the firm did its R&D in the early days when it was starved for cash. Employees used neighborhood pizza ovens and their own stoves at home to test the behavior of metals in the course of rebuilding engine parts. Many of these efforts resulted in new processes and new combinations of material that performed better than the existing ones. These added many products to SRC's line. Considerable R&D was done this way without a budget, staff, or specialized equipment.

### Competencies

The third element in a firm's capability infrastructure is "competencies." Competencies are a result of the continuous application of improvisation, leverage, and stretch to the firm's resources. Over time, the firm develops unique ways of doing things that translate into disproportionate competitive advantages for it in the marketplace by delivering a superior customer value. Interestingly enough, these unique ways cannot be replicated or duplicated by its competitor. Toyota, for example, has been known for "the Toyota way" that produced high quality that made the Toyota Camry a top-selling car. Other automakers studied "the Toyota way" carefully. They see it. They analyze it. Yet, they cannot duplicate it. Such is the peculiar nature of a competence; it cannot be copied.

# CAPABILITY DEVELOPMENT

Obviously, capability and maneuver must be aligned with one another. However, turbulence often causes misalignment between the two, and capability might lag behind the requirements of maneuver. To remedy this situation, a self-organizing system engages continuously in developing its capability. Capability development activities fall into two categories: capability planning, and, resource acquisition. Each of these is explored briefly next.

## Capability Planning

Capability planning is the process of anticipating turbulence and then specifying the kind of capability that would enable the firm to generate a generous range of maneuvers. Scenario planning is a good model for determining the kind of capability needed. Capability planning activities can be outlined as follows:

1. Constructing Scenarios for the Future: The process of constructing scenarios was discussed in Chapter 9. The same methodology is applicable in the context of capability planning. The capability plan is often based on the most likely scenario. However, should there be drastic scenarios with lesser likelihood, they should be taken into consideration. The fact that they have a low likelihood means that they still have a probability of occurring. To be ready to face the future, the firm must incorporate them in its reckoning.
2. Generating a Range of Maneuver Configurations: Given the most likely scenario and other critical scenarios, the next step is to formulate alternative maneuver designs for the firm especially strategic thrusts and business models. These configurations should be generated without being constrained by the currently existing capability. Surveying this scope of maneuver would help identify the range of moves needed for the firm to cope with turbulence.
3. Constructing the Desired Portfolio of Moves: Given the range of maneuvers, the next step is to construct the kind of portfolio of moves that can make them possible. This can be accomplished by completing the decisions called for in Exhibit 14.4.
4. Assessing Capability Gaps: At this point, we have two portfolios of moves; a desired one and an actual one. Upon comparing the two, we might discover differences or gaps between what is, and what ought to be there. Having identified the gaps, we estimate the quantities and types of resources required. The next step is to acquire these resources somehow.

## Acquisition of Resources

The second phase in capability development is the acquisition of the resources and processes that would yield portfolio of moves outlined in the capability plan. Capability acquisition often includes a set of strategies for acquiring the needed resources and the timing of the acquisition. These include:

1. Direct Purchase

2. Strategic Alliances: Pooling resources with other firms, the firm will then have access to a bigger infrastructure.

3. Leveraging Existing Resources: Leveraging existing resources is an excellent strategy to obtain extra resources and to maximize the utilization of the ones we have. Hamel and Prahalad identified five strategies for leveraging resources, namely, concentrating resources, accumulating resources, complementing resources, conserving resources, and recovering resources.[16]

   3.1. Concentrating Resources: Concentrating resources can extend their power to achieve more. Concentration can be achieved by means of "converging," "focusing," and "targeting" as follows:

   - Converging: All resources, processes, functions, and competencies must be orchestrated to "converge" on one major goal or direction.
   - Focusing: This is the avoidance of spreading resources too thin during a given time span in the pursuit of the longer-term goal.
   - Targeting: This is the selection of the "right" things on which to focus. The term "right" here designates pursuits that would have the maximum impact in terms of customer value and competitive advantage. Examples of targeting include Apple's choice of the desk-top computer or Microsoft's pursuit of WINDOWS as the area in which to concentrate resources.

   3.2. Accumulating Resources: Another way of generating leverage is accumulating resources. This can be achieved in two ways: "mining" and "borrowing."

   - Mining is the continuous search and analysis of resources with the purpose of discovering resources not fully utilized and shifting their utilization in high gear, and creating opportunities for maximizing all their utilization by finding new and different applications.
   - Borrowing is the historical way of building leverage, e.g., the use of debt. Borrowing also includes the use of resources through strategic alliances, joint ventures, licensing, and outsourcing—all are examples of how a firm can expand its resource base, without proportionate investment, by utilizing other firms' resources.

   3.3. Complementing Resources: Leverage can also be generated by building and exploiting synergy among resources. This can be achieved in ways such as: "blending," "balancing," "recycling," "co-opting," and "protecting."

   - Blending is the resourceful, imaginative interweaving of different types of resources to create or maximize a competitive advantage. Blending can be achieved through the integration of different types of technologies and functions (of R&D, production, sales, finance etc. in product development) in the effort to create value for the customer, which would translate into a competitive advantage.
   - Balancing is identifying the right proportions or amounts and types of resources in the process of creating a competitive advantage. Balancing also means proportionate emphasis on the processes that make a difference in the marketplace, e.g., strong capacity to market and distribute should be balanced against the capacity to develop and produce products.

- Recycling is the continuous extension of resources, skills, and competencies, by applying or redeploying them into a range of different fields. Examples of recycling competencies include Canon's extension of its expertise in optics to diverse applications such as cameras, copiers, ophthalmic testing equipment, and semiconductor based imaging.
- Co-opting is enlisting the support of other firms such that they will contribute to a resource pool to fight a common threat. For example, Britain's ICL, Germany's Siemens, and Amdahl in the U.S. developed a partnership to challenge the dominance of IBM in the computer business.
- Protecting is the avoidance of frontal attacks that bleed resources. Avoidance of such depletion "protects" the scarce resources that we have. An example of the application of "protecting" is Dell Computer's resort to mail order as a way of selling computers and thus avoided conformation with the expensive "computer store" distribution system that IBM utilized.

3.4. Recovering Resources: Another approach for building and maintaining leverage is the speedy recovery of resources so that they may be utilized again and again to maximize their productivity. An example of speed here is the shortening of the elapsed time between transforming cash into inventory and transforming inventory back into cash and so on.

4. Besides the above approaches, there are others such as leasing and sharing resources, such as sharing physical production and/or distribution facilities with allies.

## Timing of Resource Acquisition

A critical element in capability acquisition is the timing of the infusion of new resources. There are three points in time at which this can be done. Resources can be acquired *before* maneuvering in the marketplace. Firms that believe in advance preparation often build capability in advance. Resources can also be acquired incrementally *at the same time* as the maneuver is implemented. When uncertainty is too high or funding is not available, increments of resources can be acquired as the action takes place. The acquisition can take place *after* the current round of maneuver moves. Initially, maneuvering is undertaken using stretch, leverage, and improvisation. The resulting profits can then be used to fund the acquisition of needed resources additions, en route.

## Capability of the Multi-Business Firm

It should be stressed that the multi-business firm is essentially a constellation of single business firms or units (strategic business units or SBU's). Accordingly, it has *two sets* of capabilities. The first is the capability at the level of head office, the corporate level. The second is the capability at the SBU level, the business level as discussed in the previous section. At corporate level, the multi-business firm is essentially a portfolio of businesses. This can be visualized using the Boston Consulting Group's (BCG) matrix, known as the growth-share matrix, Exhibit 14.5.

The capability of the multi-business firm comprises a number of elements as shown in Exhibit 14.6. The central element here is the firm's capacity to create, build, and maintain a portfolio of businesses. This, in turn, rests on two further elements: financing capacity, and, managerial capacity. It is worth stressing that the term capacity here refers to a range of possible moves. Portfolio building capacity includes capacity to add new entries in the portfolio, capacity to reposition existing SBUs, and capacity to control the size of units in the portfolio. These are defined on the following page.

## Capacity to Add New Entries to the Portfolio

If the firm is in a position to add new businesses to the portfolio, it has capability. If it cannot, it does not have capability. Capacity to add depends on two further capacities: capacity to acquire other companies and capacity to develop new businesses internally. Acquisition capacity refers to the firm's ability to find acquisition targets, purchase them, and integrate them into the organization. Internal development capacity is the firm's ability to develop new business units from scratch through internal entrepreneurial ventures.

## Capacity to Position Entries within the Portfolio

Adding to the number of businesses in the portfolio is an indicator of capability but it is not enough. A crucial aspect of capacity is the ability to position entries, i.e., to move certain SBU's from one quadrant to a more desirable one in an effort to increase cash generation. For example, question marks are tomorrow's businesses. They are in an industry in the early stages of its growth. However, they have a relatively small market share. If the firm can increase the market share of these units in order to move them to the star category, this would be a good measure of capability.

## Capacity to Control the Sizes of Entries

The relative sizes of the SBUs in the portfolio have far reaching ramifications for capacity to build a viable portfolio. The presence of large size dogs clearly leads to starving the whole corporation for cash. By contrast, the existence of large size cash cows increases the cash supply. There has to be a balance in terms of size. Failing that may lead to portfolios that do not represent a healthy financial position.

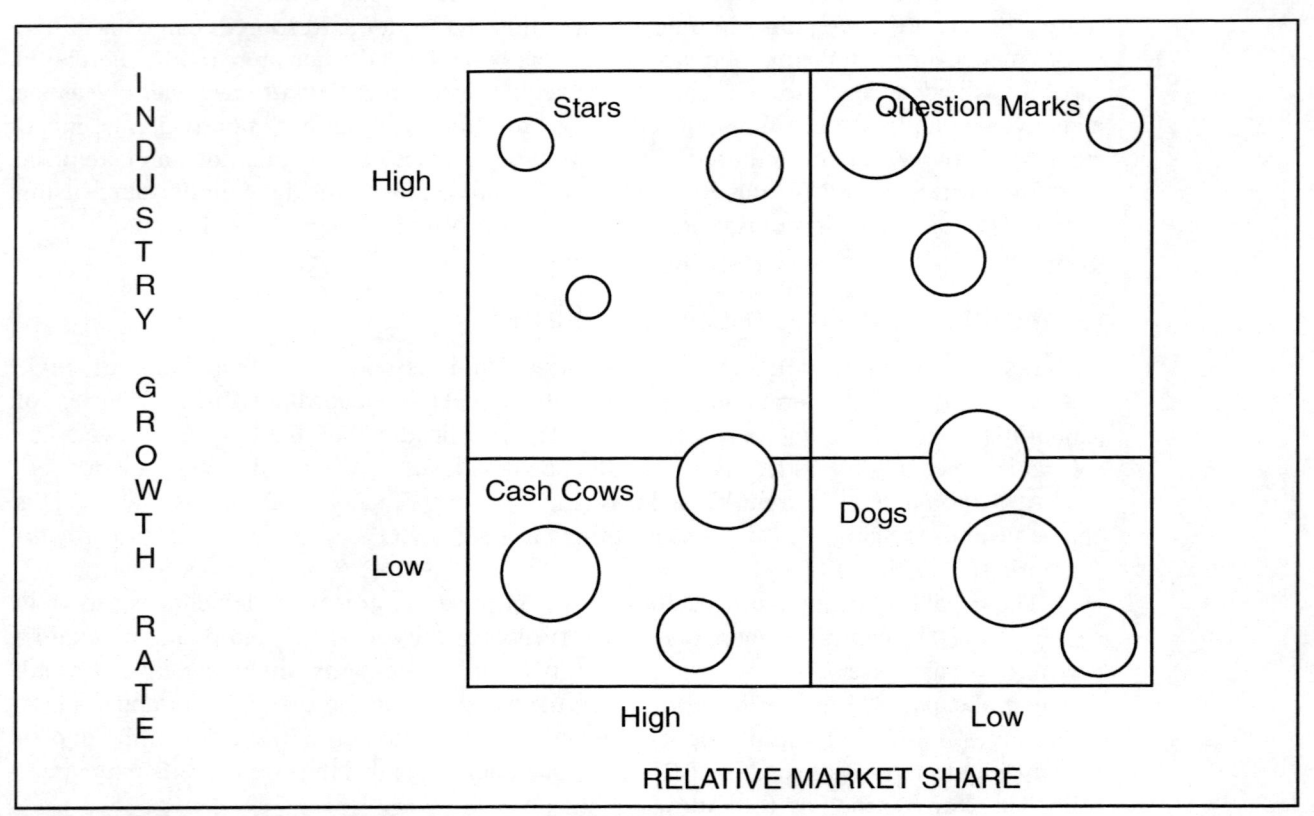

Exhibit 14.5: The BCG Growth-Share Matrix: An Application of Reduction

Capacity to control size depends on three further factors: capacity to invest, capacity to build market share, and capacity to harvest and divest. The firm has to have the wherewithal to invest in question marks so that their market share increases to become stars. Further, the firm should have the ability to enlarge the size of smaller units in the star categories so that they can become better and stronger stars. Strong stars are tomorrow's cash cows. They will fund the firm's growth in the future. Capacity to harvest refers to the firm's ability and willingness to take cash away from certain SBUs by starving them for cash on purpose. Capacity to divest refers to the firm's ability to unload businesses in the dog category. Sometimes barriers to exit exist and divestment might be difficult. This depends on the firm's ability to market these units creatively and get the best price for them rather than selling them at a loss.

The portfolio of moves here derives from two underpinning capabilities: financing capability and organizational capability. Financing capability refers to the supply of funds available to the firm to finance the moves of various SBU\s inside, around, and out of the portfolio. The supply of cash is determined by the cash generated (and used) by the various SBUs in the portfolio, cross subsidization. This is often augmented by the firm's ability to raise money from capital markets as well as funds from divestments of current cash users.

Finally, the multi-business firm must have an organizational capability. This pertains to two items: supply of CEOs for the SBUs, and structure of the relationship between the corporate office and the SBUs. The supply of CEOs for the SBUs determines the extent of the portfolio. The more the supply of CEOs, the more the firm's ability to add new SBUs and

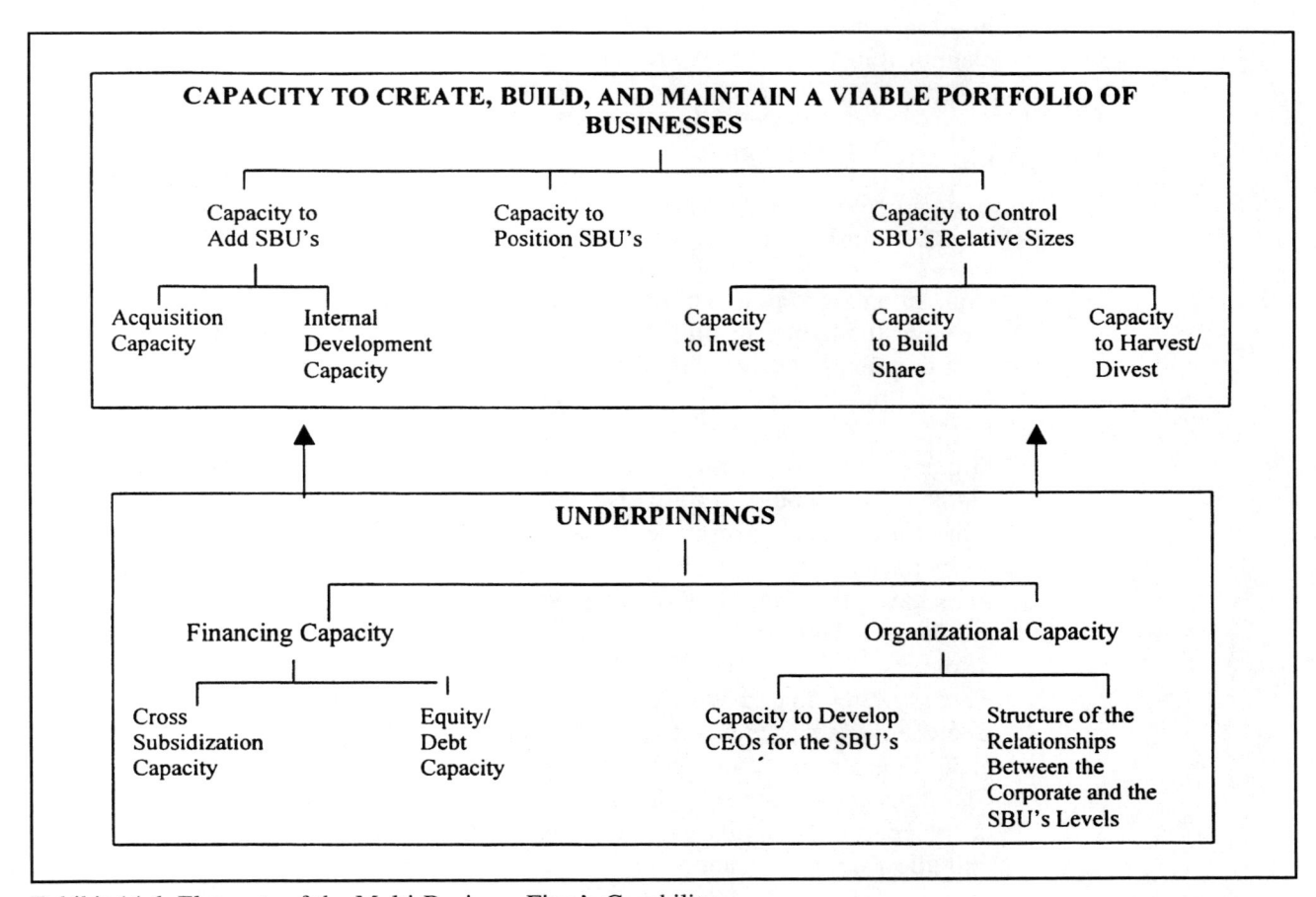

Exhibit 14.6: Elements of the Multi-Business Firm's Capability

improve existing ones. The structure of the relationships between the head office and the SBUs also affects the firm's overall capability. A structure that liberates the SBUs CEOs enables them to improve their units. This enhances the firm's overall capacity as well as the value of the portfolio. A structure, that stifles and limits SBUs CEOs, translates into inertia and rigidity that affects the portfolio in a negative manner.

# GUIDING CAPABILITY ACTIVITIES

Traditionally, capability decisions were made by the CEO and top management. Capability involves capital budgeting and allocation. These are top management prerogatives. These decisions were too important to be left to the employees. However, a self-organizing firm is continuously arranging and rearranging its capability as it arranges and rearranges its maneuver activities in the marketplace. The CEO cannot stay on top of changes in the marketplace and the commensurate changes in capability. So, how does the CEO then guide capability activities? The leader of a self-organizing firm focuses on two essential tasks:

- Discovering a semicoherent direction in the diverse initiatives that people undertake in the course of building, modifying, and deploying capability and then legitimizing the appropriate ones. These can be legitimized by formally approving them and committing funds to them
- Inducing and orchestrating strategic collaboration among the various units as they build and utilize capability. The topic of stimulating strategic collaboration was examined in Chapter 6. We revisit them briefly here:

## Creating an Environment Conducive to Collaboration for Capability Building

To create an environment conducive to collaboration with respect to capability activities, the key CEO's tasks can be briefly outlined as follows:

- Cultivating Paradigms: This includes cultivating seminal thoughts such as the principles of futuristic capability, fluidity, improvisation, stretch, and leverage.
- Building Shared Goals: The work of the CEO here involves entrenching goals such as being the lowest cost producer or the one with the most advanced capability.
- Defining Boundaryless Roles: The firm's capability comprises the individual capabilities of its various units. Although each unit will focus on building and managing its own capability, it must also have a macro perspective and assume responsibility for the firm's overall capability.
- Networking: This is crucial for ensuring that roles remain boundaryless. If all units have all the information, they will be in a better position to coordinate their various capability-building activities and eliminate duplication in the purchase of resources.
- Orchestrating Shared Workspace: Shared workspace allows information to flow freely and enables cooperative efforts in pooling intelligence and experience especially in acquiring resources and utilizing (sharing) them.
- Charging Emotions: Capability building is in essence preparation for the battle. It is an opportunity to rally various groups so that the firm may have a capability that will allow competing and winning in the marketplace.

### Inducing and Stimulating Conversation on Capability

The usual vehicle for stimulating conversation on the topic is strategic planning sessions for capability planning. In such sessions, people are drawn from different units to contemplate how to build the kind of capability that would propel the firm toward its desired strategic end-state. In strategic planning sessions, these individuals review the results of turbulence sensing and interpretation, exchange views on the strategic issues, review maneuver plans, check the current state of the firm's capability, and investigate aligning it with the requirements of the maneuver. At that time, a list of required resources and how to acquire them will be the topic of the strategic conversation.

### Marshalling Strategic Conversation to Strategic Action

The role of the CEO here is to move strategic planning conversation into actual capability building action. This involves the steps listed below:

- Developing and Cultivating Frameworks for Action like the ones presented in this chapter. It will guide the various groups as they contemplate capability decisions.
- Keeping the Vision since capability is expected to propel the firm towards the vision as the desired end-state for the firm.
- Building Collaborative Networks in order to get all groups to act together to acquire the needed capability and utilize it in an efficient manner.
- Staffing Critical Positions with knowledgeable person who can bring all concerned on side so that they may build and use capability judiciously.
- Allocating Resources: In the final analysis, capability is the application of the firm's funds, fixed and working capital. Fixed assets call for enormous long-term investments. Working capital is also affected by capability since the design and utilization of capability affect the firm's cost structure, mainly material and labor cost. The CEO can stimulate collaboration by tying capital allocation to it in the form of joint projects pertaining to capability. By allocating resources to one project or another, the CEO can steer capability activities. In the process, he/she moves conversation on capability to the action phase.

### Affirming Accountability and Governance

Capability is where the firm's assets are. The governance system provides a framework for collaboration and accountability for the firm's assets.

### Exercising Personal Influence

The personal influence of the CEO is crucial here for steering collaboration on capability. The CEO is the ultimate steward of the firm's assets and the one responsible for protecting them. This responsibility cannot be delegated. It is thus crucial for the CEO to influence capability decisions personally. This can be done in many ways including reviewing and approving capital and operating budgets, approving major capability decisions, participating in strategic planning, and coaching capability decision-makers.

# CONCLUSION

In this chapter, the capability activities of a self-organizing system were examined. A model of capability was presented as a portfolio of moves from which the moves called for by maneuver can be drawn. Capability is where the bulk of the firm's investment is made. As Abel noted,

"Using present capacities to their fullest advantage and developing new ones in anticipation of the future characterizes the high performer in all fields of human endeavor . . . Armies fight battles deploying whatever materiel and personnel they have at their disposal, and in more peaceful times develop new military capabilities in anticipation of battles still unfought.

Management as a human endeavor differs . . . in one important respect: Running the business and changing it are not sequential but parallel pursuits. Even armies are seldom on full alert all the time, at least not for limitless periods. War and peace are punctuated providing the breathing space to build and regroup. Managers enjoy no such luxury, competing today and preparing for tomorrow with no letup on either front."[17]

Capability is not just resources. It is what can be done with resources. In the final analysis capability is a robust portfolio of moves that the organization can draw from to meet an unanticipated (and anticipated) range of situations and contingencies, especially surprises. This portfolio is an ever-changing entity because environmental turbulence can render it obsolete at any moment. Hence, capability building is a continuous process. It is part of the firm's on-going effort to respond continuously to a continuously changing environment. The test of good capability is being able to respond strategically and quickly to turbulence, not only at the present time but in the future as well.

The richness of the portfolio of moves does not depend solely on resources alone. It has been shown beyond any doubt that the ingenuity of people makes a big difference. Through improvising, stretching, and leveraging people can create capability with minimal resources and sometimes without resources. However, for people to act in this manner, a certain type of organizational structure is needed. Such structure would enlist their support, energize them, and liberate them to act, and reward them for such actions. Structure is thus crucial for actualizing capability out of resources. Structure is the topic of the next chapter.

# ENDNOTES

1. Ansoff, I., and E.J. McDonnell, *Implanting Strategic Management*, 2nd Edition, New York, NY: Prentice-Hall, 1990, p. 263.
2. Stalk, G., P. Evans, and L.E. Shulman, "Competing on Capabilities: The New Rule of Corporate Strategy," *Harvard Business Review*, March–April 1992, pp. 57–69).
3. See for example, Hitt, M.A, and R.D. Ireland, and R.E. Hoskisson, *Strategic Management: Competitiveness and Globalization*, St. Paul, Min.: West, 1995.
4. Hamel, G., and C.K. Prahalad, *Competing for The Future*, Boston, MA: Harvard Business School Press, 1994.
5. Ansoff and McDonnell, op. cit., p. 261.
6. Stalk, Evans, and Shulman, op. cit.
7. Ibid.
8. Amit R., and P.J.H. Shoemaker, "Strategic Assets and Organizational Rent," *Strategic Management Journal,* January, 1993, pp. 33–46.
9. Ibid., p. 35.
10. Grant, R.M., *Contemporary Strategy Analysis: Concept, Techniques, Applications*, 2nd ed., Cambridge, Mass.: Blackwell, 1995, p. 26.
11. Hamel and Prahalad, op. cit., p. 179.
12. Ibid., p. 202.
13. Ibid., p. 202.

14. Hamel and Prahalad, op. cit.
15. Ibid.
16. Ibid., pp. 160–176.
17. Abel, D., *Managing with Dual Strategies*, New York, NY: Free Press, 1993, p. 3.

CHAPTER
# 15

# Strategic Response: Structure

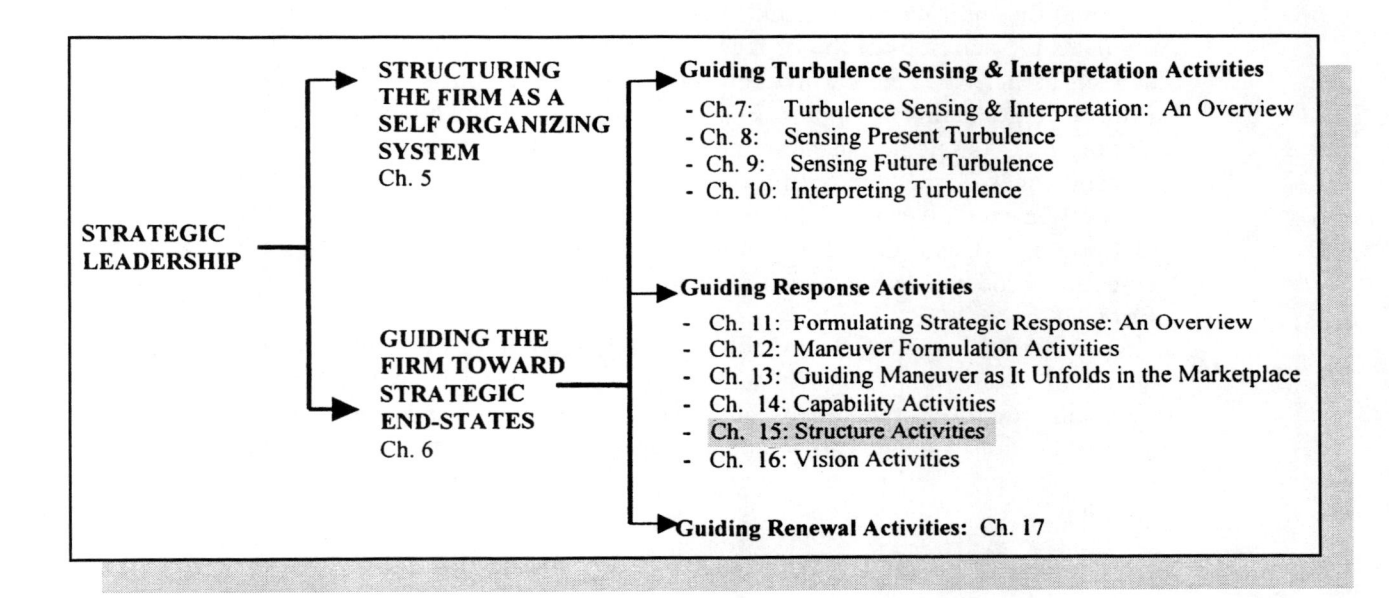

```
STRATEGIC          STRUCTURING          Guiding Turbulence Sensing & Interpretation Activities
LEADERSHIP         THE FIRM AS A         - Ch. 7:  Turbulence Sensing & Interpretation: An Overview
                   SELF ORGANIZING       - Ch. 8:  Sensing Present Turbulence
                   SYSTEM                - Ch. 9:  Sensing Future Turbulence
                   Ch. 5                 - Ch. 10: Interpreting Turbulence

                                        Guiding Response Activities
                   GUIDING THE           - Ch. 11: Formulating Strategic Response: An Overview
                   FIRM TOWARD           - Ch. 12: Maneuver Formulation Activities
                   STRATEGIC             - Ch. 13: Guiding Maneuver as It Unfolds in the Marketplace
                   END-STATES            - Ch. 14: Capability Activities
                   Ch. 6                 - Ch. 15: Structure Activities
                                         - Ch. 16: Vision Activities

                                        Guiding Renewal Activities:  Ch. 17
```

This chapter continues our exploration of the concept of strategic response. So far, we examined maneuver and capability. We now focus on the third one, structure. The choice of a particular configuration for the firm's organizational structure is a strategy in its own right. Firms compete, not just based on maneuver and/or capability, but also on structure. Structure determines the speed and agility of the firm's response. A firm that has a flat, lean, and decentralized structure can take market share away from competitors by virtue of being faster.

Structure is interwoven with maneuver and capability. Maneuver presupposes a fluid capability and a resilient organization structure. Capability affords the firm a portfolio of moves from which maneuver is drawn. Structure regulates people's freedom to actually formulate and execute such moves. Capability and structure both determine what the firm can do at any given moment. Capability without a liberating structure is a potential that is not realized. Without a liberating structure, maneuver will be less creative and imaginative.

We should keep in mind the difference between two classes of firms, the single business and the multi-business firm. In the single business firm, the structure recognizes and regulates the activities of the firm as one whole. After all, the purpose of structure is to ensure all its activities are carried out to the best of everyone's ability. In the multi-business firm, structure is more complex. Such type of firm has a two-tiered structure: the corporate and the SBU (strategic business unit) levels. A strategic business unit can be viewed as a single-business firm. At the corporate level, structure focuses on the relationship between the head office executives (the CEO and top management) and the heads (CEOs) of the SBUs. Our primary focus is on the single business firm since it is the most common case. It is the case for the independently owned companies as well as the subsidiaries of the multi-business firms.

To set the stage, we begin with an examination of the concept of organizational architecture in an attempt to survey what is involved in structuring an organization. We next analyze and categorize the self-organizing firm's activities in connection with structuring its organization. The presentation concludes with a discussion of the role of the chief executive in guiding a self-organizing firm to structure and restructure itself as it responds to turbulence.

# ORGANIZATIONAL STRUCTURE

An organization is a number of different but interdependent parts (e.g. individuals and groups). The parts are interdependent in that they perform different tasks that complement one another in the process of achieving a common goal. Structure is the configuration of this interdependence among the parts. It identifies the various parts and defines the roles of each, and the relationship among these roles in the broader scheme of things (the attainment of the common goals). Structure boils down to the regulation of relationships. Arriving at a certain configuration of structure involves arranging and rearranging three key design dimensions: horizontal, vertical, and flows.

## The Horizontal Dimension

Viewed horizontally, an organization consists of a number of units that work together side by side to help the firm arrive at a desired strategic end-state. The number of units is governed by the principle of division of labor and specialization. This principle calls for grouping and categorizing business activities based on some measure of similarity, e.g., if they pertain to a certain business function (marketing, purchasing, manufacturing, etc.), or if they pertain to a certain location (e.g. eastern region's unit). An identified group of activities is then assigned to a group of persons to be done by them on a regular basis. It becomes their specialty. Division of labor thus structures the firm horizontally. It is often referred to as differentiation because it creates different units; the difference being the unique assortment of work or activities associated with them. Differentiation thus allows business activities to be done by specialists and hence the quality of achievement would be higher than without it. The extent of differentiation determines how wide the organization will be; the greater the number of units, the wider the structure. If the units are not differentiated (compressed together), the structure will be narrow.

## The Vertical Dimension

If we scan a business organization up and down, we can see that it comprises a number of echelons. Echelons pertain to the distribution of authority. Authority is vested by law in the hands of the board of directors who in turn delegate a large portion of it to the CEO who in turn parcels it out among members of the organization to empower them to use the assets of the firm. Individual employees form the first echelon. They need to be controlled. This is done by appointing supervisors. Appointing the supervisors creates a second echelon. The number of supervisors in this echelon depends on how many employees he/she can effectively control (the span of control). Next, these supervisors need to be controlled. Therefore, a third echelon of overseers is created. Then, these overseers need to be supervised. Accordingly, a fourth echelon is introduced. This process repeats itself until we reach the top echelon, which consists of the CEO and the board of directors. The number of echelons is up to the persons who have the power to design the organization. They can make it flat (few echelons) or tall (several echelons).

## Activity Flows

Besides the vertical and the horizontal dimensions, a structure has a third feature and this is the flow of activities in it. The flow of activities is determined by the process of doing business. The value chain concept (Chapter 8) illustrates these flows. There are the primary flows and these involve the acquisition of raw inputs, transforming them into a finished products or services, and delivering these products/services to a customer segment. There are also supporting flows such as procurement, technology development, human resources, finance, accounting, and so on. These flows are often molded by procedures (manuals) for three purposes: to ensure that they are done right; to integrate the differentiated units; and, to establish accountability (who is responsible to whom, for what). Deviation from procedure is a dereliction of duties and hence it must be punished.

Procedure is a design variable. The designers of an organization can make it detailed and restricting. At the other end of the extreme, it can be minimal, leaving freedom of action to the employee. It all depends on how the designer (often the CEO) envisions the structure of the company.

An organization's structure is formed by mixing the three dimensions in various proportions. The proportions of the three factors often depend on the stage of development of the firm. A small firm often has a simple structure where the owner and a few employees do everything (minimal differentiation, minimal hierarchy, and virtually no procedure). As the firm grows, the need for division of labour emerges. The firms activities are grouped on the basis of functions (marketing, production, finance, etc.) or on the basis of process (as in the case of a job shop, e.g., machining, milling and grinding, finishing and heat treating, etc.). As the firm grows, more differentiated units appear, echelons increase, and procedures become more complex. Managing the firm becomes more difficult. Intuition and common sense are no longer adequate. Examples of these patterns of structure are illustrated in Exhibits 15.1, 15.2, 15.3, and 15.4.

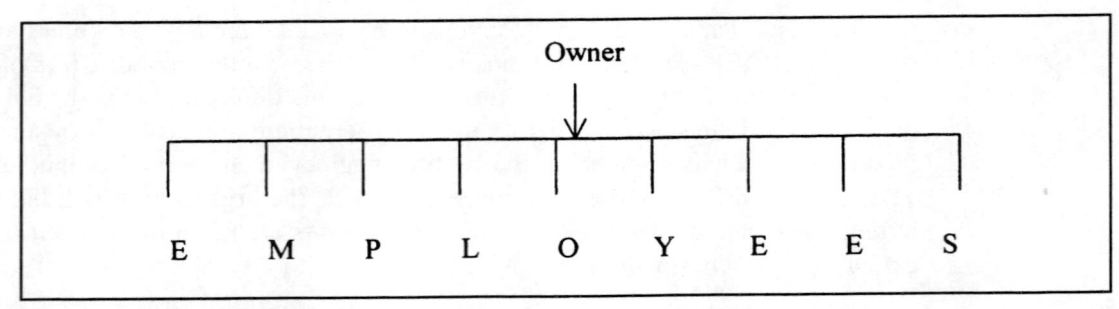

Exhibit 15.1: Simple Structure

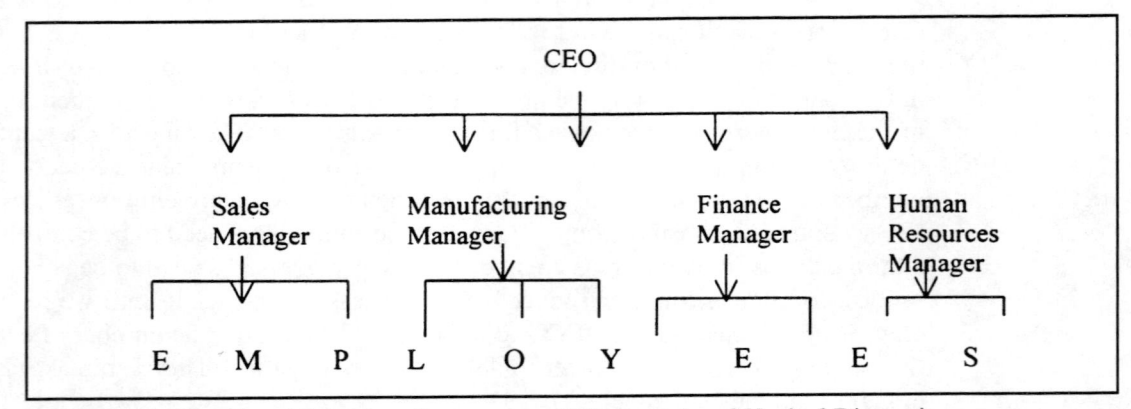

Exhibit 15.2: Functional Structure: Emergence of Horizontal and Vertical Dimensions

In the simple structure (Exhibit 15.1), the differentiation is not apparent; hierarchy is only the owner and employees. With further growth, expansion is needed. It is accomplished through division of labor and the creation of a simple functional hierarchy (Exhibit 15.2). Procedures are written down in simple rules. Further growth (more products, more geographic presence) brings more complexity; more units, more echelons, more procedures. With further growth and expansion, this process is repeated several times, we could end up with a vertical organization that comprises many levels. Simultaneously, because it has become a big organization, its horizontal dimension (e.g., number of functions, or products) and vertical dimension (number of echelons or levels) expand. To manage the vertical and horizontal relationships among the units, volumes of procedures are written to control everyone's behavior and hence the birth of bureaucracy.

When the organization becomes both vertical and horizontal, it looks like a number of chimneys, smoke stacks, or silos, e.g., marketing, manufacturing, human resources, engineering, purchasing, etc. Work moves back and forth between silos. As it does so, it becomes subject to turf fights based on specialization (e.g., production vs. sales or engineering vs. manufacturing), political alignments (various informal leaders and their groups), hierarchy (those at the bottom vs. those at the top), location (those in one city vs. another), or some other basis. The silos are controlled by the finance silo. The other silos are often in conflict with it because it tightens the control on the use of funds. More conflict arises. Top management then intervenes to settle such disputes. At this time, a different type of structure appears, the matrix organization as shown in Exhibit 15.4.

The above structures tend to be extended hierarchically and horizontally. They are also predisposed to generate volumes of procedures, generally known as bureaucracy. Hierarchy means that when employees encounter sudden turbulence, they cannot respond on the spot.

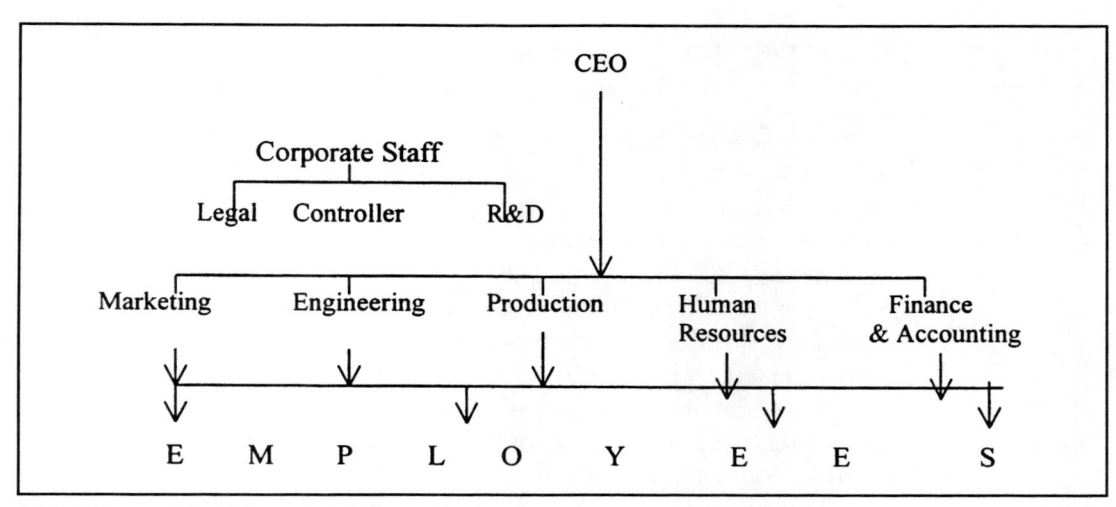

15.3: Line and Staff/Functional Organization

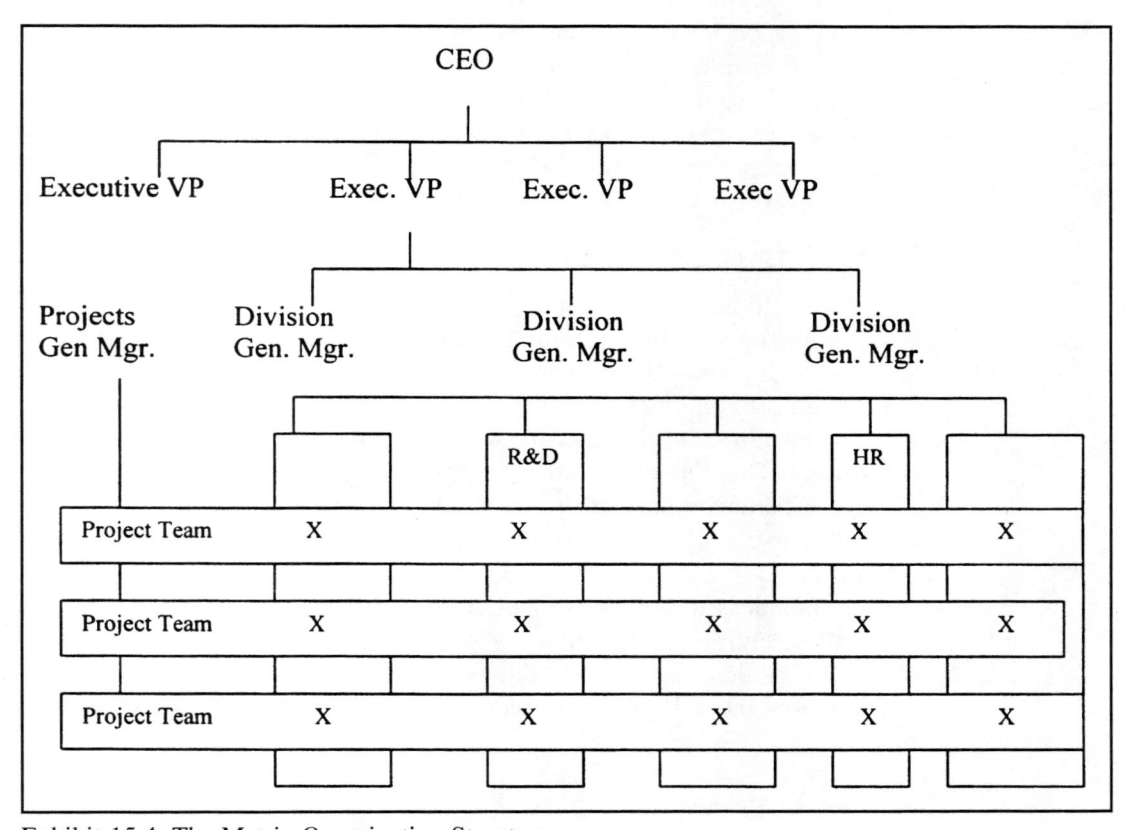

Exhibit 15.4: The Matrix Organization Structure

They have to wait for authorization. By the time the authorization arrives, it might be too late. Procedures also take time. Coordination among differentiated units (silos) takes time. When this happens, a quick response to turbulence does not occur in a timely fashion. Many firms are structured in this manner. However, they suffer the consequences of being unable to respond to customers who defect to competitors. There is a way out of this dilemma and this is the self-organizing structure presented next. It applies the principles of self-organization to the context of the business firm.

# STRUCTURE ACTIVITIES IN THE SELF-ORGANIZING FIRM

In the self-managing firm, structuring the organization is part of self-organization activities. A key attribute of self-organizing systems is that they arrange and rearrange their parts, i.e., structure as part of their resilience in responding to turbulence. In this type of organization, structure evolves out of the firm's experience with its environment. It is not designed by the CEO in advance and imposed on the people. If the CEO insists on designing the structure and driving it down the organization, two structures emerge. First, there will be a formal organization, the one represented by the organization chart drawn by the CEO and top management. It is the "official" organization structure. Second, there will be an informal organization; the one that emerges out of the dictates of reality. The informal structure often deviates significantly from the formal one so much so that it becomes formal in name only. Nevertheless, the informal organization becomes the real structure. The formal structure becomes one in name only. If this is the case, then there is no reason to have the formal organization. Let reality dictate structure.

This begs the question: how does a self-organizing system configure its structure? Complicating this question is the fact that the structure of a self-organizing system is continuously evolving. En route to a desired strategic end-state, there will be many disturbances and the system will have to change its structure in response to them. It will have to be arranged and rearranged several times. There are three main categories of activities: formation of modules (horizontal structuring), generating projects (flows structuring), distributing power to modules (vertical structuring) and coordination and integration of modules.

## Formation of Modules

As mentioned in Chapter 5, a self-organizing system exists as a distributed being, i.e., a number of loose-fitting differentiated units and not one compressed whole. Accordingly, a self-organizing firm attempts to create a structure that emphasizes empowered units with considerable autonomy guided additionally by the principles of maximizing the fringes, and growing by chunking (Chapter 6). This is accomplished by thinking of the firm as a number of modules. These modules can be snapped together to undertake various ventures. They can also be disbanded afterwards to undertake different ventures and so on. This gives the firm the ability to arrange and rearrange these modules to provide a quick, effective response to turbulence.

In business terms, the self-organizing firm is striving to arrange itself as a number of frontline entrepreneurial units or smaller businesses. The concept of organization modules needs further discussion at this point. There are four discernable modules in a business organization: the individual, the work team, the cross-functional team, and the market-scale module

### 1. The "Businessed" Employee

The primary unit of the self-organizing system is the "businessed" employee. A businessed employee is an individual who thinks and acts as a "business person," as a general manager of his/her sphere of things—a "frontline entrepreneur." Frontline entrepreneurship is essential for self-organization to take place. Only frontline entrepreneurs own into responding to turbulence quickly. A businessed employee has a corporate perspective. He or she feels responsible for the company in its entirety. He/she is aware of the cost-profit implications of his/her actions. He/she feels responsible for total customer satisfaction. The person has knowledge, skills, and competencies. He/she does not sink in the details of his/her specialization at the expense of the common good. This is the kind of employee that Patrick Kelly (PSS/World Medical) assigns the title, CEO, on his/her business card.

### 2. The Work Team Module

From the businessed employee module, a more complex module can be developed, the self-managing work team. Such work teams can be snapped together on an ad hoc basis, as the need arises to undertake projects to respond to turbulence. The work team acts as a business unit. Because it is composed of frontline entrepreneurs, work teams tend to be entrepreneurial too.

To illustrate, consider the case of Johnsonville Foods.[1] The work team consists of a dozen-person team that is empowered to do the following:

- Recruit, hire, evaluate, and fire on their own.
- Regularly recruit new skills as required and train one another when needed.
- Formulate, monitor, and amend their own budget.
- Make capital investment proposals after doing proper feasibility studies.
- Handle quality control, inspection, troubleshooting, and problem solving.
- Constant improvement of every process and product.
- Establish and monitor productivity and quality standards.
- Undertake product concepts and develop prototypes for new products and packages.
- Routinely work while being fully integrated with other teams from sales, marketing, and product development.
- Participate in corporate level strategic projects.

### 3. The Multi or Cross-Functional Module

The third building block is the cluster formed by snapping together a number of self-managing work teams drawn from various functions and specializations in the firm. The cluster module acts as a large team for the duration of the project. At the Ford Motor Company, Team Taurus was a cluster of teams drawn from many parts of the company that had the mission of developing, manufacturing, and marketing the Taurus. The cluster modules are not permanent. They form and disband depending on the need.

To illustrate, consider the cross functional teams at Titeflex.[2] The team consists of six to ten persons. The typical team has these characteristics:

- Cross-functional; it includes accounting, engineering, production, scheduling, quality assurance and the like.
- Self-managing and performs evaluations.
- Has customers.
- Deals with vendors.
- Invites in customers and vendors and goes out to visit both groups on its own initiative.
- Is involved in capital spending projects and allotment.
- Seeks out business on its own.
- Acts and behaves as a true profit and loss center.

### 4. The Market-Scale Unit Module

Cross-functional modules can be brought together to form a large module, the market-scale module. A market-scale module is almost like a small business. It is responsible for an end-to-end collection of activities to deliver a value proposition to a certain customer segment. Chrysler, for example, collapsed the silos into four market-scale modules called platforms, namely small car, large car, trucks, and Jeep. Each platform consists of several cross-functional clusters that are assembled together to create and deliver each of the four generic vehicles of Chrysler. Each platform is like a "mini automaker."

The modular design outlined above allows maximum flexibility (fluidity) in responding to turbulence, as all structures are "temporary." They can be snapped together for the duration of a certain stimulus, e.g. opportunity, threat, or problem. To illustrate, consider the case of Pepsi Cola's reorganization in the 1990s.[3] It developed what it called the right-side up structure presented in Exhibit 15.5. Pepsi inverted the structural pyramid upside down. The thesis was this, when the CEO and management are at the top of the organization chart, the employees play up to management, and in the process, they forget the customer. Pepsi's CEO wanted the employees to focus on the customer. So customers were placed at the top of the chart and management was placed at the lower levels. Closest to customers, Pepsi formed 107 market-scale modules, called "market units." Each unit's structure was also inverted with management at the bottom.

The Market Unit module was also an inverted pyramid as shown in Exhibit 15.6. Supported by a market unit manager at the bottom, there were a number of more micro modules, namely, the plant and its manager, market development unit and its manager, territory development unit and its manager, and administrative unit (office) and its manager, marketing equipment unit and its manager, territory coordinator, customer representatives, and account development representatives.

There were 13 market scale modules (Exhibit 15.5), called "business units" to support the 107 market units. Each comprised four units with their own managers: process support, human resources, planning, and customer development. These were supported by a general manager who was also placed at the lower echelon. The business unit structure is shown in Exhibit 15.7.

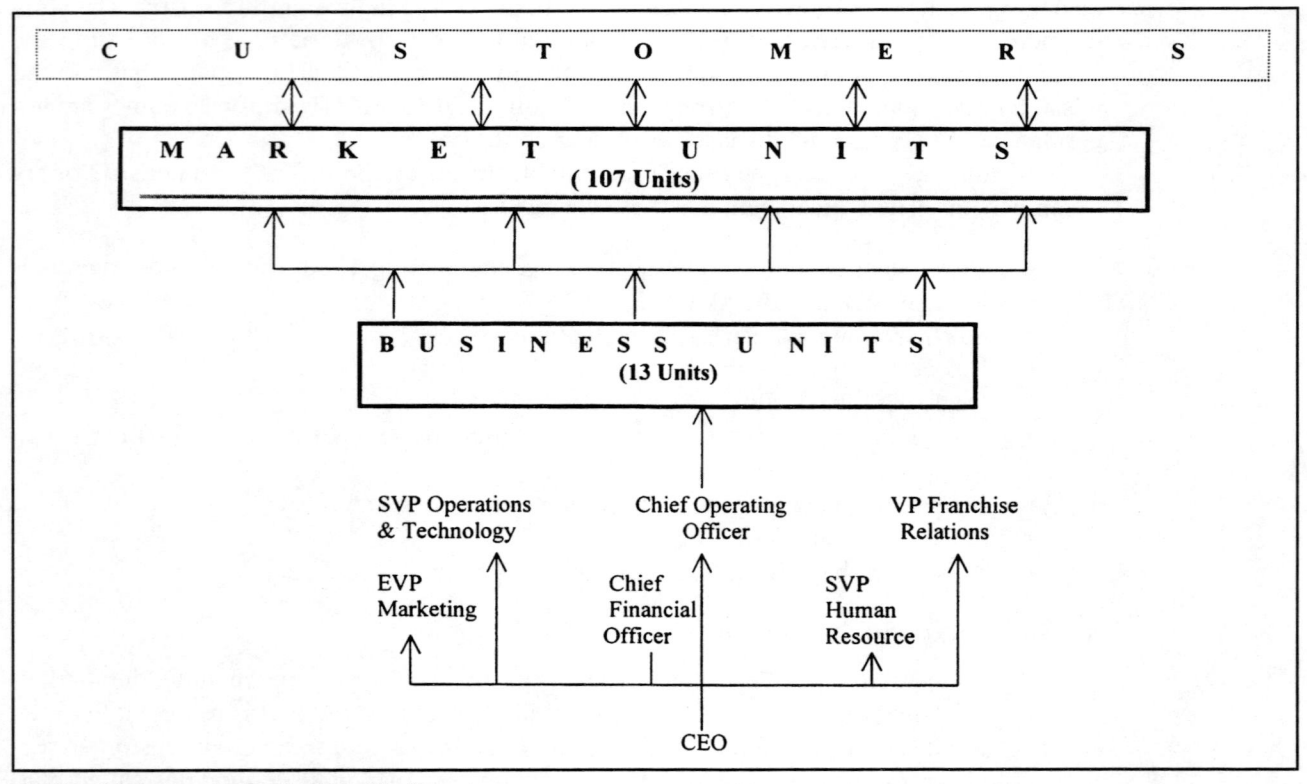

Exhibit 15.5: Pepsi's Right Side Up Structure

```
                    Territory        Customer          Account
                    Coordinator      Representative    Development
                                                       Representative
                         └───────────────┼──────────────────┘
                                         │
   Plant         Market          Territory       Administrative    Marketing
   Manager       Development     Development     Manager           Equipment
                 Manager         Manager                           Manager
     └──────────────┴───────────────┼────────────────┴────────────────┘
                                    ↑
                                Market Unit
                                Manager
```

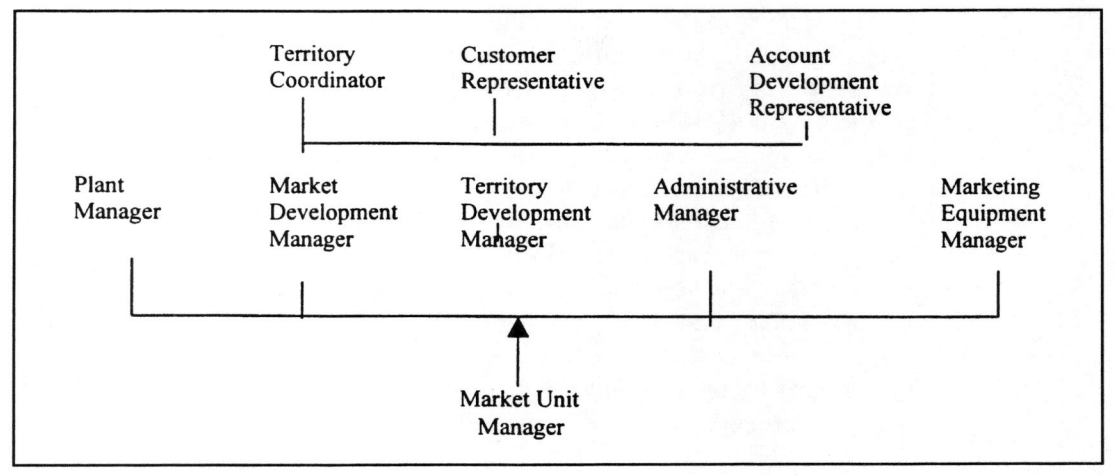

Exhibit 15.6: Structure of the Market Unit

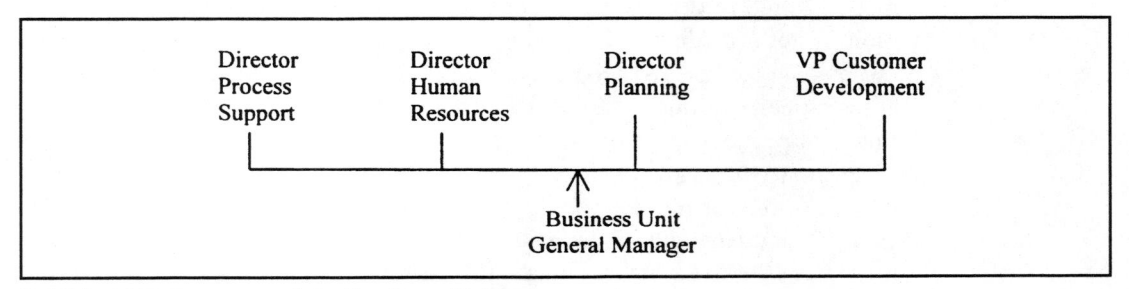

```
         Director        Director        Director      VP Customer
         Process         Human           Planning      Development
         Support         Resources
            └───────────────┴───────────────┴──────────────┘
                                    ↑
                              Business Unit
                              General Manager
```

Exhibit 15.7: Structure of the Business Unit

The fact that the self-organizing firm is a distributed being composed of differentiated, autonomous parts does not mean that there is no unity in the system. There is a sense of unity stemming from four sources. First is the invisible hand phenomenon. Second, the CEO and top management are a major integrating force. Third is the governance mechanism that assigns accountability for results. Finally, there is the appointment of coordinators and integrators.

## The Project Concept

The work of the self-organizing system encompasses all the firm's business activities, e.g., maneuvering in the marketplace, building capability, and visioning. As such, these activities are ad hoc; as part of the fluidity of the self-organizing system. They are not rigidly molded and frozen tightly through control procedures (bureaucracy). Perhaps the best way to organize such activities is the project concept. A project is an entrepreneurial venture by the organization as a whole. The venture is entrepreneurial in that it involves innovation and risk taking in the chosen action. The strategic thrust (Chapter 12), for example, is the ultimate entrepreneurial venture for the firm. This major project trickles down through the organization in the form of smaller projects for the individual modules. The project concept entrenches "adhocracy" a special effort to respond to a given situation. It is the opposite of bureaucracy. Bureaucracy aims at standardization and permanency.

The Ford Motor Company, for example, utilized the project concept to produce its successful Taurus car, "Project Taurus." At Microsoft, each version of WINDOWS was a project that was broken down into a number of subprojects. As another example, consider Komatsu, a major player in the earth moving equipment industry.[4] Its success can be attributed to the project concept. In the early 1960s, its main products, small and medium size bulldozers, were suffering from low quality and low market share. Komatsu's management launched "Project A" in 1964 which focused the organization on upgrading the quality of the bulldozer line. Told to ignore costs, disregard Japanese Industrial Standards, and build the best products, "Project A" had "spectacular results."

To focus on export, the management launched "Project B" in 1972 to develop the company's overseas markets. Project B resulted in the company having a strong position in the less developed countries, thereby establishing Komatsu as an international company. In the late 1970s, Komatsu's management started another four part project, "the V-10 Campaign," to reduce the cost by 10% while maintaining or improving quality, reducing the number of parts by over 20%, value engineering to gain economies in materials or manufacturing, and rationalization of the manufacturing system. All were achieved by the end of the decade.

A recession in the construction industry worldwide in 1979, prompted management to launch "Project F and F" (Future and Frontiers) to develop new products and new businesses which resulted in diverse new products including arc-welding robots, heat pumps, an excavation system for deep-sea sand, and amorphous silicon materials for efficient exploitation of solar energy. In 1981, Komatsu launched a new project, "Efficient Production-Oriented Choice Specifications" (EPOCHS) to improve production efficiency without reducing the number of product specifications required by the market. The purpose was to enable the firm to respond to the needs of the diverse markets it was serving without compromising its cost, quality, or product-market position. As of the mid 1980s, Komatsu set its sight higher by taking on the industry giant, Caterpillar. The overall project was "Maru-C"; Encircle Caterpillar. By the 1990s, Komatsu successfully encircled and took over Caterpillar.

For a third example, let us revisit Kolind's case again (Chapter 2). He structured Oticon as a number of projects that form and disband as the company wheels and deals in the marketplace. According to Kolind, the project, not the function or department, is the defining unit of work. At Oticon, teams form, disband, and form again as the work requires. Project leaders (anyone with a compelling idea) compete to obtain and attract the required resources and people in a "free market arena" to get their project underway. Project owners, by contrast, provide advice and support, but do not make the operating decisions. Kolind asserts, "We want each project to feel like a company, the project leader to feel like a 'CEO.' We allow a lot of freedom. We don't worry if we use more resources than planned. Deadlines are what really matter."[5]

The project structure has two major advantages. First, projects are not permanent arrangements. They are temporary snap-together arrangements of modules. Because of their short duration, projects rejuvenate people's attention span and reinvigorate them. They kindle a sense of passion in people. Permanent arrangements, by contrast, turn people's work into mundane repetitive tasks leading to loss of interest and passion. Second, projects (when successfully accomplished) give people a sense of winning. This gives them a chance to celebrate and savor the victory. This increases self-confidence and emboldens them to take on bigger undertakings. This provides the impetus for taking the initiative—a crucial condition of self-organization. Victories feed on one another and this reinforces self-organization.

## Distributing Power: Empowerment

For modules to carry on their projects, and at the same time adapt quickly to their respective environment, they must function as a sense-and-respond system. When this happens, the firm will truly function as a distributed being. Haeckel described and portrayed such a system as shown in Exhibit 15.8.[6] According to the model, organizational modules are empowered (given the authority) to perform a number of tasks that enable them to cope with

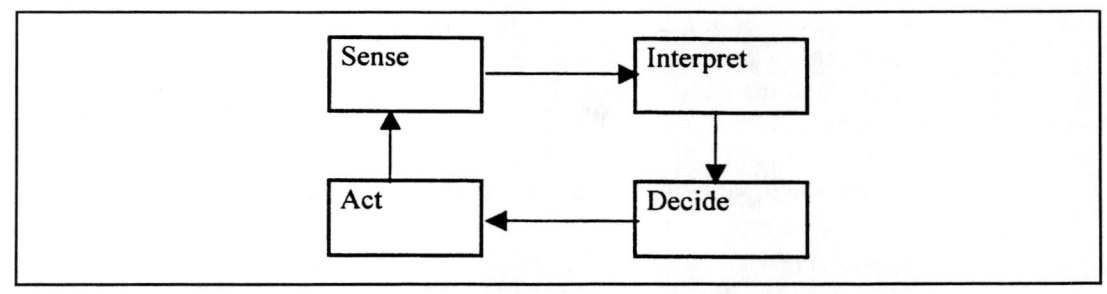

Exhibit 15.8: Haeckel's Sense-and-Respond Model

turbulence. The first task is sensing, i.e., scanning the environment (gathering information about events, developments, and trends) as receptors or points of impact for changing market conditions. Once the data are gathered, they are interpreted to pinpoint embedded opportunities, problems, and threats.

After interpretation, comes the task of deciding—generating alternatives, establishing criteria to help it select the best alternative, and actually choosing the best course of action. Once the "deciding" task is completed, the module then "acts," i.e., actually implements the decision or chosen course of action. The implementation is not the end of the cycle. Sensing starts again through monitoring results of implementation and receiving data about other stimuli driven by turbulence. These in turn are interpreted, then deciding takes place, and then implementation, and again feeding back into sensing and so on.

Being a sense-and-respond system clearly is a critical condition for a module to function as a self-organizing system. However, for a module to be a true sense-and-respond system, it must be given the authority or the power to sense, interpret, decide, and act. Waiting for detailed authorization from the higher ups disables the process of sensing and responding. In this case, the module (and the firm as a whole) will not be able to respond quickly to environmental turbulence.

Empowering the modules in the firm requires a new distribution of power. Patrick Kelly (PSS/World) called his company "a company of CEOs." Kolind (Oticon) thought of "every project leader as a CEO." From a legal standpoint, the CEO is the source of all power (as accorded to him/her by the charter of the corporation). However the sooner he/she redistributes this power to the modules, the sooner the company approaches the state of being a self-organizing system. A big portion of power must be accorded to modules; to enable them to act. The balance of the power, remaining at the top, is used for the integration of the models and for providing a sense of overall direction.

It is worth noting that empowerment is not just a word or a slogan. To be concrete, empowerment must be backed by the allocation of resources. Empowerment without resources is an empty concept. A power distribution system must be accompanied then by a supportive system for resource allocation among projects and modules.

## Coordination and Integration

A self-organizing system is a delicate balance between anarchy (differentiated horizontal units) and integration. Each part of the system is empowered to operate autonomously in its own sphere. However, if each part acts independently without concern for the other parts or the system as a whole, anarchy results. There is a need for integrating these differentiated, empowered modules. A key advantage of self-organizing systems is that they have integration and coordination mechanisms such as the invisible hand phenomenon (Chapter 5).

However, a business setting is more formal. Natural coordination is molded within a framework of accountability, a governance mechanism. As Haeckel suggested, a governance mechanism comprises three main components: governance principles, governance model, and governance process.[7] Governance principles are the seminal thoughts formulated by the leader and the people. A crucial element of these is the set of values that the leadership insists on and implements. Previously, it was shown how Jack Welch insisted on entrenching some important principles such as speed, simplicity, agility, entrepreneurship, stewardship, excellence, quality, reality, and candor.

A governance model is the hierarchy of essential accountabilities; the key things that must happen in order to carry out the mandates of the project module. A governance model specifies the "how's" of determining the key elements of structuring the responsibility for enacting the governance principles. This includes the assignment of accountability, negotiations between accountability givers and accountability holders, commitment of accountability holders, defining acceptable performance, assessment of performance, and finally acceptance or rejections of the outcome by the assignor.

The governance process is the manner in which the governance principles are embedded in the essential operating activities of the firm. It can utilize technology to keep track of the status and relationships of the commitment between people.[8] This, in turn, requires agreements that regulate the behavior of individuals and teams based on the chosen governance model. Furthermore, the governance process must also be capable of updating the governing principles themselves. As principles are tested through the governance process, some might need to be modified, changed, or even replaced with ones that are more relevant.

Besides governance, there is one more issue, i.e., boundarylessness. When modules are differentiated and empowered, they tend to focus on their own role and looking at things from one perspective, their perspective. However, a module's perspective is too narrow. To overcome this problem, a module has to approach things from two perspectives at all times. First is the perspective of the firm in its entirety. Second is the perspective of the module itself. This is what we referred to above as "busineessing" the modules. Every module will have two roles: a specialized one and then a second one involving the enhancement of the firm as a whole, the common interest. One effective approach for doing so is the appointment of integrators and coordinators. Integrators track the flow of work from project to project to ensure that they all happen on time in sequence with the right quality. The ultimate integrator is the CEO. Next are members of top management. Then, there are the special integrators like project leaders and other support personnel. In the case of the Pepsi organization mentioned above, there were 107 market scale modules, called market units. These were integrated by the next (lower level), the business units (13). The role of each business unit was to support and coordinate a number of market units. At the bottom of the inverted pyramid were the CEO and the vice presidents as the ultimate coordinators and integrator.

In sum, the activities of a self-organizing firm tend to produce a structure that has these characteristics:

- An inverted pyramid structure: At its top, frontline entrepreneurial modules organized as small businesses. They deal with customers and the marketplace directly. Below them, there is a middle level, supporting coordinators and integrators. At the bottom of the pyramid is the third level, which includes the CEO and members of top management whose job is to facilitate, enable, and integrate so that the whole firm may move in one direction.
- A flat, horizontal structure: It has a minimal number of levels. There are no deep silos or smoke stacks.
- It is boundaryless: Horizontally and vertically, all modules are integrated together and then distributed over the various project modules so that each may exist as a "small business" for the duration of a project.

- It has an entrepreneurial work pattern: Life is one project after another with the bar ratcheted up after every accomplishment.

# GUIDING STRUCTURE ACTIVITIES

One of the typical prerogatives of management in traditional organizations is the design of the firm's organizational structure. It is part of the "management must manage" paradigm. However, CEOs who opt for structuring the firm as a self-organizing system, focus on guiding the various structure activities. They realize that they cannot stay on top of a turbulent marketplace and so they let the firm's organizational structure, evolve in a self-organizing manner. They realize that the firm will arrange and rearrange its parts (structure) several times depending on the severity of the disruption by turbulence. They watch the evolving structures carefully and guide them so that they may lead to a strategic end-state that pleases the firm's stakeholders. How do they then guide the firm's activities as it structures and restructures itself over time? They do this in two ways:

1. They focus on discovering semicoherent trends in structure that suggests themselves out of the ongoing structuring and restructuring efforts. Once a semicoherent direction is spotted, they (in consultation with the various groups) legitimize it by proclaiming it as the structure of the firm; albeit a temporary one. All structures are temporary in a turbulent world.
2. They induce and orchestrate collaboration among the units so that good structures may evolve. The topic of strategic collaboration was examined in Chapter 6. The principles suggested there apply structuring the organization. We revisit them briefly here:

## Creating an Environment Conducive to Collaboration

From the outset, the CEO must create the environment that will stimulate collaboration among people in structuring the firm. This includes:

1. Cultivating Paradigms for Constructive Structures: The crucial task here is implanting seminal thoughts that can guide people as they structure and restructure the firm. The sample of CEOs examined in Chapter 3, demonstrates the importance of seminal thoughts and how these executives used them to structure the firm. Here are some examples of seminal thoughts implanted by the CEO mentioned in Chapter 3. Lars Kolind promoted these key thoughts:

- The project concept. Organizational work is to take the form of projects that are formed and dissolved as the need be.
- People as experts—autonomous units who know what to do and how to do it. Every employee has to have a "multijob"—working on a number of projects concurrently.
- The spaghetti organizational structure.
- Minimal rules and regulations—no bureaucracy.
- No walls of division of labor and specialization.

Patrick Kelly insisted that PSS/World Medical be a "company of CEOs," an organization of fully empowered individuals. His thoughts on relationships are compelling, e.g., "let the employees fire the boss." He amplified them in the form of what he calls "PSS'S TOP 20." These are shown in Exhibit 15.9.[9] At FedEx, Smith's seminal thoughts hinged on the "pitch in" principle; where people cooperate and function as one coherent group. Welch's (GE) seminal thoughts include ideas such as: entrepreneurship (empowering people), boundarylessness, and agility.

> **PSS'S TOP 20**
>
> To **SERVICE** all our customers like they are the only ones we have.
> **RECOGNIZE** our people as our most valuable asset.
> **ALWAYS** communicate without fear of retribution.
> **ENCOURAGE** ideas and creativity at all levels.
> **ENCOURAGE** self-development and individual entrepreneurship.
> **ALWAYS** strive to share the wealth.
> **ALWAYS** promote from within.
> **EARN** profits and value for our entrusted shareholders.
> **PROVIDE** an environment of trust and honesty.
> **MINIMIZE** excuses and maximize getting the job done.
> **INVOLVE** family in all social aspects of the company.
> **ENCOURAGE** and develop pride and esprit de corps.
> **ENCOURAGE** all PSS people to be shareholders.
> **TREAT** all company assets like they are your own.
> **SUGGEST** and encourage better ways of doing things.
> **MINIMIZE** paperwork and memos.
> **BE** professional at all times.
> **ANTICIPATE** and capitalize on market needs.
> **DO** what's best for all PSS.
> **RECOGNIZE** PSS as a family that cares.

Exhibit 15.9: Kelly's Governance Values for PSS

2. Building Shared Goals: If people have a shared goal, they will collaborate to achieve it. One important goal here is the discovery of a structure that can withstand wave after wave of disruption from turbulence.

3. Defining Boundaryless Roles: Helping good structure evolve is often assigned as everyone's role. Modules should not be solely concerned with structuring their own unit.

4. Networking: When all units have full information, they will be able to develop a group mind with respect to structure. When one module knows what the others are doing, it will be more inclined to integrate itself with them as they all attempt to develop an overall structure for the organization.

5. Orchestrating Shared Workspace: Sharing workspace facilitates the evolution of structure. When people work together, interdependence evolves in a coordinated manner eventually leading to a workable structure.

6. Charging Emotions: Structuring is a good opportunity to emphasize values such as flexibility, agility, and speed as effective weapons for helping the firm survive. Welch promoted certain emotions at GE when he continuously preached messages such as "change before you have to," "change before someone else makes you," or, "control your destiny or someone else will."

## Inducing and Stimulating Conversation on Structure

If structure is to be flexible and evolve continuously, conversation among modules has to be continuous. Structure is a strong determinant of the firm's survival. It should be the topic of continuous conversation in the firm. The topic of the conversation should be organizational change, to keep up with a changing environment. If conversation does not take place, the firm will be caught with an obsolete structure.

## Marshalling Strategic Conversation to Action on Structure

The role of the CEO here is to move conversation to action, i.e., implementing change in the firm's organization structure. Here are some of the possible steps to take:

1. Developing and Cultivating Frameworks for Action: Arranging and rearranging the firm's structure has to happen in a systematic way to allow good structure to emerge and to avoid change for change sake. Progressive CEOs envision certain structures and then advocate them as frameworks for reorganizing the firm, such as the flat organization or the boundaryless organization. Furthermore, they do work with the modules to develop systematic processes for changing an existing structure to the envisioned one. Often this involves intensive organization planning sessions that ensures consultation among the various units, providing external assistance (organization development consultants), and an overall process for executing organization changes.
2. Keeping the Vision: The vision is the overall destination of the firm. It has to be kept front and center during structuring efforts. The test of a good structure is whether it propels the firm towards its vision by enabling maneuver.
3. Building Collaborative Networks: Collaborative networks facilitate the emergence of structure. If isolated groups are to become a collaborative network, they need some structure to organize them as a network. Furthermore, when it is time to implement a structure, they can all pitch in to make it work.
4. Staffing Critical Positions: All matters pertaining to organizational structure are critical issues for members of the organization. They are human beings and as such they have a natural tendency to resist change. To change structure, champions are needed. The CEO can expedite the change process by appointing key persons to spark, lead and guide the change process.
5. Allocating Resources: Changing structure requires resources in terms of committing time and effort to monitor the firm's structure in light of the firm's changing environment, help new structures evolve, and then implement the envisioned structure. The CEO can orchestrate the whole process by allocating resources to one form of structure instead of another.

## Affirming Accountability and Governance

Everyone in the firm, individually and severally, must be held accountable for updating the firm's structure to ensure that it will enable the firm to find and reach strategic end-states. It should not be viewed as the job of the CEO alone. As stated earlier, the CEO cannot stay on top of things, in order to change the structure as often as needed. The CEO has an arsenal of tools here including periodic audits of collaboration with regard to structure, tracking organizational plans and their implementation, and challenging the assumptions underlying them.

## Exercising Personal Influence

The CEO's personal influence can steer collaboration towards the issue of helping constructive structures evolve. Structure is a crucial part of strategic leadership. The leader's personal involvement is crucial. This involvement can take many forms including scouting for appropriate structures, placing structure on the firm's strategic agenda, issuing directive, coaching the organization to change, preaching to people to change, and actually participating in the process of changing structure.

# CONCLUSION

This chapter examined a major subset of self-organization activities, namely, configuring the organizational structure of the firm. The presentation started with an examination of the design variables in configuring a firm's organization. Structure is a rearrangement of three main design variables: width, depth, and activity flow. These dimensions are specified with certain principles in mind. We examined these principles as they apply to the structure of the self-organizing firm. In light of these principles, four sets of structure activities were identified: formation of modules (horizontal structuring), generating projects (flows structuring), distributing power to modules (vertical structuring) and coordination and integration of modules.

The challenge for the CEO is to guide the structuring activities of empowered modules without dictating a structure or micromanaging the process. The CEO can corral and steer the various organizational initiatives by inducing collaboration among all modules in the firm so that they may, on their own, envision and implement structures that help the firm find and arrive at a desirable strategic end-state that pleases the firm's stakeholders.

# ENDNOTES

1. Peters, Tom, *Liberation Management: Necessary Disorganization for the Nanosecond Nineties*, New York, NY: Alfred Knopf, 1992, p. 237.

2. Peters, Tom, *Liberation Management: Necessary Disorganization for the Nanosecond Nineties*, New York, NY: Alfred Knopf, 1992, p. 237.

3. Harvard Business School Case, *Pepsi's Regeneration, 1990–1993*, (case no. 9-395-048, Rev. March 1996), p. 23.

4. The material here is taken from "Komatsu Limited," A Case Study, Harvard Business School (no. 9-385-277).

5. Labarre, P., "The Dis-Organization of Oticon," *Industry Week*, July 16, 1994, pp. 23–28.

6. Haeckel, S.H., "Adaptive Enterprise Design: The Sense-and-Respond Model," *Planning Review*, May/June, 1995, pp. 6–13.

7. Haeckel, op. cit.

8. Ibid., p. 10.

9. Kelly, P., *Faster Company*, New York, NY: Wiley, 1998, p. 112.

# CHAPTER 16

# Strategic Response: Vision

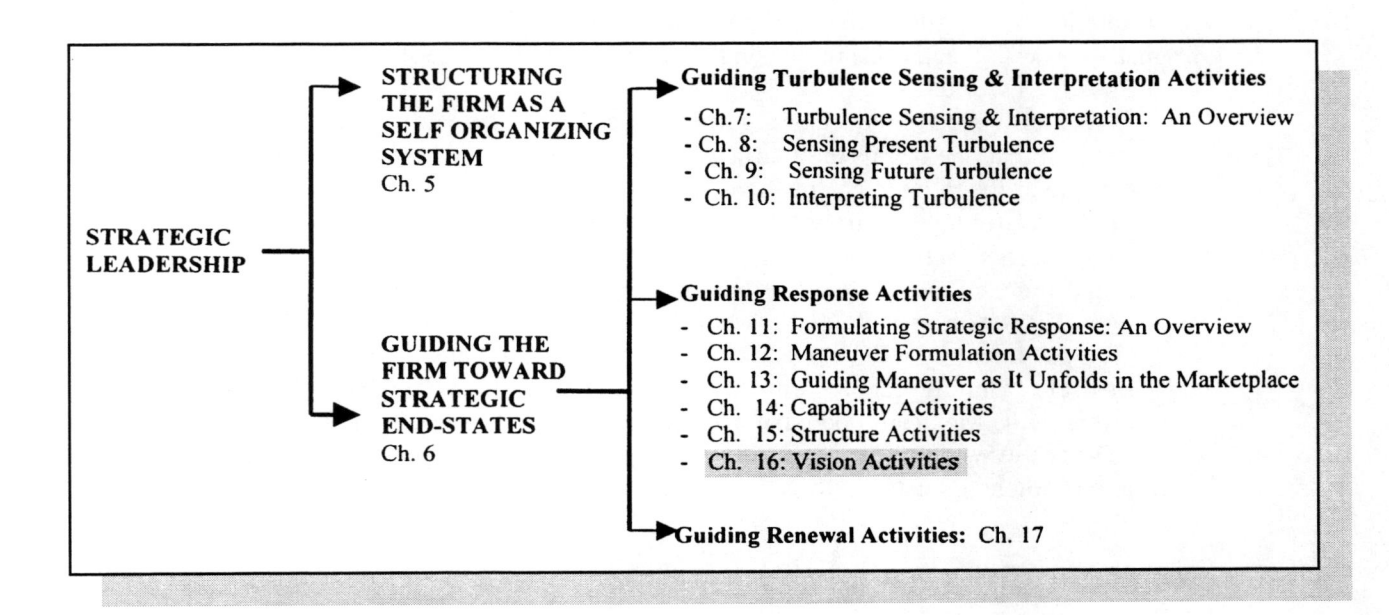

```
STRATEGIC          STRUCTURING           Guiding Turbulence Sensing & Interpretation Activities
LEADERSHIP         THE FIRM AS A           - Ch.7:  Turbulence Sensing & Interpretation: An Overview
                   SELF ORGANIZING         - Ch. 8:  Sensing Present Turbulence
                   SYSTEM                  - Ch. 9:  Sensing Future Turbulence
                   Ch. 5                   - Ch. 10: Interpreting Turbulence

                                         Guiding Response Activities
                   GUIDING THE             - Ch. 11: Formulating Strategic Response: An Overview
                   FIRM TOWARD             - Ch. 12: Maneuver Formulation Activities
                   STRATEGIC               - Ch. 13: Guiding Maneuver as It Unfolds in the Marketplace
                   END-STATES              - Ch. 14: Capability Activities
                   Ch. 6                   - Ch. 15: Structure Activities
                                           - Ch. 16: Vision Activities

                                         Guiding Renewal Activities: Ch. 17
```

A firm's strategic response to turbulence is embodied in a strategy that it formulates and implements in the market place. The strategy involves choosing a strategic destination and then plotting a path to it (maneuver), enabled by the firm's capability and structure. In the business world the desired destination is referred to as "vision." The term destination does not imply a permanent equilibrium at which the firm rests forever. In an edge of chaos environment, it is rather a transitory or a temporary moment in the history of the firm. The firm may rest at a given destination for a moment, but then turbulence makes it undesirable and the search is on again for another end-state. This goes on and on as long as the firm exists and as long as turbulence permeates its environment.

This chapter focuses on the firm's activities in searching for, choosing, and defining a vision for itself. It begins with a survey of the literature on the concept of vision. The review of the literature suggests the need for a more formal concept. We attempt to develop one and present it here. Armed with this concept, we proceed to examine the visioning process itself and present a framework that organizes its various activities. The chapter concludes with a discussion of the role of the CEO in guiding vision activities. The presentation focuses primarily on vision activities in the single business firm because it is the most frequent case in the business world.

We left vision to the end, on purpose, because of its peculiar nature. Conventional wisdom has it that one begins the journey with a clear vision and then maneuvers its way steadfastly toward it. However, business behavior suggests another interesting phenomenon. Although a firm might start with a vision, turbulence might force it to pursue another one en route. It seems that as the firm maneuvers its way in the marketplace, it comes across a defining moment every now and then. At the defining moment, the firm discovers the true nature of its business and what it wants to become. At that point, a vision is born. The following statement by CEO John Martin (Taco Bell) illustrates how a defining moment suggests itself: "Our biggest problem was that we didn't know what we were. We thought maybe we were in the Mexican food business. We thought maybe we were in the fast-food business. . . . The reality was, we are in the fast food business, and by not understanding who we were, who our potential customer was, we were just slightly missing the mark."[1]

## THE CONCEPT OF VISION

The term "vision" has become popular in the business world nowadays. Larwood *et al* counted over 1000 articles and books on the topic that have appeared in the academic press.[2] Nearly every textbook in strategic management includes some treatment of the topic. For CEOs, it has become the key instrument of leadership. As early as 1989, the concept was receiving wide recognition. Jack Welch, CEO of General Electric, affirmed the concept "Good business leaders create a vision, articulate the vision, passionately own the vision, and relentlessly drive it to completion."[3] Another CEO, Ralph Stayer observes, "Whenever executives get together, vision is the topic of the conversation."[4]

Despite its popularity and importance, Larwood *et al* found that vision ". . . remains technically a 'hypothetical construct'—one that is not directly observable and that seemingly carries meaning beyond any single or simple description."[5] Along the same lines, Collins and Porras report that there is "fuzziness" surrounding the concept ". . . one of the most overused and least understood words in the language . . . ."[6] They quote the lament of one CEO:

> "I have come to believe that we need a vision to guide us, but I can't seem to get my hands on what 'vision' is. I've heard lots of terms like 'mission,' 'purpose,' 'values,' 'strategic intent.' But no one has given me a satisfactory way of looking at vision that will help me to sort out this morass of words and set a coherent vision for my company. It's really frustrating."[7]

Abell further elaborated on this fuzziness:

> "This frequently used word (vision) too often lacks precision.... Does it mean a vision of the future business and competitive environment in which the firm will find itself? Or the future approaches the firm should follow? Or the way to go from where we are today to where we would like to be in the future? Does it apply to the situation one year from now, three to five years from now, or ten to twenty years from now? And how does the word 'vision' differ, if at all, from the words 'mission,' 'strategy,' and 'plan'?"[8]

Due to the confusion about the nature of vision, its definitions tend to reflect a range of perceptions. Here is a quick survey of attempts to define vision in the literature. Robert observed, "Each person that leads an organization, large or small, has a concept or vision of what that organization should look like sometime in the future."[9] He then proceeded to define the vision as a strategic profile: "This vision then becomes, in our terms, a Strategic Profile for the company. Such a profile becomes the target which guides the behavior of that organization and thus, its *direction* for a certain period of time."[10] He further elaborated on the concept of profile as comprising *seven* elements as follows:[11]

- Time Frame: This is a defined period in the future depending on the nature of the business.
- Driving Force and Business Concept: These are the forces that will propel the firm in the future, e.g., product, customers, technology, capability, distribution, etc. The choice of a driving force and articulating it then becomes the business concept or purpose of the organization.
- Areas of Excellence: These are the two or three activities within the company that require excellence over competitors and current achievement in order to deliver and maintain the business concept.
- Product Scope: This is the mix the current and future products that will receive more emphasis in the future.
- Market Scope: This consists of the geographic and user groups that are suited to the business concept and the product scope.
- Size/Growth Guidelines: These are the landmarks set for the firm's size and growth rate to be achieved during the strategic time frame.
- Return/Profit Guidelines: This is a specification of the numbers for profit and return over the span of the time frame.

Bennis and Nanus defined vision as "... a mental image of a possible and desirable future state of the organization."[12] Nanus in his work, *Visionary Leadership*, verbalizes the concept of vision in this fashion: "Quite simply, a vision is a realistic, credible, attractive future for your organization. It is your articulation of a destination toward which your organization should aim, a future that in important ways is better, more successful, or more desirable than is the present."[13]

Tregoe *et al* were perhaps the first to write extensively about the concept. In their book *Vision In Action*, they define it as follows: "For us vision or strategy is about what an organization wants to be in terms of products, markets, and resources or capabilities."[14] It is worth noting that they equate the terms "vision" and "strategy." They identify the main elements of the concept "vision" as follows:[15]

- Thrust or focus for future business development; the "selected" business opportunities that the firm will pursue to the exclusion of others.
- Product-Market Scope: the boundary within which future products and market choices can be made.

- Future emphasis or priority and mix for products and markets that fall within that scope.
- Key capabilities: the "strategic" resources and competencies needed to make the strategic vision happen.
- Implication for growth and return: an element of the vision is the expectation of future growth and return on the investment.

Day introduced the notion of the vision as an explicit system of what it takes to succeed: "A vision is a guiding theme that articulates the nature of the business and its intentions for the future. These intentions are based on how management collectively believes the environment will unfold, and what the business can and should become in the future. Visions are . . . explicit systems about what it takes to succeed in the future."[16]

Wilson presented a concept that he labeled as strategic vision: "A coherent and powerful statement of what the business can and should be (ten) years hence."[17] He analyzed the visions of Jack Welch of GE and Jan Carlzon of Scandinavian Airlines in an attempt to extract the components of the concept. Welch's vision for GE included six elements: (1) future focus—the business arenas for GE; (2) critical positioning, to be number 1 or number 2 in each business arena; (3) source of competitive advantage—technology and service; (4) type of organizational structure—integrated diversity; (5) management roles and structure—flat organization; and (6) culture—lean, agile, and boundaryless company. Along the same lines, Carlzon's vision for Scandinavian included three elements: (1) business concept—the "businessman's airline;" (2) organization—joint ventures to build a global network of routes; and, (3) style—empowering employees at every level to respond to customer needs.[18]

Based on such analyses, Wilson developed a conceptual framework to capture the concept of vision that comprised six main elements: business scope, business scale, product and market focus, competitive focus, image and relationships, and organization and culture. "Business scope" designates the range and mix of businesses that the company chooses to pursue—the target areas for both diversification and divestiture. The second element "business scale" bounds the desired future size of the company. A specification of scale is an important dimension of the vision. The third component is "product and market focus" and this amounts to identifying certain product lines and market niches. "Competitive focus," the fourth element, calls for choosing the basis on which the company intends to compete. The fifth component is "image and relationships," a specification of the "vital dynamics" necessary to implement the vision such as relationships with employees and other allies for the firm. Finally, the sixth element "organization and culture" designates "the structure, management systems and operating culture of the firm" as essentials for carrying out the vision.

Quigly articulates the corporate vision as: ". . . the most fundamental statement of a corporation's values aspirations, and goals. . . . It must indicate a clear understanding of where the corporation is today and offer a road map for the future."[19] He also analyzed the concept of vision and came up with three main elements: (1) values, (2) mission, and (3) goals.[20] He defined "values" as ". . . the rules or guidelines by which a corporation exhorts its members to behavior consistent with its order, security, and growth." As for "mission," Quigly defines it as the answer to the question: "What are our aspirations for the future?" He talks of the concept of the "extended mission" which includes the core mission plus related elements. The core mission answers the question: "What are we today? What do we aspire to be? What is our core competence?" The "other" elements of the mission include the following issues:

"How will we achieve our corporate aspirations as defined in our core mission? What is our internal growth strategy by major business segment? What is our internal growth strategy? What is our 'golden goose'?"

"How will we define our external growth strategy to achieve our aspirations?"

"What are our long-range financial goals? Goals answer the question: 'What is the corporation committed to achieve?' These translate the mission into a set of concrete landmarks."[21]

Abell identified five meanings for vision. He thought that ". . . vision can be manifested in at least *five* different ways, and the word 'vision' takes on a somewhat different meaning as we look from different organizational vantage points." The five different meanings appear to be five different elements that can exist side by side to form a vision.[22] These are:

- A vision of the situation or the events that have already unfolded, are currently unfolding, or are about to unfold and, in the process, produce a gap between the actual and the desirable.
- Strategic Vision: For the single business firm, it is concerned with the future definition of the business and its focus. In the multi-business firm, it embodies the future shape of the corporate portfolio and how it is to be managed.
- A vision of resources and competencies needed.
- A vision of the future organization—comprising a vision of improved organizational structure, and a vision of improved organization functioning, e.g., processes, systems, corporate culture, leadership style, etc.
- A vision of how to proceed, i.e., a vision of the path from where we are now to where we want to go, the destination.

Collins and Porras thought that a vision comprised ". . . two major components: *core ideology* and *envisioned future*. Core ideology, the yin in our scheme, defines what we stand for and why we exist. Yin is unchanging and complements the yan, the envisioned future. The envisioned future is what we aspire to become, to achieve, to create—something that will require significant change and progress to attain."[23]

Core ideology defines the enduring character of an organization that remains relatively unchanged regardless of product, market, fads, or leaders. Core ideology comprises two further components: core values and core purpose. Core values are the fundamental and lasting tenets of the firm—a short list of guiding principles. Examples of core values include Walt Disney's "imagination and wholesomeness," Proctor & Gamble's product excellence, Hewlett-Packard's respect for the individual first and foremost. By contrast, core purpose refers to the organization's reason for being, which is different from goals or business strategies. They offered some examples to illustrate the concept of purpose: 3M's "to solve unsolved problems innovatively," Hewlett-Packard's "to make technical contributions for the advancement and welfare of humanity," Nike's "to preserve and improve human life," and Sony's "to experience the joy of advancing and applying technology for the benefit of the public."

The second component, envisioned future, consists of two parts: a 10- to 30-year ambitious, daring goal; and, vivid descriptions of what it will be like to achieve such a goal. The "goal" here is different from other types of goals. It is a "bold mission," a focal end towards which major allocations of scarce resources are made. Besides the focal goal, there is the element of "vivid descriptions," the vibrant, engaging and specific descriptions of the firm's state of being upon achieving the focal goal. They presented the following vivid descriptions for Sony that were written in the 1950s: "We will create products that become pervasive around the world . . . We will be the first Japanese company to go into the U.S. market and distribute directly . . . We will succeed with innovations that U.S. companies have failed at—such as the transistor radio . . . Fifty years from now, our brand name will be as well known as any in the world . . . and will signify innovation and quality that rival the most innovative companies anywhere . . .".[24]

Kouzes and Posner broke the concept "vision" into four attributes: ideality, uniqueness, future orientation, and imagery.[25] "Ideality" means that the vision is an ideal; what ought to be as opposed to what is. "Uniqueness" refers to a state that is different—effective in distinguishing the organization from similar entities. "Future orientation" means that a vision is "located" in a future time horizon, the long term. Finally, the "imagery" attribute refers to its intellectual nature as a "conceptualization"—a mental picture of the future.

In strategic management textbooks, "vision" has been defined along similar lines. As Chakravarthy and Lorange noted, "A corporate vision articulates top management's strategic intent."[26] Mason *et al* describe vision in terms such as ". . . the concept for a new and desirable future reality that can be communicated about the organization. . . . A clear idea of where it (the firm) is going and why." They further state that a vision ". . . translates what is essentially an act of imagination into terms that describe possible future courses of action for the organization."[27] Along the same lines, Thompson and Strickland articulated the concept as follows: "A strategic vision indicates management's aspirations for the organization, providing a panoramic view of 'what businesses we want to be in, where we are headed, and the kind of company we are trying to create.' It spells out a direction and describes a destination."[28]

The sample of definitions presented above confirms the concerns about the conceptualization of vision. Various authors attempt to use different words to describe it, such as "dream," "state," "future," and the like. As they do so, different meanings appear. Driving the confusion is the difference in the perspective of the various writers. This is why Abell found five different meanings for the term. The number of vision elements varies from three (Quigly) to seven (Robert). The type and nature of elements advocated by various authors adds to the confusion. Take "corporate beliefs and values" for example. Robert asserts that ". . . corporate beliefs are not part and parcel of the strategic profile (vision)." Yet, all the others include it. This begs the question: How many elements constitute the concept of vision? How do they "hang together" to make up this thing called "vision"?

The above survey of literature suggests four main themes that underlie the concept of vision. These are:

- A vision is a "mental picture" of the firm with its various components and functions as they hang together to make a complete whole. As such, this mental picture is the state to which the firm aspires.
- The mental picture or vision shows the firm in an envisioned state of affairs for the world around it—a particular worldview, one that reflects the perceptions and biases of the people forming this worldview. The vision of the firm is predicated on this worldview. As such, this particular worldview becomes part of the total vision.
- The vision is anchored to a point in time in the future. It is as if one fast forwards a movie film to a point in the future and then pauses at a certain frame. In that frame, there will be a still picture. This still picture is the vision.
- The mental picture of the firm in the future represents a preferred future reflecting considerable ambition—bordering on the unrealistic.

## A PROPOSED CONCEPT OF VISION

In practice, every firm appears to have a vision of some sort. However, when it comes to articulating this vision, corporate practices vary considerably. Many CEOs attempted to develop a vision because it was what everyone else is doing and what the business gurus advocate. They did so without a firm grasp of what a vision is and what constitutes it. It is no surprise when one CEO complained "... I can't seem to get my hands on what a vision is."[29] In many corporate reports, the vision statement appears to be a set of general ideas bordering on platitudes. It is as if there is a "cookie-cutter" approach for wording vision statements. A Fortune article mocked this approach by presenting the vision crafter shown in Exhibit 16.1.[30]

There is a need for a more concrete concept of vision. A good approach for organizing our thoughts about the concept of vision is to analyze the processes that CEO engage in as they arrive at a vision for the firm. To illustrate, take the case of Southwest Airlines. In the boardroom of Southwest Airlines, there is a wooden plaque inlaid with a cocktail napkin that has a sketch of a three-city route. The sketch shows a triangle connecting the three cities of Dallas, San Antonio, and Houston. It was drawn long before the airline was formed—during a conversation between Rollin King, a San Antonio entrepreneur, and Herb Kelleher, a San Antonio lawyer. King foresaw that these three cities would be experiencing rapid economic and population growth and hence the market for executive travel would mushroom. The distances among them were too far to be traveled by bus but too short for a direct flight by existing airlines, which had a hub and spokes flight design. King's idea was that a new airline that would fly point-to-point such that an executive can have breakfast at home, have a morning meeting in one city, a lunch meeting in another, an afternoon meeting still in another city, and be home for supper.

Clearly, when King and Kelleher developed a vision for Southwest Air, they saw in their mind's eye a picture of a fully developed, dynamic enterprise planted in a certain setting. What did they "see" in this picture? They saw (1) an airline operating in a particular way because of (2) a certain state of affairs in its immediate environment (a worldview) that would make this particular way of operating very profitable.

In this study, the visions of a large sample of CEOs were examined. The examination did not focus on the vision statements that are presented for public relations purposes. Rather, it focused on the war stories of CEOs as they formulated a vision for the firm or led its members through a visioning process. The findings suggest that the vision of the single-business firm comprises two interdependent components: (1) a particular worldview (backdrop or setting); and (2) a vision of the firm itself within the perspective of this worldview. The vision is thus a two in one concept as shown in Exhibit 16.2. Each will be examined in some detail next.

---

"Try this Handy-Dandy Vision Crafter, an exclusive for Fortune readers. Select one to three items from each group below, add your logo, marinate overnight in Scotch and red wine, and serve with a straight face.

**OUR VISION**
**TO BE A:**
A) premier; leading; preeminent; world-class; growing
**COMPANY THAT PROVIDES**
B) innovative; cost-effective; focused; diversified; high quality
C) products; services; products and services
**TO**
D) serve the global; create shareholder value; fulfill our covenants with our stakeholders; delight our customers
**IN THE RAPIDLY CHANGING**
E) information-solutions; financial solutions; consumer solutions; financial solutions industries."

Exhibit 16.1: "Cookie-Cutter" Vision Crafter

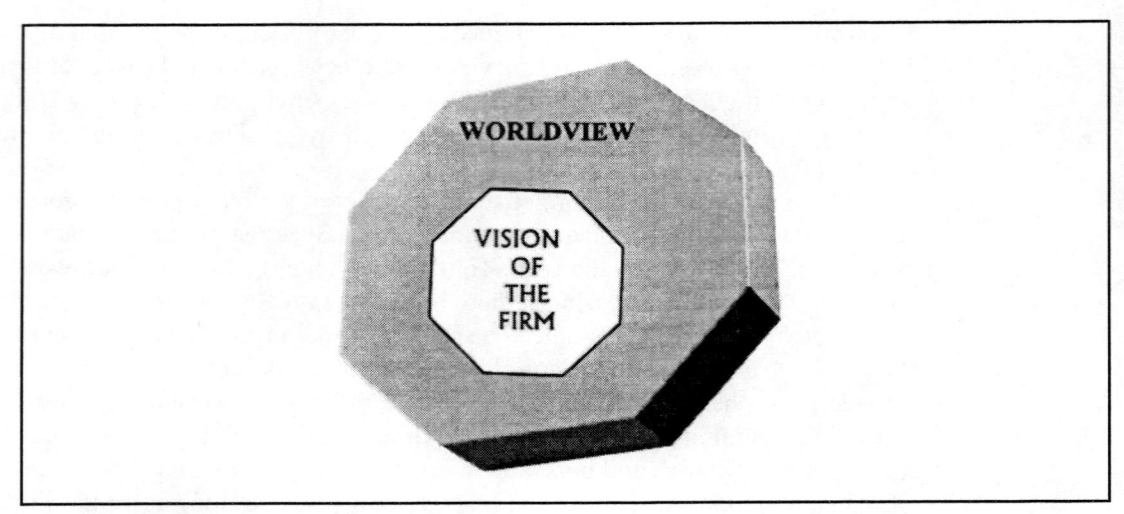

Exhibit 16.2: Vision—a Two in One Concept

## A Worldview

The first component of a vision is a particular worldview—an interpretation or a perception of the world surrounding the firm at a given point in time in the future. It is a crucial part of a firm's vision. Vision sees the firm as fitting in a certain perspective. The worldview is this perspective. Amazon.com was founded based on a certain view of the business world, a world in which the Internet as "the" marketplace; a world of "clicks" not "brick-and-mortar." The worldview, in the final analysis, is a set of assumptions, a scenario if you will, of the state of the business world in the future.

What constitutes a worldview? As shown in Exhibit 16.3, it has four main components: a view of the macro-environment, a view of the industry, a perception of a promising opportunity arena embedded in the industry, and a belief that certain key success factors are crucial for mining this opportunity arena.

### 1. View of the Macro-Environment

This view involves a perception of the state of affairs that is expected to permeate the firm's macro-environment. The concept of the macro environment and the elements that constitute it were described in Chapter 8. It includes components such as the economy, the social system, the political system, demographics, values, and life styles. A vision of the firm is always based on assumptions about the future of the macro-environment. These assumptions are essentially a scenario that the environment is expected to assume. Bezos' vision for Amazon.com assumes that the Internet will be the marketplace in the future and that electronic commerce will be the mode of exchange between buyers and sellers. These, in turn, make further assumptions about society (reading habits, education, demographics, etc.), the economy, and government, especially laws regulating e-commerce.

### 2. View of the Industry

Embedded in the vision of the macro-environment is a perception or a vision of the state of the industry in the future. After all, the industry is a subset of the macro-environment, namely, the economy. The components of the concept "industry" were described in Chapter 8. They include the key players or competitors, customers, suppliers, and substitutes, along with their respective dynamics such as the bargaining power of suppliers, customers, barri-

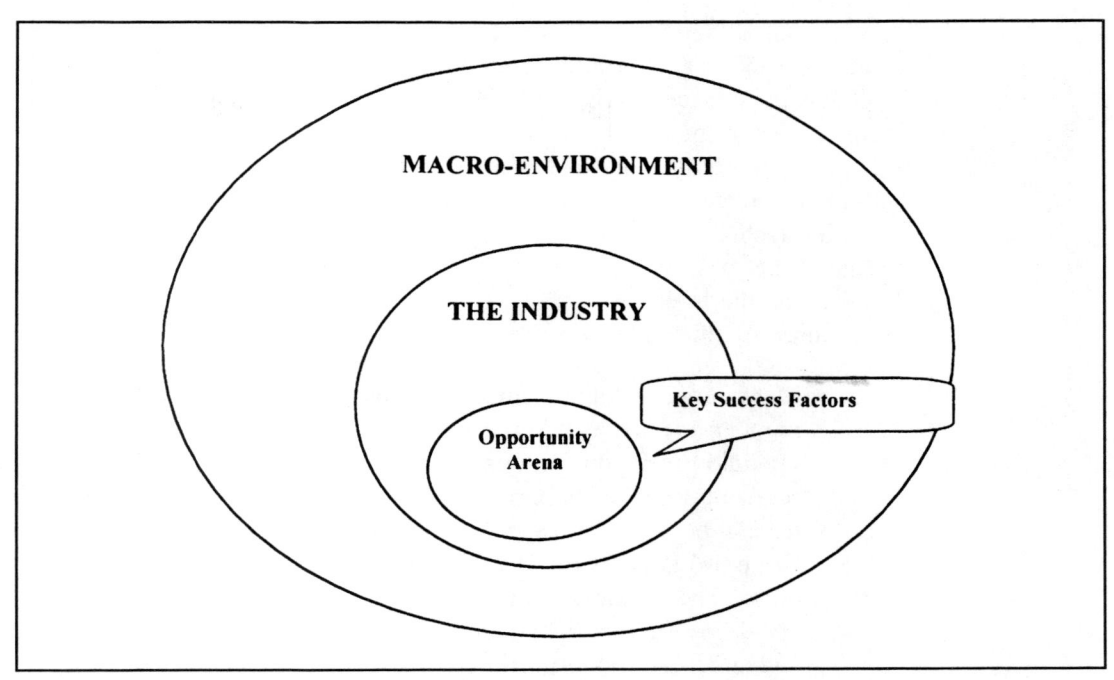

Exhibit 16.3: Components of the Worldview

ers to entry, and rivalry among the players. The vision of the firm always stems from a perception (a scenario) or a vision of these components and their dynamics. It is the perception of the industry that gives rise to the vision of the firm.

The vision of Southwest Airlines described above stemmed from a specific perception of where the airline industry was going before the firm was born. This included continued deregulation, increased demand for business travel, increased cost of operating hub and spokes design, customer alienation by major airlines (e.g., delays at airports, impersonal treatment, large-organization inertia), and the economics of the business (increased overhead and variable cost). Were it not for these assumptions, there would have been no need for a vision of a short-haul airline to be born.

## 3. Opportunity Arena

Perceptions of the environment and the industry often embody an opportunity arena, a huge market. The opportunity arena is a central component of any industry for it includes the customers around whom the industry forms. This arena contains the sustenance needed for the firm to exist and function. It is inconceivable to think of a vision for a firm without a prior concept of a particular opportunity arena that it stakes for itself. Hamel and Prahalad described this concept as follows:

> "Strategy researchers and practitioners have focused much attention on the problem of getting and keeping market share. For most companies, market share is the primary criterion for measuring the strength of a business's strategic position. But what is the meaning of market share in markets that barely exist? . . . Competition for the future is competition for *opportunity share* rather than market share. It is the competition to maximize the share of future opportunities a company could potentially access within a broad *opportunity arena* be that home information systems, genetically engineered drugs, financial services, advanced materials or something else."[31]

The term "opportunity" is so popular that people use it without defining it. As a result, it has come to mean different things to different people. The term refers to "*a mass of dollars*" existing "out there" in the market. This mass of dollars is in the hands of a number of people with common characteristics (e.g., similar demographics) who are willing and ready to spend it to satisfy a particular pressing need. Opportunities are a function of turbulence. Turbulence creates new opportunities and annihilates others. The turbulence created by information technology diminished the opportunity in the mainframe computer business, but it created the massive opportunity in the desktop computer business, local area networks (LANs), and the Internet.

An opportunity has *four* properties that can be summarized as follows:

- Magnitude: An opportunity has a mass or a dollar volume that is a function of the number of persons in a defined market segment.
- Spatial Dimension: An opportunity has a location. This location can be a particular segment or niche in the overall market. It can also be a geographic location. We now have cyberspace as a location of opportunity—electronic commerce.
- Temporal Dimension: It exists only within an unspecified time horizon or a "window." The window opens and closes. It has something like a life cycle. It starts small, grows, matures, declines, and vanishes.
- Dynamics: An opportunity often displays varying rates of change. It grows at a certain rate, accelerates at another, and declines at a different rate. Some opportunities are stable over a given time horizon. Some are erratic.

It is worth stressing that an opportunity arena is a *cluster of opportunities*. The locus of the opportunity arena is a basic human need that people are able and willing to spend money to satisfy it, e.g., the transportation need. The basic need has many aspects to it, e.g., austere transportation, luxury transportation, short-haul, long distance, etc. The need also may be satisfied by many means, e.g., air, surface, and sea. Even in surface transportation, there are the automobile, the bus, the truck, etc. When we combine the aspects of the needs along with the means of satisfying it, we end up with a whole range of opportunities that many firms can move in to fill. This range of opportunities constitutes the arena. Take for example, one means of transportation, the automobile. The auto industry by itself is an enormous opportunity arena that includes assembly, parts makers, service establishments, dealers, etc.

The typical firm stakes a certain opportunity arena as part of its vision and then proceeds to mine it by attacking the various pockets of opportunity embedded in it. The objective here is to maximize the firm's share of opportunity. For example, as of late, Amazon.com appears to have staked the Internet as its arena (whatever can be sold on the Internet). Regularly, it cherry picks one pocket of opportunity after another to exploit. Thus, in 1999, it went into selling electronics. Soon, after, it added toys.

## 4. Key Success Factors (KSF's)

The perceptions of the opportunity arena and the industry give rise to another derivative view—an interpretation of what it takes a firm to succeed in mining the opportunity arena and achieving a bigger share of it. For any firm to successfully exploit an opportunity arena, it will have to have the wherewithal to mine it. There are requirements for success. These requirements stem from the nature of the arena as well as the particulars of the industry. For example, take the opportunity arena, electronic commerce. For any firm to operate in this arena, it will have to possess a number of capabilities such as a strong presence on the Internet through a sophisticated web site, a sophisticated information system for taking orders, protecting the security of the company and its customers, economies of scale in purchasing, warehousing, order processing, and shipping. These are all examples of key success factors.

The kinds of success factors discovered at this stage are generic in nature. They are what it takes a firm, in general, to succeed. They do not pertain to any particular firm. During the formulation of the vision of the firm, a decision has to be made as to which of these key success factors is to be displayed by the firm so that it may compete successfully. Thus, certain key success factors are chosen and every effort is made to cultivate them as competencies for the firm.

## VISION OF THE FIRM

As shown in Exhibit 16.2, vision of the firm is the focal component of the overall vision. Vision of the firm is the picture to which the firm hopes to arrive, albeit for a moment. Obviously, it is predicated on its worldview, particularly the opportunity arena and the key success factors. A firm's vision is a composite of a cluster of "mini" visions as shown in Exhibit 16.4. These are:

- Purpose; the reason for being.
- Business Mode; the firm's own way of doing business.
- Competencies; unique skills that translate into superior competitive advantage.
- Character; the core values that mold the organization and shape its image.
- Outcomes; expected results that the firm must deliver to its stakeholders.

### 1. Purpose

It is inconceivable to think of a vision of a business firm without a concept of purpose. Purpose drives the formation of the vision. The purpose of a business firm is its reason for being. A firm's purpose is formulated at the time of its incorporation where it is written into its charter. At that point in time, the purpose is stated in broad terms to allow the firm considerable room to wheel and deal in the marketplace. It might be stated as to manufacture and produce a certain product (stated generically) or a service to customers in a certain industry. Behind the legal purpose lies another one, the one that actually drives the company; maximizing shareholder value. Maximizing value to shareholders is crucial because their investments keep the firm in operation. However, shareholders are not the only group that sus-

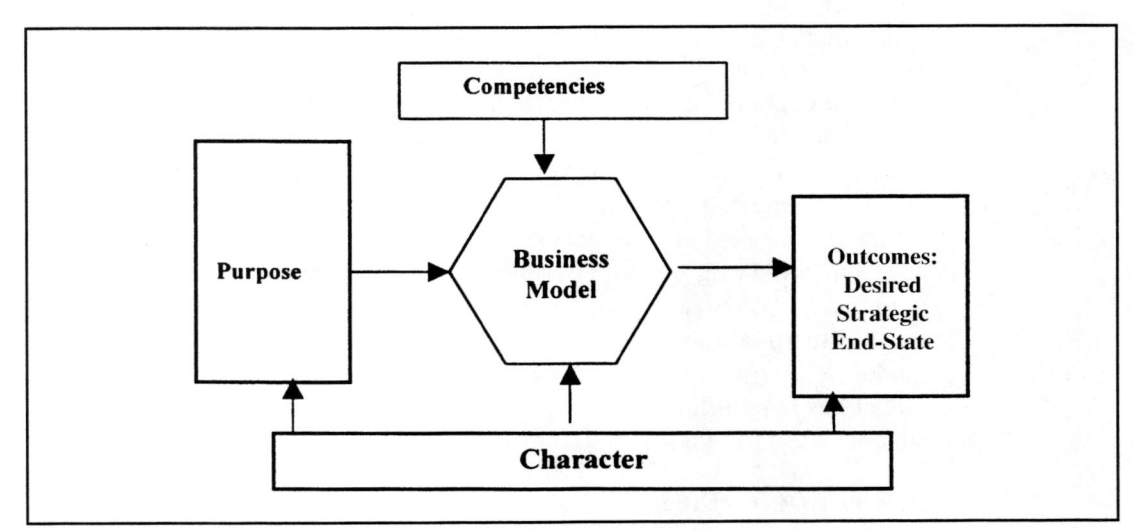

Exhibit 16.4: Elements of the Vision of the Firm

tains the firm. There are other stakeholders who also expect value from the firm, particularly its customers, employees, management, suppliers, community, and perhaps society at large.

It would seem then that creating value for stakeholders is the generic purpose for any firm. At some point in time, the generic purpose must be interpreted and stated in a specific manner to provide a concrete overarching goal for the organization. Let us examine a sample of corporate purposes to help us develop some clear thoughts about defining a firm's purpose.[32]

- Merck & Co. (pharmaceuticals) defines its reason for being as "... to provide society with superior products and services—innovations and solutions to satisfy customer needs and improve the quality of life—to provide employees with meaningful work and advancement opportunities and investors with a superior rate of return."
- Arthur D. Little (management consulting) states its purpose as "... achieving outstanding value for our clients, rewarding careers for our staff, and excellent performance for our owners."
- Intel Corporation defined its purpose as to "Do a great job for our customers, employees and stockholders by being the preeminent building block supplier to the computing industry."
- Goodyear Tires articulates its purpose as "Constant improvement in products and services to meet our customers' needs." This is the only means to business success for Goodyear and prosperity for its investors and employees.
- Leo Burnett's (advertising) purpose as articulated by the founder, Leo Burnett, "Our primary function in life is to produce the best advertising in the world bar none. This is to be advertising so interrupting, so daring, so fresh, so engaging, so human, so believable and well-focused as to themes and ideas that, at one and the same time, it builds a quality reputation for the long haul as it produces sales for the immediate present."
- Boeing (aircraft manufacturing) verbalizes its purpose as "To be the number one aerospace company in the world and among the premier industrial concerns in terms of quality, profitability, and growth."

## 2. Business Model

The concept of the business model was introduced earlier in Chapter 12 as part of the firm's maneuver. The business model defines the business of the firm and how it does business. The business model comprises four main elements: a business concept, business processes, an economic model, and a value proposition all targeted to a certain set of customers.[33] Since it was discussed earlier, there is no need to repeat a detailed description of each of these concepts here. However, we must stress that the business model that is part of the vision is somewhat different from the one that appears in maneuver. In the context of vision, the business model is more generic. For example, we might think of Amazon.com's business model as brokering between producers and customers through the Internet. However, when it comes to maneuvering, this model has to be applied to the specific competitive and customer situations the firm is facing. Every time the situation changes, the vision business model is interpreted and applied differently. One can expect that Amazon.com's business model has been reinterpreted and redesigned to suit the various businesses that it acquired, added, or acquired a stake therein.

## 3. Competencies

A critical part of a firm's vision is its concept of competencies that will distinguish it from other players in the marketplace. The concept of competencies was discussed earlier in Chapter 15 in connection with the topic of capability. Hamel and Prahalad defined a competence as "... a bundle of skills and technologies rather than a single discrete skill or technology."[34]

An intended competence must have the potential of providing the firm with a superior, disproportionate competitive advantage in the marketplace. In the context of vision, competencies derive from the discovery of the key success factors that the firm believes to be critical for doing business in the chosen arena. In the context of the worldview, key success factors are generic in nature, e.g., economies of scale. However, each firm will have a different interpretation of the concept of scale as part of its vision. For example, traditional airlines interpreted economies of scale as having a hub-and-spoke set-up to achieve high volume and maximum utilization of physical facilities. Southwest Airlines' visionaries also realized the importance of scale as a key success factor but they interpreted it differently. To them, scale meant frequent flights between two cities—intensive utilization of the aircraft and the crew. In Southwest Airline's vision, the main competence was perceived as a skill or an ability to operate the aircraft and the crew frequently between two points. This competence would translate into a competitive advantage in terms of serving its selected customer segment better and cheaper than any other airline.

## 4. Character

An integral part of a firm's vision is a concept of character or dimensions that will set it apart from others in the marketplace. These dimensions include size, scope, and core values.

### Scope of the Firm's Business

An integral part of a firm's character is its scope. The term scope refers to the range of market segments and the range of products/services it offers in each of these segments. It is the number of different market scale modules that would make up the firm in its entirety. Some firms remain focused on one product and one market segment such as Rolls Royce. Other firms choose a wide range of segments and a wide range of matched products such as GM. The choice of scope is part of the firm's identity (vision). It makes GM what it is.

### Size of the Firm

A firm's concept of itself includes a specification of the size and scale at which it intends to operate. Size is often specified in terms of sales, assets, and employment. Size is crucial for it determines the scale of the firm's operations, which can help it achieve economies of scale and position it where it wants to be in the marketplace. If the firm intends to dominate the industry, it certainly would include size as a critical factor in laying claim to its staked niche. A firm like Southwest Airlines chose a certain size as part of its vision. It did not want to be the largest hub-and-spoke airline like Northwest. Instead, it chose to distribute the firm's size as number of point-to-point operations spread throughout the marketplace. It is a distinguishing mark of Southwest Airlines concept of business. By contrast, a firm like GM believes in the importance of size as a way to dominate the market. It is part of GM's business concept.

### Core Values

Core values also define the character of the firm. These are the well-chosen values, ideals, and principles that mold employees' mindset, behaviors, and actions. They become the norms that shape the corporate culture emerge. Once a corporate culture surfaces, it exerts considerable impact on the company internally and externally. Internally, the culture is the environment within which people operate. It can be constructive, if it molds people to cooperate and pull together as a group. It can be destructive, if it creates the opportunity for conflict among people where they waste energy that could have been spent enhancing the firm's standing in the marketplace.

Core values are not just limited to ethical and moral principles, e.g., honesty, integrity, fairness, etc. They also include beliefs derived from the business model mentioned above, e.g., beliefs in "speed" (Federal Express), "empowerment" (Oticon), "innovation" (Raytheon), and so on. An example is shown in Exhibit 16.5.

## 5. Envisioned Outcomes: Desired Strategic End-State

No one envisions a company that will fail in the marketplace. Visions always reflect ambition, success expressed in terms of certain expectations or outcomes. The issue here is what kinds of outcomes. The main outcome that appears most often in vision statements is creating value for shareholders. However, this concept can be extended to include other stakeholders as well. Without a return to stakeholders, they will not come together to form the firm or continue to provide it with the resources needed for it to function as a going concern.

There are many aspects to creating value for stakeholders. These include:

- An expectation regarding level of shareholders value.
- A certain level of organizational outcomes, e.g. motivated, satisfied, accomplished people.
- An expectation of a certain level of corporate citizenship including social responsibility, ethics, environmental conservation, and the like.

In general, the envisioned outcomes should define the key parameters of a desired strategic end-state for the firm. These parameters are described in Chapter 17. They delineate the firm's strategic position, specify its financial position, set a level for its market value, and outline its societal position.

### Envisioned Outcomes (Strategic End-State) as Corporate Objectives

Envisioned outcomes play an important role in managing the firm. In the first place, they define the conditions for a strategic end-state that pleases the firm's stakeholders. They state the criteria or indices that tell the organization that the strategic end-state has been achieved. Second, they become the source of corporate objectives (i.e., objectives for the firm in its entirety) for the next round of maneuver. Corporate objectives are formulated as landmarks on the road toward the strategic end-state. When they are achieved, the firm will be a step closer to its desired end-state. As discussed in Chapter 12, corporate objectives fall into two categories: strategic objectives and financial objectives. Strategic objectives are derived directly from the envisioned outcomes. Objectives translate the vision into performance targets.

## The Difference between Vision, Mission, and Strategic Intent

At this point, one element of confusion needs clarification and this is the use of the popular terms "vision," "mission," and "strategic intent." What is the difference? There is considerable difference of opinion in the literature. While some writers view mission as part of the vision, others classify vision as part of the mission. We propose the following clarification: Vision and mission are not equivalent or subsets of one another. The vision is the longer-term destination. It is like a still picture of the firm after fast-forwarding in time to a certain point in the future. Vision is broad. It is a boundary for the firm to wheel and deal within. By contrast, the mission is a more specific task, to be achieved by the firm within a shorter time horizon. In this sense, the mission is the same as the strategic thrust. To use an

> **We Believe***
>
> That our products and services must enrich people's lives and enhance their relationships.
>
> That creativity and quality—in our concepts, products and services—are essential to our success.
>
> That the people of Hallmark are our company's most valuable resource.
>
> That distinguished financial performance is a must, not as an end in itself, but as a means to accomplish our broader mission.
>
> That our private ownership must be preserved.
>
> **The Values that guide us are:**
>
> Excellence in all we do.
>
> Ethical and moral conduct at all times and in all our relationships.
>
> Innovation in all areas of our business as a means of attaining and sustaining leadership, corporate social responsibility to Kansas City and to each community in which we operate.
>
> These beliefs and values guide our business strategies,
> our corporate behavior, and our relationships
> with suppliers, customers, communities and each other.

Exhibit 16.5: Hallmarks (Greeting Cards) Core Values[36]

analogy, the vision is like a destination. The mission is the next immediate landmark towards this destination. A vision spans a longer time horizon. The mission spans a more immediate and a shorter time horizon. The definition of mission given here makes it equal to the "strategic intent." To simplify matters, the concepts of strategic thrust, mission, and strategic intent are treated as equivalent, interchangeable terms. It is worth stressing that they are subservient to the vision.

## Vision in the Context of the Multi-Business Firm

Before Jack Welch assumed the chairmanship of GE, it had approximately 350 businesses in nearly 40 business sectors. He, however, had a different concept or a vision for GE. In 1983, he was explaining the shape of the new GE to a reporter. He took a piece of paper and drew on it three minimally overlapping circles to represent the businesses that GE will be in—what later came to be known as the three-circle concept. He labeled one "core" (lighting, major appliances, motor, transportation, turbine, and contractor equipment). On the second, he wrote "high technology" (industrial electronics, medical systems, engineering materials, aerospace, and aircraft engines). He called the third "services" (credit corporation, information services, construction and engineering services, and nuclear services). From that point onward, the three-circle configuration became the essence of the vision for GE.

The vision of the multi-business firm is different from the single business firm. The multi-business firm is a more complex enterprise for it includes several single business firms operating in different industries held from the center by corporate management. An analysis of the visions of leaders of multi-business firms suggest that it too is a two-in-one concept: a vision of context in the form of macro vision and within it a more micro vision; the vision of the multi-business firm—as shown in Exhibit 16.6.

---

*Hallmark's Core Values. Copyright © by Hallmark Cards, Inc. Reprinted by permission.

**WORLDVIEW**

```
Macro-Environment  →  Perception of Key Success Factors
       ↓                              ↓
V I S I O N   O F   T H E   F I R M

Purpose  →  Envisioned Portfolio  →  Expected Outcome
                   ↓
            Concept of Structure
```

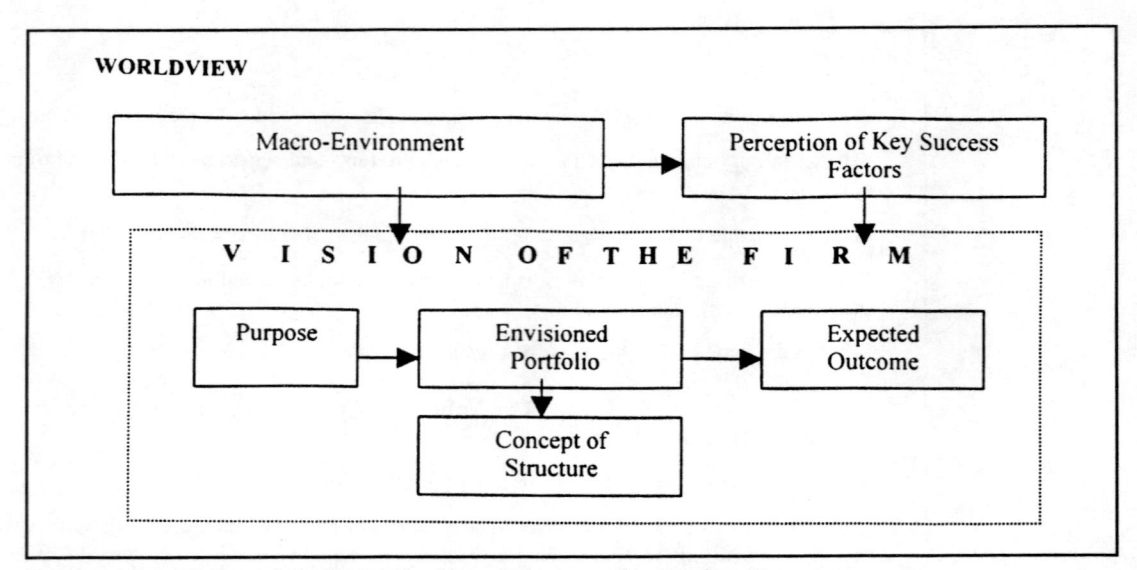

Exhibit 16.6: Vision of the Multi-Business Firm as a Two-in-One Concept

## Worldview: The Macro-Environment

The macro-environment of the multi-business firm is rather complex. Depending on the size of the firm, the scope of the vision of the macro-environment can range from one or two sectors (e.g., transportation and aerospace) to the whole economy and maybe the global economy as well. It includes the anticipated dynamics in this macro sphere. For example, in the early 1980s, Welch's vision for GE was predicated on a vision of the U.S. and global economies. He envisioned the U.S. economy as being restructured, moving from a manufacturing to a service economy. He also foresaw the emergence of a borderless world where Japan was a great threat ". . . the entire organization had to understand that GE was in a tougher, more competitive world, with Japan as the cutting edge of the new competition . . ."[37]

## Key Success Factors

The perception of the macro-environment raises a fundamental question: What are the requirements of success (key success factors) in such an environment? Here are some of the key success factors often mentioned:

- Diversity: For a multi-business firm to survive, it has to have diversity among its units. If they are all in the same industry or sector, the financial risk is greater, especially when this sector suffers a decline. However, if the firm's holdings spanned many unrelated sectors, the risk is lower.
- Scale: The larger the firm, the better the chances of surviving as a colossus in a chaotic marketplace. The scale can range from the domestic economy to the global economy.
- Resilience: A multi-business firm has to be able to spring back after a disturbance. It has to reflect the characteristics of a self-organizing system where all the units spring back to keep the whole intact.
- Speed and agility: A multi-business firm needs to be able to respond quickly to changes in the macro-environment. This would speed up resilience and reduce the risk of damage to some of its parts.

- A strong financial capability: The supply of cash (from internal or external sources) is key for building and maintaining the various units so the corporation as a whole can survive.
- A strong capability to get in and out of various businesses: The maintenance of a healthy portfolio of businesses requires an ability to find targets for adding to the portfolio as well as flexibility to exit unprofitable units.
- Managerial talent: Managing a colossus like a multi-business firm requires certain managerial talent that is rather rare. Managers have to have the breadth and depth to understand and coordinate diverse businesses.

## Vision of the Firm

Predicated on the worldview is the vision of the firm itself. This comprises four main elements. First, there is the concept of purpose for the corporation. The centerpiece is the vision of the portfolio. This portfolio needs to be supported by a concept or a configuration of a structure that would actualize the portfolio. Then, there is also the expectation of certain outcomes. As an example of the vision of the multi-business firm, consider Welch's verbalization of his vision for GE: "A decade from now, I would like General Electric to be perceived as a unique, high-spirited, entrepreneurial enterprise . . . a company known around the world for its unmatched level of excellence. I want General Electric to be the most profitable, highly diversified company on earth, with world-wide quality leadership in every one of its product lines."[38]

Exhibits 16.7 and 16.8 present further illustrations of the kind of thoughts that go into the vision of the multi-business firm. From these, we can extract elements that form a model for the vision of the multi-business firm. The first one is that of Charles Coffen, GE's CEO in the late 1890s, Exhibit 16.7. Although it was formulated in the 19th century, many parts of it are applicable to many contemporary multi-business firms. The second is that of Jack Welch, GE's CEO in the 1990s, Exhibit 16.8.

### Purpose

A fundamental element in the vision of this type of firm is a concept of purpose. Three purposes appear to be more popular. The first is maximizing shareholder value. In a way, a multi-business firm is like a portfolio of investments. As such, its ultimate purpose is to maximize the return on the investment as well as the overall value of the portfolio as measured by share prices. The second purpose is risk minimization—through diversity of the investments. The third purpose is to develop a critical mass that ensures the continuity of the firm as a profitable conglomeration. Many corporations state other purposes. These often revolve around becoming a good corporate citizen.

### Envisioned Portfolio

The centerpiece of the vision of the multi-business firm is a concept of a portfolio of businesses that will constitute the corporation. This portfolio can be represented graphically in a matrix form such as the Boston Consulting Group's Growth Share Matrix, or any of the similar models, such as the GE/McKenzie chart of the Shell Directional Policy Matrix.

An envisioned portfolio is an arrangement of four main elements:

- The number of SBU's in the portfolio: How many businesses should be in the portfolio?
- The relative size of each business: Some SBU's will be large in terms of assets, sales, and contribution to overall revenue and profits for the firm. Others will have smaller sizes and contribution but they are kept for a strategic purpose such as future potential.

1. Internal Growth:
   —Growth from within preferable to acquisition or merger.
   —GE should generate its own capital, technology, and management.
   —Debt unthinkable.
2. Constrained diversity: Design, manufacture and sale of goods related to the generation and utilization of electricity.
3. Oligopolistic competition:
   —Minimizing the number of competitors through control of entry and industry concentration.
   —Allocation of markets by region, product, and function.
   —Minimization of price competition.
   —Nonrelative growth among competitors.
   —Neutralization of government intervention.
4. Domestic saturation: The goal was to dominate the industry in the domestic market:
   —Dominate electrical science and technology.
   —Maintain fixed ratios of market share and price with competition.
   —Prevent entry of new competitors.
   —Do the above legally enough to avoid prosecution.
5. International defense: Protect its domestic market position through:
   —Domestic cross licenses with Westinghouse and other American electrical manufacturers.
   —A set of non-aggression pacts with foreign electrical manufacturers.
   —Portfolio of foreign securities.
   —The International General Electric Company.
6. Vertical centricism: The GE organizational structure resembles a wedding cake.
7. Definite chain of command.
8. Functional specialization: Inter-functional problems and opportunities almost exclusively handled by the president, thus all levels below him are primarily defined in functional terms.
9. Structural uniformity: Each organizational layer has defined authority and responsibility; all operating components at any given level of the company are of equal size; ratio type of performance measurers; a system of procedures, standards and controls.
10. Liquidity: Pay-as-you-go
11. Anticipatory relations: The pursuit of anticipatory and non-adversary relationships with government, labor, and the public.

Exhibit 16.7: CEO Coffen's Vision for General Electric[39]

- Diversity: This refers to the degree or relatedness among the businesses in the portfolio.
- The distribution of SBU's in the portfolio: This will show the degree of balance among the various types—between cash generators and cash users.

The BCG matrix is used as a model for envisioning the portfolio. It configures it in terms of cash use and cash generation. Cash generators are businesses that have a high relative market share in maturing or declining markets (cash cows). Cash users are businesses that have a small market share in a promising market (question marks) or a declining market (dogs). Some units might neither use nor generate cash, but they dominate a growing market (stars). As it turns out, a vision of a portfolio boils down to specifying the mix of cash generators to cash users, especially the numbers and relative sizes of each category. Portrayed as a BCG matrix, the vision of a portfolio is like a still picture of the businesses as they hang in the various quadrants of the matrix. Exhibit 16.9 illustrates a possible portfolio vision—a vision of cash cows, stars, question marks, and no SBU's in the "dog" quadrant.

|  | **Strategy** | **Organizational Structure** | **Human Resource Management** |
|---|---|---|---|
| **Technical** | • No. 1 or No. 2<br>• high growth businesses | • 13 businesses<br>• share best practices<br>• boundarylessness | • multiple pay systems<br>• new staffing systems<br>• development as a continuous process |
| **Political** | • integrated diversity | • no "wedding cake" hierarchy<br>• cross functional teamwork<br>• empowerment, decision making pushed to lower levels | • rewards very flexible<br>• appraisals from below as well as above |
| **Cultural** | • speed, simplicity and self-confidence<br>• ownership<br>• share best practices<br>• work-out | • shared values<br>• many cultures<br>• common vision | • human resource systems shape and mold boundarylessness<br>• new staffing and support values |

Exhibit 16.8: Welch's Vision for GE in the 1990s[40]

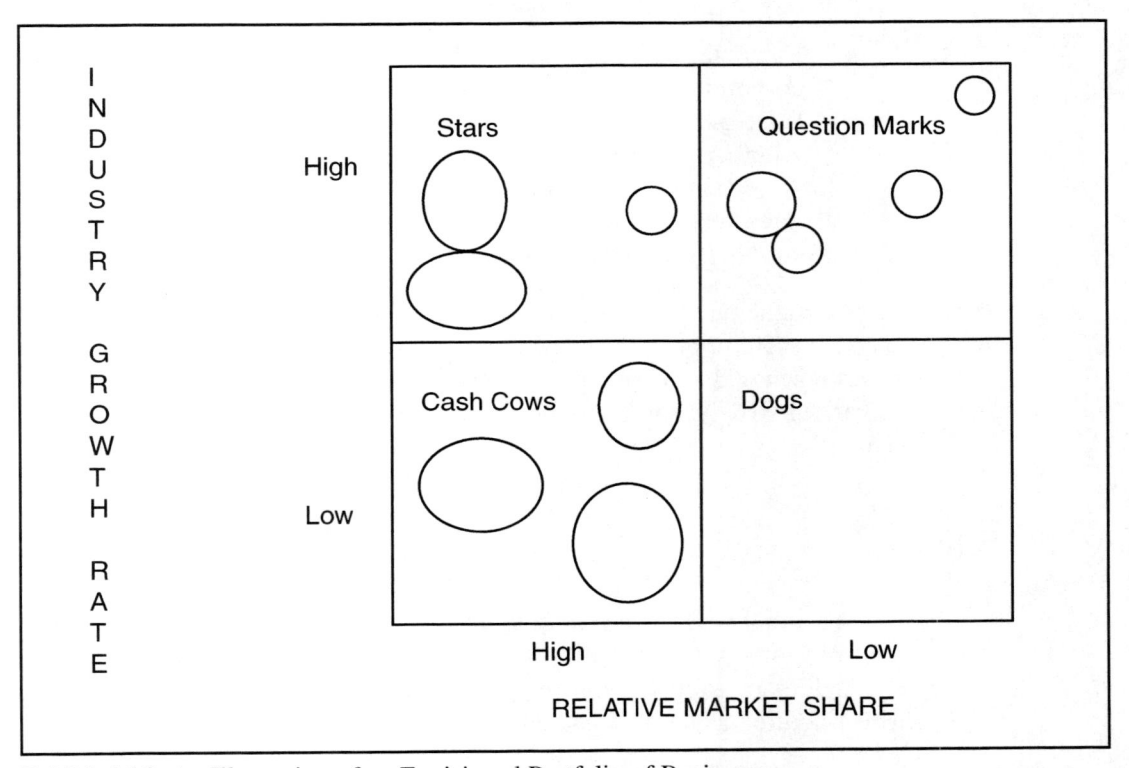

Exhibit 16.9: An Illustration of an Envisioned Portfolio of Businesses

## Concept of Structure

A portfolio of businesses is a number of businesses that have to be coordinated to act as one corporation despite their diversity. It is inconceivable to think of all these businesses without a concept of how they will hang together to achieve cohesiveness among them. This concept involves mechanisms for holding the reins since the various businesses will be granted a high degree of autonomy. The structure is often envisioned as a two-tiered one: the level of the business units and the corporate level. The centerpiece of the structure is the architecture of the relationship between the business units and the head office.

This relationship runs along a continuum. At one extreme, all the units are labeled as divisions and are run centrally by top management. The corporate level managers allocate the resources, receive financial reports from the units, and supervise them—generally managing them as if they were units in an operating company. At the other extreme, the units are treated as if they are separate businesses, i.e., totally empowered to run independently. They can even raise equity and debt capital on their own. They have their own board of directors. Sometimes corporate management is represented on these boards. Sometimes, the CEO leads, following the principle of management by exception—taking the perspective of a fund manager managing a portfolio of stocks. In between the two extremes, lie many variations, like GE under Welch. The main design issue here is control over resources in order to maximize return and shareholder value.

### Envisioned Outcomes

Like any business vision, the vision of the multi-business firm includes a concept of the outcomes that are expected to take place when the vision becomes a reality. Among the most frequently mentioned outcomes are:

- Financial outcomes, primarily return on the investment and market value of the corporation.
- Strategic outcomes, e.g., dominating a certain sector, risk distribution, strength and integrity of the portfolio as a whole.
- A certain corporate culture, particularly if corporate management becomes the integrator of all units. Welch worked hard at GE to entrench a culture of speed, simplicity, and self-confidence.

Once the outcomes are framed, the final step is to translate them into a set of corporate objectives. These objectives will then be used as guidelines for the firm's portfolio maneuver, as discussed in Chapter 12. From them a number of directives will be formulated for the various SBU's; some will be instructed to grow, others will be directed to retrench, and so on.

# VISIONING

Now that we have a clearer concept of what vision is or ought to be, we turn our attention to visioning, the activities involved in formulating a vision for the firm. First, we survey the literature on the subject. Second, we examine the vision activities in the context of a firm structured as a self-organizing system.

## Approaches for Structuring Organizational Visioning

Hickman and Silva proposed a three-step sequence as follows.[41] Step 1 is recognizing vision. This involves taking stock of the firm's executives to see who is a visionary and who is not. Such an inventory forms the talent for visioning by the organization as a whole. Step 2 is organizational introspection, i.e., in essence reviewing the current state of the environment and the organization through a process like SWOT (strengths, weaknesses, opportunities, and threats) analysis. Step 3 is scenario building, "creating the future mentally before creating it physically." The scenario building process comprises these tasks: defining the vision, determining opportunities and dangers, listing key success factors, and sequencing major events for implementing the vision.

Wilson suggested another process: (1) analyzing the company's future environment, (2) analyzing the company's resources and capabilities, (3) clarifying management values, (4) developing or revising a mission statement, (5) identifying strategic objectives, and goals, (6) generating and selecting strategic options, (7) developing the vision statement, and (8) conducting "sanity checks." He instructs that visioning is not an individual exercise. Rather, it should be a well-designed collective visioning process calling for the judicious use of diverse contributions, including informed outsiders.[42]

Nanus proposed a four-phase process for envisioning as follows.[43] The first phase is taking stock or doing a "vision audit." Part of this audit is determining what business the firm is "really" in because there may be different interpretations of the business definition, and as a result, there is a gap between the intended definition and the actual business being pursued by members of the organization. The audit also examines how the firm operates including values, objectives, strategies, and method of operation.

The second phase involves "testing reality." Two steps need to be performed. The first is identifying the various constituencies and their needs as well as the threats and opportunities facing them. The second step is targeting the vision. It includes: drawing a boundary for the vision (e.g., time, geographic, and social constraints); deciding the things that the vision must accomplish (e.g., growth, image, ethical measures); and, any special issues peculiar to the firm that must be addressed in the vision.

The third phase is considering the possibilities or defining the vision context. This step is concerned mainly with the development of alternate scenarios for the future and drawing their implications for the firm. The purpose here is to paint the future context in which the firm will operate and the strategic issues it will encounter. The fourth phase is choosing the vision. This involves synthesizing all the information gleaned from the previous steps, mapping a domain for the firm (similar to opportunity arena), generating alternative visions, choosing, and "packaging" the chosen vision.

In reviewing the literature on the topic of vision, three issues seem to dominate the debate. These are:

- Direction: Should visioning flow in a top-down, or bottom-up fashion.
- Content: What are the business decisions involved in forming a vision.
- Ownership: How to get members of the organization to own into the vision.

## 1. Direction of Visioning Activities

With respect to the flow of visioning in the firm, there are two fundamental approaches. Visioning can flow in a top-down format. Alternatively, it can proceed in a bottom-up fashion. A third possible approach is a mix between these two. We examine each below.

### The Top-Down Approach

According to this model, the CEO views vision development as an instrument for leading the organization. The CEO often treats vision formation as a leader's prerogative. Such a leader develops the vision on his/her own and then "sells" it to the people to get them to own or buy into it by a variety of means including persuasion, preaching, motivating, rewarding, propagandizing, etc. Welch represents this approach. He followed a similar process at GE. Consider his statement: "Good business leaders create a vision, articulate the vision, passionately own the vision and relentlessly drive it to completion. . . . They go up, down, and around their organization to reach people. They don't stick to the established channels. They're informal. . . . They make a religion out of being accessible. They never get bored telling their story."[44]

Undoubtedly, Welch achieved considerable success with this approach at GE. For years, the company ranked among the top ten best-managed companies in *Fortune* magazine surveys. Welch ranked among the best CEOs in the world for years. This approach, however, does not work for everyone. Most CEOs in this category develop the vision and preach it passionately, but then people pay only lip service to it, never owning into it.

There are variations of the top-down approach. A popular one is the successive enrollment of levels in the organization. Here, the CEO huddles with his/her immediate top managers. They formulate the basics of the vision as a team. Next, they enroll the next lower one. These, in turn, enroll the next lower echelon, and so on, until the lowest management echelons enroll first line employees. An example of this approach is what Craig Weatherup, Pepsi Cola CEO did in the 1990s in formulating the so-called "Right Side Up" vision for the company.[45]

Pepsi used to rely on selling the concentrate to independent bottlers who sold to various retail outlets. In 1990, Pepsi acquired all the bottlers and found itself thrust in the retailing business. As Weatherup observed, "We went from a company with 600 customers—our franchised bottlers—to 600,000 customers: those serviced through our newly acquired bottlers."[46] Weatherup realized that there was a need for a new vision for Pepsi, the new manufacturer/distributor company. What is interesting here is Weatherup's approach for creating a new vision for Pepsi. Rather than creating the vision himself, he decided to let the organization develop it under his leadership. Here is a description of the process.[47]

> "After months of data gathering and analysis, Weatherup presented his finding to his 10 direct reports in September 1990. He framed the meeting as a 'soul searching session'. . . . His primary goal was to convince his management team of the need for change. . . . He added: 'People are generally all over the map in where they want to go. I knew that this was a situation we couldn't afford the luxury of everyone flopping around. I want everybody to start the same book, on the same page, at the same time.
>
> During the first day of the meeting, Weatherup used vivid metaphors to create a sense of crisis. He described the financial, customer, and organization pain facing the organization, concluding the session with his 'freight train' speech: 'There's a freight train out there, and it is called 15% earnings. We're standing on the track, and we'd better figure out something or it will run us right over.' The management team faced accepting mediocrity—accepting, and then explaining to PepisCo management that bottling was a 5–10% business—or embarking on a journey of radical change to achieve 15% earnings growth. Weatherup asked them to 'sleep on' these alternatives and come prepared to discuss their decision in the morning.
>
> On the second day, the team began by unanimously voting to embark on a radical change program. . . . The group spent the third day brainstorming the systemic changes needed to achieve 15% annual earnings growth. To begin, they generated a list of 35 possible change levers which they distilled into 10 broad categories. After extensive discussion, each participant voted for the three most promising levers, with the five options receiving the most votes designated for further analysis.
>
> The last day of the meeting was devoted to task assignment and ground rules. Weatherup created five teams and assigned two members of his staff to each one. 'Their assignment' he recalled, was to prove that their option was the Holy Grail. They had to prove it using facts, not just that this was their passion. Weatherup also charged the teams with dedicating half of their time during the following six weeks to the task, including interviewing customers, and employees personally. Then, everyone agreed to plan and lead a meeting

---

Copyright © 1994 by the President and Fellows of Harvard College. Harvard Business School Case 9395-048. This case was prepared by Don Sull under the direction of David Carvin as the basis for class discussion rather than to illustrate either effective or ineffective handling of an administrative situation. Reprinted by permission of Harvard Business School.

in December to enroll the next level of management in the vision that emerged.... To remind his team of the situation urgency, Weatherup later gave each of them a model train with 15% painted on the side, and ten small figures standing on the track staring in terror as it approached.

Six weeks after the meeting and a host of work sessions, Weatherup's direct reports reconvened for two days in Chicago to choose among the options explored by the five teams. Wheless (one of the participants) recalled: 'The five alternatives were all false starts because they were created as individual solutions to the problem. Then we realized that you have to satisfy the customer, the employee, and the shareholder *simultaneously*.'

A vision of the future Pepsi then began to emerge. 'We realized that we had a 'wrong side up' organization, Barnes (another participant) observed, 'where the front-line performers catered to managers at the top instead of worrying about how to support customers.' The team converged on the need to turn the company 'right side up' by aligning the organization with customers' needs. Weatherup encouraged them to translate this broad consensus into a concrete vision statement.

While there was agreement on the basic thrust of 'Right Side Up,' the management team struggled over the specifics. Both concepts and language caused problems. Barnes (one of the participants) recalled: 'We agreed that we would not move forward until we were all aligned, until everyone supported it 100%. We would stop frequently for alignment checks to make sure that we had all contributed, we had all had the opportunity to be heard, and that we were all committed to support the decision. It consumed our lives. By the time we were done, we had written it, rewritten it, and argued over every word. By the time we were done, it was tattooed on our chests.'

The team then began preparing to enroll other managers in the 'Right Side Up' campaign. The first enrollment, which consisted of the 70 direct reports of the (first top management team) was kicked off with a three-day meeting in December 1990.... Members of (the top management team) then introduced the Right Side Up vision as the means to move the organization forward, and presented their finding from customer and employee interviews. They also led 'table buzz' sessions, where the participants broke into smaller groups and discussed their immediate reactions to the Right Side Up vision in short sessions.

The final day of the meeting was devoted to assigning work for the managers to complete in the three months that followed.... They were also charged with planning and leading the enrollment for the next layer in the organization.

.... Weatherup concluded each enrollment meeting with a rousing sendoff, his 'head, heart, hands' speech. In it, he explained that for change to occur, people needed to do three things: develop a conceptual understanding of the rationale, propose, and direction of change (head), internalize and commit emotionally to the new vision (heart), and begin to do the work necessary to develop new skills and ensure that the vision was realized (hands).

... After several iterations, the enrollment process culminated in 'Team 20,000,' a one-day session in which every front-line employee saw a series of presentations from top management and then broke into small groups locally to discuss the RSU (Right Side Up) vision....

To translate the Right Side Up vision into changes in employees' daily behavior, Pepsi's human resource group gathered detailed examples that illustrated the tenets of customer focus, employee empowerment, and shared values in action."

## The Bottom-Up Approach

The second approach to forming a vision is the bottom-up process where the CEO works along side the people to develop a common vision. Visions arrived at in this manner have compelling advantages. First, the vision would capitalize on the intelligence, wisdom, experience, genius, insights, and foresight of a large number of people. This might be superior to the thinking of one or few top managers. Top managers are somewhat insulated from the realities in the trenches. The employees on the firing line are not. Furthermore, top managers do not have a monopoly on wisdom. Second, a bottom-up vision has the strongest likelihood of being internalized and integrated into people's daily actions to make the actual company conform (as close as possible) to the envisioned company.

### The Top-Down/Bottom-Up Mix

In some organizations, vision is formulated via a mix between the top-down and the bottom-up approaches. Senge and Quigly proposed two possible models for this approach. Senge identified three phases for developing a shared vision: enrollment, commitment, and compliance.[48] Enrollment is the process of helping members of the organization become part of the envisioning process and the vision by choice. Commitment means that every member of the organization feels fully responsible for transforming the vision into reality. Compliance is a state, beyond enrollment and commitment, in which a member of the organization is an advocate for the vision.

Quigly outlined another process that he called "the leadership conference planning process."[49] In preparation, it begins with a determination of the leaders in the organization, selecting participants in the vision development process, and outlining what they will do in the course of formulating the vision. The process calls for three conferences with three agendas as follows:

- The first conference is concerned with establishing a framework for vision development. In this conference, vision formation is the theme. The work here involves identifying shared values, probing the future, clarifying the future game plan, and the preliminary drafting of corporate mission and goals. At the conclusion of this conference, task forces are formed to study the key thoughts and patterns (themes) that emerged from the discussion of vision in the rough.
- The second conference is dedicated to arriving at consensus. Task forces report on elaboration and specification of the themes that emerged from the first conference. Discussion ensues and general agreement is reached, at least on the fundamentals. Such agreement is essential for obtaining commitment later on. The output of this conference is a vision and the basics of a strategic plan.
- The theme of the third conference is "total commitment." The process involves discussions, presentations, and consolidation of views coupled with a specification of who is to do what. Commitments are obtained. The conference attendees become like the apostles who take the gospel to the rest of the organization.

## 2. Content: Vision Decisions

The literature seems to be unclear as to what business decisions are to be made in the course of formulating a vision. As our discussion of the concept of vision revealed, various authors prescribe various contents. Some, like Robert, include many decisions, e.g., time frame, areas of excellence, product scope, market scope, size and growth guidelines, and return and profit guidelines. Others, like Bennis and Nanus, specify content in broad terms, a desirable future without specifying what decisions have to be made in order to specify this desirable future. The issue of content remains largely undetermined and subject to considerable variation in practice. In reviewing vision statements published in annual reports, some reflect the cookie-cutter model presented in Exhibit 16.1. We prepose the content presented in Exhibits 16.2, 16.3, and 16.4.

3. Ownership

The third critical issue in visioning is the matter of ownership. For the vision to happen (i.e., the firm actually reaches its desired strategic end-state), the vision must be translated into the daily behavior of everyone in the firm. Ownership determines whether or not the vision will be enacted in daily behaviors.

Ownership largely depends on the direction of the visioning process. In the top-down approach, the CEO and top management own the vision. The employees do not. Rather, the vision is "sold" to them. They are "enrolled" into the "buy-in." Top-down visions tend to be ignored by employees for a variety of reasons. First, they do not feel that they own into it. Second, they do not reflect the realities of the marketplace because the persons who formulate it are at an organizational distance from such realities. In many cases, the employees do not buy into visions formulated at the top. Third, there may also be a question of realism. The employees on the firing line find many of these visions stand for unrealistic goals. Finally, there is the issue of platitudes. Top-down visions tend to be, like the cookie-cutter type (Exhibit 16.1). They are abstract platitudes to which the employees cannot relate.

The bottom-up approach transfers vision decisions to employees and hence they feel a sense of ownership. The vision becomes pervasive throughout the organization. Ownership ensures that the vision is acted out in daily behaviors. When this happens, the whole firm moves in the direction of the vision.

Since our concern here is the self-organizing firm, a logical question suggests itself at this point. How does visioning take place in a such a firm? Below is a proposed visioning framework.

## Visioning Activities in the Self-Organizing Firm: A Proposed Framework

In a self-organizing firm, vision activities are part of the overall self-organization activities. According to this view, it is not the sole domain of the CEO. Vision activities focus on the search for a desirable strategic end-state and articulating it by making the strategic decisions in Exhibits 16.2, 16.3, and 16.4. Every box in these exhibits represents a set of choices to be made. A vision is formulated when all these elements are specified in a clear manner.

Vision activities require strategic collaboration from members of the firm. In fact, we labeled strategic collaboration, as "strategic" because it pertains to searching for and realizing the visions. If we examine vision activities, we can clearly see that they occur along two simultaneous tracks or processes. On one hand, there are strategic decisions to be made such as the choice of an opportunity arena, delineating a niche in it, crafting a concept of business, and so on. We label this as the strategic decision-making track. This track utilizes the scenario planning process (Chapter 11) to arrive at such decisions. On the other hand, these decisions have to be made in such a way that the employees own them. The activities involved here are labeled as "the ownership track." This track comprises a process for bringing members of the organization together to make decisions as a group. Each track is highlighted next.

### The Strategic Decisions Track

This track is essentially a strategic planning process. It comprises three main phases: preparation, envisioning the future worldview, and formulating the vision of the firm.

1. Preparation

In preparing for making vision decisions, two steps must be taken at the outset. First, a time frame for the vision must be established. Is this going to be the vision for the next five years? Ten years? A time horizon serves two purposes. It puts a deadline for achieving the vision and hence the organization will be accountable for realizing it. At the same time, the horizon sets a span for extending our view of the future. It is different to peer into the future five years than ten years from now.

Second, given this time horizon, the next step is to make projections that span it. Activities here include:

- Analysis: As specified in Chapter 8, this includes macro and microanalysis.
- Scenarios construction: As outlined in Chapter 9, this involves the generation of the alternate scenarios for the firm's environment and industry for the specified time horizon.
- An issues analysis: As described in Chapter 10, this will yield a set of strategic issues. These can be valuable in nudging the firm's vision one way or the other.

2. Envisioning Future Worldview

In this phase, a view of the world (Exhibit 16.3) in which the firm will operate is firmed up. The scenarios and issues analysis should help in arriving at a picture of what the world might look like. The most likely scenarios for the industry and the environment can be used as outlines for the worldview. Such a worldview will show the various opportunity arenas open for the firm in which it can stake a strategic position. It also highlights the key success factors from which the firm must choose some, to help it play the game. The use of scenario planning is essential to determine the effect of choosing one arena versus another, or one set of key success factors instead of another.

3. Making Strategic Choices—Visionary Decisions

In light of the envisioned view of the world in the future, a number of vision decisions have to be made; again using the scenario planning process to generate alternatives and to choose from among them. We must stress that these decisions must be internally consistent. No one choice can cancel out another. Hence, there might be considerable movement back and forth to align one decision with another. The strategic decisions to be made here are:

- Share of an opportunity arena.
- A certain number of key success factors.
- A choice of purpose.
- A concept of the firm's business model.
- A specification of the firm's competencies based on the choice of the key success factors as selected above.
- A specification of the core values that will characterize the firm and set it apart from others in the industry.
- A delineation of expected outcomes.

## The Ownership Track

From a decision-making viewpoint, vision formulation appears to be a straightforward strategic planning exercise. With respect to ownership, there are two fundamental challenges for the CEO. The first is how to get the vision decisions made in such a way that employees own into them. The second is how to make an overall vision for the firm surface? A possible process is proposed below based on Quigly's concept presented earlier. The steps are as follows:

1. The CEO can start by formulating a vision project team drawn with multi-level representation. This team will be charged with the responsibility of drawing a visioning process

for the firm, assembling unit visions, and managing the schedule for the whole process so that the vision would be ready on time. This team should report directly to the CEO.

2. Next, he/she asks each first-line unit to formulate two visions (using the process of the formulation track described above): a *macro vision* for the whole company, and within it a *micro vision* for their unit. These visions are to be submitted to the vision project team.

3. Once the vision project teams assemble the units' macro visions, the CEO organizes a series of localized conferences taking a few units at a time. The purpose of each conference is to synthesize group visions into one master vision for the firm in its totality. The main task here is to arrive at a consensus because some of these visions may be radically different. The conference is a tool to reconcile these differences and arrive at some agreement on a master vision. This is not an easy task but it has to be done. The result of these conferences will be a smaller number of master visions.

4. Given the small number of master visions, the vision project team assimilates them into one master vision with the participation of the CEO. Care must be taken here to make this process objective and fair. This is not an opportunity for the CEO to manipulate the system by infusing his/her pre-established vision and hide under the guise of self-organization. However, the role of the CEO must be placed in the proper perspective. The CEO is the one ultimately responsible for the choice of a vision. His/her leanings carry a heavier weight. A CEO is paid to lead. Vision is a key leadership instrument.

5. Once the master vision synthesis is formulated, it will be treated as a tentative master vision for the firm. The next task is to bring it down the first line units again. This is accomplished through a series of localized conferences to present the master vision to them. At this point, the CEO and the vision team must be ready to deal with further objection and open-minded enough to incorporate good ideas that may materialize. It is at these conferences that people can be enrolled and committed as Senge and Quigly suggested. Hopefully, every unit will see some of its ideas in the master vision and conclude that it is the people's creation, not the CEO's.

6. Writing up the vision statement: As the master vision emerges in the hands of the vision project team, the vision ideas need to be written in the proper language. The use of attractive prose is essential. The vision statement must inspire a sense of pride. The language must be motivating. The prose must express all the components in the vision. One-sentence vision statements must be avoided, as they are too generic to serve as guides for people. A business firm's vision is too complex to be captured in one or two sentences. A vision statement has to reflect the many facets of the company. In Exhibit 16.8, Welch shows us how to capture this complexity. He put his vision in a matrix form. The wording of the vision statement cannot be platitudes. Platitudes are too generic to be implemented. Furthermore, people perceive them as insincere. Care should be taken *not* to fall into the trap of writing vision statements like those appearing in today's corporate "boiler-plate," "cookie-cutter" type of vision statements.

7. Now that the master vision is finalized, the CEO then becomes the keeper of the vision. He/she can passionately drive the organization to make it a reality.

In concluding our discussion on vision formulation, two points must be stressed. First, although the above process is lengthy and expensive, it achieves results. Employees own into the vision. They will be predisposed to act it out on a daily basis. Second, the vision process should be a continuous organizational activity. An organization does not formulate a vision and hold it constant without regard to the changing conditions in the marketplace. A vision is constant and tentative at the same time. It is constant in that it is held front and center in the present. It is tentative in that, the marketplace is turbulent. Today's vision might be obsolete or even disastrous tomorrow. Hence, a vision must be reviewed and revised continuously. The visioning exercise is thus never ending. It has to be integrated in the process of doing business so that everyone can be on the look out for better strategic end-states for the firm.

# GUIDING VISIONING ACTIVITIES

According to the vision formulation framework proposed above, the CEO entrusts the self-organizing firm to generate its vision as part of its business activities. The search for and making the vision happen is a "routine" business activity in the self-managing firm. This begs the question, what is the role of the CEO with respect to vision? The process outlined in the preceding section is based on one major premise. Visioning is a strategic collaboration activity, part of the firm's groupthink or hive-mind and swarm behavior (Chapter 5). One of the basic premises of strategic leadership is that the CEO is the person who induces and orchestrates strategic collaboration. As the person in charge of strategic collaboration, the CEO has many opportunities for corralling and steering the diverse visions of different, empowered modules. The role of the CEO thus focuses on bringing about strategic collaboration and steering it toward the best possible vision while capitalizing on every ounce of intelligence in the firm.

In a self-organizing firm, vision emerges out of the many visions of empowered modules. The framework proposed above affords the CEO several opportunities to steer them. Inducing and orchestrating strategic collaboration was presented in Chapter 6. The principles suggested in that chapter apply to the context of vision formulation as well. We revisit them below.

## Creating an Environment Conducive to Collaboration for Visioning

From the outset, the CEO must create the environment that will stimulate collaboration among people to generate, commit to, and update the firm's vision. This includes:

- Cultivating Paradigms: The crucial task here is implanting seminal thoughts to develop a groupthink or a hive-mind for the organization. The seminal thoughts can include the firm's business model, opportunity arenas, key success factors, and the like. Thoughts also can emphasize the importance of employee ownership of the vision.
- Building Shared Goals: The key goal, to be shared here, is to choose and define a destination for the firm.
- Defining Boundaryless Roles: As suggested in the proposed framework in the preceding section, the firm's vision is everyone's responsibility. Visioning should be part of everyone's role set. Each module should have two visions. The first is a vision for itself given that it is a part of the organization. The second is a broader one, a vision of the firm as a whole.
- Networking: A common vision can emerge only if all modules have all the information. Free information facilitates collaboration and working together to generate a vision for the firm.
- Orchestrating Shared Workspace: Clearly, sharing workspace can homogenize individual thoughts and visions. People who work together tend to envision things along the same lines and arrive at similar visions.
- Charging Emotions: Vision galvanizes people regardless of their differences. The vision contains the promise of the future. Visioning gives people the opportunity to

secure their own future by creating a better future for the firm. It is a time for opportunism and forming aspirations. It is a platform for generating excitement among people.

## Inducing and Stimulating Conversation on Vision

Conversation is the prerequisite for collaboration. It is important to get people to talk about vision all the time, not only to make it happen, but also to check its validity, relevance, and viability. A platform for conversation can be periodic conferences on vision, to listen to people in the trenches. Strategic planning sessions are also a good tool for stimulating conversation on vision.

## Marshalling Strategic Conversation to Vision Action

The important roles of the CEO here are:

- Developing and Cultivating Frameworks for Visioning: The concept of vision proposed here can be utilized as a framework for visioning activities. The various boxes in the diagrams tell people what decisions need to be made in the course of formulating a vision. The proposed visioning process outlined in the previous section also shows the flow of vision action in the firm, the strategic decisions and the ownership tracks.
- Building Collaborative Networks: Collaborative networks facilitate the emergence of vision. They are also needed to make the vision a reality. It is crucial to build these networks continuously.
- Staffing Critical Positions: As outlined above, visioning is a pervasive activity. It needs champions. The appointment of vision teams and leaders for such teams is crucial for making visioning activities happen.
- Allocating Resources: Visioning activities cost time and money. If people are to collaborate to generate a common vision, the CEO must allocate the necessary resources. Allocating resources also gives the CEO an effective weapon for steering vision activities.

## Affirming Accountability and Governance

Vision, being the central focus of the firm, is the responsibility of everyone. The roles of the various modules in generating visions and implementing them must be defined. People must be held accountable for performing these roles and for ensuring that the firm has a viable, valid vision.

## Exercising Personal Influence

It goes without saying that the vision is so crucial for the firm and for the CEO. Vision is the direction of the firm. The CEO is paid to set a direction for the firm. To fulfill this responsibility, the CEO must be personally involved by taking a leadership role in the visioning process. They are long-term decisions. They call for committing the firm's resources. In the proposed process, there is ample room for the CEO to exercise personal influence. There are many tools at his/her disposal including legitimizing the vision by proclaiming it, approval, issuing directives for implementation, leading the making of vision decisions, the appointment of vision project teams, allocating resources, management by walking around, preaching the vision, and so on. Visioning is perhaps the most important opportunity to practice strategic leadership.

## CONCLUSION

This chapter focused on "vision" as a fundamental aspect of the four-pronged strategy for responding to turbulence. The literature was reviewed. Ideas from the literature and from CEO practices were integrated in the form of a conceptual framework that captures the essence of vision. Some properties of vision need to be emphasized at this point:

1. The vision is a complex entity. It comprises many elements. *It cannot be captured in one or two sentences or even one or two paragraphs as we see in corporate public relations materials*. A vision is the blueprint of the desired future of the firm. As such, it has to be done in detail. Some argue that it has to be stated in short and powerful (compelling) language. However, this will produce slogans rather than true visions. The vision statement is an important strategic document. It states the long term strategy of the firm.

To illustrate this danger, consider the predicament of CEO Gerald Langeler.[50] His team began with the vision "Beat Daisy" (his biggest competitor) which left the company without a vision once Daisy was beaten. Next, he envisioned the company as a conglomerate of six businesses, which spread the company too thin; resulting in the deterioration of the six businesses. Then, he came up with the vision "the 10X Imperative." It required each operational and staff unit to explore ways and means to increase their productivity by a factor of ten within ten years. He found the words "10X Imperative" were too abstract without being inspirational, with an elusive goal, and arbitrary measurement. Inspired by another company vision statement, he arrived at the vision "change the way the world designed." Finding this to be too grand, the firm was without a vision for a while. Then, he discovered the vision as ". . . to be a company that grows and prospers by offering our customers solutions built on cooperative interactions with related companies." In desperation, he ends the description of his experience by saying, "Our current short, medium, and long-term vision is to build things people will buy." All the time, he was searching for a magic single phrase or a slogan, not a detailed vision. Since these single phrases tended to be generic, they were not achievable. As a result, he kept jumping from one to another.

2. A vision has to be ambitious and perhaps "unrealistic" in order to provide "stretch" for the organization.
3. Vision is the same as "direction." It also serves as the compass that gives the CEO and the people a sense of direction as they navigate and steer the firm in the turbulent environment, the "business world."
4. Vision is one of the functions of the self-organizing system. It should not be monopolized by the leader. Visions, that have a better chance of being acted out, emerge in a bottom-up fashion.
5. Because the firm exists in a turbulent environment, the vision is developed under conditions of ambiguity, complexity, and uncertainty. Vision thoughts are "tentative" at best. It is through vision that we probe the future. There is a chance that today's vision will become the "wrong" one for tomorrow. The vision thus has to be a *living* entity; part of a continuously changing response to a continuously changing situation.
6. Although a chosen vision is viewed as tentative, it is expected to remain stable over a time horizon. This may sound paradoxical, but such is the nature of functioning under conditions of turbulence. Vision is some order in chaos. The vision has to be held temporarily constant to provide direction. However, the firm must be always on the look out for better ones. Certainly, it should not be pursuing a vision that is out of touch with reality.

7. The vision has an essential role in strategic leadership:

- It is an instrument for measuring achievement. If the organization fulfills the vision, it has scored a victory against the forces of turbulence.
- It is a governance tool. It channels and "molds" the efforts of everyone and unifies the organization. It gives legitimacy to actions. It is a boundary to harness the diverse activities of numerous persons in an organization.
- It is a motivational tool. It is expected to inspire people to set their sights higher all the time. There is an element of stretch in good visions. Komatsu was a fledgling manufacturer of tractors in it early days. Yet, it "unrealistically" set its sights on becoming an export, global corporation, and even beating the world leader, Caterpillar. It turned its people on. They succeeded and Komatsu emerged as a world leader in the earth moving industry.

8. The vision process is difficult, demanding, and uncertain. Making the vision happen, is much more difficult. A vision will not become reality unless members of the organization internalize it and act it out minute-by-minute, hour-by-hour, day-by-day, month-by-month, and year-by-year.

9. Vision, maneuver, capability, and structure are four aspects of one thing, the strategy of the firm. It is difficult to pin point which precedes which or which drives which. Sometimes, the vision is established first and from that point onward, it will guide the other three. Other times, the vision emerges after a number of maneuver rounds. It becomes part of "self-discovery," a defining moment in the history of every firm. Sometimes, capability shapes the vision, e.g., IT capability in e-businesses. Sometimes, structure drives vision. The way the company is organized influences its concept of itself or vision. For example, the multi-divisional structure of GM shapes its vision in the automotive business, "a car for every purse and every taste."

# ENDNOTES

1. Harvard Business School, *Taco Bell Corp*, Case Study # 9-692-058 (Rev. April 20, 1994), p. 5.

2. Larwood, L., C.B. Falbe, M.P. Krieger, and P. Miesing, "Structure and Meaning of Organizational Vision, *Academy of Management Journal*, June 1995, pp. 740–786.

3. Tichy, N. and R. Charan, "Speed, Simplicity, Self-Confidence: An Interview with Jack Welch," *Harvard Business Review*, September–October, 1989, p. 113.

4. Belasco, J.A. and R.C. Stayer, *Flight of the Buffalo: Soaring to Excellence, Learning to Let Employees Lead*, New York, NY: Warner, 1993, p. 90.

5. Larwood, et al, op. cit., p. 740.

6. Collins, M.C. and J.I. Porras, "Building Your Company's Vision," *Harvard Business Review*, September–October, 1996, p. 66.

7. Collins, M.C. and J.I. Porras, "Organizational Vision and Visionary Organizations," *California Management Review*, Fall 1991, pp. 30–31.

8. Abell, D.F., *Managing With Dual Strategies*, New York, NY: The Free Press 1993, p. 219.

9. Robert, M., *Strategic Thinking: Charting The Future Direction of Your Organization*, Australia, Decision Sciences International, Ltd., 1983, p. 2.

10. Ibid., p. 2.

11. Roberts, op. cit.

12. Bennis, W. and B. Nanus, *Leaders: The Strategies For Taking Charge*, New York, NY: Harper Collins, 1985, p. 89.

13. Nanus, B., *Visionary Leadership*, San Francisco, CA: Jossey-Bass, 1992, p. 8.

14. Tregoe, B., J.W. Zimmerman, R.A. Smith, and P. Tobia, *Vision in Action*, New York, NY: Simon & Schuster, Inc., 1989, p. 12.

15. Tregoe et al., op. cit.

16. Day, G., *Market Driven Strategy*, New York, NY: The Free Press, 1990, p. 15.

17. Wilson, I., "Realizing The Power Of Strategic Vision," *Long Range Planning*, vol. 25, no. 5, 1992, pp. 18–28.

18. Wilson, op. cit., 1992, p. 21.

19. Quigly, op. cit., p. 5.

20. Quigly, op. cit.

21. Quigly, op. cit.

22. Abel, op. cit., p. 219.

23. Collins and Porras, op. cit.

24. Ibid., p. 76.

25. Kouzes, J.M. and B.Z. Posner, "Envisioning Your Future: Imagining Ideal Scenarios," *The Futurist*, May–June 1996, pp. 14–19.

26. Chakravarthy, B.S. and P. Lorange, *Managing The Strategy Process: A Framework For A Multibusiness Firm*, Englewood Cliffs, NJ: Prentice-Hall, 1991, p. 16.

27. Mason, A.J., R.O. Mason, K.E. Dickel, R.B. Mann, and R.J. Mockler, *Strategic Management: A Methodological Approach*, 4th Ed., Reading, MA: Addison-Wesley, 1995, p. 73.

28. Thompson, Jr., A.A. and A.J. Strickland III, *Strategic Management: Concepts and Cases*, Tenth Edition, Boston, MA: Irwin/McGraw-Hill, 1998, p. 27.

29. Collins, M.C. and J.I. Porras, "Organizational Vision and Visionary Organizations," *California Management Review*, Fall 1991, pp. 30–31.

30. Stewart, T.A., "A Refreshing Change: Vision Statements that Make Sense," *Fortune*, September 30, 1996, p. 195.

31. Hamel, G., and C.K. Prahalad, *Competing For The Future*, Boston, MA: Harvard Business School, 1994, p. 31.

32. Drawn from Jones, P. and L. Kahaner, *Say It and Live It: The 50 Corporate Mission Statements That Hit the Mark*, New York, NY: Currency Books, 1995.

33. Lucier, C.E. and J.D. Trosiliere, "The Trillion-Dollar Racer to 'E'," *Strategy & Business*, First Quarter, 2000, pp. 6–14.

34. Hamel and Prahalad, op. cit.

35. Ibid., p. 117.

36. Tichy, N. and R. Charan, "Speed, Simplicity, Self-Confidence: An Interview with Jack Welch," *Harvard Business Review*, September–October, 1989, p. 114.

37. Harvard Business School, "Jack Welch: General Electric's Revolutionary," Case # 9-394-065, Rev. April 12, 1994.

38. Source: James Buaughman's unpublished manuscript "Problems and Performance of the Role of Chief Executive in the General Electric Company, 1892–1974" as repotted in Tichy, N. and S. Sherman, *Control Your Destiny Or Someone Else Will, How Jack Welch Is Making General Electric the World's Most Competitive Company*, New York, NY: Doubleday, 1993, p. 270.

39. Tichy and Sherman, op. cit., p. 347.

40. Hickman and Silva, op. cit., 1984, pp. 157–173.

41. Wilson, op. cit.

42. Nanus, op. cit., pp. 218–223.

43. Tichy and Charan, op. cit., p. 113.

44. Harvard Business School, *Pepsi's Regeneration, 1990–1993*, Case # 9-395-048, Rev. March 19, 1996.

45. Ibid., p. 1.
46. Ibid., the excerpt was drawn from the content of pages 2 though 5.
47. Senge, 1990, pp. 218–223.
48. Quigly, op. cit., pp. 59–112.
49. Langeler, G., "The Vision Trap," *Harvard Business Review*, March–April, 1992, pp. 46–55.

CHAPTER
# 17

# Strategic Renewal

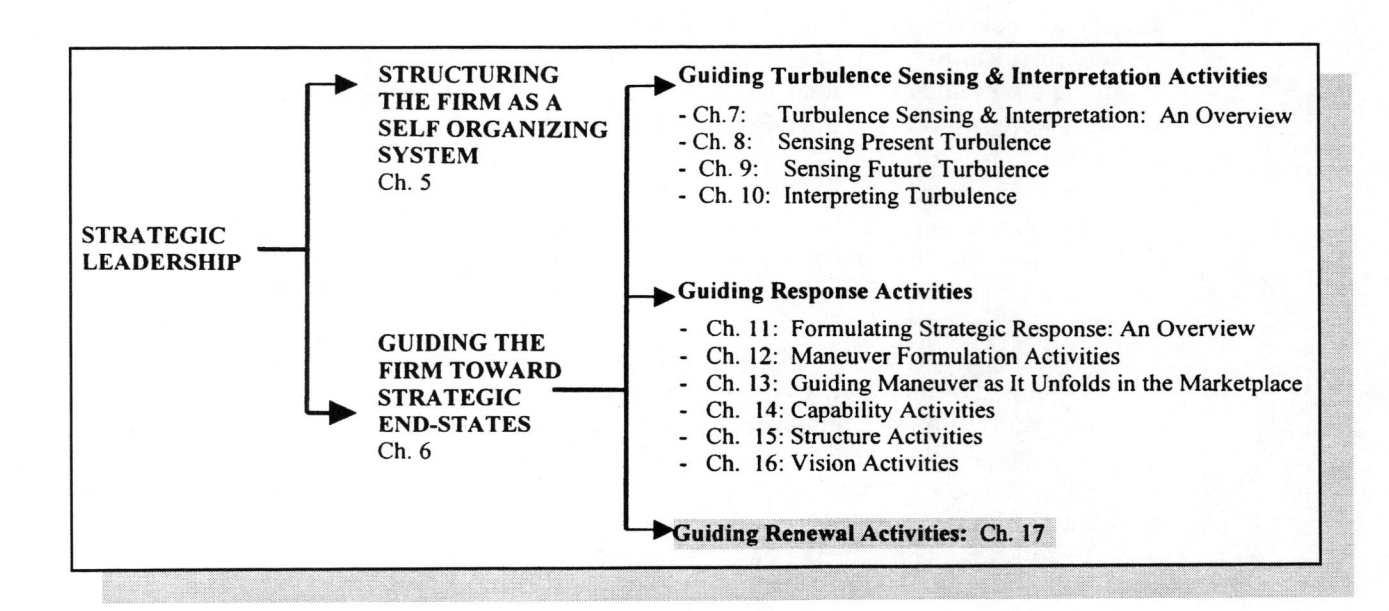

```
STRATEGIC          STRUCTURING              Guiding Turbulence Sensing & Interpretation Activities
LEADERSHIP         THE FIRM AS A
                   SELF ORGANIZING            - Ch.7:   Turbulence Sensing & Interpretation: An Overview
                   SYSTEM                     - Ch. 8:  Sensing Present Turbulence
                   Ch. 5                      - Ch. 9:  Sensing Future Turbulence
                                              - Ch. 10: Interpreting Turbulence

                                            Guiding Response Activities
                   GUIDING THE                - Ch. 11: Formulating Strategic Response: An Overview
                   FIRM TOWARD                - Ch. 12: Maneuver Formulation Activities
                   STRATEGIC                  - Ch. 13: Guiding Maneuver as It Unfolds in the Marketplace
                   END-STATES                 - Ch. 14: Capability Activities
                   Ch. 6                      - Ch. 15: Structure Activities
                                              - Ch. 16: Vision Activities

                                            Guiding Renewal Activities: Ch. 17
```

317

The major distinguishing property of a self-organizing system is its capacity to reorganize itself in response to its environment without an externally imposed direction or plan. If we analyze the system as it interfaces with its environment, we can discern two major dynamics. First, the environment of today (to which the system is currently responding) is only one transient stage in a series of never ending transformations. Today's e-economy, for example, is a temporary end-state. Before that, our economy was a manufacturing one, and preceding that, it was an agrarian economy. The environment is always evolving.

Second, the self-organizing system interfaces with its present environment through the activities of sensing and interpreting impending turbulence and making a strategic response to it. However, at the same time, it also reconfigures itself continuously to stay in alignment with its environment as it progresses from one state to another. We call this strategic renewal because it amounts to reinventing the company, its strategic stance in the marketplace, its strategy, and the redefinition of its strategic end-state. The self-organizing firm actually evolves with its evolving environment. This is what sets it apart from the traditional, command-and-control organizations. Because it is constrained by a central authority, a command-and-control firm may perform well at a given point in time, but soon finds itself obsolete when the environment assumes the next state. The current business scene is full of companies that were surprised by the e-business revolution and are currently scurrying to transform themselves.

A self-organizing system responds to its environment along two tracks. The first is a shorter-term one, undertaking a strategic response, as shown in Chapters 8 to 16. The second track is a longer term one. It deals with activities involving the renewal of the firm. At any given point in time, the focus of renewal is bringing "the next generation company." We use the term generation here as it describes technical systems such as computers for example. A computer system starts with the first configuration, and then advancements bring a second generation, and a third and so on. We know that the next generation is always around the corner. Similarly, the self-organizing firm is always working on bringing in the next generation company. As it makes the next generation company a reality, it moves on to the next generation and so on indefinitely (unless it merges with, or is acquired by, another firm or goes out of business). This is how a firm ensures its survival in an evolving environment.

To illustrate, consider the case of General Electric and how it evolved from 1981 to 1991. Exhibit 17.1 shows the change of the firm's business mix. Its manufacturing core business went down from 51% of its earnings in 1981 to 26% in 1991. By contrast, its service business increased from 19% in 1981 to 35% by 1991. Two dynamics have to be observed here. First, GE was responding to the challenges of the 1980s, e.g., globalization, foreign competition, and the restructuring of the economy from a manufacturing economy to a knowledge economy. Yet, while it was responding to these developments on a daily basis, it was also transforming itself into a new company.

|            | Percent of Earnings |       |
| :--------: | :-----------------: | :---: |
| Business   | 1981                | 1991  |
| Core       | 51%                 | 26%   |
| Technology | 30%                 | 39%   |
| Service    | 19%                 | 35%   |

Exhibit 17.1: Transformation of GE[1]

This chapter is concerned with renewal activities. It starts with an examination of the renewal phenomenon by surveying reported corporate renewal practices. Next, it attempts to define the range of renewal activities in a self-organizing firm. Finally, it concludes with a discussion of the role of the CEO in leading the firm's renewal effort. The presentation will focus on the case of the single-business firm since it is the most frequent model of business organization.

# CORPORATE RENEWAL

The decades of the 1980s and the 1990s witnessed numerous renewal efforts by many corporations. Research by Waterman and Ghoshal and Bartlett attempted to identify and catalogue corporate renewal practices. After examining several companies, Waterman observed that firms that succeeded in renewing themselves, engaged in eight main practices as follows:[2]

1. Informed Opportunism: Firms tended to remain alive to opportunity. They did not insist on implementing a detailed strategic plan right or wrong. They scouted for opportunity within the bounds of a broad direction that they chose. They kept track of rising opportunities and then moved swiftly to exploit them.
2. Direction and Empowerment: Renewing companies practice capitalizing on the intelligence of everyone in the organization. They expect creative inputs from all employees. They give up control in order to free employees to probe the environment to discover emerging opportunities.
3. Friendly Facts; Congenial Controls: As Waterman states, "The renewing companies treat facts as friends, and financial controls as liberating."[3] Renewing companies display a voracious hunger for facts to stay on top of the changing environment. They are always making comparisons, rankings, and measurements in order to move decisions away from the realm of whims and gut feel. They also maintain disciplined, real-time financial controls. Employees view these controls as benign boundaries that allow them to act and create freely, within these boundaries.
4. A Different Mirror: Renewing companies are always getting reality checks. They are curious, open, and inquisitive in the pursuit of seeing reality as it is, not as they wish it to be. In that sense, they look at themselves in a different mirror, the reality mirror; with a view toward breaking old habits and examining new possibilities for evolving in the future.
5. Teamwork, Trust, Politics, and Power: Waterman described practices here as follows:

> "Renewers constantly use words such as *teamwork* and *trust*. They are relentless in fighting office politics and power contests, and in breaking down the we/they barriers that paralyze action. There are heroic leaders, but not lone rangers: little emphasis on charisma; rather they are outstanding people, supported by others with complementary skills. Most renewing companies had a calm at the center; there was quiet intensity and determination without the helter-skelter behavior, slamming doors, shouting voices, frenetic movement, and general bedlam that poses for productive activity in stagnating companies."[4]

6. Stability in Motion: Renewing companies always manage to find a balance between change and stability. On one hand, they engage in creative destruction where they eliminate bureaucracy and procedure. They continuously remove barriers to action in an effort to induce change. At the same time, these firms do this against a base of intrinsic stability. They have a structure, but it is a fluid, self-changing one. They encourage breaking existing structures to avoid the risk of being stuck with an obsolete structure. People are encouraged to

seek forgiveness, not permission. They have budgetary systems, but budgets are used as a framework to stimulate creativity, not to constrain action.

7. Attitudes and Attention: Renewers tend to display certain attitudes, particularly viewing change as an opportunity, not a threat. They expect the best from people, realizing fully that people do live up to expectations. They give attention because they have a bias for action. Words are backed by commensurate behavior. Ideas come alive. This is how they are able to bring about concrete change.

8. Causes and Commitment: As Waterman observed, "Renewing organizations seem to run on causes."[5] Causes are very crucial for renewal. As people pursue a cause, they change to stay with the cause. This change adds up to renewal. Renewing companies, therefore, constantly review their causes in light of the issues suggested by the changing world around them. They also have a habit of turning tedious issues into overarching purposes, or noble causes. Causes are useless unless they translate into a commitment. Renewing companies always commit to their cause by allocating the needed resources and nurturing a cause during its life cycle.

Ghoshal and Bartlett studied a number of firms that adapted well to the business environment.[6] They suggested that these firms view themselves as a portfolio of processes, streams, or flows in the firm that occur contemporaneously. These are: the entrepreneurial process, the integration process, and the renewal process.

1. The Entrepreneurial Process: The entrepreneurial flow of activities is concerned with scouting for opportunities and exploiting them. This is supported by other activities such as developing the employees and supporting their initiatives. At the same time, top management establishes a stretching opportunity horizon and defines standards in terms of entrepreneurial results, i.e., how many new opportunities were exploited successfully.

2. The Integration Process: Activities in this stream focus on developing competencies and on coordinating the various operations in an entrepreneurial undertaking. At the same time, managers work on linking dispersed knowledge, skills, and best practices in the organization. Top management reinforces integration by institutionalizing a set of common norms and values to support collaboration and trust throughout the organization.

3. The Renewal Process: Renewing companies engrain this process at the various levels of the organization. At the trenches, the focus is continuous improvement and scouting for innovations. At the middle level, the attention is on managing the balance between short-term performance and long-term ambitions and vision. Top management's attention is on creating an overarching corporate purpose and ambition while challenging current achievements and paradigms.

Now that we know about how successful companies renew themselves, we attempt to develop a framework that organizes the elements of the renewal process.

# RENEWAL ACTIVITIES OF THE SELF-ORGANIZING FIRM

Our analysis of the activities of self-organizing firms resulted in a framework that comprises three main categories of activities. These are: connecting with the changing business environment, envisioning the next generation company, and becoming the next generation company. The framework is presented in Exhibit 17.2.

```
┌─────────────────────────────────────────────────────────────┐
│   ┌─────────────────────────────────────────────────────┐   │
│   │ Connecting with the Changing Environment:           │──▶│
│   │ Continuous Reality Checks                           │   │
│   └─────────────────────────────────────────────────────┘   │
│         │         ▲        │         ▲                      │
│         ▼         │        ▼         │                      │
│   ┌──────────────┐   ┌──────────────────┐                   │
│   │ Envisioning  │   │ Transformation:  │                   │
│   │ the Next     │──▶│ Becoming the Next│──▶                │
│   │ Generation   │   │ Generation       │                   │
│   │ Company      │   │ Company          │                   │
│   └──────────────┘   └──────────────────┘                   │
│   ············································▶              │
│              T    I    M    E                               │
└─────────────────────────────────────────────────────────────┘
```

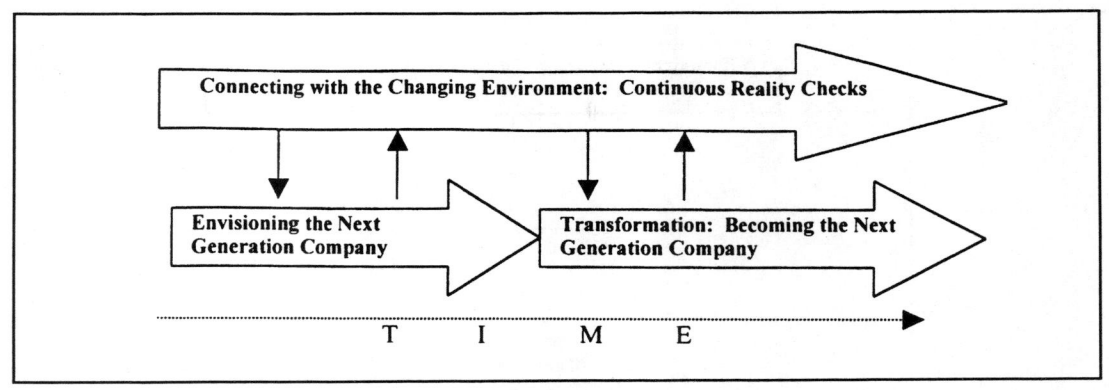

Exhibit 17.2: A Framework for Corporate Self-Renewal

## CONNECTING WITH THE CHANGING ENVIRONMENT

The first step in strategic renewal is plugging into the changing business environment. Connecting with the firm's environment encompasses four main activities:

- Mapping the unfolding environment.
- Mapping the firm's evolving strategic configuration.
- Mapping unfolding strategic end-states.
- Assessing unfolding end-states.

### Mapping the Unfolding Environment

Renewal is premised on the need for a change. To demonstrate the need for change, one must demonstrate that the environment has changed. The way to do this is to map the emerging landscape of the business environment. Therefore, the first step is to connect with the changing environment in order to provide a context for renewal. As we evaluate the performance of the firm's configuration in light of environmental change, we will be in a better position to decide whether the configuration needs to be changed and to what extent. In Chapter 8, we examined many methods for mapping the firm's environment such as environmental analysis, industry analysis, market analysis, and competitor analysis.

To illustrate, consider the unfolding environment in the retailing field right now. What is transpiring is the e-business landscape where retailers like Amazon.com are altering the face of retailing. Even a cursory search of the Web can show the extent to which the retailing landscape has changed. Virtually every product and many services are traded on the Net from parts and raw material to finished goods. Traditional brick-and-mortar retailers are quickly discovering that their business configuration is becoming obsolete. Many have undertaken renewal activities such as adding an e-business unit. Some might eventually become purely e-business.

### Mapping the Firm's Strategic Configuration

To be grounded in reality, we also need to obtain an up-to-date snapshot of the firm's strategic stance in the marketplace, its strategic configuration. The firm's business configuration is the way its components hang together at any point in time. A business configuration is a composite of seven interlocking elements as shown in Exhibit 17.3.

A business configuration comprises the following elements:

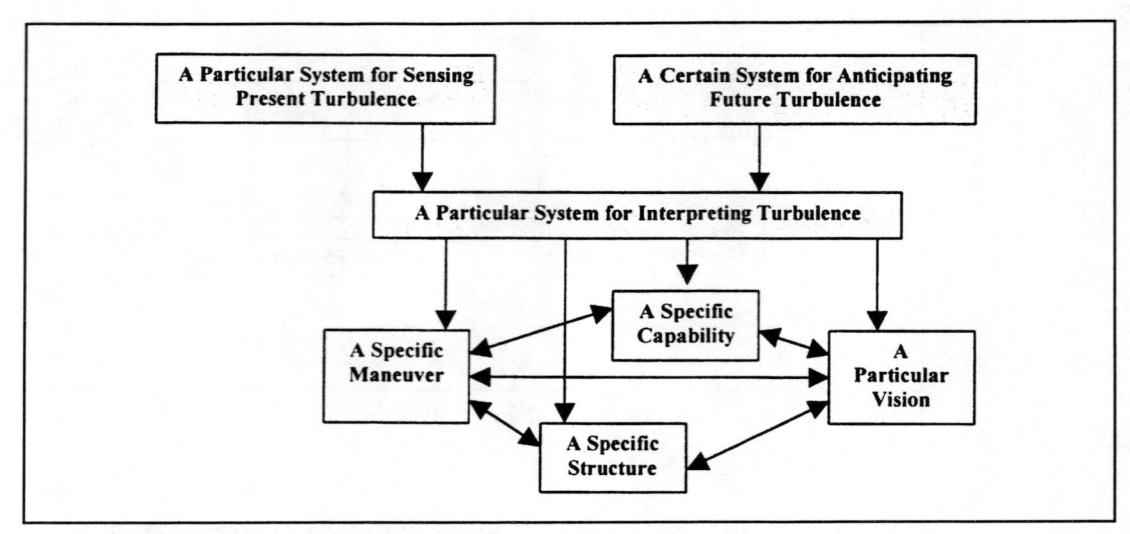

Exhibit 17.3: The Strategic Configuration of a Self-Organizing Firm

- The Chosen Configuration for Sensing Present Turbulence: Every firm has its own system for gathering intelligence data about its environment and industry. It utilizes certain frameworks for searching and organizing such data, e.g., the ones presented in Chapter 8. Furthermore, the process is carried by an organization, a system that assigns intelligence and surveillance data to various members of the organization with the understanding that they are to be carried out continuously.
- The Chosen Configuration for Sensing Future Turbulence: This is the process for anticipating the future (e.g., scenarios construction) and the organization for it. As part of self-organization, this responsibility has to be defined, distributed, and assigned to various members so that it is performed on a continuous basis.
- The Chosen Configuration for Turbulence Interpretation: This is the specific system for developing strategic issues and extracting them from turbulence data, the issues analysis process. Included in this configuration is assigning the organization the responsibility for conducting issues analysis on behalf of the firm, i.e., the individuals and groups who are entrusted with the tasks of developing the issue pool, conducting impact analysis, cross impact analysis, and so on as described in Chapter 10.
- The Chosen Configuration of the Firm's Maneuver: This is the firm's maneuver platform, including its particular strategic thrust, its specific business model, and its system of moves. Part of this configuration is the organizational structure for formulating and implementing maneuver.
- The Chosen Configuration of the Firm's Capability: This is the specific collection of the firm's resources, processes, and the chosen manner of using them (e.g., stretch and leverage practices) along with the organization for capability planning and upgrading.
- The Chosen Configuration of the Firm's Structure: This is the particular shape of the organization structure that the firm chose for itself, including modules, networks, hierarchy, governance mechanism, and work flow pattern (projects).
- The Chosen Configuration of the Firm's Vision: This encompasses the specific vision decisions, including the opportunity arena, purpose, business model, character, competencies, expected outcomes, and so on as described in Chapter 16.

We have to obtain a last-minute snapshot of our strategic configuration because it changes in the course of doing business. If we do not capture this change, we will be working with the configuration thinking that it is "X," but in reality, it is "Y." Generally, the configuration is formulated during the course of a certain encounter with turbulence. However, at the end of the encounter, the configuration might not be the same as the one intended in the plans. As the firm struggles with turbulence, modifications to the initial configurations will be made on the fly. As these incremental modifications add up, we can end up with a configuration that might not resemble the initial one. Such is the reality of operating in a turbulent world. Accordingly, we must pause, after each episode of confronting turbulence, to map the emerging configuration. This step is crucial. In order for the system to renew itself, it has to know how things stand. The renewal process is essentially the process of creating the next generation configuration.

## Mapping the Firm's Strategic End-State

The next step in connecting with reality is to identify and assess the strategic end-states that the firm arrives at. If we are to plot these end-states and correlate them with the evolving strategic configurations, we will be in a position to see the relationship among them. Is our configuration producing satisfactory end-states given our tracking of the changing environment? If it is, then we are on the right track so to speak. The firm is evolving with its evolving environment. This ideal however is rare. Most of the time, one or more of these three items is out of alignment. This will be the trigger for the renewal effort.

An important question suggests itself at this point: What constitutes a strategic end-state? How does one assess an end-state? Previously, we defined a strategic end-state as a profitable, defensive, and strategic position in the marketplace. We can elaborate further by defining it as shown in Exhibit 17.4. There are four major but interdependent components of

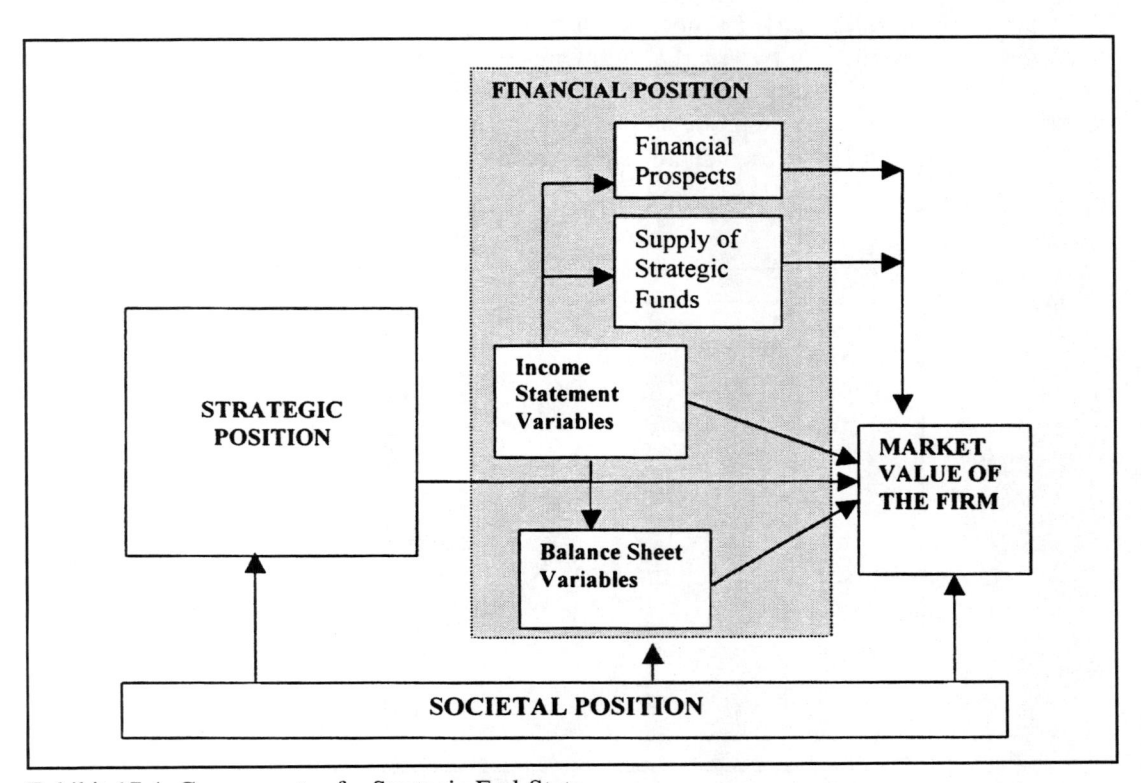

Exhibit 17.4: Components of a Strategic End-State

an end-state. The first one is the strategic position of the firm. This leads to the second, its financial position, which in turn affects its market value. Underlying all of them is the firm's societal position, which legitimizes its presence as a socio-economic unit.

## 1. Strategic Position

The term strategic position refers to the nature and dimensions of the niche that the firm occupies in the marketplace. The nature and dimensions of the strategic position depend on whether the firm is a single business or a multi-business firm. In the case of the single business firm, the strategic position is the number of market segments it serves and the product entries in each one of these segments. By contrast, the strategic position of the multi-business firm represents the range of industries it is in and the strategic positions of its business units (SBUs) in these industries. We will focus here on the single business firm since it is the most common case; keeping in mind that the multi-business firm is a conglomeration of single businesses (units, divisions, or subsidiaries).

The strategic position of the single business firm is a complex concept that encompasses six elements: (1) product-market position, (2) entrenchment, (3) freedom of action, (4) future readiness, and (5) competencies. Each of these variables must be read and ascertained. Their sum total represents the feedback from the marketplace. They tell whether the firm is on the right track or not. These are shown in Exhibit 17.5.

### 1.1. Product-Market Position

The market position is the "territory" that the firm occupies in the industry. Market position can be measured qualitatively in the form of: (1) a product-market matrix, and (2) a Boston Consulting Group's (BCG) Growth-Share Matrix. The product-market matrix (Exhibit 17.6) shows what products the company has and in what segments they exist. The market can be segmented based on a variety of criteria, e.g., income, lifestyle, or use. The spread (the X's) of the firm in the matrix represents the firm's market position. It illustrates a full product-market scope; an entry in each market segment. If, by contrast, the firm has two products in two market segments, the matrix would have revealed a limited market scope.

Market position can also be assessed by using BCG Growth-Share Matrix. This time, the entries are products. The x-axis represents the relative market share for each product; the product's market share as a fraction of the competing product with the largest market share.

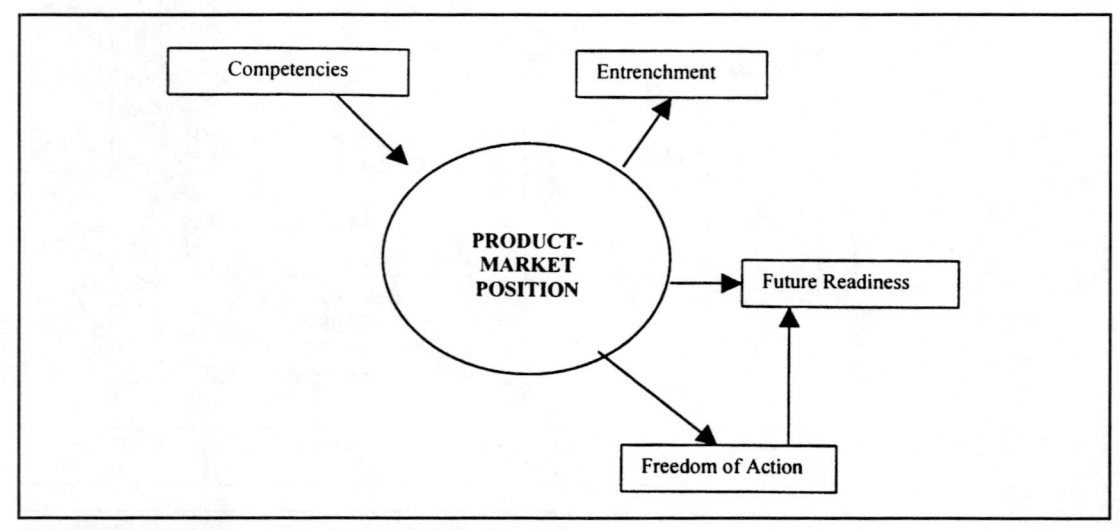

Exhibit 17.5: Components of Strategic Position

| Product | Market Segment ||||| 
| | Segment A | Segment B | Segment C | Segment D | Segment E |
|---|---|---|---|---|---|
| Product 1 | Version/Model 1 | Version/Model 2 | | | |
| Product 2 | Version/Model 1 | Version/Model 2 | Version/Model 3 | Version/Model 4 | Version/Model 5 |
| Product 3 | | Version/Model 1 | Version/Model 2 | | |
| Product 4 | | | | | Version/Model 1 |
| Product 5 | Version/Model 1 | Version/Model 2 | Version/Model 3 | Version/Model 4 | Version/Model 5 |

Exhibit 17.6: An Illustration of Market Position as Product-Market Scope

The y-axes represent the growth rate in the market for the product. The areas of the various circles represent the sales volume of the respective products. The BCG product matrix is shown in Exhibit 17.7. The distribution of the products in the quadrants would show where the firm's market position is in terms of growing or declining markets. If the products are in the star quadrant, the firm's strategic position is strong. If they fall in the "cash cow" or "dog" quadrants, then the firm's position is primarily in maturing or declining markets.

### 1.2. Entrenchment

Market position is simply the spread of the firm's product entries over a range of market segments. Equally important is the strength of this position. The strength can be assessed in terms of entrenchment. Entrenchment is measured by how expensive and difficult it would be for a competitor to dislodge the firm from a market segment(s). There are four aspects to entrenchment. When these aspects are assessed, they will tell how deeply entrenched the firm is. The four aspects are: (1) products relative position in the market place, (2) the overall position of the firm in its industry, (3) deterrents, and (4) positioning.

#### 1.2.1. Relative Position of the Firm's Individual Products

The Boston Consulting Group's Growth-Share Matrix can be used to indicate entrenchment by exposing the relative position of its various products. The matrix can be utilized in two ways as follows. First, if we construct it using products as entries in the four quadrants (Exhibit 17.7), it would tell how deeply entrenched the firm is. If the firm's products are in the star and cash cow category, then, as a whole, it is deeply entrenched. Star and cash cow products have the highest market share and this is a good measure of entrenchment. By contrast, if most of the products fall in the question marks and dog product categories, this will indicate lack of retrenchment since these products have a small market share, and hence, a weak market presence.

Second, if we construct the matrix using all the firms in the industry (Exhibit 17.8), it can tell us how deeply entrenched the firm is relative to its competitors. This time, we enter the firm and its competitors in the four quadrants. If our firm, as a whole, is a star, it is deeply entrenched since it falls in the high-growth/high market-share category. If it is a cash cow, it is also deeply entrenched. If the firm falls in the question marks or the dog category, its entrenchment is not established.

#### 1.2.2. The Overall Position of the Firm in Its Industry

Another way of portraying entrenchment is to examine the firm's overall position in its industry in relation to its competitors. A good device in this regard is the business position

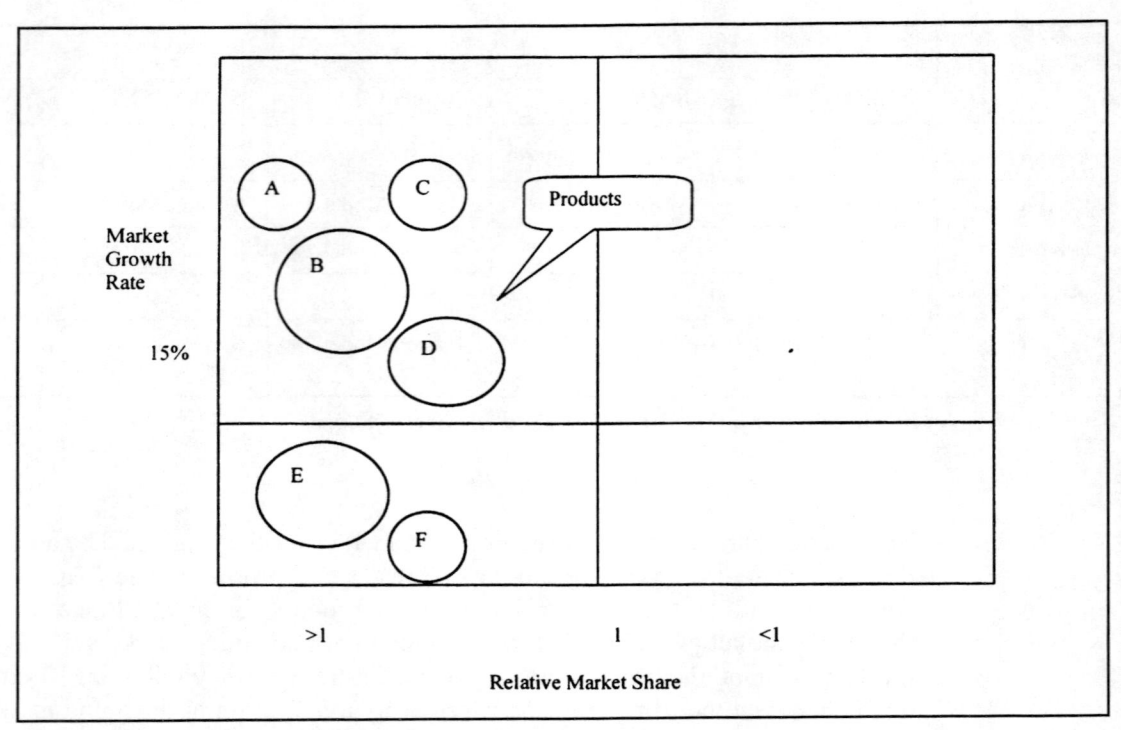

Exhibit 17.7: A Products BCG Matrix

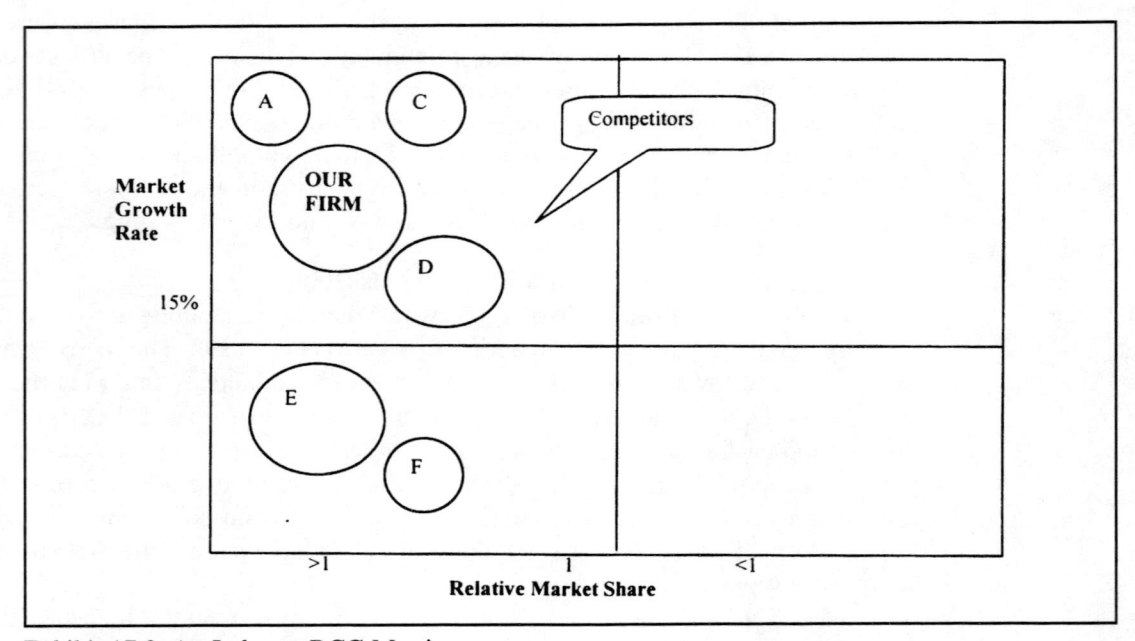

Exhibit 17.8: An Industry BCG Matrix

screens presented in Exhibit 17.9. The screen is a variant of a tool known as attractiveness analysis or GE's business screen. It locates the firm and its competitors on a two-dimensional graph. The x-axis represents the business strength of the firm, which comprises three intervals: strong, medium, and weak. The second dimension represents the industry's attractiveness and it has three intervals: high, medium, and low. Measures of competitive position include: market share, relative market share (firm's sales divided by the sales of its next biggest

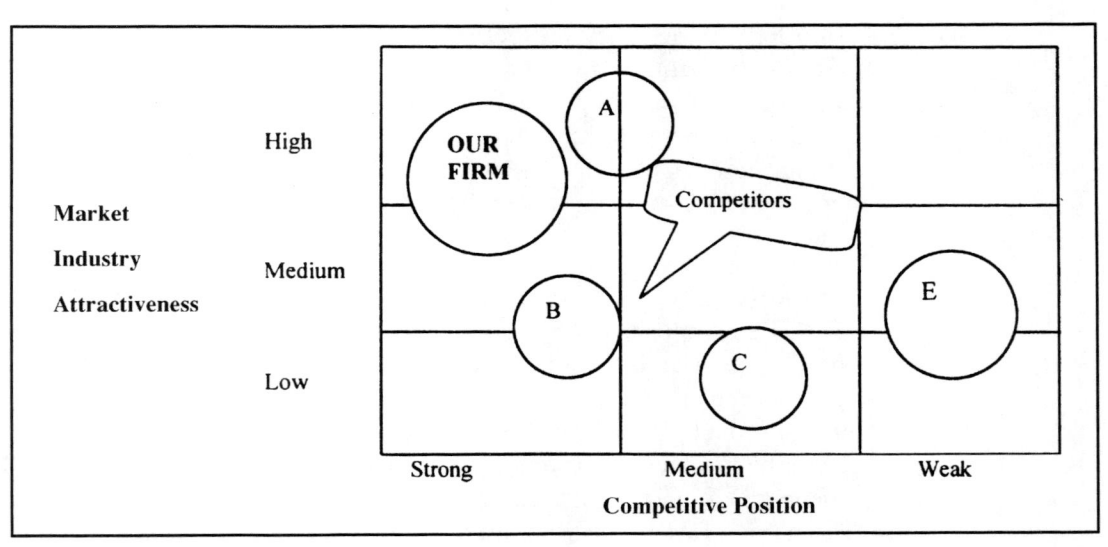

Exhibit 17.9: Business Position Screen

competitor), market share trends, level of capacity utilization, cost of raw material, sales force quality, distribution coverage, price competitiveness, relative product quality, number of accounts making 80% of the company's sales, relative R&D strength, relative ROI (firm's ROI divided by the leading competitor's ROI), and relative value added per employee (firm's value added per employee divided by leading competitor's value added per employee). A scale of 1–5 is contracted for each one of these measures. Our firm is then rated on each one of these measures and the average of all ratings would be the firm's measure of competitive position. This procedure is then repeated for each of the firm's strong competitors.

The y-axis can be quantified in a similar manner. The measures of attractiveness include: market size, growth per year, seasonality, bargaining power of suppliers, bargaining power of buyers, market structure (e.g., dominated by few like an oligopoly or widely scattered like perfect or monopolistic competition), intensity of retaliatory activities, contribution margins, stage in life cycle (maturity of the industry), degree of differentiation, customer characteristics and demographics, and unionization of workforce. Again a scale of 1–5 is constructed for each measure and the firm's market is rated accordingly. The average is then calculated. This average score of market attractiveness will then be used as the measure of market attractiveness and is entered on the y-axis.

The entries in the nine cells are the competing firms in such a market. If the firm falls in the cells that show weak position and unattractive markets, then the firm lacks entrenchment and its strategic position is deemed weak and unacceptable to stakeholders. The letters represent the names of all competitors. The circles represent sales volumes.

### 1.2.3. Deterrents

A firm's entrenchment can also be assessed in terms of the strength of deterrents that it enjoys in the face of competition. Deterrents include barriers to entry and intellectual property protection. Barriers to entry include scale of investments, production, and marketing needed to dislodge or dislocate the firm. It is difficult to think of dislodging a firm like GM or IBM because of the huge scale of investment needed in fixed assets. Another type of barrier is the strong relationship that the firm enjoys with suppliers, customers, and distributors. Such relationships translate into commitments that are not extendable to competitors (e.g., preferential treatment, discounts or rush orders), and thus provide some protection for the firm.

Intellectual property protection provides a good deterrent. Patent and copyright laws inhibit competitors from encroaching on a firm's position for a number of years. During that time, the firm can proceed, more or less freely, to exploit a temporary monopoly. In some situations, there are ways of getting around intellectual property protection. Principles underlying the design of the patented product can be altered in superficial ways to justify another patent for a similar product. Intellectual property protection is thus a relatively weak deterrent.

### 1.2.4. Positioning

This is a composite of two main positions: the individual positioning of the firm's products (product positioning) in the minds of customers, and, the positioning of the firm (company positioning) in the minds of the members of the industry (buyers, suppliers, competitors, etc.). Product positioning refers to where the product lies with respect to the dimensions that shape the product's perception in the customers' minds. For example, let us assume that the dimensions of perceiving a car are: advanced technology, quality, luxury, price, and styling. The name "BMW" is at the high end of each dimension. The name Hyundai, by contrast, might occupy the lower end, in the minds of car buyers. Positioning is a crucial measure of strategic position for it indicates the firm's entrenchment in the market. Eventually, positioning translates into sales.

Company positioning refers to where the firm lies if all the firms in the industry were arranged in an array along certain criteria. For example, IBM spent a great deal to achieve the positioning of "The Computer Company." Intel achieved the positioning of being the number one microprocessor company. The name Microsoft connotes a certain positioning in the software industry relative to other software firms. Company positioning is a crucial measure of strategic position. It is a measure of entrenchment. It translates into better product positioning. A chip made by Intel somehow achieves a better positioning than those made by other manufacturers. The reason is the institutional positioning that Intel achieved over the years.

### 1.3. Freedom of Action

A good indicator of strategic position is freedom of action. This refers to being in a position to undertake new initiatives to defend, enhance, or expand the firm's product-market scope and its business position. If the firm is "stuck" in a certain position and it is unable to reposition itself, its strategic position is not a healthy one. The opposite is true. Freedom of action is measured qualitatively by the firm's ability to respond to pressing change in the marketplace. If the firm can respond to pressing events in real time, i.e., as a market change occurs, then it has freedom of action, and it is deemed to be in a good strategic position. Freedom of action can be visualized by displays such as the one shown in Exhibit 17.10. If it takes the firm a long time to address pressing market changes, then it is inflexible and its strategic position is therefore threatened.

### 1.4. Future Readiness

The health of strategic position can be indicated by how well the firm is poised to face its future. Being poised to face the future can be indicated by three main factors. First, having a strong position in "tomorrow's products," i.e., products that are in the early stages of their life cycle and products in the growth cycle. Second, if the firm has sufficient reserves (resources, cash, and cash like), then it can use them to undertake initiatives to respond to whatever challenges the future may present. Third, the firm is unencumbered by problems and threats inherent in today's position.

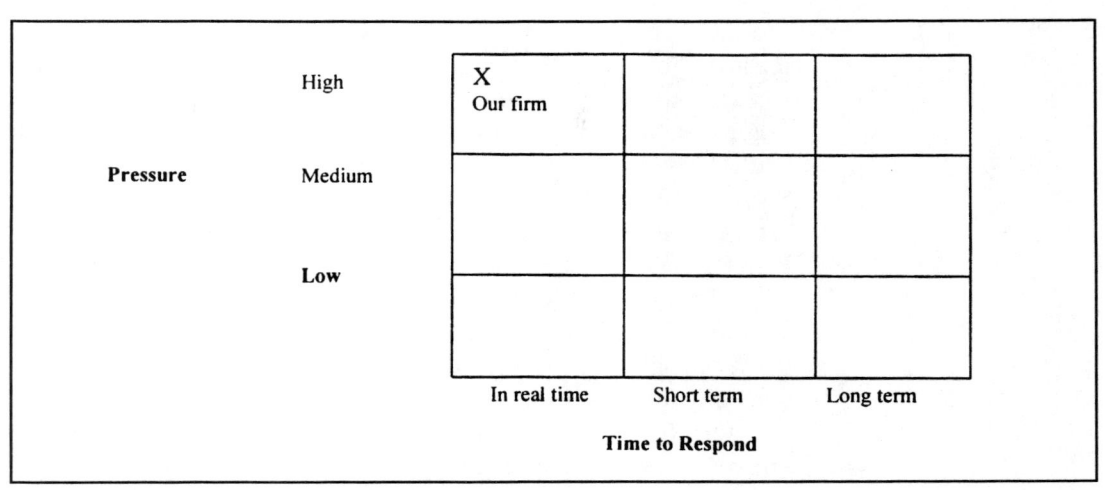

```
                    High    | X           |             |            |
                            | Our firm    |             |            |
                            |             |             |            |
          Pressure   Medium |             |             |            |
                            |             |             |            |
                            |             |             |            |
                    Low     |             |             |            |
                            |             |             |            |
                              In real time   Short term   Long term
                                        Time to Respond
```

Exhibit 17.10: Firm's Freedom of Action

### 1.5. Competencies

The concept of competencies was discussed in connection with capability (Chapter 14). It refers to the unique skill that a firm has in doing things. Competencies translate into disproportionate advantages in the marketplace. Their presence or absence is an indicator of the health of the firm's strategic position. They drive the product-market position.

## 2. Financial Position

The firm's financial position comprises a number of factors, namely, income statement variables, balance sheet variables, financial prospects, and supply of strategic discretionary funds.

### 2.1. Income Statement Variables

The income statement variables are the usual items that appear in such statements as measured by the appropriate accounting methods. Of critical importance here are the variables of sales, cost of goods sold, selling expenses, administrative expenses, and net income. The sales figure represents feedback from customers. If the firm is creating and delivering value for customers, this figure will show it. The expense categories indicate the effectiveness and efficiency of the firm's business activities. The bottom line, net income, is crucial, for it is the indicator of the firm's ability to create value for stakeholders particularly shareholders.

### 2.2. Balance Sheet Variables

The market value of the firm is present in the balance sheet variables. These variables represent the values of the firm's assets, liabilities, and shareholders/owners equity. In the final analysis, the rock bottom value of the firm equals its assets minus its liabilities, all adjusted to reflect current market conditions. The interplay between income statement and balance sheet variables is clear. The more activities in the income statement variables, the higher the values of the balance sheet variables.

To facilitate the monitoring of income statement and balance sheet variables, a number of indices can be used:

- Activity: Activity refers to assets turnover; as measured by ratios like inventory turnover, total assets turnover, receivables turnover, and the like.

- Liquidity: Liquidity refers to the convertibility-to-cash of the firm's assets. It is measured by ratios such as the current ratio and the acid test. Liquidity means that the firm would be able to meet its financial obligations. Failure to meet obligations, (e.g., payables, wages, and debt service), means that the firm is insolvent. This could lead to bankruptcy proceedings.
- Profitability: It is measured by ratios such as gross margin to sales, return on sales, earnings before taxes to sales, return on total assets, and many more.
- Efficiency: Efficiency indicates the utilization of resources. It is assessed by the ratio of the value of inputs to outputs. It is measured by ratios such as cost of goods sold to sales, gross margin to sales, selling expenses to sales, administrative expenses to sales, and many others. Efficiency is a crucial indicator of how well the company uses its resources to maximize their productivity.
- Financial Structure: This refers to the proportions of the various types of financing utilized, especially debt and equity. It is measured by ratios such as debt to equity, debt to total assets, equity to total assets, and the like. Financial structure is a key indicator of financial soundness. If the firm is financed by mostly debt, management loses control. The cost of debt becomes excessive and erodes profitability, especially at times of inflation and high interest rates. Debt service increases the cost of doing business.

The balance sheet variables embody two further important factors: financial prospects and supply of strategic funds. These are discussed next.

2.3. Financial Prospects

From the income statement and balance sheet variables, another important indicator can be computed, the financial prospects for the firm. These prospects influence the firm's market value. They boil down to a prediction of whether the firm will succeed or fail. Altman and LaFleur developed a measure, the z score, for predicting success and failure.[7] The z score can be computed as follows:

$z = 1.2\ X1 + 1.4\ X2 + 3.3\ X3 + 0.6\ X4 + 1.0\ X5$, where
$X1$ = ratio of working capital to total assets.
$X2$ = retained earnings to total assets.
$X3$ = earnings before interest and taxes to total assets.
$X4$ = market value of equity to book value of total liabilities.
$X5$ = Sales to total assets.

As can be seen from the equation above, the factor with the heaviest impact on probability of bankruptcy is $X3$, the ratio of earnings before interest and taxes to total assets. A z score below 1.8 indicates a high probability of going bankrupt. A z score above 3.0 indicates a low probability of bankruptcy. A score between 1.8 and 3.0 shows the firm as being in the gray area.

2.4. Supply of Strategic Discretionary Funds

Another important indicator embedded in the balance sheet and income statement variables, is the supply of strategic funds available for undertaking strategic projects. If the firm is a net cash generator, it will have funds available to finance initiatives to protect, maintain, or expand its market position. The quality of the firm's cash flows is a good measure of the supply of strategic funds. If the dominant source is cash from operations, as opposed to debt or equity, the supply of funds would be a sound, healthy one. Besides the supply of funds from operations, there are two more sources, the debt capacity and the potential for selling equity. These indicate the size of potential strategic funds available.

## 3. Market Value

One of the most critical elements of an end-state is the firm's market value. It is especially crucial for shareholders and the financial markets. This value is an index of how well it is doing in terms of creating value for two important constituencies: customers and stakeholders. There are many approaches for assessing the value of a company. The value of a firm can be as simple as the value of its shares in the financial markets on a given day. There are other variations of the concept of value that measure the effectiveness of the firm's leadership, such as the market value added, MVA (the difference between the capital the investors put into a company and the money they can take out) and economic value added, EVA (the after tax net operating profit minus the cost of capital). Clearly, the firm's market value is a function of its financial and strategic positions.

## 4. Societal Position

In the final analysis, the soundness of the firm's end-state depends on its societal position. A corporation is a legal person and a citizen. Its actions bring about certain socioeconomic and political consequences that can enhance or destroy its strategic and financial positions and its market value. Consider the vulnerability of the position of tobacco companies as we enter the 21st Century. Currently, they are being sued by various governments to compensate them for health cost. The product has been declared a health hazard. The same goes for firms that pollute the environment and destroy it.

## Assessing Unfolding End-States

Once an end-state is mapped, the next step is assessment. Assessment boils down to determining how the end-state came about and the extent to which it pleases the firm's stakeholders. There are three important variables to consider here. First is the behavior of the non-controllables, the changing environment itself. Did they behave as we anticipated them in our scenarios? Second is the behavior of our organization. Did it behave in a self-organizing manner? Finally, there is the desirability of the transpiring end-state. Does it please stakeholders?

To help with the assessment processes, the instrument presented in Exhibit 17.11 was constructed. The y-axis represents the behavior of the firm as it carried out the planned configuration. It has two categories: system behaved as planned, and the system did *not* behave as planned. The x-axis is reserved for the behavior of the non-controllables, the forces of turbulence. This also has two intervals: non-controllables behaved as anticipated, and non-controllables behaved in a surprising manner, i.e., *not* as expected.

The z-axis is reserved for plotting the desirability of the emerging end-state. There are two possible ends to this dimension: the end-state is desirable, or, it is *not* desirable. Desirability is assessed based on four criteria:

- Stakeholders' expectations—the extent to which the emerging end-state meets or exceeds such expectations.
- Past record—whether or not it exceeds previous achievement levels.
- Industry comparisons—whether or not it exceeds those of similar companies in the industry.
- Economic conditions—whether or not the emerging end-state is reasonable in light of the prevailing economic conditions. What is unacceptable at times of economic growth might be satisfactory at times of recession.

The graph shows eight cells representing different combinations of the three variables. Each cell can be labeled as shown in Exhibit 17.11. Such a label becomes a descriptor of the

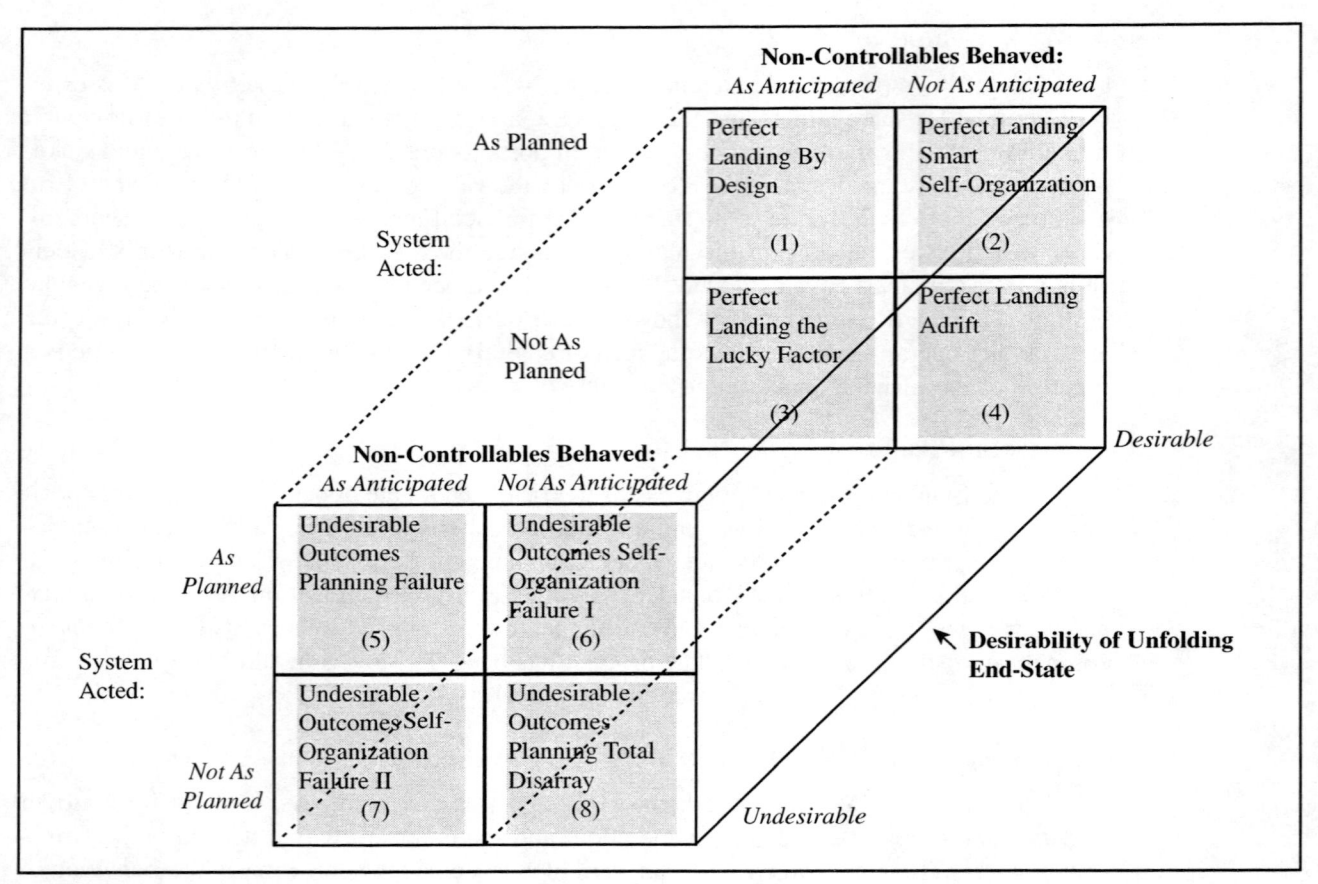

Exhibit 17.11: An Illustration of the Assessment of Results

end-state at which the firm arrived. The assessment involves slotting the end-state into one of the eight cells. The eight cells can now be assigned assessment labels to reflect our sentiments toward the emerging end-state. It is worth noting that placing the unfolding pattern in one of the cells is a judgment call. The assessment process should not be a mechanical, "paint by numbers" approach.

Placing an unfolding end-state in one of the eight cells is half the assessment. The other half is explaining it, or how it came about. Each of the eight cell labels summarizes a possible explanation of how the pattern was arrived at. Such an explanation would be helpful in finding out the main cause(s) behind a given end-state. This would be useful in suggesting the extent of the renewal action to be taken.

The eight assessment possibilities can be described as follows:

- Perfect Landing by Design: Cell (1) represents a perfect world in which a desirable end-state is taking place as planned and the world is behaving as anticipated in our constructed scenario. It is time to celebrate achievement and attack the future with confidence.
- Perfect Landing; Smart Self-Organization: In cell (2), the firm has achieved a desirable end-state although the unfolding realities surprised the firm and thwarted its plans. Nevertheless, self-organization allowed the firm to respond creatively to a surprising turn of events. Opportunities were exploited. Problems and threats were successfully dealt with. Here again, it is time to celebrate. It is also time to analyze our turbulence anticipation process (scenarios construction).

- Perfect Landing, the Luck Factor: In cell (3), the end-state is desirable. However, it was arrived at by luck. The firm is not behaving as planned although the world is unfolding as expected. The firm succeeded despite itself. In this case, there is a lot of room for soul searching—including investigations into the organizational structure, the portfolio of action sets, and the way the system of maneuvers is conceived.
- Perfect Landing, Drifting: Cell (4) represents a situation where the firm arrived at a desirable end-state although it was not behaving as planned and the world unfolded in a surprising manner. The firm is adrift, but it has landed safely. Serious, comprehensive investigation and realignment are needed.
- Undesirable Outcomes; Planning Failure: This is the situation represented by cell (5). The end-state is undesirable although the firm acted as planned and the world unfolded as expected. It would seem that the main cause is miscalculations during planning time.
- Undesirable Outcomes; Failure of Self-Organization I: Cell (6) represents a situation in which the firm behaved as planned, but it could not cope with a world unfolding in a surprising manner. The fact that it could not cope is in itself a failure of self-organization. A successful self-organizing system always adapts quickly to surprise and arrives at an acceptable state. This type of self-organization failure is labeled as type I.
- Undesirable Outcomes; Failure of Self-Organization II: In cell (7), the emerging end-state is undesirable and the firm did not behave as planned although the world is turning out as envisioned. This is a higher degree of self-organization failure. This is why it is labeled type II. More radical restructuring of the firm is needed urgently.
- Undesirable Outcomes; Total Disarray: Cell (8) represents a situation where everything has gone wrong. The unfolding end-state is undesirable. The firm did not behave as planned. The turbulence is radically new and surprising. The firm is in a state of disarray, a crisis. Nothing is going right for it internally or externally.

## ENVISIONING THE NEXT GENERATION COMPANY

As of this point, we have tracked our changing environment, our strategic configuration, and our strategic end-states as they unfold. We are now in a better position to think about the future and the next generation company. The next step in renewal, therefore, is envisioning. Envisioning involves two main things: envisioning the trajectory of the environment, and envisioning the next generation company.

### Envisioning the Trajectory of the Changing Environment

The environment of the firm (i.e., its industry segment and overall industry), is like an object hurled into space, the domestic and global economy. It often assumes a path or a trajectory in this universe. The path is unknown, but it can be pieced together one frame at a time. For example, the trajectory of manufacturing in the 20th Century moved from manual, to mechanical, to automation, and now to hi-tech. For another, consider retailing: small shops, large retailers (department stores), discounting chains (K-Mart), and now e-tailing (selling on the Internet). If the firm is to renew itself, it has to come to grips with this trajectory somehow.

Renewal is about putting the firm in a trajectory that is consistent with the (envisioned) trajectory of its environment. Envisioning the environment is best accomplished through the mapping of alternate futures, or scenarios construction as presented in Chapter 9. The scenario construction process should be a continuous one since the environment is changing continuously. The more surprising the environment, the lesser the time span for the scenarios and the more often they have to be constructed. As scenarios are developed, the most likely scenario suggests itself. It can then be viewed as the direction of the environment. The trajectory of the environment will then be a series of most likely scenarios sequenced over a certain period. This will provide a moving picture or a trajectory of the environment.

## Envisioning the Next Generation Company

With the trajectory of the environment in hand, the next step is to envision the next generation company, the future version of our firm. The chassis of the next generation company is a strategic configuration that is aligned with the emerging direction of the environments. Alignment here means that the firm will have many opportunities to exploit and emerge to a desirable strategic end-state. The focus of the renewal effort will be on envisioning the next generation strategic configuration, particularly broadly outlining its specifications (Exhibit 17.3). This outline will be the direction for the renewal effort. The expectation is that everyone will work to make this configuration a reality. This should not distract the organization from pursuing today's configuration and from exploiting today's opportunities. The future configuration is a different track altogether, but it starts today.

## TRANSFORMATION: BECOMING THE NEXT GENERATION COMPANY

With the envisioned environment and the next generation strategic configuration, the next set of activities involve bringing it about, despite the pressing issues of today. The challenge for the organization is to weave the next generation configuration into present operations so that they may evolve into it. A critical issue is the pacing of the transformation. Melon and Helgrin suggested a conceptual scheme that may shed some light on this issue.[8] They identified two continua for change: proactive-reactive change, and, continuous-revolutionary change. Using this scheme, four quadrants emerge, each suggests an option for transforming the firm as shown in Exhibit 17.12. It is up to the leadership and the organization to choose the most suitable one.

The four options for transforming the firm are as follows:

1. The Proactive Revolutionary Option: Here the changeover from the current to the next generation configuration is swift and massive. It is a breakaway with the present. It happens before the future is here. The risk is that the firm is being transformed in advance based on a speculation of what shape the environment will assume. The pace of change might induce resistance from various members of the organization. The advantage, however, is that the firm will be the first to take advantage of the evolving, new environmental conditions.

|  | Revolutionary Renewal | |
| --- | --- | --- |
| Proaction | 1<br>Proactive Revolutionary | 2<br>Reactive Revolutionary |
|  | 3<br>Proactive Incremental | 4<br>Reactive Incremental | Reaction
|  | Continuous Renewal | |

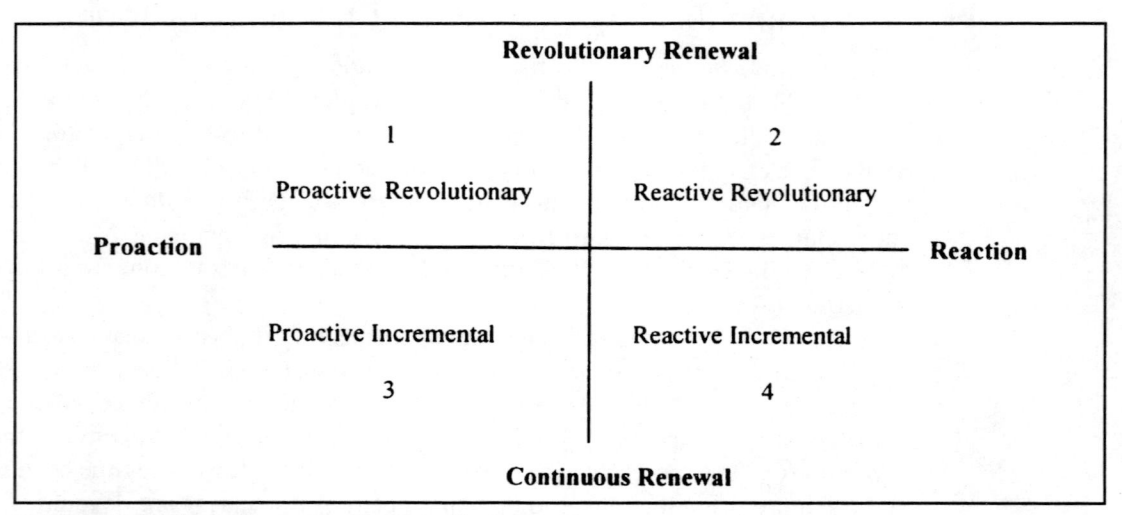

Exhibit 17.12: Transformation Strategy Options

2. The Reactive Revolutionary Option: In this case, the transformation occurs after or as the environment itself changes. The firm might follow a wait-and-see approach and bring in the next generation company when it judges that the time is right. Waiting is an advantage. It minimizes the risk of betting on an uncertain environment. However, firms that transformed themselves in a proactive manner will occupy the best positions. It will be expensive to catch up with them.
3. The Proactive Incremental Option: This is a cautious approach. It minimizes the bet by making the changeover gradual. At the same time, the firm will be ready when the new environment materializes. Furthermore, resistance to change will be minimized.
4. The Reactive Incremental Option: Here the firm changes gradually to the new configuration, but after it becomes more certain about the shape of the evolving environment. Again, this option minimizes the risk of upset due to the pace of change and betting on an uncertain future. The main disadvantage is that the firm will be forced to accept what is left by the competitors that pursued the proactive option.

## Renewal Platforms

Once a transformational option is chosen, the next challenge is to proceed with the transformation. The concept of platform provides a good insight into the renewal process.[9] A platform is a collection of resources and skills that is designed in a generic way and as such, it is capable of creating a variety of innovative outputs. It is a popular concept in the automotive industry where a platform is built with general parameters, but then it generates a family of models and features thus allowing an automaker to create passenger cars, sports, and SUV models from it. Along the same line, the firm can be laid out as a set of platforms. Since these platforms are capable of innovative variety, they enable the firm as a whole to evolve with its evolving environment. Naturally, there will be a time when a platform will become obsolete. However, by that time, the changing environment would have evolved into a discernible trajectory. Then, more up-to-date platforms can be designed.

This leads to another question: How does one apply the platform concept in the context of renewal? There are four basic platforms that a firm must have. These are: the business model platform, the process platform, the resource platform, and the organization platform.

1. The Business Model Platform

This platform can create a variety of derivative, novel business models over time. To illustrate, consider Amazon.com. It started with one platform, an e-business model for selling books. This was the time when the e-business revolution was in the early stages. However, as the e-business revolution spread, Amazon.com started developing other business models from this platform. It used it as a business model for selling toys, electronics, and a whole range of products and services. A firm can have as many business model platforms as it needs depending on the degree of diversification in its products and markets. Renewing companies insist on having an inventory of potential business models that can be rolled out as the environment unfolds.

Jonash and Sommerlette catalogued these platforms into four levels.[10] A level I platform is an exploratory platform designed to probe little known opportunities, that may be promising in the future. A level II platform is one that developed a technology or an innovation the impact of which is yet to be assessed. With some development, this technology can be a source of products. The level III platform is a center of expertise that is producing innovation and creativity. It is a source of new products for the near future. Finally, the level IV platform is one that is turning out successful business models that are strengthening the firm's strategic position. Clearly, a renewing firm will need to have a portfolio of these levels. The first two levels represent tomorrow's growth engines. In all likelihood, they will evolve to become the backbone of the next generation company. They need to be seeded and fertilized so that they can become the next generation company. Level III and IV pertain primarily to today's growth engines.

2. The Process Platform

Process is the skeleton of the firm's activities. It is the chassis on which business models are hoisted. Process variety produces business model variety. If the process evolves, so will the business models. Hence, the more versatile the process platforms are, the more flexible the firm can become, and this would help the firm to evolve with its changing environment. In the case of Amazon.coms, process refers to sourcing products, taking orders through the company's website, collecting payments, filling the orders, and delivery. Some traditional retailers, like Sears, missed the beginning of the e-business revolution because the brick-and-mortar platform did not allow them to do business online. Now, they are renewing their business process to include an e-business operation. Renewing companies always ensure that they have an inventory of next generation process candidates so that the firm may deploy them as the environment evolves.

3. The Resource Platform

The resource platform is the configuration of the firm's resources. When the resource platform is versatile, it can support more processes and business models as well as sustain their development. A resource platform includes the firm's resources, suppliers, competencies, partners, allies, and perhaps customers if they aid the firm to become a reliable supplier to them.

The crucial challenge is to have next generation resources available as time goes by to enable the next generation company to evolve. Jonash and Sommerlatte suggested a number of guidelines for developing next generation resources.[11] These include:

- Resisting the temptation to see resources in purely budgetary terms, rather they should be viewed from the perspective of the future as investment in renewal.
- Leveraging existing resources, even if they are proprietary, in order to obtain futuristic resources.
- Eliminating barriers, particularly those in the way of suppliers and customers to share resources with the firm and share the firm's resources.
- Investing in platforms' human resources and competencies, for they are the engines of renewal.
- Getting the most of intellectual capital, the source of innovation and renewal.
- Developing innovation, resource, and asset management plans by utilizing traditional valuation methods and qualitative assessment to assess the contribution of the various renewal projects.

4. The Organization Platform

In the final analysis, the engine that powers the preceding three platforms is the organization platform. This platform provides the structure that would enable people to work in the other platform to create next generation business models, processes, and resources. Ghoshal and Bartlette suggested a possible configuration for this platform.[11] An adaptation of their concept is presented in Exhibit 17.13. The renewing firm can be structured as a matrix of three levels and three processes. The three levels are frontline entrepreneurs, facilitators (middle managers acting as resource persons), and strategic leadership (top management). The three processes are the entrepreneurial, integration, and renewal.

There is one more element in the organization platform, a culture of continual change and learning. The key values here are: entrepreneurship, loving change, driving change, innovation, and learning. A learning organization is one that is open to its environment, ven-

| ORGANIZATIONAL PROCESSES | ORGANIZATIONAL LEVELS |||
|---|---|---|---|
|  | **Frontline Entrepreneurs** (Market Level) | **Facilitators** (Middle Level) | **Strategic Leadership** (Top Management) |
| **The Renewal Process** | Ensuring continuous improvement and innovation within units | Managing the tension between short-term performance and long-term ambition | Creating overarching corporate purpose and ambition while challenging embedded assumptions |
| **The Integration Process** | Attracting and developing competencies and managing operational interdependencies | Linking dispersed knowledge, skills, and best practices across units | Institutionalizing a set of norms and values to support cooperation and trust |
| **The Entrepreneurial Process** | Creating and pursuing new opportunities | Developing individuals and reviewing and supporting their initiatives | Establishing a stretching opportunity horizon and performance standards |

Exhibit 17.13: The Organizational Platform

turesome, and willing to take risks and to make mistakes. However, mistakes are viewed as success delayed. It is in this spirit that Jack Welch advocated the policy of rewarding successes and failures. In a way, rewarding failure encourages people to try and try again until they hit the right target. Renewal requires such a philosophy because the environment is not so well defined that the firm can size it up in a precise fashion. It is veiled in the confusion of turbulence. Unfortunately, the only way is to hit and miss. Tom Peters (the well-known management guru) publicized the saying, "Ready, Fire, Aim." The message is that we cannot see the target, let alone aim it. The time spent aiming can be used to make several probes in the hope that one of them will hit the target. Then, we will know where it is.

# GUIDING STRATEGIC RENEWAL ACTIVITIES

Guiding the firm towards strategic end-state is the core of the CEO's job. As the preceding analysis revealed, every firm is a composite of three firms. The firm as we see it today, which evolved from the firm of yesterday, is now evolving to the next generation company. As Bob Lutz (former president of Chrysler) described Chrysler in 1994, "we are not the firm we used to be, and we are not yet the firm we want to be." It seems that the CEO has to guide two sets of activities: those pertaining to bringing about a desirable strategic end-state today (today's performance), and those of renewal or migration to the next generation company. Balancing these two streams is essential. Emphasizing present performance at the expense of tomorrow's ambition will be too shortsighted. Focusing on the next generation company at the expense of today's performance is not desirable. Stakeholders want to see results now. Fortunately, today's performance and tomorrow's ambition are not mutually exclusive. Rather, they are concurrent. However, they have to be placed in the proper perspective.

Migrating to the next generation company involves numerous activities as mentioned above. For the CEO to corral and steer these activities, the practical vehicle is strategic collaboration. Renewal is a self-organizing activity in the final analysis. All parts of the firm have to co-evolve in relation to one another, and as they do so, the firm itself evolves. The principles of inducing and orchestrating strategic collaboration were discussed in Chapter 6.

They are revisited here in the context of renewal. To organize thoughts about the work of the CEO in this regard, Exhibit 17.14 was prepared. It outlines the key categories of renewal activities and the stages involved in inducing and orchestrating strategic collaboration among individuals and groups in the organization to perform such activities. The empty cells can be filled with various tasks that the CEO performs to lead the renewal effort. An overview of these tasks is presented next.

## Creating an Environment Conducive to Renewal Collaborative Action

For renewal collaborative action to germinate, it needs the right environment. The CEO is the key figure for creating such an environment. The following is only a partial list of the possible CEO tasks in this regard:

1. Cultivating Renewal Paradigms: Implanting renewal collaborative action in the organization's mindset is crucial. Collaboration for renewal must be part of the culture and the organization psyche of the firm. The thoughts encompass the categories of renewal activities, i.e., connecting with the changing environment, envisioning the next generation company, and transformation. Here are some examples. To emphasize getting a reality check, Jack Welch (GE) promoted the thought "face reality as it is." Such a thought stresses the need to have reality checks instead of living in a perceived world of our own making. With respect to envisioning tomorrow's firm, he preached the thought, "change before you have to." He describes ideal GE leaders as persons who "Stimulate and relish change . . . are not frightened or paralyzed by it. See change as an opportunity, not just a threat."

| CEO TASKS TO INDUCE AND ORCHESTRATE RENEWAL COLLABORATIVE ACTION | RENEWAL ACTIVITIES | | |
|---|---|---|---|
| | Connecting with a Changing Environment | Envisioning the Next Generation Company | Becoming the Next Generation Company |
| Creating an Environment Conducive to Renewal Collaborative Action | | | |
| Inducing and Stimulating Strategic Renewal Conversation | | | |
| Marshalling Strategic Conversation to Strategic Collaborative Action, Making the Transition | | | |
| Acknowledging and Rewarding Strategic Renewal Collaborative Action | | | |
| Affirming Accountability for Renewal and Enshrining Renewal in the Governance Mechanism | | | |
| Exercising Personal throughout the Collaboration Process | | | |

Exhibit 17.14: Inducing and Orchestrating Strategic Collaboration for Renewal

With respect to transformation, Welch always stressed revolutionary, not slow change. He always narrated the parable of the frog in the boiling water. It goes like this. If you put a frog in boiling water, it will jump out quickly and survive. However, if you put it in cold water and then increase the water temperature gradually, the frog will continue to stay in the water until a time when the water boils and the frog will die without realizing the water was becoming deadly.

2. Making Renewal a Shared Goal: For collaborative renewal to take place, it has to be entrenched as a shared goal for all individuals and groups. At Amazon.com, CEO Bezos urges ". . . employees to run scared every day."[12] He makes renewal a shared goal by making this proposition to the organization: "We still have the opportunity to be a footnote in the e-commerce industry."[13]

3. Defining Boundaryless Roles: For renewal to encompass the company in its entirety, it has to be a common role for every individual and group in the firm. Not only do they have to act in a boundaryless manner at the present, they also have to behave in the same manner with respect to renewal. Every person and group must assume the two roles of serving the company of today and bringing in the next generation company without being constrained by specialization or job descriptions.

4. Orchestrating Shared Workspace: This is crucial for bringing people together to develop a groupthink mindset. A prominent feature of this groupthink is collaboration to make the firm evolve into the next generation company.

5. Charging Emotions: Collaboration is triggered and sustained by individual emotions. Nothing can charge emotions like the fear of the future and the uncertainty it evokes. The renewal emotion is a balance between the fear of an unknown future and the optimism of facing it together by attacking it together. Renewal is an opportunity to excite members of the organization and create the attitudes conducive to change. Andy Grove always created the emotion of paranoia, the fear appeal. Welch created the emotion of loving change as a friend, a source of opportunity and hope.

## Inducing and Stimulating Renewal Conversation

Given the right environment for collaboration in renewal, the next step is to make "the next generation company" the topic of every day's conversation. Renewal conversation has to be part of the routine conversation protocol. It is not enough to talk about today's problems. The future ushers itself in on a daily basis. If it is left out of the daily agenda, we will be surprised (mostly unpleasantly) when it becomes full blown. The CEO can stimulate renewal conversation by undertaking actions like those listed below:

- Clarifying and articulating a vision of the next generation company and a strategy for making it happen.
- Developing shared understanding of the environment of tomorrow and the need to think about the next generation company.
- Placing renewal on top of the strategic agenda. Upon observing the emergence of the e-business revolution, Jack Welch instructed every unit to come up with a breakthrough e-business idea, as a top priority.
- Championing new options for the next generation company to serve as a proposal to be debated by various groups. This ought to make renewal a topic for conversation and exchange among various groups.
- Stimulating advocacy for various concepts of the next generation company and alternative paths to get there. The debate among advocates is bound to create enough attention and conversation.

## Marshalling Conversation to Collaborative Renewal Action

The work of the CEO here focuses on moving conversation to actual renewal action as a part of the firm's current business activities. The purpose here is to phase in the transformation into the next generation company. There are many tasks to be done here as follows:

1. Developing and Cultivating Frameworks for Action: To help members of the organization transform the firm into the next generation company, the CEO needs to develop (individually or jointly with the organization) frameworks for guiding the processes of connecting with the changing environment, envisioning the firm of the future, and transforming it. The frameworks presented in this chapter serve as examples.
2. Building Renewal Collaborative Networks: Networks have to be in place to facilitate collaboration on renewal. Networks are important in connecting with the environment, envisioning the next generation company, and making the transformation. The task of renewal is so massive. It needs the energy and intelligence of everyone in the organization. Networks tend to mobilize energy and intelligence and make things happen.
3. Driving Creative, Entrepreneurial Renewal: Envisioning and bringing about the next generation company is an act of entrepreneurship. Therefore, the CEO must insist on genuine entrepreneurial results so that the firm may disconnect from an obsolete business configuration.
4. Designating Renewal Champions: For renewal to happen, it has to have champions in the organization. These can be the leaders of the next generation company's project leaders. To drive renewal throughout the organization, the CEO needs to designate and appoint these champions. Failing to do this may result in today's projects overshadowing the projects that will bring forth the next generation company.
6. Removing Barriers to Renewal: The worst barriers to renewal include: emphasis on short-term results, bureaucracy that inhibits entrepreneurship, and lack of resources to fuel the next generation company's projects. The CEO must work to remove these barriers.
7. Allocating Resources for Renewal Projects: Resources should be apportioned between current pursuits and projects for bringing about the next generation company. The danger here is the pursuit of the present will consume the firm's resources, leaving none for the future. The firm's capital budgeting and strategic planning sessions are excellent opportunities for allocating resources for the future.
8. Transferring Renewal Decision-Making Powers: Clearly, to move conversation to actual renewal actions, the power to make the necessary decisions has to be transferred to members of the self-organizing firm. This does not mean that the CEO does not exercise any influence on the evolutionary course of the firm. The CEO is not excluded at all. These decisions are made under his/her watchful guidance. The CEO has numerous opportunities for corralling and steering these decisions.
9. Approval of Renewal Direction: The CEO can help move conversation into action by approving or concurring with the various visions of the next generation company and ways to bring it about. It is the main tool for orchestrating collaborative renewal.
10. Issuing Directives for Implementing Renewal Visions: As the various visions of the next generation emerge and the projects to bring it about are planned, the CEO still has further chances to influence the direction of collaboration, namely, issuing the directives for the organization to proceed in that direction.

## Acknowledging and Rewarding Collaborative Renewal Action

Renewal collaborative behavior must be reinforced. The work of the CEO here involves identifying when genuine collaborative renewal is taking place and celebrating such achievement. At the same time, the various individuals and groups (who championed renewal visions and projects and brought them about) must be recognized and celebrated.

## Fusing Renewal into Accountability and Governance

Collaborative renewal must become part of the firm's accountability and governance scheme. It is just as important as accountability for today's performance. CEO's work here involves auditing the firm's overall strategic renewal effort, keeping score (who is doing what with whom to renew the company), challenging assumptions, visions and paradigms, raising the bar (a more ambitious and overarching vision of the next generation company), and holding court especially when people (as a self-organizing group) fail to perceive the future, imagine it, and make it happen.

## Exercising Personal Leadership of the Renewal Effort

In the final analysis, the CEO is the one accountable for what the firm has evolved into, and to what state it will migrate in the future. Renewal is a personal responsibility that cannot be delegated, even though the CEO lets the firm function as a self-organizing system. It is understandable then that the CEO exercises personal influence to corral and steer collaborative renewal. The CEO can exert personal influence in many ways including setting the example (be the first to fuse the future into the present, be the first to avoid placing all emphasis on short-term results, and the like), coaching (working with individual and groups on renewal practices), preaching (continually persuading and pressing people to be futuristic in their thinking and action), and management by walking around (to see personally if the future is placed in the proper perspective along with today's pressing issues).

# CONCLUSION

In this chapter, we dealt with the topic of how a self-organizing system renews and reinvents itself *en route* as it struggles with turbulence day by day. Renewal was placed in the perspective of the progression of a firm's life. We viewed the firm as a composite of three "personalities" at any point in time. The first personality is a function of the past. The second is function of the present. The third is a function of the future, the next generation company. Renewal was defined as bringing the next generation company today; at some speed dictated by the realities of the firm's situation. We stressed the message that the future is just as important as today. It should never be overshadowed by today's issues no matter how pressing they may be. The future will be here eventually. Not evolving with it or into it can cost the firm its existence.

Renewal was presented in this chapter as one of the natural functions of self-organization. A self-organizing system has the capacity to renew itself without an externally imposed plan or directive. It is part of its resilience property where it naturally organizes and reorganizes itself in the course of evolving with its evolving, turbulent environment. Like all self-organization activities, renewal is also a collaborative effort. Collaboration is also a natural process in a self-organizing system because all parts of the system have a shared purpose that makes them interdependent, and this is surviving and thriving in a turbulent environment.

The chapter concluded with an exploration of the work of the CEO with regard to renewal. Like all other activities of the firm, the CEO must guide it by corralling and steering numerous individual and collaborative initiatives of members of the system. Guidance by the CEO boils down to inducing and orchestrating strategic collaboration so that all concerned may work together to make the firm evolve into the next generation company. The CEO works to create the appropriate environment for collaborative renewal efforts, to stimulate ample conversation on the topic of the future and an appropriate vision of the next generation company, to move conversation into tangible renewal action, enshrine renewal into the accountability and governance system, reinforce renewal effort, and exerting personal influence throughout the renewal process.

This chapter also concludes the book. In this book, we presented a different proposition for running the business firm in the e-business age, the digital age. The e-business age calls for a radical change in the way the CEO manages the firm. All signs point out in one direction: a new paradigm where the CEO runs the firm as a self-organizing system. The CEO actually lets go because the alternative of managing the firm personally through heroic leadership is no longer humanly possible. In the e-world, business is conducted at the speed of thought. It is so turbulent that the CEO (and a small top management team) cannot stay on top of things; only those in the firing line can. In the e-organization, decision-making power and resources have to be transferred to them.

The fact that the firm is operating as a self-organizing system, however, does not absolve the CEO from the responsibility to stakeholders, namely bringing the firm to a strategic end-state that pleases them. In fulfilling this responsibility, the CEO in the digital age switches from micromanagement to virtual leadership. He/she focuses on guiding or corralling and steering empowered people by inducing and orchestrating strategic collaboration among them so that they may pursue a promising direction, a viable strategic end-state.

Peter Drucker suggested the model of the conductor of a symphony orchestra as a paradigm for managing the contemporary firm. The conductor leads a number of competent professionals without micromanaging them during the concert. However, the analogy needs some further tightening. The conductor and members of the orchestra operate under conditions of certainty. During a given concert, all players have the same score. They adhere to it. Acoustic and lighting conditions remain unchanged. The audience remains largely unchanged throughout the concert. The CEO does not enjoy such certainties. Rather, he/she deals with "ephemerals" all the time. Every element in the firm has its own mind. We expand the conductor's analogy further to make it reflect the realities of running a firm:

> The CEO is like the conductor of a symphony orchestra where the players are accomplished specialists who compose their own score as they play and as a result the score changes in an unpredictable manner as the orchestra plays. The instruments are invented and reinvented as the orchestra plays. Members of the audience come and go unpredictably and change their requests of the orchestra without notice. The auditorium where the orchestra plays is changing. The walls change in a surprising manner sometimes disappearing altogether. Lighting conditions change without notice from dim to clear. Oddly enough, the conductor conducts, the players play harmoniously as an orchestra should, music is made, the audience enjoys and pays for the concert, the orchestra makes money and pays the bills, and the show goes on.

# ENDNOTES

1. Tichy, N.M. and S. Sherman, *Control Your Destiny or Someone Else Will: How Jack Welch is Making General Electric the World's Most Competitive Corporation*, New York, NY: Doubleday, 1993, p. 15.
2. Waterman, Jr., R.H., *The Renewal Factor: How the Best Get and Keep the Competitive Edge*, New York, NY: Bantam Books, 1987, pp. 5–17.
3. Ibid., p. 8
4. Ibid., p. 10.
5. Ibid., p. 12.

6. Ghoshal, S. and C.A. Bartlett, *The Individualized Corporation: A Fundamentally New Approach to Management*, New York, NY: Harper Collins, 1997, Chapter 7.

7. Altman, E.I. and J.K. LaFleur, "Managing a Return to Financial Health," *Journal of Business Strategy*, Summer 1981, pp. 31–38.

8. Melin, L. and B. Hellgren, "Patterns of Strategic Processes: Two Change Typologies," in Thomas, H., D. O'Neal, R. White, and D. Hurst, eds., *Building the Strategically-Responsive Organization*, New York, NY: John Wiley & Sons, 1994, p. 251.

9. Jonash, R. S. and T. Sommerlatte, *The Innovation Premium*, Cambridge, MA: Perseus Book, 1999.

10. Ibid.

11. Ibid.

12. Ghoshal and Bartlett, op. cit.

13. Sellers, P. "Bezos on Buffett," *Fortune Magazine*, November 22, 1999, p. 220.

14. Ibid., p. 220.

# APPENDIX I

# A Research Note

The strategic leadership model underlying this work is the product of a research project that began in the early 1980s. In those days, North American corporations were suffering not only from a worldwide recession but also from business practices that made them weaker in the face of Japanese competition. Peters and Waterman found many companies that were excelling despite these hardships. They wrote about them in their well-known work, *In Search of Excellence*.[1] These companies were run by imaginative leaders who managed in unique, innovative ways.

Inspired by Peters and Waterman's work, this study was designed to focus on the practices of the CEOs who departed from the traditional mold. These CEOs introduced radical concepts of corporate leadership. They redefined their role and function to allow their firms to cope with the new realities in the business world. For example, Ralph Stayer (Johnsonville Foods) decided to step back and transferred ownership of problems and strategic decisions to the employees. He let them lead the company.[2]

From that point onward, an intensive search was undertaken to find such CEOs from a variety of sources including:

- Books written by CEOs about their experience in leading their corporations.
- Books written about CEOs, e.g., biographies.
- Books written by management consultants and academics about CEOs.
- Case studies from the Harvard Business School's collection.
- Speeches and addresses by CEOs.
- Corporations' annual reports, letters to shareholders, as well as SEC filings such as Form 10-K.
- Articles by and about CEOs in business periodicals such as *Fortune, Business Week,* the *Wall Street Journal, Harvard Business Review, CEO Magazine, Strategy & Business*, and the like.
- Video documentaries about various CEOs and their companies.
- Various databases.
- Websites of corporations, business media, and management consulting firms.

The unit of study for this research is the CEO, namely the avant-garde CEO, the one whose management practices are judged as non-traditional. A CEO was judged as avant-garde if the business media reported him or her as such. To illustrate, Exhibit 1 contains a small sample of names.

Researching CEOs directly is impossible due to the confidential nature of their activities. To overcome this obstacle, the research strategy for this project was to redefine the study unit as the "reported practice" of a CEO. The terms "practice" and "reported" were defined as follows. A "practice" was defined as a policy or an approach that the CEO used consistently during his/her reign in running his/her company. Example of practices include: establishing a clear vision for the company, defining a focus or a strategic thrust for the firm, empowering employees, flattening the organization, inculcating specific values, and the like.

A "reported" practice is one that is described by a CEO (his/her own book or article), those who write about CEOs, e.g., business media reporters (in *Fortune, Business Week,* etc.) consultants, academics (written case studies, research studies, books, etc.), business "gurus," (e.g., Tom Peters) and the like. If one article or book described ten practices about a certain CEO, these were treated as ten reports although they pertain to one CEO. A CEO's name can appear several times in the database, e.g., when each of his/her practices is isolated and entered separately, or when separate portions of his/her practices are reported by more than one writer (e.g., two practices were written about in *Fortune* and three others were reported in *Business Week*). A practice of a particular was entered only once in the database. For a reported practice to be admissible in this study, it had to be corroborated by a second source

| CEO's Name | Company |
|---|---|
| Jack Welch | General Electric |
| Ralph Stayer | Johnsonville Foods |
| Lars Kolind | Oticon |
| Jack Stack | Springfield Remanufacturing |
| Fred Smith | FedEx |
| Herb Kelleher | Southwest Air |
| Jeff Bezos | Amazon.com |
| John Chambers | Cisco Systems |
| Bill Gates | Microsoft |
| Craig Wetherup | Pepsi |
| Luciano Benetton | Benneton |
| George Willis | Lincoln Electric |
| Dee Hock | Visa |
| Ed McCracken | Silicon Graphics |
| William Pollard | Service Masters |
| Patrick Kelly | PSS/World Medical |
| Bob Lutz | Chrysler |
| Marshal Collins | British Airways |
| John Martin | Taco Bell |

Exhibit 1: Examples of CEOs Researched

(e.g., a report in that appeared first in the *Wall Street Journal* and later on in *Business Week*) unless the writer was the CEO himself/herself. Data gathering in this manner started in 1984. It continues to this day.

The raw data for this study were thus the reported practices. Each reported practice was given a code reflecting its topic, the CEO, and the source where it was reported. This facilitated sorting practices by topic, CEO, or source. When the database reached 12,000 practices and 600 CEOs, the task of data analysis began.

Given all these collected practices, the challenge was to organize them to find out if a particular model underlies them. If such a model can be unearthed, it can then serve as a representation of the work of the contemporary CEO. A qualitative research method known as Grounded Theory provided an insight. Strauss and Corbin described grounded theory as follows: "A grounded theory is one that is inductively derived from the study of the phenomenon it represents. That is, it is discovered, developed, and provisionally verified through systematic data collection and analysis of data pertaining to that phenomenon. Therefore, data collection, analysis, and theory stand in a reciprocal relationship with each other."[3]

A variant of grounded theory was developed for this study. The research procedure was as follows: Single practices were grouped into elemental categories based on similarity or proximity to one another, e.g., all reports about establishing a vision were grouped in one category and the category was labeled as "established a vision." Since practices were coded by CEO also, a category was constructed when 60% of the CEOs in the database followed it. Each category was assigned a code and it was added to the practice's code. The resulting categories were labeled first level categories.

First level categories (or concepts as they are called in Grounded Theory procedure) were next sorted out into new groups (broader categories or second level categories) based on their proximity to one another, i.e., pertaining to one major task (broad category). For example, categories pertaining to strategy were put in one group. Along the same lines, those pertaining to structuring the organization were placed in one group. This process was repeated and new broad categories emerged, namely, second level categories.

The next step was to relate second level categories to one another. To unearth the relationships among them, a number of links were explored. Thus, if a category preceded another category, they were sequenced as such. For example, if establishing focus occurred before structuring the organization, this precedence was preserved. Similarly, if two categories occurred simultaneously, they were plotted as such, e.g., the case of adding capability and at the same time structuring the organization. Along the same line, if one category was viewed as the cause or effect of another, they were arranged in light of this relationship. For example, putting resources and decision power in the hands of those close to the customer led to flattening the organization. If the relationship was circular, the respective categories were arranged accordingly, as in the case of vision and strategy when they tended to drive one another.

When various second level categories were plotted graphically according to their relationships, they formed mini-frameworks. They showed how a number of them hang together to form a group of CEO practices or tasks. A mini-framework was viewed as a third level category and was given a new label, e.g., structuring the firm as a self-organizing system.

Finally, third level categories were related to one another based on precedence, simultaneity, and cause-and-effect. When this was done, a master framework suggested itself and this is the strategic leadership model presented in Chapter 4. At the end of all this categorization, there were two almost concurrent major (broadest) categories: (1) structuring the firm as a self-organizing system; and, (2) guiding the firm toward strategic end-states.

Validity testing is an important part of any research. In grounded theory, validation is accomplished by checking the resulting model against the same data set from which it was derived. This was accomplished by writing fifty of short cases or narratives about CEOs in the database. Examples of these are the ones presented in Chapter 2. The cases seemed to confirm the model. The respective CEOs' tended to structure their firm (or organize the people) as a self-organizing system and then they focused on guiding the workings of this system. In this regard, the model appears satisfactory. It does mirror the reality as contained in these short cases.

A second validation procedure was followed. The model was checked against *new* data, new reports about CEOs' practices in business periodicals, new books by CEOs, Harvard Business School case studies, and the like. For example, when Patrick Kelly, CEO, and founder of PSS/World wrote a book about his practices in leading this company, he reported that he structured it as a "company of CEOs." Each employee actually carried a business card identifying him or her as "CEO of PSS/World."[4] A phrase like "a company of CEOs" clearly indicates that Kelly structured the company as a self-organizing system. This attests to the validity of the model produced by this research. Published books by CEOs and others repeatedly show that the findings of this study are corroborated by subsequent CEO practices.

There is no research study without limitations. This one has its share. First, this study has a bias. It focuses only on *avant-garde* CEOs, the pioneers, the trailblazers. Thus, the model presented here is not representative of *all* CEOs. Second, this study did not follow the strict discipline of "scientific" inquiry that lives up to the precision of physical science. The sample is not a proper probability sample. There is no quantification and hence quantitative methods were not used. The study followed qualitative research methodology taking advantage of the flexibility it accords. No claim is made here that this study represents the ultimate in scientific rigor. There was, however, considerable meticulousness in gathering practices, verifying them from more than one source, investigating relationships, and organizing concepts into frameworks.

Third, the data collected for this study were second-hand, mainly reports by CEOs and observers of CEOs (business reporters, consultants, etc.). Using second-hand data poses problems of its own. People (including CEOs) could have embellished things when they report them after the fact. Observers could have misinterpreted or misread things. This is all possible. However, the alternative is to follow a large number of CEOs daily for a long time, record their actions, and analyze the firm in detail. Unfortunately, cost and practical considerations eliminated this avenue.

Fourth, there is considerable subjectivity in coding and categorizing the data, determining relationships among concepts, and organizing them in the form of a conceptual framework or a model. All these decisions are subjective no matter how meticulous the researcher is. It is possible that another researcher using this same data set, or one similar to it, could have ended up with a different arrangement or conceptual framework. There is a reliability concern here. Subjectivity is part of any research effort.

Fifth, the findings of this study represent a snapshot of the present era, which is one in a series of punctuated chaos in the business world. It reflects the current wave of chaos (e-commerce, e-corporation, the Net culture, the digital organization, etc.). Perhaps the next restructuring or upheaval in the business world will cause a new reconfiguration of the CEO's work. Should this happen, the model of this study will become obsolete. That is why this study is an on-going project. It does not stop at this point in time. Data collection continues. Validation continues.

# ENDNOTES

1. Peters, T. and R.H. Waterman, *In Search of Excellence*, New York, NY: Harper & Row, 1982.

2. Belasco, J.A., and R.C. Stayer, *Flight of the Buffalo: Soaring To Excellence, Learning To Let Employees Lead*, New York, NY: Warner Books, 1993.

3. Strauss, A. and J. Corbin, *Basics of Qualitative Research: Grounded Theory Procedures and Techniques*, Newbury Park, CA: Sage Publications, 1990, p. 23.

4. Kelly, P., *Faster Company: Building the World's Nuttiest Turn-on-a-Dime Home-Grown Billion-Dollar Business*, New York, NY: Wiley, 1998.

# Selected Bibliography

Abell, D.F., *Managing With Dual Strategies*, New York, NY: The Free Press, 1993.

Abell, D.F., and J.S. Hammond, *Strategic Market Planning: Problems and Analytical Approaches*, Englewood Cliffs, NJ: Prentice-Hall, 1979.

Ackoff, R.A., *The Democratic Corporation*, New York, NY: Oxford University Press, 1994.

Altman, E.I. and J.K. LaFleur, "Managing a Return to Financial Health," *Journal of Business Strategy*, Summer 1981.

Alsop, S., "E or Be Eaten," *Fortune*, November 8, 1999, pp. 86–87.

Amara, R. and A.J. Lipinski, *Business Planning for an Uncertain Future: Scenarios & Strategies*, New York, NY: Pergamon Press, 1983.

Amit, R., and P.J.H. Shoemaker, "Strategic Assets and Organizational Rent," *Strategic Management Journal*, January, 1993.

Annison, M.H., Managing the Whirlwind: Opportunities in a Changing World, Englewood, CO: Medical Group Publishing, 1993.

Ansoff, H.I., and E.J. McDonnell, *Implanting Strategic Management*, 2nd ed., New York, NY: Prentice Hall, 1990.

Ansoff, H.I., *The New Corporate Strategy*, New York, NY: John Wiley & Sons, 1988.

Ascher, W. and W.H. Overholt, *Strategic Planning and Forecasting: Political Risk and Economic Opportunity*, New York, NY: John Wiley & Sons, 1983.

Ashkenas, R., D. Ulrich, T. Jick, and S. Kerr, *The Boundaryless Organization: Breaking the Chains of Organizational Structure*, San Francisco, CA: Jossey-Bass, 1995.

Ashkenas, R., D. Ulrich, T. Jick, and S. Kerr, *The Boundaryless Organization: Breaking the Chains of Organizational Structure*, San Francisco, CA: Josey-Bass, 1995.

Bagby, M., *Rational Exuberance: The Economic Power of Generation X*, New York, NY: Dutton Plume, 1997.

Bardwick, J.M., *In Praise of Good Business: How Optimizing Risk Rewards Both Your Bottom Line and Your People*, New York, NY: John Wiley & Sons, 1998.

Barney, J.B., *Gaining and Sustaining the Competitive Advantage*, Reading, MA: Addison-Wesley, 1997.

Bartlett, C. and S. Ghoshal, "Beyond Strategic Planning to Organizational Learning: Lifeblood of the Individualized Organization," *Strategy & Leadership*, November/December, 1997.

Baufre, A., *An Introduction To Strategy With Practical Reference To Defense, Politics, and Diplomacy In the Nuclear Age*, Translated by R. H. Barry, New York, NY: Frederic A. Praeger, Publishers, 1965.

Belasco, J.A. and R.C. Stayer, *Flight of the Buffalo: Soaring To Excellence, Learning To Let Employees Lead*, New York, NY: Warner Books, 1993.

Belasco, J.A., *Teaching the Elephants To Dance: Empowering Change in Your Organization*, New York, NY: Crown Publishing, 1990.

Bennis, W. and B. Nanus, Leaders: *The Strategies For Taking Charge*, New York, NY: Harper Collins, 1985.

Bennis, W., *Managing People Is Like Herding Cats*, South Bravo, Utah: Executive Excellence Publishing, 1997.

Blanchard, K. and T. Waghorn, *Mission Possible*, New York, NY: McGraw-Hill, 1997.

Boroush, M.A. and C.W. Thomas, "Alternative Scenarios for the Defense Industry After 1995," *Planning Review*, May/June 1992.

Bower, J.L., C.A. Bartlet, H. Uyterhoven, and R.E. Walton, *Business Policy: Managing the Strategic Process*, 8th Ed., Chicago, Ill.: Irwin, 1995.

Bower, J.L., C.A. Bartlet, C.R. Christensen, A.E. Pearson, and K.E., Andrews, *Business Policy: Managing the Strategic Process*, 7th. Ed., Chicago, Ill.: Irwin, 1991.

Brown, K., *Guidelines For Managing Corporate Issues Programs*, Report No. 795, New York, NY: The Conference Board, 1981.

Brown, L.S., and K.M. Eisenhardt, *Competing on the Edge: Strategy as Structured Chaos*, Boston, MA: Harvard Business School Press, 1998.

Callahn, C.V. and B.A. Pasternack, "Corporate Strategy in the Digital Age," *Strategy & Business*, Second Quarter 1999.

Camillus, J.C., R.T. Sessions, and R. Webeb, "Visionary Action: Strategic Processes in Fast-Cycle Environments," *Strategy & Leadership*, November/December, 1997.

Carlzon, J., *Moments of Truth*, Cambridge, MA: Ballinger, 1987.

Chakravarthy, B.S. and P. Lorange, *Managing The Strategy Process: A Framework For A Multibusiness Firm*, Englewood Cliffs, NJ: Prentice-Hall, 1991.

Citrin, J.M. and T.J. Neff, "Digital Leadership," *Strategy & Business*, First Quarter, 2000, pp. 42–46.

Clifford, D.K., and R.E. Cavanagh, *The Winning Performance: How America's High Growth Midsize Companies Succeed*, New York, NY: Bantam Books, 1985.

Collins, J.C, and J.I. Porras, *Built To Last: Successful Habits of Visionary Companies*, New York, NY: HarperBusiness, 1994.

Collins, M.C. and J.I. Porras, "Organizational Vision and Visionary Organizations," *California Management Review*, Fall 1991.

Collins, M.C. and J.I. Porras, "Building Your Company's Vision," *Harvard Business Review*, September–October, 1996.

Cronin, M.J., *The Internet Strategy Handbook: Lessons from Internet Success Stories*, Boston, MA: Harvard Business School Publishing, 1996.

Cusumano, M.A. and R.W. Selby, *Microsoft Secrets: How the World's Most Powerful Software Company Creates Technology, Shapes Market, and Manages People*, New York, NY: The Free Press, 1995.

Dauphinais, G.W., and C. Price, *Straight from the CEO: The World's Top Business Leaders Reveal Ideas that Every Manager Can Use*, New York, NY: Simon & Schuster, 1998.

Davis, S. and C. Meyer, "An Economy Turned on its Head: Why You Must Be Knowledge-Based to Compete in the Today's World," *Strategy & Leadership*, November/December, 1997.

Day, G., *Market Driven Strategy*, New York, NY: The Free Press, 1990.

De Geus, A., *The Living Company: Habits for Survival in a Turbulent Business Environment*, Boston, MA: Harvard Business School Press, 1997.

Dell, M., *Straight from Dell*, New York, NY: Harper Business, 1999.

Dickie, B.N. "The CEO Agenda" in *The CEO Survival Kit*, New York, NY: Booz-Allen & Hamilton, 1998.

Dilenschneider, R.L., *A Briefing For Leaders: Communication As the Ultimate Exercise of Power*, New York, NY: Harper Business, 1991.

Downes, L. and C. Mui, *Unleashing the Killer App: Develop Digital Strategies that Help You Dominate the Market*, Boston, MA: Harvard Business School Press, 1998.

Drucker, P., *Management Challenges for the 21st Century*, New York, NY: Harper Business, 1999.

Drucker, P., *On the Profession of Management*, Boston, MA: Harvard Business School Press, 1998.

Drucker, P., *Post-Capitalist Society*, New York, NY: Harper Business, 1993.

Drucker, P., *The New Realities*, New York, NY: Harper & Row, 1990.

Duncan, W.L., *Manufacturing 2000: Get A Jump on the Future*, New York, NY: AMACOM, 1994.

Dunlap, A.J., *Mean Business: How I Save Bad Companies and Make Good Companies Great*, New York, NY: Fireside Publishing, 1996.

Fahey, L. and R.M. Randall, *Learning from the Future: Competitive Foresight Scenarios*, New York, NY: John Wiley & Sons, 1998.

Fahey, L. and R.M. Randall, *The Portable MBA in Strategy*, New York, NY: Wiley & Sons, 1994.

Farkas, C.M. and P. De Backer, *Maximum Leadership: The World's Leading CEOs Share Their Five Strategies for Success*, New York, NY: Henry Holt, 1996.

Farkas, C.M. and P.De Backer, *Maximum Leadership: The World's Leading CEOs Share Their Five Strategies for Success*, New York, NY: Henry Holt, 1997.

Fradette, M. and S. Michaud, *The Power of Corporate Kinetics: Create a Self-Adapting, Instant Action Enterprise*, New York, NY: Simon & Schuster, 1998.

Frangos, S.J. and S.J. Bennett, *Team Zebra*, Essex Junction, VT: Oliver Publishing, 1993.

Freiberg, K. and J. Freiberg, *Nuts: Southwest Airlines' Crazy Recipe for Business and Personal Success*, Austin, Texas: Bard Press, 1996.

Furey, T.R. and S.G. Diorio, "Making Reengineering Strategic," *Planning Review*, July–August, 1994.

Gates III, W.H., *Business @ the Speed of Thought: Using a Digital Nervous System*, New York, NY: Warner Books, 1999.

Geneen, H., *Managing*, New York, NY: Doubleday, 1984.

Ghemwat, P., *Strategy and the Business Landscape: Text and Cases*, Reading, MA: Addison Wesly Longman, 1999.

Ghoshal, S. and C.A. Bartlett, *The Individualized Corporation*, New York, NY: HarperCollins, 1997.

Goldstein, S., "Exploit Discontinuities To Grow," *Strategy & Leadership*, September/October, 1996.

Gould, M., A. Cambell, and M. Alexander, *Corporate Level Strategy: Creating Value in the Multibusiness Company*, New York, NY: John Wiley & Sons, 1994.

Grant, R.M., *Contemporary Strategy Analysis: Concept, Techniques, Applications*, 2nd ed., Cambridge, Mass.: Blackwell, 1995.

Gunter, R., J. Kluge, R.D. Kempis, R. Diederichs, and F. Bruk, *Simplicity Wins: How Germany's Mid-Sized Companies Succeed*, Boston, MA: Harvard Business School Press, 1995.

Haeckel, S.H., "Adaptive Enterprise Design: The Sense-and-Respond Model," *Planning Review*, May/June, 1995.

Hamel, G., and C.K. Prahalad, *Competing For The Future*, Boston, MA: Harvard Business School, 1994.

Hammer, M., and J. Champy, *Reengineering the Corporation: It's Time to Rethink Your Assumptions*, New York, NY: Harper Business, 1993.

Hammer, M., *Beyond Reengineering*, New York, NY: Harper Collins, 1996.

Handy, C., *The Age of Paradox*, Boston, MA: Harvard Business School Press, 1994.

Handy, C., *The Age of Unreason*, Boston, MA: Harvard Business School Press, 1990.

Handy, C., *The Gods of Management: The Changing Work of Organizations*, New York, NY: Oxford University Press, 1995.

Hargrove, R., *Mastering the Art of Creative Collaboration*, New York, NY: McGraw-Hill, 1998.

Harmon, R.L., *Reinventing the Business: Preparing Today's Enterprise for Tomorrow's Technology*, New York, NY: The Free Press, 1996.

Harvard Business Review, Command Performance: The Art of Delivering Quality Service, Boston, MA: Harvard Business School Press, 1994.

Hasslebein, F., M. Goldsmith, and R. Beckhard, *The Organizations of the Future*, San Francisco, CA: Jossey-Bass, 1997.

Hasselbein, F., M. Goldsmith, and R. Beckhard, *The Leader of the Future*, San Francisco, CA: Jossey-Bass, 1996.

Hax, A.C. and N.S. Majluf, *The Strategy Concept & Process: A Pragmatic Approach*, Englewood Cliffs, NJ: Prentice-Hall, 1991.

Herschell, G.L. and R.D. Lewis, *Selling on the Net*, Lincoln Wood, IL: NTC Publishing, 1997.

Hey, K.R. and P.D. Moore, *The Caterpillar Doesn't Know: How Personal Change Demands Organizational Change*, New York, NY: The Free Press, 1998.

Hickman, C.R. and M.A. Silva, *The Future 500: Tomorrow's Organizations Today*, New York, NY: New American Library, 1987.

Hickman, C.R., and M.A. Silva, *Creating Excellence: Managing Corporate Culture, Strategy, and Change in the New Age*, New York, NY: New American Library, 1984.

Hitt, M.A, and R.D. Ireland, and R.E. Hoskisson, *Strategic Management: Competitiveness and Globalization*, St. Paul, Min.: West, 1995.

Hope, H. and T. Hope, *Competing in the Third Wave*, Boston, MA: Harvard Business School Press, 1997.

Huey, J., "The New Post-Heroic Leadership," *Fortune*, Vol. 129, No. 4, February 21, 1994.

Ibrahim, B. and K. Argheyd, *Strategic Management*, New York, NY: McGraw-Hill, 1992.

Inkpen, A. and N. Choudhary, " The Seeking of Strategy Where It Is Not: Towards A Theory of Strategy Absence," *Strategic Management Journal*, May 1995.

Jacobs, G. and R. Macfarlane, *The Vital Corporation: How American Business Large and Small Double Profits in Two Years or Less*, Englewood Cliffs, NJ: Prentice-Hall, 1990.

Jager, R.D. and R. Oritz, *In the Company of Giants: Candid Conversations with the Visionaries of the Digital World*, New York, NY: McGraw-Hill, 1997.

James, G., *Business Wisdom of the Electronic Elite: 34 Winning Management Strategies*, New York, NY: Times Business, 1996.

Jasinowski, J., and R. Hamrin, *Making It in America: Proven Paths to Success from 50 Top Companies,* New York, NY: Simon & Schuster, 1995.

Jones, P. and L. Kahaner, *Say It & Live It: 50 Mission Statements That Hit The Mark*, New York, NY: Doubleday, 1995.

Kanter, R.M., *On the Frontiers of Management*, Boston, MA: Harvard Business School Press, 1997.

Kanter, R.M., *When Giants Learn to Dance*, New York, NY: Simon & Schuster, 1989.

Kanter, R.M., *World Class: Thriving Locally in the Global Economy*, New York, NY: Simon & Schuster, 1995.

Kantz, P.C., a letter to the editor, *Fortune*, April 24, 1988.

Kearns, D.T., and D.A. Nadler, *Profits in the Dark: How Xerox Reinvented Itself and Beat Back the Japanese*, New York, NY: Harper Business, 1992.

Kelly, K., *Out of Control: The New Biology of Machines, Social Systems and the Economic World*, Reading, MA: Addison Wesley, 1994.

Kelly, P., *Faster Company: Building the World's Nuttiest Turn-on-a-Dime Home-Grown Billion-Dollar Business*, New York, NY: Wiley, 1998.

Kelly, S., and M.A. Allison, *The Complexity Advantage: How the Science of Complexity Can Help your Business Achieve Peak Performance*, New York, NY: McGraw-Hill, 1999.

Kiernan, M.J., *Get Innovative or Get Dead: Building Competitive Companies for the 21st Century*, Vancouver, B.C.: Douglas & McIntyre, 1995.

Kotter, J.P., *Leading Change*, Boston, MA: Harvard Business School Press, 1996.

Kouzes, J.M. and B.Z. Posner, "Envisioning Your Future: Imagining Ideal Scenarios," *The Futurist*, May–June 1996.

Kouzes, J.M. and B.Z. Posner, *The Leadership Challenge: How To Keep Getting Extraordinary Things Done in Organizations*, San Francisco, CA: Jossey-Bass, 1995.

Krass, P., *The Book of Leadership Wisdom: Classic Writings by Legendary Business Leaders*, New York, NY: John Wiley & Sons, 1998.

Kuhn, T.S., *The Structure of Scientific Revolutions*, Chicago, Ill.: University of Chicago Press, 1970.

Kurtzman, J., *Future Casting*, Palm Springs, CA: ETC Publications, 1984.

Larwood, L., C.B. Falbe, M.P. Krieger, and P. Miesing, "Structure and Meaning of Organizational Vision," *Academy of Management Journal*, June 1995.

Labarre, P., "The Disorganization of Oticon," *Industry Week*, July 16, 1994.

Langeler, G., "The Vision Trap," *Harvard Business Review*, March–April, 1992.

Lele, M.M., "Selecting Strategies That Exploit Leverage," *Planning Review*, January–February, 1992.

Low, J. and T. Siesfeld, "Wall Street Considers Non-Financial Performance More Than You Think," *Strategy & Leadership*, March/April, 1998.

Lucier, C.D. and J.D. Torsilieri, "The Trillion-Dollar Race to 'E'," *Strategy & Business*, First Quarter 2000, pp. 6–14.

Lutz, R., *Guts*, New York, NY: John Wiley & Sons, 1998.

Mariotti, J.L., *The Shape Shifters: Continuous Change for Competitive Advantage*, New York, NY: Van Nostrand Reinhold, 1998.

Marriot, J.W. and K.A. Brown, *The Spirit to Serve: Marriot's Way*, New York, NY: Harper Collins, 1997.

Martin, J., *Cybercorp: The New Business Revolution*, New York, NY: AMACOM Books, 1996.

Mason, D.H. and R.G. Wilson, "Future Mapping: A New Approach To Managing Strategic Uncertainty," *Planning Review*, May/June 1987.

McKenna, R., *Real Time: Preparing for the Age of the Never Satisfied Customer*, Boston, MA: Harvard Business School Press, 1997.

Melhon, T., *The New Partnership: Profit by Bringing Out the Best in Your People, Customers, and Yourself*, Essex Junction, VT: Oliver West Publications, 1994.

Melohn, T., *The New Partnership: Profit by Bringing Out the Best in Your People, Customers & Yourself*, Essex Junction, VT: Omneo, 1994.

Mendell, J.S., "The Practice of Intuition," in J. Fowles (ed.), *Handbook of Futures Research*, Westport, CT: Greenwood Press, 1978.

Miller, A., *Strategic Management*, 3rd ed., Boston, MA: Irwin-McGraw-Hill, 1998.

Mills, D.Q., *Rebirth of the Corporation*, New York, NY: John Wiley & Sons, 1991.

Mintzberg, H. and J.B. Quinn, *The Strategy Process: Concepts, Contexts, Cases*, 3rd ed., Upper Saddle River, NJ: Prentice-Hall, 1996.

Moore, J.F., *The Death of Competition: Leadership & Strategy in the Age of Business Marketplaces*, New York, NY: Harper Business, 1996.

Morris, E., "Vision and Strategy: A Focus for the Future," *Journal of Business Strategy*, Fall 1987.

Morrison, I., "The Second Curve: Managing the Velocity of Change," *Strategy & Leadership*, November/December, 1997.

Nadler, D.A., *Profits in the Dark: How Xerox Reinvented Itself and Beat Back the Japanese*, New York, NY: Harper Collins, 1992.

Nanus, B., *Visionary Leadership*, San Francisco, CA: Jossey-Bass, 1992, p. 8.

Nielson, G.L., B.A. Pasternack, and A.J. Viscio, "Up the (E) Organization: A Seven-Dimensional Model for the Centerless Enterprise," *Strategy & Business*, First Quarter 2000, pp. 52–57.

O'Toole, J., *Leading Change*, San Francisco, CA: Jossey-Bass, 1995.

O'Connor, R., *Planning Under Uncertainty: Multiple Scenarios and Contingency Planning*, A Research Report from the Conference Board, New York: The Conference Board, 1978.

Ohmae, K., *The Mind of the Strategist, Gain Competitive Advantage through Analysis and Insight*, New York, NY: McGraw-Hill, 1982.

Ostroff, F., *The Horizontal Organization: Redesign Your Company to Better Deliver Value*, New York, NY: Oxford University Press, 1999.

Parker, G.M., *Cross-Functional Teams*, San Francisco, CA: Jossey-Bass, 1994.

Pascale, R.T., *Managing On the Edge: How the Smartest Companies Use Conflict to Stay Ahead*, New York, NY: Simon and Schuster, 1990.

Pasternack, B.A. and A.J. Viscio, "The Centerless Corporation: A Model for Tomorrow," *Strategy & Business*, Third Quarter, 1998.

Perry, L.T., R.G. Scott, and W.N. Smallwood, *Real Time Strategy: Improvising Team Based Planning for a Fast-Changing World*, New York, NY: John Wiley & Sons, 1993.

Peters, T. and R.H. Waterman, *In Search of Excellence*, New York, NY: Harper & Row, 1982.

Peters, T., and N.K. Austin, *A Passion for Excellence*, New York, NY: Random House, 1985.

Peters, T., *Thriving On Chaos: Handbook For A Management Revolution*, New York, NY: Harper & Row, 1987.

Peters, Tom, *Liberation Management: Necessary Disorganization for the Nanosecond Nineties*, New York, NY: Alfred Knopf, 1992.

Pollard, C.W., *The Soul of the Firm*, New York, NY: Harper Business, 1996.

Porter, M., *Competitive Strategy*, New York: NY: Free Press, 1980.

Porter, M., *Competitive Advantage*, New York, NY: The Free Press, 1985.

Price Waterhouse Change Integration Team, *Better Change: Best Practices for Transforming Your Organization*, Homewood, IL: Irwin, 1995.

Puris, M., *Comeback: How Seven Straight-Shooting CEOs Turned Around Troubled Companies*, New York, NY: Time Business Random House, 1999.

Putnam, H.D., *The Winds Of Turbulence: A CEO's Reflections on Surviving and Thriving on the Cutting Edge of Corporate Crisis*, New York, NY: Harper Collins, 1991.

Quigly, J.V., *Vision: How Leaders Develop It, Share It & Sustain It*, New York, NY: McGraw-Hill, 1993.

Quin, S. and R. Evans, "The New Business Leader: Socrates with a Baton," *Strategy & Leadership*, September/October, 1997.

Robert Tomasko, a keynote address to the International Strategic Leadership Conference, Strategic Leadership Forum, Atlanta, GA, 1996.

Robert, M., *Strategic Thinking: Charting The Future Direction of Your Organization*, Australia, Decision Sciences International, Ltd., 1983.

Rogers, D., *Waging Business Warfare: Lessons from the Military Masters in Achieving Corporate Superiority*, New York, NY: Chales Kribber's Sons, 1987.

Rommel, G., Klue, J, R.D. Kempis, R. Diderichs, and Bruck, F., *Simplicity Wins: How Germany's Mid-Sized Industrial Companies Succeed*, Boston, MA: Harvard Business School Press, 1995.

Rowe, A.J., R.O. Mason, E.E. Dickel, R.B. Mann, and R.J. Mockler, *Strategic Management: A Methodological Approach*, (4th ed.), Reading, MA: Addison-Wesley Publishing Company, 1994.

Schendel, D.E. and C.W. Hofer (editors), *Strategic Management: A New View of Business Policy and Planning*, Boston, MA: Little, Brown, and Company, 1979.

Schrifer, A., "The Future: Trends, Discontinuities, and Opportunities," *Strategy & Leadership*, November/December, 1997.

Schwartz, P., "Composing a Plot for Your Scenario," *Planning Review*, May/June. 1992.

Schwartz, P., *The Art of the Long View*, New York, NY: Bantam-Doubleday-Dell, 1991.

Senge, P.M., *The Fifth Discipline: The Art and Practice of the Learning Organization*, New York, NY: Doubleday, 1990.

Seybold, *Cutomer.Com: Develop and E-Business Strategy that Attracts and Keeps Customers*, New York, NY: Times Business, Random House, 1998.

Silva, M. and R. McGrann, *Overdrive: Managing in Crisis Filled Times*, New York, NY: John Wiley & Sons, 1995.

Simon, H., *Hidden Champions: Lessons from 500 of the World Best Unknown Companies*, Boston, MA: Harvard Business School Press, 1996.

Simon, H., *Hidden Champions: Lessons from 500 of the World's Best Unknown Companies*, Boston, MA: Harvard Business School Press, 1996.

Slater, R., *Jack Welch and the GE Way*, New York, NY: McGraw-Hill, 1999.

Slyotzky, A.J., *Value Migration*, Boston, MA: Harvard Business School Press, 1996.

Slywotsky, A.J. and D.J. Morrison, *The Profit Zone: How Strategic Business Design Will Lead You to Tomorrow's Profits*, New York, NY: Time Books, 1997.

Stack, J., *The Great Game of Business: Unlocking the Power and Profitability of Open-Book Management*, New York, NY: Doubleday, 1992.

Stalk, G., and T. Hout, *Competing Against Time*, New York, NY: The Free Press, 1990.

Stalk, G., P. Evans, and L.E. Shulman, "Competing on Capabilities: The New Rule of Corporate Strategy," *Harvard Business Review*, March–April 1992.

Stewart, T., *Intellectual Capital*, New York, NY: Bantam Doubleday Dell Publishing, 1997.

Stewart, T.A., America's Most Admired Companies: Why Leadership Matters, *Fortune*, March 2, 1998.

Strauss, A. and J. Corbin, *Basics of Qualitative Research: Grounded Theory Procedures and Techniques*, Newbury Park, CA: Sage Publications, 1990.

Tapscott, D., "Strategy in the New Economy," *Strategy & Leadership*, November/December, 1997.

Tapscott, D., *Growing Up Digital: The Rise of The Net Generation*, New York, NY: McGraw-Hill, 1998.

The Virtual Organization, *Challenges: Ontario Business: Issues and Opportunities*, Spring, 1996.

Thomas, H., D. Oneil, R. White, and D. Hurst, *Building the Strategically Responsive Organization*, Chichester, UK: John Wiley & Sons, 1994.

Thompson, Jr., A.A. and A.J. Strickland III, *Strategic Management: Concepts and Cases*, Tenth Edition, Boston, MA: Irwin/McGraw-Hill, 1998.

Tichy, N. and R. Charan, "Speed, Simplicity, Self-Confidence: An Interview with Jack Welch," *Harvard Business Review*, September–October, 1989.

Tichy, N.M., and S. Sherman, *Control Your Destiny Or Someone Else Will: How Jack Welch Is Making General Electric The World's Most Competitive Company*, New York, NY: Doubleday, 1993.

Tornow, W.W., M. London, and CCL Associates, *Maximizing the Value of 360-Degree Feedback: A Process for Organizational Development*, San Francisco, CA: Jossey-Bass, 1998.

Trout, J. and S. Rivkin, *The New Positioning: The Latest on the World's #3 Business Strategy*, New York, NY: McGraw-Hill, 1996.

Tyson, K.W.M., "Perpetual Strategy: A 21st Century Essential," *Strategy & Leadership*, November/December, 1997.

Viscio, A.J. and B.A. Pasternack, "Toward a New Business Model," *Strategy & Business*, Second Quarter, 1996.

Voss, H., "Virtual Organizations: The Future Is Now," *Strategy & Leadership*, July/August 1996.

Waldrop, M.M., *Complexity: The Emerging Science at the Edge Of Order and Chaos*, New York, NY: Simon & Schuster, 1992.

Wallace, J. *Overdrive: Bill Gates and the Race to Control Cyberspace*, New York, NY: John Wiley & Sons, 1997.

Waterman, R.H., *The Renewal Factor*, New York, NY: Bantam Books, 1987.

Waterman, R.H., *What America Does Right: Learning from Companies that Put People First*, New York, NY: WW Norton & Company, 1994.

Weaver, P.H., *The Suicidal Corporation*, New York, NY: Simon & Schuster, 1988.

Wetherbe, J.C., *The World On Time: The 11 Management Principles that Made FedEx and Overnight Sensation*, Santa Monica, CA: Knowledge Exchange 1996.

Wheatley, M.J., and M. Keliner-Rogers, "Self-Organization: The Irresistible Future Of Organizing," *Strategy & Leadership*, July/August, 1996.

Wheelen, T.L., and J.D. Hunger, *Strategic Management and Business Policy: Entering the 21st Century Global Society*, 6th ed., Reading, MA: Addison-Wesley, 1998.

Wilson, I, "The Five Compasses of Strategic Leadership," *Strategy & Leadership*, Vol. 24, no. 4, July–August, 1996.

Wilson, I.H., "Scenarios" in J. Fowles (ed.), *Handbook of Futures Research*, Westport, CT: Greenwood Press, 1978.

Wilson, I., "Realizing The Power Of Strategic Vision," *Long Range Planning*, vol. 25, no. 5, 1992.

Wilson, I., "Teaching Decision Makers to Learn from Scenarios: A Blueprint for Implementation," *Planning Review*, May/June, 1992.

Yasuda, Y., *40 Years, 20 Million Ideas*, Cambridge, MA: Productivity Press, 1991.

Youngblood, M.D., "Leadership at the Edge of Chaos: From Control to Creativity," *Strategy & Leadership*, September/October, 1997.

Zand, D.D., *The Leadership Triad: Knowledge, Trust, and Power*, New York, NY: Oxford University Press, 1997.